W9-CZX-495

ELITES IN AMERICAN HISTORY

TECHNICAL COLLEGE OF THE LOWCOUNTRY
LEARNING RESOURCES CENTER
POST OFFICE BOX 1288
BEAUFORT, SOUTH CAROLINA 29901-1288

ELITES IN AMERICAN HISTORY

The Civil War
to the New Deal

Philip H. Burch, Jr.

TECHNICAL COLLEGE OF THE LOWCOUNTRY
LEARNING RESOURCES CENTER
POST OFFICE BOX 1288
BEAUFORT, SOUTH CAROLINA 29901-1288

HOLMES & MEIER PUBLISHERS, INC.
New York ● London

First published in the United States of America 1981 by
Holmes & Meier Publishers, Inc.
30 Irving Place
New York, N.Y. 10003

Great Britain:
Holmes & Meier Publishers, Ltd.
131 Trafalgar Road
Greenwich, London SE10 9TX

Copyright © 1981 by Philip H. Burch, Jr.
All rights reserved

Library of Congress Cataloging in Publication Data

Burch, Philip H
  Elites in American history.

  Includes indexes.
  CONTENTS: v. 1. The Federalist years to the Civil
War.—v. 2. The Civil War to the New Deal.—v. 3. The
New Deal to the Carter administration.
  1. Business and politics—United States—History.
2. United States—Officials and employees—Appointment,
qualifications, tenure, etc.—History. 3. Elite (Social
sciences)—United States—History. I. Title.
  JK467.B87   322'.e'0973   80-11287

  ISBN 0 8419-0594-0 (v.1)
  ISBN 0 8419-0704-8 (v.1 pbk.)
  ISBN 0 8419-0595-9 (v.2)
  ISBN 0 8419-0705-6 (v.2 pbk.)
  ISBN 0 8419-0565-7 (v.3)
  ISBN 0 8419-0566-5 (v.3 pbk.)

Manufactured in the United States of America

LEARNING RESOURCES CENTER
POST OFFICE BOX 1288
BEAUFORT, SOUTH CAROLINA 29901-1288

To L. Ethan Ellis,
Bennett M. Rich,
and Abe Yeselman, three men
it has been my pleasure
to know at Rutgers

Contents

Tables and Chart

Preface and Acknowledgments

This work was begun in the early 1960s in an effort to explore some of the linkages between business and government as revealed by an examination of the makeup of the boards of directors of America's large corporations. This, I later discovered, was an approach which had not yet been employed in a thorough, systematic fashion, primarily because the requisite business directories were not available over a long period of time to be mined by various able historians and other social scientists. In part because of my orientation and training as a political scientist, my initial labors were confined to the post-1941 period, and focused largely on the federal recruitment process. However, as my work continued, the question naturally arose, what was the politico-economic linkage pattern in the preceding period? So I carried this general line of analysis back to the turn of the century, for most of which period a number of good business directories were available (along with a substantial set of secondary works); then to the late 1860s, for which years only *Poor's Railroad Manual* was available (to be supplemented by a wide variety of secondary sources); and finally, in one last major research effort, back through the pre-Civil War decades to 1789, for which years I had to rely largely on non-primary material, particularly biographical studies of high federal officials.

The initial aim of this study was to make a systematic analysis of the socio-economic background of the top appointive officials in the federal government over time in the hope that the data might be put to good use by other social scientists. Another equally important purpose was to employ these recruitment findings to make a rough general assessment of the distribution of power in the country and thereby shed some light on the "elitist" versus "pluralist" controversy which has been raging among political scientists and sociologists in recent decades. The analysis of major issues and events was undertaken somewhat later in an effort to show that there may be a significant relationship between the background of various high federal officials and their governmental actions, although it

xi

should be stressed that the latter acts do not constitute any kind of statistically sound sample, but are simply intended to demonstrate (rather than prove) that there is some connection between the two.

Because of the highly controversial nature of this work, I have deliberately eschewed much use of the voluminous archival material often mined by historians, preferring instead, aside from business directories, to rely almost exclusively on secondary sources, because, unlike the latter, the papers and correspondence of high federal officials cannot readily be checked.

The author of any such lengthy work owes a great deal to other people. I would like to express my special thanks to Tom Ferguson, now of M.I.T., for his highly supportive efforts during the critical late stages of this study. The author is also indebted to G. William Domhoff of the University of California (Santa Cruz); Michael Levy of Texas A. & M.; Ernie Reock, director of the Rutgers Bureau of Government Research and Services; Al Barnes, another stellar friend at the Bureau; and my two older children, Carol and David Burch, for their substantial aid and encouragement. Although I am not a member of this profession, I received considerable help from various members of Rutgers' fine history department, especially Sidney Ratner, Richard L. McCormick, Gerald Grob, Lloyd Gardner, Warren Susman, David Oshinsky, and Rudy Bell. Some of my political science colleagues were also supportive, notably Josef Silverstein, Steve Bronner, Anthony Champagne, Stanley Friedelbaum, Richard Mansbach, and Richard Wilson. None of these scholars is, of course, responsible for any errors contained in this study.

In addition, the author secured much sound counsel from two other people at Rutgers, Marlie Wasserman and J. Carl Cook. The staff at the Rutgers University Library was unfailingly helpful during the many years of research involved in this undertaking. The able and ever-cheerful Claire Luma did an extraordinary job of typing this manuscript, all on an overtime basis. I am also grateful to those sweet squash players at Rutgers for providing a welcome break in many a long workday.

CHAPTER I

Introduction

As indicated in the introduction to Volume I of this work, the approach taken in this historical study of American politico-economic relations is one which focuses primarily on the role of various influential elites, largely because of the many problems involved in trying to deal with such important, but often elusive, concepts as class, power, decision-making, and the dispensation of governmental benefits (and burdens) over time. This is not to say that such critical considerations as the distribution of power in a society, the allocation of economic benefits to different segments of the population, and the relation of elite groups to the class structure of a country are slighted, but rather that a systematic analysis of the socio-economic background and affiliations of America's political elite may provide the most rewarding and reliable way of getting at such matters, particularly when it is combined, as it is here, with an analysis of various major governmental actions.

Indeed, although remarkably few sound elite studies have been conducted to date, especially in economically advanced countries,[1] this kind of research can do much to illuminate such crucial areas and issues as the number and relative power of different elite groups, their possible ties with one another, their socio-economic make-up and rates of change, the manner of their recruitment, and their relations to other classes and less organized segments of the citizenry.[2] Such study can also shed considerable light on the extent to which there has been much equality of opportunity to hold high governmental office in the United States.[3]

There is yet another reason for concentrating heavily on the social and economic ties of a nation's political elite, and that is to place governmental officials (and their chief advisors or confidants) in a more revealing setting than has generally been done to date. For despite the emphasis placed on the economic basis of politics by Charles A. Beard, the vast majority of American scholars have been content to merely refer to various governmental officers as a former successful lawyer or an important businessman, without delving into their economic ties or those of their close kin or key business associates. And this is a grievous error. Where did such figures fit into the economic structure of the country at the time they were appointed or elected to high public office? Were they, in effect, "Establishment" men, political mavericks, or ardent reformers, as Samuel J. Tilden, the 1876 Democratic presidential candidate, was commonly thought to be? Without more pertinent data and discerning analysis, it is impossible to tell (as the old adage goes, "you can't tell the players without a program"). Moreover, it is a basic premise of this study that a President may well be judged by the administrative, diplomatic, and judicial company he keeps—that is, by the type of men he picks to serve as his chief officers and advisors. In short, an in-depth analysis of a nation's top decision-makers should reveal much about the locus of power in a society.

In this work the term *governmental elite* is used primarily to mean the occupants of the nation's major Cabinet, diplomatic, and Supreme Court posts.[4] In the post–Civil War to New Deal period the key diplomatic positions include not only the prestigious posts of Minister (or Ambassador) to Great Britain and France, but also to Germany, for that country had certainly come of economic and military age by 1870.

The data collected for this largely positional analysis of high administrative, diplomatic, and judicial figures stress the economic ties of an official (or his close kin) at or near the time of his appointment to a federal post, particularly his primary business or occupational position, his major directorship ties, and, where relevant, certain key civic associations.[5] These links are probably more important than a person's distant social origins since they represent his most recent, presumably predominant, economic allegiance.

These vital data, which have never been systematically mined over a long span of time, were gathered for most 20th-century officials from such generally reliable sources as *Who's Who in America,* the *Directory of Directors in the City of New York* (which contains data on a number of concerns located in other places), and the primary national business directories published during all or part of this period, mainly *Poor's* and *Moody's*.[6] From the Civil War to the turn of the century, similar data have been culled from such sources as *Poor's Manual of Railroads* (which extends back to 1868), the *Dictionary of American Biography,* the *National Cyclopaedia of American Biography,* and a substantial number of historical studies and political biographies. This information, which is listed in systematic tabular form in two appendices presented at the end of this volume, is analyzed in considerable depth and detail in the text to see whether there are any key institutions, corporate clusters, or politico-economic alliances that have played a prominent role in the overall federal recruitment and decision-making process at various points in time.

A major distinction is also made, to the extent possible (given the paucity of reliable data prior to 1900), between what might for the time be described as big business on the one hand and small or medium-sized firms on the other. For despite the many problems involved, the reader is entitled to know whether the firms found to be closely linked to certain high federal officials were large- or small-scale enterprises. And perhaps equally significant is a determination as to whether they were controlled by managerial or wealthy entrepreneurial interests, for which purposes the author has generally relied, in the absence of sound stockownership data, on an analysis of the make-up of the boards of directors of the companies in question.[7] It is on the basis of such information that an assessment has been made, where the data permitted, of the economic elite or non-elite status of all high federal officials from the Civil War to the New Deal.[8]

Also, it should be noted that the author, unlike many social scientists, does not look upon the partners in the emerging corporate law firms after the Civil War as detached professional men. While this description may have fitted most attorneys up to the 1860s, this state of affairs was, as Beryl Levy has pointed out, substantially altered, with the railroad-spurred advent of the Industrial Revolution, by the growth of the big-city law firms and their increasingly close links with major corporate and financial clients.[9] Thus while most lawyers practicing on their own, or with just a few partners or associates, are treated here as professional men, the top figures of the big firms in the post–Civil War years must be regarded as either the allies or agents of important economic interests.

Another subject which is emphasized in this work concerns elite family links. This area has been largely ignored by American social scientists, perhaps because the very concept of such ties runs counter to the nation's democratic ethos. However, if scholars were to take a close look at this topic, they could not help but be impressed by the frequency with which key family ties appear to play a vital role in a person's rise to high public office.[10]

Although this analysis of politico-economic relations in America concentrates primarily on the corporate and kinship ties of high governmental officials, major long-recognized political considerations are not overlooked. Due note of other prior governmental service, various key party posts held, and pertinent geographic and ethnic factors is made in both the text and the biographical background tables found at the end of this volume. In other words, it is readily conceded that many appointments to high governmental office are made wholly or largely for political reasons. Yet a substantial number also appear to have been the result primarily of economic influence.[11]

Since the socio-economic background of people usually has a marked effect on their actions, it is imperative to look at the role of high federal officials from yet another standpoint—namely, that of possible conflicts of interest in American government. As the generally conservative Bar

Association of the City of New York rightly pointed out in its report on *Congress and the Public Trust,* the term *conflict of interest* should be viewed in a broad light as meaning the assumption of an obligation on the part of a public official to do more than merely abstain from lining his pockets (or those of family or friends); even more importantly, he should try to avoid being placed in any position which would result in the impairment of his independent judgment, so that all governmental decisions can be made in what is generally termed the "public interest."[12] It was with this in mind that the New York bar association came to the conclusion that members of Congress should not serve as officers, directors, trustees, or partners in any commercial enterprise, a recommendation the author would extend, for the same reasons, to all high administrative, diplomatic, and judicial officials. Indeed, some feel that the real problem with the appointment of businessmen (or other wealthy or "friendly" figures) to high posts in government is not so much overt corruption (which, as a rule, occurs only sporadically), but the intrusion of improper (pro-business) bias into the formulation and implementation of governmental policy.[13]

Because of the strong possibility that the appointment of pro-corporate federal officials may have a profound effect on the governmental decision-making process, an analysis is also made of a selected set of major events in the 1861–1933 period in an effort to see what, if any, relationship exists between the socio-economic background of high governmental authorities and their actions in office.[14] In short, this study may provide a rough test of the relative impact of the federal recruitment pattern on the government's policy-making process.

For example, in the first volume of this work it was shown that about 95 percent of the top posts in the federal government in the pre–Civil War period were held by economic elite figures. In fact, during the Federalist years all of the major Cabinet, diplomatic, and Supreme Court officers were either wealthy or well-connected men. Though America was an overwhelmingly agrarian nation, many of these early high federal officials had primarily urban business links, such as with Philadelphia financier (and later land speculator) Robert Morris. Although President Washington was a large Virginia landholder with a pro-entrepreneurial outlook, the dominant force in his administration was probably that exerted by the extremely able Alexander Hamilton, a New York lawyer who had married well, had a number of influential socio-economic ties, particularly with New York and Philadelphia interests, and was the founder of the first major financial institution in his home city, the Bank of New York, a prominent concern in America's business community even today. The power wielded by such interests in these early years can also be seen in the appointment of various elite leaders, such as John Jay and James Wilson (an attorney for Robert Morris), to the U.S. Supreme Court.

With the rise of the Jeffersonian Republicans to power in 1801, there were some noteworthy changes in the make-up of the federal government. For instance, there was much greater representation of agrarian interests, especially those of big Southern planters. This was, of course, most clearly revealed by the background of the three men—Jefferson, Madison, and Monroe—who held presidential office during the first 24 years of this period, which has been described, somewhat misleadingly, both as the "era of good feeling" and the "Virginia dynasty." But this shift in politico-economic power was also manifested through the selection of such major Cabinet and diplomatic officers as Robert Livingston and his brother-in-law, John Armstrong, two rich Hudson Valley landholders who served as Minister to France under Jefferson, and Georgia's William H. Crawford and South Carolina's John C. Calhoun, who served as Secretary of the Treasury and Secretary of War under James Monroe. Yet there was a strong mercantile faction in the Jeffersonian Republican party too, although it never possessed as much influence as such interests did under the preceding Federalist regimes, and the merchants who were associated with it were generally viewed as mavericks or economic "newcomers."

As to the Supreme Court, a somewhat different situation prevailed during much, if not all, of the Jeffersonian Republican years, for although a majority of the men who served on this body were of this political persuasion, the Court was, in fact, dominated by the extraordinary intellect and character of its longtime (1801–1835) Chief Justice, John Marshall, who had been appointed just before the end of the Adams administration. Marshall, like many Supreme Court Justices, was an elite figure. He came from a wealthy (landholding) family in Virginia and had married into one of the richest families in the state. In addition, Marshall had been employed for many years by Philadelphia's influential financier, Robert Morris, who had substantial business and real estate operations in the South, which ties were further strengthened by the fact that Marshall's younger brother had married Morris's daughter. John Marshall had also served as a political agent or confidant of New York's entrepreneurially oriented Alexander Hamilton. Hence it is not surprising that in most of the major politico-economic cases brought before the Court in these early years, this body ruled in favor of property interests.

The Jacksonian era (1829–1841) has been described by many historians, especially Arthur M. Schlesinger, Jr., as the age of the "common man," as an age of political, if not economic, equalitarianism, as a period in which the people triumphed over property. In short, it is widely believed to have been a time in which the Western frontiersmen and the urban working class emerged as major political forces and, under the leadership of Andrew Jackson, seized the reins of power from the wealthy figures who had long dominated the federal government. But in more recent years a second school of historians, led primarily by Edward Pessen and Bray Hammond, has come up with a very different line of analysis, which is frequently referred to as the entrepreneurial interpretation of Jacksonian democracy. They contend that the fiery Jackson did not really represent the working men of America so much as he did another set of emerging elite forces. This controversy has raged for a considerable time now, with both sides still far apart.

Though rarely employed, the basic approach taken in this study of American politico-economic relations, that of examining the background and business ties of the nation's top federal officials, sheds a good deal of light on this dispute. For instance, this analysis, which is presented in detail in Volume I, reveals that Jackson himself was, despite certain early financial scrapes, a wealthy elite (landholding) figure by the time he entered the White House, and that he was closely allied with the "haves" rather than the "have-nots" of Tennessee society. Even more important, there was little change in the elite (or non-elite) status of Jackson's major Cabinet and diplomatic officials compared to those of the preceding Jeffersonian Republican regimes. These officers included such well-connected men as New York's Martin Van Buren, who was the leader of an entrepreneurially oriented political group known as the Albany Regency; Lewis Cass, a large landowner and bank stockholder from Michigan; Louis McLane, who had numerous economic elite ties in his native state of Delaware; and Benjamin F. Butler, another member of the Albany Regency who was a director of banks in both Albany and New York City.[15] Moreover, all six of the Supreme Court Justices who were appointed by Andrew Jackson during his eight years in office were elite figures, the most prominent of whom was Chief Justice Roger B. Taney, a former Maryland lawyer who had served at various times on the board of several state banks and had been the first general or senior counsel for the Baltimore and Ohio Railroad before becoming a member of Jackson's Cabinet in 1831. On the basis of such background data, it would certainly seem that the historians who have viewed Old Hickory as the political leader of a new set of elite forces are probably much closer to the mark than those who have portrayed him as the champion of America's urban and rural masses.

That this is true may also be seen by taking a look at the one overriding issue of this era, Jackson's famous "war" against the second Bank of the United States. This epic struggle has generally been described in one of three ways. Some analysts claim that it was basically a battle which pitted the debt-ridden farmers and urban working classes against the alleged "monied aristocracy"; another group of writers has depicted it essentially as the inexorable clash of two strong-willed men, the impetuous Andrew Jackson versus the haughty, patrician president of the Bank of the United States, Nicholas Biddle; and still other scholars maintain that it represented primarily a conflict between rising entrepreneurial interests, especially the newer state banks, and a long-entrenched economic elite, centered especially in Philadelphia, which was then clearly the nation's financial capital. There is some truth to each of these contentions. But judging from the highly elitist background of most of Jackson's major Cabinet officers (not to mention his many well-connected diplomatic and judicial appointees) and the pioneering work of Bray Hammond, who has argued that financial interests in other cities, particularly New York, played a prominent behind-the-scenes role in this affair, it would appear that it was rival elite forces which were largely responsible for Jackson's relentless drive to destroy the Bank of the United States.

The two pre–Civil War decades were likewise dominated by elite interests. Indeed, except for the Buchanan administration, all of the major Cabinet and diplomatic officers (for whom sufficient pertinent background data are available) to serve under these Presidents were elite figures, and in Buchanan's case 75 percent of his top officials had various key socio-economic links. For instance, aside from the probably atypical Harrison-Tyler administration and the rather inept Fillmore regime, the position of Secretary of the Treasury was held by such influential men as Robert J. Walker, a wealthy Mississippi lawyer, planter, and land specu-lator who had married a member of one of Philadelphia's most prominent families; William Meredith, a Philadelphia lawyer who was related to several well-connected families in the urban Northeast; James Guthrie, a Louisville lawyer who was a director of both a bank and a railroad in Kentucky; and Howell Cobb, a Georgia lawyer who was one of the largest planters and slaveholders in the South. In like manner, the Supreme Court was dominated throughout this 20-year period by such incumbent jurists as Chief Justice Roger B. Taney, a former Maryland bank and railroad lawyer; James M. Wayne, a Georgia lawyer and big landowner whose close kinsmen were involved in several railroad concerns in the South; Peter V. Daniel, who had married a daughter of Virginia's Edmund Randolph and was a former member of the long-powerful Richmond Junto; and such later appointees as New Hampshire's Levi Woodbury, who was a member of his home state's potent Concord Regency and whose father-in-law was one of the richest merchants in Maine. In short, there was relatively little difference in the predominantly elite nature of the federal recruitment process between the two pre–Civil War decades and the preceding administrations, except that, because of the steadily increasing importance of the slavery issue, sectional considerations began to assume a more critical role in many decisions made by high-level officials.

As one might expect, a number of the major issues and events that took place during this period involved either land or land-related slavery questions. For instance, in the 184(, much of the pressure for America's annexation of the recently created Republic of Texas, which had been part of Mexico, came from influential politico-economic figures, particu-larly in the South, where there was widespread fear that this country would, at Britain's urging, adopt a law abolishing slavery. In addition. a number of people in the United States were heavily involved in land speculation and securities schemes in this large, primarily American-settled territory. For example, when, after some abortive efforts, the annexation act was approved in the first part of the pro-Southern Polk administration, one of the President's chief advisors was his Secretary of the Treasury, Robert Walker, an entrepreneurially oriented Mississippi lawyer and planter who, before he assumed Cabinet office, had been deeply enmeshed in land speculation activities in the Texas territory. Thus there is considerable doubt as to whether this action was taken solely to promote the nation's public interest.

A number of the other major acts approved later in this period revolved around or directly impinged upon the issue of slavery. In 1850 when the problem arose as to how to treat America's war-acquired territories of California, Utah, and New Mexico, emotions rose to a white heat over the right of Congress to decide whether slavery should be excluded from these regions. Southern extremists talked openly of secession and possible armed conflict if slavery were banned from these lands without significant concessions made to protect their interests. High-minded Northern leaders, many of whom had supported the newly formed Free Soil party in the 1848 election, vehemently opposed any Congressionally sanctioned extension of slavery into these areas, pointing to a "higher law" than the Constitution itself. In an adroit effort to avoid such a confrontation, Kentucky's able and ambitious Henry Clay conceived of a shrewd measure, known as the Compromise of 1850, which provided for the immediate admission of California into the Union as a free state, the organization of territorial governments in New Mexico and Utah without reference to the question of slavery (thereby permitting these units to resolve this issue for themselves at a later date), the adoption of a more stringent fugitive slave law, and the abolition of the domestic slave trade in the nation's capital. Clay's plan appealed to both conservative Southern planters and many Northern businessmen, particularly textile merchants and manufacturers, whose trade depended on the maintenance of normal peacetime relations. Yet there was a great deal of opposition to this proposal, especially on the part of the "radical" free-soil men, the so-called Conscience Whigs, and fiery Southern secessionists like Jefferson Davis and John C. Calhoun, which bitter conflict alarmed most of America's commercial and industrial leaders, a sizable number of whom were "Cotton Whigs" whose motto was 'peace at any price.'

At this critical juncture a momentous debate took place on the floor of Congress, with many impassioned speeches made on both sides of this plan. Without a doubt, the greatest of these was made by New England's immensely gifted orator, Daniel Webster, who rose to the occasion and delivered a stirring appeal which helped to turn the tide against the forces of secession. For this dramatic effort Webster has been credited by many authorities with having performed an extraordinary feat of courageous leadership.

However, there is another interpretation that can be placed upon Webster's role as the ardent advocate of the Compromise of 1850. According to this line of analysis, he acted primarily, not as an idealistic or farsighted statesman defending the course of national unity, but rather as the spokesman of Northeastern business interests, the "Cotton Whigs", who placed the preservation of normal trade relations above the plight of a cruelly exploited and enslaved people. As two historians have noted, Webster was the hero of the Northern businessmen. "For these he preached Union; for these he surrendered the fugitive slave."[16]

A few years later, during the first part of the pro-Southern Pierce administration, another important measure was passed which dealt largely with the issue of slavery and its possible extension into some of the relatively undeveloped Midwestern sections of the United States, the Kansas and Nebraska territories. Most Americans had thought that this question had long been firmly settled by an 1820 Congressional agreement known as the Missouri Compromise. It decreed that Missouri would be admitted into the Union as a slave state and Maine, to counterbalance, as a free state, but that the pernicious institution of slavery would also be thereafter banned in all parts of what was once known as the Louisiana Territory.

This tranquil state of affairs was rudely shattered in 1854 when Illinois Senator Stephen A. Douglas introduced a Congressional bill which provided for the governmental organization of the Great Plains area into two territories—Kansas and Nebraska—based, apparently at the insistence of Southern spokesmen, on the principle of "popular sovereignty," a proposed act that would clearly render the Missouri Compromise null and void. Despite the angry storms of protest aroused in the North and the heated debate generated in Congress itself, the Douglas forces, with the strong backing of many Southern leaders and President Pierce and various top figures in his administration, soon won approval of this controversial plan, which, though Douglas did not so intend, regrettably led to much bloody conflict in the two hotly disputed territories, for in a sense it represented the opening round in the Civil War.

Various explanations have been offered over the years as to why the politically ambitious Douglas initiated and vigorously promoted a governmental measure which was almost bound to disrupt the politico-economic status quo, particularly concerning the explosive issue of slavery. Among the arguments advanced are charges that Douglas had strong pro-Southern sympathies or, more likely, that his action stemmed largely from his political calculations that the bill would, by securing the support of both the South and the Northern frontiersmen, greatly enhance his prospects for the Presidency. Yet there is another, often overlooked reason why Douglas strove so hard to open up this vast area. And that has to do with his own entrepreneurial activities and his more than cordial relationship with various western railroads, which association was revealed a few years earlier when he vigorously promoted the nation's first big land grant for a railroad, the Illinois Central. However, judging from David Potter's recent research in particular, the primary reason Douglas made this controversial move was that he was in league with certain major railroad leaders who were extremely eager to build one or more routes to the Pacific Coast and thereby open up the Great Plains to agricultural and commercial development.[17] Douglas was in strong accord with these plans, so long, as it was agreed, that at least one line would have Chicago as its eastern terminus, for it was here that Douglas had amassed some of his largest landholdings, which were sure to appreciate tremendously in value if Chicago became a great railroad nexus. Hence Douglas felt he had much to gain from the territorial and transportation expansion envisioned under the provisions of the Kansas-Nebraska Act.

By far the most important action taken during the last part of this period was the Dred Scott decision, which famous Supreme Court case involved the legal status of a Missouri slave who had lived briefly in the North under his master, an Army physician, but was later returned to his state of origin. The plaintiff's lawyers argued that by virtue of his onetime residence in another (non-slave) state Dred Scott had become a citizen of the United States, with all the rights and privileges that pertain thereto— clearly an explosive issue for major slaveholders interested in maintaining the politico-economic status quo. In a highly controversial ruling the Taney-led Court decreed that Scott was not actually an American citizen and that his legal status was instead determined by the laws of the state in which he then dwelled, Missouri. In short, although the nation's many dedicated abolitionists had hoped to secure a verdict favorable to their cause, the judgment was one which backed the South and the odious institution of slavery.

The most puzzling aspect of this case was not the verdict (which might have been predicted given the pro-Southern make-up of the Court), nor the affirmative role of the abolitionists and their attorneys, but rather the reason why the defendant, John F. A. Sanford, a former St. Louis merchant now living in New York City, chose to carry this fight all the way to the U.S. Supreme Court. Many authorities have claimed that Sanford was acting, for other members of his family, hopefully to aid the abolitionist cause. Yet it is by no means certain that he was so motivated. Indeed, according to one analysis of this affair, Sanford did not really wish to contest this case in federal court, but was "badgered" into doing so by some (unspecified) people with a political, rather than a personal, interest in the proceedings.[18] The question is, who exerted the pressure? Many scholars believe that it was certain zealous abolitionist leaders, such as Sanford's kinsman, Dr. Calvin Chaffee. But given Sanford's background, it seems much more likely that he was influenced by various major business figures in the North, who were probably fearful about either the ultimate political consequences of a quiet pro-abolitionist settlement out of court or the potentially explosive concern of many large Southern slaveholders if this gnawing question were not soon satisfactorily resolved. In fact, a substantial number of Northern businessmen were, to use a colloquial expression, going to great lengths to "keep the lid on" the slavery issue. And, although it is rarely noted, Sanford was very much a part of the Northern, particularly New York City, business community, as may be seen from the fact that he served on the board of three major railroads in the United States (the most prominent of which was the Illinois Central system) and two sizable financial institutions in New York City. The officers and directors of these and other Northern companies were no doubt well aware of what a fierce civil war would do to trade relations in many sections of the country, and may have counseled Sanford accordingly. Thus Sanford may well have been acting in the Dred Scott case as the representative of various Northern business interests, which were attempting to keep the long-simmering division over slavery from erupting into a bloody internecine conflict. But in the end all such efforts failed, partly because of the weak, if not inept, leadership of the much-troubled Buchanan administration.

Notes

1. For a survey of the work of historians, political scientists, sociologists, and economists in this general area, see the first part of the Introduction to Volume I of this study.

2. For an incisive discussion of these questions, see T. B. Bottomore, *Elites and Society* (Middlesex, England: Penguin Books, Ltd., 1964), *passim.*

3. Because of the immense difficulties involved in trying to ascertain in any precise manner the relative ability or expertise of those people chosen to hold high office over the years, the author has decided to eschew this obviously important matter. Another reason for skirting this subject is that skill or intelligence is often closely related to a person's socio-economic background. Similarly, the author does not intend to deal with the perplexing questions of ambition and personality, given the present inchoate state of research in these areas, and the fact that there is no way to apply these terms to officials in times past.

4. By major Cabinet officer, the author means all but the Postmaster General (the position was not accorded Cabinet status until 1829). With a few exceptions this study will not deal with members of Congress, partly because of the problem posed by the sheer weight of numbers, and also because they are elected on a state or district basis and not from any national pool of political aspirants. Nor will much attention be given to the nation's top

military leaders, for, aside from the early post–Civil War years, their importance was relatively minor. Another set of officials who will receive scant treatment are the top figures of the independent regulatory agencies because only two were created prior to the New Deal.

5. Because of the light it may shed on the distribution of politico-economic power at the time, due note is made of any figure who is known to have been formally offered, but chose not to accept, appointment to an important Cabinet, diplomatic, or judicial post, for in certain cases the actual occupant of this office was a second or third choice of the President and his chief advisors. The role of major party fundraisers and presidential campaign managers is also discussed to the extent that the data, often spotty, permit.

6. Although theoretically a person is elected to a board of directors (or trustees), the term *appointed* has generally been employed in this study because it more accurately describes this process.

7. The earliest (annually compiled) national business directory that contains much information on industrial corporations is *The Manual of Statistics,* which was published from 1878 to 1924. Unfortunately, prior to 1900, this volume did not provide very good coverage of the many manufacturing concerns in operation, so it is difficult to deal systematically with such enterprises in the late 19th century. Also, up to about this time bank directories rarely included the overall make-up of the boards of directors of such institutions, except in one series for selected large cities.

8. Since no widely accepted definition of the term *economic elite* has been established by American scholars, the author was forced to rely largely on his knowledge and experience in this area, and the rough scale he has employed is, of necessity, a relative one, pitched to fit the then-current level of economic development in the country. A person associated with a sizable financial institution or industrial firm in a major metropolitan center, such as Minneapolis or St. Paul, would, for example, be classified as a national economically elite figure, whereas a man who served on the board of the Stroudsburg National Bank or Scranton Trust Co. would not be so viewed. The determination of an official's personal or family wealth was a much more difficult matter. Here the author was compelled to rely on relevant statements found in various published sources—hardly an ideal approach, but the best possible under the circumstances. A breakdown of the occupational and elite (or non-elite) status of every major Cabinet and diplomatic official of each administration from 1861 to 1933 and every Supreme Court Justice appointed during this period is presented in the appendices found at the end of this volume.

9. See Beryl H. Levy, *Corporation Lawyer: Saint or Sinner?* (Philadelphia: Chilton 1961), p. 43.

10. Of course, a family may occasionally have what is known as a "black sheep," but such aberrations do not diminish the overall importance of family ties, particularly in elite circles.

11. In those cases where both political and economic considerations may have been involved, some understandable differences of opinion may arise as to their proper relative weighting, although these hopefully will be resolved by further study.

12. See the Association of the Bar of the City of New York, *Congress and the Public Trust* (New York: Atheneum, 1970), pp. 39–40.

13. See Edwin M. Epstein, *The Corporation in American Politics* (Englewood Cliffs, N.J.: Prentice-Hall, 1969), p. 35. As one scholar has recently observed, "it is much easier for businessmen, where required, to divest themselves of stocks and shares as a kind of *rite de passage* into government service than to divest themselves of a particular view of the world and the place of business in it." See Ralph Miliband, *The State in Capitalist Society* (New York: Basic Books, 1969), p. 59.

14. The major issues and events examined in this work do not, of course, constitute a representative sample of all important political actions (how could this be determined?), but

were selected simply to show through illustration that there may indeed be a connection between the socio-economic background of governmental leaders and their decisions made in office. Nor is it claimed that the treatment of issues and events represents an in-depth analysis of these topics. Space did not permit more than a brief summary, although most of the case studies are based on the work of a number of scholars. But, hopefully, enough evidence has been presented to make a persuasive case regarding these relationships, or at least spark other researchers to pursue these matters further.

15.   However, unlike the preceding presidents, Jackson also had an influential informal set of governmental advisors, which famous group has long been known as his Kitchen Cabinet. In contrast to his top federal officials, most, though not all, of these men were non-elite figures who held strong anti-Bank views, and thus provided a considerably different outlook in the Jackson administration.

16.   See Thomas C. Cochran and William Miller, *The Age of Enterprise* (New York: Macmillan, 1942), p. 87.

17.   See David M. Potter, *The Impending Crisis, 1848–1861* (New York: Harper & Row, 1976), pp. 145–76, especially 168–70.

18.   See Vincent C. Hopkins, *Dred Scott's Case* (New York: Fordham University Press, 1951), p. 179.

TECHNICAL COLLEGE OF THE LOWCOUNTRY
LEARNING RESOURCES CENTER
POST OFFICE BOX 1288
BEAUFORT, SOUTH CAROLINA 29901-1288

CHAPTER 2

The Civil War and Reconstruction Years

The period covered by the Civil War and Reconstruction years has usually been described as a great watershed in the nation's history. In fact, many authorities, following the lead of Charles and Mary Beard, have referred to it as "the Second American Revolution," for it certainly ushered in many sweeping changes in the political, economic, and social life of the United States.[1] Clearly the war represented a victory of the more urban and populous North over an essentially agrarian South. But a number of noted historians have also portrayed this era as one which, with the destruction of the powerful landed slaveholding interests of the South, marked the transition from a predominantly mercantile economy to industrial capitalism. As Louis Hacker, perhaps the primary exponent of this view, has declared, "industrial capitalism was now in control of the state" and, in effect, manipulated this governmental mechanism for its own ends—to be precise, for a higher protective tariff, major internal improvements, and favorable fiscal policies, including provision for a system of (privately-owned) national banks.[2] Some other writers have even gone so far as to argue that in the immediate postwar years influential Northern capitalists took full advantage of their newly acquired politico-economic position and thoroughly exploited the economic resources of a militarily prostrated South.[3]

While there is some truth to these assertions (at least with reference to the political influence of the South), there is also much that is false or misleading. For instance, these accounts generally give the impression that manufacturing concerns dominated the economic scene in America in the early postwar years. Such was simply not the case. Indeed, aside from a few atypical combines (the most conspicuous of which was probably the Standard Oil Co.), it was not until almost the turn of the century that big manufacturing firms came into being, either through mergers or sound enterpreneurial and managerial development. As late as the 1890s "most manufacturing establishments were organized either as partnerships or closely held corporations, and only a few had capitalizations in excess of

$5 million.''[4] In the early post–Civil War years a $10-million company was considered uncommonly large. When the Carnegie (Steel) Co. was first organized in 1872, it was only a $700,000 concern, and even when it was reorganized as a much-expanded enterprise in 1881, it was capitalized at just $5 million.[5] At the same time there were at least 41 railroads in the United States which, according to *Poor's Railroad Manual,* had a capital value of $15 million or more.[6] Thus, contrary to what many have been led to believe, big manufacturing firms did not suddenly emerge as a major force in American economic (and political) affairs in the early post-Civil War years.[7] Most of the large industrial concerns that did exist produced basic goods, primarily food and clothing, for a still largely agrarian nation.[8] Indeed, it was the vast railroad construction undertaken during this critical period which ultimately provided the vital transportation network necessary for the creation of broad regional and national markets and the shipment of key raw materials such as coal.

In short, these years were a time of tremendous railroad development. In the first post–Civil War decade alone, more than 40,000 miles were built in the United States, almost twice the amount of track laid down in the 1850s.[9] This expansion continued throughout the latter part of the 19th century, sweeping virtually all before it, including many thousands of unfortunate Indians who happened to stand in the way of powerful, and sometimes ruthless, railroad forces.[10] Hence it is with good reason that this entire era (1850–1900) is frequently referred to as the Railroad Age, for this industry so dominated the economic and political affairs of the nation that few enterprises, even when aggregated on a group basis, provided any kind of serious competition or possessed, to use John Kenneth Galbraith's phrase, much countervailing power.[11] So compelling was the railroads' pressure—and, many would add, the transportation needs of the time—that the first federal charter issued since the second Bank of the United States was created in 1816 was granted to the Union Pacific Railroad in 1862 for the purpose of building a major transcontinental line across the western part of the country.[12] To further stimulate railroad development, particularly in the Great Plains and Rocky Mountain areas, the federal government embarked on a much-expanded railroad land-grant program, through which well over 100,000,000 acres of land were given, under certain conditions, to various rail enterprises between 1862 and 1871, more than four times the amount of land allotted to such concerns in the 1850s.[13] Much of this was later sold to settlers (many of whom were brought or attracted to the West by railroad promotional efforts) at substantially marked-up prices.[14] Thus, with this kind of aid and entrepreneurship, railroading became a major enterprise in the United States in the post–Civil War years. Indeed, although many people have overlooked this development, the railroads soon emerged as America's first "big business."[15]

The funds for this massive expansion came from various sources. Much of the money was raised informally by close-knit groups of wealthy men in such Eastern cities as Boston, Philadelphia, and New York. One of the most famous of these was known as the "Forbes group," which set of influential, interrelated Brahmins dominated the affairs of the Chicago, Burlington and Quincy Railroad (and several other western lines) for many years.[16] Another important source of funds was the commercial banks in the United States, which, thanks to the passage of the National Banking Act of 1863 (which authorized federal charters), had grown considerably in number from about 1,600 in 1861 to well over 2,500 by the latter part of the 1870s.[17] Yet another vital mechanism for raising funds for railroad construction was provided by the much smaller set of private (primarily investment) banks in America. These often-overlooked firms played a key role by securing, mostly through the sale of securities, much of the capital needed for these vast undertakings, and also for sustaining the huge Union Army during the Civil War itself. For instance, Jay Cooke & Co. became famous through its work with the federal government during this bitter conflict, as a result of which its top official became known as "the financier of the Civil War." Other banks rose to positions of power and prominence in later years through their relations with various major railroads. Some of these ties took on an extremely close-knit character, such as those forged between the Atchison, Topeka & Sante Fe system and Kidder, Peabody & Co. (and to a lesser extent, the British banking house of Baring Brothers).[18] Thus by several means substantial funds were raised for railroad development in the postwar period.

Another important association established during this time of great economic growth was that linking the business community and the legal profession. Before the Civil War there were, of course, a number of lawyers who represented various business interests, but since most such concerns were fairly small, the amount of money derived from this kind of practice was, as a rule, relatively modest. For example, according to one reliable source, in the early years of the century, when Edmund Randolph was widely acknowledged to be the leading lawyer in the (then) wealthy state of Virginia, he was barely able to make a decent living from his legal practice.[19] And in the 1840s when Daniel Webster was at the peak of his powers and considered the foremost trial attorney in the country, he rarely managed to earn over $20,000 a year. Yet by 1873, with the tremendous growth in business enterprise, Massachusetts' Caleb Cushing, who was far from Webster's legal peer, was able to take in over $200,000 a year. So the Civil War decade apparently marked a turning point in the role of many American lawyers, from that of independent practitioner to highly paid legal aide and adviser to wealthy corporate interests, particularly major railroad enterpreneurs and executives.[20]

The emergence of these new forces also had an enormous effect on the overall operation of government and the general level of political morality in the postwar period. More than a few officials, tempted by the massive profits made either during the war by unscrupulous contractors or in later years by big railroad (or other) companies, were induced, for the proper consideration, to do the bidding of various powerful business figures. A substantial number of persons sought office, not with any thought of providing public service, but for pure partisan advantage or merely to enrich themselves.[21] Many historians have, in fact, referred to the latter part of this period as the start of a "gilded age" in which avaricious and immoral magnates ruled supreme. Certain other critics have, primarily in retrospect, described it in even hasher terms, as the age of the "robber barons" (a somewhat misleading term, for it tends to obscure the fact that most of the "robber barons" were railroad men).[22] But whatever the phrase, it is clear that the post–Civil War period was one in which wealthy railroad interests exercised a pervasive, and often corrupt, influence over governmental affairs in the United States.[23]

The Lincoln Administration

In the momentous presidential contest of 1860 the unheralded Abraham Lincoln won the Republican nomination over several prominent rivals, and then emerged as the victor in the bitterly fought general election over three other candidates, the most conspicuous of whom was his longtime political foe, Stephen A. Douglas.[24] Much has been written about Lincoln, almost all of it extolling him as an able and inspiring chief executive in time of grave national crisis. Most scholars agree with this judgment. But because he was caught up in the awful maelstrom known as the Civil War and exhibited great qualities of leadership in this searing struggle, many Americans are (erroneously) inclined to look upon Lincoln as a staunchly progressive figure who fought unceasingly to free the slaves. However, as various historians have pointed out, Lincoln was not really an abolitionist and probably won the Republican nomination and the general election only because he was viewed as a moderate, particularly on the slavery issue.[25] Judging from his professional activity, political record, and primary backers, Lincoln was also probably a conservative on economic matters. He was, for instance, regularly employed as one of the attorneys for the Illinois Central Railroad from its formative years in the early 1850s up to the time he was nominated as the Republican presidential candidate in 1860.[26] Indeed, although Lincoln had a variety of clients, he derived a good deal of his income from the Illinois Central, which was one of the five largest railroads in the United States, and had many friends and dedicated supporters among its high officials.[27] Thus it might be more accurate to view Lincoln as a railroad lawyer rather than as a "rail-splitter," his more popular image.[28]

Lincoln's chief campaign officials were also men who were clearly

linked with railroads and related entrepreneurial activities. One of this top
strategists was Chicago lawyer Norman B. Judd, the shrewd Illinois state
party chairman who spent many hours in the late 1850s promoting
Lincoln's candidacy, and then at the 1860 national convention formally
nominated Lincoln as the Republican standard-bearer.[29] Though comparatively little has been written about Judd, a look at some early business
directories reveals that he was intimately associated with various major
railways in the West. For example, in 1856 he served as president of the
Peoria and Bureau Valley Railroad, a 47-mile line which was closely
affiliated with the much larger Chicago and Rock Island Railroad.[30]
Moreover, up to the early 1860s Judd acted as an attorney for and director
of the Chicago and Rock Island Railroad, the Chicago and Milwaukee
Railroad, and the Mississippi and Missouri Railroad.[31]

Another key figure in Lincoln's well-planned pre-convention and presidential election campaign was his longtime friend, state court judge David
Davis.[32] Since Davis had served on the Illinois bench for over a decade,
he was not formally linked with any business enterprises during this
period. However, before donning the judicial robes, Davis had been
active in the promotion of one of the many east-west lines that fed into the
Illinois Central Railroad. Furthermore, in the early 1850s Davis had
bought, through friends, about 8,500 acres close to the main line of this
great transportation facility.[33] In addition, his Illinois cousin, Levi Davis,
served either as secretary or director of the Terre Haute, Alton and St.
Louis Railroad from at least 1856 through 1865.[34] Although this fact has
not been stressed by some historians, it was in considerable part through
the efforts of these two men that Lincoln won the Republican nomination
in 1860, after which, as a result of a split in the Democratic ranks, he
emerged as the victor in the general election.[35]

As his Secretary of State, Lincoln chose, largely for political reasons,
his former primary presidential rival, New York Senator William H.
Seward, who had long been recognized as one of the more militant
abolitionist leaders (his "radical" stance had probably cost him the
Republican nomination). Seward has generally been portrayed as an able
and ambitious man who, with the steady aid and advice of New York's
shrewd lobbyist-party boss, Thurlow Weed, devoted much of his life to
high public office, serving as governor of his home state from 1838 to 1842
and later (from 1849 to 1861) as a U.S. Senator. As to his legal or business
activities, Seward has been described by his biographer, G. G. Van
Deusen, as a man who, though he disliked the legal profession and its
many petty details, practiced law, except during his years as governor, up
to the early 1840s (and perhaps even later), when he became engrossed in
certain upstate real estate operations, particularly with the Holland Land
Co.[36] While it is true that Seward was on intimate terms with upstate New
York party boss Thurlow Weed, a politician with close ties to various
business interests, there was considerably more to Seward's role in
New York state affairs than has been revealed to date by either popular or

serious writers.[37] As Van Deusen and others have pointed out, although Seward had secured a good deal of money through inheritance and invested heavily in a number of railroad and real estate ventures, he still fell into substantial debt at times, from whence he was usually extricated by his longtime friend and New York City attorney, Richard M. Blatchford.[38] Indeed, in the early 1840s Blatchford, a wealthy lawyer with much experience in business matters, was virtually forced to take over the handling of Seward's financial affairs, and managed, with the help of Weed, to keep Seward economically afloat over the years only through the extension of sizable loans, some of which were made after Seward became Secretary of State.[39]

But the relationship between Seward and Blatchford was more than one of mere friendship and mutual political goals, for Blatchford was no ordinary attorney. Although Van Deusen, for one, has depicted Seward's law practice as of little or no importance in the post–Jacksonian era, the fact is that Seward, though an Auburn resident and lawyer, was a full-fledged partner of Richard M. Blatchford up to 1850 and continued in a less active, but still significant association with him up to late 1860.[40] Blatchford was probably one of the first great corporation lawyers in New York City (in the sense of acting primarily as an out-of-court business advisor), and represented such prominent concerns as the Bank of America (of New York City), the Bank of North America, Adams Express Co., Wells, Fargo & Co., and the Girard Trust Co. (of Philadelphia).[41] Moreover, Blatchford served as a director, and later high officer, of the New York Central Railroad from 1861 (either just before or after Seward's appointment as Secretary of State) to 1867, when the Vanderbilt interests took over control of the line.[42] Thus, while Seward may have been a militant or "radical" on the slavery issue, it would appear, in light of these associations, that he was a conservative on most economic matters.[43]

As his first Secretary of the Treasury, Lincoln chose another prominent Republican leader from the North who had been very active in the abolitionist movement, Salmon P. Chase, a Cincinnati lawyer. Chase, who was politically ambitious, had served as a United States Senator from 1849 to 1855 and then as governor of Ohio up to the early 1860s when he briefly returned to the Senate. Perhaps equally significant, Chase had long been involved in the anti-slavery crusade, to such an extent, in fact, that he was frequently referred to as "the attorney general for runaway slaves." Chase was able to devote so much time to this cause primarily because in the mid–1840s, after the death of his first two wives, he married the wealthy daughter of one of the founders and early major landholders of Cincinnati, which union provided a sufficient economic base for him to lend his time and talent to abolitionist affairs.[44] And it was largely in recognition of the widespread acclaim he achieved through these activities that President Lincoln felt compelled to appoint him to this key post.

Once in office, Chase quickly established an unusually close working relationship with the influential Jay Cooke, who had, by the start of the Civil War, become one of Philadelphia's leading financiers. The linkage was first forged some years earlier in Ohio, largely through Cooke's brother, Henry, who had served as the editor of the primary Republican newspaper in the state, the *Ohio State Journal,* which had long been a vigorous backer of Chase in his various political endeavors.[45] Because of great fiscal strain placed upon the federal government by the Civil War, this association soon ripened into one in which Jay Cooke & Co., a newly formed and perhaps maverick firm, became the principal investment banker for the Treasury Department, handling the sale of many of the government bond issues during this critical period.[46] Though subject to much criticism, particularly from firms which resented Cooke's favored position, this arrangement continued until the middle of 1864 when, following a long-simmering dispute with Lincoln, Chase resigned from office, thereby creating a breach in the Republican party ranks.[47]

As his successor, Lincoln selected a well-known Maine political leader and Portland lawyer, William P. Fessenden.[48] Fessenden had first served briefly as a Congressman in the early 1840s and then for a much longer period (1854–1864) as a U.S. Senator, during which years he had gained a reputation for being a rather outspoken and independent figure. Though perhaps not as closely linked to business interests as many other Cabinet officials in this period, Fessenden took a conservative stance on most financial matters, in part because of his strong socio-economic ties.[49] As Secretary of the Treasury, Fessenden did attempt, to his credit, to maintain a more distant and objective relationship with Philadelphia financier Jay Cooke than did his predecessor. However, Fessenden apparently did not find this high administrative office to his liking and resigned in March in 1865 to resume his role as a U.S. Senator from Maine.[50]

Lincoln's first Attorney General was another prominent Republican who had been a serious early contender for the presidential nomination in 1860, Edward Bates of Missouri. Like Lincoln, Bates was a former state legislator and judge who had served only briefly in Congress (back in the late 1820s), but who, as a lawyer, had managed to play an active part in Missouri politics over the years. This was probably due to the fact that he was closely affiliated, socially and professionally, with the wealthy business and landed interests of St. Louis. To be more precise, he represented primarily, according to his biographer, the banking and mercantile class of the city.[51] Toward the end of Lincoln's strife-ridden first term, Bates resigned from office, largely because of dissension within the Cabinet. At this point Lincoln turned to a lesser-known figure from Kentucky, Louisville lawyer James Speed.[52] Speed had only limited governmental experience (two brief stints in the state legislature), but his brother, Joshua, was one of Lincoln's closest friends. It should also be noted that James Speed served as a director of the Louisville and Nashville Railroad up to 1865, another possible indication that Lincoln preferred men of a conservative stripe on economic matters.[53]

Primarily because of a political agreement made during the presidential nominating proceedings, Lincoln selected Pennsylvania Republican boss Simon Cameron as his first Secretary of War. Cameron had served for a number of years in the United States Senate (originally as a Democrat), but by 1860 his strength lay chiefly in the firm grasp he had secured on state party affairs, which enabled him to control a sizable bloc of delegates at the national convention. Cameron was known to be a rather ruthless figure who was not averse to using his power to build up his interests as a central Pennsylvania businessman. His enterprises extended into many areas, the most conspicuous of which were banking and railroading. Indeed, by the mid or late 1850s he held a dominant position in three railroads—the Northern Central Railway, the Lebanon Valley Railroad, and the Susquehanna Railroad—and at least two banks in the Harrisburg area.[54] However, Cameron proved to be a distinct disappointment as head of a major Cabinet agency in time of war, and was gracefully eased out of office in December 1862 by the expedient action of appointing him American Minister to Russia, a post viewed by most knowledgeable people as a form of political exile. He was replaced by a much more able and dedicated man, Edwin M. Stanton, who had first demonstrated his fitness for high office in the middle and closing years of the (Democratic-controlled) Buchanan administration by serving initially as special counsel for the government in certain highly complex claims cases, and then in 1860–1861 as U.S. Attorney General. Stanton was a former Steubenville, Ohio and Pittsburgh lawyer who, though he still maintained the latter affiliation through a partnership, had devoted much of his time since 1856 to practicing in federal court in Washington, D.C.[55] In the mid-1850s Stanton had also married the daughter of a wealthy Pittsburgh merchant, Lewis Hutchison. But this family link was apparently of little or no importance in Stanton's appointment as Cameron's successor, for in time of major civil conflict the North could ill afford to have another inept executive in charge of the War Department.

As his Secretary of the Navy, Lincoln wanted very much to have a New Englander, for otherwise there would be no representation of this region in his Cabinet. After considerable deliberation and consultation, he finally chose a longtime Connecticut political leader, Gideon Welles, who, though he had never held a major governmental post, had taken a very active role in state and local politics. Welles was the son of a well-to-do Connecticut merchant who devoted much of his time in the pre–Civil War period to serving as an editor or high official of two Hartford newspapers. As one might expect given his wealth and background, Welles was a conservative on most economic issues, and, in fact, sat on the board of the Hartford National Bank from 1855 to 1860. Indeed, it would appear that Welles may have owed his appointment to the intervention and support of some important northeastern businessmen with whom he was on close terms. For instance, although his biographer makes no mention of the matter, his Cabinet selection was strongly backed by the influential chairman of the Republican National Committee, New York governor and wealthy entrepreneur Edwin D. Morgan, whose cousin and partner, George D. Morgan, was Welles's brother-in-law.[56] Thus it is possible that the politico-economic power of certain New York City interests was partially responsible for the appointment of New England's only representative in Lincoln's Cabinet.

As part of an informal agreement entered into at the Republican National Convention in Chicago, Lincoln selected as his first Secretary of the Interior, Caleb B. Smith, the man who had made the motion to second his presidential nomination and helped throw Indiana into Lincoln's column. Smith was a longtime Indiana political leader whose most recent federal posts had been as a Congressman (1843 to 1849) and as a Mexican claims commissioner (1849 to 1851). He had not, however, held any important governmental positions in the ten years preceding the Civil War. During this decade he practiced law in Cincinnati for three years (1851–1854) and then became president of the Cincinnati and Chicago Railroad, a position he filled until 1858, when this line fell into severe financial difficulty. Smith then returned to Indiana to resume his work as an attorney. As Secretary of the Interior, Smith proved to be a rather lazy and inept figure, who was often away from Washington for long periods. He was finally induced to resign in late 1862 through the offer of a federal judgeship.

As his successor, Lincoln chose another Indiana attorney, John P. Usher, who had already been acting for the better part of a year as Assistant Secretary of the Interior, in which capacity he had been forced to make a number of major decisions in the absence of the derelict Smith.[57] Usher had only limited governmental experience, having served briefly in the early 1850s as a state legislator and then in 1861–1862 as Indiana's attorney general, but he was a close personal friend and professional acquaintance of President Lincoln and some of his most intimate advisors. As a lawyer and part-time Washington lobbyist, Usher was also very much involved with various newly formed railroad enterprises in the West in the late 1850s (and perhaps even the early 1860s), chief of which was apparently the Leavenworth, Pawnee and Western Railroad in the hotly contested Kansas territory.[58] In addition, he had a substantial interest in the affairs of the Terre Haute and Richmond Railroad through his brother-in-law, Demas Deming, and his warm friend and former law partner, William D. Griswold, both of whom served on the board of this concern during all or part of this period.[59] Indeed, according to his biographers, the promoters of the first line, in particular, were extremely anxious to place one of their agents or allies in a high post in the Department of the Interior since this agency exercised important powers over railroad development in the United States.[60] And they certainly seem to have achieved their goal with the appointment of Usher, for he did much to aid the rail line, which, following certain financial difficulties, was temporarily renamed the Union Pacific Railroad–Eastern Division. His actions at Interior ranged from employing Union Pacific men to act as federal commissioners in negotiating with various Indian tribes about land along the railroad's right-of-way to providing military protection for railroad survey crews which were being harassed by Indian tribes along the Platte River.[61] If Usher's tenure as Secretary of the Interior did not constitute overt malfeasance in office, it at least vividly demonstrated the dangers involved in appointing a man with his economic interests to such a critical Cabinet post.

As American Minister to Great Britain (a key position during the Civil War years), Lincoln chose a distinguished Boston Brahmin, Charles Francis Adams, former President John Quincy Adams's son, who was generally considered a moderate anti-slavery spokesman, at least in comparison to such zealots as Massachusetts Congressman Charles Sumner. Adams was probably best known as an author and historian, for he had served only two years (1859–1861) in Congress, and much earlier for a five-year span as a state legislator. Interestingly, in 1860 he had been a strong backer of one of Lincoln's chief Republican opponents, William H. Seward, who worked hard to secure his appointment.[62] Unlike his famous father and grandfather, this patrician was well-fixed financially, having married a daughter of one of Boston's richest merchants, Peter Chardon Brooks, who served as a high official of the Massachusetts Hospital Life Insurance Co. and as a director of the Cabot Manufacturing Co. up to his death in 1848.[63] Also, shortly before his departure for Great Britain, Adams's son, John Quincy Adams II, married into the wealthy Crowninshield family, one member of which, Francis B. Crowninshield, was president of the Boston and Lowell Railroad and a director of the Old Colony Railroad (up to 1865) and the Suffolk Bank of Boston. With these kinds of connections, Adams was clearly the most elite figure to serve in this capacity since the early 1840s when his brother-in-law, Edward Everett, held this prestigious post.

Lincoln's Minister to France, William L. Dayton, was a well-known New Jersey lawyer who had held various important governmental posts over the years, the most recent of which were as a U.S. Senator (1842–1851) and as New Jersey's attorney general (1857–1861). He was a member of one of the apparently less affluent branches of the wealthy landholding, pro-mercantile Dayton family, but because of inadequate research his socio-economic status is still unclear. The same, however, cannot be said of Lincoln's Minister to Prussia (Germany), for this emissary was former Illinois Republican party chairman and Chicago lawyer Norman Judd, who was closely linked with a number of railroads in the West, particularly the Chicago and Rock Island. Judd would have preferred a Cabinet seat, but in jockeying for such a position encountered stiff opposition from Lincoln's best friend and long-trusted advisor, David Davis, another case of elite figures at odds in American politics.[64]

Though the Lincoln administration must be judged primarily in terms of its conduct of the war and handling of the slavery issue (in which areas it is usually given high ratings), it should also be pointed out that this regime did much to advance the cause of business enterprise in the United States, partly because of the exigencies of the war (and, some would add, the elimination of the agrarian opposition of the South) and partly because of the basically conservative nature of the government. For instance, it passed the Morrill Tariff Act of 1861, which raised import duties to their 1846 levels, and it continued to revise the tariff rates upward throughout war years, both to generate much-needed revenue for the Union Army and to protect Northern industry from foreign competition. In addition, despite considerable indifference and opposition in various financial circles, it enacted the National Bank Act of 1863, which, through the chartering of (privately-owned) national banks and the substitution of national bank notes for the many different kinds of script that had previously been used, made it much easier to carry on business affairs.[65]

Another major measure adopted during these trying times was that providing for the construction, with sizable cash and land-grant subsidies, of the long-debated transcontinental railroad, a venture which clearly was not essential to the conduct of the Civil War.[66] Indeed, to get some idea of the extent to which the Lincoln administration favored railroad development, especially in the West, one need only compare the magnitude of the land grants made to rail lines by the various presidential regimes which were in power during the critical third quarter of the century:[67]

Administration	Total Amount of Public Acreage Awarded to Railroads
Fillmore (1850–1853)	8,198,593
Pierce (1853–1857)	19,678,179
Buchanan (1857–1861)	—
Lincoln (1861–1865)	74,395,801
Johnson (1865–1869)	34,001,297
Grant (1869–1877)	19,231,121

Thus more land was given out by the Lincoln administration than any other three regimes combined, a perhaps not surprising finding when one considers that Lincoln was backed at the 1860 Republican National

Convention by major railroad forces in the West.[68] What's more, railroad influence can even be discerned in the appointment of the governmental directors selected by the administration to oversee the operations of the Union Pacific Railroad. For example, in 1865 three of the five governmental directors of this important line were associated, directly or indirectly, with other, presumably friendly, railroad interests.[69] Two of the governmental directors of the Union Pacific Railroad—Springer Harbaugh and Jesse Williams—were outside directors of the Pittsburgh, Fort Wayne and Chicago Railway, and another governmental director, Charles T. Sherman, had a brother, Ohio Senator John Sherman, who served in 1865 as a director of the Atlantic and Great Western Railway and the next year was elected to the board of the first-named Pittsburgh-to-Chicago line. Given this sort of selection, it was no wonder that relatively little effective federal supervision was exercised over the affairs of America's first transcontinental rail line, a fact later demonstrated in the Credit Mobilier scandal.[70]

The Andrew Johnson Administration

With Lincoln's assassination in April 1865, just one month after the start of his second term, a major change took place in American government, for this heinous act automatically made Andrew Johnson, a pro-Union Democratic leader from Tennessee, President of the United States. While Johnson and Lincoln had similar humble origins, there were significant differences between the two men, the most conspicuous of which related to their occupational and economic status. Johnson, who was a longtime Greeneville, Tennessee tailor, was clearly a plebeian figure, whereas Lincoln had, as a well-established lawyer, moved up into the elite ranks, primarily through his connections with the Illinois Central Railroad and other important interests in the West.[71] Despite his lack of social status, Johnson had held a number of prominent governmental posts over the years, such as U.S. Congressman (1843–1853), governor of Tennessee (1853–1857), U.S. Senator (1857–1862), and most recently, on a wartime emergency basis, military governor of Tennessee (1862–1865). He had been chosen as Lincoln's running mate in 1864 largely because he was an anti-slavery (and anti-secessionist) Democratic leader from a pivotal Border state, in a rather obvious effort to strengthen the pro-Union cause, without any thought that he would ever be thrust into the Presidency.

Finding himself in a delicate political position in time of grave national crisis, Johnson chose to retain as many of Lincoln's Cabinet officers as he could. One of these was Secretary of State William H. Seward, who had served quite effectively in this capacity under Lincoln and furthermore had a formidable base of political support in the New York Republican machine led by Albany lobbyist and party chieftain Thurlow Weed. As indicated earlier, Seward was also on intimate political and professional terms with his former law partner, New York City attorney Richard Blatchford, who had many ties with various prominent business interests, the most important and recent of which was as a director and high official of the New York Central Railroad from 1861 to 1867, when the emergent Vanderbilt forces assumed control of the company. In addition, during the Johnson administration one of Seward's sons (William H., Jr.) became involved with the organization and operation of a rail line in upstate New York, serving, from 1867 on, as treasurer of the Southern Central Railroad.[72] A year later he became one of the incorporators of the economically expansionist Isthmus Canal Co.[73] Thus, although Seward apparently avoided overt corporate connections himself, his pro-business orientation was probably revealed through the links maintained by various close friends and family members.[74]

Johnson's Secretary of the Treasury was another holdover from the preceding regime, although this official, Indiana's Huge McCulloch, was a very late Lincoln appointee. McCulloch was an able and experienced financial figure, who had served for about twenty years as the manager of the Fort Wayne branch of the State Bank of Indiana (a quasi-state institution designed to operate in many respects like a central bank), and then was made president of the parent concern, which post he held from 1856 to 1863. Because of his long record of conservative and sound business practice, he was appointed in the latter year as U.S. Comptroller of the Currency, from which position he later rose to Cabinet rank. Yet it should also be pointed out that McCulloch was a close friend of Philadelphia financier Jay Cooke, and they generally worked well together.[75] Moreover, shortly after McCulloch stepped down as a Cabinet officer in 1869, he agreed to become head of the London office that Cooke decided to establish at this time, another sign of a good working relationship.

Johnson's first Attorney General, James Speed, was another carryover from the latter part of the Lincoln administration. As previously noted, Speed was a former Louisville lawyer who had relatively little governmental experience (two terms in the Kentucky state legislature) before his appointment to the Cabinet in late 1864. Like a number of Lincoln supporters, he was associated with various business interests, the most important of which was his linkage as a director (up to some time in 1865) of the Louisville and Nashville Railroad. Speed, however, resigned from office in July of 1866 when President Johnson, in the midst of an increasingly bitter controversy with the Republican-controlled Congress, called inopportunely for the creation of a third party in American politics, an abortive move which simply produced more rancor and dissension. His replacement was an Ohio figure, Henry Stanbery, about whom, unfortunately, little is known other than the fact that he was a former Cincinnati (and Lancaster, Ohio) lawyer who had once served (from 1846 to 1853) as state attorney general.[76] Stanbery held this post until March of 1868 when he resigned, in time of grave constitutional and political crisis, to become chief counsel for the defense in the impeachment proceedings which had been initiated against the President by a vindictive Congress dominated by Radical (anti-slavery) forces. After the Senate, in a stormy session, fell one vote short of formally removing the President from office, the much-harassed Johnson appointed a new Attorney General, William M. Evarts, who, because of the illness of Henry Stanbery, had served ably as one of the primary defense attorneys in this unprecedented and highly partisan affair. Evarts, who was a close friend of Secretary of State William H. Seward, was a member of a prominent New York City law firm which dealt mainly with large corporate interests and wealthy clients, such as apparently the Astor family.[77] Thus one might surmise from Evarts's role in the late 1860s that certain major business forces were opposed to the spirited attempt by the Radical Republicans to unseat the President.

Though he would later rue the day, Johnson decided, upon taking office, to retain Edwin M. Stanton as his Secretary of War. Stanton was a former Washington (D. C.) and Pittsburgh lawyer with some recent wealthy family ties, who had served well under Lincoln during most of the critical Civil War years. However, in the rancorous Reconstruction era Stanton cast his lot increasingly with the Radical Republicans who were vehemently opposed to Johnson's conciliatory attitude toward the South, which they believed should be severely punished for its bloody secessionist action. Stanton's hostile reaction to Johnson's postwar reunification policy led ultimately to his suspension from office in August 1867 when he refused, with substantial support from Congress, to submit his resignation, as requested by a now thoroughly aroused President. As an interim successor, Johnson chose, in an effort to bolster his political position, the still enormously popular Civil War hero, General Ulysses S. Grant, who, after much inept leadership, had proved to be the dogged military commander needed to bring this terrible conflict to a successful end. By mutual agreement, Grant retained his position as the U.S. Army's commanding general after entering the Cabinet, a rare dual mixture of high military and civilian authority. But Stanton would not resign his departmental post. Indeed, in early 1868, buttressed by the Senate's refusal to approve his suspension from office, Stanton strongly urged Grant to give up his interim post, advice the pliable war hero readily followed, whereupon Johnson picked another lesser-known Army officer, Adjutant General Lorenzo Thomas, to act temporarily as Secretary of War. This strained state of affairs continued until the impeachment proceeding was resolved in the President's favor. Then, having finally secured Stanton's resignation from the federal government, Johnson, acting on the advice of his former defense counsel, William M. Evarts, selected another longtime Army officer, John M. Schofield, to serve as his Secretary of War for the remainder of the administration.

As his Secretary of the Navy, President Johnson decided, upon assuming office in 1865, to retain Connecticut's Gideon Welles, in keeping with his general practice regarding Cabinet officers. Welles was, as pointed out earlier, a former Hartford political leader and newspaper editor who had various prominent socio-economic ties, the most notable of which was his pre–Civil War (1855–1860) association as a director of the Hartford National Bank. He may also have partially owed his appointment at the outset of the Lincoln administration to the intercession and support of wealthy New York entrepreneur (and then Governor) Edwin D. Morgan, whose former business partner was Welles's brother-in-law. Over the years Welles proved to be an able and conscientious executive who, like Seward, could generally be relied upon by the President. Thus Welles was a loyal supporter of the much-troubled Johnson regime.

When Secretary of the Interior John P. Usher resigned under pressure in early 1865, he was replaced, pursuant to a move made by President Lincoln shortly before his death, by James Harlan, another man from the Midwest. Harlan was a longtime Iowa City (and Mount Pleasant) lawyer who had served in the U.S. Senate, both in the mid-1850s and the 1860s. Although not widely noted, he was closely associated with the powerful railroad-oriented wing of the Republican party in Iowa, known as the "Des Moines Regency," up to the late 1860s when he broke with this business-dominated group in a major electoral struggle and became a more progressive spokesman. Indeed, according to one source, Harlan had been a lobbyist for Thomas C. Durant, one of the organizers and high officials of the Union Pacific Railroad, and, as Secretary of the Interior, reportedly favored this line's construction plans over those of one or more rival routes.[78] But Harlan held office for only about a year and a quarter, for following the resignation of two other Cabinet members over Andrew Johnson's perhaps ill-conceived call for the creation of a centrist third party, he too decided to leave the administration because of his increasing disagreement with the President. He was succeeded in office by Orville H. Browning, a longtime Quincy, Illinois lawyer whose only major governmental experience was his brief service as a U.S. Senator in the early 1860s. In the pre–Civil War period he had been closely associated with at least one Illinois enterprise, the Northern Cross Railroad (a company headed by his law partner, Nehemiah Bushnell), a concern that was merged into the much larger Chicago, Burlington and Quincy system in 1857, after which time Browning's connection with the line becomes unclear.[79] Upon his departure from the Senate in 1863, Browning did not return to Illinois, but remained in Washington, where with several politically well-established figures he formed a new firm to engage in both the practice of law and extensive lobbying before various governmental agencies.[80] It was from this background, which smacked of influence-peddling, that Browning moved into the position of Secretary of the Interior, a post he held for the duration of the Johnson administration.[81]

As American Minister to Great Britain, Johnson decided to retain Boston Brahmin Charles F. Adams, who had served in this capacity throughout the trying Civil War years. As noted earlier, Adams was, unlike his father, a very wealthy man, having established the family's fortune by marrying a daughter of one of Boston's richest merchants, Peter C. Brooks. And his son, John Quincy Adams II, had married into the affluent Crowninshield clan, some of whose members had turned from mercantile pursuits to railroads and other business endeavors. Adams's links with the Boston business world became even more firmly secured in 1865 when his brother-in-law, Peter C. Brooks, Jr., was made a vice-president of the elitist Massachusetts Hospital Life Insurance Co. (he was elected president of this concern five years later). Adams held diplomatic office until May 1868 when, following the settlement of a number of complex, primarily war-related issues, he felt compelled to resign. As his successor, the President picked Reverdy Johnson (no kinsman), a longtime Baltimore lawyer who had served as Attorney General under Zachary Taylor and more recently (1863–1865) as a U.S. Senator from Maryland. Johnson was probably even more closely tied to the business community than his predecessor since he had been employed for almost forty years as counsel for the Baltimore and Ohio Railroad. Moreover, he had married into the politically and socially prominent Bowie family of Maryland, two members of which were associated (one as president) with the considerably smaller Baltimore and Potomac Railroad. Thus, except perhaps for textile and tariff matters, there would appear to have been little change in the economic nature of our diplomatic representation in London during the Johnson administration.

America's Minister to France during the first part of the Johnson regime was New York's John Bigelow, a former newspaperman (co-owner and editor of the *New York Post*) who had served as the U.S. Consul-General in that country from 1861 to 1865. Bigelow was appointed to this ambassadorial post primarily because of the substantial support and influence exerted in his behalf by his close friend and political ally, Secretary of State William H. Seward.[82] However, Bigelow soon became tired and disillusioned with his diplomatic position and resigned in late 1866. His replacement was former (1861) Secretary of the Treasury and onetime (1845–1853) U. S. Senator John A. Dix, another New Yorker who had devoted most of his time since the early 1850s to various legal and business interests, chief of which were railroads. For example, in the span of little more than a dozen years he served as president of the Chicago and Rock Island Railroad (in 1853–1854), president of the Mississippi and Missouri Railroad (from 1854 to at least 1859), and head of the Union Pacific Railroad (1863–1867). The selection of Dix would hence seem to indicate that neither President Johnson nor William Seward were hostile to railroad forces in the United States.[83]

Key Issue and Action of the Johnson Administration

The major conflict which beset the Johnson administration—the Radical Republicans' bitter opposition to the President's moderate or conciliatory Reconstruction policy toward the South—has until recently been characterized, in keeping with the Beards' view of the Civil War, as the climax of many years of economic rivalry between the industrial North and the agrarian South, as one in which the Radical leaders, acting as the agents of wealthy Yankee business interests, attempted to impose a reign of predatory capitalism on the prostrate South.[84] This line of analysis, which was given its most detailed and explicit treatment in Howard K. Beale's *The Critical Years,* has been repeated in many different ways over the years.[85] Yet a close look at the primary participants in this epic controversy shows that this interpretation of the early Reconstruction years is incorrect. Thaddeus Stevens, for example, is generally conceded to have been one of the most prominent and militant Radical leaders in Congress in the postwar period. However, despite the many efforts to depict him in other terms, Stevens was basically a small-town (Gettysburg, Pennsylvania) lawyer turned local businessman.[86] And while he had a couple of contacts with Thomas A. Scott of the Pennsylvania Railroad and a few ties with representatives of two other rail lines, these rather meager connections scarcely transformed Stevens into an agent or spokesman for major industrial interests.[87] Another key Radical figure was Massachusetts Congressman Charles Sumner. But although this man had been brought up in a Boston Brahmin social milieu, he did not have close ties to the city's powerful economic establishment in later life, in part because of his staunch abolitionist stand over the years. Indeed, he was reportedly shunned, if not ostracized, by many of the area's Cotton Whig merchants and industrialists.[88] Among Johnson's early Cabinet members, the most avowedly Radical official was probably Secretary of War Stanton, a man whose relations with the business world are still unclear (and need further study). As a matter of fact, of all the postwar Radical leaders in power during the Johnson years, only one or two could really be identified as persons with important economic links.[89]

What's more, many of the Cabinet officers who remained loyal, dedicated supporters of President Johnson throughout his troubled years were Republican leaders known to be on good, if not intimate, terms with various major segments of the Northern business community. For example, his Secretary of State, William H. Seward, who was once considered a Radical spokesman, never wavered in his allegiance to Johnson, most likely largely because of his longtime legal and political ties with wealthy corporation lawyer Richard M. Blatchford, who served as a director or high executive of the New York Central Railroad up to 1867. Another Johnson stalwart was Secretary of the Navy Gideon Welles, a business-oriented Connecticut figure whose brother-in-law, George D. Morgan, was a director of the Equitable Life Assurance Society and a former partner of New York business and Republican leader Edwin D. Morgan, who graced still other boards.[90] Johnson's second Secretary of the Interior, Orville H. Browning, and his Secretary of the Treasury, Hugh McCulloch, also had a close relationship with various railroad and banking interests. Furthermore, Johnson's chief defense counsel during his impeachment proceedings (and later Attorney General) was a well-known Wall Street lawyer, William M. Evarts, whose firm represented a number of important interests, including the Astor family.[91] And almost equally prominent in Johnson's defense was Boston lawyer (and former Supreme Court Justice) Benjamin R. Curtis, who had close links with that city's Brahmin business establishment, as evidenced by the fact that he served as a vice-president of the Massachusetts Hospital Life Insurance Co. both before and after his appointment to the High Court.[92]

Hence there would seem to have been a good deal of support for President Johnson in many Northern business circles.[93] As Robert Sharkey pointed out in his recent study of the Reconstruction period, most of the major mercantile and financial figures in New York were very much behind Andrew Johnson's overall political program, just as they backed the hard-money policies of his Secretary of the Treasury.[94] Professor Sharkey also claimed that the economic measures proposed by the Radicals were generally deemed to be detrimental to New York business interests. Many of the Radical leaders were, in fact, soft-money men and staunchly opposed to the Johnson administration's anti-inflationary fiscal program.[95] While some acquisitive Radical politicians or their unscrupulous allies may have been intent on extracting substantial economic benefits from the South during the Reconstruction period, as the Beards and other writers have alleged, most business leaders in the North merely wanted to reestablish normal trade relations with the lower half of the country and therefore threw their weight behind the more conciliatory policies of President Johnson, which were designed essentially to bind up the wounds of the nation. Thus it seems fair to say that while the Civil War may have ushered in a new era, and in this sense constituted a "Second American Revolution," the Republican party in the late 1860s and early 1870s was far from a monolithic body, faithfully carrying out the orders of its wealthy and highly cohesive capitalist masters. Instead, it was composed of a number of diverse, and sometimes rival, forces.[96]

The Grant Administration

Toward the end of the strife-ridden Johnson regime, the Republican party, sensing that a decisive electoral victory was within its grasp, managed to unite behind the acclaimed Civil War hero, Ulysses S. Grant, as its presidential candidate. Grant was obviously chosen for his name and popular appeal, for although few people know where he stood on major political or economic issues, he had become widely idolized throughout the North. However, Grant's qualifications for the Presidency were quite meager, for he had spent virtually his entire life, since graduating from West Point in 1843, as an officer in the United States Army, and therefore had little governmental, financial, or (non-military) administrative experience. But such shortcomings were of scant concern to Grant's principal political boosters, who may have cynically viewed his lack of knowledge and expertise as an asset. Grant, in fact, would appear to have been quietly groomed and promoted for this post, particularly in certain Northern business circles.[97] As the former commander of the Union Army in the latter stages of the Civil War, he also had the support of most Radical Republicans. In addition, thanks to his substantial financial backing, Grant had a sizable political warchest at his disposal, at least one far greater than the Democrats were able to amass.[98] With these assets, he was able to score a smashing victory over his Democratic opponent, former New York Governor Horatio Seymour, a compromise candidate put forward by the conservative, business-dominated Eastern wing of the Democratic party.[99]

Upon assuming the reins of executive leadership, President Grant, after making one brief, rather misleading interim appointment and one abortive overture, finally chose as his Secretary of State, New York City lawyer Hamilton Fish.[100] This patrician had held a number of major governmental posts in the course of his career, the most important of which were as governor of New York (1848–1850) and as a U.S. Senator (1851–1857). But by the time of his appointment, Fish had been out of politics for well over a decade. Hence it is quite possible that his selection stemmed largely from other considerations, such as his key social and economic links. Fish's mother was a member of the wealthy Stuyvesant family, and his father, up to his death, had been involved in both banking and railroad enterprises in New York state. Fish himself served as an officer or director, mostly the latter, of the New Jersey Railroad (or its successor parent company) from 1851 until at least 1872, the New York Life Insurance and Trust Co. from 1854 through 1877 (the last of his Cabinet years), and the Bank for Savings in the City of New York from 1860 to 1869.[101] Moreover, his brother-in-law, John Kean, sat on the board of the Central Railroad of New Jersey from 1874 through 1877.[102] And despite Fish's disclaimer that he would only serve for a short period of time, he held this key post throughout virtually all of Grant's eight years in office. Thus, although the Grant administration is commonly thought of as an era of the rapacious "spoilsmen," it would appear that the State Department was still primarily in the hands of sound, respectable business interests.[103]

Grant initially attempted to appoint a rich New York City merchant, Alexander T. Stewart, as his Secretary of the Treasury, partly as a reward for his big campaign contribution.[104] But this nomination ran into a wall of protest in the Congress, where certain important figures, who were allegedly annoyed because they hadn't been consulted in advance, maintained that a law, enacted back in 1789, prohibited anyone connected with trade or commerce from serving in such a capacity—a provision that could also have been applied (though no attempt was made to do so) to all financial figures.[105] As a result of this opposition, the President was soon forced to abandon Stewart's selection. Then, largely at the insistence of the vociferous Radical forces in Congress, Grant picked a well-known Massachusetts politician, George S. Boutwell, for this key post. Though Boutwell once had some trusteeship (or overseer) ties with Brahmin-controlled Harvard College in the mid-1850s, he was essentially a self-made man who had climbed up the political and legal ladder in his home state by dint of his own efforts. Although Boutwell does not appear to have been closely linked to any noteworthy business interests, he was not unfavorably viewed by economic leaders.[106] As a fairly independent and conservative figure, Boutwell served as Secretary of the Treasury until the end of Grant's first term of office, when, having come under increasing fire for his cautious and unimaginative policies, he decided to resign.

As his successor, Grant selected Boutwell's longtime friend and former (1869–1873) chief aide in the Treasury Department, William A. Richardson, who had served as a state judge in Massachusetts for thirteen years. Richardson did not have much experience in financial matters and was not, in fact, especially well regarded in some economic circles.[107] However, one reason for his elevation to Cabinet office may lie in the fact that Richardson had some significant ties to the Boston business community, for his brother (and former law partner), Daniel S. Richardson, had long served as president of the Vermont and Massachusetts Railroad (from at least 1865 through 1874) and as a director of the Boston and Lowell Railroad (from the late 1850s through 1874).[108] Yet Richardson did not prove to be a very successful Secretary of the Treasury, and resigned about a year after his appointment under a cloud of scandal, a not uncommon occurrence in the Grant administration.

At this point President Grant turned to a Southerner, Kentucky's Benjamin Bristow, who had built up a politically reformist record for ability and integrity in office that was perhaps unmatched in the early postwar period.[109] Bristow was originally a small-town (Elkston and Hopkinsville) Kentucky lawyer who had remained loyal to the North and shortly after the Civil War had been appointed, thanks partly to his old friend and fishing companion Attorney General James Speed, U.S. Attorney for the district of Kentucky.[110] After four years of meritorious work in this capacity, he was appointed U.S. Solicitor General, a post he held until almost the end of Grant's first term in office, when he resigned to return to the more remunerative practice of law. However, at the suggestion of Iowa railroad entrepreneur Grenville M. Dodge, Bristow was soon asked to become president of the newly formed California and Texas Construction Co. by the head of its parent company (the Texas and Pacific Railway), the able and ambitious Thomas A. Scott, who was also the chief executive of the Pennsylvania Railroad. Scott was then engaged in a frantic effort to expand his operations across the country in the face of vigorous opposition on the part of Collis P. Huntington, the prime mover behind the Central and Southern Pacific lines. Within a year Bristow tired of this post and returned to Louisville, where he quickly became counsel to a number of railroad enterprises.[111] Thus when Bristow was asked in mid-1874 to take over as Secretary of the Treasury, he had a background marked by an unusual mixture of political reform and railroad-oriented activity.[112] Bristow served for two years in this important capacity, and during his tenure he won considerable support and praise as a dedicated public servant and possible presidential candidate. But when in June 1876 he failed to obtain the Republican party nomination for this high office, despite the backing of many reformers, he abruptly resigned from the Cabinet in bitter disappointment.

Bristow was succeeded for the remaining nine months of the Grant administration by Lot M. Morrill, an Augusta, Maine lawyer and longtime political leader who had held a seat in the United States Senate since the start of the Civil War. Although he was from a primarily agrarian state, Morrill was quite acceptable to most financial interests in the country, largely because of his conservative views and associations. For instance, he had been a member of the board of the Somerset and Kennebec Railroad in the mid–1850s, and his brother, Anson P. Morrill, had been a director of the Androscoggin and Kennebec Railroad before the Civil War and had later become a high official of the Maine Central Railroad (he was also the owner of a big woolen mill in the state). In addition, his former law partners, James W. Bradbury and Richard D. Rice, had been involved at different times with various major railroads. In fact, Rice, though merely an Augusta lawyer, had served first as a director (in the late 1860s) and then as vice-president (up to the mid–1870s) of the Northern Pacific Railroad, a recently created giant enterprise financed largely by northeastern capitalists that extended from Lake Superior to the Puget Sound.[113] Thus business interests probably had good reason to have considerable confidence in Lot M. Morrill as Secretary of the Treasury.

As his first Attorney General, Grant made an unusual choice, the distinguished Massachusetts lawyer and jurist Ebenezer Hoar, who, unlike many well-established figures, had been a staunch abolitionist leader in the pre–Civil War period. Moreover, in contrast to the usual pattern, Hoar had devoted the bulk of his career (sixteen out of the previous twenty years) to the state judiciary.[114] Yet Hoar had certain elitist links, for he served as a fellow of Harvard College from 1857 to 1868, and thereafter as president of the board of overseers of this prestigious institution. In addition, he was a close relative and frequent correspondent of his departmental predecessor, Wall Street lawyer William M. Evarts, a man with many business connections.[115] Hoar only held this post for a little over a year when, because of the increasing bitter opposition of the fiery Ben Butler (a non-elite figure) and other Radical leaders, he was suddenly dismissed from office.

He was replaced, in an obvious political maneuver, by a long time Georgia lawyer and, surprisingly, former Confederate Army officer, Amos T. Akerman, a rather minor figure with very limited (1869–1870) experience as a governmental official. Akerman was chosen primarily because President Grant needed substantial Southern backing for his controversial Santo Domingo treaty, which was then pending in the Senate, and spokesmen for this region demanded some sort of Cabinet recognition in return for their support. Akerman remained in office for only about a year and a half because he managed to antagonize certain powerful Western railroad interests by submitting a report to the Secretary of the Interior that disallowed some of their dubious land-grant title claims. Infuriated by this ruling, a number of major railroad magnates, led by Jay Gould and Collis P. Huntington, launched a massive assault on Akerman, which finally resulted in his removal from office in June 1872.[116]

He was succeeded by George H. Williams, a Portland, Oregon lawyer, who had held a seat in the United States Senate from 1865 to 1871. Williams also had a substantial amount of judicial experience, having served as chief justice of the Oregon territory from 1853 to 1857, and before that as an Iowa judge. But a more likely reason for his selection was that the Pacific Coast area had been demanding Cabinet recognition for some years, and the choice of Williams relieved this pressure. Another important set of economic considerations was that Williams was reported to be on friendly terms with railroad forces in the Far West and that he was the attorney for the Alaska Improvement Co., a concern in which Grant was a stockholder himself.[117] Williams acted as Attorney General for well over three years, during which period the Grant administration was rocked by one scandal after another. All these revelations finally took their toll, for Williams stepped down from office in April 1875.

As his successor, the President chose Edwards Pierrepont, a New York City lawyer who had relatively limited governmental experience, having served briefly (1869–1870) as U.S. Attorney for the southern district of New York and for a somewhat longer period in the pre–Civil War era as a New York City judge. But Pierrepont's primary support for this post may have come from another source, for he had at least one major link with the business community; he had served in the early 1870s as an officer and director of the newly formed Texas and Pacific Railway, a concern headed by Thomas A. Scott of the Pennsylvania Railroad, which wanted very much to expand its operations across the continent.[118] Pierrepont acted as Attorney General for only about a year when, in the spring of 1876, he was suddenly called upon, because of another scandal in the administration, to take over as American Minister to Great Britain.

At this point, Grant asked his recently appointed Secretary of War, Alphonso Taft, to assume the duties of Attorney General. Taft was a longtime Cincinnati lawyer who had served for seven years as a municipal judge in the early postwar period. Yet he, too, had significant socio-economic ties, for he sat on the board of the Little Miami Railroad from at least 1856 to 1868, and before the Civil War had been a director of the Cincinnati and Hillsboro Railroad and the Marietta and Cincinnati Railroad.[119] Thus Alphonso Taft, who was the founder of the famous Taft political dynasty, was, like many postwar Cabinet officials, closely linked with railroad interests.

As his first Secretary of War, Grant picked, after some equivocation, his close friend and chief military aide during the Civil War, James A. Rawlins. Initially apparently, the President did not plan to appoint Rawlins to this post because he was in poor health, but when pressured by Rawlins and his avid supporter, former Civil War general and railroad entrepreneur Grenville M. Dodge, Grant readily agreed to give Rawlins this important office.[120] Rawlins, however, had tuberculosis and died about six months after taking this job. President Grant then persuaded one of the Civil War's most famous officers, General William T. Sherman, to assume the reins of departmental leadership while he searched for a more permanent successor.[121] This person turned out to be a relatively minor Civil War figure and prewar Keokuk, Iowa lawyer named William W. Belknap, whose only recent governmental experience had been as U.S. Collector of Internal Revenue for the state of Iowa, hardly an impressive post. Belknap, who soon became part of Grant's coterie of unsavory political associates, remained in office for over six years, during which time his department was beset by a series of scandals, some of which involved Belknap himself. When these revelations finally came to light in early 1876, this corrupt and mediocre official quickly resigned from office in an attempt to avoid impeachment proceedings. He was replaced by the aforementioned Alphonso Taft, the former Cincinnati judge and lawyer, who had been closely affiliated, up to recently, with a number of railroad enterprises in the southern part of Ohio.[122] Taft served in this capacity for only a few months when he was suddenly asked to take over for Attorney General Edwards Pierrepont, who had agreed to replace another diplomatic official who had resigned under a cloud of scandal. In his selection of Taft's successor, Grant again succumbed to dubious political pressure by appointing Pennsylvania's J. Donald Cameron. This man had never held any kind of public office and was chosen largely because he was the son of state party boss and U.S. Senator Simon Cameron, a rather unscrupulous figure in his own right. The younger Cameron had acted as the manager of his father's many business interests, the most important of which roles were as president (up to 1874) of the Northern Central

Railway—a line closely linked with, if not controlled by, the Pennsylvania Railroad—and as a director of both the Wilmington and Weldon Railroad (from 1870 to 1875) and the Wilmington, Columbia, and Augusta Railroad (from 1869 through 1877).[123] Thus although Grant's initial appointments to this Cabinet post were basically military or political figures, his later selections were men who had major economic ties.

As his first Secretary of the Navy, President Grant picked another person who had never previously held public office, Philadelphia merchant and entrepreneur Adolph E. Borie. Like some of Grant's other Cabinet nominees, Borie had been a substantial contributor to the General's 1868 electoral campaign, which political largess he could well afford. In addition to running his large dry goods business, he had served as president of Philadelphia's prestigious Bank of Commerce from 1848 to 1860 (and thereafter as a director), and in the postwar years he was a director of the Philadelphia Savings Fund Society and the Philadelphia and Reading Railroad.[124] But Borie, who reportedly had been reluctant to accept the post, soon discovered that he was ill-suited for such work and resigned within a matter of months.

After offering this position to two other rather obscure Philadelphia figures, Grant finally succeeded in getting a New Jersey lawyer, George M. Robeson, to take over as Secretary of the Navy.[125] Unlike Borie and Cameron, Robeson had some prior governmental experience, the most notable and recent of which was as state attorney general (1867–1869). Of even more importance perhaps was the fact that he had served since 1867 as a director of the Belvidere Delaware Railroad, a New Jersey concern apparently run by the same potent interests (the Stockton and Stevens families) which controlled the Camden and Amboy Railroad and various other lines in the state.[126] Though not an especially able executive, Robeson managed to hold this post for the duration of the administration, no mean feat considering the high turnover and turbulent nature of the ill-starred Grant regime.

As his Secretary of the Interior, Grant selected a highly regarded Ohio lawyer and political leader, John D. Cox. This comparatively young man, who apparently had no major socio-economic ties, had established a notable record first as a Civil War officer and then as governor of Ohio (1866–1868), in which latter capacity he showed himself to be a staunch foe of the party spoilsmen. Indeed it was over this issue that the strong-willed Cox soon clashed with the President, who, as a friend of many unsavory politicians, was quite indifferent, if not hostile, to the need for civil service reform, which conflict led in late 1870 to Cox's angry resignation from the Cabinet.

As his successor, Grant picked another Ohio figure who had a very different background, Columbus Delano. This onetime (1831–1850) Mt. Vernon, Ohio lawyer had held a seat in Congress on two separate occasions (1847–1849 and 1865–1869). In the first half of the pre–Civil War decade he had also been a partner in a (probably small) New York City banking firm known as Delano, Dunlevy & Co., and in the mid-1850s he had sat on the board of the Springfield, Mt. Vernon and Pittsburgh Railroad. More recent evidence of Delano's pro-business allegiance may be found in the fact that both the Secretary of the Interior and his son, John, served, from 1873 through 1875, as directors of the Western and Atlantic Railroad, a (Georgia) state-owned facility operated under a special lease arrangement by various private interests, one of which groups had placed Delano and his son on the board as a means of strengthening its political position.[127] Apparently undisturbed by this conflict of interest, Delano held on to his Cabinet post until the fall of 1875 when, in the wake of some disturbing charges involving influence-peddling on the part of his son, he finally resigned.[128]

At this rather late date in the administration, Delano was succeeded as Secretary of the Interior by another wealthy Republican stalwart, Zachariah Chandler, a former Detroit businessman and longtime (1857–1875) U.S. Senator. Chandler had amassed a considerable fortune fairly early in life through a profitable dry goods trade and various other endeavors, the most prominent of which were banking and real estate.[129] Thereafter, he devoted much of his time to governmental affairs, although he continued to maintain frequent contact or close ties with a number of important figures in the business world, such as Jay Gould.[130] Though not a railroad man, Chandler would thus seem to have been a Cabinet official who was acceptable to both major political and economic forces in the country.

Apparently at the urging of Massachusetts Congressman Charles Sumner, President Grant picked a well-known Boston historian, John L. Motley, to act as American Minister to Great Britain. Motley had very little governmental or diplomatic experience, although he had written extensively on various European countries. Like many of his predecessors, he was a wealthy patrician with numerous family ties to Boston's economic and political establishment. His father, for example, had been a prominent merchant who had served first as a director (1823–1853) and then as a vice-president (1854–1860) of the Brahmin-dominated Massachusetts Hospital Life Insurance Co.[131] Furthermore, his niece had married the son of the (now deceased) textile magnate Abbott Lawrence, who had held this prestigious diplomatic post himself some years earlier. Thus Motley was merely another in a long line of elite Boston figures to represent the United States at the Court of St. James. However, the haughty Motley frequently refused to follow instructions from the State Department and often treated people in a rather cavalier fashion, so that within a short period he was summarily removed from office.

After a prolonged search, Grant selected a longtime Ohio lawyer and Congressman, Robert C. Schenck, to serve as Motley's successor.[132] Schenck had some diplomatic experience in the early 1850s, but the bulk of his time over the years had been devoted to domestic matters.[133] He was, moreover, a man who often displayed a marked interest in various business enterprises. For instance, in the mid-1850s he had been a vice-president of an apparently abortive major railroad venture known as the American Central Railway.[134] Indeed, shortly before he was offered this diplomatic post, Schenck had, as a "lame duck" Congressman, accepted a position on the legal staff of the Northern Pacific Railroad, a concern then largely financed, and probably indirectly dominated, by Jay Cooke. Upon consulting Cooke's brother and receiving assurances that the job would be held open for him pending his return from Great Britain, Schenck agreed to assume the position.[135] Schenck served as emissary for almost five years when some belated revelations about his involvement in an unethical stock market venture led to his abrupt removal from office.[136] Upset by this experience, President Grant picked a more financially established figure, former Attorney General and New York lawyer Edwards Pierrepont, to take over as American Minister to Great Britain for the duration of the administration. A wealthy patrician, Pierrepont had little need to engage in dubious economic activity, although he was as closely linked with railroad interests as many other high governmental officials in the postwar period.

As American Minister to France, Grant picked a former Galena, Illinois lawyer and U.S. Congressman, Elihu B. Washburne, who had no prior diplomatic experience, but had been a close personal friend and political supporter of both Lincoln and President Grant (a Galena neighbor), and who had a wealthy wife of French descent. Through his wife (the former Adele Gratiot), Washburne was related to the rich and influential Chouteau family of St. Louis, one member of which sat on the board of the Illinois Central Railroad in the late 1850s (he succeeded kinsman John F. A. Sanford, who died right after the Dred Scott decision), and another served as a director of the Syracuse, Binghamton and New York Railroad in the mid- and late-1860s.[137] Perhaps even more important, Washburne was a member of an unusual family that was quite active in the political and economic affairs of the north central section of the country. Two of his brothers (who dropped the "e" from their last name) were millionaires in their own right, with major holdings in timberlands, flour mills, and railroad development. Both brothers, Cadwallader C. and William D. Washburn, had been high officials of the Minneapolis Mill Co., which they had organized back in 1856.[138] In addition, William D. Washburn served as a director of the Minnesota Valley Railroad in the mid-1860s and the Lake Superior and Mississippi Railroad in the early 1870s, as president of the Minneapolis and Duluth Railroad in the early 1870s, and as first vice-president (1870–1875) and then president of the Minneapolis and St. Louis Railroad (the last three of these lines were interlinked). Thus, although many accounts treat Elihu Washburne as essentially a political figure, it is clear that he had considerable wealth and many key socio-economic ties which helped to ease any financial burden he may have incurred during his eight years of service as American Minister to France.[139]

In summary, the Grant administration seems to have been run by a mixture of able and incompetent (or unscrupulous) people. Some were former Civil War associates of the President who had no elite links; however, many others were pro-business figures with whom the President had originally little or no acquaintance. Most major Cabinet and diplomatic posts were, moreover, marked by a high rate of turnover, for because of the ignorance or ineptitude of the President, the administration was in an almost constant state of turmoil.[140] But amidst all the confusion and corruption of the Grant administration, one thing is abundantly clear— namely, that the key posts in the federal government were being taken over increasingly by men closely aligned with the emergent economic forces of the country, chief of which were the powerful railroad interests.

Supreme Court Appointments and Actions

The Supreme Court was also subjected during this period to a great deal of railroad influence, primarily through the recruitment process. At the outset of this stormy era, the Chief Justice was a longtime occupant of this office, Maryland Democrat Roger B. Taney, who had been elevated to this post by Andrew Jackson back in 1836. Before he became a member of Jackson's Cabinet, the wealthy Taney had been a director of several banks in Maryland and had served briefly as senior counsel for the Baltimore and Ohio Railroad. After presiding over the High Court for many troubled years, Taney died in October of 1864, presenting President Lincoln with an opportunity to pick a Chief Justice more to his liking. After some hesitation, Lincoln finally decided upon his former Secretary of the Treasury, Salmon P. Chase, a well-known abolitionist leader and onetime Cincinnati lawyer who had both considerable ability and strong political backing, particularly in Radical circles. Chase had some prominent socio-economic ties preceding his appointment to the Supreme Court, most notably with Philadelphia financier Jay Cooke, and he formed still more shortly before his elevation to this key post through the marriage of his daughter, Kate, to Rhode Island Senator and wealthy businessman William Sprague, whose economic fortune, built largely on textiles, was reputed to be close to $25 million.[141] Indeed, by 1869 Sprague's textile empire was reported to employ about 10,000 workers, an enormous total for that time.[142] The Sprague interests also extended into the realm of railroads, for William Sprague served in the late 1860s as a director of the New Orleans, Mobile and Chattanooga Railroad, and his brother, Amasa, was elected to the board of the newly formed Kansas Central Railroad in the early 1870s.[143] Apparently, Chase himself never severed his informal close links with Jay Cooke, and as time progressed, he became increasingly interested in various large railroad enterprises, even to the point of angling for the presidency of such mammoth concerns as the Union Pacific Railroad and later the Central Pacific Railroad (for some reason, he believed he could hold these positions without resigning from the Supreme Court).[144] Thus, while a Supreme Court Justice, Chase was clearly a pro-corporate figure.

Chase died in 1873, after serving only nine years as Chief Justice, a short stint compared to his 19th century predecessors. In typically fumbling fashion, President Grant offered this key post to a number of persons before he finally came up with one who could gain Senate approval and was willing to assume the office (some extremely ambitious people had still higher goals).[145] This man was Morrison R. Waite, a longtime Toledo, Ohio lawyer, who had very little governmental experience, but who had won considerable acclaim for his work as one of the American representatives during the recent British-American claims negotiations in Geneva. Waite had devoted most of his adult life to private law practice. Many of his clients were wealthy corporate interests, a fact that has led some observers, such as Gustavus Myers and Fred Rodell, to describe him as a "railroad" lawyer or "big business" attorney, a charge which other authorities view as misleading or unfair.[146] Yet a look at the record shows that Myers and Rodell were closer to the truth than many are willing to admit, since Waite served as a director of the Toledo Gas Light and Coke Co. from 1854 to 1874, the Toledo National Bank (and its economic predecessor) from apparently 1855 to 1874, and as a board member of the Toledo Street Railway Co. for an indeterminate period starting in the early 1860s.[147] Furthermore, Waite represented at various times the Cleveland and Toledo Railroad, the Michigan Southern and Northern Indiana Railroad, and the Lake Shore Railway, and he also served from 1868 to 1874 as a director and vice-president of the Dayton and Michigan Railroad.[148] In addition, Waite's close friend and former law partner, Samuel M. Young, was a member of the board of directors of the Cleveland and Toledo Railroad up to 1869, and later (starting in 1874) became a director of the Columbus and Toledo Railroad. Since Waite served as a vice-president, rather than just an outside director, of a major rail line for a significant number of years before his appointment as Chief Justice, it does not seem unfair to describe him as a longtime railroad and corporate lawyer.

When Lincoln assumed the reins of presidential leadership, the Supreme Court was still dominated by pro-slavery interests (albeit by a narrow margin). It was composed of Chief Justice Taney and four Southern jurists—John Catron, James Wayne, Peter Daniel, and John Campbell (mostly wealthy planter-business figures)—and four Northern jurists—John McLean, Samuel Nelson, Robert Grier, and Nathan Clifford (the last-named was a fairly recent appointee with major socio-economic ties, particularly to railroads).[149] But because of death or resignation, there were three Court vacancies to be filled in the early 1860s.

Lincoln's first selection was Noah Swayne, a longtime Columbus, Ohio lawyer, whose only previous governmental experience had been as U.S. attorney for the district of Ohio back in the 1830s. Swayne reportedly had excellent ties with the business and financial world, whose support of the Northern war effort was considered essential at this point by President Lincoln.[150] Swayne, in fact, went to substantial lengths to secure the backing of important figures in economic circles, such as New York corporate attorney Samuel J. Tilden and Western railroad executive William B. Ogden, president of the Chicago and Northwestern Railroad, who had known Swayne for about 25 years.[151] Indeed, as John Schmidhauser has put it, "the strong intervention by the President of the Chicago and Northwestern Railroad . . . with the Lincoln administration in behalf of Noah Swayne coincided with the rapid growth of corporate influence at all levels of government in the Civil War and post-Civil War era."[152] Swayne's main economic supporters were not to be disappointed, for, according to two authorities, he soon emerged ". . . as their grand champion in the face of popular protest against railroading and its financing."[153]

Lincoln's second selection, made to fill the vacancy created by the death of Virginia's Peter Daniel, was a very different sort of man, since he apparently had no significant socio-economic ties and was the first justice to be appointed from a state west of the Mississippi River. This man, Keokuk, Iowa attorney Samuel F. Miller, was generally considered to be the most able lawyer in this part of the country at the time of his elevation to the Supreme Court, a factor that had to rank high in Lincoln's calculations, even though Miller had never held any major judicial or governmental office.[154] Unlike many other jurists in the post–Civil War period, Miller had a deep humanitarian instinct (he was strongly opposed to capital punishment) and had an open, if not even skeptical, attitude toward corporate and financial interests.[155] Not surprisingly, in his many later years on the Court Miller tried vigorously to block the development of the due process clause of the Fourteenth Amendment as a protective device for the business community—an ultimately futile effort given the pro-corporate pattern of appointments to this tribunal in the postwar era.[156] Because of his stand on this and other issues, Leo Pfeffer has described Miller as a "poor man's John Marshall."[157]

Lincoln's third nominee to the Supreme Court was another Midwesterner, former Illinois judge and attorney David Davis, whose selection (following that of Miller) as a replacement for Alabama's John A. Campbell marked an irreversible shift in the distribution of power in this important body away from the agrarian South. Davis was an extremely close friend of Lincoln and had served as one of his chief political strategists in his quest for the Presidency. As another major point in his favor, Davis had presided for fourteen years as an Illinois state judge, in which post he had established a sound record. He had also been a Bloomington (Illinois) lawyer and a substantial real estate speculator over the years, at one time purchasing, through friends, approximately 8,500 acres along the right-of-way of the Illinois Central Railroad.[158] In addition, he had a cousin, Levi Davis, who was closely linked with a major enterprise in the state, the St. Louis, Alton and Terre Haute Railroad, of which he served as an officer or director from at least 1856 through 1877. Because of his background, Justice Davis apparently took a fairly conservative position on most major economic issues, although he proved to be a staunch defender of civil liberties on the high Court in the postwar period.

The last appointment Lincoln made to the Supreme Court was that of Stephen J. Field, a former New York City lawyer who in 1849 had moved to California where he embarked on a mercurial career as an attorney, a real estate speculator, and (starting in 1857) a judge of the state supreme court. Field's elevation to this newly created seat on the U.S. Supreme Court came about partly for legal and geographic reasons (he was reportedly the ablest jurist in the Far West). Furthermore, he was strongly backed by California governor and Central Pacific Railroad executive Leland Stanford, who was a close friend of Field and, perhaps equally important, an acquaintance of President Lincoln, whom he implored to make this appointment.[159] Lincoln was also urged to place Field on the Supreme Court by his older brother, New York City lawyer David Dudley Field, who had warmly supported Lincoln's candidacy in 1860, and who represented many wealthy business figures in the East, including, later in the decade, the notorious Jay Gould.[160] In light of these links, it is not surprising that Field was a zealous defender of private property and corporate interests during his nearly 35 years on the High Court.[161]

The next major judicial appointment was not made until early 1870 when President Grant, within a space of about thirty days, elevated two Easterners to the Supreme Court, both of whom were widely regarded as pro-railroad men. The first of these jurists was Pennsylvania's William Strong, a former Reading (1832–1857) and Philadelphia (1868–1870) lawyer who had served for over a decade (1857–1868) as a judge of the state supreme court and at one time (1847–1851) as a Congressman.[162] Strong also had some notable economic ties, the most important of which were (up to presumably 1857) as a director of the Lebanon Valley Railroad and as one of the two attorneys for the Philadelphia and Reading Railroad.[163] The second selection was that of Newark, New Jersey lawyer Joseph P. Bradley, who had no judicial experience (though his father-in-law was a former state supreme court justice), but did have a great deal of support from such pro-corporate figures as Secretary of State Hamilton Fish, Secretary of the Navy George Robeson, New Jersey Senator John Stockton, and former Senator Frederick T. Frelinghuysen.[164] Bradley was, in fact, more closely linked to the business community than many of his colleagues on the High Court, for he served as president of the New Jersey Mutual Life Insurance Co. (in the late 1860s), as a board member of the Second National Bank of Newark from the mid-1860s through 1876, and as a director of the Morris and Essex Railroad and the Camden and Amboy Railroad from at least 1865 to 1870 (his legal tie with the latter line is reported to have extended back over a much longer period, more than twenty years).[165] Thus Bradley was clearly on intimate terms with various powerful corporate and railroad interests prior to his appointment to the U.S. Supreme Court.

The last man placed on this high tribunal during the Reconstruction period was a rather obscure figure named Ward Hunt. Since 1865 he had served as a New York state judge, and before that as a Utica lawyer, but in neither of these capacities had he compiled a very impressive record. He had, however, established some noteworthy economic ties, having served as a director of the Mohawk Valley Railroad briefly in the early 1850s, and considerably later (in 1868–1872) as a board member of the Schenectady and Utica Railroad (a medium-sized line which was apparently never completed).[166] But, according to most reliable accounts, Hunt was selected primarily because he was a longtime friend and political lieutenant of New York's imperious Republican boss, Roscoe Conkling.[167] In short, Hunt was not an especially strong or able person, and his contribution to the Court was reduced even more by the fact that he suffered from ill health much of the time he was on the bench.

During this period the Supreme Court made a number of major decisions, some of which revealed a great deal about American politico-economic relations. Among the most important were the so-called legal tender cases.[168] In the first of these (*Hepburn v. Griswold*) the Supreme Court ruled by a narrow margin in early 1870 that while "greenbacks," a form of currency which had no official gold or specie backing, could rightly be issued by Congress during the Civil War as an emergency measure, this body did not have the power to continue this practice during normal peacetime conditions. This decree, which was written by Chief Justice Chase (who, while Lincoln's Secretary of the Treasury, had become very friendly with various banking interests, particularly Jay Cooke), was greeted with delight by the nation's lending institutions, which had feared that the many debts owed them would be repaid with the depreciated greenbacks.

However, it raised a storm of protest among the debtor segments of society and numerous business concerns which had borrowed for expansion purposes, or were planning to do so. It was apparently with this latter influence in mind that President Grant, when presented with two openings on the Supreme Court in 1870, selected William Strong and Joseph Bradley to serve as Associate Justices, for both were known to be "soft" on the money issue, and their presence on the bench soon resulted in a complete reversal of the previous ruling (see *Knox v. Lee* and *Parker v. Davis*). The question is, why did these two jurists support the controversial greenbacks? And the answer, according to several studies, is that both Strong and Bradley had been primarily railroad lawyers before their elevation to the High Court, and many of these companies had rapidly expanded their activities in recent years, or were about to do so; this required substantial money, much of it borrowed.[169] These firms obviously preferred to pay their future financial obligations in (possibly depreciated) paper currency instead of gold.

Thus, in summary, it is clear that despite the great turmoil of the Civil War and Reconstruction years, the highly elitist character of the recruitment pattern of high federal officials in the United States continued to prevail, though to a lesser degree—around 81 percent, compared to the prewar total of over 95 percent—a drop created mainly by the actions of Andrew Johnson. But the nature of the elites changed in a number of ways. For instance, close to 65 percent of the major Cabinet, diplomatic, and Supreme Court officers now had college educations. Though this was but a moderate increase over the figure for the pre–Civil War era, it was far in excess of the proportion of the population attending college in the country. Yet only about 58 percent of these top officials had a considerable amount of significant governmental experience, in contrast to roughly 92 percent in the prewar years. This last set of figures points up a marked shift in the nation's politico-economic relations, for a substantial number of high officials after 1860 were recruited essentially from outside the government. Aside from a few military men, almost all of these "outsiders" were businessmen and pro-corporate laywers; furthermore, the vast majority of these men were closely associated with railroad companies. Also, this period witnessed the political demise of the Southern planters and mercantile interests, for they were never thereafter an important force in national affairs.

This economic transformation is perhaps best reflected in the make-up of the Lincoln administration. Although not widely emphasized, Lincoln was a fairly wealthy lawyer who had been linked with certain railroads in the Midwest, especially the Illinois Central. And many of the men he appointed to major Cabinet and diplomatic office had either strong railroad or financial ties. Thus, perhaps not surprisingly, it was during the Lincoln administration that the greatest amounts of land were granted, as promotional measures, to railroads in the United States, primarily in the West. This general appointment and policymaking trend continued into the bitterly divided Johnson administration and, in even more conspicuous manner, into the scandal-ridden Grant regime. The political influence of railroad forces also extended to the selection of Supreme Court Justices, as may be seen by the pressure generated in behalf of Noah Swayne and Stephen Field in the early 1860s, and in the more direct railroad connections of William Strong and Joseph Bradley, who were appointed in 1870. These actions had some desired results, such as in the controversial legal tender cases. Hence by 1876 the railroad industry had clearly emerged as the dominant politico-economic force in the nation.

Notes

1. See Charles A. Beard and Mary R. Beard, *The Rise of American Civilization* (New York: Macmillan, 1927), Vol. II, pp. 52–121.

2. See Louis M. Hacker, *The Triumph of American Capitalism* (New York: Columbia University Press, 1940), pp. 339–400, especially 339–40 and 361. A less sweeping and more discerning work, Cochran and Miller's *The Age of Enterprise,* presents a somewhat similar view, in part because its immediate pre–Civil War chapter is entitled "The Early Railroad Age" and one of its first post–Civil War chapters is described as "The Triumph of Industrial Enterprise."

3. For a discussion of this controversial theme, see B. P. Gallaway, "Economic Determinism in Reconstruction Historiography," *Southwestern Social Science Quarterly* (December 1965), pp. 247–49.

4. See Vincent P. Carosso, *Investment Banking in America: A History* (Cambridge, Mass.: Harvard University Press, 1970), p. 42.

5. See Joseph F. Wall, *Andrew Carnegie* (New York: Oxford University Press, 1970), pp. 309 and 360. In 1882 when the Standard Oil Co. first entered into its famous monopolistic trust agreement, it reportedly had an overall capital value of a little over $70 million, an enormous figure for that day, but one which was clearly atypical of industrial operations in the post–Civil War decades. And four years earlier, when it was already acknowledged that the Standard Oil Co. controlled approximately 90 percent of the refining facilities in the United States, this investment represented a total outlay of only about $33 million, an aggregate substantially exceeded by the physical plants and assets of the New York Central Railroad and many other major rail lines. For more on the Standard Oil Co., see Harold F. Williamson and Arnold R. Daum, *The American Petroleum Industry: The Age of Illumination, 1859–1899* (Evanston, Ill.: Northwestern University Press, 1959), especially pp. 429 and 550.

6. The overall amount of money invested in railroads far exceeded that put into industrial development in the early post–Civil War years. For instance, according to the 1880 census, America's railroads were capitalized at over $2 billion, textile mills at $373 million, and iron and steel manufacturing plants at $231 million. See William Miller (ed.), *Men in Business* (Cambridge, Mass.: Harvard University Press, 1952), p. 331.

7. The only non-transportation corporation to come out of the Civil War as a truly large-scale enterprise was the Western Union Telegraph Co., which had been molded through a series of mergers dictated by the North's need for better communications during this great conflict. See Burton J. Hendrick, *The Age of Big Business* (New Haven, Conn.: Yale University Press, 1919), p. 9.

8. For an incisive analysis of these economic developments, see Alfred D. Chandler, Jr., "The Beginnings of 'Big Business' in American Industry," *Business History Review* (Spring 1959), pp. 1–31.

9. To get some idea of the magnitude of railroad construction during this period, one need only note that nearly half the iron produced in the United States was utilized for this purpose. See Albert W. Niemi, Jr., *U.S. Economic History: A Survey of the Major Issues* (Chicago: Rand McNally College Publishing, 1975), p. 87. For a general overview of this topic, see George R. Taylor and Irene D. Neu, *The American Railroad Network* (Cambridge, Mass.: Harvard University Press, 1956), *passim*.

10. The often ugly role played by railroad interests in the subjugation of the Great Plains Indians has rarely been treated by American historians. Yet, according to various accounts, some big railroad enterprises took a very active part in clearing vast sections of the West of Indians who, though acting primarily in self-defense, were deemed a threat to the construction and successful operation of the country's recently chartered major transcontinental rail lines. For example, Grenville M. Dodge, one of the early promoters and prime movers of the Union Pacific Railroad, secured official approval as a Civil War general (and still active businessman) to direct a massive military campaign designed to either annihilate or forcibly "pacify" the Indians along the proposed route of this facility. Also, unknown to many, Buffalo Bill earned his nickname by slaughtering thousands of bison whose meat was needed for the small army of construction workers engaged by his employers, the builders of the Kansas-Pacific Railroad, an occupation that had the important side effect of destroying a significant part of the food supply of the Great Plains Indians. See Stanley P. Hirshson, *Grenville M. Dodge: Soldier, Politician, Railroad Pioneer* (Bloomington: Indiana University Press, 1967), pp. 110–27, especially pp. 115 and 125; and Richard O'Connor, *Iron Wheels and Broken Men* (New York: G. P. Putnam's Sons, 1973), p. 195.

11. In his comprehensive survey of American economic history Edward C. Kirkland has set the beginning of the Railroad Age at 1850, a date close to the mark, and he has also noted that there was a decline in the construction of new rail lines around 1900, by which time important new forces had clearly emerged. With regard to the first date, Kirkland has probably rightly singled out Stephen A. Douglas (the ambitious Illinois Senator, land speculator, and shrewd promoter of the nation's railroad land-grant program) as the first statesman of the Railroad Age. See Edward C. Kirkland, *A History of American Economic Life* (New York: F. S. Crofts, 1932), pp. 371, 385, and 387.

12. This legislation, which provided for the appointment of five government directors, called for the construction of a major rail line between the Missouri River and a subsequently prescribed point in Utah. At about the same time the Central Pacific Railroad was organized in California, under the direction and control of four prominent mercantile and entrepreneurial figures (Charles Crocker, Mark Hopkins, Collis P. Huntington, and Leland Stanford), to build, with federal support and approval, the westernmost leg of this vital transcontinental route. This was a case where, by governmental decree, firm agreement was required, at least as to a common junction, between these two railroads. However, it should not be assumed that railroad interests always worked together simply because they were a part of the same industry, for these forces sometimes waged bitter battles over such matters as rates, rights-of-way, terminal points, and governmental aid.

13. A few rail lines also got special construction subsidies in the form of loans, which were only grudgingly and belatedly repaid. The Union Pacific Railroad received an aggregate of $27 million in federal funds and the Central Pacific got a total of $25 million, sizable sums in those days. However, these railroads were required to carry the mail, American troops, and federal property at reduced rates for a long period of time, so that the government secured substantial benefits from this provision. The question of who ultimately gained the most from the government's land-grant program, the railroads or the general public, is a complex one which has not been resolved to this day. Some lines certainly did well. For instance, according to one authority, the Illinois Central Railroad netted, within 25 years of its award, over $25 million from the sale of its land, a figure just $1 million short of its original construction cost. See Edward C. Kirkland, *A History of American Economic Life,* p. 390.

14. Although it is difficult to make an accurate and objective assessment of the railroad

land-grant program, one possible measure might be to compare it with the distribution of benefits derived from the Homestead Act of 1862, which was passed primarily to aid many hard-pressed settlers who were eager to have some land they could till. Judged by this standard, the railroads would seem to have done much better than the small farmers and frontiersmen, for these major enterprises received more than twice as much land from the federal and state governments as the western homesteaders. See Morton Keller, *Affairs of State* (Cambridge, Mass.: Harvard University Press, 1977), p. 387.

15. See, for instance, Alfred D. Chandler, Jr. (ed.), *The Railroads: The Nation's First Big Business* (New York: Harcourt, Brace & World, 1965), *passim;* and also his later, more detailed study, *The Visible Hand,* pp. 81–187.

16. The central figures in this key enterpreneurial complex were John Murray Forbes, his brother, Robert B. Forbes, Thomas H. Perkins (who was John Murray Forbes's uncle), John P. Cushing (a first cousin of J. M. Forbes), William Sturgis (whose uncle married T. H. Perkins's sister), and another close kinsman, Charles E. Perkins. Almost all the prominent families in Boston were probably related, in some fashion, to one or more members of this elite group. For a detailed analysis of its involvement in western railroad development and its many overlapping links, see Arthur M. Johnson and Barry E. Supple, *Boston Capitalists and Western Railroads* (Cambridge, Mass.: Harvard University Press, 1967), *passim;* and Mary C. Crawford, *Famous Families of Massachusetts* (Boston: Little, Brown, 1930), Volumes I and II, *passim.*

17. For more on the intimate links which existed between certain commercial banks and railroad concerns in the latter decades of the 19th century, see Paul B. Trescott, *Financing American Enterprise: The Story of Commercial Banking* (New York: Harper & Row, 1963), pp. 117–30.

18. See Vincent P. Carosso, *Investment Banking in America,* pp. 29–36.

19. See Fowler Hamilton, "The Lawyer and Business," *Fortune* (October 1948), p. 180.

20. See Beryl H. Levy, *Corporation Lawyer: Saint or Sinner?* (Philadelphia: Chilton, 1961), p. 43.

21. It was in this era that the Tweed ring rose to the heights of its notorious powers. It systematically looted the New York City treasury of millions of dollars before it was finally crushed by a vigorous investigation and prosecution directed by outraged local leaders.

22. The term *robber barons* is believed to have been coined by the Midwestern reformer, Carl Schurz, in 1882. However, this provocative phrase did not gain widespread currency until 1934 when Matthew Josephson published a book called *The Robber Barons.* Some of the magnates treated by Josephson were probably more constructive figures than he was willing to concede, men such as railroad builder James J. Hill. But many are acknowledged to be fairly accurate appraisals. For three more conservative articles on the subject, see Thomas Cochran, "The Legend of the Robber Barons," *Pennsylvania Magazine of History and Biography* (July 1950), pp. 307–21; Hal Bridges, "The Robber Baron Concept in American History," *Business History Review* (Spring 1958), pp. 1–13; and John Tipple, "The Anatomy of Prejudice: Origins of the Robber Baron Legend," *Business History Review* (Winter 1959), pp. 511–22.

23. The most glaring example of such venal influence came to light shortly after the Civil War with the Crédit Mobilier scandal. In this affair a number of shares in the Union Pacific Railroad were distributed to various important members of Congress as a largely preventive measure designed to squash or forestall a possible probe into certain corrupt construction practices, which because of governmental subsidies probably involved federal funds. The political careers of several prominent officials were badly tarnished, if not ruined, as a result of these revelations.

24. Douglas, who was clearly viewed as a pro-Southern leader, had substantial support in many parts of the country, especially in New York business circles which apparently felt

that Lincoln's election might lead to a civil war and economic disaster. Among Douglas's chief backers were financier August Belmont, the 1860 chairman of the Democratic National Committee, real estate magnate William B. Astor, Erastus Corning, and Dean Richmond, the last two of whom were high officials of the New York Central Railroad. Although these men all backed Douglas throughout the presidential campaign, a number of important New York City businessmen shifted over to Lincoln. However, the bulk of the city's mercantile community remained loyal supporters of Stephen A. Douglas. For more on this matter, see Philip S. Foner, *Business and Slavery: The New York Merchants and the Irrepressible Conflict* (Chapel Hill: University of North Carolina Press, 1941), pp. 169–207; and Robert W. Johannsen, *Stephen A. Douglas* (New York: Oxford University Press, 1973), pp. 702 and 732–33.

25. Actually, Lincoln was basically a conservative on most major issues. See David Donald, *Lincoln Reconsidered* (New York: Alfred A. Knopf, 1959), pp. 19–36; Richard Hofstadter, *The American Political Tradition* (New York: Alfred A. Knopf, 1948), pp. 93–136; and Kenneth M. Stampp, *The Era of Reconstruction, 1865–1877* (New York: Alfred A. Knopf, 1966), pp. 24–49, especially p. 44.

26. Lincoln was not the general counsel for this concern, but one of a number of local attorneys retained to handle much of its business (about 40 cases in all) in his section of the state. In addition, the Illinois Central apparently employed Lincoln as a lobbyist to help obtain its charter from the state legislature in 1850. At times Lincoln represented various other lines such as the Chicago and Alton, the Ohio and Mississippi, and the Chicago and Rock Island, although he was also hired on numerous occasions by aggrieved citizens to bring suit against railroad interests. However, unlike the very ambitious Stephen A. Douglas (whom Illinois Central officials may not have fully trusted), Lincoln did not engage in any major stockownership or land speculation activities. See John W. Starr, Jr., *Lincoln and the Railroads* (New York: Dodd, Mead, 1927), pp. 57–72, 80, and 117–25; John J. Duff, *A. Lincoln: Prairie Lawyer* (New York: Rinehart, 1948), pp. 210 and 312–17; John P. Frank, *Lincoln as a Lawyer* (Urbana: University of Illinois Press, 1961), p. 25; Benjamin P. Thomas, *Abraham Lincoln* (New York: Alfred A. Knopf, 1952), p. 156; and Edwin S. S. Sunderland, *Abraham Lincoln and the Illinois Central Railroad* (New York: privately printed, 1955), pp. 16–17. Sunderland was a senior partner in a leading Wall Street law firm which served as general counsel to this big rail line through much of the post–World War II period.

27. In one much-discussed case, Lincoln billed the railroad $5,000 for his services, an enormous sum for those days (it was 3½ times the annual salary of the governor of Illinois), and one for which he was forced to go to court to collect. See Edwin S. S. Sunderland, *op. cit.,* pp. 20 and 24, and Carlton J. Corliss, *Main Line of Mid-America: The Story of the Illinois Central* (New York: Creative Age Press, 1950), pp. 110 and 121. Also, for reference to a number of Lincoln's other corporate clients, see Reinhard H. Luthin, *The Real Abraham Lincoln* (Englewood Cliffs, N.J.: Prentice-Hall, 1961), p. 158.

28. Such ties were even found in his wife's more elitist Southern family. For instance, Mrs. Lincoln's sister's father-in-law, John L. Helm, served as president of the Louisville and Nashville Railroad from 1854 to 1860, when he was ousted by a dissident economic group.

29. For more on Judd's efforts to boost Lincoln, see Stephen B. Oates, *With Malice Toward None: The Life of Abraham Lincoln* (New York: Harper & Row, 1977), pp. 170 and 175.

30. See the *U.S. Railroad Directory, 1856,* p. 139. A majority of the directors of this line also served in a similar capacity with the Chicago and Rock Island Railroad, and Azariah C. Flagg (a former member of the Albany Regency) held administrative positions in both concerns.

31. See the U.S. *Railroad Directory, 1856,* pp. 139 and 158; *The Capitalist's Guide and*

Railway Annual for 1859 (New York: published by Samuel T. Callahan, 1859), pp. 75 and 198; and *Ashcroft's Railway Directory for 1862.* According to the *Dictionary of American Biography* (Vol. 5, p. 230), Judd was also associated with the Michigan Southern and Northern Indiana Railroad and the Pittsburgh, Fort Wayne and Chicago Railroad sometime between 1848 and 1860.

32. Lincoln, it should be remembered, was not a well-known national figure at this time, having served only one term in Congress back in the late 1840s, so that despite the acclaim he achieved through the famous Lincoln-Douglas debates, he entered the presidential race a distinct underdog (William H. Seward was the initial heavy favorite). Hence it took considerable effort and ingenuity for him to win the Republican nomination.

33. See Willard L. King, *Lincoln's Manager, David Davis* (Cambridge, Mass.: Harvard University Press, 1960), pp. 21–22 and 101, and also Paul W. Gates, *The Illinois Central Railroad and Its Colonization Work* (Cambridge, Mass.: Harvard University Press, 1934), pp. 59 and 112.

34. See the *U. S. Railroad Directory, 1856,* p. 140, and *Ashcroft's Railway Directory: 1865* (New York: John W. Amerman, printer, 1865), p. 116.

35. One insight into the array of forces which helped Lincoln gain the Republican nomination may be gleaned from the fact that Lincoln also had considerable help from railroad interests in certain other western states. For example, according to one account, presidential affairs were of great importance in Iowa, particularly for the backers of the Mississippi and Missouri Railroad. Because Lincoln was known to favor the construction of a transcontinental railroad, many of the people involved in the promotion of this line strongly supported his candidacy. Indeed, at one point in the proceedings, when the Republican nomination was still very much in doubt, Lincoln's influential ally, Norman B. Judd, asked Grenville M. Dodge, an Iowa political leader and major railroad man, to come to Chicago (the convention site) to help swing his state's wavering delegation to the Lincoln cause. See Stanley P. Hirshson, *Grenville M. Dodge,* pp. 34–35.

36. See Glyndon G. Van Deusen, *William Henry Seward* (New York: Oxford University Press, 1967), pp. 29–30, 39, 88, and 145. Unfortunately, this account is not very clear about Seward's later legal activities. Indeed, virtually the only reference to Seward's subsequent work as a lawyer is a brief note (p. 262) on his action as counsel in a patent case for Chicago manufacturer Cyrus McCormick in 1856. The general impression conveyed in this analysis is that although Seward was frequently in financial difficulty because he held many important but low-paying governmental positions, he derived much of his income, even in the 1850s, from his speculative land ventures.

37. According to his biographer, Weed had substantial holdings in railroads and many other enterprises. More important from a political standpoint, he was able to raise a great deal of money from business sources, especially those in New York City, for major campaign purposes. For example, in the fall of 1839, just one week before the state legislative elections when party fortunes were in doubt, he made an emergency appeal to Whig merchants in New York City. The response was immediate and enthusiastic. Various businessmen wrapped $8,000 in a handkerchief, chartered a steamboat, and took a night trip up the Hudson to bring the needy funds to Albany. See Glyndon G. Van Deusen, *Thurlow Weed: Wizard of the Lobby* (Boston: Little, Brown, 1947), pp. 77, 85, 107, 220–25, 246, 287, and 290.

38. Seward's father was a doctor, merchant, and land speculator who, by the time of his death in 1849, had amassed a fortune of over $300,000. Also, Seward's father-in-law, Elijah Miller, had given up the practice of law to become an enterpreneur who devoted much of his time to the promotion and management of the Auburn and Syracuse Railroad, one of New York's early upstate lines.

39. See Glyndon G. Van Deusen, *William Henry Seward,* pp. 50, 53, 87–88, 264, and 403.

40.   Though listed as "of counsel" in the 1850s, Seward was reported to have received substantial sums for his work with the firm in 1853 (and perhaps other years during the pre–Civil War decade). The Blatchford-Seward concern was the original partnership of what is today, after much growth (and many name changes), one of Wall Street's greatest law firms—Cravath, Swaine & Moore. Seward's nephew, Clarence, served as a partner in this concern from 1854 until his death in 1897. See Robert T. Swaine, *The Cravath Firm and its Predecessors, 1819–1947* (New York: privately printed, 1947), *passim,* especially pp. ix and 117.

41.   See Robert T. Swaine, *op. cit.,* pp. 2, 27, 140, and 151.

42.   See the *Annual Report of the State Engineer and Surveyor of the State of New York . . . from the Reports of the Railroad Corporations for the Year ending September 30, 1861* (Albany: Weed, Parsons & Co., 1862), p. 166, and *Ashcroft's Railway Directory: 1866,* p. 46. Blatchford also served on the board of the much smaller Saratoga and Whitehall Railroad from 1860 to 1865. In addition, Seward's son, William H. (Jr.), was made treasurer and director of the newly formed Southern Central Railroad in 1867.

43.   Among Seward's other close friends and political supporters in major economic circles were Samuel B. Ruggles, a prominent New York City merchant and entrepreneur, and New York Governor and businessman Edwin D. Morgan, who served around 1860 on the board of the United States Trust Co., Manhattan Fire Insurance Co., and Bank of Commerce (of New York City). For more on Ruggles's relations with Seward and later involvement in the so-called Pacific Railroad lobby, see D. G. Brinton Thompson, *Ruggles of New York* (New York: Columbia University Press, 1946), pp. 28–29 and 106–07.

44.   Unfortunately, there is no sound study of this able, but complex individual. However, according to various reliable accounts, Chase did not practice much law (other than in antislavery cases) after 1848, apparently because of his newly acquired affluence. Gustavus Myers claims that Chase served as a director of the Lafayette Bank in Cincinnati from about 1834 to 1844 (see his *History of the Supreme Court of the United States* [New York: Burt Franklin, 1912], p. 492). But this association was probably of such a distant nature by 1860 as to be of doubtful significance. And the fact that it was terminated so early would seem to indicate that Chase had attained enough economic security and prestige to apply his energies almost entirely to state and national political affairs.

45.   See Henrietta M. Larson, *Jay Cooke: Private Banker* (Cambridge, Mass.: Harvard University Press, 1936), pp. 102–03. Larson maintains that it was part of the Cookes' plan to secure an important Cabinet post for Chase. According to another source, by 1864 Jay Cooke had invested close to $100,000 in Chase's political career. See Clarence H. Cramer, *American Enterprise: Free and Not So Free* (Boston: Little, Brown, 1972), p. 168.

46.   Jay Cooke & Co. was not created until 1861, and apparently was generally regarded as an interloper or "outsider" in the business community. From 1843 to 1857 Cooke had been a partner in the well-established Philadelphia banking house of E. W. Clark & Co. In the immediate pre–Civil War period (1858–1861) Cooke branched out on his own and, like many Americans, turned his hand to various railroad ventures, the most prominent of which was the Sunbury and Erie line, a concern headed by his brother-in-law, William G. Moorhead. In 1863, at the height of his politico-economic power, Cooke played an important part in the organization and early operation of the First National Bank of Philadelphia. See Henrietta M. Larson, *op cit.,* pp. 88, 93, and 139.

47.   In November 1863 Chase's daughter married Rhode Island Senator William Sprague, who had reportedly amassed a fortune of close to $25 million in the textile business, and had served up to the early 1860s as a director of the Hartford, Providence and Fishkill Railroad. Since this link was forged toward the end of Chase's term as Secretary of the Treasury, it probably had little or no effect on the government's fiscal program. With regard to Sprague's wealth, see Thomas G. Belden and Marva R. Belden, *So Fell the Angels* (Boston: Little, Brown, 1956), p. 43.

48. Lincoln's first choice for this post was a Youngstown businessman and recent governor of Ohio, David Tod, who served on the board of the Cleveland and Mahoning Railroad up to at least the early 1860s. However, he was forced to decline because of ill health.

49. Fessenden had married the daughter of James Deering, one of Portland's wealthiest merchants. He had also made a number of business and real estate investments over the years, most of which had turned out quite well (although his association with the proposed Atlantic and St. Lawrence Railway had proved to be disappointing and apparently soured him on such activity). Clearly, he was not hostile to business, for he was on friendly terms with such major magnates as John Murray Forbes of Boston. See Charles A. Jellison, *Fessenden of Maine: Civil War Senator* (Syracuse, N.Y.: Syracuse University Press, 1962), pp. 15, 47–50, 140, and 249.

50. Fessenden was replaced by Indiana's Hugh McCulloch, who had been serving as U.S. Comptroller of the Currency. Since Lincoln was assassinated about one month later, this official will be discussed in more detail in the next section of this chapter. Actually, this important Cabinet post was first offered to New York Senator and wealthy entrepreneur Edwin D. Morgan, who had recently been a director of a number of banks and railroads. His cousin and former longtime business partner, Gerald D. Morgan, sat on the board of the Equitable Life Assurance Society, and his uncle, E. A. Bulkeley, was the first (1853–1872) president of the Aetna Life Insurance Co. Because of major factional problems, however, Morgan chose to remain in the United States Senate.

51. See Marvin R. Cain, *Lincoln's Attorney General: Edward Bates of Missouri* (Columbia: University of Missouri Press, 1965), pp. 4–6, 11, 17, and 19, and Timothy W. Hubbard and Louis E. Davids, *Banking in Mid-America: A History of Missouri's Banks* (Wash.: Public Affairs Press, 1969), p. 80. Indeed, one recent scholar has referred to Bates, who was a longtime Whig, as an archconservative. See Michael Lee Benedict, *A Compromise of Principle* (New York: W. W. Norton & Co., 1974), p. 60.

52. According to various American history texts, Bates acted as Attorney General up to some time in 1863, at which point he was replaced by Pennsylvania's Titian J. Coffey, Bates's longtime friend and chief aide in the department. This is incorrect, for according to official records, Bates served up to the end of November 1864, and Coffey merely filled in briefly as an interim official.

53. See, for instance, the *U.S. Railroad Directory, 1856*, p. 103, and *Ashcroft's Railway Directory for 1865*, p. 131. When Speed was first elected to the board of this company, it was headed by Mrs. Lincoln's sister's father-in-law, John L. Helm, although he was forced out of this position in 1860.

54. See Lee F. Crippen, *Simon Cameron: Ante-Bellum Years* (Oxford, Ohio: Mississippi Valley Press, 1942), pp. 12, 113, and 125; and Erwin S. Bradley, *Simon Cameron: Lincoln's Secretary of War* (Philadelphia: University of Pennsylvania Press, 1966), pp. 33, 53–57, and 103. Cameron also had some important holdings in certain iron and coal enterprises and one or more newspapers in the central part of the state. Another sign that Cameron was closely associated with railroad interests may be found in the fact that the man he chose to serve as his first Assistant Secretary of War was Thomas A. Scott, a vice-president of the Pennsylvania Railroad.

55. Stanton was a partner of former judge Charles Shaler, who, as one source has put it, ". . . had retired from the bench to share in the big cases and big fees provided by a region where business and its profits were expanding gigantically. . . . Shaler had the necessary business, political and social connections, but needed a good court man to work with him." (See Fletcher Pratt, *Stanton, Lincoln's Secretary of War* [New York: W. W. Norton, 1953], p. 44.) Unfortunately, the precise nature of the relations of Stanton or his partner with various prosperous clients is still unclear because of the skimpy treatment given to this topic by political biographers. According to one source, Stanton had long served as general

counsel for the Central Ohio Railroad, which around 1860 was merged into the much larger Baltimore and Ohio line, whose president, John W. Garrett, reportedly carried great weight with Stanton. See Edward Hungerford, *The Story of the Baltimore and Ohio Railroad, 1827–1927* (New York: G. P. Putnam's Sons, 1928), Vol. I, p. 351, and Vol. II, p. 47.

56.   Morgan wrote directly to Lincoln urging Welles's appointment as a Cabinet officer. (See James A. Rawley, *Edwin D. Morgan: Merchant in Politics, 1811–1883* [New York: Columbia University Press, 1955], p. 129.) Welles's most recent biographer, John Niven, made brief reference to this relationship, but said nothing more about Morgan's efforts in Welles's behalf; he merely noted that the former's firm handled the latter's investments. (See John Niven, *Gideon Welles: Lincoln's Secretary of the Navy* [New York: Oxford University Press, 1973], p. 74.) Morgan served on the board of the United States Trust Co. and National Bank of New York City until at least 1860, and he had been a director of the Hudson River Railroad (and one other major railroad) up to the late 1850s, around which time he was elected governor of New York.

57.   Lincoln's first Postmaster General was a prominent Republican and abolitionist leader named Montgomery Blair, who had held various local government posts in Missouri in the 1840s and had served as a St. Louis lawyer up to 1853 when he moved to the Washington area, where he continued his legal and political activities. Blair was a wealthy man, in part because he had married the daughter of former (entrepreneurially oriented) Jacksonian Cabinet member and U.S. Supreme Court Justice Levi Woodbury. Because of the political suspicion that beset the Lincoln administration with the approach of the next presidential election, Blair resigned as Postmaster General in September 1864, and was replaced by William Dennison, a former (1859–61) governor of Ohio and longtime Columbus lawyer and businessman. Like many men of this period, Dennison was heavily involved in railroad affairs. He served in the mid-1860s as a director of the Columbus and Indianapolis Central Railway, the Central Ohio Railroad, and the Columbus and Xenia Railroad.

58.   In the late 1850s Usher also represented the Indiana, Ohio and Ft. Wayne Railroad and the Lake Erie, Wabash and St. Louis Railroad in different court actions. See Elmo R. Richardson and Alan W. Farley, *John Palmer Usher: Lincoln's Secretary of the Interior* (Lawrence: University of Kansas Press, 1960), p. 15. Unfortunately, neither the first railroad nor the Leavenworth line was listed in any of the business manuals published in the pre–Civil War period, so it is difficult to know what figures, other than their chief executives, were associated with these entrepreneurial efforts.

59.   See the *U.S. Railroad Directory, 1856*, p. 132; and *Ashcroft's Railway Directory for 1865*, p. 104. Griswold also served in the prewar period as president of the Evansville and Crawfordsville Railroad, and later as head of the Western Division of the Ohio and Mississippi Railroad.

60.   See Richardson and Farley, *op. cit.*, p. 17.

61.   See Richardson and Farley, *op. cit.*, pp. 50–62, particularly p. 62. This study clearly demonstrates that in his conduct of office Usher grossly favored railroad interests over those of the Indians.

62.   See Martin B. Duberman, *Charles Francis Adams, 1807–1886* (Boston: Houghton Mifflin, 1961), p. 256.

63.   Adams's brother-in-law, Peter C. Brooks, Jr., followed in his father's footsteps and served, starting in 1865, as a vice-president of the first company. He was also a longtime member of the board of the Chicopee Manufacturing Co.

64.   See Reinhard H. Luthin, *The Real Abraham Lincoln*, p. 245. Additional evidence of business influence at work in this administration can be found in the background and economic associations of other ministers picked in the early 1860s, such as those appointed to Japan and the Papal States.

65.   This system was conceived essentially by Secretary of the Treasury Salmon P.

Chase. Many state banking interests opposed it. Chase's close friend and financial supporter Jay Cooke initially had misgivings about the plan too. However, Cooke, unlike a large number of business and financial leaders, soon became convinced of its utility and worked assiduously to promote its passage (see Henrietta M. Larson, *Jay Cooke,* pp. 137–39). Substantial credit for the passage of this measure should also be given to Boston Congressman and merchant Samuel Hooper, who was the son-in-law of wealthy Brahmin businessman William Sturgis, a former longtime partner of textile magnate William Appleton, and a vice-president of the Massachusetts Hospital Life Insurance Co. In addition, Hooper had served for many years as a director of the Eastern Railroad and the Merchants Bank of Boston.

66. The passage of the Homestead Act of 1862 is usually cited as another notable achievement of the Lincoln administration. However, while it is true that this legislation helped to open up the West to many settlers, it was a boon to the railroads too, for they were much interested in the promotion of land sales and the overall economic and agricultural development of the region, which would generate considerable passenger and freight traffic.

67. See Lewis H. Haney, *A Congressional History of Railways in the United States from 1850 to 1877* (Madison, Wisc.: Democrat Printing, 1910), p. 14. No railroad land grants were awarded during the Buchanan years, primarily because of the sharp adverse impact of the financial panic and recession of the late 1850s.

68. Curiously, little research has been done on this important topic. However, according to the biography of an influential New York businessman, there was a "Pacific Railroad lobby" at work during this period, and one of its prime movers was apparently William H. Seward's close friend and political supporter, Samuel Ruggles. See D. G. Brinton Thompson, *Ruggles of New York,* pp. 106–07.

69. A sizable number of the non-governmental directors of the Union Pacific Railroad were also officers or directors of the Chicago and Rock Island Railroad, a line that had, up to recently, retained Lincoln's campaign manager, Norman B. Judd, as its general counsel.

70. With regard to the Civil War, it is interesting to note that one of Lincoln's first commanders of the Union Army was George B. McClellan, a West Point–trained former (1846–57) Army officer who, upon returning to civilian life in the late 1850s, had served first as chief engineer and vice-president of the Illinois Central Railroad (from 1857 to 1860) and then briefly (1860–61) as president of the Ohio and Mississippi Railroad. When, because of his excessive caution, he was relieved of his command in November 1862, he was replaced briefly by a woeful choice, General Ambrose Burnside, another former Army officer who had served in the immediate pre–Civil War years as treasurer of the Illinois Central Railroad. As a still popular military figure, McClellan was the Democratic party's presidential candidate in 1864. He was vigorously backed for the nomination by various influential conservative forces within the party, particularly the New York Central Railroad–dominated political machine (the now-transformed Albany Regency), financier August Belmont, Wall Street lawyer Samuel L. M. Barlow, and the Stockton-controlled Camden and Amboy Railroad in New Jersey. On McClellan's candidacy, see Edward C. Kirkland, *The Peacemakers of 1864* (New York: Macmillan Co., 1927), pp. 112–13; and Joel H. Silbey, *A Respectable Minority: The Democratic Party in the Civil War Era, 1860–1868* (New York: W. W. Norton & Co., 1977), *passim;* and George T. McJimsey, *Genteel Partisan: Manton Marble, 1834–1917* (Ames, Iowa: Iowa State University Press, 1971), pp. 38 and 50.

71. Probably because of his background, Johnson initially supported a number of measures that would have resulted in the breakup of most of the large estates in the South, but for various reasons he soon gave up the struggle. See Kenneth M. Stampp, *The Era of Reconstruction, 1865–1877,* pp. 51–70.

72. See Henry U. Poor, *Manual of the Railroads of the United States for 1868–69* (New York: H. V. & H. W. Poor, 1868), p. 202. One of Seward's old friends and former Auburn (1831–42) law partners, Nelson Beardsley, was a director of the Michigan Southern and

Northern Indiana Railroad in 1868, during which year he was also elected to the board of the Southern Central Railroad. Even more important, Seward's nephew, Clarence, was a longtime partner in the New York City law firm then known as Blatchford, Seward & Griswold (now Cravath, Swaine & Moore).

73. See Ernest N. Paolino, *The Foundations of the American Empire: William Henry Seward and U.S. Foreign Policy* (Ithaca, N.Y.: Cornell University Press, 1973), p. 132.

74. The most important diplomatic action taken during the Johnson years was, of course, the purchase of Alaska, a (then) vast wasteland which Russia had finally decided was a bad economic venture. It thus initiated high-level negotiations with Secretary of State Seward, who managed to secure governmental approval of this transaction, despite cries of its being ''Seward's folly,'' largely because of the low asking price. Although Alaska seemed to offer scant hope of financial return, its purchase was apparently pushed by Seward and some of his entrepreneurially oriented business friends and allies in New York City, chief of whom may have been Samuel Ruggles, who, prior to the laying of the Atlantic cable, had been much involved in the promotion of an intercontinental telegraph system across Alaska and Russia (see Ernest N. Paolino, *op. cit., passim*). However, this probably should not be described as a strongly expansionist act, for Russia was extremely eager to get rid of this property and dispensed considerable money to help win support for the measure from various important people, both in and out of government.

75. See Henrietta M. Larson, *Jay Cooke,* p. 199, and Robert P. Sharkey, *Money, Class and Party: An Economic Study of Civil War and Reconstruction* (Baltimore: Johns Hopkins Press, 1959), p. 247. Additional evidence that Cooke and McCulloch were on friendly terms even before the latter's appointment as Secretary of the Treasury may be seen in the fact that at one point in 1864 McCulloch seriously considered resigning as Comptroller of the Currency to accept the presidency of Jay Cooke's newly formed Fourth National Bank of New York City. See Fritz Redlich, *The Mold of American Banking* (New York: Hafner Publishing Co., 1951), Part II, p. 113.

76. According to John and LaWanda Cox, Stanbery was a former conservative Whig whose appointment as Attorney General was strongly urged by Lancaster, Ohio lawyer (and two-time Cabinet member) Thomas Ewing, who was one of Andrew Johnson's closest informal advisors. Ewing was the father-in-law of the famous Civil War general, William T. Sherman, whose brother, John, was a United States Senator and a director of the Pittsburgh, Ft. Wayne and Chicago Railway. Ewing's son, who was a Washington lawyer, was reportedly offered two Cabinet posts (Attorney General and Secretary of War) by Johnson, but chose not to accept. See John H. and LaWanda Cox, ''Andrew Johnson and His Ghost Writers: An Analysis of the Freedmen's Bureau and the Civil Rights Veto Messages,'' *Mississippi Valley Historical Review* (December 1961), p. 462; and the *Dictionary of American Biography,* Vol. III, pp. 238–39.

77. Harvey O'Connor's book on the Astor family contains numerous references (especially on page 115) to this firm's three senior partners, Evarts, Joseph H. Choate, and Charles F. Southmayd. Also, shortly before his appointment as Attorney General, Evarts served, along with a number of other New York figures, as one of the incorporators of the Isthmus Canal Co., which was organized in an early abortive effort to build a much-desired waterway across Panama. See Harvey O'Connor, *The Astors* (New York: Knopf, 1941) and Ernest N. Paolino, *op. cit.,* pp. 132–33.

78. See Stanley P. Hirshson, *Grenville M. Dodge,* pp. 121–22 and 128–42; for more on Harlan's political ties, see Leland L. Sage, *William Boyd Allison* (Iowa City: State Historical Society of Iowa, 1956), p. 64.

79. See Maurice G. Baxter, *Orville H. Browning* (Bloomington: Indiana University Press, 1957), pp. 9, 54, 57, 256, and 259; and the *U.S. Railroad Directory, 1856,* p. 138. Unfortunately, the latter source has an incomplete entry for the Northern Cross Railroad; none of its outside directors are listed. Browning invested an unspecified amount of money

in the Northern Cross, and later drew up the papers for the merger of this line into the Boston-controlled Chicago, Burlington and Quincy Railroad. Baxter described Browning as a "railroad attorney" who was in the employ of the Chicago, Burlington and Quincy from 1869, when he resigned from the Cabinet, until his death in 1881. But judging from Browning's background and affiliations and his entry in the *Dictionary of American Biography* (Vol. II, pp. 175–76), he may have been involved with this big concern even earlier, in either the late 1850s or the mid-1860s. Further research may resolve this matter.

80. For one rather euphemistic account of this activity, see Maurice G. Baxter, *op. cit.*, p. 106. For a more realistic assessment, see the entry on Browning in the *Dictionary of American Biography*.

81. Though treated last here because of its fairly recent origin, the position of Secretary of the Interior was actually one of the most important in the Cabinet in this era of substantial western land and railroad development. It is in this light that the pattern of pro-railroad appointments should be evaluated.

82. See Margaret Clapp, *Forgotten First Citizen: John Bigelow* (Boston: Little, Brown, 1947), pp. 228 and 124, in particular. Bigelow was actually nominated, largely at the urging of Seward, in the last months of the Lincoln administration, but since he did not formally take office until shortly after Johnson assumed the Presidency, he has been treated as a part of the latter regime.

83. America's first Minister to Prussia (Germany) in the Johnson administration was Indiana lawyer and political leader Joseph A. Wright, who had served in this capacity in the pre–Civil War (1857–61) period, and before that as governor of his home state. Unfortunately, Wright, about whom little is known, died about a year and a half after taking office. He was succeeded by the famous historian and onetime (Massachusetts) Democratic leader, George Bancroft, who had been both Secretary of the Navy and American Minister to Great Britain in the Polk administration. Bancroft was by the late 1860s a fairly wealthy New York City figure with substantial railroad stockholdings. Moreover, his nephew, J. C. Bancroft Davis, had been on the board of the Erie Railroad since at least 1865. For more on Bancroft's investments, see Russell B. Nye, *George Bancroft* (New York: Knopf, 1944), pp. 227 and 293.

84. See Charles A. Beard and Mary R. Beard, *The Rise of American Civilization*, Vol. II, pp. 52–121.

85. See Howard K. Beale, *The Critical Years: A Study of Andrew Johnson and Reconstruction* (New York: Harcourt, Brace, 1930), *passim*. For a more recent exposition of this nature, see George R. Woolfolk, *The Cotton Regency: The Northern Merchants and Reconstruction, 1865–1880* (New York: Bookman Associates, 1958), *passim*. Woolfolk claimed that the Radicals represented primarily a politico-economic alliance of Boston and Philadelphia capitalists who were bent on exploiting the South and who, in the process, managed to thwart the more moderate policies espoused by New York mercantile interests, whose basic goal was to restore normal trade relations. However, Woolfolk presented little empirical evidence to back up his assertions.

86. Through his own industry and accumulated capital, Stevens had become the owner of the Caledonia Iron Works in south central Pennsylvania, but this was a fairly small concern (it had little more than 200 workers), which was often unprofitable and had only limited access to important outside markets. See Richard N. Current, *Old Thad Stevens* (Madison; University of Wisconsin Press, 1942), p. 122.

87. One scholar, who holds a contrary view, claimed, for instance, that Stevens ". . . was not only the embodiment of Pennsylvania capitalism himself, but also a go-between for others of that ilk." He also maintained, on the basis of rather skimpy evidence, that there was "a very real connection between Radicalism and railroads and iron." (See Richard N. Current, *op. cit.*, pp. 226–27.) The author does not agree with these assertions, although he concedes that Stevens was a Pennsylvania ironmaster with a strong vested

interest in a high protective tariff. For another, more accurate assessment of Stevens' politico-economic role, see Fawn M. Brodie, *Thaddeus Stevens: Scourge of the South* (New York: W. W. Norton & Co., 1959), especially pp. 169–71. Brodie claims that a Confederate raid, which destroyed Stevens' foundry in 1863, probably caused this Republican leader to take a vengeful attitude toward the South after the Civil War. Stevens was an economic radical in one sense, for he originally proposed to confiscate all large (over 200-acre) Southern farms and divide this land among the recently freed blacks, a program which soon died for lack of support.

88.   See David Donald, *Charles Sumner and the Coming of the Civil War* (New York: Alfred A. Knopf, 1960), *passim,* and Lawrence Lader, *The Bold Brahmins: New England's War Against Slavery, 1831–1863* (New York: Dutton, 1961), pp. 160 and 190. According to the latter work, there was a noticeable split in the ranks of the Boston business community with regard to the interrelated issues of slavery and western expansion, with some leaders, who had substantial railroad investments in the Midwest, favoring the free-soil movement, while the city's textile merchants and manufacturers took a strongly pro-Southern stance and were bitterly opposed to the abolitionist cause.

89.   For an overall analysis of these figures, see Hans L. Trefousse, *The Radical Republicans: Lincoln's Vanguard for Racial Justice* (New York: Alfred A. Knopf, 1969), *passim.* Perhaps the most prominent businessman in the Radical ranks was Zachariah Chandler, a former Detroit dry goods merchant. However, having amassed a sizable fortune, Chandler would appear to have severed most of his major business affiliations and devoted himself largely to politics.

90.   Even Johnson's diplomatic appointments would indicate that he had substantial support from the business community, for, after the impeachment controversy had been resolved, the President picked Baltimore and Ohio Railroad lawyer Reverdy Johnson to serve as American Minister to Great Britain, and his second Minister to France was New York lawyer-businessman John A. Dix, who had been president of several major rail lines. Edwin D. Morgan, who was then a U.S. Senator, did vote for Johnson's impeachment, but his action was apparently dictated by political pressure and expediency (and would reportedly have been different if he had thought that Johnson would really be removed from office). See James A. Rawley, *Edwin D. Morgan,* pp. 228–29.

91.   As a Republican, Evarts apparently felt that Johnson was much at fault for creating this bitter situation, but agreed to serve as a defense attorney partly for professional reasons.

92.   Several other lawyers were involved in this crucial case, but Evarts and Curtis were clearly the primary attorneys for the defense.

93.   Shortly after the Civil War an attempt was made to create a new National Union party, designed to unite conservative Democrats and like-minded Republicans behind President Johnson, in opposition to the Radical Republicans. Some of the top figures in this movement were William H. Seward, New York Republican boss Thurlow Weed, Edwin D. Morgan, Gideon Welles, Hugh McCulloch, Orville H. Browning, and Dean Richmond, the president of the New York Central Railroad, who was the head of the Democratic party in New York state. But Richmond died suddenly and, partly because of his demise, the plan apparently collapsed. See Glyndon G. Van Deusen, *William Henry Seward,* pp. 454–60; LaWanda Cox and John H. Cox, *Politics, Principle, and Prejudice, 1865–1866* (Glencoe, Ill.: Free Press, 1963), pp. 1–406; and Alvin F. Harlow, *The Road of the Century* (New York: Creative Age Press, 1947), pp. 180–81.

94.   See Robert P. Sharkey, *Money, Class, and Party,* pp. 272 and 275. Sharkey also argued (see p. 289) that the warm reception given to the visiting Andrew Johnson in the summer of 1866 ". . . by such men as A. T. Stewart, Moses Taylor, A. A. Low, William H. Vanderbilt, William B. Astor, and others made it quite clear that the monied interests of New York were in sympathy with the President." One should not infer, however, from this

statement that Andrew Johnson, a former Tennessee tailor, had any close links with these Northern business leaders. Their interests simply happened to coincide.

95.   A sizable number of the Radical spokesmen were either minor entrepreneurs or representatives of rapidly expanding industries who desired easy credit and high tariffs, whereas the conservative hard-money men backing President Johnson's program were primarily well-established Eastern merchants, commercial bankers, and textile manufacturers. Indeed, if the Reconstruction program had simply paved the way for a massive Yankee-directed economic takeover of the South, most of this region's railroads would have quickly fallen into Northern (or Carpetbagger) hands. But this did not occur on any significant scale. On the contrary, the historical record clearly reveals that Northern capital was channeled principally into Western railroads, both before and after the Civil War.

96.   Sharkey rightly criticized the Beards, not for their emphasis on economic forces, but for their failure to make a more discerning analysis of the various divergent or conflicting economic groups in the country. As a rule, the Beards relied on a gross aggregate analysis which stressed such frequently misleading categories as capitalist and agrarian classes without making any distinction as to size or type of operation. Sharkey noted that the Beards often confused (or glossed over) the diverse interests of industrial and financial forces, although the former generally favored a high protective tariff and easy credit over the years, while the latter leaned strongly toward free trade and sound money. See Robert P. Sharkey, *op. cit.*, pp. 293 and 299.

97.   In December 1867, for example, Republican party boss Thurlow Weed arranged an important meeting, called ostensibly by New York merchant A. T. Stewart, banker Moses Taylor, Cornelius Vanderbilt, and other prominent citizens, for the express purpose of taking Grant's candidacy out of the hands of politicians and putting it under more conservative or reliable control. Among the other key figures at this affair were investment banker Levi P. Morton, merchant Moses Grinnell, railroad man Daniel Drew, and William B. and John Jacob Astor, Jr. Also, shortly after the Civil War Grant had been plied with gifts from various wealthy friends. In New York he was given a total of $100,000 to pay the mortgage on his Washington home, and in Boston fifty businessmen presented him with a library which cost about $75,000. See William B. Hesseltine, *Ulysses S. Grant* (New York: Dodd, Mead, 1935), pp. 63 and 102.

98.   Jay Cooke's brother, Henry, is reported to have acted as the Republican party's principal angel in this campaign, although many other wealthy figures were undoubtedly involved. And in 1872, when Grant ran successfully for reelection, Jay Cooke himself is alleged to have contributed about one-quarter of the total campaign funds. Cooke's relationship with Grant was clearly a very cordial one throughout the President's first term of office, though he probably had been closer to some Cabinet officers in the two preceding administrations, for he now had many formidable rivals, even in Philadelphia, where the hostile, patrician Drexel interests were a potent politico-economic force. In the late 1860s and early 1870s Cooke branched out ambitiously into railroading and became immersed in the affairs of the Lake Superior and Mississippi Railroad and the Northern Pacific Railway, particularly the latter, which, when it fell into severe financial difficulty in 1873, led abruptly to Cooke's bankruptcy. The demise of Cooke's banking establishment marked the end of Philadelphia's reign of fiscal supremacy in the nation, which probably reached its peak under Nicholas Biddle and the second Bank of the United States. As a result, no Secretaries of the Treasury have been recruited from Philadelphia in the post–Civil War period. For more on the Cookes' fundraising activities, see George Thayer, *Who Shakes the Money Tree?* (New York: Simon and Schuster, 1973), pp. 34–35, and William B. Hesseltine, *op cit.*, p. 126.

99.   Seymour, who was both born and married well, had been associated with many business enterprises over the years. In the latter part of the 1850s (between his two stints as governor) he served as a director of the Demoine Navigation and Railroad Co. and, both then and in the late 1860s, he sat on the board of the Blossburgh and Corning Railroad. In

addition, he was head of the Fox and Wisconsin Improvement Co. (a major canal company) up to 1862, when he was elected governor again, at which point his younger brother, John F. Seymour, took over as president. The latter Seymour also served as a director of the New York Central Railroad in the late 1850s (see the *U.S. Railroad Directory, 1856,* p. 38). Horatio Seymour was on very close terms with such prominent politico-economic leaders as Dean Richmond, Erastus Corning, John V. L. Pruyn, and Samuel J. Tilden (all primarily railroad figures), and New York banker August Belmont. When a more liberal Democratic candidate, the idealistic (onetime Republican) Horace Greeley, won the party's presidential nomination in 1872, August Belmont resigned, apparently in disgust or protest, as chairman of the Democratic National Committee, a post he had held for twelve years. He was, interestingly, succeeded by August Schell, a Tammany Hall chieftain, who was a vice-president of the Lake Shore and Southern Michigan Railway and a director of the New York Central and Hudson River Railroad, both Vanderbilt-controlled lines. See Stewart Mitchell, *Horatio Seymour of New York* (Cambridge, Mass.: Harvard University Press, 1938), *passim.*

100.   In a most unusual maneuver, Grant initially asked his longtime Illinois friend Elihu Washburne to become Secretary of State for an extremely short period (less than a week), apparently so that he would have some prestige when he was appointed shortly thereafter as American Minister to France. (Because of the dubious nature of this action, Washburne will be described in this chapter only in his role as a diplomat.) Grant then offered the post of Secretary of State to Iowa Congressman James F. Wilson, who was a key figure in the railroad-dominated Des Moines Regency, but this Republican leader declined to serve for financial reasons (a low governmental salary and high expenses). For more on Wilson's pro-railroad views and associations, see Leland L. Sage, *William Boyd Allison,* pp. 33, 65, and 89–90, and Stanley P. Hirshson, *Grenville M. Dodge,* pp. 176–77.

101.   In his biography of Fish, Allan Nevins makes brief reference to two of these ties, although he erred in saying that Fish was a vice-president of the Camden and Amboy Railroad between 1864 and 1872 (Fish's links were with the New Jersey Railroad, a somewhat smaller line). It is impossible to tell from Poor's *Manual of the Railroads of the United States* whether Fish continued to serve as a director of the latter concern after 1872, but Nevins's book indicates that he did not. See Allan Nevins, *Hamilton Fish* (New York: Dodd, Mead & Co., 1937), pp. 95–96, and also his *History of the Bank of New York and Trust Company* (New York: privately printed, 1934), appendix, p. vi.

102.   See Henry V. Poor, *Manual of the Railroads of the United States* (New York: H. V. & H. W. Poor, 1875–78) for the appropriate entries. Also of note, Fish's sister, Susan, had married Daniel LeRoy, whose sister was the second wife of Daniel Webster. And one of the Secretary of State's sons, Stuyvesant Fish, was with the major New York banking house of Morton, Bliss & Co. from 1872 to 1877. Its senior partners were officers or directors of many railroads (and probably other enterprises) in the early and mid-1870s.

103.   As his first Assistant Secretary of State, Fish chose New York City lawyer (and onetime minor diplomatic official) J. C. Bancroft Davis, after being given firm assurances that the latter's recent directorship tie with the Jay Gould–dominated Erie Railway was due entirely to his efforts to protect innocent stockholders from the financial machinations of this unscrupulous Robber Baron. But Davis's association with the Erie Railway predated Gould's takeover of the line, and he also sat (up to at least 1869) on the board of the Towanda Coal Co., a small concern headed by Gould, so there is some question about the nature of their relationship. Davis was a socially well-established figure, being the son of former Massachusetts Governor John Davis, the nephew of historian-diplomat George Bancroft, and the son-in-law of the late New York City financier James Gore King (who was the son of former Federalist leader Rufus King).

The other two persons to serve as Assistant Secretary of State under Fish were Charles Hale, a Boston Brahmin former newspaperman and diplomatic official, whose mother was a sister of the wealthy onetime Minister to Great Britain Edward Everett, and John L.

Cadwalader, a member of a prominent Philadelphia family, who was, up to his appointment in 1874, a partner in Bancroft Davis's New York law firm.

104. By this time, the mercantile house of A. T. Stewart was the largest dry goods distributor in the country, with (perhaps exaggerated) sales of $50 million a year. See Alfred D. Chandler, Jr., *The Visible Hand,* p. 218.

105. See, for instance, Harry E. Resseguie, "Federal Conflict of Interest: The A. T. Stewart Case," *New York History* (July 1966), pp. 294–99.

106. See William B. Hesseltine, *Ulysses S. Grant,* p. 147. Jay Cooke, for example, was reportedly fearful that a hostile New Yorker would be appointed, so the selection of Boutwell was acceptable to him. See Henrietta M. Larson, *Jay Cooke,* p. 200.

107. For a number of important figures, he was clearly preferable to some other possible choices. Jay Cooke, for instance, ". . . feared that another Philadelphia banker, closely allied to the rival Drexel & Childs, would be the nominee, and instructed his brother, Henry, to 'bring everything to bear upon General Grant' to defeat the move." See William B. Hesseltine, *op. cit.,* p. 312.

108. See *The Capitalist's Guide and Railway Annual for 1859, Ashcroft's Railway Directory for 1865,* and *Poor's Manual of the Railroads of the United States.* Henceforth, when the author refers to a federal official's former or still extant railroad ties, he will not bother to give any documentation unless it is from a source other than *Poor's Railroad Manual* (as it is popularly known).

109. This post was first offered, interestingly, to one of Philadelphia's leading bankers, Anthony J. Drexel, and then to Quaker City industrialist Joseph Patterson, but neither could be persuaded to accept. See Keith Ian Polakoff, *The Politics of Inertia* (Baton Rouge: Louisiana State University Press, 1973), p. 18.

110. See Ross A. Webb, *Benjamin Helm Bristow* (Lexington: University Press of Kentucky, 1969), p. 51. Another point in Bristow's favor was that he was a cousin of John L. Helm, a former governor of Kentucky and onetime (1854–1860) president of the Louisville and Nashville Railroad, who was the father-in-law of Mrs. Lincoln's half-sister, Mrs. Ben Hardin Helm.

111. These included the Louisville and Nashville Railroad, the St. Louis and Southeastern Railway, and the Pullman's Palace Car Co. See Ross A. Webb, *op. cit.,* pp. 125 and 132.

112. As Secretary of the Treasury, Bristow came under heavy attack by certain Western railroads when, in an almost unprecedented move, he instituted proceedings against those lines which had failed to repay the federal government for the generous building loans extended to them.

113. See the *Dictionary of American Biography,* Vol. 13, p. 199, and the appropriate entries in *Poor's Railroad Manual.* With regard to Bradbury, see Gustavus Myers, *History of the Supreme Court of the United States,* pp. 478–79.

114. In the last half of the 1850s Hoar did practice law in Boston, part of the time with a wealthy Brahmin, Horace Gray, who was later appointed to the U.S. Supreme Court by President Chester A. Arthur.

115. See Brainerd Dyer, *The Public Career of William M. Evarts* (Berkeley: University of California Press, 1933), p. 9 and *passim.* Hoar, who, according to Baltzell, was a member of one of Boston's top 50 families, was himself quite friendly with such major railroad men as John Murray Forbes. See E. Digby Baltzell, *Puritan Boston and Quaker Philadelphia* (New York: Free Press, 1979), p. 464; Moorfield Storey and Edward W. Emerson, *Ebenezer Rockwood Hoar* (Boston: Houghton Mifflin, 1911), *passim;* and Mary C. Crawford, *Famous Families of Massachusetts,* Vol. I, pp. 49 and 103.

116. See Allan Nevins, *Hamilton Fish,* p. 591.

117. See the *Dictionary of American Biography,* Vol. 1, p. 134, and William B. Hesseltine, *Ulysses S. Grant,* p. 262.

118.   Pierrepont was also reportedly a substantial contributor to Grant's 1868 presidential campaign, but we do not know whether this act was repeated in 1872, and if so, what effect it had on Pierrepont's later appointment as Attorney General. See William B. Hesseltine, *op. cit.*, pp. 126 and 130.

119.   The family's fortunes had also been bolstered greatly by the recent marriage of one of Taft's sons (Charles P.) to the daughter of David Sinton, reputedly one of the richest men in Cincinnati.

120.   See Stanley P. Hirshson, *Grenville M. Dodge,* pp. 173–74, and William B. Hesseltine, *op. cit.,* p. 140.

121.   Sherman had been a career Army officer up to 1853, when, apparently in economic need, he turned his hand, without notable success, to various lesser business and legal pursuits before he accepted the more suitable position of superintendent of a military college in 1859. His Ohio brother, U.S. Senator John Sherman, was not only a major political leader, but had several important economic ties, the most conspicuous of which were as a director of the Pittsburgh, Fort Wayne and Chicago Railway in the late 1860s and as a director (until 1866) of the Atlantic and Great Western Railway.

122.   See, for instance, Ishbel Ross, *An American Family: The Tafts—1689–1964* (Cleveland: World Publishing, 1964), p. 13.

123.   Cameron also served for many years as president of the family-dominated Bank of Middletown (Pennsylvania) and as a director of the various other, primarily lesser, enterprises.

124.   Borie also sat on the board of the Philadelphia Contributionship for the Insurance of Houses from Loss by Fire, a fairly small concern long associated with that city's socio-economic elite. According to one authority, Borie was a member of one of Philadelphia's top 50 families. See E. Digby Baltzell, *Puritan Boston and Quaker Philadelphia,* p. 460.

125.   According to William B. Hesseltine, Grant first turned to two Philadelphia businessmen, George H. Stuart and Lindley Smyth (spelled Smith in Hesseltine's book), but neither man found the office very attractive. See William B. Hesseltine, *Ulysses S. Grant,* p. 160.

126.   For more on the influence of the Stockton family, in particular, see Stephen Hess, *America's Political Dynasties* (Garden City, N.Y.: Doubleday, 1966), pp. 393–416.

127.   See John F. Stover, *The Railroads of the South, 1865–1900: A Study in Finance and Control* (Chapel Hill: University of North Carolina Press, 1955), pp. 85–86. This account merely claims that John S. Delano was added to one of the groups competing in the early 1870s for this governmental lease, whereas, in fact, both Columbus Delano and his son served on the board of directors from 1873 through 1875. See the pertinent entries in *Poor's Railroad Manual.*

128.   The Assistant Secretary of the Interior during much of the time Delano was in office was a Bellaire, Ohio banker named Benjamin R. Cowen, who, despite his essentially small-town background, had certain significant business ties, the most prominent of which was as a trustee (i.e., director) of the fairly large Wisconsin-headquartered Northwestern Mutual Life Insurance Co. from 1868 through 1877. (See Harold F. Williamson and Orange A. Smalley, *Northwestern Mutual Life: A Century of Trusteeship* [Evanston, Ill.: Northwestern University Press, 1957], p. 336.) For want of space and lack of adequate biographical data, the author will not make a systematic analysis of these second-tier positions, except for the State Department, until almost the turn of the century, when these posts became more important, and more pertinent primary and secondary material are available.

129.   See Mary K. George, *Zachariah Chandler* (East Lansing: Michigan State University Press, 1969), p. 3. Chandler reportedly severed all connections with his former primary business in 1869, although he continued to be a major stockholder in a number of Detroit

enterprises. He apparently was not heavily involved in railroad development, perhaps because most of the larger lines in Michigan were controlled by outside interests.

130. See, for instance, Mary K. George, *op cit.,* p. 275. Actually, Jay Gould was not a major "behind-the-scenes" power in the Grant administration, for he had established a bad reputation, both in and out of government, and, aside from his notorious attempt to corner the gold market, probably exerted significant influence only intermittently. Also, there were a number of other important rival business figures who were constantly striving to secure access to various high federal officials, which efforts frequently served to offset those of Gould.

131. See Gerald T. White, *A History of the Massachusetts Hospital Life Insurance Company* (Cambridge: Harvard University Press, 1955), pp. 170 and 173. Motley's father may have served on various other important boards, but since this concern is one of the few in the Boston area for which complete officer and directorship data are available, it is probably being referred to disproportionately in this study. Hopefully, more research will correct this problem.

132. Grant first offered this post to U. S. Senator Frederick T. Frelinghuysen, a New Jersey lawyer who had many key socio-economic ties, the most prominent of which was as a director of the Central Railroad of New Jersey and, up to an 1864 merger, the Great Western Railroad (a line now known as the Wabash Railroad). When this patrician refused to accept, Grant turned to Indiana Senator Oliver P. Morton, about whom little is known. However, his nomination had to be withdrawn for political reasons.

133. One of the things that allegedly attracted Schenck to President Grant was his skill at poker, a game the General loved to play. See William B. Hesseltine, *Ulysses S. Grant,* p. 231.

134. See the *U.S. Railroad Directory, 1856,* p. 172.

135. See William B. Hesseltine, *op. cit.,* p. 231.

136. As Minister, Schenck had lent his name to the Emma Silver Mining Company's ". . . advertised list of directors in return for an annual salary of $2,500 and the offer to carry $10,000 worth of stock in his name one year free of charge, with guaranteed dividends." Schenck assured many British citizens that the concern was a good investment, when, in fact, about 84 percent of the money put into this venture was lost in one year alone. See Allan Nevins, *Hamilton Fish,* pp. 651–52 and 814.

137. For the economic ties of other members of the Chouteau-Gratiot family, see the appropriate entry in Appendix A, and for a description of Washburne's marital links, see Gaillard Hunt, *Israel, Elihu and Cadwallader Washburn* (New York: Macmillan Co., 1925), pp. 177–80. It is also interesting to note that J. Pierpont Morgan, who was just beginning his illustrious career as a New York banker, served as a vice-president and director of the Syracuse, Binghamton and New York Railroad in the late 1860s.

138. Cadwallader C. Washburn was reported, by the mid-1870s or early 1880s, to have been the largest single owner of mill property in the world. See Gaillard Hunt, *op. cit.,* p. 384, and Stephen Hess, *America's Political Dynasties,* p. 138.

139. As his Minister to Germany, Grant chose to retain Brahmin historian and onetime high federal official George Bancroft, who had been appointed in the latter part of the Johnson regime. Bancroft was by this time a wealthy, rather conservative man with substantial stockholdings in railroads and various other enterprises. He served in Germany until the summer of 1874, when he was replaced by his nephew, former (1869–1874) Assistant Secretary of State J. C. Bancroft Davis, who had married into the (Rufus) King family and, prior to his appointment to this departmental post, had served as a director of the Erie Railway.

140. The administration's major economic policies were likewise characterized by frequent change and indecision, as there were numerous splits within the business commu-

nity over such issues as hard versus soft money. As Irwin Unger has pointed out, the bulk of the older established interests in the country strongly desired a stable currency, while many industrial entrepreneurs and Western railroad men preferred an inflationary policy (or at least one providing easy credit). Similarly, there were deep divisions in the business world about the tariff program, even among railroad executives. For more on this matter, see Irwin Unger, *The Greenback Era* (Princeton, N.J.: Princeton University Press, 1964), *passim*.

141. See Thomas G. Belden and Marva R. Belden, *So Fell the Angels*, pp. 42–43.

142. See Irwin Unger, *The Greenback Era*, p. 147.

143. In addition, in the late 1850s William Sprague had sat on the board of the Hartford, Providence and Fishkill Railroad, a line then headed by his cousin, Byron Sprague. In the post–Civil War period William Sprague and his brother, Amasa, were also heavily involved in Western real estate speculation, which led them to become staunch advocates of easy credit.

144. About a year after becoming Chief Justice, Chase also wrote to Jay Cooke suggesting that he be made a silent partner in the latter's firm, which tactless, if not improper, request Cooke skillfully evaded by offering Chase a position with his London branch of operations, a geographically incompatible post for Chase to hold. Furthermore, in 1869 the brazen Chase mailed a letter to Cooke indicating that he would like to be placed on the board of directors of the Northern Pacific Railroad, another dubious solicitation that came to naught. See Thomas G. Belden and Marva R. Belden, *op. cit.,* p. 171, and Ellis P. Oberholtzer, *Jay Cooke: Financier of the Civil War* (Philadelphia: George W. Jacobs, 1907), Vol. II, pp. 102 and 130.

145. Grant first offered the Chief Justiceship to New York lawyer and U.S. Senator Roscoe Conkling, an ambitious and imperious man who dominated the state Republican machine in the 1870s and apparently had no important formal socio-economic ties. However, Conkling, who had his eyes set on the Presidency, refused to serve. Grant then submitted the name of his Attorney General, George H. Williams, a former Oregon lawyer of no special note (and some hint of scandal), who was vigorously rejected by the Senate. Stung by this turn of events, Grant turned to Massachusetts lawyer and onetime Cabinet officer Caleb Cushing, who had recently served with considerable distinction at the Geneva arbitration proceedings called to resolve economic disputes over depredations committed by the British during the Civil War. But Cushing was an elderly Democrat and was suspected of having Southern sympathies, so the Senate blocked his appointment too. Grant is also reported to have offered the Chief Justiceship to Wisconsin Senator Timothy P. Howe, Indiana Senator Oliver P. Morton, and Secretary of State Hamilton Fish, although he did not formally nominate any of them.

146. See Gustavus Myers, *History of the Supreme Court of the United States,* pp. 531–39, and Fred Rodell, *Nine Men: A Political History of the Supreme Court from 1790 to 1955* (New York: Random House, 1955), p. 162. Rodell maintains that Grant passed over the able Associate Justice Samuel F. Miller and named a second-rate railroad lawyer from Ohio as Chief Justice. Waite's two biographers, on the other hand, take a much more roseate view of the matter. For instance, Bruce Trimble, has rather innocently claimed that Waite ". . . was a plain man, of much wisdom, and few pretenses." And Peter Magrath, while acknowledging that Waite had certain noteworthy railroad ties, nevertheless asserts that he was not a "railroad attorney" in the usual sense of the word, for as he argues, with some but not total justice, ". . . after the 1850s no business lawyer worth his salt could avoid involvement in railroad cases. Railroads became an integral part of the nation's business life and lawyers inevitably were caught up in their affairs." See Bruce R. Trimble, *Chief Justice Waite: Defender of the Public Interest* (Princeton, N.J.: Princeton University Press, 1938), p. 2, and C. Peter Magrath, *Morrison R. Waite* (New York: Macmillan, 1963), p. 52.

147. See Bruce R. Trimble, *op. cit.,* pp. 50–51. Trimble also refers to Waite's participa-

tion in the organizational plans for the creation of the Toledo, Wabash and Western Railroad, but makes no mention of his involvement in other railroad enterprises.

148. See C. Peter Magrath, *op. cit.*, pp. 50–51. Contrary to Magrath's claim of 1871, *Poor's Railroad Manual* reveals that Waite was first appointed a vice-president of the company in 1868, after having served for many years as an outside member of the board of directors.

149. Although Clifford was appointed by Buchanan, the bulk of his judicial service occurred during the Civil War and Reconstruction years (hence his description here). As Gustavus Myers has pointed out, two of Justice Clifford's children married (one by the late 1850s, the other by the mid-1860s) into the family of Maine business magnate John B. Brown, who was the longtime head of the Portland Sugar Co. and a director (and presumably large stockholder) of a number of important rail lines—the Atlantic and St. Lawrence Railroad (from probably at least 1856 through 1877); the Portland and Kennebec Railroad and its successor company, the Maine Central Railroad (at least 1865 through 1877); the Toledo, Peoria and Warsaw Railroad (at least 1865 through 1877); the Portland, Saco and Portsmouth Railroad (the late 1860s); and the Erie Railroad (starting in 1875). See the appropriate entries in the 1867–1877 issues of *Poor's Railroad Manual* and Gustavus Myers, *op. cit.*, p. 479. Two of the other three Northern justices, Grier and Nelson, did not have such key ties, although the former was probably an elite figure of lesser (pro-mercantile) status. Both Grier and Nelson served on the High Court until the early 1870s.

150. See Henry J. Abraham, *Justices and Presidents* (New York: Oxford University Press, 1974), p. 108. Also, according to Gustavus Myers (*op. cit.*, p. 497), Swayne had represented a number of business enterprises in Ohio, particularly banks and insurance companies.

151. See Leon Friedman and Fred L. Israel (eds.), *The Justices of the United States Supreme Court, 1789–1969* (New York: Chelsea House Publishers, 1969), Vol. II, p. 991; and John P. Frank, "The Appointment of Supreme Court Justices: Prestige, Principles and Politics," *Wisconsin Law Review* (March 1941), p. 179.

152. See John R. Schmidhauser, *The Supreme Court: Its Politics, Personalities, and Procedures* (New York: Holt, Rinehart & Winston, 1960), p. 57.

153. See Leon Friedman and Fred L. Israel, *op. cit.*, Vol. II, p. 996. Later evidence of Swayne's pro-railroad orientation may be found in the fact that his son, Wager, served in the early and mid 1870s (shortly after being admitted to the bar) on the board of the Atlantic and Lake Erie Railroad, the Toledo, Tiffin and Eastern Railroad, and the Mansfield, Coldwater and Lake Michigan Railroad.

154. See Henry J. Abraham, *Justices and Presidents*, p. 108. Judging from various other studies, Miller was not closely allied with such avowed pro-railroad spokesmen as Grenville M. Dodge, William B. Allison, or any leader associated with that potent political faction soon known as the Des Moines Regency. Miller's Keokuk law practice has been devoted largely to land-claims litigation.

155. See Charles Fairman, *Mr. Justice Miller and the Supreme Court, 1862–1890* (Cambridge, Mass.: Harvard University Press, 1939), pp. 426–27. At one point in his career, exasperated by the blatant pro-business bias displayed by many of his colleagues on the Supreme Court, Miller is said to have remarked that "it is vain to contend with judges who have been, at the bar, the advocates of railroad companies, and all the forms of associated capital, when they are called upon to decide cases where such interests are in contest." See Fred Rodell, *Nine Men*, p. 146.

156. See Leon Friedman and Fred L. Israel, *op. cit.*, Vol. II, p. 1021.

157. See Leo Pfeffer, *This Honorable Court* (Boston: Beacon Press, 1965), p. 167.

158. See Willard L. King, *Lincoln's Manager, David Davis*, p. 101. According to one

reliable source, Davis was a millionaire, presumably at the time he was appointed to the Supreme Court. See J. G. Randall and David Donald, *The Civil War and Reconstruction* (Lexington, Mass.: D. C. Heath, 1969), p. 659.

159.   See Henry J. Abraham, *op. cit.,* p. 111; John P. Frank, *op. cit.,* p. 180; Carl B. Swisher, *Stephen J. Field: Craftsman of the Law* (Washington, D.C.: Brookings Institution, 1930), pp. 116 and 243–45; and Norman E. Tutorow, *Leland Stanford: Man of Many Careers* (Menlo Park, Cal.: Pacific Coast Publishers, 1971), p. 283.

160.   For more on this clientele tie, see Walter K. Earle, *Mr. Shearman and Mr. Sterling and How They Grew* (New York: privately printed, 1963), pp. 13–21. Stephen Field first practiced law with his brother in New York City in the 1840s, before branching out on his own in California. Field had another more famous brother, Cyrus, who as head of the Atlantic Telegraph Co. had much to do with the laying of the first trans-Atlantic cable shortly after the Civil War. Cyrus Field later expanded into other business ventures, some of them undertaken with his friend and neighbor Jay Gould.

161.   President Johnson had only one opportunity to fill a seat on the High Court, that had been left vacant by the death of John Catron. But because of the hostility of Radical forces in Congress, his nominee, Ohio attorney Henry Stanbery, was not acted upon by the Senate.

162.   Because of great pressure from Pennsylvania forces, Grant initially chose former Secretary of War Edwin M. Stanton for this key post, but he died four days after being confirmed by the Senate. Grant then nominated Attorney General Ebenezer R. Hoar, an able Boston Brahmin, but this selection ran into a wall of bitter opposition in the Radical-dominated Senate and was rejected.

163.   See Gustavus Myers, *History of the Supreme Court of the United States,* p. 517; Leon Friedman and Fred L. Israel, *op. cit.,* Vol. II, p. 1154; and the *U.S. Railroad Directory, 1856,* pp. 56 and 61. Other sources, which have some gaps, do not show Strong as serving in either of these capacities, so the author has assumed that these ties were severed in 1857.

164.   Bradley's nomination was strongly opposed, in a revealing example of elite infighting, by Pennsylvania Senator and Republican party boss Simon Cameron, the Pennsylvania Railroad's reputed primary spokesman in Congress. This line had long nursed a bitter grudge against the Camden and Amboy Railroad and its political allies for blocking its plans to secure a new right-of-way across New Jersey. (See Leon Friedman and Fred L. Israel, *op cit.,* Vol. II, pp. 1185–86.) The fact that it was unable to prevent Bradley's appointment indicates that the power of the Pennsylvania Railroad in national affairs has been overrated.

165.   See Leon Friedman and Fred L. Israel, *op. cit.,* Vol. II, p. 1183; the *Newark City Directory* in the post–Civil War period; and on the last point, Charles Fairman, "Mr. Justice Bradley's Appointment to the Supreme Court and the Legal Tender Cases," *Harvard Law Review* (April 1941), p. 982.

166.   See, for instance, Leon Friedman and Fred L. Israel, *op. cit.,* Vol. II, p. 1222, and David M. Jordan, *Roscoe Conkling of New York* (Ithaca, N.Y.: Cornell University Press, 1971), pp. 18 and 108.

167.   See, with regard to the first tie, Edward Hungerford, *Men and Iron: The History of the New York Central* (New York: Thomas Y. Crowell, 1938), pp. 69–70, and Frank W. Stevens, *The Beginnings of the New York Central Railroad* (New York: G. P. Putnam's Sons, 1926), pp. 252–53.

168.   A later, perhaps equally important ruling, which is not so amenable to economic analysis, was that laid down in the Granger cases, first and foremost of which was *Munn v. Illinois.* In this set of decisions the Court upheld the action taken by various western states, because of merchant and farm protest, providing for a significant amount of governmental regulation of railroad rates and practices. Surprisingly, the decision was written by Chief Justice Waite, a former Ohio lawyer and railroad official, reportedly with considerable help

from Associate Justice Bradley, a longtime New Jersey railroad attorney. Justice Miller also strongly supported these state measures, though probably for different reasons. Several of the other Justices followed one of these two leads. However, two pro-railroad jurists, Field and Strong, vehemently disagreed with this verdict. A possible reason for this split in the railroad ranks on the Court is that some of the Justices may have feared that this agrarian-backed movement would lead to an irresistible groundswell of support for federal regulation of the railroads, and they may have preferred to see the matter handled by the states, which might be more susceptible to railroad pressure. Also, much of the regulatory activity was directed at Western rail lines, which were of comparatively little concern to Eastern jurists, regardless of their economic orientation.

169. See, for instance, Sidney Ratner, "Was the Supreme Court Packed by President Grant?", *Political Science Quarterly* (September 1935), pp. 343–58, and for a more conservative, probably overly sanguine view, see Charles Fairman, "Mr. Justice Bradley's Appointment to the Supreme Court and the Legal Tender Cases," *Harvard Law Review* (April 1941), pp. 977–1034 and (May 1941), pp. 1128–55. Bradley continued to serve on the board of the Second National Bank of Newark during his early years on the Court, but this was apparently a less important affiliation than his longstanding tie with the Camden and Amboy Railroad. It should also be noted that some of Lincoln's Supreme Court appointees were either closely associated with or friendly to railroad interests.

CHAPTER 3

Hayes through Cleveland

The two decades following the Civil War and Reconstruction years were marked by a return to close two-party competition in national politics and the continued striking economic growth of the country. Much of this latter development occurred in the railroad sector, which almost completely overshadowed all other areas of activity. Indeed, because of an enormous, perhaps excessive, surge in construction, the amount of track in operation in the United States virtually doubled between 1877 and 1887, and underwent a like jump in the next ten years, reaching a total of over 240,000 miles by 1897.[1] Even by this last date, when large-scale industrial enterprise is supposed to have emerged as a major force in American life, the physical plant (i.e., assets) of the railroads far exceeded that of manufacturing. In fact, before the 1890s industrial securities were almost unknown in the United States, aside from the coal and textile fields, and many coal companies were, as big shippers, closely allied with the railroads.[2]

To get a better idea of the extent to which railroad enterprises dominated the economic scene even in the late 1890s, one has merely to look at the comparative size of the larger railroad and industrial concerns. Outside of transportation, there were, judging from available data, at best five companies which had assets of over $100 million in 1897. They are shown in Table 1.[3]

TABLE 1

America's 5 Largest Industrial Enterprises in 1897

Rank	Company	1897 Assets (millions)
1.	Standard Oil Co.	$147.2
2.	U.S. Leather Co.	136.2
3.	Western Union Telegraph Co.	128.4
4.	American Sugar Refining Co. (the old so-called sugar trust)	116.1
5.	Carnegie Steel Co.	101.4 (a 1900 figure)

Such modern-day giants as the Anaconda Copper Mining Co. had assets of only about $38 million, and the Westinghouse Electric & Manufacturing Co. had just $18 million. On the other hand, there were many railroads that had assets of more than $100 million. Most of them far exceeded the size of any industrial enterprise, as seen from Table 2.

TABLE 2

America's 12 Largest Railroads in 1897

Rank	Company	1897 Assets (millions)
1.	Southern Pacific (Rwy.) Co.	$522.0
2.	Atchison, Topeka & Sante Fe Rwy.	415.4
3.	Pennsylvania RR (and its subsidiary, Pennsylvania Co.)	340.2
4.	Northern Pacific Rwy.	321.0
5.	Erie Railroad	296.6
6.	Southern Railway	287.3
7.	Chicago, Burlington & Quincy RR	265.4
8.	Union Pacific Railway	230.0
9.	Chicago & Northwestern Rwy.	222.9
10.	Reading (RR) Co.	206.0
11.	New York Central & Hudson River RR	194.1
12.	Illinois Central Railroad	172.2

Thus one railroad alone—the Southern Pacific—was almost as large as four of the five biggest industrial concerns combined.[4]

However, it should not be assumed that the railroads represented a monolithic force in American business and politics. On the contrary, there was often tremendous rivalry and conflict among various powerful entrepreneurs and executives in this vital field. As a result, by the early 1880s many of the major rail lines in the country had fallen under the sway of one or another set of highly competitive corporate or kinship groups, chief of which were the nouveau-riche Vanderbilt interests, the John M. Forbes–led Boston Brahmin elite, the economic forces of New York financier Jay Gould and his ally Russell Sage, the Pennsylvania Railroad (an essentially management-dominated concern), and the Southern Pacific–Central Pacific system, which was controlled by the so-called Big Four (a team composed of Collis P. Huntington, Leland Stanford, Charles Crocker, and Mark Hopkins).[5] The Vanderbilt system consisted initially of the Harlem Extension Railroad, the New York Central and Hudson River Railroad, the Lake Shore and Michigan Southern Railway, and a few other lines in the densely populated Northeast. They were so profitable that the founder of this famous dynasty was able to amass about $100 million by the time of his death in 1877, a vast sum generally viewed as the first of the great American fortunes.[6] Vanderbilt's entrepreneurial heirs managed to expand the family's range of operations still further into the north central section of the country through the acquisition of a sizable stake in other important railroads, such as the Chicago and Northwestern, with the result that their reported holdings ultimately reached a total of 21,000 miles of railway.

The major transportation enterprises controlled by the close-knit Boston Brahmin group were, curiously enough, not in the New England area, but in the Middle and Far West. Its principal economic interests were centered during all or part of the late 19th century in three big companies—the Atchison, Topeka, and Sante Fe Railway, the Chicago, Burlington and Quincy Railroad, and the Union Pacific Railroad (although this last-named concern was dominated at times by other forces).[7]

The third large railway network was that assembled by the rapacious New York entrepreneur, Jay Gould, whose first famous coup was his takeover in the late 1860s of the Erie Railway, a concern he so thoroughly exploited (perhaps plundered would be a better word) that there was an extensive investigation and judicial proceeding which culminated in his removal from corporate office, a rich but badly discredited man. Having been thwarted in this endeavor, Gould shifted his attention and resources to the western part of the United States, where by the early 1880s he had put together a much larger complex of railroads, the major components of which were:[8]

	Mileage (1881)	Assets (millions)
International & Great Northern RR	776	$ 28
Missouri, Kansas & Texas Rwy.	1,286	76
Missouri Pacific Rwy.	904	62
St. Louis, Iron Mountain & Southern RR	719	56
Texas and Pacific Rwy.	1,392	45
Union Pacific Rwy.	4,619	200
Wabash, St. Louis and Pacific Rwy.	3,348	122
Total	13,044	$589

In addition, Gould secured control of the massive Western Union Telegraph Co., a concern which long represented one of his most valuable holdings.

The fourth huge transportation enterprise was the Pennsylvania Railroad, which company was headed in the post–Civil War period by a series of able and farsighted executives who were eager to expand its operations, primarily by indirect means (other corporate entities), into the southern and especially the western portions of the country. Under the leadership of Thomas A. Scott, this company engaged in a titanic struggle in the early and mid-1870s to secure a transcontinental connection through a then closely linked line, the Texas and Pacific Railway, for its essentially northeastern rail business. In his efforts to obtain federal aid for this endeavor, Scott encountered considerable resistance from other railroad forces and ultimately met defeat, but only after an epic battle that affected many of the most important politico-economic interests in the nation.

The fifth great railroad system was forged in the Far West by the "Big Four," an entrepreneurial group led chiefly by Collis P. Huntington, which exercised firm control over both the Central Pacific and Southern Pacific railways (these concerns were merged in 1885, with the latter emerging as the parent unit).[9] This network completely dominated rail travel in the Pacific Coast area. As Richard O'Connor has put it, so thoroughly did this combine monopolize transportation in the region ". . . that from the mid-1870s to 1910 the profit margins of almost every business and industry on the Coast were controlled, not by market conditions, but by the dictates of the railroad."[10] As ambitious men, Huntington and his associates were not content with this range of operations, but strove to extend their enterprise eastward, thereby precipitating a bitter clash with the powerful forces led by Thomas A. Scott and his Pennsylvania Railroad backers.[11]

The development of these major railroad systems required a great deal of capital, some of which was provided by the entrepreneurs themselves. The Boston Brahmin group had, for instance, amassed considerable money from previous mercantile ventures, and Commodore Vanderbilt had accumulated a sizable fortune from his pre–Civil War steamboat business. But much capital had to be generated by other means, and while there were many commercial banks in the country, most were fairly small and hence limited in their financial resources. As a result, various investment banks rose to prominence by serving as key fundraising agencies, in the process of which they, quite understandably, worked closely with the railroads, and often informally with one another.[12] Perhaps the most important of these was Drexel, Morgan & Co., which was formed in 1871 (just before the collapse of Jay Cooke & Co.) through the merger of the prestigious Drexel firm of Philadelphia and the more recently created (J. P.) Morgan concern of New York City. The latter house, however, soon emerged as the dominant party in this relationship, and by 1879 had established a critical tie with the Vanderbilt railroad empire and other major forces.[13] Similarly, in Boston Kidder, Peabody & Co. developed such close links with the Atchison, Topeka and Sante Fe Railway that it took ". . . an almost proprietary interest in the line."[14]

Another source of funds that began to assume some importance toward the latter part of this 20-year period were the various life insurance companies, most of which were not created until about the middle of the century. A sizable number were chartered in the 1840s; the most prominent of these were the New York Life Insurance Co. and the Mutual Life Insurance Co. of New York. But many others were not organized until almost the Civil War or shortly thereafter, as may be seen by the following selective list of (now famous) firms and their dates of incorporation— Equitable Life Assurance Society (1859), John Hancock Mutual Life Insurance Co. (1862), Travelers Insurance Co. (1865), Metropolitan Life Insurance Co. (1866), and the Prudential Insurance Co. of America (1875). Initially, most of these concerns were restricted by law as to their investment authority, which was frequently confined to real estate mortgages and government bonds. However, after 1870 these strictures were gradually loosened, so that by the late 19th century certain insurance companies were investing considerable funds in corporate securities. In fact, by around the turn of the century the "big three" of the industry— Mutual, Equitable, and New York Life—had between 40 and 50 percent of their investments in railroad stocks and bonds.[15]

Another important relationship which continued to evolve during this period was that between the legal and business communities. Not only were lawyers more highly valued and rewarded by major entrepreneurs in the post-Reconstruction years, but the links between these two sets of figures became increasingly close-knit and formalized through the appointment of trusted attorneys to many boards of directors. And the basis on which the lawyers (or law firms) were picked by businessmen was not always legal ability; sometimes it was family ties. For example, the law firm regularly retained by J. P. Morgan & Co. (to use its later name) in the latter part of this period was Bangs, Stetson, Tracy and MacVeagh, one of whose senior partners, Charles E. Tracy, was J. P. Morgan's brother-in-law.

Many of these economic and legal forces were pitted against one another in the election of 1876. After a lengthy convention battle in which all the major contenders were eliminated, the Republicans finally settled on a relatively unknown candidate who was acceptable to most factions, Ohio Governor Rutherford B. Hayes, who was a former Cincinnati and Fremont lawyer, United States Congressman, and high-ranking Civil War officer. The Democrats united behind a wealthy New York City lawyer, Samuel J. Tilden, who had built up a reputation as a political reformer in the early 1870s by directing the proceedings that led to the destruction of a notoriously corrupt ring run by Tammany Hall boss William M. Tweed, and then largely on the basis of this record and acclaim he had been elected governor of New York.

The 1876 presidential race was unique in American history, for while Tilden won the popular vote by a comfortable margin (over 260,000), the electoral count was much closer, with Tilden initially holding a 19-vote edge. But 20 votes in the South were bitterly contested on the grounds of fraud or irregularities. After considerable discussion it was agreed that the validity of these votes, and thus the outcome of the election, would be decided by a special 15-man commission created to deal with this dispute. Enormous pressures were brought to bear on governmental officials, both in and out of Washington, in the course of which, according to C. Vann Woodward, a major compromise was arrived at whereby critical Southern Democratic support would be thrown to Hayes in return for his tacit approval of certain measures strongly desired by various influential figures. These reportedly included a promise to end all repressive Reconstruction policies, the passage of a bill which would provide federal subsidies for the construction of the Texas and Pacific Railway (a concern headed by Pennsylvania Railroad president Thomas A. Scott), and as a later amendment, a favorably revised federal reimbursement scheme for the Central Pacific and Union Pacific railways (lines controlled by Collis P. Huntington and Jay Gould).[16] As a result of these negotiations, all 20 votes were, by a narrow (8–7) margin, awarded to Hayes, who thereby became President of the United States, albeit under dubious circumstances.

Because of the importance of the issue and the need to gain a sound perspective on the alignment of forces within the Democratic party in the post–Civil War years, it is essential at this point to provide a partial corrective to the way in which Hayes's opponent, Samuel J. Tilden, has generally been treated by American historians. For instance, in his pioneering account of these electoral proceedings, C. Vann Woodward has, like many writers, depicted Tilden as basically a governmental reformer, although one who had been a railroad attorney (and corporate speculator) in the past.[17] This emphasis on the past is, however, largely erroneous, for Tilden was, in fact, the most closely railroad-connected person ever to run for President of the United States. And contrary to numerous claims, Tilden had severed only a few of his major rail affiliations by 1876. He served, for example, on the board of the Pittsburgh, Fort Wayne and Chicago Railroad (from at least 1865 through 1876), the St. Louis, Alton and Terre Haute Railroad (for a like period), the Cleveland and Pittsburgh Railroad (from 1869 through 1876), and the New York, Boston, and Montreal Railway and one of its Vanderbilt-controlled predecessor concerns, the Harlem Extension Railroad (from at least 1869 to 1876).[18] Indeed, Tilden may well have been, as his friendly biographer put it, ". . . the foremost railroad lawyer in the nation."[19] In short, Tilden was not really an idealistic political leader in the mold of Horace Greeley. He was instead the conservative heir to the leadership of the railroad-dominated state Democratic organization, which mantle passed into his hands in 1866 upon the death of New York Central Railroad president Dean Richmond. Hence it seems fair to say that Tilden was not a crusading reformer locked in epic combat with such magnates as Thomas A. Scott and Jay Gould, but rather the spokesman for a different set of railroad interests, which were hostile to the efforts of the Pennsylvania Railroad and certain western lines to improve their positions with the financial help of the federal government (which massive subsidy plan ultimately failed, but not for want of trying).[20]

The Hayes Administration

As President of the United States, Hayes was not a very impressive figure. He was basically a product of good economic and political fortune. Though his father died when he was very young, he had a wealthy and devoted uncle, Sardis Birchard, an Ohio merchant and entrepreneur, who took him under his wing and provided him with substantial financial support throughout much of his life. After some indecision, Hayes embarked on a legal career, first in Fremont, Ohio (1845–1850), and then for the duration of the pre–Civil War period in Cincinnati, where by the mid-1850s he was a partner in a law firm, one member of which, Richard M. Corwine, served as a solicitor and director of the Cincinnati and Chicago Railroad.[21] During the Civil War Hayes achieved a certain amount of fame as a Union Army officer, and soon after the cessation of hostilities he was elected to Congress. This brief service was followed by two separate stints (1868–1872 and 1876–1877) as governor of Ohio, in which role he compiled a mildly reformist, though essentially conservative, record. Although in the post–Civil War years he reportedly did not practice much law, Hayes was comfortably fixed, primarily as a result of his investments in real estate and apparently railroads, plus a sizable inheritance from his uncle (who died in 1874). In fact, he listed himself in the Fremont city directory as a "capitalist," albeit on a small scale.[22] Thus while not a well-known political leader, Rutherford B. Hayes entered the White House with considerable financial security, a number of notable local socio-economic ties, and a general pro-business outlook.[23]

As his Secretary of State, President Hayes chose a well-known New York City lawyer, William M. Evarts, who had been Attorney General in the last nine months of the much-troubled Andrew Johnson administration, and had also served in other special governmental capacities from time to time, such as defense attorney for President Johnson in his impeachment proceedings, and more recently as counsel to the Republican party during the bitter Tilden-Hayes electoral dispute. But Evarts was primarily what might best be described as a Wall Street lawyer, for he had been a member of one of the city's top corporate law firms—Evarts, Choate & Southmayd—since before the Civil War. Over the years Evarts had represented many of the most important economic interests in the country, including the Ohio and Mississippi Railroad (in 1866), the Union Pacific Railroad (in the early 1870s), and the Chicago and Northwestern Railway in the famous Granger cases.[24] Although apparently he had never sat on a railroad board, Evarts did serve as a director of the fairly large Consolidation Coal Co. from 1872 to 1877.[25] His law partner, Charles F. Southmayd, was perhaps even more closely linked with the forces of wealth, since he was the longtime attorney for the Astor family and in 1875 was appointed to the board of the New York Life Insurance and Trust Co., which included several members of the Astor family.[26] In sum, there would seem to be little doubt that Evarts was on very friendly terms with various corporate interests.[27]

For the chief financial post in the Cabinet, Hayes picked his Ohio friend and presidential campaign advisor, John Sherman, who had long been regarded as the state's most distinguished Republican leader. Sherman had held a seat in Congress for six year before the Civil War and then served as a United States Senator for sixteen years, during which period he gained much experience in economic affairs. Unfortunately, relatively little is known about Sherman's non-political life except for the fact that he had been a Mansfield, Ohio lawyer for well over three decades and that he was the brother of the famous Civil War general, William T. Sherman. However, a look at the postwar railroad directories reveals that he sat on the board of the big Pittsburgh, Fort Wayne and Chicago Railway from 1866 through 1881, and briefly before that was a director of the Atlantic and Great Western Railway.[28] Thus, though far from a Wall Street lawyer, Sherman had at least one major economic tie which he maintained throughout his years as a Cabinet officer.

As his Attorney General, Hayes deliberately chose a New Englander, Charles Devens, a Massachusetts lawyer who had served during most of the post–Civil War period as, first, a state superior court judge (1867–1873) and then a supreme court justice (1873–1877). But Devens was not very well known. Indeed, aside from geographic considerations and his judicial background, Devens was probably appointed to this high post primarily because he was an intimate friend and former law partner of Brahmin political leader George F. Hoar, who was, in turn, a kinsman (first cousin) and close associate of Secretary of State William M. Evarts, a New York City attorney with many corporate connections.[29] In short, as one historian has noted, Devens had links with the Boston oligarchy.[30]

As Secretary of War, Hayes selected a Midwestern Republican leader and Keokuk, Iowa lawyer, George W. McCrary, who had shown considerable ability in serving as a state legislator (1861–1865) and a U.S. Congressman (1869–1877). Yet McCrary was also widely viewed as a railroad spokesman, in part because he had been a member of the board of the Des Moines Valley Railroad up to 1868 (that is, until about the time he entered Congress).[31] But the primary reason for this charge stemmed from the fact that McCrary was a dedicated supporter of the Des Moines Regency, a political faction headed by railroad executive and entrepreneur Grenville M. Dodge, who had served since 1869 as a director of the

Union Pacific Railroad and since 1872 as chief engineer of the Texas & Pacific Railway, two concerns heavily involved in the behind-the-scenes maneuvers that led up to the great compromise of 1877, which reportedly helped put Hayes into office.[32] Indeed, according to at least one reliable source, McCrary was "sponsored" by General Dodge and the railroad interests he represented at this time—namely, Jay Gould of the Union Pacific, and Thomas A. Scott, president of both the Pennsylvania Railroad and the Texas & Pacific Railway.[33] When McCrary resigned in late 1879 to accept a federal judgeship, he was replaced by another Midwesterner, Alexander Ramsey, who had much in common with his predecessor. Ramsey was a longtime St. Paul lawyer who had served for many years (1863–1875) as a U.S. Senator and for two terms (1849–1853 and 1859–1863) as governor of Minnesota. Like McCrary, Ramsey had a long record of association with various railroad enterprises, ranging from a close link with the Minnesota and North Western Railroad before the Civil War, to the promotion of the Northern Pacific Railroad in the early 1860s, and finally to his service as a director of the recently organized Western Railroad of Minnesota in 1879 (and perhaps preceding years), a fairly small line that was leased to and later absorbed by the Northern Pacific Railroad.[34] Hence it seems fair to conclude that during the Hayes administration the War Department was run by a pro-railroad official.

President Hayes made a most unusual move in selecting his Secretary of the Navy in that he picked someone from the country's interior, Indiana's Richard Thompson, a rather obscure figure who was thereafter whimsically referred to as "the Ancient Mariner of the Wabash."[35] Thompson was chosen largely out of deference to Indiana's influential Senator Oliver P. Morton, who, prior to his death in 1877, generally looked upon Thompson as his trusted agent in all proceedings. Thompson was also a longtime Terre Haute lawyer, who, according to his biographer, served as attorney for the Terre Haute and Indianapolis Railroad (and its predecessor concern) from the late 1840s to sometime in the 1870s.[36] In addition, unknown to many historians, Thompson sat, up to 1880, on the board of the Jeffersonville, Madison and Indianapolis Railroad, which line was controlled by an arm of the Pennsylvania Railroad and was headed by the latter's able chief executive, Thomas A. Scott.[37] So, indirectly, the Pennsylvania Railroad had a representative in Hayes's Cabinet, though the President and other high officials may not have been aware of it. Thompson held office until almost the end of the administration, when he was suddenly forced to resign under a cloud of scandal because he had foolishly accepted a lucrative position with an American subsidiary of a French-owned Panama Canal company, a post he apparently believed was not incompatible with his role as Secretary of the Navy. He was succeeded in the closing months of the regime by a Clarksburg, West Virginia lawyer and entrepreneurial figure, Nathan

Goff, Jr., who had served as U.S. attorney for his state for well over a decade and had, perhaps more importantly, many key politico-economic links.[38]

As his Secretary of the Interior, President Hayes made another unexpected choice, Missouri newspaperman Carl Schurz, who was the longtime leader of the liberal Republican movement in the Midwest. Schurz had served as a U.S. Senator from 1869 to 1875, but had held only one other major public office (and that was briefly back in the early 1860s). Unlike most Cabinet members, Schurz was an immigrant to the United States, having fled his native Germany following the abortive Revolution of 1848. Upon settling in the Midwest, he became a spokesman for the many German-Americans living in that part of the nation and a strong advocate of various moderate or progressive causes. Not surprisingly, Schurz was a man of modest means with no major socio-economic ties. And perhaps because of this background, his term as Secretary of the Interior was marked by numerous reforms and improvements in governmental policy, particularly with regard to the treatment of the nation's Indians.[39]

As American Minister to Great Britain, President Hayes, at the urging of his close advisors, chose someone from Pennsylvania, an important state that had thus far been overlooked in the award of high federal posts. For this prestigious position, Hayes picked a Philadelphian, John Welsh, who, though he had a rather common name, was actually one of this city's most prominent merchants. He had served on the board of the Philadelphia National Bank since 1857 (as had his father for 50 years before him) and the Philadelphia Contributionship for the Insurance of Homes for Loss by Fire (long an elite-dominated institution) from 1866 through 1879.[40] The elderly Welsh resigned in the latter part of 1879, after less than two years of service, because of poor health. Following a brief search for a successor, President Hayes selected a Boston Brahmin academic and literary figure, James Russell Lowell, who had been acting as American Minister to Spain.[41] Though Lowell had eschewed a business life, he was, as a result of various family ventures, independently wealthy, and many of his kinsmen were involved in a host of major economic enterprises. For example, one cousin, John A. Lowell, was a longtime high official or director of a number of textile mills and a director of the Suffolk Bank (from 1822 to 1881) and the Massachusetts Hospital Life Insurance Co. (from 1834 to 1878), while another kinsman, John Lowell Gardner, was appointed in 1878 to the board of the big Chicago, Burlington and Quincy Railroad.[42] In short, both of America's Ministers to Great Britain during the Hayes administration were clearly elite figures.

As Minister to France, Hayes picked a close friend, distant kinsman, and firm political ally, Edward F. Noyes, who as head of the Ohio delegation at the 1876 Republican national convention had placed Hayes's name in nomination as the party's candidate for the Presidency.[43] Noyes was a former Civil War hero and Cincinnati lawyer who had been elected governor of Ohio in the early 1870s between Hayes's two stints in state executive office. But unlike many high-ranking diplomatic officials, Noyes apparently had no major socio-economic ties (although there has not been enough research to be certain on this point). Hence, on the basis of the available evidence, one can only conclude that close personal and political links were the primary reasons for Noyes's appointment to this key post.

After considerable delay, President Hayes finally chose a rather unusual man to serve as American Minister to Germany. This was Bayard Taylor, a Pennsylvania writer and translater who had acted briefly in the early 1860s as secretary of the legation at the U.S. Embassy in Russia, but who otherwise had held no governmental office of any note. Taylor was, however, very knowledgeable about the German language and culture, for he had also been (non-resident) professor of German literature at Cornell University from 1870 to 1877. Unfortunately, Taylor died soon after he arrived in Germany, whereupon President Hayes persuaded an even more distinguished scholar, Andrew D. White, who was the founder and first president of Cornell, to take over as his chief diplomatic representative in Berlin. While White made his mark mainly as an academic, he was actually much more than that. He had substantial wealth, much of it inherited from his father, who was a Syracuse banker and, up to his death in 1860, a sizable stockholder and director of both the New York Central Railroad and the considerably smaller Buffalo and State Line Railroad.[44] In addition, Andrew D. White himself sat briefly on the board of the New York Central Railroad in the mid-1860s, shortly before he became president of Cornell University.[45] Thus, while President Hayes relied more than his predecessors on literary and academic figures to serve as diplomatic emissaries, a number of these men were (or had been) linked, directly or indirectly, with major economic enterprises.

Perhaps the most important and revealing event of the Hayes administration was the way in which it responded to the railroad strikes of 1877, which wave of unrest and disorder represented the first large-scale action taken by organized labor in the United States. It started because of a rash of wage cuts imposed by many Eastern rail lines as a result of a recession. This action touched off a series of bitter clashes that led to the destruction of considerable property and delay in the shipment of goods, and culminated in several places in substantial violence. A number of governors thereupon made formal requests for federal troops to help restore law and order. After extensive discussion with certain members of his Cabinet (most of whom were pro-business figures and two were still active railroad directors), Hayes somewhat reluctantly responded by sending Army units into selected states where conditions seemed badly out of hand.[46] Although these forces played, by presidential order, only a limited role, it was in many respects a decisive one. This intervention probably also set a bad precedent, for it clearly represented a form of federal strikebreaking and did little to alleviate the basic grievances of the railroad workers of the nation.

The Brief Ill-Fated Garfield Regime

In 1880, because of Hayes's refusal to seek a second term, the Republican party encountered considerable difficulty in agreeing upon a presidential candidate, although there were several prime contenders. The most formidable were former President Ulysses S. Grant, a now tarnished figure closely linked with political spoilsmen and scandal; Maine's brilliant orator and ambitious Congressional spokesman, James G. Blaine, who had been a disappointed aspirant in 1876; and Ohio's venerable Republican leader, John Sherman, who had served as Hayes's Secretary of the Treasury. But a deadlock developed at the national convention and a "dark horse" compromise candidate emerged in the person of Ohio's amiable but undistinguished Congressman, James A. Garfield, a former Hiram, Ohio and Washington, D.C. lawyer with no prominent socioeconomic ties. Garfield was acceptable to all major factions and the party's principal financial backers.[47] The Democrats had similar problems in selecting their presidential candidate. After failing to rally behind one of two nationally known figures, Samuel J. Tilden and Delaware's patrician Senator Thomas F. Bayard (who was warmly supported by New York banker August Belmont), the party followed a well-established political pattern and settled upon a Civil War hero and career Army officer, General Winfield S. Hancock.[48] Despite the fact that Hancock had little experience in (non-military) federal affairs, the race turned out to be exceedingly close in terms of popular preference, with Garfield winning by less than 10,000 votes, although the electoral count was more decisive.

In an effort to restore party unity, Garfield chose one of his major political rivals as his Secretary of State, the ambitious James G. Blaine, who had twice lost out in his presidential drive, mainly because of grave suspicions about his financial dealings. Blaine, who was born into a family of modest means, had been a Maine newspaperman in the pre–Civil War period. But he soon discovered his great gift for oratory and politics and thereafter devoted himself largely to governmental affairs, serving first as a Maine Congressman (from 1863 to 1876) and then as a U.S. Senator (1876–1881). In the course of his political career Blaine gained numerous friends and supporters, including certain wealthy businessmen, some of whom gave him frequent advice on investments and economic ventures.[49] In addition, he served briefly, around 1880, as a director of the Richmond and Allegheny Railroad (a recently organized enterprise headed by New York banker F. O. French), and only a few months after he was appointed Secretary of State, he was elected to the board of the newly formed West Virginia Central and Pittsburgh Railway (which was controlled by

Blaine's most intimate financial advisor, Stephen B. Elkins, and his father-in-law, Henry G. Davis).[50] Thus, although Blaine had been criticized primarily for his previous dubious dealing with the Little Rock and Fort Smith Railway, he was much more closely linked with two other railroads around the time of his appointment to Cabinet office.[51]

After an unsuccessful effort to recruit a well-known Midwestern leader, President Garfield chose Minnesota's William Windom to act as his Secretary of the Treasury, primarily because of growing Western resentment of the alleged power of Wall Street and Eastern financial interests.[52] Windom was a longtime Winona lawyer who had served for eleven years (1858–1869) as a Congressman and then for a like period (1870–1881) as a U.S. Senator. But Windom had also been affiliated with the Northern Pacific Railway, for he sat on the board of this big rail line from 1869 to 1874. In the latter year Windom apparently felt compelled to sever this connection because of his appointment as chairman of a special Senate committee dealing with the railroads. However, this action should not be taken to mean that Windom had begun to assume a more critical stance vis-à-vis the railroads, for a few months after he became Secretary of the Treasury, he joined with several other high-ranking federal officials to form part of a stockownership syndicate to underwrite the construction of the West Virginia Central and Pittsburgh Railway.[53] Hence it would appear that in Windom Garfield had found a Western Cabinet executive who was on friendly terms with railroad (and probably other business) forces in the nation.

For the position of Attorney General, Garfield chose a Harrisburg, Pennsylvania lawyer, Wayne MacVeagh, who had relatively little experience in governmental affairs, having served only briefly (1870–1871) as American Minister to Turkey.[54] MacVeagh was a rather unusual person in that while he was a son-in-law of Pennsylvania Republican boss Simon Cameron, he did not appear to approve of the latter's brand of unsavory politics and never became a cog in his party machine.[55] Yet MacVeagh was clearly a railroad attorney in his own right, for he served as a director of the Northern Central Railway from 1875 to 1877 and thereafter as its general counsel, which enterprise had by this time been taken over from its former owners (the Cameron family) by the Pennsylvania Railroad.[56]

In an astute bow to American history, Garfield selected as his Secretary of War, Chicago lawyer and political neophyte Robert T. Lincoln, who was the son of the martyred Civil War President. Robert T. Lincoln, however, had a much more narrow and "elitist" law practice than his father, for it was made up largely of wealthy business clients such as the Pullman's Palace Car Co., Marshall Field & Co., and certain Chicago utilities.[57] In fact, according to one source, Lincoln was elected to the board of directors of the Pullman's Palace Car Co. just a year before his appointment to Cabinet office.[58] In short, Robert Lincoln was one of Chicago's leading corporate lawyers.

As his Secretary of the Navy, Garfield chose a Southerner, William H. Hunt, whose prior governmental service had been limited to three years as a judge of the U.S. Court of Claims in Washington and an even briefer stint as Louisiana's attorney general.[59] Unfortunately, very little is known about the obscure Hunt other than that he came from an influential New Orleans family and had been a successful (primarily commercial) lawyer.[60] In light of his modest political record, one might well conclude that his selection was dictated largely by geo-political considerations, for he was the sole representative of his region in the Cabinet.

After much consultation and maneuver, Garfield picked a longtime Iowa lawyer and political leader, Samuel J. Kirkwood, to serve as his Secretary of the Interior. Kirkwood had held numerous important offices over the years, chief of which were governor of Iowa (from 1860 to 1864 and again in 1876–1877) and U.S. Senator (1866–1867 and 1877–1881). As such, he was, almost of necessity, on intimate terms with various key figures in the railroad-dominated Des Moines Regency. Moreover, Kirkwood had served as president of the newly formed Chicago, Omaha and St. Joseph Railroad from 1870 to 1875, when this line fell into severe difficulty, and Kirkwood decided to seek high political office again.[61] In short, it was largely as a result of the support and pressure of such influential Regency leaders as William B. Allison (a well-known business and railroad ally) that Kirkwood was awarded a seat in Garfield's Cabinet.[62]

Thus, although the Garfield administration was destined to be exceedingly short-lived and Garfield himself apparently had few important economic ties, it is clear that his chief aides and advisors were primarily men with various business links. Of the six major Cabinet officials, five had significant recent (or still extant) railroad connections—Blaine, Windom, MacVeagh, Lincoln, and Kirkwood. And the sixth post in the Cabinet, which was ultimately awarded to a relatively unknown Southerner, had been first offered to a wealthy New York City banker and Congressman, Levi P. Morton.[63] Hence it may be said that Garfield's administration was one in which conservative forces were in near total control.

The Arthur Administration

With the assassination of President Garfield shortly after he took office, the reins of executive authority passed automatically to New York's Chester A. Arthur, who had been nominated as ʼ1e Republican vice presidential candidate in 1880 in an effort to allay the hostile feelings of state party boss (and longtime Grant supporter) Roscoe Conkling, and to help carry New York state in the upcoming election. Arthur was for many years a (non-elite) New York City lawyer. He became quite active in politics and soon established himself as one of Conkling's most able and important lieutenants. As a result, he was rewarded in 1871 with the often highly lucrative post of Collector of Customs at the port of New York, a heavily patronage-ridden office he administered, to his credit, with considerable efficiency and probity until the latter part of the decade, when he and various other members of the Conkling machine were summarily removed by the Hayes administration as part of a business-backed reform move. Arthur also later showed surprising strength and independence, as well as more than a little ambition, when he accepted the vice-presidential nomination over the angry protests of his imperious party leader, Roscoe Conkling (who soon fell from power, largely because of his own arrogance and certain major political miscalculations).[64]

Not surprisingly under the circumstances, all the incumbent Cabinet members submitted their resignations to President Arthur in the fall of 1881 so that he might select his own chief administrators and advisors. Although he had never before held such a critical national post, Arthur displayed a good deal of initiative and self-confidence, for he soon replaced all but one of Garfield's top officials, and that individual was Secretary of War Robert T. Lincoln, a pro-business figure with whom Arthur quickly established a warm personal and working relationship. As another plus, Lincoln had a name which, because of his father, was almost sacrosanct in American politics.

As his Secretary of State, President Arthur chose a well-known New Jersey political leader, Frederick T. Frelinghuysen, who had served on two separate occasions (1866–1869 and 1871–1877) as a United States Senator, and before that (1861–1866) as New Jersey attorney general. But Frelinghuysen was, perhaps even more importantly, a Newark lawyer with many key socio-economic ties. He had sat on the board of the Central Railroad of New Jersey (from at least 1856 up to 1881), the Howard Savings Institution of Newark (from 1857 through 1885), and the Mutual Benefit Life Insurance Co., another Newark-based concern (from 1878 through 1885).[65] His brother-in-law, John N. A. Griswold, a New York City merchant and entrepreneur, served as a director of the big Boston-controlled Chicago, Burlington and Quincy Railroad from 1874 through 1885. Thus in many respects Frelinghuysen bore a marked similarity to Grant's Secretary of State, Hamilton Fish, for both were metropolitan New York lawyers who graced the boards of (different) New Jersey railroads and had numerous other important economic and family ties.[66]

After one unsuccessful effort to appoint a prominent New York City business and political leader as Secretary of the Treasury, President Arthur picked a longtime New York state judge and former legislator, Charles J. Folger, to serve as his chief fiscal advisor.[67] Folger apparently had few, if any, links to wealthy corporate interests, but rather, like Arthur himself, had been closely associated with the state party machine which had been dominated for well over a decade by Republican boss

Roscoe Conkling. Despite his comparative lack of financial experience, Folger proved to be a fairly capable Secretary of the Treasury and held office until his death in September 1884. His place was taken temporarily by former (1882–1884) Postmaster General and (1869–1882) federal judge Walter Q. Gresham, who, being ill-suited for the post, soon stepped down from office (in October 1884). At this late date in the administration, President Arthur turned to a much more seasoned official, former (1865–1869) Secretary of the Treasury and (1863–1865) Comptroller of the Currency Hugh McCulloch, who had recently been appointed to the U.S. Tariff Commission. McCulloch had originally been an important bank executive in Indiana. After holding the first two federal posts, he was made a partner in Jay Cooke & Co. and then, following the collapse of this concern in 1873, he became the head of his own New York City banking firm. Also, shortly before going on the Tariff Commission, McCulloch had been appointed to the board of the Northern Pacific Railway, the Richmond and Allegheny Railroad, and the Bowery Savings Bank of New York City—three posts which indicate that this key Cabinet office was again in safe hands.

For his Attorney General, President Arthur selected a longtime Philadelphia lawyer, Benjamin H. Brewster, who was already working for the government in a special ad hoc capacity, handling, with the help of another lawyer, the investigation and prosecution of the so-called Star Route fraud case (a federal mail contract scandal). Though apparently an able man, Brewster did not have much governmental experience, since his only previous post was that of Pennsylvania attorney general (in 1867–1868). Brewster was probably chosen for this Cabinet position for several reasons, one of which was the fact that he had served for many years as chief counsel for Pennsylvania state party boss Simon Cameron and various members of his family, some of whom were still involved in a number of business and railroad ventures.[68] Since his predecessor, Wayne MacVeagh, had married Cameron's daughter, it might be said that this post was kept within the family.[69]

As head of the Navy Department, President Arthur picked a man, New Hampshire's William Chandler, who appeared to represent New England, a region that had claimed a Cabinet seat in most administrations since Washington's first term in office. A onetime New Hampshire legislator, Chandler proved to be an astute politician and in 1865 received an appointment as Assistant Secretary of the Treasury. Two years later he stepped down from this post and opened up what might loosely be termed a Washington "law office," although, as his biographer readily admits, his work was in practice largely that of a lobbyist.[70] He reportedly acted as the chief legislative agent for the Union Pacific Railroad from the late 1860s to the early 1880s, in addition to representing various other interests, such as the Northern Pacific Railway from 1869 to 1873, when Jay Cooke was closely associated with this line, and by the mid-1870s, Jay

Gould.[71] Chandler was also an active and high-ranking party official, having served throughout most of the post–Civil War period as New Hampshire's Republican National Committeeman and in both the 1868 and 1872 presidential election campaigns as secretary of the Republican National Committee. Hence Chandler was both a major lobbyist and politician, although there is some question as to what economic interests he represented in the nation's capital.

As Secretary of the Interior, President Arthur followed an established precedent and chose a prominent figure from the Far West, Colorado's Henry Teller, who had held a seat in the U.S. Senate for the last six years. Teller was a longtime Central City (Colorado) lawyer who had a wide range of business interests, chief of which were mining and railroading. He had served as president of the Colorado Central Railroad from 1871 to 1876 (and before that as a director), and was for a considerable period of time the Colorado attorney for the Union Pacific Railroad.[72] Predictably, he acted as a firm ally of these enterprises while in the U.S. Senate.[73] And it would seem safe to assume that he did likewise as Secretary of the Interior, albeit perhaps in more discreet fashion. In short, the Union Pacific Railroad apparently had two representatives in Arthur's Cabinet.

In contrast to these many administrative shifts, President Arthur chose to retain a number of key diplomatic officials. He made no change, for instance, in our representation to Great Britain; Boston's wealthy academic, James Russell Lowell (a Hayes appointee), continued to act as American Minister to that country. Similarly, Arthur decided to retain the newly commissioned Levi P. Morton as U.S. Minister to France. Morton, who was undoubtedly on friendly terms with the President, had served for two years (1879–1881) as a New York Congressman. But he was best known as a New York City banker, for his firm (Morton, Bliss & Co.) ranked by this time as one of the top investment banking concerns in the nation. He had also been closely linked with various large railroads, since he served on the board of the Milwaukee and St. Paul Railroad (from 1869 to 1874), the Union Pacific Railroad (in the early 1870s), the Burlington, Cedar Rapids and Northern Railroad (in the mid-1870s), and the Delaware and Hudson Railroad (from 1877 to 1881).[74] Thus, although Morton has usually been depicted as little more than a loyal supporter and financial "angel" of the Conkling-led New York state Republican organization, he was clearly an important business figure in his own right.

As American Minister to Germany, President Arthur chose, after some delay, a prominent Western political leader and Nevada City, California lawyer, Aaron Sargent, who had served two separate stints (1861–1863 and 1870–1873) as a California Congressman and then a six-year term as a U.S. Senator. In these roles Sargent was known primarily as a loyal ally of the Central Pacific Railroad and, above all, a close friend of this rail line's dominant entrepreneurial figure, Collis P. Huntington, to whom Sargent may have owed his appointment as Minister.[75] Sargent held office for approximately two years when, because of a series of diplomatic incidents, he became persona non grata to German Chancellor Bismarck and was recalled from his post. He was replaced in the closing months of the administration by a maverick Iowa leader, John A. Kasson, who had served on three occasions (1863–1866, 1873–1877, and 1881–1884) as a Congressman and during the Hayes regime as American Minister to Austria-Hungary (a post generally regarded as a form of political exile). Kasson was a Des Moines lawyer who had once been on good terms with the state's party hierarchy, but since 1866 had become anathema to many of the top figures in the railroad-dominated Des Moines Regency.[76] Nevertheless, thanks to his long-established popularity with the electorate, Kasson had been returned repeatedly to Congress and in late 1884 was, largely as a result of his friendship with President Arthur and Secretary of State Frelinghuysen, appointed American Minister to Germany.

Thus, although the names of most of the Cabinet members (and some of the high diplomatic officials) changed during the Arthur administration, there was comparatively little alteration in the overall politico-economic make-up of the federal government. Of the six major Cabinet posts, five were filled by pro-railroad and business spokesmen, the one exception being Secretary of the Treasury Charles J. Folger. Hence it is not surprising that little federal action was initiated during this period, for the business forces of the country had a largely laissez-faire outlook, which meant that, apart from a protective tariff and the provision of sound, stable money, it generally desired a passive government.[77]

Cleveland's First Administration

Despite his substantial business backing, President Arthur was unable to win his party's nomination for a second term in office in 1884. He lost out to James G. Blaine, Maine's longtime Republican leader who had served briefly as Secretary of State under Garfield, was a brilliant public speaker, and a political tactician who had built up a tremendous following in the GOP's ranks and had considerable support in various important economic circles around the country. Blaine, however, was still viewed by many prominent business and governmental figures as a man of highly dubious ethics, in part because of his questionable financial dealings with an Arkansas railroad some fifteen years earlier.[78] The Democrats, on the other hand, nominated a largely unknown, but completely honest conservative candidate in the person of Grover Cleveland, who had served briefly as mayor of Buffalo (1882–1883) and then as a Tilden-backed governor of New York.[79] Cleveland had been a partner in a fairly prominent Buffalo law firm for a number of years and reportedly counted among his clients the Buffalo, Rochester and Pittsburgh Railroad, the Lehigh Valley Railroad, the Standard Oil Co., and the Merchants' and

Traders' Bank of Buffalo.[80] In the ensuing campaign, which was marked by charges of scandal and one classic political faux pas (the claim that the Democratic party stood for "Rum, Romanism, and Rebellion"), Cleveland emerged triumphant, but only by a popular vote margin of about 23,000, an extremely close contest which may have been decided by Cleveland's rocklike image of integrity.[81]

As the first Democratic president in nearly thirty years, considerable interest was aroused as to the type of men this New York leader would recruit for his Cabinet. In a not unexpected move, President Cleveland chose as his Secretary of State one of his former chief political rivals, Delaware's longtime Senator, Thomas F. Bayard, who ranked second only to Cleveland as a party leader. Bayard belonged to what might be called the "gentry" class in American society (a declining breed in the post–Civil War era). His family had large landholdings and many key kinship ties in the eastern part of the country.[82] Yet this should not be taken to mean that Bayard, a Wilmington lawyer, had no critical links with the business community, for he was on extremely close terms with New York City financier (and major Democratic party fundraiser) August Belmont, who since 1872 had been Bayard's principal political backer.[83] Moreover, although Bayard had never been formally linked with any particular segment of American business, it would appear that he was either a substantial stockholder or director of the West Virginia Central and Pittsburgh Railway when this line was first established in the early 1880s.[84] Therefore, it seems safe to say that Bayard was a spokesman for conservative forces in American politics.[85]

For the key post of Secretary of the Treasury, Cleveland made what some have described as a rather unusual choice. Daniel Manning had no formal governmental experience and had only recently been appointed to a managerial position in a fairly small Albany bank (though he had previously served as a director of this and one other commercial bank in the city). Manning was essentially a political figure, having worked his way up through the organizational ranks (partly by running the party's long-established newspaper) to become a close friend and trusted lieutenant of New York Democratic leader Samuel J. Tilden, a wealthy railroad lawyer. Though not a major business figure, Manning did serve on the board of the Albany and Susquehanna Railroad in the early 1880s, first as a regular director and then in a special "public" or municipal capacity.[86] Actually, Manning was reportedly reluctant to accept this post, but was finally persuaded to do so by Tilden, who privately assured him that he would always be available to give him sound fiscal advice.[87] Indeed, according to Tilden's biographer, "Manning was pathetically dependent on the aged Tilden's judgment for every step he took" in Washington.[88] Manning, however, became seriously ill after about two years in office and was forced to step down from the Cabinet. He was replaced by one of his top aides in the department, former Albany and New York City lawyer

Charles S. Fairchild, who had already demonstrated his political and administrative mettle as state attorney general under Tilden in the late 1870s. Fairchild was no ordinary figure, but had many ties with important men and institutions in New York state. He had married the niece of former (1868) Democratic presidential candidate Horatio Seymour, a Tilden ally, who had various railroad links over the years.[89] In addition, Fairchild's father (Sidney T. Fairchild) had served for many years as an upstate attorney for the New York Central Railroad and also sat until the late 1880s on the board of the Erie and Pittsburgh Railroad (a medium-sized line controlled by William L. Scott, a relatively unknown Pennsylvania Congressman closely associated with the Vanderbilts) and the Union Trust Co. of New York City (a concern dominated by the Vanderbilt interests).[90] Thus there is little doubt that during the first Cleveland administration this Cabinet post was held by men who were on intimate terms with major railroad and financial forces in New York.

As his Attorney General, President Cleveland deliberately chose a Southerner for geo-political reasons. Augustus H. Garland was a longtime Little Rock lawyer who had served for the last eight years as a U.S. Senator, and prior to that (1874–1876) as governor of Arkansas, a state often overlooked in the federal recruitment process. Like many prominent figures of his day, Garland had at one time been closely linked with a fairly sizable railroad enterprise, for he sat on the board of the Memphis and Little Rock Railway shortly before (1873–1874) he was elected governor of Arkansas.[91] Garland was also involved as a major stockholder in certain other business concerns, one of which later created a minor scandal during his term as Attorney General.[92] Hence he was another Cabinet member who was clearly sympathetic to the emerging economic forces of early industrial America.

After some hesitation, Cleveland chose, in part because of sectional considerations, a wealthy New England patrician, William C. Endicott, to serve as his Secretary of War.[93] Endicott was a former Salem, Massachusetts lawyer who was appointed a state supreme court judge in 1873, a position he held until 1882, when he was forced to step down from office because of a siege of bad health. Endicott was probably picked primarily because of his key socio-economic ties, particularly those his family had forged over the years through intermarriage with various members of Boston's highly inbred business elite.[94] For example, his late uncle, Francis B. Crowninshield, had served, up to his death in the late 1870s, as president of two New England railroads and as a director of the Suffolk Bank (of Boston). Moreover, Endicott himself had married into the rich and socially prominent Peabody family, one member of which, George Peabody, had established a well-known international banking firm that counted J. P. Morgan's father among its senior partners.[95] Thus, though never formally part of the business community, Endicott was certainly on close terms with Boston's economic elite, which at this time ranked second only to that of New York.

As his Secretary of the Navy, Cleveland picked an able and ambitious attorney, William C. Whitney, who since the Civil War had been making his mark in New York City, most notably by serving (as a Tilden ally) as municipal corporation counsel from 1875 to 1882. Upon stepping down from this position, Whitney had thrown himself, first, into the promotion of Cleveland's gubernatorial candidacy, and then, with even greater vigor, into the direction of this conservative Democrat's presidential drive, for which efforts he was rewarded with a Cabinet post. Whitney was also awarded this important office because of the great value Cleveland placed on his advice and friendship. Yet, like many other leaders, Whitney had major socio-economic ties which were of considerable help in his career and probably had a significant effect on his views and actions in public life. Though rarely noted, Whitney served briefly on the board of the New York, Ontario and Western Railway (in 1879–1880) and the New York, Chicago and St. Louis Railway (in 1882–1884), which was controlled by the Vanderbilt forces.[96] In addition, Whitney had married the daughter of a prominent Ohio political and economic figure, Henry B. Payne, whose primary business interest was apparently in railroads. Payne served, for example, as a director of the large Vanderbilt-dominated Lake Shore and Michigan Southern Railway from 1869 to 1883 (and prior to that, one of its predecessor concerns), the Cincinnati, Wabash and Michigan Railway from 1880 through 1889, and two other lines. And, as has been emphasized in various works, Whitney's brother-in-law, Oliver H. Payne, was for many years an officer or director of the Standard Oil Co., which link provided Whitney with access to the Rockefeller interests. Indeed, Whitney could hardly have had better business connections.

As his Secretary of the Interior, President Cleveland selected a second well-known Southerner, Mississippi's Lucius Q. C. Lamar, who had been a U.S. Senator for the last eight years and on two prior occasions (1857–1860 and 1873–1877) had held a seat in Congress. Though of a distinguished family with deep Georgia roots, Lamar was basically a small town (Oxford, Mississippi) lawyer who supplemented his rather modest income by serving as a law professor at the University of Mississippi in the immediate pre– and post–Civil War years. Although attempts have been made to portray Lamar in rather idealistic terms, it should be noted that he sat on the board, as corporate attorney, of the Mississippi Central Railroad from 1867 to 1874, and on that of its successor company, the New Orleans, St. Louis and Chicago Railroad, from 1874 to 1876 (when it fell into severe financial difficulty and was absorbed by the larger Illinois Central system).[97] Not surprisingly, during many of his years in Congress Lamar was widely regarded as a spokesman for certain major railroad interests.[98] However, Lamar was appointed to the U.S. Supreme Court in early 1888, at which point he was replaced by a Wisconsin political leader, William F. Vilas, who had been acting as Cleveland's Postmaster General. Vilas was a well-fixed Madison lawyer who had various profitable business interests, one of the largest being his sizable stake in a number of lumber companies in the northern part of the state.[99] Vilas's most important affiliation was probably that, starting in 1874, of Wisconsin attorney for the big (Vanderbilt-controlled) Chicago and Northwestern Railway.[100] In short, both men who served as Secretary of the Interior during the first Cleveland administration had marked railroad links.[101]

In the realm of foreign affairs, Cleveland chose a longtime Vermont lawyer and Democratic political leader, Edward J. Phelps, to act as American Minister to Great Britain. In some respects Phelps was a rather unusual selection, for he had little formal diplomatic or governmental experience. He was, however, regarded as an extremely able lawyer, as evidenced by the fact that he was elected president of the American Bar Association in 1880 and a year later was appointed a Yale College law professor. Earlier in his career Phelps had been fairly closely associated with certain railroad enterprises. He served on the board of the Rutland and Burlington Railroad up to 1865 and, probably as a result of a corporate merger, as a director around 1870 of the Harlem Extension Railroad (a northern New York line controlled by the Vanderbilt interests).[102] Unfortunately, little else is known about Phelps, so, aside from his undoubted legal ability, the reasons for his appointment remain obscure.[103]

As American Minister to France, President Cleveland picked a well-known Baltimore lawyer, Robert M. McLane, who had been actively involved in Maryland government and politics in recent years, first as a Congressman and then as governor of the state. He had also secured some diplomatic experience in the pre–Civil War period by serving as our Ambassador to Mexico and as U.S. Commissioner to China. McLane was the son of a wealthy, prominent political leader, Louis McLane, who had been a Jacksonian Cabinet officer, a two-time representative to Great Britain, and, from 1837 to 1848, president of the Baltimore and Ohio Railroad. In much of the 1850s and 1860s, Robert McLane had lived in California, where at one point he was regularly retained as counsel for the Western Pacific Railroad. Upon his return to Maryland, he quickly aligned himself with the so-called Old Guard of the state Democratic party and, with the help of its leaders, climbed up the legislative and executive ranks to become, largely at the urging of Senator Arthur P. Gorman (a pro-railroad figure who served as Cleveland's de facto presidential campaign manager), an important diplomatic official.[104]

Finally, as Minister to Germany Cleveland chose a prominent Ohio Democratic leader and Cincinnati lawyer, George H. Pendleton, who had served for the previous six years as a U.S. Senator and sometime before that (1857–1865) as a member of Congress. Pendleton was, probably for political reasons, a well-known spokesman for the Midwestern "soft-money" interests (one of the few such figures appointed to a high post by the Cleveland administration), and was widely, albeit erroneously, regarded as the "father" of civil service reform in America. However, like many other officials, he had a number of marked socio-economic ties. His brother, Elliott H. Pendleton, was a Cincinnati merchant and banker, and he himself served as president of the Kentucky Central Railroad from 1870 to 1877 (and for three years thereafter as a director). In addition, his nephew sat on the board of his fairly sizable rail line from the early 1870s through 1889, presumably representing the family interests. Hence it would seem that, despite his reputation as a reformer and "soft-money" man, Pendleton was an elite figure.

In retrospect, then, it is clear that the Cleveland administration was dominated by pro-business, and more specifically pro-railroad, leaders—to a greater extent, in fact, than some of the preceding Republican regimes.[105] Relatively little new legislation of major note was enacted during this period of continued corporate ascendancy.[106] The most important measure adopted during these years was the Interstate Commerce Act of 1887, which provided for the first federal regulation of railroads. This law was passed after almost two decades of protest by various farm and shipping groups against certain much-criticized railroad practices. However, by this time, according to one authority, many railroad figures, such as the New York Central's Chauncey Depew, were also in favor of such legislation as one way of eliminating rate wars and establishing more stable economic relations, so long as there was an independent commission created to administer the process, subject to judicial review.[107] Curiously, judging from the available literature, the Cleveland administration itself did not play a very prominent part in these negotiations and maneuvers, preferring to leave the initiative to a number of concerned Congressional leaders. But whatever the pressures or sequence of events, the Interstate Commerce Commission was, for a variety of reasons (some legislative, others judicial), an extremely weak body during its early years and hardly posed a serious threat to railroad entrepreneurs and executives.[108]

The Benjamin Harrison Administration

In 1888 President Cleveland decided to seek reelection on the basis of his record in office, which might best be summarized as "honesty and frugality in government." He was pitted against Indiana's Benjamin Harrison, a man who, although he had held office for only six years as a U.S. Senator, had a name that was well known in American politics, for his grandfather, William Henry Harrison ("Old Tippecanoe"), was the first Whig President in American history. Aside from the tariff issue, the two candidates held relatively similar views. But in another narrow race characteristic of this period, the conservative Democratic incumbent was defeated (although he actually won the popular vote).[109]

The new President was a well-fixed Indianapolis lawyer who had apparently studiously avoided any direct or formal ties with major business enterprises. Yet Harrison was known to be friendly toward such interests. He was, for instance, on intimate terms with an influential group of corporate and railroad spokesmen in the U.S. Senate, which was led by such figures as Iowa's William B. Allison and Rhode Island's Nelson W. Aldrich.[110] Moreover, Harrison had various sizable stockholdings, and at one point in the late 1880s even wrote to Northwestern railroad magnate James J. Hill to ask this able executive (who had much inside knowledge about business matters) to invest a good deal of his money for him, presumably in safe or promising railroad stock.[111] Thus the business forces of the nation probably had good reason to feel confident about Benjamin Harrison.

As his Secretary of State, President Harrison chose, largely because of political imperative, Maine's James G. Blaine, who had been the Republican standard-bearer in 1884 and was still the most popular figure in the party, even though he had decided not to seek the nomination in 1888.[112] Blaine was an extremely ambitious man who had served for many years (from 1863 to 1881) in the U.S. Senate and House of Representatives, during which time he had compiled a rather mixed record, at times tinged by scandal. He had briefly been Secretary of State once before (under Garfield in 1881), and, having been out of office for the last eight years, apparently hoped to use this Cabinet post as a way to advance his cause in the years ahead. The pro-business Blaine had served as a director of the West Virginia Central and Pittsburgh Railway from June of 1881 to 1885, and was reappointed to this board in January 1891, while he was Secretary of State.[113] The dubious nature of Blaine's tangled relationships with various major business leaders was probably most sharply revealed in his close association with his longtime friend and political supporter, steel magnate Andrew Carnegie, who managed to get Blaine to use his influence as Secretary of State to help land lucrative contracts for his company with several foreign countries.[114] Blaine was forced to step down from office in June 1892, primarily for political reasons (Harrison was growing uneasy over his Secretary of State's patent presidential aspirations). After vainly trying to recruit a prominent Northern businessman (the New York Central's Chauncey Depew) for this position, Harrison turned to a well-seasoned diplomatic official, former Indiana newsman, lawyer, and Republican party leader John W. Foster, who directed the department for the duration of the administration.[115]

For the top fiscal post in the Cabinet, President Harrison tried to recruit Iowa's longtime Senator William B. Allison, but to no avail.[116] Wishing to pick a man from the western part of the country, Harrison turned next to a more available figure, former Minnesota Senator, Congressman, and lawyer William Windom, who, like Blaine, had served briefly in the Cabinet under Garfield. Although Windom had returned for a short time (1881–1883) to the Senate, he thereafter devoted much of his time to quietly building up a New York City law practice (a matter glossed over in his selection), and reportedly acquired substantial amounts of real estate and railroad securities.[117] In the late 1880s Windom served as president of a small, newly formed railroad in Minnesota (the Winona and Southwestern Railway), still another indication that he was not hostile to such interests.[118] When the aged Windom died in early 1891, he was replaced by a former Ohio governor (1879–1883) and Congressman (1871–1879), Charles Foster, who was a longtime friend of the President. Foster has generally been described as a prominent Fostoria, Ohio merchant (1890 population of 6,171), but he was also associated, more significantly, with various railroad enterprises over the years. He served, for example, as an officer or director of the Lake Erie and Louisville Railway (and its successor company, the Lake Erie and Western Railway) from about 1870 to 1883, as a director of the Ohio Central Railroad in the late 1870s and early 1880s, and, perhaps most revealingly, as a director of the Columbus, Hocking Valley and Toledo Railway from 1890 through 1893 (that is to say, during his term of office as Secretary of the Treasury). In short, Foster was clearly a pro-railroad official.

In filling the chief legal post in his administration, President Harrison made a choice which can be explained in neither economic nor political terms. He selected, primarily for personal reasons, his longtime (1874–1889) Indianapolis law partner, William H. H. Miller. This was a somewhat surprising move, for Miller had never held a governmental position and apparently had not even been casually involved in either state or local politics. Moreover, judging from the available (unfortunately sparse) data, he had no major socio-economic ties. So Miller was almost assuredly chosen because of strong personal and professional considerations.

As his Secretary of War, Harrison selected a second New Englander, former (1878–1880) Vermont Governor Redfield Proctor, mainly because he was an early supporter of the President at the Republican national convention. Proctor was a longtime high official (and presumably major stockholder) of the Vermont Marble Co., which, although reportedly the largest company of its kind in the world, was nevertheless a fairly small concern, at least compared to many railroads of this era.[119] Proctor also served in the late 1880s as president of the Clarenden and Pittsford Railroad, an even smaller operation. Given the size of these firms, it seems unlikely that Proctor was chosen because of his economic background or affiliatons, although he undoubtedly had a pro-business bias. Instead, Proctor was probably selected primarily because he was "an original Harrison man" at a critical early juncture in the latter's presidential drive.[120] Proctor held office until late 1891 when he resigned to run for the

Senate. He was quickly replaced by a wealthy entrepreneur, Stephen Elkins, who had first made his political and economic mark in the southwestern part of the country, as a New Mexico lawyer, major mine owner, bank president, and political leader (he was a longtime Blaine supporter). Yet even more important, in 1875 he married the daughter of a rich West Virginia businessman, Henry G. Davis, and moved to the East to join his father-in-law in his many economic enterprises. These interests centered largely in coal, lumber, and railroads, and were of such magnitude that they employed, in all, about 5,000 men by the late 1880s.[121] Elkins served as a vice-president of his father-in-law's West Virginia Central and Pittsburgh Railway from 1881 through 1893 (that is, through his term as a Cabinet officer), and in the early 1890s he also sat on the board of the St. Louis Southwestern Railway (a big concern that may have been controlled by the Gould forces). Hence Elkins was obviously an elite figure.

Largely for political reasons, President Harrison chose a relatively unknown New York City lawyer (and former state and federal official), Benjamin F. Tracy, as his Secretary of the Navy. A serious split had developed at the very outset of the administration between the President and New York's powerful state party boss, Thomas C. Platt. Harrison sought (as it turned out, unsuccessfully) to heal this breach by appointing Tracy, who was a longtime friend and political ally of Platt, to this important Cabinet office. In fact, Platt's son (Frank) had since 1885 been a partner in Tracy's New York City law firm.[122] Tracy, it is true, did have some corporate links. But these were mostly of a minor nature or of significance only in terms of what they reveal about Tracy's political ties, for the most prominent board on which he served was that of the American Loan and Trust Co. (of New York City), a concern that also included Thomas C. Platt as a director.[123] Therefore, the best assessment that can be made of Tracy's selection as Secretary of the Navy is that it was basically a political, rather than an economic, appointment.

In selecting his Secretary of the Interior, President Harrison adhered to the usual practice and picked a Midwesterner, St. Louis lawyer John W. Noble, about whom, unfortunately, relatively little is known. Noble had scant governmental experience, having served only as U.S. attorney for the eastern district of Missouri from 1867 to 1870. According to one presumably reliable source,[124] as an attorney he represented a number of large corporate and railroad interests in the Southwest over the years (although the author has not found any evidence to this effect in *Poor's Railroad Manual*). However, his brother, Henry C. Noble, had served on the board of the Columbus and Hocking Valley Railroad up to 1881. Thus, it is difficult to arrive at a well-informed judgment as to why, geography aside, this Missouri leader was selected, although it would appear that Noble was friendly to some railroad interests.

As America's first Secretary of Agriculture to hold office for any length of time, President Harrison selected, after considerable pressure, a Wisconsin Republican, Jeremiah M. Rusk, who had served for the previous seven years as governor of his state, as a U.S. Congressman during much of the preceding decade, and in various lesser capacities. Rusk was, in private life, a successful businessman, who had apparently demonstrated the requisite qualities of executive drive and entrepreneurship. But the primary reason for his appointment to this recently created Cabinet post was probably because he was a trusted ally of the dominant triumvirate of the state Republican party, particularly Philetus Sawyer and John C. Spooner, both of whom had been much involved with important railroad and lumber interests over the years.[125] With this backing, it seems unlikely that Rusk was a dedicated spokesman for the hard-pressed farmers his department was supposed to represent.[126]

As our major diplomatic emissary to Great Britain, President Harrison chose a well-known Illinois figure, Robert T. Lincoln, who, even though he had not been a political supporter of the new chief executive, enjoyed much prestige as the son of the famous Civil War President. Lincoln had served as Secretary of War under Garfield and Arthur, but otherwise his governmental experience was quite limited. He had spent most of his adult years with a Chicago law firm, in which capacity he had represented a number of wealthy corporate and railroad interests.[127] As one might expect, these relations also extended into Lincoln's social life; as one authority has put it, the Lincolns " . . . were a part of the elite of Chicago and counted as their friends the families of George M. Pullman, Potter Palmer, Marshall Field, and others who made up the list of the most prominent families of the city."[128] It is then clear that Lincoln was on intimate terms with many important men in the nation's higher circles.

At the suggestion of Secretary of State James G. Blaine, President Harrison selected an influential New York City newspaperman, Whitelaw Reid, to serve as American Minister to France. Though Reid lacked formal governmental or diplomatic experience, as the longtime editor and publisher of the *New York Tribune,* he had paid close attention to foreign affairs throughout most of the postwar period. The primary reason for Reid's appointment was probably the strong support he had given to the President and the Republican party, especially in the late 1880s. Reid was hardly a neutral economic or professional figure. Rather he was a man with marked ties to certain major business institutions and leaders. He had, for example, been president of the Mergenthaler Linotype Co. and a director of the Mercantile Trust Co. (of New York City) before his ambassadorial appointment. He had also married into one of America's wealthiest families, that of Darius O. Mills, a Western mining magnate turned Eastern entrepreneur. Most likely because of his substantial stockholdings, Mills sat on the board of the Bank of New York, the Metropolitan Trust Co., the Farmers Loan and Trust Co. (of New York City), the huge Lake Shore and Michigan Southern Railway, the Duluth and Iron Range Railroad, and the Minnesota Iron Co.[129] Thus, Whitelaw Reid was more than an influential journalist; he was a representative of the nation's top economic interests. Reid returned from France in early 1892 to help direct President Harrison's reelection drive. His diplomatic replacement was a Boston business leader, T. Jefferson Coolidge. This man, who had married into the wealthy Appleton family, had been a longtime executive of several New England textile concerns, and had also served as a director of the Chicago, Burlington and Quincy Railroad, the Kansas City, Fort Scott and Memphis Railroad, the Massachusetts Hospital Life Insurance Co., the newly formed Old Colony Trust Co., and a number of other major enterprises.[130] Hence Reid's successor was even more closely linked with America's major economic forces.

As U.S. Minister to Germany, President Harrison chose a man who had a more noteworthy record of governmental service, but who was, nonetheless, a big business figure, New York City financier William W. Phelps. This wealthy scion and longtime Republican party supporter (especially of James G. Blaine) had held a seat in Congress on two occasions (1873–1875 and 1888–1889) and had acted briefly (in 1881–1882) as American Minister to Austria-Hungary. However, he had devoted most of his adult life to managing his family's many business interests and investments, in the process of which he served, through 1893, on the board of such prominent concerns as the Delaware, Lackawanna and Western Railroad, the National City Bank, the Farmers Loan and Trust Co., and the United States Trust Co. (the last three were New York City firms). Thus, all three of America's major ambassadors (to use the title employed after 1893) during the Harrison administration were essentially big business representatives with scant experience in diplomatic affairs, a gap apparently of little account in an age of increasing corporate influence.

According to most historians, the Harrison regime was devoid of important accomplishments in both domestic and foreign affairs. This was probably due to the fact that it was dominated by business interests, which, aside from such questions as the tariff (which was boosted to new heights during these years), strongly believed in laissez-faire. Indeed, Matthew Josephson has described the Harrison administration as one symbolized by the "Businessmen's Cabinet."[131] This statement is true, but it could also be applied equally well to all the other presidential regimes of this period, especially that of the Bourbon Democrat, Grover Cleveland.

Cleveland's Second Administration

In 1892, after four years of enforced political retirement, Cleveland reemerged as his party's standard-bearer, largely at the behest of a group of Northern businessmen led by his close friend and chief political advisor, William C. Whitney.[132] These men were fearful of the threat posed to their longtime dominance of Democratic affairs by the growing strength of the agrarian-based ("easy money") Populist movement in the western and southern sections of the country, and some weak or expedient politicians in the Northeast, such as New York Senator David B. Hill, who was Cleveland's major rival for the party's presidential nomination. Thanks in part to a sizable Democratic war chest (for one of the few times in modern American history, it was considerably larger than that raised by the Republican party) and the masterful management of his campaign by businessman-lawyer William C. Whitney, Cleveland won by a fairly substantial margin over his rather ineffectual opponent, the incumbent Benjamin Harrison, and thus became the first man to serve two non-consecutive terms as President of the United States.

However, the Grover Cleveland who entered the White House in early 1893 was not the same figure, in terms of legal ties, as the former governor (and Buffalo lawyer) who had assumed the reins of executive leadership in 1885. Upon returning to private life in 1889, Cleveland had become associated with a prominent New York City law firm, Bangs, Stetson, Tracy and MacVeagh, of which his close friend (and Whitney's onetime assistant municipal corporation counsel) Francis Lynde Stetson was a senior partner. This association is of considerable importance because this law firm had emerged by the late 1880s as the chief legal arm of the now-powerful House of Morgan (which concern dropped the Drexel name from its title in 1894 and simply became known as J. P. Morgan & Co.).[133] Some scholars claim, on the basis of questionable data, that Cleveland was not a regular partner in the firm (sharing in all its decisions and monetary returns), but merely "of counsel," a much more restricted affiliation, which apparently meant little more than the use of common office and clerical facilities.[134] Yet this assessment would appear to be in error, for according to one of this firm's later partners (who certainly should have known), Cleveland was actually a partner (or was so viewed by "insiders") in Bangs, Stetson, Tracy and MacVeagh during his four years of presidential "exile." So by the start of his second term, Cleveland was more than a mere "bourgeois" lawyer or statesman, to use Richard Hofstadter's phrase, but one closely linked with the House of Morgan.[135]

After two unsuccessful attempts to appoint well-known Democrats as Secretary of State, President Cleveland, somewhat surprisingly, offered this position to a longtime Midwestern U.S. Circuit Court judge, Walter Q. Gresham.[136] Gresham had been a high-ranking Republican party leader (and administrative official under President Arthur), but for various reasons had bolted to the Democratic cause in 1892, carrying his home state of Indiana with him, a political favor that was not forgotten by the incoming Cleveland regime.[137] Though he apparently had no significant socio-economic ties and had only limited financial resources, Gresham was viewed in a mixed light. Many archconservative Republicans looked upon him as an unduly liberal or independent figure. Yet, despite this reputation, he was, according to one authority, a person who, as a federal judge, had rendered valuable service to the business community over the years by his rulings protecting railroads from strikes and boycotts.[138] Gresham died after holding office for about two years, during which period no crucial action was taken in the realm of foreign affairs. He was succeeded by a longtime Boston corporate lawyer, Richard Olney, who had been acting as Cleveland's second-term Attorney General. Since Olney's most important influence in the government was exerted during his first two years in Cabinet office, little need be said here other than to note that he maintained unusually close ties with major business interests.

Cleveland initially offered the post of Secretary of the Treasury to one of the top fiscal executives in his first administration, Charles S. Fairchild, who had been serving for the last few years as president of the New York Security and Trust Co., but he could not be induced to reenter the Cabinet. Stung briefly by this rebuff, Cleveland turned to one of the most respected leaders of the party, Kentucky's John G. Carlisle, who had served for thirteen years (1877–1890) in Congress, close to half of them as Speaker of the House, and more recently (1890–1893) as a U.S. Senator. Carlisle was a longtime Covington, Kentucky lawyer, who apparently had no major corporate links and only moderate personal resources. Nonetheless, according to one authority, he was regarded as generally friendly to the business community, and in recent years had stood firmly against the rising tide of Populist and "easy money" sentiment that had swept through much of the West.[139] Hence in Carlisle the economic leaders of the nation had a man of substantial ability and experience who, while not their ready agent, was someone in whom they had considerable confidence.

After one unsuccessful effort, President Cleveland selected, at the suggestion of his advisors, Richard Olney, a Boston corporation lawyer, whom he had met only once before (and who had very little governmental experience), to serve as his Attorney General.[140] Olney was a very able and strong-willed individual, who, having spent almost all of his adult life working for various major economic interests, generally took a marked pro-business position on public issues. Indeed, so close were his business links that contrary to the impression created by certain writers, he did not bother to sever many of these connections upon assuming Cabinet office.[141] He served on the board of the big Boston and Maine Railroad (and one of its predecessor concerns, the Eastern Railroad) from 1879 through 1897, the Boston-controlled Chicago, Burlington and Quincy Railroad from 1889 through 1897, and the Brahmin-dominated Old Colony Trust Co. from its incorporation in 1890 through 1897.[142] Thus Olney was deeply enmeshed in the affairs of a number of important railroad and business enterprises even while he was serving as the President's chief legal advisor.[143] But with the death of Walter Gresham, Olney resigned as Attorney General to take over the reins as Secretary of State. He was promptly replaced by a longtime Ohio lawyer, Judson Harmon, who had previously served for close to a decade (1878–1887) as a Cincinnati municipal court judge, a worthy post, but hardly one to lead directly to high federal office. More recently, Harmon had been linked with certain railroad interests, for he had been a member of the board of the Cincinnati, Washington and Baltimore Railroad from 1887 to 1889 (at which time it was merged into the larger Baltimore and Ohio system) and the Ohio Southwestern Railroad in 1893–1894. In addition, he had served as general counsel for the Baltimore and Ohio Southwestern Railroad from 1890 to 1894. In short, Harmon was another pro-railroad figure.

Although not initially so inclined, President Cleveland ultimately picked, largely because of personal pressure, one of his longtime friends and chief political aides, Daniel S. Lamont, to serve as his Secretary of War. Lamont had worked his way up the Democratic party ladder over the years, to the point where, thanks mainly to the backing of Daniel Manning and William C. Whitney, he was appointed private secretary to the President during his first term in office. After leaving this White House post in 1889, Lamont found employment in the business world of New York City, initially in conjunction with some of the wealthy Whitney's municipal traction interests. He also served in various other, apparently unrelated corporate capacities, such as a board member of the New York Security and Trust Co. and the Continental National Bank (of New York City).[144] One of Cleveland's most important and highly trusted Cabinet officers, Lamont obviously reflected the business point of view and most likely counseled the President accordingly.[145]

After making what was evidently a token offer to a prominent New Englander (John Quincy Adams), Cleveland selected as his Secretary of the Navy a conservative Southerner, Hilary A. Herbert, who had served for the last sixteen years as an Alabama Congressman. Herbert was a longtime Montgomery lawyer whose firm had reportedly built up one of the largest practices in the entire state.[146] Little is known about the interests his firm represented. However, one of his clients was the Montgomery branch of the now largely New York–based mercantile firm of Lehman Brothers, and Herbert was a very close friend of one of its founding partners, Mayer Lehman.[147] Hilary Herbert was thus a geopolitical Cabinet selection who was clearly favorably disposed toward corporate interests.

As his first Secretary of the Interior, President Cleveland selected another Southerner, Hoke Smith, who, although he had never held governmental office, had long played an important "kingmaker" role in Georgia state politics and had been an ardent Cleveland supporter at the 1892 Democratic national convention.[148] Though linked through his wife to one of Georgia's most prominent planter families (he married the niece of Buchanan's Secretary of the Treasury, Howell Cobb), Smith was primarily a representative of what some have referred to as the "new South," in that he had a number of noteworthy ties to business interests. Smith was, in fact, a wealthy Atlanta lawyer, who in 1887 had become the owner and publisher of the *Atlanta Journal,* reputedly in part to increase his political power. Although as a newspaperman he sometimes took an anti-railroad stance, he served on the board of the Georgia, Carolina and Northern Railroad from at least 1890 up to 1893 and as a director of the big Capital City Bank of Atlanta for a like period. In addition, his brother and law partner, Burton Smith, had married the daughter of one of the most influential politico-economic leaders in the state, John B. Gordon, who was an integral part of Georgia's so-called Bourbon Triumvirate.[149] Smith was, then, closely allied with conservative business enterprises and, perhaps as a consequence, had helped lead the fight in Georgia against the Populist movement and its (1892) presidential candidate, James B. Weaver. Smith eventually grew tired of Washington affairs and stepped down from office in the latter part of 1896. He was replaced by a Midwesterner, David R. Francis, who had already held two major public posts, mayor of St. Louis (1885–1887) and governor of Missouri (1888–1892). Probably equally important, Francis was a well-established St. Louis merchant who had also acted as a vice-president of the Mississippi Valley Trust Co. (up to 1896) and as a director of the Merchants-Laclede National Bank of St. Louis. Further, his father-in-law, John D. Perry, had been president and then a director of the Kansas Pacific Railway (from 1867 to 1878), and had more recently served as a board member of the Illinois and St. Louis Railroad and Coal Co. (1880–1888) and the Mississippi Valley Trust Co. (up to at least 1897). Thus, if anything, Francis was more closely linked to the business community than the man he replaced.

For Secretary of Agriculture, Cleveland followed the example of his predecessor and picked a man from the Midwest, Nebraska's J. Sterling Morton, who was a well-known newspaperman, publicist, and Democratic party leader. Although Morton had rarely held electoral office, he had served in various appointive posts over the years, chief of which was as president of the state board of agriculture in 1873–1875 (and before that as a board member). This position presumably weighed heavily in his favor as a candidate for Cleveland's Cabinet. Yet, while Morton had been extremely active in farm and civic affairs in Nebraska, he really did not represent agrarian interests so much as he did those of several major railroads in the West, for as a reading of his biography makes clear, Morton was, from the early 1870s up to his appointment to Cabinet office, primarily a paid lobbyist and propagandist for certain (mainly Boston-controlled) railroad enterprises, especially the big Chicago, Burlington and Quincy line.[150] Moreover, one of Morton's sons (Paul) was closely associated with a number of business concerns about this time, serving as a director of the Colorado Fuel and Iron Co. from 1890 to 1895, as a board member of the Indiana, Illinois and Iowa Railroad from 1893 up to 1896, and then as a vice-president of the Atchison, Topeka and Santa Fe Railway.[151] It is a revealing commentary on the politico-economic nature of the Cleveland administration that it would appoint a railroad lobbyist-publicist as Secretary of Agriculture when these businesses were under bitter attack by farmers.[152]

In the diplomatic realm, President Cleveland appointed one of the nation's most prominent Democratic leaders, Delaware's Thomas F. Bayard, as American Ambassador to Great Britain.[153] Bayard had been out of public life for the last four years. Earlier he had served for a long time (1869–1885) in the U.S. Senate, had twice been a prime presidential candidate (with the strong support of the now-deceased August Belmont), and had essentially capped his career by acting as Secretary of State in Cleveland's first administration. Bayard was a wealthy patrician and longtime Wilmington lawyer who belonged to what might best be described as the "gentry" class in American politics, and as such, he was one of the last of a declining breed. Although the Bayards had long-established ties to New York's social elite, even extending indirectly to "the" Mrs. William Astor, Bayard's daughter had married a representative of a very different order, industrialist Samuel D. Warren, whose family owned and operated a major (paper) manufacturing enterprise in New England.[154] Though these relations may have had little effect on Bayard's actions as a diplomatic official, they signified the changing nature of America's political economy in the late 19th century.

As Ambassador to France, President Cleveland selected a loyal Louisiana Democrat, James B. Eustis, who had served on two separate occasions (1877–1879 and 1885–1891) in the U.S. Senate and had been a strong supporter of Cleveland's 1892 presidential drive.[155] Eustis was a longtime New Orleans lawyer. From 1879 to 1884 he had also been a professor of law at the University of Louisiana (now Tulane). He had, moreover, numerous important family ties, for he had married the daughter of a wealthy planter and his father had many years earlier been chief justice of the Louisiana supreme court. Yet, judging from available (perhaps inadequate) data, Eustis had no major business connections, so he would seem to have been primarily a political selection whose roots were in the old pre-industrial order.

Finally, as American Ambassador to Germany, Cleveland chose a relatively unknown New Jersey figure, Theodore Runyon, who had no experience in national or diplomatic affairs. He had, however, held a number of state and local governmental posts, the most prominent of which was as chancellor of New Jersey from 1873 to 1887. Runyon was also a longtime Newark lawyer who had served up to the early 1870s as an officer or director of a number of local economic enterprises. And although a high state official for many later years, he continued to sit on the board of the Newark Gas Light Co. up to the mid-1890s.[156] Runyon died in early 1896, and was succeeded by Edwin F. Uhl, a former Grand Rapids, Michigan lawyer and banker who had been serving as Assistant Secretary of State since the start of the second Cleveland administration.[157] Though a pro-business figure, Uhl apparently had no key corporate ties in recent years. Thus, in contrast to his Cabinet, Cleveland appointed few major ambassadors who were closely associated with important business interests.

The most critical and controversial actions of the Cleveland administration were clearly in the realm of domestic affairs, particularly in its handling of the Pullman strike of 1894. This dispute originated in June of that year when, following the financial panic of 1893 and its ensuing depression, the Pullman's Palace Car Co. (which since 1899 has simply been known as the Pullman Co.) attempted to reduce the wages and work hours of its employees, while holding the rents and other charges imposed in its essentially company-owned town at their previous, fairly substantial levels. The workers strenuously objected by going out on strike. When the request of the newly formed American Railway Union for impartial arbitration of these grievances was summarily rejected by the paternalistic George M. Pullman, the union voted to boycott all trains that carried Pullman (sleeping) cars in the country. The railroads in the Chicago area, acting collectively through the General Managers Association, which represented the twenty-four lines going into or out of the city, reacted quickly by vigorously backing the position of Pullman, with whom a sizable number of railroad entrepreneurs and executives were on close economic terms. They feared that anything less than total support would be viewed as a sign of weakness and greatly strengthen the rapidly growing union, led by the militant Eugene V. Debs. As a result, an acrimonious dispute, which was initially confined to a single company, exploded into an, at times, violent and destructive general strike affecting all railroads operating in and around Chicago and other western parts of the country, thereby disrupting much traffic and interstate commerce. Although no intervention was requested by Illinois' humane and objective Governor, John Peter Altgeld, the federal government decided, largely at the instigation of Attorney General Richard Olney, whose views carried great weight with President Cleveland (who had recently been associated with J. P. Morgan's law firm), to take swift and decisive action. It appointed a special counsel, Chicago lawyer Edwin Walker, to institute legal proceedings against the strike leaders and, contrary to constitutional provision, sent in federal troops to restore "law and order," which latter (probably unnecessary) step, in effect, broke the strike.

In analyzing this set of events, great emphasis has been placed by historians of various persuasions on the importance of Olney's former railroad and other corporate connections in shaping his views and actions in this bitter dispute. For instance, since the early 1930s it has been stressed that Edwin Walker, the attorney appointed by Olney to act as the government's special counsel in this matter, was the longtime (1870–1894) Illinois lawyer for the Chicago, Milwaukee and St. Paul Railroad, and it was later pointed out that he was the law partner of A. J. Eddy, who was a member of the General Managers Association's legal committee.[158] But there was actually much more to Olney's involvement in railroad affairs than has been revealed up to recently. Thanks largely to the research of Gerald Eggert, it has now been shown that Olney continued to serve as a director and general counsel of both the Chicago, Burlington and Quincy Railroad and the Boston and Maine Railroad throughout his terms of office as, first, Attorney General and then Secretary of State. This meant that he was in frequent touch with the officials of these enterprises, the first set of which, in particular, had a sizable stake in the outcome of these proceedings.[159] Indeed, Olney continued to draw substantial money from the big Chicago, Burlington, and Quincy line—more, in fact, than his annual salary as Attorney General—up to August of 1894, by which time the Pullman strike had been effectively broken (and Olney apparently thought it best to call a halt to these payments, although he thereafter served gratis, to the extent that his federal duties permitted, as director and counsel for these two railroads).[160] Moreover, Olney was also evidently on very close terms with George M. Pullman, for although this wealthy magnate had no connection with the Chicago, Burlington and Quincy concern, he did sit on the board, along with Olney (and William C. Whitney's brother and brother-in-law), of the Boston and Maine Railroad, so these men presumably had more than a nodding acquaintance.[161] One might therefore contend that the Cleveland administration's highly biased intervention in the Pullman strike, with its disastrous impact on organized labor, was the almost inevitable outgrowth of the extremely close politico-economic relations which characterized American government in the post–Civil War period.[162]

Supreme Court Appointments and Actions

In the late 19th century the Supreme Court was marked by a similar dominance by big business interests, particularly major railroad enterprises. For instance, in 1877 the recently appointed Chief Justice was Morrison R. Waite, a former Toledo lawyer, much of whose practice had been devoted to the representation of railroads. He had served first as a director (starting in the late 1850s) and then as a vice-president (from 1868 to 1873) of the Dayton and Michigan Railroad, and had a number of ties with local business concerns. One of his sons, Christopher C. Waite, was also closely linked with various railroads throughout the time his father presided over the Supreme Court. He was secretary and treasurer of the Cincinnati and Muskingum Valley Railroad from 1875 to 1881, assistant to the president of the New York, Lake Erie and Western Railway in

1881–1882, vice-president of the Cincinnati, Hamilton and Dayton Railroad (which had taken over the Dayton and Michigan line) from 1882 through 1888, president of the considerably smaller Dayton and Union Railroad from 1883 through 1888, and a director of the Chicago and Atlantic Railway for the same period.[163] Thus, despite certain claims to the contrary, Chief Justice Waite was basically a pro-railroad figure.[164]

After fourteen years of service on the High Court, Waite died in the first part of 1888. Following a rather frustrating search for a successor, President Cleveland picked a relatively unknown Chicago corporation lawyer, Melville W. Fuller, to become Chief Justice.[165] Fuller had practiced law in this city since 1856, but it was not until 1866, when he married the daughter of William F. Coolbaugh, president of the big Union National Bank of Chicago (who had served as a director of the Burlington and Missouri River Railroad and was shortly thereafter appointed to the board of the Chicago, Rock Island and Pacific Railroad), that his legal and financial fortunes picked up and he began to establish an important and lucrative clientele.[166] Included were Chicago businessmen Marshall Field and John W. Doane (both of whom served on the board of the Pullman's Palace Car Co.), the Union National Bank, the Merchants Loan & Trust Co., and the Chicago, Burlington and Quincy Railroad.[167] In short, Fuller was closely linked with various major economic interests, and, as Chief Justice, he presided over a Court which, not coincidentally, went far toward providing business enterprise with a carefully devised set of constitutional guarantees and defenses for private property and corporate rights through what many regard as a strained interpretation of the Fourteenth Amendment.

Four previously appointed Associate Justices served on the Court until the early 1880s. These were William Strong, a former Pennsylvania lawyer and state supreme court justice (who had once represented the Philadelphia and Reading Railroad and certain other lesser concerns); Ward Hunt, a onetime Utica, New York lawyer and state judge (who was a close friend of party boss Roscoe Conkling, and who had been linked with at least one railroad in the post–Civil War period); Maine's Nathan Clifford; and Ohio's Noah H. Swayne. The last two jurists still had indirect (family) ties with various railroad enterprises. For instance, Swayne's son, Wager, had served as a director of the Atlantic and Lake Erie Railroad, the Toledo, Tiffin and Eastern Railroad, and the Mansfield, Coldwater and Lake Michigan Railroad in the mid-1870s. And the father-in-law of two of Justice Clifford's children, Portland entrepreneur John B. Brown, was a board member of the New York, Lake Erie and Western Railroad in the mid-1870s and a longtime director of the Atlantic and St. Lawrence Railroad and the Maine Central Railroad.

The other three Supreme Court incumbents all served till sometime in the 1890s. Justice Samuel F. Miller, who unlike many of his colleagues had no known railroad or business ties, sat on the high Court until

October 1890. Justice Joseph P. Bradley, who was a former Newark, New Jersey lawyer and director of both the Camden and Amboy and Morris and Essex railroads, served until early 1892. In a span of unparalleled length, the able archconservative Justice Stephen J. Field, who was a close friend of railroad magnate Leland Stanford, graced the high Court up to almost the turn of the century, during which period he had a profound effect on many proceedings. It should probably also be noted that his more famous, entrepreneurially minded brother, Cyrus Field, was a director of the (Vanderbilt-controlled) New York Central and Hudson River Railroad, the (Gould-controlled) Manhattan Railway, and the (Gould-dominated) Western Union Telegraph Co. from around 1880 until his death in 1892.[168] Clearly, a majority of the men who sat on the High Court at the outset of this (1877–1897) era were pro-business (particularly pro-railroad) figures, and several of them served for considerable lengths of time.

The first new Justice to be appointed during this period was a person of a very different stripe. Kentucky's John Marshall Harlan apparently had no major economic affiliations. Nor had he held many governmental offices over the years, although he had often been a candidate for important state posts. However, he was widely recognized as an extremely able Louisville lawyer and as a prominent Republican party leader in Kentucky, who was closely allied with Benjamin H. Bristow. In fact, he acted as Bristow's campaign manager in the latter's efforts to win the Republican presidential nomination in 1876. This drive aborted, and it was largely as a result of Harlan's critical late shift over to the Hayes camp that this Kentucky leader was rewarded with a Supreme Court appointment.

The other Justice chosen by Rutherford B. Hayes was a relatively unknown transplanted Northerner, William B. Woods, who since the Civil War had been living in the South, where for eleven years (1869–1880) he had served as a U.S. Circuit Court judge. Though he had practiced law briefly in Alabama in the late 1860s (and extensively prior to the Civil War in Newark, Ohio), Woods was primarily a judicial figure with no major socio-economic ties. Reportedly, he was picked to appease the South, for he was the first Justice to be appointed from that region in the postwar era.

When Woods died in the spring of 1887, he was replaced by another Southerner, Lucius Q. C. Lamar, who, unlike Woods, had deep social and economic roots in this region, including among his many prominent kinsmen former Supreme Court Justice John A. Campbell. Over the years Lamar had held a number of important governmental posts, first as a Mississippi Congressman (1857–1861 and 1872–1877), then as a U.S. Senator (1877–1885), and most recently as Secretary of the Interior in the first Cleveland administration. As a political leader in the post-Civil War era he had also done much to heal badly strained North-South relations.

In private life, Lamar was a longtime Oxford, Mississippi lawyer and large plantation owner who had once served for almost a decade (1867–1876) as a director of the Mississippi Central Railroad and its successor company, the New Orleans, St. Louis and Chicago line. Like his predecessor, Lamar sat on the High Court for only a short period (five years) before he died in June 1893.

In keeping with political practice, he was succeeded by still another Southerner, Tennessee's Howell E. Jackson, who had served both as a U.S. Senator (1881–1886) and as a judge of the U.S. Circuit Court of Appeals (1886–1893). But Jackson was also a financially well-established figure who as a Memphis lawyer had built up a substantial practice, devoted largely to corporate, railroad, and banking affairs.[169] In addition, his father had been a big plantation owner in Tennessee, and his father-in-law had a 3,000-acre thoroughbred horse farm near Nashville.[170] Jackson held office for even less time (2½ years) than his two immediate predecessors, for he died unexpectedly in the summer of 1895.

At this juncture, having already picked a Southerner for a recent opening on the Court, President Cleveland selected a well-regarded Northerner, Rufus W. Peckham, a former Albany, New York lawyer, to take Jackson's place on the bench. Peckham actually had considerable experience in this area, having served on the New York state supreme court from 1883 to 1886 and more recently (1886–1895) as a judge of the New York Circuit Court of Appeals. He therefore seemed eminently qualified for this high post. However, it should also be noted that Peckham served on the board of the big Mutual Life Insurance Co. from 1884 up to almost his last years on the High Court, which long-term association probably affected his views on many public issues (particularly those dealing with the governmental regulation of business) for two reasons.[171] First, by sitting on this board for a long time, Peckham came into considerable contact with a number of prominent business leaders, more than a few of whom were officers or directors of major railroads, such as Stuyvesant Fish, president of the Illinois Central. And perhaps even more important, the Mutual Life Insurance Co. had, thanks to a gradual liberalization of New York state law, invested a substantial amount of money in railroad securities, a policy with which Peckham presumably agreed.[172] Thus, it seems safe to say, Peckham was not an impartial jurist, but rather one who sided strongly with corporate interests.[173]

The only Supreme Court Justice appointed during Garfield's brief term of office was Ohio's Stanley Matthews. He had been nominated to the Court in the latter part of the Hayes administration, but for several reasons (one of which was a charge of nepotism) had met with a distinctly cool reception.[174] However, despite a storm of protest from various farm and "anti-monopoly" groups, he was approved by the narrowest of margins in early 1881. Matthews was a longtime Cincinnati lawyer who had held a number of governmental posts over the years, only one of which was of much prominence, that of U.S. Senator in the late 1870s. Of probably greater note is the fact that he had acted as attorney for the Cincinnati, Hamilton and Dayton Railroad from 1868 to 1878, and as a director of the fairly small Knoxville and Ohio Railroad from at least 1877 to 1881. Yet the most controversial aspect of Matthews' appointment was that he had served in recent years as Midwestern counsel for railroad magnate Jay Gould, a man with a most unsavory financial reputation.[175] Matthews held judicial office for approximately eight years, during which period many of his critics' fears were fortunately not realized. He died in 1889.

To fill this opening on the Court, President Harrison picked, at the urging of the two U.S. Senators from Kansas, a longtime high judicial figure from their state, David J. Brewer.[176] Brewer had served from 1870 to 1884 as a Kansas supreme court justice and for the last five years as a judge of the U.S. Circuit Court of Appeals. Hence he appeared to be fully qualified for this key post. But Brewer, too, was tied in certain ways to important business interests, for, as has frequently been noted, he was a nephew of the long-incumbent Justice, Stephen J. Field, and New York entrepreneur Cyrus Field, who sat, up to his death in 1892, on the board of the Manhattan Railway, New York Central and Hudson River Railroad, and Western Union Telegraph Co. In addition, Brewer himself served, along with many business (and railroad) executives, on the board of the big Northwestern Mutual Life Insurance Co. from 1872 to the end of his judicial career, a long-term link that reinforced his rightist thinking.[177]

The first Supreme Court Justice to be appointed by President Arthur was a well-known New Englander, Horace Gray, who had practiced law in Boston early in his career (from 1851 to 1864, the last seven years as a partner of Grant's first Attorney General, Ebenezer R. Hoar). But Gray's most important work was as a jurist, for he had served for seventeen years (1864–1881) on the Massachusetts supreme court, the last eight years as its Chief Justice. Obviously an experienced and highly qualified official, Gray was also the scion of a wealthy mercantile family. His grandfather, Salem shipowner William Gray, was widely regarded as one of the richest men in New England in the first part of the century. Over the years this family had become thoroughly integrated, through marriage and other associations, into Boston's socio-economic elite. The Justice's half-brother, John C. Gray, served as a vice-president of the Brahmin-dominated Massachusetts Hospital Life Insurance Co. both before the Civil War and in the latter part of the century. And probably even more importantly, he had, with the support and encouragement of Horace Gray, managed to establish one of the leading corporate law firms in the Boston area, Ropes and Gray (as it is still known today). Not surprisingly, a number of this jurist's kinsmen sat on various railroad boards around this time, one of the most prominent of which was the Chicago, Burlington and Quincy. Thus, while not directly linked to any major business enterprises, Justice Gray was clearly favorably disposed toward entrepreneurial and corporate interests.

The other Supreme Court Justice appointed by President Arthur was New York's Samuel Blatchford, who, like Horace Gray, had spent many years (1867–1882) on the bench before his elevation to the High Court.[178] While apparently well qualified, Blatchford was also an elitist figure with numerous key socio-economic ties. His father, Richard M. Blatchford, had been an influential New York City attorney, one of William H. Seward's closest advisors and former law partner, and, up to 1867, an officer or director of the (pre-Vanderbilt) New York Central Railroad. Moreover, Blatchford had married a member of the wealthy Boston Appleton family, which had been involved in a host of major textile and other entrepreneurial activities. Yet perhaps of greater significance was the fact that Blatchford himself had been associated with the Seward and Blatchford (Auburn and New York City) law firm for twenty-five years before taking up his judicial career, and that his son, Samuel Appleton Blatchford, was a partner in this concern up to 1884, during which period it had evolved into a prominent Wall Street law firm known in the late 1880s as Seward, Da Costa and Guthrie (and today as Cravath, Swaine and Moore). There is, then, little doubt that Blatchford was a pro-business jurist.

Blatchford died in 1893, after serving a little over eleven years on the High Court. Following a bitter and highly partisan battle (during which two of President Cleveland's judicial nominees were arbitrarily rejected by the Senate as a result of the opposition of New York Democratic leader David B. Hill), Blatchford was finally succeeded by Louisiana's Edward D. White. He was a longtime New Orleans lawyer who had held for brief periods a number of governmental posts, the most recent of which was U.S. Senator (1891–1894).[179] Although a somewhat accidental selection, White was nonetheless an elite figure about whom, unfortunately, little is known other than that both he and his wife came from wealthy Louisiana families and he had been president of a large sugar refinery in the South.[180] Among his legal clients was the New Orleans branch of Lehman Brothers. In fact, White was such a close friend of this influential family that until his Supreme Court appointment he rarely visited New York City without stopping to see Mayer Lehman.[181]

Two other Supreme Court Justices were appointed in the early 1890s. One of these men, Michigan's Henry B. Brown, had considerable experience on the bench, having served as a U.S. district court judge for fifteen years. Brown was a former Detroit lawyer who, like many of his colleagues, had married well and thereby become quite wealthy.[182] Up to 1875 he had been a partner of a prominent Detroit attorney, Ashley Pond, who, shortly after Brown's appointment to federal office, became a director and general counsel of the Vanderbilt-controlled Michigan Central Railroad, which posts he held until 1906.[183] Thus Brown would appear to have been a pro-business figure.

The other Supreme Court Justice selected about this time was Pennsylvania's George Shiras, Jr. This appointee had almost no prior judicial or governmental service, but was a longtime Pittsburgh lawyer with many key socio-economic ties. His father was a wealthy local merchant who had amassed enough money to retire by the age of 32. And Shiras himself had married the daughter of a prominent Pittsburgh manufacturer.[184] He was also a cousin of James G. Blaine. However, Shiras's most important contacts were developed through his work as a highly successful corporate lawyer, for his chief clients were the big iron, coal, and steel companies of western Pennsylvania and the Baltimore and Ohio Railroad, with the bulk of his income probably coming from the former.[185] Indeed, Shiras was probably the first American Supreme Court Justice to have represented primarily industrial interests rather than railroad forces.[186]

In looking back over this twenty-year period—in fact, the entire post-Civil War era—it is clear that enormous changes were taking place in both the make-up and the actions of the Supreme Court. Although a number of essentially corporate (or entrepreneurially minded) lawyers served on the High Court in earlier, more agrarian times, John R. Schmidhauser is quite right in describing the postwar years as a period in which corporate wealth attained great power on this body, for pro-business, especially pro-railroad, lawyers were appointed to the Court on a sharply increased scale, to the point where they came to dominate most of its proceedings.[187]

Given this marked trend, it is not surprising that, despite the efforts of such objective jurists as Samuel F. Miller, the Court began to extend the scope of the due process clause of the Fourteenth Amendment from the basic protection of the civil rights of the recently freed Negroes (its original, though never well-implemented intent) to a constitutional defense of all private and corporate property in America. This clause proved to be a potent weapon in the battle waged by various vested interests against the attempts of the federal government to effectively regulate the nation's rapidly expanding industrial economy.[188] Also, toward the end of this period the business-oriented Court handed down a remarkably strained decision concerning a federal income tax which the more liberal Democratic forces in Congress, led by Nebraska's gifted orator William Jennings Bryan, had managed to pass in 1894 in exchange for their acceptance of a major boost in the protective tariff. In this case *(Pollack v. Farmers' Loan and Trust Company)* the archconservative Supreme Court overturned a 99-year-old precedent, which held that the only direct taxes (which must be apportioned among the states strictly on the basis of population) were capitation and land taxes. It ruled by a 5–4 margin that this new act was unconstitutional, as it too, in their view, was a "direct" tax, thereby setting back this form of progressive legislation for almost two decades.[189]

Finally, it should be noted that during this period the Court began to rule consistently in favor of railroad interests in a series of decisions. One, in effect, reversed the decision laid down in the *Granger* cases by proclaiming that the "reasonableness" of railroad rates could no longer be left exclusively to the discretion of state authorities, but was henceforth subject to (more conservative?) judicial review. Even more telling evidence of the influence of railroad forces at work can be found in the fact that of the sixteen cases heard by the Supreme Court under the Interstate Commerce Act between 1887 and 1906, this august body ruled, in all but one instance, in favor of the railroads.[190] Such a set of judicial decrees was hardly happenstance.

This same set of socio-economic forces was also heavily represented, as shown earlier, in the various presidential administrations during this (1877–1897) period. Overall, about 87 percent of the major Cabinet and diplomatic officials had one or more important socio-economic ties (of which roughly 20 percent were of an indirect, generally family, nature). This was a significant increase over the Civil War and Reconstruction era. What's more, there was relatively little difference in this regard between the four Republican regimes and the two (Cleveland) Democratic administrations. Yet there was a noticeable drop in the proportion of high officials who had a college education, a little over 57 percent (in contrast to approximately 65 percent in the Civil War and Reconstruction years), which decline would indicate a growth in the power and prestige of the self-made American businessmen.[191] Although corporate influence was on the rise in both parties, it should not be assumed that the Republican and Democratic leaders of the country represented, as some Marxists would have it, the same set of politico-economic interests, a mere case of Tweedledum and Tweedledee. Certain businessmen carried much more weight in one party than the other, a not unimportant consideration in an age when political access was often crucial. For instance, many merchants, bankers, and railroad men who derived much of their income from international trade (or preferred lower-priced foreign products) were closely allied with the Democratic party, while most manufacturers were, for the opposite reason, staunch Republicans.[192] This would appear to have been the major line of cleavage between the two parties in the Gilded Age, when the farmers and the urban working class were still ineffective forces in American politics.

Notes

1. Alfred D. Chandler is probably right in saying that the American railroad network was, in terms of its basic framework, practically completed by the 1890s, even though the overall railroad mileage of the nation continued to grow at a much lesser pace up to almost World War I. See Alfred D. Chandler, Jr. (ed.), *The Railroads: The Nation's First Big Business* (New York: Harcourt, Brace & World, 1965), p. 11.

2. For an incisive treatment of this topic, see Thomas R. Navin and Marian V. Sears, "The Rise of a Market for Industrial Securities, 1887–1902," *Business History Review* (June 1955), pp. 106–111. As they point out, while there were some big coal companies, the typical textile concern was fairly small. The Pullman's Palace Car Co. was actually the only large manufacturing company listed on the New York Stock Exchange in the late 1880s, and its business was devoted entirely to supplying the growing railroad industry. The other half-dozen big manufacturing firms were privately owned. See Herman E. Krooss, *American Economic Development,* 3rd ed. (Englewood Cliffs, N.J.: Prentice-Hall, 1974), pp. 187 and 194.

3. There were three other fairly large concerns—the American Bell Telephone Co. (now known as AT&T, which had assets of only $60.8 million in 1897), the People's Gas Light & Coke Co. (a Chicago utility that had assets of $63.7 million), and the Pullman's Palace Car Co. (assets of $63.5 million). Thus, of the eight biggest non-transportation companies, three were public utilities, and one could almost be classified as a railroad enterprise. For all but the Carnegie Steel and Standard Oil entries, see the miscellaneous corporation section of the 1898 *Poor's Railroad Manual.*

4. Another revealing indicator of the great changes that took place in American life after the Civil War can be found in the fact that in 1881 the top post in the Northern Pacific Railway was assumed by a representative of various Eastern business interests, Henry Villard, who was the son-in-law of the fiery abolitionist leader, William Lloyd Garrison.

5. In his study of Jay Gould, Julius Grodinsky refers to three other major railroad empires, in the early 1870s, but by the latter part of this decade the "Big Four" had also emerged as a potent force in national affairs. (See Julius Grodinsky, *Jay Gould* [Philadelphia: University of Pennsylvania Press, 1957], p. 115.) There were, of course, other big systems which were controlled by influential interests, such as the Baltimore and Ohio Railroad, a line dominated by the Garrett family. But these were not of the same order of magnitude as those twelve huge rail networks.

6. See Gustavus Myers, *History of the Great American Fortunes* (Chicago: Charles H. Kerr & Co., 1909), Vol. II, p. 99.

7. For a detailed analysis of these relationships, see Arthur M. Johnson and Barry E. Supple, *Boston Capitalists and Western Railroads* (Cambridge, Mass.: Harvard University Press, 1967), pp. 107–26 and 156–330.

8. See Julius Grodinsky, *Jay Gould,* p. 354; and the 1882 *Poor's Railroad Manual.* The author did not include all the companies listed by Grodinsky as under the control of Jay Gould because some were of only medium size, and there was considerable doubt about whether certain others (especially a few Eastern lines) were really part of his economic empire.

9. For more on the growth of these lines, see Oscar Lewis, *The Big Four* (New York: Alfred A. Knopf, 1938), *passim.*

10. See Richard O'Connor, *Iron Wheels and Broken Men* (New York: G. P. Putnam's Sons, 1973), p. 241. According to this writer, the Southern Pacific did not lose a single court battle up to the late 1870s, which may indicate that its power extended even to the judiciary.

Many judges were quite friendly to railroad interests during this period, sometimes for reasons that are not hard to discern. For instance, U.S. Circuit Court Judge John F. Dillon, who reportedly ruled frequently in favor of the railroads, was a longtime member of the board of the Northwestern Mutual Life Insurance Co., where he associated with various prominent railroad and business leaders. In addition, his uncle, Sidney Dillon, had served as the chief legal counsel for railroad magnate Jay Gould.

11.   Though Huntington failed to achieve his objective, for many years he was also head of the Chesapeake and Ohio Railway in the East. Other major railroad men began to emerge in the latter part of this twenty-year period. The most important of these were Edward H. Harriman, who was elected president of the Illinois Central Railroad in 1887 (and later acquired control of the Union Pacific Railroad), and James J. Hill, who became a dominant figure in the affairs of the Great Northern Railway and the Northern Pacific Railway. But neither was a potent force in American business and politics until sometime in the 1890s.

12.   As Vincent Carosso has rightly noted, the greatest demand for investment banking services came from the railroad industry. As time progressed, this relationship became extremely close and highly institutionalized, with many bankers being appointed as directors (or finance committee members) of railroads in the latter part of the century. See Vincent P. Carosso, *Investment Banking in America*, pp. 29 and 32.

13.   Initially the Drexel family reportedly directed the operations of both their Philadelphia and New York City offices. However, before long the initiative had passed to J. P. Morgan, and in 1894 the firm was reorganized to reflect this fact (through the deletion of the Drexel name).

14.   Carosso, *op. cit.*, p. 34.

15.   See Morton Keller, *The Life Insurance Enterprise, 1855–1910* (Cambridge, Mass.: Harvard University Press, 1963), pp. 13 and 158–60.

16.   See C. Vann Woodward, *Reunion and Reaction* (Boston: Little, Brown, 1951), *passim*. For a more recent study which places greater weight on political factors in this controversy, see Keith Ian Polakoff, *The Politics of Inertia: The Election of 1876 and the End of Reconstruction* (Baton Rouge: Louisiana State University Press, 1973), *passim*.

17.   See C. Vann Woodward, *op. cit.*, pp. 16 and 136. For a more accurate assessment of Tilden, see H. Wayne Morgan, *From Hayes to McKinley: National Party Politics, 1877–1896* (Syracuse, N.Y.: Syracuse University Press, 1969), pp. 75 and 78.

18.   Additional evidence of Tilden's marked pro-railroad orientation may be seen in the fact that his close friend and campaign manager Abram S. Hewitt served as a director of the Illinois Central Railroad (up to 1872), the Atlantic and Great Western Railroad (in the early 1870s), the Long Island Railroad (from 1868 through 1876), and both the Atlanta and Charlotte Air-Line Railway and the Dubuque and Sioux City Railroad (in the mid-1870s). Tilden and Hewitt also shared a sizable stake in a number of industrial concerns, such as the Trenton Iron Co., Franklin Coal Co., and Phoenix Park Coal Co. In a biographical study Allan Nevins portrays Hewitt as primarily an Eastern ironmaster, when, in fact, with the shift of this industry westward following the Civil War, he had become increasingly involved in various railroad enterprises. See Allan Nevins, *Abram S. Hewitt* (New York: Harper, 1935), *passim*.

19.   See Alexander C. Flick, *Samuel Jones Tilden: A Study in Political Sagacity* (New York: Dodd, Mead & Co., 1939), p. 74. According to this source (p. 161), Tilden represented more than half of the railroads in the middle atlantic and north central sections of the country on various occasions between the early 1850s and late 1860s. Although Flick indicates that Tilden's railroad role had ceased or sharply diminished by 1876, this was clearly not the case.

20.   Another possible reason for the opposition of Jay Gould to Tilden's candidacy may stem from a seemingly unrelated action. When Tilden, acting as the legal agent of many outraged business and civic leaders, helped smash the Tweed ring, which had been plunder-

ing the New York City treasury, he also destroyed one of Gould's chief political allies, Tammany Hall boss William Marcy Tweed. The existence of this probably mutually profitable link can be seen in the fact that both Tweed and his top aide, Peter B. Sweeny, served on the board of the Gould-dominated Erie Railway in the late 1860s and early 1870s, when the Gould forces were ousted from this line and Tweed and Sweeny were indicted for municipal graft and corruption. See, for example, *Poor's Railroad Manual* for 1869–1870 and 1870–1871, and also Alexander B. Callow, Jr., *The Tweed Ring* (New York: Oxford University Press, 1966), p. 219.

21.   See Harry Barnard, *Rutherford B. Hayes and His America* (Indianapolis, Ind.: Bobbs-Merrill, 1954), p. 184, and the *U.S. Railroad Directory, 1856*, p. 104.

22.   See Harry Barnard, *op. cit.,* pp. 212, 234, 250–51, and 257, Elisabeth P. Myers, *Rutherford B. Hayes* (Chicago: Reilly & Lee, 1969), p. 48, and also Matthew Josephson, *The Politicos* (New York: Harcourt, Brace, 1938), p. 221.

23.   Hayes's brother-in-law, William A. Platt, was a wealthy Columbus businessman who sat on the board of a number of banks and railroads (one of the latter being the Scioto Valley Railroad). Another kinsman, close friend, and trusted political advisor of the President was Ohio Senator and Cincinnati lawyer Stanley Matthews, who served as general counsel for the Cincinnati, Hamilton and Dayton Railroad (from at least 1856 to 1878) and as a director of the Knoxville and Ohio Railroad (from at least 1877 up to 1881). Matthews was also the Midwestern attorney for the Gould railroad interests. See Harry Barnard, *op. cit.,* pp. 122 and 307, and *Poor's Railroad Manual* for the appropriate years.

24.   See Chester L. Barrows, *William M. Evarts* (Chapel Hill, N.C.: University of North Carolina Press, 1941), pp. 253–59, and Benjamin R. Twiss, *Lawyers and the Constitution: How Laissez Faire Came to the Supreme Court* (Princeton, N.J.: Princeton University Press, 1942), pp. 66, 94, and 99. In the latter work Evarts's association with vested interests is described in a chapter entitled "The Prince and the Sweatshops." Evarts has since been severely criticized for continuing to practice law while serving as Secretary of State, particularly in his first year of office when he reportedly handled a substantial number of cases (see Barrows, *op. cit.,* p. 348).

25.   See *Poor's Railroad Manual* for the years 1873–1874 through 1876–1877.

26.   See Harvey O'Connor, *The Astors* (New York: Alfred A. Knopf, 1941), pp. 163–164, and Allan Nevins, *History of the Bank of New York and Trust Company,* appendix, p. vi. The brother of the other senior partner, Boston attorney Charles F. Choate, had also long served as a director and general counsel of the Old Colony Railroad, and was in 1877 elected president of this big line.

27.   As his Assistant Secretary of State, Evarts initially chose Frederic W. Seward, the son of former Secretary of State William H. Seward, who had served in a similar capacity under his father in the 1860s. Since then he had become a New York legislator and upstate lawyer. When Seward stepped down from office in 1879, he was replaced by John Hay, who had once acted as President Lincoln's personal secretary and later as secretary of the American legation in Paris. In the first half of the 1870s Hay had worked as a journalist for the *New York Tribune,* but shortly after his marriage to the daughter of Cleveland railroad man Amasa Stone, he moved to that city and became a business aide to his father-in-law. Stone served on the board of the Cleveland, Tuscarawas Valley and Wheeling Railway from 1873 through 1881 and as an officer or director of the (now Vanderbilt-controlled) Lake Shore and Michigan Southern Railway (and one or more of its predecessor lines) from the mid-1850s through 1881.

28.   At the time of his appointment to Cabinet office, the first company had assets of almost $40 million, which ranked it as the second largest line in the state (not formally controlled by another corporate unit).

29.   See Harry Barnard, *op. cit.,* p. 417. Evarts's father died early, and the Hoar family forged an extremely close relationship with young Evarts in an effort to fill this gap. See

George F. Hoar, *Autobiography of Seventy Years* (New York: Charles Scribner's Sons, 1903), Vol. II, p. 16, and Brainerd Dyer, *The Public Career of William M. Evarts* (Berkeley: University of California Press, 1933), *passim.*

30. See H. Wayne Morgan, *From Hayes to McKinley,* p. 13.

31. See either *Ashcroft's* or *Poor's* railroad directories for the early post–Civil War years (both of these sources added an extra vowel to McCrary's name).

32. For more on Dodge's many important economic and political activities, see Stanley P. Hirshson, *Grenville M. Dodge,* p. 203 and *passim.*

33. See Harry Barnard, *op. cit.,* p. 417, and also Arthur M. Schlesinger, Jr. and Fred L. Israel (eds.), *History of American Presidential Elections* (New York: Chelsea House Publishers, 1971), Vol. II, p. 1426.

34. See Henry Cohen, *Business and Politics in America from the Age of Jackson to the Civil War* (Westport, Conn.: Greenwood Press, 1971), pp. 176 and 185, Eugene V. Smalley, *History of the Northern Pacific Railroad* (New York: G. P. Putnam's Sons, 1883), p. 95, and the 1880 *Poor's Railroad Manual,* pp. 835–36. Unfortunately, this source does not list the directors of the Western Railroad for any previous years.

35. See Kenneth E. Davison, *The Presidency of Rutherford B. Hayes* (Westport, Conn.: Greenwood Press, 1972), pp. 97 and 112. This post was first offered to Maine's Senator Eugene Hale, who was the son-in-law of Detroit's wealthy business and political leader, Zachariah Chandler. But Hale preferred to keep his seat in the Upper House.

36. See Charles Roll, *Colonel Dick Thompson: The Persistent Whig* (Indianapolis: Indiana Historical Bureau, 1948), p. 134. This writer took a very sanguine view of Thompson's legal and business activities. However, in the *Dictionary of American Biography* (Vol. IX, Part 2, p. 468), Thompson is described in much less flattering terms, as little more than a railroad lobbyist.

37. See, for example, the 1878 *Poor's Railroad Manual,* pp. 340 and 679.

38. According to a presumably reliable source, Goff may have owed his appointment to the influential support of West Virginia's Stephen B. Elkins and his father-in-law, Henry G. Davis, who was a close friend of Goff's father. See Oscar D. Lambert, *Stephen Benton Elkins* (Pittsburgh, Pa.: University of Pittsburgh Press, 1955), p. 131, and Charles M. Pepper, *The Life and Times of Henry Gassaway Davis* (New York: Century, 1920), pp. 39 and 258.

39. See Kenneth C. Davison, *op. cit.,* pp. 183–93. As a research topic, it would be interesting to compare Schurz's record as Secretary of the Interior with that of many of his more business-oriented predecessors and successors, for the administration of the big land-grant program, which affected the railroads, fell under the jurisdiction of this department.

40. For more on this second concern, see E. Digby Baltzell, *Philadelphia Gentlemen* (Glencoe, Ill.: Free Press, 1958), p. 74. Welsh also served as a director of the Lehigh and Susquehanna Railroad in the late 1860s (and possibly later years), and his son, J. Lowber Welsh, sat on the board of the Syracuse, Geneva and Corning Railroad (up to 1876) and the New York, Lake Erie and Western Railroad (from 1875 through 1879).

41. The post was first offered to New York businessman and real estate magnate John Jacob Astor III, who chose not to accept, whereupon it was preferred to Secretary of State Evarts's close friend and kinsman, Massachusetts Senator George F. Hoar, who also declined to serve. The latter then recommended that it be given to his Brahmin supporter, James Russell Lowell. See Chester L. Barrows, *William M. Evarts,* p. 393.

42. For more on this famous family, see Ferris Greenslet, *The Lowells and Their Seven Worlds* (Boston: Houghton Mifflin, 1946), *passim,* and especially with regard to John A. Lowell, pp. 219–222.

43. For Noyes's kinship ties with Hayes, see Elisabeth P. Myers, *op. cit.,* p. 46.

44. See the *U.S. Railroad Directory, 1856, pp. 32 and 38, and F. H. Stow, The Capitalist's Guide and Railway Annual for 1859*, p. 67.

45. See *Ashcroft's Railway Directory for '°66*, p. 46. Judging from this and other earlier directories, it would appear that White succeeded his uncle (Hamilton White) on this big railroad board.

46. Unfortunately, President Hayes did not investigate field conditions and merely accepted the word of the governors as to the nature and magnitude of the problem. One Cabinet member, Secretary of War George McCrary (a longtime railroad supporter), apparently took a very active part in these proceedings and upgraded the description of many of the reported events from "riot" to "insurrection," which may have helped tip the balance in favor of federal intervention. Also, just a few days before the request for federal troops in 1877, the law firm of Secretary of State Evarts received a $2,500 fee for legal services from the Vanderbilt-controlled Lake Shore and Michigan Southern Railway. And Secretary of the Treasury John Sherman still served on the board of the Pittsburgh, Fort Wayne and Chicago Railway, one of the major parties involved in this dispute. See Gerald G. Eggert, *Railroad Labor Disputes* (Ann Arbor: University of Michigan Press, 1967), pp. 28, 30, and 50, and for another somewhat harsher view of this affair noting Evarts's and Devens's friendly relations with certain railroads, see Robert V. Bruce, *1877: Year of Violence* (Indianapolis, Ind.: Bobbs-Merrill, 1959), *passim*, especially pp. 210–11.

47. Garfield's record as a private attorney has been neglected by all of his biographers. Apparently the bulk of his practice was carried on in Washington, where he spent much of the preceding eighteen years as a member of Congress. However, there are still many gaps or contradictions. For instance, Richard Bates claims that the law did not constitute Garfield's principal occupation, but later states that his legal fees amounted to a considerable sum over the years. See Richard O. Bates, *The Gentleman from Ohio* (Durham, N.C.: Moore Publishing, 1973), pp. 33–34.

48. August Belmont was a close friend and strong backer of Delaware's Thomas Bayard, and was quite cool to the candidacy of wealthy railroad lawyer Samuel Tilden, which shows that even within one major business center economic leaders do not always band together, but frequently divide into various factions. For more on this division, see Herbert J. Clancy, *The Presidential Election of 1880* (Chicago: Loyola University Press, 1958), *passim*, and Irving Katz, *August Belmont* (New York: Columbia University Press, 1968), *passim*.

49. According to his biographer, Blaine speculated freely in the stock market, especially in Western railroads, and had sizable holdings in coal and iron lands and in real estate, the value of much of which rose sharply in the post–Civil War years. See Davis S. Muzzey, *James G. Blaine* (New York: Dodd, Mead, 1934), p. 233.

50. See Charles M. Pepper, *The Life and Times of Henry Gassaway Davis*, pp. 97–98, and David S. Muzzey, *op. cit.*, pp. 145 and 233. Other evidence of Blaine's pro-railroad leanings may be found in the fact that when Ohio's Senator Thurman introduced a bill in 1877 calling for the recapture of the funds owed the federal government by the Union Pacific and Central Pacific railroads, Blaine opposed the measure so strenuously that he was referred to as "Jay Gould's errand boy."

51. As his Assistant Secretary of State, Blaine chose a relatively unknown former government reporter, Robert R. Hitt, who had served for the previous seven years as secretary of the American legation in Paris. Shortly after stepping down from this sub-Cabinet post in December 1881, Hitt was appointed to the board of the Louisville, New Albany and Chicago Railway.

52. This post was first offered to Iowa Senator and Des Moines Regency leader William B. Allison, but for some reason this Republican business and railroad spokesman decided not to serve. See Leland L. Sage, *William Boyd Allison*, pp. 170–73.

53. See Charles M. Pepper, *op. cit.*, pp. 97–99.

54. Garfield is reported to have first offered this post to New York judge Charles J.

Folger, a loyal ally of state party boss Roscoe Conkling, with the hope of winning the support of this politically hostile leader, who had supported Grant in 1880. But after consulting with various close advisors, Folger declined the position.

55. MacVeagh, who was a brother of a wealthy Chicago merchant, was also closely associated with Philadelphia banker Wharton Barker, who had been one of Garfield's strongest political backers. See Robert C. Olson, "Advocate of Reform: A Biography of Wayne MacVeagh" (unpublished dissertation, Pennsylvania State University, 1969), pp. 38 and 133–37.

56. MacVeagh did not become a member of the board of the Northern Central Railway until the Camerons were no longer personally associated with this line. However, despite their political differences, Cameron is still reported to have frequently consulted the able MacVeagh before making many of his major investments. See Edward S. Bradley, *Simon Cameron, Lincoln's Secretary of War*, p. 412.

57. See, for instance, John S. Goff, *Robert Todd Lincoln* (Norman: University of Oklahoma Press, 1969), p. 98.

58. See Stanley Buder, *Pullman: An Experiment in Industrial Order and Community Planning, 1880–1930* (New York: Oxford University Press, 1967), p. 191. H. Wayne Morgan also claims that by 1880 Lincoln had already made a fortune from railroads. See H. Wayne Morgan, *From Hayes to McKinley: National Party Politics, 1877–1896*, p. 122, and also the *Dictionary of American Biography*, Vol. VI, Part 1, p. 267.

59. This seat was first offered to New York's well-connected banker and Congressman, Levi P. Morton, who was closely allied with state party boss Roscoe Conkling, who urged him to reject the position.

60. See Thomas Hunt, *The Life of William H. Hunt* (Brattleboro, Vt.: E. L. Hildreth & Co., 1922), pp. 72–79 and 116–25.

61. According to his biographer, Kirkwood was head of the Iowa and Southwestern Railway during this five-year period. But the author has found no such line listed in *Poor's Railroad Manual*. See *Poor's Railroad Manual* for the appropriate years and Dan E. Clark, *Samuel Jordan Kirkwood* (Iowa City: State Historical Society of Iowa, 1917), pp. 323–25.

62. See Leland L. Sage, *William Boyd Allison*, pp. 169–73.

63. The President later appointed Morton, who had many railroad ties, to act as American Minister to France. But since Garfield's regime was short-lived, Morton served mainly under his successor, Chester A. Arthur, and will thus be treated in more detail as the latter's emissary.

64. In the early 1880s the leadership of the state Republican party was taken over by Thomas C. Platt, one of Conkling's chief lieutenants. But Platt was a man of a different mold. Unlike his predecessor, he was very much involved in various major enterprises, serving as president of the Southern Central Railway and as a director of the Chesapeake, Ohio and Southwestern Railroad (a concern headed by California magnate Collis P. Huntington).

65. Frelinghuysen also served as counsel (and director in the early 1870s and possibly other years) of the Morris Canal and Banking Co., and as a board member of the Great Western Railroad of Illinois up to 1865, when this line was merged into the Toledo, Wabash and Western Railway.

66. Frelinghuysen's first top aide in the State Department was J. C. Bancroft Davis, a onetime director of the Erie Railroad and son-in-law of former New York City financier James Gore King, who had held this post twice before. Frelinghuysen's second Assistant Secretary of State was his son-in-law, New York City attorney John Davis (who was no relation to Bancroft Davis).

67. President Arthur tried desperately to get New York entrepreneur, major party

fundraiser, and former governor and U.S. Senator Edwin D. Morgan to assume this post. But the elderly Morgan, who had apparently recently taken over the New York, Lake Erie and Western Railroad (the old Erie Railway), could not be so persuaded, although he did recommend Folger for the position. This was the second time that Morgan had been offered this position. See James A. Rawley, *Edwin D. Morgan,* pp. 234–36 and 262–63.

68. See Erwin S. Bradley, *Simon Cameron, Lincoln's Secretary of War,* pp. 214 and 301, and Eugene C. Savidge, *Life of Benjamin Harris Brewster* (Philadelphia: J. B. Lippincott, 1891), pp. 56–59. Although the Cameron family had by this time withdrawn from many of its previous economic activities, Cameron's son and primary business manager, J. Donald Cameron, still served on the board of the Washington, Columbus and Augusta Railroad.

69. Brewster also had strong kinship ties, for he had married the daughter of former (1845–1849) Secretary of the Treasury Robert J. Walker, who, though a Mississippian, had married into the powerful Bache-Dallas clan of Philadelphia.

70. See Leon Burr Richardson, *William E. Chandler, Republican* (New York: Dodd, Mead, 1940), p. 82.

71. See Leon Burr Richardson, *op. cit.,* pp. 83, 119, 163, 245, and 427, and David J. Rothman, *Politics and Power: The United States Senate, 1869–1901* (Cambridge, Mass.: Harvard University Press, 1966), p. 193. According to the first source, Chandler's early lobbying was done for the Union Pacific Railroad, Eastern Division (or as it was later known, the Kansas-Pacific Railway), but this would seem to be an error, for he worked primarily for the completely separate Union Pacific Railroad (see Stanley P. Hirshson, *Grenville M. Dodge,* p. 172). Curiously, Chandler was not on good terms with the railroads in his home state of New Hampshire.

72. See Elmer Ellis, *Henry Moore Teller: Defender of the West* (Caldwell, Idaho: Caxton Printers, 1941), pp. 79–87. Teller's place on the Colorado Central board was later taken by his brother and law partner, Willard Teller.

73. See Elmer Ellis, *op. cit.,* pp. 85 and 121.

74. In addition, his partner, George Bliss, was a director of the New York, Lackawanna and Western Railroad, the Morris and Essex Railroad, and the Cincinnati, Indianapolis, St. Louis and Chicago Railway.

75. See Oscar Lewis, *The Big Four,* pp. 190 and 243, R. Hal Williams, *The Democratic Party and California Politics, 1880–1896* (Stanford, Cal.: Stanford University Press, 1973), pp. 66–69, and David Lavender, *The Great Persuader* (Garden City, N.Y.: Doubleday, 1970), p. 135. Leland Stanford and Sargent were not, however, on close terms and later became serious political rivals within the state party organization in California.

76. See Edward Younger, *John A. Kasson* (Iowa City: State Historical Society of Iowa, 1955), *passim,* and Stanley P. Hirshson, *Grenville M. Dodge,* pp. 132–34.

77. The most significant measure adopted during these years was the so-called Pendleton Act, which provided for a modest amount of civil service reform. It was passed primarily because of the great public outcry created by the assassination of President Garfield by a disgruntled office seeker.

78. Although a good deal was made of this matter for a number of years, Blaine was actually much more closely linked later with certain other rail lines, the most notable of which was probably the West Virginia Central and Pittsburgh Railway (of which he was still a director in 1884). This enterprise was controlled by the family of one of Blaine's best friends and most intimate advisors, Stephen B. Elkins, who was Blaine's campaign manager against Cleveland.

79. Cleveland's chief opponents for the Democratic nomination were Ohio Senator Allen Thurman (whose "mushy" monetary position was viewed as suspect by many Eastern banking interests), Pennsylvania Congressman Samuel Randall (a high-tariff man distrusted

by shippers and railroad officials), and Delaware's patrician Senator Thomas F. Bayard (who was handicapped by being from a small state and not having sufficient Southern support).

80.   See Allan Nevins, *Grover Cleveland: A Study in Courage* (New York: Dodd, Mead, 1934), p. 77. The author does not see how Cleveland could have represented the Buffalo, Rochester and Pittsburgh Railway before becoming President, since this company was not created, via the merger of various lesser firms, until October 1885. He also has considerable doubts as to Cleveland's reported relationship with the Standard Oil Co. and Lehigh Valley Railroad. However, Cleveland's law partner, Wilson S. Bissell, did serve as an officer or director of several small (or subsidiary) lines, the most significant of which was the Buffalo and Southwestern Railroad. In addition, it should be noted that Cleveland's first (1869–1871) law partner, Albert P. Laning, acted as western New York counsel for the New York Central Railroad apparently up to his death in 1881, and that Cleveland himself handled a number of cases for the New York Central.

81.   One curiosity of this electoral contest is that both the titular manager of Cleveland's 1884 campaign, Connecticut Senator William H. Barnum, and the more able de facto director, Maryland Senator Arthur P. Gorman, served on the board of the West Virginia Central and Pittsburgh Railway, along with Blaine himself. Obviously, these particular associations do not shed any light on the alignment of forces in the country at this time, but merely show the marked overall railroad orientation of many important governmental figures.

82.   For an extended discussion of this once-famous family, see Stephen Hess, *America's Political Dynasties,* pp. 272–98. He claims that the Bayards had ". . . linked fortunes through marriage with the Washingtons of Virginia; the Carrolls, Howards, and Wirts of Maryland; . . . the Kembles, Kirkpatricks, Stevens, and Stocktons of New Jersey; and the Stuyvesants, DeLanceys, Jays, Livingstons, Pintards, and Schuylers of New York."

83.   See Irving Katz, *August Belmont,* especially pages 214–15, 244, 266, and 272–74, and Perry Belmont, *An American Democrat* (New York: Columbia University Press, 1940), *passim.* Such was their relationship that in the mid-1870s Belmont's oldest son, Perry, went to live with Bayard and served as his assistant during one session of Congress.

84.   See David J. Rothman, *Politics and Power,* p. 209, and Charles M. Pepper, *The Life and Times of Henry Gassaway Davis,* pp. 97–99, 137, 158, 253, 265, and 271.

85.   As his (first) Assistant Secretary of State, Bayard chose a former Tennessee lawyer, James D. Porter, who had served in several different roles in the postwar period; as a state judge (1870–1874), as governor of Tennessee (1875–1879), as president of the big Nashville, Chattanooga and St. Louis Railroad, and as a director of the Tennessee Coal, Iron and Railroad Co. Porter resigned from office in the latter part of 1887, and he was replaced by a well-known New York City attorney, George L. Rives, whose father was a member of the board of the Bank of New York. Rives was related through his recently deceased wife to New Jersey businessman John Kean, who had served as a high official of the Central Railroad of New Jersey until the early 1880s, and in the mid and late 1880s as a director of the Lehigh and Wilkes-Barre Coal Co.

86.   Both J. Pierpont Morgan and his father-in-law, New York City attorney Charles Tracy, sat on the board of this upstate enterprise. Morgan also served, probably because of his well-established link with the Vanderbilt interests, as a director of the New York Central and Hudson River Railroad.

87.   See H. Wayne Morgan, *From Hayes to McKinley,* p. 240.

88.   See Alexander C. Flick, *Samuel Jones Tilden,* p. 491. This relationship apparently lasted until Tilden's death in August 1886.

89.   See Stewart Mitchell, *Horatio Seymour of New York* (Cambridge, Mass.: Harvard University Press, 1938), p. 382 and the Seymour genealogy in this book's appendix.

90.   See the *National Cyclopaedia of American Biography,* Vol. II, p. 406, and Wheaton

J. Lane, *Commodore Vanderbilt* (New York: Alfred A. Knopf, 1942), pp. 268 and 273. Moreover, Allan Nevins claims that Scott, a northwestern Pennsylvania Democrat and major entrepreneur, was one of Cleveland's best political friends. As a Congressman, Scott was a low-tariff man who at one point in the late 1880s wrested control of the state party organization away from Philadelphia's protectionist Samuel J. Randall. Unfortunately, very little has been written about Scott. However, a look at *Poor's Railroad Manual* reveals that, in addition to his Erie and Pittsburgh link, he served on the board of the Lake Shore and Michigan Southern Railway, the Michigan Central Railroad, the Chicago and Northwestern Railway, the Chicago, St. Paul, Minneapolis and Omaha Railway, and the Chicago, St. Louis and Pittsburgh Railroad—all but one of which (the last) were Vanderbilt-controlled lines. Two other close friends and informal advisors of Cleveland during his first term of office were Abram S. Hewitt (a wealthy iron and railroad figure who had acted as Tilden's 1876 presidential campaign manager) and Francis Lynde Stetson (a New York City lawyer, about whom more will be said later). With reference to these three men, see Allan Nevins, *Grover Cleveland,* pp. 239 and 289.

91.   See the 1874–1875 *Poor's Railroad Manual,* p. 232. In describing this member of Cleveland's Cabinet, Allan Nevins merely asserted that Garland ". . . felt too much sympathy with the interests which were exploiting the national domain." See Allan Nevins, *Grover Cleveland,* p. 198.

92.   Shortly before his appointment as Attorney General, Garland was given, without so much as a token payment, 500,000 shares of the newly formed Pan-Electric Co. and was named the company's general counsel. See John Brooks, *Telephone: The First Hundred Years* (New York: Harper & Row, 1975), p. 88.

93.   According to Allan Nevins (*Grover Cleveland,* p. 196), Cleveland was wavering between Endicott and another better-known Brahmin, John Quincy Adams, Jr. (whose brother was then president of the Union Pacific Railway). At the urging of Cleveland's close friend and trusted advisor Francis Lynde Stetson, he ultimately picked Endicott.

94.   Although Matthew Josephson claims in *The Politicos* (p. 376) that Endicott had been a director of one or more railroads before he became Secretary of War, the author has not found any evidence to this effect, and believes that Josephson may have this person confused with William Endicott, Jr. (an apparently distant relative). However, according to the *Insurance Yearbook,* William C. Endicott was a member of the board of the New England Mutual Life Insurance Co. in 1889, and may have so served in previous years (although the author has not found any earlier sources which would clarify this matter).

95.   Some idea of the close bond between these two families can be gathered from the fact that one member of the wealthy Peabody clan served as best man at J. P. Morgan's wedding in 1865. See Edwin P. Hoyt, Jr., *The House of Morgan* (New York: Dodd, Mead, 1966), pp. 109–11.

96.   Although Whitney's biographer placed considerable stress on Whitney's emerging New York City traction interests, he made no mention of his major intercity railroad affiliations, which the author believes were of much greater importance. See Mark D. Hirsch, *William C. Whitney: Modern Warwick* (New York: Dodd, Mead, 1948), *passim.* According to Hirsch (p. 223), Whitney's friends and associates, presumably acting at his order or suggestion, created the Metropolitan Traction Co., which may have been the first "holding company" organized in the United States.

97.   See *Poor's Railroad Manual,* and James B. Murphy, *L. Q. C. Lamar: Pragmatic Patriot* (Baton Rouge: Louisiana State University Press, 1973), pp. 91–94. Murphy claims (p. 94) that Lamar's work as a corporate lawyer was short-lived and that he was basically a dedicated federal official.

98.   See, for instance, C. Vann Woodward, *Origins of the New South, 1877–1913* (Baton Rouge: Louisiana State University Press, 1951), pp. 17–18, and Horace S. Merrill, *Bourbon Leader: Grover Cleveland and the Democratic Party* (Boston: Little, Brown, 1957), p. 76.

For a description of the railroad land-grant reclamation controversy between Lamar and his more zealous Land Commissioner, W. A. J. Sparks, which resulted in the latter's abrupt resignation from office, see John B. Rae, "Commissioner Sparks and the Railroad Land Grants," *Mississippi Valley Historical Review* (September, 1938), pp. 211–30, especially 226–27.

99.   Vilas's father was also a wealthy and successful business figure (mainly banking and real estate) who within a year of his arrival in Wisconsin reportedly built the most elegant residence in the entire state. According to one source, "so busy was he with these various [economic] enterprises that he made no serious effort to pursue his profession of law." See Horace S. Merrill, *William Freeman Vilas: Doctrinaire Democrat* (Madison: State Historical Society of Wisconsin, 1954), p. 8.

100.   See Horace S. Merrill, *William Freeman Vilas*, pp. 22, 35–36, 60, and 66. Vilas apparently never sat on a railroad board prior to his appointment to federal office. But at times he represented certain lesser lines, such as the Wisconsin Central Railroad. Actually, the railroad forces were not highly unified in Wisconsin and jockeyed for position (and power) within the same party, as may be seen from the fact that Vilas was closely allied with the Chicago and Northwestern, while the longtime head of the state Democratic organization, Alexander Mitchell, was president of the rival Chicago, Milwaukee and St. Paul Railway.

101.   It should also be noted that a new Cabinet post, Secretary of Agriculture, was created in the last days of the Cleveland administration. Its first occupant, Norman J. Colman, a former Missouri lawyer and newspaperman, served for only about a month in this capacity, and hence warrants little treatment.

102.   See, for instance, *Ashcroft's Railway Directory for 1865*, p. 22, and the 1870–1871 *Poor's Railroad Manual*, p. 470.

103.   The author cannot account for Phelps's apparent lack of corporate activity after 1870. It may simply have been a reflection of his professional integrity or the lack of major business enterprise in his home state. Yet in 1890, shortly after his return to the United States, Phelps was appointed to the board of the newly formed (or reorganized) Chicago Junction Railways and Union Stock Yards Co., the chairman of which was Chauncey Depew, president of the New York Central and Hudson River Railroad. This later step would certainly seem to indicate that Phelps was not hostile to corporate interests.

104.   See John R. Lambert, *Arthur Pue Gorman* (Baton Rouge: Louisiana State University Press, 1953), pp. 92–93 and 117, and Frank R. Kent, *The Story of Maryland Politics* (Hatboro, Pa.: Tradition Press, 1968), *passim*. Gorman was, up to this time, on friendly terms with the Baltimore and Ohio Railroad and, as pointed out before, sat on the board of the West Virginia Central and Pittsburgh Railway. Other signs of McLane's general economic orientation may be found in the fact that one of his brothers (James L.) served briefly in the late 1880s on the board of the Baltimore and Ohio Railroad, and another brother (Louis) was a director of the much smaller Seaboard and Roanoke Railroad from 1884 through 1889.

105.   Horace Merrill is obviously right in describing Cleveland as a "businessmen's president." He maintains that, under the guidance of such men as Samuel J. Tilden and Daniel Manning (and, the author would add, William C. Whitney), the Democratic party in the North was molded into a highly conservative set of forces, led primarily by powerful railroad, banking, and mercantile interests, probably in that order of importance. See Horace S. Merrill, *Bourbon Leader: Grover Cleveland and the Democratic Party*, pp. 51, 71, and 101.

106.   Perhaps because of the influence of railroad and banking interests in the Democratic party, the Cleveland administration did make a strenuous attempt to reduce the high protective tariff that had been built up by strong industrial pressures over the years. But

because of the vigorous opposition of the heavily Republican manufacturing forces in Congress, these efforts were not very successful.

107. See Gabriel Kolko, *Railroads and Regulation, 1887–1916* (Princeton, N.J.: Princeton University Press, 1965), pp. 7–44. The railroad forces were not in complete agreement on this issue. There were some staunch industry opponents of this measure, such as Charles E. Perkins, president of the Chicago, Burlington and Quincy line, and many railroad executives disagreed as to the precise type of regulation required. For more on this matter, see Edward A. Purcell, Jr., "Ideas and Interests: Businessmen and the Interstate Commerce Act," *Journal of American History* (December 1967), pp. 561–78.

108. See, for instance, George H. Miller, *Railroads and the Granger Laws* (Madison: University of Wisconsin Press, 1971), p. 170, and Clarence H. Cramer, *American Enterprise: Free and Not So Free* (Boston: Little, Brown, 1972), p. 497. Cramer claims that, up to 1906, the ICC was largely a data-collection agency, with no meaningful enforcement powers. And another authority has gone so far as to say that the original Interstate Commerce Act of 1887 was ". . . deliberately drawn up as a weak and ineffective measure, more designed to hush the voices of the 'radicals' of that day than to provide real control." See Leland L. Sage, *William Boyd Allison*, p. 297.

109. To gain considerable insight into the forces allied with Cleveland, one need only note that his two de facto campaign managers in 1888 were Maryland's pro-railroad Senator, Arthur P. Gorman, and Ohio Senator Calvin Brice, who served as president of the Lake Erie and Western Railroad, vice-president of the East Tennessee, Virginia and Georgia Railway, the Duluth, South Shore and Atlantic Railway, and the Memphis and Charleston Railroad, and as a director of the Georgia Pacific Railway, the Richmond and Allegheny Railroad, the Richmond and Danville Railroad, Kentucky Central Railroad, Richmond and West Point Terminal Railway and Warehouse Co., and Pacific Mail Steamship Co.

110. See Harry J. Sievers, *Benjamin Harrison: Hoosier Statesman* (New York: University Publishers, 1959), pp. 207–08. Allison, who was closely linked with the Des Moines Regency and once served on four railroad boards in the Midwest, was the longtime chairman of the Senate Appropriations Committee as well as the Republican party caucus leader. The affluent Aldrich was the head of the Senate Finance Committee. This clique coordinated its activities in the Senate through various informal meetings, which in the 1890s were held regularly at the home of Michigan's recently elected Senator, James McMillan, a wealthy Detroit industrialist and entrepreneur. Other important members of this group included Wisconsin Senator (and former railroad lawyer and director) John C. Spooner, Connecticut Senator Orville H. Platt, who was allied with the Rockefeller interests, and Maine Senator Eugene Hale, who had married the daughter of Detroit millionaire and former Cabinet official Zachariah Chandler. See David J. Rothman, *Politics and Power: The United States Senate, 1869–1901, passim;* Leland L. Sage, *William Boyd Allison*, pp. 64, 89–90, 159–60, 246–47, and 276; Stanley P. Hirshson, *Grenville M. Dodge, passim;* and Horace S. Merrill and Marion G. Merrill, *The Republican Command, 1897–1913* (Lexington: University Press of Kentucky, 1971), pp. 29, 32–34, and 71.

111. See Harry J. Sievers, *op. cit.*, p. 310, and also his later study, *Benjamin Harrison: Hoosier President* (Indianapolis: Bobbs-Merrill, 1968), p. 168.

112. As his Assistant Secretary of State, Blaine chose a Boston attorney, William F. Wharton, who had served as a director of the Brahmin-controlled Atchison, Topeka and Santa Fe Railway from 1885 to 1889. During his four years in office Wharton sat on the board of the Madison Square Garden Corp., which counted J. P. Morgan among its directors. Though neither association constituted an overt conflict of interest, both indicate where Wharton's interests and sympathies lay.

113. Also, in 1889 Blaine's son, Emmons, married the sister of Cyrus H. McCormick II, who was the head of the big McCormick Harvesting Machine Co. (which later became an integral part of the International Harvester Co.).

114.   See Joseph F. Wall, *Andrew Carnegie* (New York: Oxford University Press, 1970), p. 648.

115.   See Chauncey M. Depew, *My Memories of Eighty Years* (New York: C. Scribner's Sons, 1924), pp. 133 and 138. Foster had held a number of fairly important diplomatic posts, the most prominent of which were as Minister to Mexico (1873–1880), Russia (1880–1882), and Spain (1883–1885).

116.   The primary reason Allison reluctantly rejected this prestigious post was because of a strong fear that his successor in the Senate might be one of his most hated rivals, William Larrabee, a man whose views on railroad regulation were anathema to Allison's best friends and loyal supporters, Grenville M. Dodge (a longtime railroad entrepreneur still closely associated with the Union Pacific system) and Boston Brahmin Charles E. Perkins (president of the Chicago, Burlington and Quincy Railroad). See Leland L. Sage, *William Boyd Allison*, p. 239, and Harry J. Sievers, *Benjamin Harrison: Hoosier President*, p. 12.

117.   See the *Dictionary of American Biography*, Vol. X, Part 2, p. 383.

118.   Windom also served on the board of the Northern Pacific Railway from 1869 to 1874, when, perhaps for political reasons, he stepped down from this position.

119.   For the statement regarding the size of the Vermont Marble Co., see the *Dictionary of American Biography*, Vol. VII, Part 1, p. 246. For the first available financial data on this firm, see *The Manual of Statistics: 1900*.

120.   See Harry J. Sievers, *Benjamin Harrison: Hoosier President*, p. 18.

121.   One can get some idea of the size of the Davis-Elkins operations in West Virginia by noting that a decade later, in 1901, the value of their three coal companies was $34.8 million (and this was exclusive of their railroad and other holdings). See Oscar D. Lambert, *Stephen Benton Elkins*, pp. 32, 50, 66, 80, 109, and 249.

122.   See Benjamin F. Cooling, *Benjamin Franklin Tracy* (Hamden, Conn.: Archon Books, 1973), pp. 41–42 and *passim*.

123.   Platt was a major business figure in his own right, for he was president of the Southern Central Railroad, the Addison and Pennsylvania Railroad, the United States Express Co., and (briefly) the Tennessee Coal, Iron and Railroad Co. He was also a director of the Chesapeake, Ohio and Southwestern Railroad (a big line headed by California magnate Collis P. Huntington).

124.   See the *Dictionary of American Biography*, Vol. VII, Part 1, p. 539.

125.   See Dorothy G. Fowler, *John Coit Spooner: Defender of Presidents* (New York: University Publishers, 1961), pp. 26–119, especially p. 54; Richard N. Current, *Pine Logs and Politics: A Life of Philetus Sawyer, 1816–1900* (Madison: State Historical Society of Wisconsin, 1950), pp. 184–85, 243–44, and 251; and Harry J. Sievers, *Benjamin Harrison: Hoosier President*, p. 20. The first book portrays Spooner as a former railroad lawyer, who, following an economic change and his election to the U.S. Senate in 1885, began to take a broader public view of governmental affairs—a rather strained interpretation.

126.   Harrison's Postmaster General was a wealthy, prominent Philadelphia merchant, John Wanamaker, who had been a big Republican party fundraiser during the 1888 presidential campaign. Wanamaker was probably the richest and best-known economic figure in the entire administration, certainly more so than Fostoria, Ohio dry goods merchant, Charles Foster, or Vermont "marble king," Redfield Proctor. Yet he received the least important and prestigious place in the Cabinet, perhaps because he had no major (or non-Philadelphia) business ties, or, alternatively, because he was a relative newcomer to the city's monied circles. Also, it should be noted, by way of comparative analysis, that very few retail trade executives have been appointed to high federal posts over the years, particularly in the post–Civil War period.

127.   See the *Dictionary of American Biography*, Vol. VI, Part 1, p. 267. According to Lincoln's biographer, these included the Pullman (Palace Car) Co., Marshall Field & Co.,

and several major Chicago utilities. *Poor's Railroad Manual* also indicates that, starting in 1890, his law firm was retained by the Railroad Equipment Co., a concern that depended largely on one line of sales. When Lincoln returned from Great Britain a few years later, he was appointed to the board of many big business firms in the Chicago area, a sign that he was well regarded by such interests.

128. See John S. Goff, *Robert Todd Lincoln,* p. 151.

129. He had also served in a similar capacity with the Chicago and Northwestern Railway up to 1888. In addition, his son, Ogden Mills, was a director of the New York, Lake Erie and Western Railroad (from 1884 through 1892) and the Chicago and Eastern Illinois Railroad (in the late 1880s). No mention is made of any of these links in either Royal Cortissoz's or Bingham Duncan's biography of Whitelaw Reid.

130. Moreover, his son, T. Jefferson Coolidge, Jr., was president of the Old Colony Trust Co. and a director of the recently organized General Electric Co. and the Manhattan Trust Co. (of New York City). The last link is of particular interest because it was about this time that important intercity directorship ties began to be forged with other kinds of business concerns than the railroads.

131. See Matthew Josephson, *The Politicos,* p. 440.

132. According to Allan Nevins, Henry Villard, head of the Northern Pacific Railroad, called on Cleveland early in 1892 and secured his initially reluctant consent to the promotion of his candidacy. See Allan Nevins, *Grover Cleveland,* pp. 480–81.

133. This association came about largely because one of the other senior partners in the firm, Charles E. Tracy, was J. P. Morgan's brother-in-law. Upon his death in 1887, Morgan turned for legal advice and service to Francis Lynde Stetson, who probably already handled much of his work, and who in the mid and late 1890s served on various railroad boards in league with the Morgan interests. This firm, which has continued to act as general counsel for the House of Morgan over the years, was, because of certain shifts among the top partners, later known as Stetson, Jennings and Russell, and in more recent times as Davis, Polk and Wardwell.

134. See, for instance, Allan Nevins, *Grover Cleveland,* pp. 443 and 450, and Rexford G. Tugwell, *Grover Cleveland* (New York: Macmillan Co., 1968), p. 172.

135. See Edwin S. S. Sunderland, *Abraham Lincoln and the Illinois Central Railroad* (New York: privately printed, 1955), p. 41. Sunderland was at this time a senior partner in Davis, Polk, Wardwell, Sunderland & Kiendl. Hofstadter's much cited appraisal of Cleveland as a bourgeois leader is taken from his famous book, *The American Political Tradition* (New York: Alfred A. Knopf, 1948, p. 148). In this work he described Cleveland, rather harshly, as ". . . a taxpayer's dream, the ideal bourgeois statesman for his time; out of heartfelt conviction he gave to the interests what many a lesser politician might have sold them for a price."

136. This key post was first offered to Cleveland's political friend and advisor, William C. Whitney, and then to Delaware's long-established Senator (and onetime Secretary of State), Thomas F. Bayard. But Whitney was busily engrossed in numerous business ventures, and Bayard, having already held this office, chose instead to take a prestigious diplomatic mission. In 1893 Whitney was a director of the medium-sized New York and Northern Railway, the considerably larger Boston and Maine Railroad, and two New York City institutions, the Plaza Bank and the Western National Bank. His brother-in-law, Charles T. Barney, also served on the board of the Northern Pacific Railroad (which was headed by Cleveland booster Henry Villard).

137. The first man to serve as Assistant Secretary of State in this regime was the product of a distinguished Massachusetts family, Josiah Quincy, who was a still young Boston lawyer. However, he resigned after only six months in office, and was replaced by Edwin F. Uhl, a longtime Grand Rapids, Michigan lawyer and banker (and recent mayor of this city).

In early 1896 Uhl was appointed Ambassador to Germany, and a career diplomat, William W. Rockhill, took over this State Department post.

138. See Gerald G. Eggert, *Railroad Labor Disputes,* pp. 36 and 137, and also his *Richard Olney* (University Park: Pennsylvania State University Press, 1974), p. 53. However, Gresham had also taken some decisive steps against certain dubious railroad interests. In one case he removed one of Jay Gould's friends from his position as a receiver for a big bankrupt rail line, thereby earning the emnity of such forces.

139. See Gerald G. Eggert, *Richard Olney,* p. 53. Once a silverite, Carlisle had shifted over to the conservative opposition and was regarded as a renegade by many "easy money" men—as some put it, "the Judas from Kentucky." See C. Vann Woodward, *Origins of the New South,* p. 271.

140. Apparently William C. Whitney had urged the appointment of Olney, with whom he had served on the board of the Boston and Maine Railroad since 1891. Olney's brother, Peter, a New York City attorney, was also a good friend and legal advisor of Whitney and had worked closely with this powerful Democratic party figure in New York politics since the early 1870s. In fact, he acted as an intermediary in these appointment proceedings. See Gerald G. Eggert, *Richard Olney,* pp. 48–49, and Geoffrey Blodgett, *The Gentle Reformers: Massachusetts Democrats in the Cleveland Era* (Cambridge, Mass.: Harvard University Press, 1966), p. 12. Actually, this post was first offered to Delaware Senator George Gray, but this wealthy Wilmington lawyer (and railroad director) chose not to accept.

141. Allan Nevins, for instance, stated that Olney had been a director of the Chicago, Burlington & Quincy as late as 1889, thus conveying the false impression that this association was terminated at, or some time before, his appointment to the Cabinet. And even Matthew Josephson, who was certainly no apologist for business, led his readers to believe that these directorship ties were probably dissolved prior to Olney's entry into the federal government. See Allan Nevins, *Grover Cleveland,* p. 615; and Matthew Josephson, *The Politicos,* p. 524.

142. Olney also reportedly worked as a lawyer for the Atchison, Topeka and Santa Fe Railway during much of this period, and he aided in the organization of the General Electric Co. in the early 1890s. On the first point, see Gerald Eggert, *Richard Olney,* pp. 33–34.

143. According to Cochran and Miller, Olney was so intimately associated with various railroad magnates that he accepted the Attorney Generalship only after getting permission from Charles E. Perkins, president of the Chicago, Burlington and Quincy Railroad. Of this appointment, Perkins' corporate superior (and Boston kinsman), John Murray Forbes, noted that "of course we shall lose the benefit of constant and early counsel with Olney, but I think we can get more good out of him on great points for his being at headquarters [the nation's capital] where he may have a chance to do good work for all railroads against Interstate Commerce meddling and paternalism generally." See Thomas C. Cochran and William Miller, *The Age of Enterprise,* p. 172; Gerald Eggert, *Richard Olney,* p. 50; and Richard C. Overton, *Burlington Route* (New York: Alfred A. Knopf, 1965), pp. 239–40.

144. Gerald Eggert claims (on the basis of material contained in Lamont's private papers) that in 1893 Lamont was a director of no less than fifteen corporations. The author has only been able to find public evidence concerning a few of these companies, apparently primarily because late 19th century industrial directories were very sketchy. For more on Eggert's findings, see his *Railroad Labor Disputes,* p. 137, and also his *Richard Olney,* p. 53.

145. Lamont was often referred to as "Mr. Assistant President" during Cleveland's two administrations. Because of this relationship, Matthew Josephson wrote in *The Politicos* (p. 523), "Lamont is Secretary of War; but military duties do not occupy enough of his time. He glides from the Post Office to the White House, to the corridors of the Senate, back to the Treasury Department, where, at times, he seems to supersede Carlisle."

146. See Hugh B. Hammett, *Hilary Abner Herbert* (Philadelphia: American Philosophical Society, 1976), p. 61.

147. See Allan Nevins, *Herbert H. Lehman and His Era* (New York: Charles Scribner's Sons, 1963), pp. 13 and 20. Herbert Lehman was, in fact, named after his father's friend and legal counselor, Hilary Herbert. Although Lehman Brothers had not yet moved into investment banking, it had already become a fairly important concern, as may be seen by the fact that Mayer Lehman sat on the board of the big American Cotton Oil Co. in the mid-1890s.

148. See Horace Montgomery (ed.), *Georgians in Profile* (Athens: University of Georgia Press, 1958), p. 304.

149. See Dewey W. Grantham, Jr., *Hoke Smith and the Politics of the New South* (Baton Rouge: Louisiana State University Press, 1958), pp. 17, 23, and 39, and C. Vann Woodward, *Origins of the New South*, pp. 14–18.

150. See James C. Olson, *J. Sterling Morton* (Lincoln: University of Nebraska Press, 1942), pp. 182–354. Not surprisingly, the Cabinet officer with whom Morton formed the closest ties was Boston railroad lawyer Richard Olney, who represented at least two of these companies.

151. Another son, Joy Morton, had also become head of a large salt company (which since 1910 has been known as the Morton Salt Co.) and sat on the board of the American Trust and Savings Bank in Chicago.

152. As the first Postmaster General of his second administration, Cleveland chose his close friend and former (1873–1883) law partner, Wilson S. Bissell, who was, according to Gerald Eggert (see his *Richard Olney*, p. 53), one of the leading railroad attorneys in western New York. He served, for example, as an officer or director of the medium-sized Buffalo and Southwestern Railroad from 1878 to 1895 (the last six years he was president of this line), and as a board member of the Geneva, Ithaca and Sayre Railroad from 1886 to 1888 and the much larger Buffalo, Rochester and Pittsburgh Railway from 1890 to 1892. Bissell resigned in 1895, and was replaced by William L. Wilson, a West Virginia Congressman and Charleston lawyer (with apparently no major economic ties), who had led the fight for tariff reform for the Cleveland forces in the House of Representatives.

153. In 1893 the title of the chief diplomatic representative to all important countries was changed from Minister to Ambassador.

154. See, for instance, Harvey O'Connor, *The Astors,* p. 194. About a decade later, Bayard's son married a member of the Du Pont family, which union clearly represented a blending of the new and old orders in Delaware.

155. Allan Nevins claims, less charitably, that the primary reason for Eustis's appointment was that, having recently been voted out of office, he needed the job. See Allan Nevins, *Grover Cleveland*, p. 517.

156. See the *Newark City and Business Directory: 1894–95* (Newark, N.J.: Holbrook Newark Directory, 1894), p. 879.

157. Uhl did serve briefly in the mid-1870s as a director of the Detroit, Eel River and Illinois Railroad, but this was not a very sizable concern, nor was it a recent connection.

158. See Allan Nevins, *Grover Cleveland,* p. 616, Almont Lindsey, *The Pullman Strike* (Chicago: University of Chicago Press, 1942), p. 154, Gerald Eggert, *Railroad Labor Disputes*, p. 162, and also his *Richard Olney*, p. 136.

159. See Gerald Eggert, *Railroad Labor Disputes,* p. 138 and his *Richard Olney*, pp. 50–51 and 152. For confirmation from other sources, see Richard C. Overton, *Burlington Route*, pp. 239–40, and *Poor's Railroad Manual* for the appropriate years. Olney's past and present corporate affiliations probably had much to do with the general ineffectiveness of the federal government's antitrust program at this time, for Olney (who had recently represented the whiskey trust in a suit initiated by his departmental predecessor) permitted the sugar trust case to go to court in such deplorably weak form that it was quickly dismissed by the U.S. Supreme Court. See Gerald Eggert, *Richard Olney*, pp. 87–100, and Allen Nevins, *Grover Cleveland*, p. 722.

160.   See Richard C. Overton, *Burlington Route*, p. 240, Gerald Eggert, *Railroad Labor Disputes*, p. 138, and his *Richard Olney*, p. 152. Since two of the big lines in the Chicago area were Vanderbilt-controlled systems (the Chicago and Northwestern Railway and the Chicago, St. Paul, Minneapolis and Omaha Railway), and President Cleveland had been associated from 1889 to 1893 with the New York City law firm of Bangs, Stetson, Tracy and MacVeagh, general counsel for the House of Morgan (which was closely linked with the Vanderbilt interests), it might be worthwhile to delve further into this set of relationships.

161.   Of further interest is the fact that when Olney died in 1917 the single most valuable block of stock in his estate was his holding in the Pullman Co. (which then amounted to about $80,000). Eggert was unable to determine when this purchase was made, but thinks it may have been in 1892 when the Boston and Maine Railroad gave Pullman a monopolistic sleeping-car franchise with the line and invited him to sit on its board. See Gerald Eggert, *Richard Olney*, p. 347.

162.   It should also be noted that Olney's top aide, Solicitor General Lawrence Maxwell, was closely linked with railroad interests, for he had served from 1887 through 1894 as general counsel for the Cincinnati, Hamilton and Dayton Railroad, had been retained periodically by the Ohio and Mississippi Railway, and was elected to the board of the Cincinnati, New Orleans and Texas Pacific Railway in October 1894 (several months before he resigned from the Justice Department as a result of a personal clash with Olney). In addition, one of the two generals in charge of the federal troops dispatched to restore law and order in Chicago, Nelson A. Miles, had married the daughter of Ohio Senator John Sherman, who was a longtime director of the Pittsburgh, Fort Wayne and Chicago Railway. For more on Miles's ties, see Gerald Eggert, *Railway Labor Disputes*, pp. 149 and 270–71.

163.   Much of this information can be found in less precise form in C. Peter Magrath, *Morrison R. Waite*, pp. 50–51, and Gustavus Myers, *History of the Supreme Court of the United States*, pp. 531–38. Myers' study is clearly a much underrated work, its polemical nature and various errors notwithstanding.

164.   According to his friendly biographer, Peter Magrath (see p. 52), Waite was not a "railroad attorney" in the usual sense of the word. However, most of Waite's associations, and many of those of his family and friends, would certainly seem to indicate that he was favorably disposed toward such interests, although in some cases he ruled against the railroads. For example, one of his closest friends (and onetime law partner), Samuel M. Young, was a fairly prominent businessman who served up to 1881 on the board of the Columbus and Toledo Railroad.

165.   Fuller was actually Cleveland's fourth choice for this post. The other three were never formally proposed because of various major recruitment problems. One lawyer who coveted this position was Fuller's political mentor, William C. Goudy, who was the general counsel for the Vanderbilt-controlled Chicago and Northwestern Railway. However, Cleveland felt he was too openly associated with such interests to be named Chief Justice, so Fuller was nominated instead. For more on these proceedings, see Leo Pfeffer, *This Honorable Court*, pp. 205–08.

166.   See Leon Friedman and Fred L. Israel (eds.), *The Justices of the United States Supreme Court, 1789–1969*, Vol. II, p. 1475. The influential Coolbaugh had been slated to become Secretary of the Treasury under Tilden if the Democrats had won in 1876. Coolbaugh (who, in a deeply depressed state, committed suicide the following year) was at this point a member of the board of the Equitable Life Assurance Society of New York City, and considered to be the leading banker in the West. See Willard L. King, *Melville Weston Fuller* (New York: Macmillan Co., 1950), pp. 64 and 83.

167.   See, for instance, Willard L. King, *Melville Weston Fuller*, pp. 68 and 94. Fuller is also reported to have represented Chicago merchant Franklin MacVeagh, who was an uncle of a senior partner in the New York City law firm of Bangs, Stetson, Tracy and MacVeagh, with which Cleveland was associated between his two presidential terms.

168. Cyrus Field's links to both the Morgan-Vanderbilt and Gould interests are not easy to explain, since these great forces were hostile to each other. As it turned out, the overly trusting Field was virtually ruined financially by Gould in the late 1880s, and only managed to survive with the help of the House of Morgan. For more on this matter, see Samuel Carter III, *Cyrus Field: Man of Two Worlds* (New York: G. P. Putnam's Sons, 1968), pp. 317, 325, 330–31, and 336–56.

169. See Leon Friedman and Fred L. Israel (eds.), *The Justices of the United States Supreme Court, 1789–1969,* Vol. II, p. 1608.

170. For a study that describes some of Jackson's many social, economic, and political ties, see Roger L. Hart, *Redeemers, Bourbons & Populists* (Baton Rouge: Louisiana State University Press, 1975), pp. 12, 51, and 63–66. According to Gustavus Myers' *History of the Supreme Court of the United States* (p. 597), Jackson and his brother, William, were reputed to be the two richest men in Tennessee.

171. See Stephen B. Clough, *A Century of American Life Insurance: A History of the Mutual Life Insurance Company of New York, 1843–1943* (New York: Columbia University Press, 1946), p. 350. Peckham served in this capacity until 1905 when, as a result of much public criticism created by a governmental investigation of certain large insurance companies, he apparently felt compelled to step down from the board of this concern, which by the late 1890s had become very closely linked with the House of Morgan. See Leo Pfeffer, *This Honorable Court,* p. 225.

172. See Stephen B. Clough, *op. cit.,* p. 183. According to this source, the proportion of the Mutual Life Insurance Company's assets invested in railroad securities rose sharply from 4.8 percent in 1881 to a rather striking 41.4 percent by 1906, from which trend one may infer that its railroad holdings in 1895 were quite large. It should also be noted that Peckham's brother, Wheeler, who was a New York City attorney, was a longtime director of the Buffalo, Rochester and Pittsburgh Railway, the vice-president of which concern, Adrian Iselin, Jr., was a high official of the Morgan-dominated Guaranty Trust Co. of New York.

173. Henry Abraham has, for instance, asserted that Peckham was the confidant of tycoons such as James J. Hill (president of the Great Northern Railway), George F. Baker (president of the First National Bank of New York and J. P. Morgan's closest friend and ally), Cornelius Vanderbilt (board chairman of the New York Central and Hudson River Railroad), William Rockefeller (John D.'s brother), James Speyer (a New York City investment banker), and J. P. Morgan. See his *Justices and Presidents,* p. 136, and George Wheeler, *Pierpont Morgan and Friends: The Anatomy of a Myth* (Englewood Cliffs, N.J.: Prentice-Hall, 1973), p. 255.

174. Hayes and Matthews were extremely close friends and former college classmates. Mrs. Hayes's brother (Joseph Webb) had also married Matthews' sister.

175. See Henry J. Abraham, *Justices and Presidents,* p. 127, and C. Peter Magrath, *Morrison R. Waite,* p. 244.

176. One of these Senators, Preston B. Plumb, served (like Rufus Peckham) on the board of the Mutual Life Insurance Co. of New York, so he was probably on friendly terms with a number of Eastern financial leaders who probably wanted to see that the "right" sort of people were appointed to the High Court. See Stephen B. Clough, *op. cit.,* p. 350.

177. See, for instance, Harold F. Williamson and Orange A. Smalley, *Northwestern Mutual Life: A Century of Trusteeship* (Evanston, Ill.: Northwestern University Press, 1957), pp. 122–23 and 336. Although this board met much less often than most others (only once a year and on various special occasions) and Brewer may have viewed this largely as a civic endeavor, the fact remains that he came into friendly contact with a sizable number of leading businessmen over a considerable period of time, which was almost bound to color his judicial outlook. For a summary analysis of Brewer's pro-business rulings, see Leon Friedman and Fred L. Israel (eds.), *The Justices of the United States Supreme Court, 1789–1969,* Vol. II, pp. 1517–33.

178. This post was first offered to New York Senator and Republican party boss Roscoe Conkling, and Vermont Senator George F. Edmunds, a Burlington attorney and onetime railroad director. But both refused to accept for various personal reasons.

179. Cleveland's first choice for this post was New York City lawyer William B. Hornblower, who was a nephew of Supreme Court Justice Joseph P. Bradley and a recently appointed trustee of the New York Life Insurance Co. However, he failed to gain sufficient support because New York Senator David B. Hill found him "personally [i.e., politically] offensive." President Cleveland then picked Wheeler H. Peckham, another New York City attorney and a longtime director of the Buffalo, Rochester and Pittsburgh Railway, who was a brother of the aforementioned Rufus Peckham. But he met a similar fate.

180. See C. Vann Woodward, *Origins of the New South,* p. 271.

181. See Allan Nevins, *Herbert H. Lehman and His Era,* p. 20. Largely because of their close ties, Lehman Brothers managed the joint fortune of White and his wife.

182. See Charles A. Kent, *Memoir of Henry Billings Brown* (New York: Duffield, 1915), pp. 53 and 61, and Leon Friedman and Fred L. Israel (eds.), *The Justices of the United States Supreme Court,* Vol. II, p. 1554. Brown, Fuller, Shiras, and White have been classified by William Miller as lawyers with close ties to big business. See his "American Lawyers in Business and in Politics," *Yale Law Journal* (January, 1951), p. 68.

183. Although little information exists concerning Brown's relations with Pond after 1875, it seems safe to assume that they continued to have close ties. For more on Brown's pre-1875 legal and business activities, see Gustavus Myers, *History of the Supreme Court of the United States,* p. 592, and Charles A. Kent, *op. cit.,* p. 71.

184. In addition, Shiras's brother, Oliver, was a Dubuque, Iowa attorney, who was a friend of Republican leader William B. Allison and the law partner of Congressman David B. Henderson, another high figure in the railroad-dominated Des Moines Regency. See Leland L. Sage, *William Boyd Allison,* pp. 59 and 97, in particular.

185. See George Shiras 3rd, *Justice George Shiras, Jr. of Pittsburgh* (Pittsburgh: University of Pittsburgh Press, 1953), pp. 76–77, and Henry J. Abraham, *Justices and Presidents,* p. 140. Prior to his appointment to the high Court, Shiras also served briefly on the board of the fairly large Safe Deposit & Trust Co. of Pittsburgh, and his seat was quickly taken by his son, William K. Shiras. Moreover, the elder Shiras was a member of the exclusive, industrially dominated Duquesne Club of Pittsburgh, where he mingled easily with many of the region's leading businessmen. For an incisive analysis of this socially elite institution, see E. Digby Baltzell, *The Protestant Establishment: Aristocracy and Caste in America* (New York: Random House, 1964), pp. 362–66.

186. As evidence of this alignment, Shiras was appointed, over the opposition of Pennsylvania party boss Matthew Quay, with the strong support of such influential iron and steel magnates as Andrew Carnegie, a close friend of Shiras. See George Shiras 3rd, *op. cit.,* pp. 89–90, and Joseph F. Wall, *Andrew Carnegie,* pp. 644 and 712.

187. While agreeing with Schmidhauser's general line of analysis, the author has nonetheless arrived at substantially higher totals with regard to the number of primarily corporate lawyers (and like-minded figures) appointed to the High Court in the postwar era, even allowing for the different way in which our time periods are delineated. For instance, Schmidhauser found, from 1862 to 1888, only three Supreme Court Justices whom he classified as essentially corporate lawyers, whereas the author maintains that there were no less than six (Waite, Fuller, Bradley, Brewer, Matthews, and Shiras), and there were at least five others (such as Blatchford, Clifford, Field, Gray, and Swayne), who, through family or other ties, were closely linked with business interests. See John R. Schmidhauser, *The Supreme Court: Its Politics, Personalities, and Procedures,* pp. 30–62, and also his article, "The Justices of the Supreme Court—A Collective Portrait," *Midwest Journal of Political Science* (February 1959), pp. 1–57.

188. For an incisive analysis of this judicially contrived alteration of the Fourteenth

Amendment, see Ernest S. Bates, *The Story of the Supreme Court* (Indianapolis: Bobbs-Merrill Co., 1936), pp. 204–08, and Alpheus T. Mason and William M. Beaney, *American Constitutional Law* (New York: Prentice-Hall, 1954), pp. 380–87.

189.   For a scathing critique of this case, see Edward S. Corwin, *Court over Constitution* (Princeton, N.J.: Princeton University Press, 1938), pp. 171–209.

190.   See Thomas C. Cochran and William Miller, *The Age of Enterprise*, p. 170. Even though the time period specified in this book extends nine years beyond that covered in this chapter, many of the jurists treated here continued to serve up to or after 1906, so the above statement basically reflects their views and actions.

191.   There was no appreciable change in the proportion of major Cabinet and diplomatic officers who had a considerable amount of governmental experience; it held firm at around 60 percent.

192.   For example, Northwestern railroad magnate James J. Hill was a Cleveland Democrat apparently because he was forced to pay about 50 percent more for steel rails than he would have if there had been no protective tariff. See Albro Martin, *James J. Hill and the Opening of the Northwest* (New York: Oxford University Press, 1976), p. 307. For more on this subject, see Tom E. Terrill, *The Tariff, Politics, and American Foreign Policy, 1874–1901* (Westpost, Conn.: Greenwood Press, 1973), *passim*, and John M. Dobson, *Politics in the Gilded Age* (New York: Praeger Publishers, 1972), p. 122.

CHAPTER 4

McKinley, Theodore Roosevelt and Taft

The era between the years 1897 and 1913 was marked by momentous change, both politically and economically, especially the latter. Indeed, this period has frequently been described as one characterized by "the rise of finance capitalism," which is both an accurate and a somewhat misleading phrase.[1] It is true, of course, that various financial figures came to play a much increased role in American business, but this term obscures the fact that other important shifts were taking place in the overall economic structure of the nation.

Perhaps the best way to summarize this period is to say that it was an age when big industry came into being. As indicated in the first part of Chapter 3, while there were only about five manufacturing firms in the country which had assets of more than $100 million in the late 1890s (in contrast to roughly twenty-five railroads), this total had grown to over twenty by 1913. Although most of these companies were not as large as many of the big rail lines, they were major enterprises in their own right, as may be seen by a glance at the list of the nation's top fifteen firms, outside of railroads and finance, provided in Table 3.[2] Some of these concerns reached huge proportions mainly by natural growth, others by a process of mergers (especially after 1895), more than a few of which were engineered by influential entrepreneurs or financiers such as the great J. P. Morgan, who played a key role in the creation of the such as the great J. P. Morgan, who played a key role in the creation of the enormous United States Steel Corp. in 1901—America's first billion-dollar corporation.[3] The vast majority of these companies were dominated by ambitious, newly rich families such as the Guggenheims (who controlled the American Smelting & Refining Co.) or by major economic interests. The most glaring example of the latter was the House of Morgan's hegemony over the United States Steel Corp.[4]

It should also be noted that a number of powerful financial forces, especially that headed by J. P. Morgan, had been involved in a series of railroad mergers and reorganizations some years earlier (primarily in the mid- and late-1890s), out of which evolved a set of gigantic rail lines, the largest of which are listed in Table 4:

TABLE 3

America's 15 Largest Industrial Enterprises around 1913

Rank	Company	1913 or late 1912 Assets ($ millions)
1	United States Steel Corp.	1,635.9
2	American Telephone & Telegraph Co.	656.0
3	Standard Oil Co. of N.J.	357.0
		(860.4 in 1911)*
4	Amalgamated Copper Co. (now Anaconda)	198.2
5	International Mercantile Marine Co.	194.2
6	American Smelting & Refining Co.	189.8
7	United States Rubber Co.	185.8
8	Western Union Telegraph Co.	168.3
9	Consolidated Gas Co. of N.Y.	165.2
10	Pullman Co.	158.5
11	Armour & Co.	156.2
12	Swift & Co.	151.2
13	American Tobacco Co.	143.9
14	General Electric Co.	131.9
15	International Harvester Co.	129.9
		(242.9 in 1912)*

*The figures in parenthesis represent the maximum size of these companies prior to recent antitrust action.

TABLE 4

America's 15 Largest Railroads around 1913

Rank	Railroad	1913 or 1912 Assets* ($ millions)
1	Pennsylvania	940.1
2	Union Pacific	902.7
3	Southern Pacific	892.1
4	Chicago, Milwaukee & St. Paul	751.5
5	Atchison, Topeka & Sante Fe	697.1
6	New York Central & Hudson River	686.5
7	Northern Pacific	658.8
8	Baltimore & Ohio	645.1
9	Great Northern Railway	643.9
10	New York, New Haven & Hartford	490.4
11	Chicago, Burlington & Quincy	484.9
12	Southern Railway	484.4
13	Erie Railroad	476.6
14	Chicago & Northwestern	413.6
15	Chicago, Rock Island & Pacific	364.7

*If the assets of two closely affiliated companies—the Atlantic Coast Line Co. and the Louisville & Nashville Railroad—were combined, this economic aggregate would rank among the nation's top ten railroads.

In addition, there were important shifts in the locus of control of a surprising percentage of these rail lines after the early 1890s, with the emergence of several new major railroad magnates and the decline or disappearance of other long-established forces. The wealthy, close-knit Boston Brahmin interests had, for instance, been compelled to relinquish their grip on the Atchison, Topeka and Santa Fe Railway, and then, shortly after the turn of the century, were eased out of their control of the Chicago, Burlington and Quincy. These losses marked the end of this elite group as railroad leaders. Moreover, the hated Jay Gould had died in 1892, and while various members of his family retained a firm hold on the Missouri-Pacific Railway and other lesser Western lines throughout most of this period, his offspring did not have his extraordinary ability and drive, and thus became a much-reduced force in national economic affairs. Similarly, California magnate Collis P. Huntington, who was the long-dominant and last-surviving figure in the "Big Four," died in 1900, and control of both the Union Pacific and Southern Pacific railroads passed into the hands of a rising financier from the East, Edward H. Harriman. Though he lived only another nine years, Harriman made his weight felt in many business circles around the nation.[5] Another relatively new figure to emerge during this period was the lesser known, but probably equally important, James J. Hill, who was largely responsible for the development of the Great Northern Railway and later became allied with the House of Morgan in a bitter struggle to ward off efforts by the acquisitive E. H. Harriman to add the Northern Pacific to his string of railroad enterprises.[6] And, though closely linked with both the Vanderbilt and the Hill interests, the House of Morgan was itself deeply immersed in the affairs of a number of major rail lines, for it controlled such big systems as the Erie and Southern railroads.[7]

With a few exceptions, the nation's financial institutions were considerably smaller than either the railroad or industrial concerns. Indeed, at the start of this period the only fiscal enterprises of a truly sizable sort were the three largest life insurance companies—the Mutual Life Insurance Co., New York Life Insurance Co., and Equitable Life Assurance Society of New York (each of which had assets of over $200 million in 1897)—and one recently expanded commercial bank, the National City Bank of New York.[8] But while these firms were quite large and continued to grow at a rather remarkable rate (New York Life reached a total of $720 million by 1913 and Mutual Life over $600 million), the big life insurance companies were subject to certain statutory restrictions as to their fiscal, especially their investment, practices and thus played a less prominent role in business affairs than one might otherwise expect.[9]

Instead it was the investment and commercial banks which served as the key agents in raising much-needed capital, creating corporate mergers, and in this manner promoting the economic growth of the country. And the importance and success of these endeavors was determined mainly not by the size and nature of these institutions (most, in fact, were fairly small), but by the unusual ability and character of the men who directed their operations.

By far the most influential of these men was the legendary J. P. Morgan, who, having initially centered his attention on railroads, had begun in the 1890s to branch out into numerous other lines of activity. In league with his close friend and business associate George F. Baker (the longtime president and dominant stockholder of the First National Bank of New York), he soon fashioned an enormous network of economic power, which understandably revolved primarily around his own firm of J. P. Morgan & Co., but also extended in the first part of the century to many other financial concerns, foremost of which were:[10]

Financial Institution	*Early 1913 Assets* *($000,000)*
Astor Trust Co. (originally incorporated as the Astor National Bank)	$ 23
Bankers Trust Co. (which was created in 1903 and later absorbed the friendly Manhattan Trust Co.)	190
Chase National Bank (which did not become a Rockefeller concern until 1930)	124
First National Bank of New York (a staunch ally of J. P. Morgan)	142
Guaranty Trust Co. (which had recently absorbed the friendly Morton Trust Co. and Fifth Avenue Trust Co.)	247
Liberty National Bank (a second-tier institution, like the Astor Trust Co.)	29
Mutual Life Insurance Co.	599
National Bank of Commerce (of which J. P. Morgan was a vice-president until 1903 and thereafter a director)	195
Subtotal (excluding Mutual Life)	$ 950
Total	$1,549

Partly because of these links and fiscal resources, the House of Morgan wielded great influence in American business around the turn of the century. Indeed, the imperious J. P. Morgan (who died in 1913, thus in a sense marking the end of an epoch) was probably the most powerful banker ever to grace the national economic scene. In fact, one authority has, for this reason, referred to this period as the "Morgan era."[11]

Yet there were also certain potent independent, if not rival, forces at work in the American business community. The most prominent of these was another New York City-based faction which might best be described as the Rockefeller (or Stillman-Rockefeller) complex.[12] The bulk of the money behind this key group came originally from the highly lucrative operations of the mammoth Standard Oil Co. With the gradual retirement of the great John D. Rockefeller from active business during this period, the major leadership in this circle was provided by William Rockefeller, John D.'s brother, who had a wide range of entrepreneurial interests, and James Stillman, who was the longtime head of the big Rockefeller-dominated National City Bank.[13] Indeed, these leaders were bound not only by business ties, but socially by the marriage of Stillman's two daughters to the two sons of William Rockefeller.[14] This elite group also controlled, or had an important stake in, several other sizable financial institutions in New York City, such as the Farmers' Loan and Trust Co., Hanover National Bank, and probably the United States Trust Co. (these three concerns had overall 1913 assets of about $330 million).[15] And it established close links with a number of other influential figures who were not in the "Morgan camp," the most notable of whom was railroad magnate E. H. Harriman.[16]

Another group of a very different type should be mentioned at this point, and that is the National Civic Federation. This organization was created in 1900 in an effort to foster better relations between labor and management, a matter of growing concern in certain major business circles. The outlook of the corporate component of this group was that of moderate or "enlightened" conservatism on most important politico-economic issues, particularly in contrast to the more militant, if not reactionary, line espoused by the National Association of Manufacturers, an organization dominated by medium and small business and devoted largely (after 1902) to crushing organized labor.[17] Perhaps the most unusual feature of the National Civic Federation (NCF) was its governing body, for it was run by an executive committee of from 45 to 50 members, roughly one-third of whom were representatives of various employers, one-third representatives of American wage earners (all of these were labor union officials), and one-third were supposed to be representatives of the general public. However, despite this seemingly fair and well-balanced structure, the NCF was really dominated by big business, for many representatives of the "general public" were actually closely linked with one or more large companies. For instance, in 1903 ten of the sixteen "public" members had such economic affiliations, and in 1910 nine of the seventeen "public" representatives were drawn from corporate circles (although some also had prominent civic ties).[18] Thus, most likely unknown to many of its wage-earner members, the National Civic Federation was probably not as impartial as it purported to be, but rather was a useful pro-business body for influencing the federal government and public policy.

A knowledge of these economic interests is important because the presidential election of 1896 was one of the major turning points in American political history. In this year the long-depressed agrarian forces of the West managed to wrest control of the Democratic party from its Bourbon-dominated Eastern wing and, inspired by the impassioned oratory of Nebraska's William Jennings Bryan, nominated this charismatic figure as the party's first progressive candidate for President of the United States in the post–Civil War era. The ensuing campaign was fought largely over domestic to the extraordinary pre-convention efforts of Cleveland business (and political) leader Mark Hanna, who was the first and perhaps the most influential "president-maker" in American history, the Republicans put up Ohio's amiable, though hardly distinguished, Governor and former Congressman, William McKinley.[19] The ensuing campaign was fought largely over domestic fiscal policy, particularly over the question of "hard" versus "soft" money, with the former vigorously supported by most major business interests in the country (including many who had backed Cleveland in the past), and the latter advocated by debt-ridden farmers and certain silver mining forces in the West.[20] Although handicapped by a lack of funds, Bryan swept almost all the southern and western states, but it was not enough. McKinley, buttressed by a well-endowed political war chest and severe economic pressure exerted by business in the Northeast, where labor was still quite weak, won by a fairly comfortable margin, thereby keeping the nation in "safe" economic hands.[21]

The McKinley Administration

Like several Republican Presidents before him, McKinley had few noteworthy economic connections. He was instead primarily a politician who was best known for his many years of service in Congress (from 1877 to 1883 and 1885 to 1891), where he had proved to be a dogged defender of a high protective tariff, and as governor of Ohio (1892–1896).[22] He was also a longtime Canton, Ohio, lawyer, whose career had been aided early by his marriage to the daughter of James A. Saxton, one of the city's most prominent businessmen, who had interests in banking, newspaper publishing, and various other enterprises. As a well-established local citizen, McKinley himself served on the board of the Central Savings Bank of Canton in the mid-1890s. But McKinley's rise to national power was due largely to the unremitting efforts of a number of wealthy friends and political supporters, chief of whom were the aforementioned Mark Hanna and another Cleveland businessman, Myron T. Herrick. These two men had entree into important economic circles.[23] Not only did they provide much of the guidance and financial wherewithal to ensure McKinley's success as a presidential candidate, but they had even, at an earlier point when he was governor, been primarily responsible for rescuing McKinley from a potentially embarrassing (and probably politically disastrous) bankruptcy.[24] Thus McKinley was much indebted to certain influential figures in the business world.

After considerable deliberation and consultation with key advisors, McKinley chose the following men as his chief Cabinet officers at the outset of his administration:

Secretary of State	John Sherman, Ohio (1897–1898)	U.S. Senator (1861–1877 and 1881–1897) and Secretary of the Treasury (1877–1881) Longtime Mansfield, Ohio lawyer Director of Pittsburgh, Fort Wayne and Chicago Rwv. (1866–1898); son-in-law, Colgate Hoyt, a director of the Missouri, Kansas & Texas Rwy. (1890–1898) and Spanish-American Iron Co. (at least 1897 on)
Secretary of Treasury	Lyman J. Gage, Ill. (1897 through 1901)	No significant governmental experience President of First National Bank of Chicago (1891–97), vice-president (1882–1891); also a former president of the American Bankers Association
Attorney General	Joseph McKenna, Cal. (1897–1898)	Judge, U.S. Court of Appeals (1892–1897) and California Congressman (1885–1892) Former Fairfield and Benicia, California lawyer
Secretary of War	Russell Alger, Mich. (1897–1899)	Governor of Michigan (1885–1887); also state Republican party leader Wealthy Michigan businessman (lumber and other enterprises) Director of several Detroit banks, Mansitique Rwy. (1889–1899), and U.S. Express Co. (at least 1897 on)
Secretary of Navy	John D. Long, Mass. (1897 through 1901)	U.S. Congressman (1883–1889) and governor of Massachusetts (1880–1883) Longtime Boston lawyer Director of United States Trust Co., Boston (early 1901 on)
Secretary of Interior	Cornelius N. Bliss, N.Y. (1897–1899)	No formal governmental experience, though active in Republican party affairs Longtime head of N.Y.C.

		textile concern of Bliss, Fabyian & Co.; also high official of Fourth National Bank of New York (at least 1891–1897, a director thereafter)
		Director of Equitable Life Assurance Society (1884–1899), Central Trust Co. of New York (at least 1891–1899), Home Insurance Co. (late 1890s and perhaps earlier), and American Cotton Co. (late 1890s)
Secretary of Agriculture	James Wilson, Iowa (1897 through 1901)	U.S. Congressman (1873–1877 and 1883–1885); member of Iowa Railroad Commission (1878–1883)
		Longtime Iowa farmer; head of agricultural experiment station at Iowa State College (1891 on)

In summary, of the seven initial members of McKinley's Cabinet, three were prominent businessmen, two of whom, Gage and Bliss, had no formal governmental experience.[25] The third, Michigan lumber king Russell Alger, had at least one significant economic link with a big Eastern enterprise, the United States Express Co., a firm controlled by New York Republican party boss, Thomas C. Platt (who was often at odds with McKinley). A fourth official, Secretary of State John Sherman, was also associated with major business interests through his longtime relationship with Ohio politico-economic leader Mark Hanna (who until recently had been one of his chief backers) and his directorship tie with the Pittsburgh, Fort Wayne and Chicago Railway, which was headed by New York City financier Charles Lanier, a close friend and firm ally of J. P. Morgan.[26] Furtheremore, three of these officials—Alger, Bliss, and Sherman— maintained a number of their corporate affiliations throughout their years as high-level federal executives.

The other three Cabinet members were much less directly linked with business forces. Massachusetts' John Davis Long was largely a geo-political and personal selection, for he was the only New Englander in the Cabinet and an old Congressional friend of President McKinley. He was, however, related through his mother and other family members to a number of Boston Brahmins and no doubt was thoroughly integrated into this close-knit group, as seen by the fact that he was appointed to the board of the United States Trust Co. of Boston in early 1901 (over a year before he resigned from federal office).[27] Attorney General Joseph McKenna (of California) had long been an intimate friend and loyal political supporter of railroad magnate Leland Stanford, and although this man had died several years earlier, it is unlikely that McKenna's basic economic views had shifted significantly in the interim.[28] Iowa's James Wilson, who was a well-known farmer and head of the agricultural experiment station at Iowa State College, was probably the furthest removed from business influence. Yet even he was on friendly terms with such potent pro-railroad leaders as William Boyd Allison, one of the major kingpins in the Des Moines Regency.[29]

With the passage of time, certain changes were made in McKinley's Cabinet. By rough order of importance, these were as follows:

Secretary of State	William R. Day, Ohio (April–September 1898)	Assistant Secretary of State (1897–1898)
		Partner, Canton law firm of Lynch and Day (1872–1897)
		Director of City National Bank of Canton (at least 1893 through 1898)
	John Hay, Ohio (1898 through 1901)	Ambassador to Great Britain (1897–1898); also Assistant Secretary of State (1879–1881)
		Former writer and journalist; also overseer of many investments, including those of rich (deceased) father-in-law, Amasa Stone (1883–1897)
		Director of Western Union Telegraph Co. (1880–1900) and Cleveland, Lorain & Wheeling Railroad (1884–1885)
Attorney General	John W. Griggs, N.J. (January 1898–March 1901)	Governor of New Jersey (1896–1898)
		Paterson, N.J. lawyer (1871 on); also president of Paterson National Bank (1894–1901)
		Director of Morris County Railroad (1891–1895)
	Philander C. Knox, Pa. (April 1901 on)	No significant governmental experience
		Partner in Pittsburgh law firm of Knox and Reed (1877 on)
		Director of Pittsburgh

		National Bank of Commerce, Union Trust Co., and Union Savings Bank (up through 1903) and Pittsburgh and Lake Erie Railroad (1897 through 1901); also former general counsel for Carnegie Steel Co.
Secretary of War	Elihu Root, N.Y. (August 1899 through 1901)	U.S. Attorney for southern district of N.Y. (1883–1885) Longtime New York City lawyer (most recent firm, Root, Howard, Winthrop & Stimson) Director of National Bank of North America (at least 1888–1901), Bank of New Amsterdam (at least 1888–1901), State Trust Co., N.Y.C. (at least 1899–1900), Morton Trust Co. (1900 on), Louisville, New Albany & Chicago Railroad (1885–1889), and Hannibal & St. Joseph Railroad (1879–1883)
Secretary of Interior	Ethan A. Hitchcock, Mo. (February 1899 through 1901)	U.S. Ambassador to Russia (1897–1898) Longtime St. Louis businessman; president of Crystal Plate Glass Co. (1888–1895, when merged into Pittsburgh Plate Glass Co.); also president of Chicago & Texas Railroad and predecessor concerns (1876–1898, when merged into Illinois Central Railroad) Director of Pittsburgh Plate Glass Co. (1895–1900) and Merchants Bank, St. Louis (at least 1888–late 1890s)

Although most of these men had little or no formal governmental experience, all had significant ties to one or more business enterprises, many of which were large companies. Moreover, most of these officials had other indirect economic connections. For example, William Day's longtime law partner, William A. Lynch, had served as a director of the Connotton Valley Railroad in the early 1880s, as an officer of the Pittsburgh, Akron and Western Railroad in the early 1890s, and as president of the Canton and Massillon Electric Railway in the mid-1890s.[30] And his successor, John Hay, who was a longtime board member of the big Western Union Telegraph Co., had even more important indirect links with the business world, for his brother-in-law, Samuel Mather, was a key figure in Pickands, Mather & Co. (a major Ohio mining concern), president of the Minnesota Steamship Co. (an iron ore–carrying company), vice-president of the American Steel Barge Co., and a director of the Morgan-dominated Federal Steel Co. and almost all the big banks in Cleveland.[31] Thus Hay, who served longer as Secretary of State than either Sherman or Day, was clearly on intimate terms with big business.

Some analysts might argue that New Jersey's John W. Griggs, who took over as Attorney General in early 1898, did not fit into this pattern. He was a lawyer who had been involved with small- and medium-sized enterprises, for the bank he headed had rather limited resources and the railroad with which he had been affiliated was puny compared to many of the larger lines in the country. However, this assessment does not take into account the fact that he was a close friend of McKinley's Vice President, Garret A. Hobart, to whom he may well have owed his appointment.[32] Unlike most running mates, Hobart had a number of important economic connections, some of which he maintained, even as Vice President, up to his death in November of 1899. For example, he served as a director of the Morgan-dominated Liberty National Bank of New York City (from at least 1892 to 1899), the New York Life Insurance Co. (1896–1899), the Lehigh and Hudson Valley Railroad (1881–1898), and, before his election, the American Cotton Oil Co. and the New York, Susquehanna and Western Railroad. So Griggs may have linked, through Hobart, to the business community.

Griggs's successor as Attorney General, Pittsburgh lawyer Philander C. Knox, was much more closely tied to such powerful forces.[33] He had been a member of the board of three big banks in which the Mellon family apparently had a sizable stake, as well as that of the largely Vanderbilt-owned Pittsburgh and Lake Erie Railroad. In addition, his law partner, James H. Reed, had served since 1897 as president of the Pittsburgh, Bessemer and Lake Erie Railroad (a line evidently controlled by the Carnegie interests) and, from 1891 to 1898, as a director of the Lake Shore and Michigan Southern Railway (which had long been dominated by the Vanderbilt-Morgan complex). Indeed it would have been hard to find a man with more close links to major segments of the business world than Philander Knox.

Of the six later-selected officials in McKinley's Cabinet, only one, Elihu Root, had no noteworthy indirect ties.[34] Root was an extremely able

New York corporate lawyer who had been appointed Secretary of War in 1899 in a much-needed effort to improve the management of this department which, under his amiable but inefficient predecessor, had evinced many glaring weaknesses during the Spanish-American War. Over the years Root had established numerous close clientele and directorship links with various banks and railroads, the most recent of which was forged with the newly formed Morton Trust Co. after he entered McKinley's Cabinet.[35] He had also been retained since the early 1880s by the Havemeyer interests, which dominated the American Sugar Refining Co. (the so-called sugar trust), and the New York City transit enterprises controlled by Cleveland's former Cabinet member, William C. Whitney, and Thomas Fortune Ryan, a relative newcomer in Eastern business circles.[36] In short, Elihu Root was closely associated with many potent economic forces.

Like most of the other men appointed to McKinley's Cabinet at some point after the start of the regime, his second Secretary of the Interior, Ethan A. Hitchcock, had only limited governmental experience—a brief stint as Ambassador to Russia—but had numerous major socio-economic ties. In addition to his own long-established links (the most important of which was his directorship affiliation with the Pittsburgh Plate Glass Co. up to 1900), Hitchcock had an older brother, Henry, who was a prominent St. Louis lawyer, a director of the Mississippi Valley Trust Co., and a former board member of the Continental Trust Co. of New York City. Thus, both men who served as Secretary of the Interior in the McKinley administration were intimately connected with the nation's business interests.

As a matter of fact, this statement can be extended to most members of McKinley's Cabinet, be they appointed at the beginning or later in the administration. Of the thirteen men to hold such posts under McKinley, the vast majority had one or more key links with various large economic enterprises, many of which were supplemented by the ties of close kinsmen or trusted associates.[37] Hence it seems fair to say that the McKinley administration was heavily dominated by corporate influence.

Much the same set of forces would appear to have played a substantial part in the selection of America's major ambassadors during this period, as shown by the following brief biographical descriptions:

Ambassador to Great Britain	John Hay, Ohio (1897–1898)	Assistant Secretary of State (1879–1881); also held number of minor diplomatic posts in late 1860s Former writer and journalist; also overseer of various sizable investments (through his marriage to a daughter of Cleveland businessman Amasa Stone)

		Director of Western Union Telegraph Co. (1880–1900) and Cleveland, Lorain & Wheeling Railroad (1884–85)
	Joseph H. Choate, N.Y. (1899 through 1901)	Little prior governmental experience Longtime partner in New York City law firm of Evarts, Choate, Sherman and Leon (and predecessor concerns); attorney for the Rockefeller and the Astor interests Director of New York Life Insurance and Trust Co. (1898 on)
Ambassador to France	Horace Porter, N.Y. (1897 through 1901)	Private secretary to President U. S. Grant (1869–1872) New York vice-president of Pullman Palace Car Co. (1872–1896) Director of Equitable Life Assurance Society (1872–1897), Atlanta, Knoxville & Northern Railroad (1897 through 1901), and St. Louis and San Francisco Railway (1880–1889)
Ambassador to Germany	Andrew D. White, N.Y. (1897 through 1901)	Ambassador to Russia (1892–1894); also U.S. Minister to Germany (1879–1882) President of Cornell University (1867–1885) Apparently no recent economic connections

From the above data, it is clear that most of America's top diplomatic officials during the McKinley administration were closely associated with important economic interests, and that two, Choate and Porter, had little or no recent governmental experience, particularly in the realm of foreign affairs. John Hay was obviously an elite figure through both his marriage and directorship ties. His successor as Ambassador to Great Britain, Joseph H. Choate, was probably on even more intimate terms with business leaders, for as a member of a prominent Wall Street law firm (whose now-retired senior partner, William M. Evarts, had served as

Hayes's Secretary of State) he had regularly represented a number of rich and well-established forces, chief of which were apparently the Astor and Rockefeller families.[38] Moreover, Choate had a brother, Charles, who, as a Boston lawyer, was a board member of the New York, New Haven and Hartford Railroad, and either an officer or director of a number of Brahmin-dominated financial institutions such as the New England Trust Co. and the Massachusetts Hospital Life Insurance Co. McKinley's Ambassador to France, Horace Porter, also had close ties to the business world and little experience in diplomatic affairs. His appointment was rather unusual because he was not a corporate chief executive, but a former (1872–1896) vice-president of the Pullman Palace Car Co. Porter, a major political fundraiser, was probably selected because of his other economic connections, the most recent of which were his directorship links with the big Equitable Life Assurance Society and the Atlanta, Knoxville and Northern Railway (the latter was a line headed by Henry McHarg, who was a vice-president of the Bank of Manhattan). America's Ambassador to Germany, Andrew D. White, had the fewest formal contacts with business leaders and the greatest amount of diplomatic experience (aside perhaps from John Hay) of any high official in the McKinley administration. Yet it should not be assumed that he was an impartial public figure, for he came from a wealthy family which had once been closely associated with the New York Central Railroad (see Chapter 3) and, as the first president of prestigious Cornell University, counted many of the nation's top entrepreneurs and executives among his friends and loyal supporters. In sum, then, the major diplomatic officials of the McKinley administration were, like the President's Cabinet, primarily men with intimate ties to influential business interests.

Major Action of the McKinley Administration

By far the most important act of the McKinley administration was its decision to intervene in Cuba's bitter civil war, which had been raging since 1895 between the long-established Spanish colonial government and a sizable segment of the native population who were demanding independence from their oppressive rulers. This fierce conflict was given extensive coverage by the American press, and thanks to the lurid and biased reporting of certain widely read newspapers, particularly William Randolph Hearst's New York *Journal* and Joseph Pulitzer's New York *World,* a vast swell of public opinion was created calling for United States action to end the conflict and grant political freedom to the Cuban people. As one might expect, this internecine struggle had led to the wanton destruction of many sugar fields, refining facilities, and other property, much of which was owned by American interests, and precipitated a tremendous decline in the commercial exchange between the United States and Cuba.[39] Yet these economic losses apparently did not generate a substantial amount of pressure within the business community (except for certain sugar concerns) for American intervention in Cuban affairs, in part because many of the entrepreneurs and executives with a major stake in the country feared that such action would force Spanish authorities to confiscate their holdings.[40] And perhaps because of business opposition (which did not shift until late in this political debate), President McKinley did not succumb until April 1898 to the growing public and Congressional clamor for such measures which, following the accidental blowup of an American battleship, led to war with Spain over the strife-torn island of Cuba.[41]

Although most major businessmen were initially against a military confrontation with Spain, once this "splendid, little war" was won with almost incredible ease, the attitude of many industrial and financial leaders changed sharply. Bolstered by the doctrines expounded by Admiral Mahan, they became much more imperialistic. The nation's economic well-being, it was now argued, was intimately tied to an expanding volume of exports, particularly of manufactured goods, and this in turn depended on the control of various major foreign markets, some of which lay in Central and South America and others in such distant lands as China.[42] Given the marked pro-business make-up of the McKinley administration, it is not at all surprising that the United States took an overtly expansionist line in its negotiations with the vanquished Spanish government. Instead of being content with the award of a naval base and commercial trading station in the Philippines, the McKinley regime decided that it would accept nothing less than the cession of the entire archipelago, which was viewed as providing an important stepping stone to the presumably lucrative Oriental market. A temporary military government was also established in Cuba under the direction of Secretary of War Elihu Root, charged with the responsibility of restoring order in this blighted land and providing for its overall economic development. Root and other officials construed this mandate as an invitation to American capital and corporate interests to take over many Cuban facilities and resources.[43] Although initially restricted by the Teller resolution, which disclaimed any intent by the United States to exercise control over the island, the McKinley administration managed to circumvent this clause through the adoption of the so-called Platt Amendment, which severely limited Cuba's treaty-making powers and, much to the relief of outside investors, gave the American government the right to intervene, under certain conditions, in Cuban affairs. Thus, as a result of the Spanish-American War and later business pressure, the United States expanded its economic and military reach to other areas, in part for the purpose of providing various domestic enterprises with a lucrative foreign market.

Theodore Roosevelt's Administration

With the assassination of President McKinley in September 1901, the complexion of the federal government changed in significant ways, for this unexpected event thrust the reins of executive power and leadership into the hands of New York's ambitious and ebullient Theodore Roosevelt. A wealthy patrician who apparently had never cared to practice law or work in the rarely highlighted world of business, Roosevelt had sufficient resources to devote much of his life to the more exciting realm of public affairs. Through a combination of considerable luck, drive, and ability, he had risen rapidly in politics from such comparatively minor positions as U.S. Civil Service board member (1889–1895) and New York City Police Commissioner (1895–1897) to two much more important posts, Assistant Secretary of the Navy (1897–1898) and, following his acclaim as leader of the "Rough Riders" in the Spanish-American War, Governor of New York (1899–1901). Roosevelt then won the vice-presidential nomination in part because he had proved to be so independent and troublesome to New York state party boss Thomas C. Platt that the latter, in his desire to get rid of Roosevelt as governor, exerted substantial pressure at the Republican national convention to have him selected, much to Mark Hanna's dismay, as McKinley's running mate in 1900.

Having accidentally risen to the pinnacle of political power in the United States, Roosevelt soon established a reputation as a dynamic and progressive leader who strove to give a "square deal" to the general public and to provide, for the first time, meaningful control over the growth and influence of big business in American life. He lashed out against the "malefactors of great wealth" in the country and vigorously backed a number of major reform measures. Because of his actions against certain vast business combines, he was extolled by both the contemporary press and many later historians as the "great trustbuster." For instance, John Morton Blum, taking a favorable view, has portrayed Roosevelt as a political pragmatist and "conservative progressive" who found his natural allies (and presumably, principal supporters) among the nation's farmers, small businessmen, and "upper-class mechanics."[44] Gabriel Kolko, on the other hand, maintains that contrary to his much-cited intent "to speak softly and carry a big stick," Roosevelt often engaged in strong political rhetoric (which sometimes sounded quite radical), but was rather weak and ineffective in action, and that he actually had fairly close relations with important forces in the business world.[45] Given these disparate views of Roosevelt, where does the truth lie?

One way of getting at this matter is by examining the economic background and business affiliations of various members of the so-called Oyster Bay Roosevelts, of which family Theodore Roosevelt was the first member to achieve political fame.[46] As Stephen Hess has pointed out, the primary interest of the Oyster Bay clan had always been in Wall Street rather than in Washington—that is to say, in business rather than public affairs.[47] For example, as New York City bankers, both Theodore Roosevelt's father and his uncle, James A. Roosevelt, were closely associated in the late 1870s with the Dubuque and Sioux City Railroad, a concern whose board included such other prominent figures as J. P. Morgan and Abram S. Hewitt (who had served as Samuel Tilden's 1876 presidential campaign manager).[48] Moreover, James A. Roosevelt was a director, from 1888 to his death in 1898, of the Vanderbilt-dominated New York, Chicago and St. Louis Railway. Also, around the turn of the century two of President Roosevelt's close kinsmen and major financial advisors, his first cousin, W. Emlen Roosevelt, who had taken James A. Roosevelt's place as head of the family banking concern, and his brother-in-law, Douglas Robinson, a New York stockbroker, served on the following major corporate boards:[49]

W. Emlen Roosevelt	Astor National Bank (or Trust Co.), 1899–1906
	Chemical National Bank, N.Y.C., at least 1894 through 1909
	Gallatin National Bank, N.Y.C., at least 1893 through 1909
	New York Life Insurance & Trust Co., 1893 through 1909
	Union Trust Co., N.Y.C., at least 1894 through 1909
	Buffalo, Rochester and Pittsburgh Railway, 1891 through 1909
	Mobile and Ohio Railroad (a subsidiary of the Morgan-dominated Southern Rwy.), 1900 through 1909
	New York, Chicago and St. Louis Railroad, 1900–1907
	Mexican Telegraph Co., at least 1894 through 1909
	Central and Southern American Telegraph Co. 1905 through 1909
Douglas Robinson	Astor National Bank (or Trust Co.), 1902 through 1909
	Atlantic Mutual Insurance Co., N.Y.C., 1902 through 1909

Many of these concerns were either controlled by or closely linked with Morgan (or Vanderbilt-Morgan) interests. For example, in 1902 the president of the Astor National Bank was George F. Baker, the chief executive of the First National Bank of New York City and J. P. Morgan's staunchest ally. And in 1909 the Astor Trust Co., as it was then known, was headed by Edmund C. Converse, who was also president of the Morgan-dominated Bankers Trust Co.; in addition, three Morgan partners graced its board of directors. Similarly, in 1909 the board of the Central and South American Telegraph Co. included such important figures as William P. Hamilton (J. P. Morgan's son-in-law), Charles Lanier (a longtime business associate of J. P. Morgan and a director of the National Bank of Commerce in New York and the Southern Railway), and William D. Sloane (who had married into the Vanderbilt family). Thus the Oyster Bay Roosevelts had long been firmly linked with the Morgan and Vanderbilt forces, to such an extent that it probably, perhaps even unconsciously, affected the outlook of President Roosevelt himself.[50]

Another even better way of assessing the economic orientation and affiliations of the Roosevelt administration is through an examination of the background and major associations of the chief Cabinet members who held office at the outset or early part of this important regime:

Secretary of State	John Hay, Ohio (September 1901–July 1905)	Secretary of State and Ambassador to Great Britain in the McKinley administration
		Former writer and journalist; also overseer of many investments, including those of rich (deceased) father-in-law, Amasa Stone
		Director of Western Union Telegraph Co. (1880–1900) and member, through other kinship ties, of a number of wealthy families
Secretary of Treasury (successor to Lyman J. Gage)	Leslie M. Shaw, Iowa (January 1902–March 1907)	Governor of Iowa (1898–1902)
		Partner in Denison, Iowa law firm of Shaw and Kuchnle; also former president of Bank of Denison
		Apparently no notable directorship ties
Attorney General	Philander C. Knox, Pa. (September 1901–June 1904)	U.S. Attorney General (April–September 1901)
		Partner in Pittsburgh law firm of Knox and Reed (1877–1901)
		Director of Pittsburgh National Bank of Commerce, Union Trust Co. of Pittsburgh, and Union Savings Bank (up to 1904), and the Pittsburgh and Lake Erie Railroad (1897–1901); also former general counsel for Carnegie Steel Co.
Secretary of War	Elihu Root, N.Y. (September 1901–February 1904)	Secretary of War (1899–1901)
		Longtime New York City corporate lawyer (1867 on)
		Director of Morton Trust Co. (1900–1904), Continental Insurance Co. (1902 through 1904), Western National Bank (1903), and a number of other banks and railroads before 1900

Secretary of Navy (successor to John D. Long)	William H. Moody, Mass. (May 1902–June 1904)	Mass. Congressman (1895–1902); also U.S. attorney for eastern district, Mass. (1890–1895) Haverhill, Mass. lawyer (1878 on) Director of Shoe and Leather National Bank, Boston (1891–1893)
Secretary of Interior	Ethan A. Hitchcock, Mo. (September 1901–March 1907)	Secretary of Interior (1899–1901); Ambassador to Russia (1897–1899) Longtime St. Louis businessman; president of Crystal Plate Glass Co. (1888–1895, when merged into Pittsburgh Plate Glass Co.); also president of Chicago and Texas Railroad and predecessor concerns (1876–1898) Director of Pittsburgh Plate Glass Co. (1895–1900 and 1905 on) and Merchants Bank, St. Louis (through early and mid-1890s)
Secretary of Agriculture	James Wilson, Ia. (1901 through 1909)	Secretary of Agriculture (1897–1901); U.S. Congressman (1873–1877 and 1883–1885); former member of Iowa Railroad Commission (1878–1883) Longtime Iowa farmer; head of agricultural experiment station, Iowa State College (1891–1897) Apparently no notable directorship ties

Thus, of the seven major Cabinet members at the time of McKinley's assassination, Roosevelt retained a total of five, and all but one of these—Secretary of Agriculture James Wilson—had one or more ties with important business interests, some of which were supplemented (or reinforced) by those various close kinsmen or economic associates. For example, in addition to his own former investment or entrepreneurial links, John Hay had a wealthy brother-in-law, Samuel Mather, who was a longtime high official in the Ohio iron ore concern of Pickands, Mather & Co., a former director of the Morgan-dominated Federal Steel Co. (until its merger into the U.S. Steel Corp.), and a still active board member of almost all the major banks in Cleveland and the big Lackawanna Steel Co.[51] As a large employer, Mather served also on the executive committee of the National Civic Federation, which heavily business-weighted body represented something approaching a politico-economic establishment in the first part of the century. Furthermore, in 1902 John Hay's daughter married one of financier William C. Whitney's sons, thereby linking the Hays with another rich and influential family (which was already associated, by a similar union, with the Vanderbilts).[52] Until his death in 1904 Whitney served as a director of a number of important firms such as the Mutual Life Insurance Co., Morton Trust Co., National Bank of Commerce, Cuba Co., and Consolidated Gas Co. of New York (the first three of these were Morgan-dominated enterprises). Hence by the early 1900s Secretary of State John Hay was intimately associated with some of the most powerful forces in the country.

Roosevelt's Attorney General, Philander Knox, was likewise closely linked with major business interests, primarily through regular business and professional affiliations rather than elitist family ties. Knox was a well-established Pittsburgh lawyer who had served as general counsel for the Carnegie Steel Co. until its merger into U.S. Steel in 1901, as a board member of the medium-sized (Vanderbilt-controlled) Pittsburgh and Lake Erie Railroad from 1897 to 1901, and as a director of three Mellon-dominated banks in Pittsburgh for various lengths of time up through 1904 (that is, while he was holding Cabinet office).[53] Indeed, Knox's relations with the rising Mellon forces were of such an intimate nature that one objective observer has referred to him as "Andrew Mellon's man Friday."[54]

Roosevelt's Secretary of War, Elihu Root, who was a longtime friend and political advisor of the President, was also deeply involved in corporate and financial affairs. As a prominent Wall Street lawyer, Root had long represented such major concerns as the American Sugar Refining Co., the traction interests controlled by William C. Whitney and Thomas Fortune Ryan, and a number of New York City banks. Although Root had apparently severed some of his earlier links, he managed to forge several others while holding Cabinet office (though he probably did not attend many board meetings). He served, for example, as a director of the Continental Insurance Co. from 1902 to 1905, the Mutual Life Insurance Co. in 1904–05, the Morgan-dominated National Bank of Commerce from 1903 to 1905, and, perhaps most important of all, the Morton Trust Co., which was headed by J. P. Morgan's friend, Levi P. Morton. Without a doubt, Elihu Root was on intimate terms with various key financial forces on Wall Street, although these did not include the Stillman-Rockefeller complex.

In similar, though less marked fashion, Ethan A. Hitchcock, the man Roosevelt chose to retain as Secretary of the Interior, was closely linked to business interests, primarily in the St. Louis area. As the former president of both a manufacturing firm and a railroad company, Hitchcock had forged many strong economic ties over the years. Hitchcock was especially wedded to one corporate enterprise, for not only did he apparently reluctantly sever his directorship affiliation with the Pittsburgh Plate Glass Co. after assuming Cabinet office, but he resumed this relationship in 1905, about two years before he resigned from his high federal post. Such action would indicate a marked bias in favor of industrial and probably financial interests.

It is true that the two major Cabinet officials whom Roosevelt appointed early in his administration—Secretary of the Treasury Leslie M. Shaw and Secretary of the Navy William H. Moody—had much less significant ties to the business world than most of those the President decided to retain.[55] Shaw was a former Midwestern small-town (Denison, Iowa) lawyer and banker, who had served as governor of his state since 1898, and apparently had no key socio-economic links. However, he was a close friend and loyal political supporter of many of the leaders of the railroad-dominated Des Moines Regency, such as U.S. Senator William Boyd Allison, who had, in fact, helped secure this high post for him.[56] The other newly appointed Cabinet official, William H. Moody, was a longtime Boston-area lawyer who had served as U.S. attorney for the eastern district of Massachusetts from 1890 to 1895, and then for seven years as a Congressman.[57] Moody was from an old, well-established Massachusetts family that had been involved, first, in mercantile activities, and later, with the wealthy Lawrence, Lowell, and Appleton interests, in various pre–Civil War textile enterprises. In fact, Moody himself had served briefly in the early 1890s as a director of the fairly small Shoe and Leather National Bank of Boston. Thus, though both Shaw and Moody had some links with economic (or politico-economic) interests, these were clearly of a less important nature than those held by the Cabinet officials who were carried over from the McKinley administration.

The same cannot be said of many of the Cabinet appointments Roosevelt made in the ensuing years, when he was at the height of his political popularity and authority. That this is true can be seen from the following summary descriptions of later-selected Cabinet members (which set of officials was expanded to a total of eight through the business-backed creation of the Department of Commerce and Labor in early 1903):[58]

Secretary of State	Elihu Root, N.Y. (July 1905–January 1909)	U.S. Secretary of War (1899–1904) New York City corporate lawyer (1867–1899 and 1904–1905)

		Director of Morton Trust Co. (1900–1905), Western National Bank of N.Y.C. (1903), National Bank of Commerce (1904–1905), Mutual Life Insurance Co. (1904–1905), and a number of other banks and railroads before 1900
	Robert Bacon, N.Y. (January–March 1909)	Assistant Secretary of State (1905–1909)
		Partner, J. P. Morgan & Co. (1894–1903); partner, E. Rollin Morse & Brother, Boston (1883–1894)
		Director of National City Bank of N.Y.C. (1897–1902), Bank for Savings in NYC (1903 through 1909), Manhattan Trust Co. (1905 through 1909), Federal Steel Co. (1898–1903), National Tube Co. (1899–1903), U.S. Steel Corp. (1903–1905), Amalgamated Copper Co. (1899–1903), North American Co. (1901–1905), Northern Securities Co. (1902–1905), Northern Pacific Rwy. (1896–1901), Erie Railroad (1901–1905), and Hocking Valley Rwy. (1901–1905)
Secretary of Treasury	George B. Cortelyou, N.Y. (March 1907–March 1909)	U. S. Postmaster General (1905–1907); Secretary of Commerce and Labor (1903–1904); secretary or clerk to Presidents Cleveland and McKinley (1895–1903); clerk and stenographer, U.S. Customs Service (1887–1895)
		No significant business experience or directorship ties
Attorney General	William H. Moody, Mass. (July 1904–December 1906)	Secretary of Navy (1902–1904), in which

		capacity Moody was described in the preceding biographical table
	Charles J. Bonaparte, Md. (December 1906–March 1909)	Secretary of Navy (1905–1906); member of U.S. Board of Indian Commissioners (1902–1904) Baltimore lawyer (1874–1902) Director of Real Estate Trust Co., Baltimore (1899–1900) and member of executive committee of National Civic Federation (1900–1908)
Secretary of War	William H. Taft, Ohio (February 1904–June 1908)	President of U.S. Philippine Commission (1900–1904); U.S. Circuit Court judge (1892–1900); U.S. Solicitor General (1890–1892); Ohio superior court judge (1887–1890) Dean of University of Cincinnati Law School (1896–1900); Cincinnati lawyer (1880–1887)
	Luke E. Wright, Tenn. (July 1908–March 1909)	Ambassador to Japan (1907–1908); Governor General of Philippines (1904–1907); member of U.S. Philippine Commission (1900–1904) Memphis lawyer (1868–1900) No direct corporate ties
Secretary of Navy	Paul Morton, Ill. (July 1904–July 1905)	No significant governmental experience (though father had served as Secretary of Agriculture under Cleveland) Vice-president of Atchison, Topeka & Santa Fe Rwy. (1896–1904) Director of Iowa Central Rwy. (1901 through 1905), Great Western Cereal Co. (1904), Commercial National Bank of Chicago (1902–1904), Indiana, Illinois & Iowa Railroad (1893–1895 and 1899–1901), and Colorado Fuel & Iron Co. (1890–1895)

Charles J. Bonaparte, Md.
(July 1905–December 1906)

Member of U.S. Board of
Indian Commissioners
(1902–1904)
Baltimore lawyer (1874–1902)
Director of Real Estate Trust
Co., Baltimore (1899–1900)
and member of executive
committee of National Civic
Federation (1900 through
1906)

Victor H. Metcalf, Cal.
(December 1906–December
1908)

U.S. Secretary of Commerce
and Labor (1904–1906);
California Congressman
(1899–1903)
Longtime partner in Oakland
(Cal.) law firm of Metcalf
and Metcalf
Director of First National
Bank, Oakland (early 1900s)
and California Bank,
Oakland (mid- and late-
1890s)

Truman H. Newberry, Mich.
(December 1908–March 1909)

Assistant Secretary of Navy
(1905–1909)
President of Detroit Steel &
Spring Co. (1887–1901);
vice-president of Michigan
State Telephone Co.
(1904–1905)
Director of Packard Motor
Car Co. (1903 on),
Cleveland-Cliffs Iron Co.
(early 1900s on), and Union
Trust Co. (1896–1909), and
State Savings Bank, Detroit
(through early 1900s)

Secretary of
Interior

James R. Garfield, Ohio
(March 1907–March 1909)

Commissioner of
Corporations, U.S.
Department of Commerce
and Labor (1903–1907);
member of U.S. Civil
Service Commission
(1902–1903)
Partner in Cleveland law firm
of Garfield and Garfield
(1888–1902)
No direct corporate ties

Secretary of Commerce and Labor	Victor H. Metcalf, Cal. (July 1904–December 1906)	See Secretary of Navy entry
	Oscar S. Straus, N.Y. (December 1906–March 1909)	U.S. Minister to Turkey (1887–1889 and 1898–1900); member of Permanent Court of Arbitration, Hague (1902–1906) Longtime high official, L. Straus & Sons, NYC mercantile concern Director of New York Life Insurance Co. (1894–1906) and high official of National Civic Federation (1900–1906)

Thus of the eleven Cabinet members Roosevelt chose after he was firmly secure in the Presidency, seven had direct ties to business interests, most of which were of a highly significant nature.[59] For example, Elihu Root, who was recalled from his lucrative New York City law practice to serve as Secretary of State upon the death of John Hay in July 1905, had a long history of close corporate connections. And he had established several new links in the relatively brief period (sixteen months) between major Cabinet appointments. The most important of these were his directorships with two Morgan-dominated institutions, the National Bank of Commerce and Mutual Life Insurance Co. As a matter of fact, Root not only represented J. P. Morgan & Co., but the great Pierpont Morgan personally, handling a wide range of matters, including the famous Northern Securities case.[60]

Although Root's replacement as Secretary of State, Robert Bacon, served in this capacity for merely six weeks at the end of the administration, he had acted, for over 3½ years as the second-ranking figure in the State Department, and thus merits considerable attention.[61] Bacon, who prior to 1905 had no experience in foreign affairs, was an old friend of President Roosevelt from their Harvard College days and had come to know Root through various contacts in the New York City business world, for Bacon had been a partner for nearly ten years in J. P. Morgan & Co. (from which he had resigned in 1903 because of a siege of bad health). In this connection he had served as a director of the Rockefeller-dominated National City Bank of New York, the Federal Steel Co. and National Tube Co. (both of which were, after 1901, subsidiaries of the U.S. Steel Corp.), the Erie Railroad, Northern Pacific Railway, North American Co., and several other enterprises that were either controlled by or affiliated with the House of Morgan and its economic allies. In addition, Bacon sat on the board of the U.S. Steel Corp. from 1903 to

1905, the Bank for Savings in the City of New York from 1903 through 1909, and the Manhattan Trust Co. from 1905 through 1909.[62] In short, Bacon continued to maintain fairly close ties with prominent businessmen associated with the last two firms while he was serving as Assistant Secretary of State, a dubious practice.

Two other Cabinet members were closely linked to business interests largely through what might be described as national civic Establishment ties. Charles J. Bonaparte, who served first (in 1905–1906) as Secretary of the Navy and then (1906–1909) as Attorney General, was a wealthy Baltimore lawyer with major real estate holdings in and around the city.[63] Although Bonaparte had little significant governmental experience prior to his appointment to high federal office, he had been much involved in the civil service reform movement, which activity commended him to Roosevelt, who strongly supported this worthy cause.[64] However, it would appear that Bonaparte's most important connection was as a "public" member of the executive committee of the business-dominated National Civic Federation, along with such notables as Charles Francis Adams (a Boston "publicist" who served on the board of the Westinghouse Electric & Mfg. Co.), John G. Milburn (a New York City lawyer whose partner, Lewis C. Ledyard, was a vice-president of the American Express Co. and a director of the Boston and Maine Railroad, Great Northern Paper Co., and United States Trust Co. of New York), and James Speyer (a New York City banker who sat on the board of the Baltimore and Ohio Railroad, Guaranty Trust Co., Lackawanna Steel Co., and Union Trust Co. of New York). Roosevelt's last Secretary of Commerce and Labor, former New York City merchant Oscar S. Straus, was also a former (1900–1906) high official in the elitist National Civic Federation, and he served for an even longer period (1894–1906) as a director of the big New York Life Insurance Co.[65] Although Roosevelt's biographers have paid scant attention to the politico-economic role played by the National Civic Federation in administration affairs, this group seems to have exerted considerable influence in the recruitment of certain high federal officials and, directly or indirectly, on the formulation of public policy during these stormy years.[66]

The other two Cabinet members with obvious links to business interests, Paul Morton and Truman H. Newberry, both served as Secretary of the Navy, and for relatively brief periods. They also had elitist family ties which clearly reinforced their overall economic orientation. Morton had, as indicated, a number of notable corporate connections (some of which were maintained during his time in public office), and a brother, Joy, who was a high official of the International Salt Co., a vice-president of the Great Western Cereal Co., and a director of the Corn Products Co., the American Trust & Savings Bank of Chicago, and the North American Trust Co. of New York City. Similarly, Newberry, who, like Morton, had no prior governmental experience, had been a high official of the Detroit

Steel & Spring Co., and the Michigan State Telephone Co., and a board member of the Packard Motor Car Co., the (Mather-dominated) Cleveland-Cliffs Iron Co., and Railway Steel Spring Co. of New York City. Furthermore, he came from a family that was deeply immersed in a web of socio-economic relationships which might well be called Detroit's first real business aristocracy—the Algers, McMillans, Newberrys, and Joys. These families had once been heavily involved in major railroad and other related enterprises, but in more recent years, sensing the industrial trend, they had moved into such comparatively new activities as manufacturing and public utilities.[67] So both Morton and Newberry were elitist choices.

What's more, three other members of Roosevelt's Cabinet—William Howard Taft, Luke E. Wright, and James R. Garfield—had important indirect (family) ties to corporate interests, although at least two of these officials were picked largely for other reasons. Secretary of War Taft had an extensive record of governmental experience, having served as Solicitor General in the early 1890s, as a U.S. Circuit Court judge during the rest of the decade, and as head of the newly formed U.S. Philippine Commission from 1900 to 1904, in which last capacity he had received considerable acclaim for his management of governmental affairs. As a result primarily of his handling of this knotty problem, Taft was rewarded with a Cabinet post.[68] However, the Taft family, which strongly supported William Howard's political career, was also a very wealthy clan with numerous major socio-economic ties. Taft's half-brother, Charles, had married the daughter of one of the richest men in Ohio (David Sinton). He later bought a controlling interest in the *Cincinnati Times-Star* and served as a director of the Little Miami Railroad (from 1891 through 1908), the Cincinnati Gas & Electric Co. (from 1903 through 1908), and the Cincinnati & Suburban Bell Telephone Co. (from at least 1904 through 1908).[69] Around the turn of the century, Charles Taft's daughter married the son of Melville E. Ingalls, a well-established Ohio railroad executive who had served as president of the Cleveland, Cincinnati, Chicago & St. Louis Railway and its predecessor line from 1880 through 1908 (during much of this period it was controlled by the Vanderbilt-Morgan complex), as president of the Morgan-dominated Chesapeake and Ohio Railway from 1889 to 1899, and as a board member of the Cincinnati, New Orleans & Texas Pacific Railway (from 1896 through 1908) and the Equitable Life Assurance Society of New York (from 1891 to 1905). In fact, both Ingalls and William Howard Taft himself held high posts in the National Civic Federation from 1907 through 1909. Another of Taft's brothers, Henry, was a partner in a prominent Wall Street law firm, then known as Strong and Cadwalader, which represented such well-known concerns as Speyer & Co. and the Manhattan Trust Co.[70] In this capacity Henry Taft served on the board of the (privately-owned) National Railroad Co. of Mexico in the early 1900s, and from 1906 on as a director of the Morgan-dominated Mutual Life Insurance Co. In short, while William Howard Taft himself was primarily a governmental figure, various members of his family had many links with influential economic forces.

James R. Garfield, who was picked in 1907 to succeed Ethan A. Hitchcock as Secretary of the Interior, was probably chosen both because of his name (he was a son of former President James A. Garfield) and because of the recognition he had achieved as head of the Bureau of Corporations of the Department of Commerce and Labor between 1903 and 1907. Garfield had also been a fairly prominent Cleveland lawyer who had practiced, up to 1902, in partnership with his brother, Harry, who sat on the board of the Cleveland Trust Co. from 1895 to 1909 (about which time he became president of Williams College). Perhaps even more important, James R. Garfield had married the daughter of a former major railroad executive, John Newell, who had served, up to his death in 1894, as president of the big Lake Shore and Michigan Southern Railway and the smaller Pittsburgh and Lake Erie Railroad (both lines were controlled by the Vanderbilt-Morgan complex), and as a director of the Cleveland, Lorain and Wheeling Railroad.[71] Thus it would appear that Garfield, both as a Cabinet official and as Commissioner of Corporations, was favorably disposed toward economic interests.

Hence of the eleven Cabinet members chosen after Roosevelt was firmly entrenched in power, all but one—George B. Cortelyou (who served in two major federal posts)—had significant socio-economic ties.[72] And only a few did not have some sort of key corporate linkage.[73] It would seem therefore that John Morton Blum was far off the mark when he asserted that ". . . Roosevelt throughout his Presidency took care to find important posts for labor leaders, Grand Army men, Hungarian-Americans, Jews, Catholics, and Methodists."[74] Some, of course, might contend that the accuracy of this statement depends to a considerable extent on one's definition of an "important" post. But clearly, no matter how viewed, the *most* important posts in the Roosevelt administration did not go to labor leaders, Hungarian-Americans, or any other representatives of the middle or lower classes. Even the one (token?) Jew and Catholic appointed to the Cabinet were wealthy elite figures, for both Oscar Straus and Charles Bonaparte were members of the executive committee of the business-dominated National Civic Federation, and Straus was a longtime director of the big New York Life Insurance Co.

Further insight into Roosevelt's overall politico-economic relations can be gleaned from the fact that one of the President's most important informal advisors was George W. Perkins, a rather remarkable man who served as a vice-president of the New York Life Insurance Co. up to 1905, as a partner in J. P. Morgan & Co. from 1901 to 1910, as a high official during all or most of this period of the United States Steel Corp., International Harvester Co., and Chicago, Burlington & Quincy Railroad, and as a director much of this time of the National City Bank of New York (a Stillman-Rockefeller concern), the New York (Security and) Trust Co.,

Northern Securities Co., and Morgan-dominated International Mercantile Marine Co.[75] Thus, through Perkins later became an influential force in the Progressive party (until its demise in 1916), it is difficult to look upon him as anything other than a big business figure—in fact, as J. P. Morgan's chief governmental emissary, whose advice to Roosevelt and other political leaders was essentially that of an "enlightened" conservative.[76]

That important business interests carried considerable weight in the Roosevelt administration can also be seen from the following summary analysis of the backgrounds and socio-economic ties of the major diplomatic officials chosen by the President after his assumption of the reins of executive leadership in 1901.[77]

Ambassador to Great Britain	Whitelaw Reid, N.Y. (May 1905 through 1909)	Former U.S. Minister to France (1889–1892) Longtime publisher of *New York Tribune;* also either officer of director of Mergenthaler Linotype Co. (mid-1880s through 1909) No other formal corporate ties (though many held by father-in-law, Darius O. Mills)
Ambassador to France	Robert S. McCormick, Ill. (May 1905–March 1907)	Ambassador to Russia (1902–1905); Minister to Austria–Hungary (1901–1902) No major business association (but a member of rich McCormick family, which had long dominated the International Harvester Co. and its predecessor concern) No formal directorship ties
	Henry White, N.Y. (March 1907–November 1909)	Longtime American career diplomat No major business affiliation (although married into wealthy, well-established New York family) No formal directorship ties
Ambassador to Germany	Charlemagne Tower, Pa. (December 1902–June 1908)	Ambassador to Russia (1899–1902); Minister to Austria-Hungary (1897–1899)

Vice-president of Finance Co.
  of Pa. (1887–1891); also high
  official of Minnesota Iron
  Co. (1882–1887) and
  president of the Duluth and
  Iron Range RR (1882–1887)
Director of Northern Pacific
  Rwy. (1896–1897), Duluth
  and Iron Range RR
  (1888–1897), Philadelphia,
  Reading and New England
  RR (and predecessor
  concern, 1889–1898), and
  Lehigh Coal & Navigation
  Co. (1891–1897)

David J. Hill, N.Y.
(June 1908 through 1909)

Minister to Netherlands
  (1905–1907) and Minister to
  Switzerland (1903–1905);
  also Assistant Secretary of
  State (1898–1903)
President of University of
  Rochester (1888–1896) and
  of Bucknell University
  (1879–1888)
No formal corporate ties

Although only one of these important emissaries, Charlemagne Tower, a wealthy mining, railroad, and financial figure, had many formal ties to corporate interests, most of them were linked in other ways, usually by family connections, to influential economic forces.[78] New York newspaper publisher Whitelaw Reid was a prominent person in his own right, but he owed much of his wealth and status to the fact that he had married the daughter of the rich Western mining magnate Darius O. Mills, who, after moving to the East, had served as a director of such major enterprises as the Bank of New York, Erie Railroad, Farmers Loan and Trust Co., International Paper Co., Lackawanna Steel Co. (with, up to 1909, John Hay's brother-in-law, Samuel Mather), Lake Shore and Michigan Southern Railway, Mergenthaler Linotype Co., Morton Trust Co., New York Central and Hudson River Railroad, Southern Pacific Railroad, and the United States Trust Co. of New York City. Similarly, the first man Roosevelt appointed to act as American Ambassador to France, Robert S. McCormick, was a member of the famous Chicago family that had long dominated the affairs of one of the large companies which in 1903 was merged into the International Harvester Co. While this concern was still run largely by members of the McCormick family, it had also come, since its recent reorganization, into what might be called ''the Morgan orbit,'' for George W. Perkins became chairman of its finance committee in 1906, and its board of directors included such potent forces as George F. Baker, Morgan's closest "outside" ally, Elbert H. Gary, board chairman of the United States Steel Corp., and Charles Steele, a partner in J. P. Morgan & Co. In addition, in 1903 McCormick's son, Joseph, had married the daughter of Mark Hanna (who died in 1904, but many of his business interests were taken over by his son or brothers).[79] When McCormick, a previously experienced official, stepped down from this post in 1907, he was replaced by a man who, though a career diplomat, was another elitist figure. Henry White had married into one of New York's most prestigious and well-established families, the Rutherfords, who had close ties with such old families as the Stuyvesants and (Gouverneur) Morrises, and one of whose members served on the board of the Morton Trust Co. from 1904 through 1910.[80] So most of Roosevelt's chief diplomatic officials had a marked pro-business bias, like many of his Cabinet members.

Major Actions of the Roosevelt Administration

By all odds, the most important diplomatic act of the Roosevelt administration was its involvement in the establishment of the new nation of Panama and America's concomitant acquisition, by hastily framed treaty, of the Panama Canal Zone, a ten-mile-wide stretch of land which was to be used for the construction and operation of a transoceanic canal much desired by influential military and economic interests in the United States. The history of this issue extended back well into the 19th century. It revolved around two possible routes, one through the isthmus of Panama, where work had actually been started by a French company over 20 years earlier, and the other through Nicaragua, which project was ardently supported by many potent forces in the United States, particularly mercantile interests in the South.[81] In fact, up to late 1901, most high-ranking officials in both Congress and the administration were firmly committed to the Nicaraguan route. If such a measure were approved by American authorities (and in early 1902 one passed the Lower House by a vote of 308–2), it would have resulted in heavy losses for the major stockholders of the now reorganized French company, which had already made a big investment in the Panama Canal project, estimated to be as high as $40 million. However, thanks in no small part to the strenuous efforts of two extraordinarily able lobbyists, New York lawyer William Nelson Cromwell and French entrepreneur Philippe Bunau-Varilla, this concern managed to reverse the situation and helped secure the enactment of a law that called for the construction of a canal through the isthmus of Panama if suitable arrangements could be made within a reasonable time with the Republic of Colombia, which had long controlled this relatively small but valuable territory.

Unfortunately for the United States, because of certain dubious clauses Colombia refused to ratify the so-called Hay-Herran treaty, which was negotiated by responsible diplomatic officials of the two countries. Faced with this unexpected setback, the impetuous President Roosevelt was prepared to intervene militarily, but was saved from such an overtly imperialistic venture by a carefully contrived revolution which was arranged largely by a small group of conspirators closely linked with the Panama Railroad (a subsidiary of the New Panama Canal Co.) and canal lobbyists Philippe Bunau-Varilla and William Nelson Cromwell, who reportedly had received assurances from both Roosevelt and Secretary of State John Hay that the United States would, if required, act to prevent Colombia from suppressing the revolt.[82] As a result primarily of this externally aided coup, the Republic of Panama was established in late 1903, despite the bitter protests and futile actions of Colombian officials. The newborn nation was immediately accorded de facto recognition by the Roosevelt administration, and shortly thereafter its government signed a treaty granting the United States the right (for an agreed upon price) to build and operate in perpetuity a canal through a formally ceded ten-mile zone of the swampy isthmus.

Judging from all accounts, the man who did most to bring about this sequence of events was New York attorney William Nelson Cromwell, who was the real founder of the Wall Street law firm of Sullivan and Cromwell.[83] Some observers have attributed Cromwell's vast political access and influence to the fact that he had given a sizable amount of money ($60,000) to the last Republican presidential campaign fund.[84] However, Cromwell had power far beyond that usually established through such channels and reportedly carried great weight with Mark Hanna, a key figure early in these proceedings.[85] Cromwell was associated with a number of concerns through which he had a variety of links to people in high public office. For example, he sat on the board of the North American Co., along with such prominent men as George R. Sheldon, a New York financier who served as treasurer of the North American Co. and a director of the Panama Canal Co. of America, Postmaster General Henry C. Payne, and Robert Bacon, a partner in J. P. Morgan & Co. and one of President Roosevelt's most intimate friends (who two years later was appointed Assistant Secretary of State under Elihu Root). Cromwell, moreover, served as a director of the American Cotton Oil Co., which counted the following well-connected businessmen among its board members.[86]

Harris C. Fahnestock	A vice-president of the First National Bank of N.Y.C. and director of the Southern Rwy.
Charles Lanier	A close friend of J. P. Morgan; president of the Pittsburgh, Fort Wayne & Chicago Rwy.; vice-president of the Central

	and South American Telegraph Co.; and a director of the Mutual Life Insurance Co., National Bank of Commerce of N.Y.C., Niagara Falls Power Co. (which was headed by Darius O. Mills, the father-in-law of Roosevelt's next Ambassador to Great Britain), and the Western Union Telegraph Co. (of which concern Secretary of State John Hay was a director till 1900)
Joseph Larocque	A Wall Street lawyer and a director of the Niagara Falls Power Co. and the Morton Trust Co. (of which Secretary of War Elihu Root was still a board member)
J. Kennedy Tod	A New York financier closely allied with James J. Hill, and a director, among other concerns, of the Buffalo, Rochester & Pittsburgh Rwy. (President Roosevelt's cousin, W. Emlen, was a director of this line and its vice-president was Adrian Iselin, Jr., a high official of the Guaranty Trust Co. of N.Y.C.)[87]

Thus Cromwell had at least one direct link and several indirect ties to important officials in the Roosevelt administration.

But Cromwell was more than a lawyer who merely represented and advised the Panama Railroad (or its apparently largely French-owned parent company); he was also a member of the board of directors of this line, whose officers and employees were deeply involved in the artfully arranged Panamanian revolution.[88] And there were a number of fairly prominent Americans who served either as executives or directors of this concern, such as its president, J. Edward Simmons (who was reportedly Mark Hanna's New York City banker and a director of the Panama Canal Co. of America), Vernon H. Brown (who was a member of the board of the Hanover National Bank and Atlantic Mutual Insurance Co., of which latter firm President Roosevelt's brother-in-law, Douglas Robinson, was a director), Robert M. Gallaway, president of the Merchants National Bank of New York and a director of both the Erie and Southern railroads), and

James H. Parker (who was a member of the board of the Western National Bank of the United States, along with Secretary of War Elihu Root).[89] Hence, although we do not know the make-up of the board of the parent company (the New Panama Canal Co.) or the major stockholders in any of these interrelated enterprises, there would seem to have been substantial American economic interest in the promotion and development of the Panama Canal.[90]

At about this time President Roosevelt took an unusual step in the domestic area when, after some indecision, he worked to resolve a major labor dispute in 1902, an action that added much to his reputation as a governmental leader. A bitter strike had erupted in the hard coal fields of Pennsylvania between the long-aggrieved miners (who in 1900 had secured their first pay raise in twenty years) and the nation's large anthracite operators, the most important of which was the Reading (Railroad) Co., whose chief executive took an extremely rigid and benighted attitude toward the rights of America's workingmen.[91] As the months wore on without a solution and winter approached, there was increasing fear among business and political leaders about the growing labor unrest and the possible adverse consequences of the strike on the upcoming elections. Still, the coal operators remained adamant, and the President appeared to be at a loss as to what to do. Then in October 1902, after consulting with Massachusetts Governor W. Murray Crane, Roosevelt vigorously asserted himself and exerted sufficient pressure, in part through a threat to take over and operate the mines with militia, to get the owners to agree to a plan whereby the dispute would be submitted to an arbitration commission. These proceedings ultimately resulted in a settlement that was moderately favorable to the strikers.[92]

For his role in this affair, President Roosevelt has since received considerable praise as a fair-minded, if not progressive, statesman. But this assessment is in many ways misleading, for not only was he backed in this matter by such influential men as Mark Hanna (a National Civic Federation leader) and J. P. Morgan, but Roosevelt actually got his idea for resolving the conflict from another pro-business figure, Governor Crane, whose brother, Zenas, was a director of the Vanderbilt-Morgan–dominated Chicago and Northwestern Railway and AT&T's New York and New Jersey Telephone Co.[93] Moreover, Crane himself was appointed to the board of AT&T and GE one year later when he stepped down from public office.[94] Given this source of advice and support, it would seem that Roosevelt's intervention in the bitter coal strike of 1902 was essentially a conservative action.

In the domestic realm Roosevelt is probably best known for his outspoken views and well-publicized stance against the nation's rapidly growing business and industrial combines, which assertions and activity have since earned him the reputation for being America's first great "trustbuster.''[95] Yet, in point of fact, only 44 antitrust cases were initiated during the entire 7½ years of the Roosevelt administration, in contrast to a total of 80 in the four-year regime of his supposedly more conservative successor, William Howard Taft.[96] And no more than ten of these were directed against truly large companies.[97] Most were instituted against such comparatively small and unknown concerns as the People's Ice and Fuel Co. and the Amsden Lumber Co. Thus, while Roosevelt's antitrust record compares quite favorably with that of McKinley (who took almost no action in this area), it would hardly seem to justify his reputation as a "great trustbuster."[98]

What's more, President Roosevelt made a curious distinction between what he described as "good trusts" and "bad trusts." The latter enterprises were, in his judgment, either controlled by unscrupulous "malefactors of great wealth" or were created by unethical practices that led to monopolistic conditions. On the other hand, the "good trusts" were those which resulted from natural growth or those that acted fairly and sold their products at reasonable prices to the American consumer.[99] However, this is a misleading, moralistic distinction that Roosevelt, because of his socio-economic background, may well have believed, but which simply does not stand up under close scrutiny. It would be more accurate to say that, with one understandable exception (the Northern Securities Co, which will be discussed shortly), Roosevelt's "bad trusts" were basically "non-Morgan trusts," such as the Rockefeller-controlled Standard Oil Co., the Harriman-dominated Union Pacific Railroad, and the American Tobacco Co, which was headed by the legendary James B. Duke.[100] Conversely, Roosevelt's "good trusts" usually turned out to be big Morgan-controlled companies, such as the U.S. Steel Corp. and International Harvester Co., neither of which grew primarily by natural means, but were largely the product of massive mergers.[101] Yet no action was taken against either of these giant concerns (although some federal officials were so inclined), partly because of Roosevelt's implicit trust in Morgan-backed firms and the quiet, though highly effective pressure applied by such influential Morgan men as George W. Perkins and Elbert H. Gary, board chairman of the U.S. Steel Corp.[102] Indeed, the only time Roosevelt moved against a major Morgan-dominated concern was in the Northern Securities case, and this suit was instituted early in his administration at a time when he may have felt he needed to establish a bold public image as a fearless trustbuster, and involved a huge, recently created railroad holding company, which even Mark Hanna believed was in flagrant violation of the Sherman Antitrust Act.[103] Thus, as Matthew Josephson and Gabriel Kolko have suggested, Theodore Roosevelt was essentially an astute conservative, who by his flamboyant and seemingly radical tactics took the wind out of the sails of William Jennings Bryan and other progressive (or disaffected) forces in the United States.[104]

The Taft Administration

When Roosevelt stepped down from the Presidency in 1908, honoring his promise not to seek another full term, he essentially handpicked his successor, Ohio's William Howard Taft. Having served for four years as a devoted and highly trusted Cabinet member, Taft was a logical choice to carry the Republican party banner against the Democrats' William Jennings Bryan in the upcoming national election, for it was widely believed that he had ". . . no suspicious ties to Wall Street or the trusts, a sterling reputation for integrity, and a solid political base in the strategically important Midwest."[105] In fact, Henry Pringle claims that Taft ". . . was unique among the great lawyers of his day in that the brand of 'corporation attorney' could never be placed upon him."[106] Pringle also rightly asserts that Taft had little liking for private practice and never handled many cases, an economic path made possible by his family's recently amassed fortune. Indeed, Taft toiled for only about six years as a Cincinnati attorney before devoting himself to public service, and if he had been permitted to follow his true desires, he would probably have pursued a judicial career. However, various members of his family were firmly, if not avidly, dedicated to the promotion of his presidential candidacy. For instance, his older and extremely wealthy half-brother, Charles Taft, devoted almost a year of his life (and a substantial amount of money) to building up Taft's political prospects in 1908 and, in effect, masterminded his entire pre-convention campaign.[107] The family was eminently successful in ths endeavor, though much of the credit for Taft's election must be given to the vigorous backing provided by his good friend Theodore Roosevelt.

Yet it should be noted that while Taft himself did not sit on any corporate boards during this period, he did serve, from 1907 through 1913, as an officer or executive committee member of the business-dominated National Civic Federation, an affiliation which may have affected his judgment on various major issues. In addition, certain members of his family were, as indicated earlier, closely linked with important economic interests. His brother, Henry Taft, was a partner in a major Wall Street law firm then known as Strong & Cadwalader, which had long represented such prominent concerns as the New York banking house of Speyer & Co., the New Jersey Zinc Co., and the Manhattan Trust Co.[108] He also served at various times on the board of the National Railroad Co. of Mexico (most likely as the legal agent of Speyer & Co.), the American-Hawaiian Steamship Co., and the Morgan-dominated Mutual Life Insurance Co. The new President's wealthy half-brother, Cincinnati newspaper publisher Charles Taft, was a director of the (medium-sized) Little Miami Railroad, the Cincinnati & Suburban Bell Telephone Co. (in which AT&T had a 30 percent stake), the First National Bank of Cincinnati, and the large Columbia Gas & Electric Co.[109] In addition, Charles Taft's daughter had married the son of railroad executive Melville E. Ingalls, who served up to 1912 as president of the Vanderbilt-controlled Cleveland, Cincinnati, Chicago, & St. Louis Railway (and in the 1890s as head of the Chesapeake and Ohio Railway), and as a director of the Cincinnati, New Orleans and Texas Pacific Railway, the First National Bank of Cincinnati, and up to recently the Equitable Life Assurance Society of New York City. Thus the Taft family was intimately associated with a number of major eco . mic enterprises.[110]

Taft's pro-business orientation was even more clearly reflected, in part because of a skewed informal advisory process, in the initial make-up of his Cabinet, as seen by the following brief biographical sketches:[111]

Secretary of State	Philander C. Knox, Pa. (1909–1913)	U.S. Senator, Pa. (1904–1909); U.S. Attorney General (1901–1904)
		Former (1877–1901) partner in Pittsburgh law firm of Knox and Reed
		Director of Union Trust Co. and Union Savings Bank of Pittsburgh (through 1913), Pittsburgh National Bank of Commerce (up to early 1900s), and the Pittsburgh and Lake Erie RR (1897–1901); also general counsel to Carnegie Steel Co. (up to 1901)
Secretary of Treasury	Franklin MacVeagh, Ill. (1909–1913)	No significant governmental experience
		Head of Franklin MacVeagh & Co., large Chicago wholesale grocery concern (1871–1909)
		Director of the Commercial National Bank of Chicago (1881–1909) and an employer representative on the executive committee of the National Civic Federation (1900–1909; a public member thereafter)
Attorney General	George W. Wickersham, N.Y. (1909–1913)	No significant governmental experience
		Member of New York City law firm of Strong & Cadwalader (1887–1909)

		Director of Mexican Central Railway, Ltd. (1909), Interborough-Metropolitan Co. (1906–1909), American-Hawaiian Steamship Co. (1906–1909), and the National Railroad Co. of Mexico (1904–1905)
Secretary of War	Jacob M. Dickinson, Ill. (March 1909–May 1911)	Assistant U.S. Attorney General (1895–1897); member of Tennessee Superior Court (1891–1893)
		General solicitor or counsel, Illinois Central Railroad (1899–1909); general attorney, Louisville & Nashville Railroad (1897–1899)
		Director of Bon Air Coal & Iron Co., Tenn. (1902–1910)
Secretary of the Navy	George von L. Meyer, Mass. (1909–1913)	U.S. Postmaster General (1907–1909); Minister to Russia (1905–1907) and Italy (1900–1905)
		Longtime member of Linder & Meyer, Boston mercantile firm
		Director of Old Colony Trust Co. (1897–1908), Provident Institution for Savings, Boston (1897–1913), Amoskeag Manufacturing Co. (through 1913), and Ames Plow Co. (at least 1905 through 1913)
Secretary of the Interior	Richard A. Ballinger, Wash. (March 1909–March 1911)	U.S. Commissioner of General Land Office (1907–1908); mayor of Seattle (1904–1906); Washington Superior Court judge (1894–1897)
		Longtime partner in Seattle law firm of Ballinger, Ronald, Battle & Tennant
		Director of Scandanavian-American Bank, Seattle (1900–1909)

Secretary of Agriculture	James Wilson, Iowa (1909–1913)	U.S. Secretary of Agriculture (1897–1909); onetime Iowa Congressman and member of Iowa Railroad Commission
		Longtime Iowa farmer; head of agricultural experiment station, Iowa State College (1891–1897)
		Apparently no notable corporate ties
Secretary of Commerce and Labor	Charles Nagel, Mo. (1909–1913)	St. Louis city councilman (1893–1897); state legislator (early 1880s)
		Partner in St. Louis law firm of Nagel, Kirby & Shepley (1905–1909); St. Louis lawyer (early 1870s on)
		Officer or director of American Diesel Engine Co. (1904–1906)

In short, of the eight major Cabinet officers initially chosen by William Howard Taft, all but one—Secretary of Agriculture James Wilson, an Iowa (actually Des Moines Regency) figure, who was carried over from the preceding Roosevelt and McKinley administrations—were closely linked with important national or regional business interests. For instance, Secretary of State Philander C. Knox, a former Attorney General and U.S. Senator from Pennsylvania, had served up to 1901 as general counsel to the Carnegie Steel Co. and as a board member of the Vanderbilt-dominated Pittsburgh and Lake Erie Railroad, and continued to be intimately associated, even while holding high federal office, with the formidable Mellon forces through his directorship affiliation with two Mellon-controlled banks in Pittsburgh, the Union Trust Co. and Union Savings Bank.[112] Although reportedly picked primarily to give the South a seat in the Cabinet, Taft's Secretary of War, Jacob M. Dickinson, a onetime Nashville, Tenn. lawyer, was likewise linked with the business community, largely through his decade of recent service as general counsel for the Illinois Central Railroad (in which line E. H. Harriman still held a substantial stake, along with certain other prominent Eastern interests).[113] Taft's Secretary of the Navy, George von L. Meyer, who unlike most members of Taft's Cabinet had held a number of prominent governmental posts, was, if anything, even more closely associated with major New England economic interests, for, as a well-established Brahmin (he had married a member of the wealthy Appleton family), he sat on the board of the Old Colony Trust Co. up to 1908, the Provident

Institution for Savings in Boston up through 1913, and for a like period the Amoskeag Manufacturing Co. and the Ames Plow Co., all of which were dominated by elitist forces.[114] Taft's Secretary of the Interior, Seattle's Richard A. Ballinger, was apparently more a geo-political choice than an economic selection, since he was the only representative of the Far West in the Cabinet and had worked diligently in Taft's behalf as a Republican party organizer, orator, and fundraiser in the 1908 presidential election. In addition, he was an old friend from Williams College years of his predecessor, James R. Garfield, under whom he had served as Commissioner of the U.S. General Land Office.[115] But Ballinger also had some important economic ties, for he was primarily a corporate lawyer who had been a director of the fairly large Scandinavian-American Bank of Seattle from 1900 to 1909 (during which period he held both federal and local office). And finally it should be noted that while Taft's Secretary of Commerce and Labor, Charles Nagel, was reportedly awarded this high post principally because of his strenuous efforts in support of Taft's presidential candidacy, he too was associated with certain business interests, mainly as a prominent St. Louis lawyer, but also partly through his former (1904–1906) affiliation with the American Diesel Engine Co., a concern headed by Adolphus Busch, who was president of the Anheuser-Busch Brewing Association and a director of the American Car & Foundry Co., Kansas City Southern Railway, North American Co., and St. Louis Union Trust Co.[116]

Two of Taft's Cabinet members would appear to have been picked more because of their secondary ties than their primary affiliations. Secretary of the Treasury Franklin MacVeagh was the longtime head of a large Chicago wholesale grocery concern (an unusual background for such a high financial official) and a former (1881–1909) director of the Commercial National Bank of Chicago, which major firm was founded and long run by his father-in-law, Henry F. Eames. Also of considerable importance in MacVeagh's selection was the fact that he served as an employer representative on the executive committee of the big business-dominated National Civic Federation from 1900 to 1909 (he continued to be associated as a "public" member of this body through 1913).[117] Perhaps of even greater significance were his family ties to influential economic interests in the East. His brother, Philadelphia lawyer Wayne MacVeagh, who had been Garfield's Attorney General, was a trustee of the Morgan-dominated Mutual Life Insurance Co. from 1908 through 1913. And his nephew, Charles MacVeagh, was a longtime partner in the Wall Street law firm of Stetson, Jennings & Russell, which was general counsel to J. P. Morgan & Co., and had served some years earlier as an officer or director of the Bethlehem Steel Corp., Federal Steel Co., and several other companies which were merged into the giant U.S. Steel Corp. in 1901. More recently, he had been elected to the board of the big (Wisconsin-based) Allis-Chalmers Co., the head of which was Elbert H.

Gary, the chairman of the U.S. Steel Corp. Hence it seems fair to infer that Franklin MacVeagh was chosen Secretary of the Treasury for other reasons than his long-term association with a large wholesale grocery concern.[118]

Taft's Attorney General, George W. Wickersham, would also appear to have been picked primarily because of his indirect ties. At various times during the decade prior to his appointment, Wickersham did serve on the board of several sizable companies, but only one of these—the Interborough-Metropolitan Co. (a big transit holding company)—was controlled by important business interests.[119] Probably of greater weight was the fact that he was a member of a major Wall Street law firm then known as Strong & Cadwalader, one of whose senior partners was the President's brother, Henry Taft, who apparently exchanged directorship ties with Wickersham on two occasions in the preceding decade, and also served from 1906 through 1913 on the board of the Morgan-dominated Mutual Life Insurance Co.[120] Although Henry Pringle maintains that William Howard Taft did not consult to any great extent with his New York lawyer-brother, it seems unlikely that the President would select a longtime partner of Henry Taft, who had been one of his strongest political boosters, to serve as his Attorney General without the advice and support of his kinsman.[121] Not only that, according to one presumably reliable source, it was Taft's brother who, at the request of the President, managed to persuade Richard A. Ballinger to forsake his lucrative Seattle law practice and accept the position of Secretary of the Interior.[122] In light of these links and activity, it would certainly appear that Henry Taft played a significant role in the appointment of Attorney General George W. Wickersham (and perhaps other important figures in the administration).[123]

Only two Cabinet members resigned before the end of the (one-term) Taft administration. The background of the men chosen to succeed them again revealed the pro-business leanings of the President and his chief advisors, for both were well-established corporate lawyers. When Secretary of the Interior Richard Ballinger was, in effect, forced out of office in early 1911 following the bitter Ballinger-Pinchot conservation controversy, he was replaced by Walter L. Fisher, a partner in the Chicago law firm of Matz, Fisher and Boyden and a fairly new member of the Federal Railroad Securities Commission. But even more importantly, Fisher had been quite active in the national conservation movement. He was a close friend and supporter of recently ousted Gifford Pinchot and was apparently appointed in an attempt to placate this famous forester's many zealous followers. While Fisher himself had no major formal corporate ties, the same cannot be said of his two leading law partners, Rudolph Matz and William C. Boyden, for the former served as a director of the Chicago Savings Bank and Trust Co. and the big Boston-based United Shoe Machinery Corp., and the latter sat on the board of the

Western Trust & Savings Bank of Chicago (and its successor concern, the Central Trust Co.). These ties suggest that Fisher, the nationally known conservationist, was probably also favorably disposed toward business interests.

The other man to replace a member of Taft's Cabinet (Secretary of War Jacob Dickinson) was a rising young Wall Street lawyer, Henry L. Stimson, who had acted as U.S. attorney for the southern district of New York from 1906 to 1909, but had otherwise devoted most of his time to the maintenance of an essentially corporate practice. In fact, he had been a member of Elihu Root's law firm up to 1901, at which point Root embarked on his extensive and highly successful federal career and the concern was reorganized as simply Winthrop & Stimson. Its business clientele included such sizable concerns as the National Bank of North America, the National Sugar Refining Co., and the Mutual Life Insurance Co., and Bronson Winthrop, Stimson's longtime close friend and law partner, served on the board of the Morton Trust Co. from 1908 to 1910 (when it was merged into the Guaranty Trust Co.).[124] And, judging from at least one account, the influential Elihu Root, whom Stimson looked upon as a "second father," had much to do with Stimson's promotion to this important Cabinet post.[125]

Most of America's chief diplomatic officials during the Taft administration were also closely linked to major business interests. Taft retained as his Ambassador to Great Britain, New York's wealthy newspaper publisher Whitelaw Reid, whose rich father-in-law, Darius O. Mills, was, up to his death in 1910, affiliated through directorship ties with a number of giant economic enterprises, most of which his son, Ogden Mills, in effect, inherited.[126]

Taft did choose to appoint a new Ambassador to France. For this mission he selected New York's Robert Bacon, a former partner in J. P. Morgan & Co., who had served for several years as Assistant Secretary of State under Elihu Root (and briefly at the end of Roosevelt's administration as Secretary of State). Though he had devoted the last few years to public life, Bacon was essentially a business figure, for while he had severed the bulk of his corporate links when he assumed high federal office in 1905, he nevertheless saw fit to serve on the board of the Manhattan Trust Co. up to 1909 and the Bank for Savings in the City of New York up through 1912, in which year he resigned from this diplomatic post.[127] President Taft thereupon appointed an old Ohio friend and loyal political supporter, Myron T. Herrick, as Ambassador to France. While Herrick had been governor of Ohio in 1904–1905, he likewise was primarily a businessman, since he was the longtime head of one of Cleveland's major banks (the Society for Savings), board chairman of the Wheeling and Lake Erie Railroad (from 1900 through 1913), vice-president of the National Carbon Co. (from 1902 through 1913), and a director of the Quaker Oats Co. (from 1901 through 1913).[128]

Taft's first Ambassador to Germany, David J. Hill, was, like Whitelaw Reid, a carryover from the Roosevelt regime, but was a man of a very different stripe in that he was a former college president (Bucknell and the University of Rochester), who upon stepping down from his academic posts had served in various high diplomatic capacities. When he resigned from office in 1911, he was replaced by a once-prominent economic figure, John G. A. Leishman, who had been a top executive in the Carnegie Steel Co. up to the late 1890s, at which point, following a split between Carnegie and Henry Clay Frick, he turned his hand to governmental matters.[129] Thus Taft's chief diplomatic emissaries were also drawn largely from the business world.

With the exception of one area of activity—ironically, antitrust—the record of the Taft regime was marked by its support of conservative causes.[130] Nowhere was this better demonstrated than in the so-called Ballinger-Pinchot controversy. This bitter dispute revolved around the approval by Secretary of the Interior Ballinger (a former Seattle lawyer) of the allegedly fraudulent Cunningham coal claims, which were reportedly backed by a potent, though somewhat nebulous, Guggenheim-Morgan financial syndicate.[131] In this conflict between the conservationists, led by nationally known United States forester Gifford Pinchot, and a number of important conservative (or pro-business) figures in the administration, the most prominent of whom was Richard Ballinger, Taft sided strongly with the latter forces and eventually felt compelled to dismiss the zealous Pinchot from the federal government. After much heated exchange, this matter was ultimately resolved largely in favor of the conservationists, with the cancellation of the Cunningham coal claims and Ballinger's early (politically dictated) retirement from office. But this was only because of the great mass of adverse publicity generated by this dispute, which compelled the Taft administration to take such action, much against its will.[132]

Another major issue in the Taft administration which deserves considerable attention is its unusual record of antitrust activity. As indicated earlier, not only did the Taft regime—or to be more precise, Attorney General George Wickersham—undertake more action in this area than did that of Roosevelt, but it also instituted more suits against truly large concerns, such as the American Sugar Refining Co. and Missouri-Pacific Railway. Furthermore, in the latter part of Taft's term the government filed antitrust charges against two huge firms which were closely linked with the House of Morgan, against which the Roosevelt regime had refused to move—namely, the United States Steel Corp. and the International Harvester Co.[133] And this unprecedented action so provoked certain figures, particularly George W. Perkins, J. P. Morgan's chief governmental intermediary (who still served as an officer or director of the International Harvester Co., Erie Railroad, International Mercantile Marine Co., New York Trust Co., and U.S. Steel Corp.), that he and other affected economic leaders threw tremendous weight behind the Progressive party candidacy of the now aroused Theodore Roosevelt in 1912, an ambitious but futile effort that badly split the Republican party and resulted in the election of the Democratic nominee, Woodrow Wilson.[134]

Supreme Court Appointments and Actions

From 1897 to 1913 the Supreme Court was likewise dominated by conservative interests, although more so probably in the first part of this period than in its latter stages. The Court's conservatism stemmed partly from the fact that until 1910 the Chief Justice was Melville W. Fuller, a former Chicago corporate lawyer who had been appointed by President Cleveland in 1888. Fuller, as indicated earlier, had built up a lucrative practice, in the process of which he was greatly aided by his marriage to the daughter of William F. Coolbaugh, who up to his death in 1877 was president of Chicago's largest bank and generally considered to be the leading banker in the West.[135] Moreover, in the course of his career he regularly represented such prominent entrepreneurs and enterprises as Marshall Field (who, in addition to his own major mercantile establishment, was a substantial stockholder in the Pullman Palace Car Co.), John W. Doane (president of the Merchants Loan and Trust Co. of Chicago), Erskine W. Phelps (who was a close friend of President Cleveland), Franklin MacVeagh (a Chicago merchant who was appointed Secretary of the Treasury in 1909), and the Chicago, Burlington & Quincy Railroad.[136] In light of his earlier economic ties, it is not surprising that Fuller proved to be a conservative bulwark during his many years on the High Court.

The marked pro-business bias of the Supreme Court is even better revealed by a look at the background of the other members of this important body at the outset of the McKinley administration. With the exception of Edward D. White, who later became Chief Justice (and hence will be treated separately), these officials, presented by length of service during this period, were as follows:

John M. Harlan, Ky.
(till December 1911)

Associate Justice, U.S. Supreme Court (1877–1911)

Former Frankford and Louisville, Kentucky lawyer

No direct (or even indirect) corporate ties

David J. Brewer, Ka.
(till March 1910)

Associate Justice, U.S. Supreme Court (1889–1910); judge, U.S. Circuit Court of Appeals (1884–1889); Kansas supreme court justice (1870–1884)

Onetime (pre-1870) Leavenworth, Kansas lawyer

Trustee of Northwestern Mutual Life Insurance Co. (1872–1910)

Rufus W. Peckham, N.Y. (till December 1909)	Associate Justice, U.S. Supreme Court (1895–1909); New York state judge (1883–1895)
	Albany, N.Y. lawyer (1859–1883)
	Trustee of Mutual Life Insurance Co. (1884–1905)
Henry B. Brown, Mich. (till May 1906)	Associate Justice, U.S. Supreme Court (1890–1906); U.S. district court judge (1875–1890)
	Former (1859–1875) prominent Detroit corporate lawyer (specialty, maritime law)
	No formal business or directorship ties
George Shiras, Jr., Pa. (till February 1903)	Associate Justice, U.S. Supreme Court (1892–1903)
	Former (1858–1892) Pittsburgh corporate lawyer
	Director of the Safe Deposit & Trust Co., Pittsburgh (1891–92)
Horace Gray, Mass. (till September 1902)	Associate Justice, U.S. Supreme Court (1881–1902); Massachusetts supreme court justice (1864–1881)
	Former (1851–1864) Boston lawyer
	No formal corporate links (but many elite family ties)
Stephen J. Field, Cal. (till December 1897)	Associate Justice, U.S. Supreme Court (1863–1897); California supreme court justice (1857–1863)
	Former (1849–1857) Marysville, California lawyer
	No formal corporate ties (but two brothers once had elitist links)

Thus most of the Associate Justices sitting on the High Court during the first part of this sixteen-year period were closely affiliated, directly or indirectly, with influential economic interests. Indeed, Kentucky's John Marshall Harlan would seem to have been the one conspicuous exception to this general pattern. Some Justices were, in fact, still formally connected with major corporate enterprises. For instance, Justice Brewer, who was a nephew of the archconservative Stephen J. Field, sat on the board of the big Northwestern Mutual Life Insurance Co. from 1872 up to his death in 1910, even though this company began to invest heavily in railroad securities in the 1890s, to the point where such holdings soon drawfed all others in its investment portfolio.[137] Similarly, Rufus W. Peckham served as a trustee of the Mutual Life Insurance Co. from the early 1880s up to 1905 (when many such concerns came under heavy attack for financial malpractice), during which period railroad stocks and bonds grew from a small fraction of its invested assets to a very substantial 41.4 percent.[138] Given the lengths of these links, it would have been difficult for any official to avoid having his views on economic and governmental matters affected by such business contact.[139]

What's more, at least two of the other Justices sitting on the Supreme Court in the first part of this period had their previous pro-business legal affiliations supplemented by family ties of a similar nature. For instance, not only had George Shiras, Jr. been a longtime Pittsburgh lawyer who represented many big iron, coal, oil, railroad, and banking interests in western Pennsylvania, but when he was appointed to the High Court one of his sons (William) took his place as a director of the fairly large Safe Deposit and Trust Co. of Pittsburgh.[140] And although Boston's Horace Gray had not served in a nonjudicial capacity since 1864, he came from a wealthy Boston family which was related to the Lowells, Peabodys, and Gardners, to name but a few close-knit clans. In addition, his younger half-brother, John C. Gray, helped found one of Boston's most prominent corporate law firms, then known as Ropes, Gray and Loring, all of whose (still active) senior partners had important economic ties.[141] Thus it seems fair to say that the Supreme Court was dominated around the turn of the century by elitist figures.[142]

The first (and only) Justice to be replaced during the first part of this period—that is to say, during the McKinley years—was California's aged archconservative Stephen J. Field. In keeping with established geopolitical tradition, President McKinley chose California's Joseph McKenna as his successor. As indicated earlier, McKenna was a good friend of the President and had served in 1897–1898 as his first Attorney General. Earlier he had been a federal judge and a U.S. Congressman. Unlike many of his colleagues on the High Court, McKenna was essentially a former small-town (Fairfield and Benicia, California) lawyer. However, like his predecessor, Justice Field, he had been a longtime close associate of railroad magnate Leland Stanford up to the latter's death in 1893, so that although McKenna proved to be less rigid and doctrinaire than Field, and was, at times, even amenable to progressive legislation, he was basically a conservative jurist.

Though he held office for 7½ years, McKinley's colorful successor, Theodore Roosevelt, only had the opportunity to appoint three Supreme Court Justices. All had noteworthy business or family ties as well as a considerable amount of governmental experience, as may be seen from the following biographical summaries:

Oliver Wendell Holmes, Mass. (December 1902 through 1913)	Justice, Massachusetts Supreme Court (1883–1902)
	Member of Boston law firm of Shattuck, Holmes & Munroe (1873–1882)
	No formal business connections (but numerous elite family ties)

William R. Day, Ohio
(February 1903 through 1913)

Judge, U.S. Circuit Court of Appeals (1899–1903); Secretary of State (April–September 1898); Assistant Secretary of State (1897–1898)

Member of Canton l~~ f~ .1 of Lynch and Day (1872–1897)

Director of City National Bank of Canton (at least 1893 up to 1900)

William H. Moody, Mass.
(December 1906–November 1910)

U.S. Attorney General (1904–1906); Secretary of Navy (1902–1904); Massachusetts Congressman (1895–1902); U.S. attorney for eastern district, Massachusetts (1890–1895)

Haverhill, Mass. lawyer (1878–1902)

Director of Shoe & Leather National Bank, Boston (1891–1893)

The first of these men, Oliver Wendell Holmes, was by far the most able and influential. He left an indelible mark on American jurisprudence, albeit largely through a series of vigorous dissents registered in various important cases, particularly in the realm of civil rights. Holmes was unlike his predecessor, Horace Gray, in that, though a Boston Brahmin (whose mother was a member of the wealthy and well-established Jackson family), his father was a longtime professor of medicine at Harvard and a noted man of letters who implanted an unusual streak of independence and integrity in his son which, much to the dismay of some business interests, often enabled him to rise above the socio-economic bounds and biases of his class.[143]

The second Supreme Court Justice selected by Roosevelt was Ohio's William R. Day, who had been one of President McKinley's closest friends and key political advisors, and had served in two high federal posts early in his administration before being appointed a U.S. Circuit Court judge in 1899.[144] Unlike the patrician Holmes, Day had some notable economic links, chief of which was his directorship tie with the City National Bank of Canton from at least 1893 to 1900.[145] In addition, as pointed out earlier, Day's former (1872–1897) law partner, William A. Lynch, had been a board member of a number of medium-sized railroads in the Midwest in the latter part of the 19th century. As one might expect with this background, Day compiled a rather conservative record on the High Court, for he adhered to an unrealistic narrow interpretation of the federal government's right to regulate commerce in an era of increasingly complex economic relations.

Roosevelt's third appointee to the Supreme Court, William H. Moody, was a somewhat unusual choice in that he was another New Englander. But he had been strongly backed for this high post by the President's longtime close friend, Massachusetts Senator Henry Cabot Lodge.[146]

Like his predecessor, Michigan judge and attorney Henry B. Brown, Moody had a good deal of governmental experience, having recently held two Cabinet positions (Secretary of the Navy and Attorney General), and before that he had served as a Massachusetts Congressman and U.S. attorney for the eastern district of his home state. Moody had also once been a successful corporate lawyer whose clients included numerous paper, transit, and other public utility concerns in this region. In addition, he had served briefly in the early 1890s as a director of the fairly small Shoe & Leather National Bank of Boston.[147] Perhaps because of his extensive governmental experience, which may have done much to dilute the effect of his former pro-business ties, once on the Court Moody took a rather moderate stance toward progressive measures. Unfortunately, because of serious illness, Moody served for so short a period (less than four years) that it is impossible to tell whether this represented his real judicial outlook.[148]

During the single term of Roosevelt's successor, William Howard Taft, an unusual number of changes were made on the Supreme Court because of the death or illness of six of its members. The most important of these occurred in 1910 when Chief Justice Melville W. Fuller died after 22 years of service on this high tribunal. After much deliberation and consultation, President Taft decided to fill this key post with one of the Court's sitting judges, Louisiana's Edward D. White, who had been appointed to this body in 1894 and had since proved to be a staunch conservative on most major issues. Prior to his elevation to the Court, White had relatively limited governmental experience. He had served briefly in the early 1890s as a United States Senator, and earlier as a state government official. Instead he had been primarily a New Orleans lawyer who in his later years became a member of a very prominent firm (White, Parlange and Saunders), which had built up one of the most successful practices in the city.[149] In addition, the conservative White had been born into a wealthy, well-established family (his father had once been governor of Louisiana) that had sizable sugar plantation and refinery holdings, from which White received considerable income throughout his career. Thus the only Chief Justice to be appointed from the Deep South in the post–Civil War period was obviously an elite figure, though most of his ties were apparently with state or regional interests.

The vast majority of Taft's other appointees to the Supreme Court were also of a distinctly conservative nature, as revealed through the following brief biographical summaries:

Horace H. Lurton, Tenn. (1910 through 1913)	Judge, U.S. Circuit Court of Appeals (1893–1910); Tennessee Supreme Court justice (1886–1893)
	Law school dean and professor, Vanderbilt University (1898–1910); Clarksville, Tenn.

	lawyer (late 1860s–1886); president of the Farmers and Merchants Bank, Clarksville (late 1870s to apparently 1886) No other formal business ties
Joseph R. Lamar, Ga. (1910 through 1913)	Georgia Supreme Court justice (1903–1905); also former state legislator Longtime Augusta, Ga. lawyer No formal corporate ties
Charles Evans Hughes, N.Y. (1910 through 1913)	Governor of New York (1907–1910); counsel for Armstrong insurance commission investigation (1905–1906) Member of New York law firm of Hughes, Rounds & Schurman and predecessor concerns (1887–1891 and 1893–1907); professor of law, Cornell University (1891–1993) No formal corporate ties
Willis Van Devanter, Wyo. (1910 through 1913)	Judge, U.S. Circuit Court of Appeals (1903–1910); Interior Department official (1897–1903); Chief Justice, Wyoming Supreme Court (1889–1891) Longtime Cheyenne, Wyoming lawyer; partner in Wyoming law firm of Lacey and Van Devanter (1891–1897) No formal corporate ties
Mahlon Pitney, N.J. (1912 through 1913)	Chancellor of New Jersey (1908–1912); member of N.J. Supreme Court (1901–1908); N.J. Congressman and state legislator (1895–1901) Morristown and Dover, N.J. lawyer (early 1880s to 1901) Officer and director of Cranbury Iron Co., 1882–1889; director of the East Tennessee & Western North Carolina Railroad (1902–1908); many elite family ties

However, these capsule portraits do not indicate the various important indirect (or more covert) ties that a number of these jurists had either prior to or after their appointment to the Supreme Court. For instance, Joseph R. Lamar was a descendant of two of Georgia's most distinguished and affluent families (the Lamars and the Ruckers, who at one time owned at least a dozen large plantations), and in his later years as a lawyer represented two large railroads in the South, the Georgia Railroad and Banking Co. and the Central of Georgia Railway.[150] Similarly, while Wyoming's Willis Van Devanter had served as a high federal official for a number of years, he had also been frequently retained, as a member of a prominent Cheyenne law firm, by the powerful Union Pacific Railroad in the 1890s, and his brother-in-law and former law partner, John W. Lacey, served on the board of the Cheyenne Light, Fuel & Power Co. (a concern headed by state party boss and rancher-businessman Francis Warren) up to 1906, when it was merged into a larger enterprise.[151] Taft's last appointee, Mahlon Pitney, would appear to have been merely a former New Jersey government official, who, according to one presumably reliable source, had been associated at some distant point in the past with a minor concern known as the Cranbury Iron Co.[152] But a closer look at Pitney's background and socio-economic ties reveals that his brother, John O. H. Pitney, was a senior partner in one of Newark's top law firms (Pitney, Hardin & Skinner), a longtime officer or director of P. Ballantine & Sons (a brewery), and that he had served for some time on the board of the National Newark Banking Co. and the Mutual Benefit Life Insurance Co. Moreover, John Pitney's father-in-law, Robert F. Ballantine, had, up to his death in 1905, been president of P. Ballantine & Sons, a vice-president of Newark's Howard Savings Institution, and a board member of the Mutual Benefit Life Insurance Co. and the Farmers Loan & Trust Co. of New York City.[153] Perhaps because of these links, Mahlon Pitney proved to be a strongly pro-business (and anti-labor) figure on the high Court.[154]

However, there was one person in this group who, despite his New York City legal background, was not on intimate terms with influential economic interests prior to his appointment, and that was Charles Evans Hughes. This able individual had recently served for several years as governor of New York, a post he had won largely as a consequence of the vigorous (and well-publicized) manner in which he had conducted two major state investigations dealing with gas and insurance company practices. Before that he had been a member of a fairly prominent New York City law firm known as Hughes, Rounds & Schurman (originally Carter, Hughes & Dwight). And while this firm did a considerable amount of business with various large companies (mostly dry goods concerns, importers, and commission merchants), its senior partners, unlike those of most other Wall Street firms, apparently did not serve on any important corporate boards of directors.[155] Nor did Hughes have any key kinship ties. It is not surprising, therefore, that as an Associate Justice he compiled a moderate, if not liberal, record in his early years on this high tribunal.

Given this overall judicial alignment, it was inevitable that the bulk of the decisions rendered by the Court on the increasingly important matter of labor and management relations would favor business interests. And so it was during this period. In fact, there were three major anti-labor rulings handed down during these years—*Lochner* v. *New York,* in which it proclaimed that the states could not impose laws regulating the number of hours men might be required to work in a period of time; *Adair* v. *United States,* in which the Court invalidated laws banning "yellow-dog" contracts, which forced employees either to withdraw from or not to join labor unions; and a case in which the Court struck down, on narrow technical grounds, the Federal Employers' Liability Act of 1906, which would have provided financial compensation to workers for injuries due to an employer's negligence.[156] Indeed, labor scored only one significant victory during this period, in the case of *Muller* v. *Oregon* in which the Court, perhaps overwhelmed by the famous massive brief prepared by attorney Louis Brandeis, felt compelled to uphold a state law limiting the number of hours women could work in factories to a maximum of ten hours a day. In short, largely because of its make-up, the Supreme Court continued to hand down verdicts which ran counter to the needs and desires of the great majority of the people.[157]

Relatively little was also done in other areas of American government to meet the pressing economic problems of the time, the various "reformist" measures and flamboyant tactics of the Roosevelt administration notwithstanding. Given the elitist background and affiliations of the top administrative and diplomatic officials of these three Republican regimes, it would have been surprising if it had been otherwise. In all, nearly 92 percent of the chief Cabinet officers and diplomatic representatives of these three administrations had one or more key family or business ties, a slightly higher total than that found for the preceding twenty-year period. Moreover, although they had about the same amount of governmental experience, there was a significant increase in the proportion of such officials who had a college education (over 72 percent), which would also seem to indicate that the federal recruitment process was becoming more elitist. In fact, a substantial proportion (70 to 80 percent) of these appointees were big city figures, and a rather surprising number (ranging from a third to a half) had ties with influential New York City enterprises, many with Morgan-dominated concerns, or the business-dominated National Civic Federation.[158] Hence there can be little doubt that potent economic interests carried great weight in government circles during this period.

Notes

1. See, for instance, Thomas C. Cochran and William Miller, *The Age of Enterprise*, pp. 181–210. These two scholars actually apply this term to the period from 1893 to 1913, whereas the author is dealing with a somewhat shorter span, but not enough to make a significant difference.

2. The financial aggregate for Standard Oil would have been considerably larger (over

$600 million) were it not for the federal government's recent antitrust action against this huge firm, which led to the creation of four other sizable concerns—the Standard Oil Co. of California, the Standard Oil Co. of Indiana, the Standard Oil Co. of New York, and the Atlantic Refining Co.

3. For more on this topic, see Glenn Porter, *The Rise of Big Business, 1860–1910* (New York: Crowell, 1973), particularly p. 40. This was also clearly an age in which heavy metals and mining predominated over many other lines of activity, such as chemicals, automobiles, and (aside from the Standard Oil Co.) petroleum. For example, the General Motors Corp. had assets of only $58.5 million in 1913, the Gulf Oil Corp., $42.6 million, and the E. I. du Pont de Nemours & Co., $74.8 million.

4. In the absence of supporting stockownership data, which did not become available on an extensive scale until after 1940, one is forced to rely on an analysis of the make-up of the board of directors (or executive committee) to ascertain the locus of control in a corporation. Employing this approach, it is clear that the United States Steel Corp. was dominated by trusted agents and allies of the House of Morgan early in the century. For example, in 1909 thirteen of the twenty-four directors were, by conservative count, closely linked with this key complex.

5. Harriman had scored his first coup some years earlier when he secured control of the financially troubled Illinois Central Railroad (the management of which he left largely to trusted subordinates). Although the Harriman interests relinquished direction of the Southern Pacific around 1913, they have continued to dominate the affairs of the Union Pacific Railroad up to the present.

6. Hill probably does not deserve to be described as a "robber baron," for apparently he was primarily interested in the sound construction and operation of a major rail line, and he did not amass a huge fortune, at least not one on the same scale as more acquisitive magnates. During these years the New York Central and Chicago and Northwestern lines continued to be controlled by the Vanderbilt interests (who were closely allied with the House of Morgan), while the Pennsylvania Railroad remained an essentially management-dominated concern run largely for its wealthy Philadelphia stockholders.

7. For example, in 1913 the outside directors of the Erie Railroad were George F. Baker (president of the First National Bank, J. P. Morgan's staunchest ally, and a director of the U. S. Steel Corp.), Elbert H. Gary (board chairman of the U. S. Steel Corp.), William P. Hamilton (J. P. Morgan's son-in-law), Charles A. Peabody (president of the probably Morgan-dominated Mutual Life Insurance Co. and a director of two big Morgan-controlled banks, the Guaranty Trust Co. and the National Bank of Commerce), George W. Perkins (a longtime business associate or ally of J. P. Morgan and a director of the U. S. Steel Corp.), Charles Steele (a partner in J. P. Morgan & Co. and a director of both the U. S. Steel Corp. and the Morgan-dominated International Mercantile Marine Co.), Francis L. Stetson (J. P. Morgan's "attorney general"), and six other businessmen, at least three of whom were friendly to the Morgan interests. For more on the Southern Railway, see John F. Stover, *The Railroads of the South, 1865–1900: A Study in Finance and Control* (Chapel Hill: University of North Carolina Press, 1955), p. 253, and also this company's board of directors. Rival forces led by William Rockefeller (John D.'s brother) apparently controlled several other railroads, such as the Chicago, Milwaukee and St. Paul. But these were much less numerous than the Morgan-dominated lines.

8. Through a merger consummated in 1897, the assets of National City Bank jumped from $37 million in 1896 to $110 million in the next year, thereby making it the biggest bank in the United States. The Northwestern Mutual Life Insurance Co. also moved into the $100 million asset category in 1897, but this was the only other concern that had resources of this magnitude. The Metropolitan Life Insurance Co. had assets of no more than $36 million at this time, and the Prudential Insurance Co. of America had even less, $24 million.

9. In fact, at least two of the largest insurance companies were closely allied with, if not

subordinate to, certain majoɪ banks in New York City. See Herman E. Krooss and Martin R. Blyn, *A History of Financial Intermediaries* (New York: Random House, 1971), pp. 112–13.

10.   See Frederick Lewis Allen, *The Great Pierpont Morgan* (New York: Harper, 1949), pp. 270–71; Vincent P. Carosso, *Investment Banking in America*, pp. 142–43; Edwin P. Hoyt, Jr., *The House of Morgan* (New York: Dodd, Mead, 1966), p. 363; Matthew Josephson, *The Robber Barons* (New York: Harcourt, Brace, 1934), p. 409; and Thomas W. Lamont, *Henry P. Davison* (New York: Harper, 1933), *passim*. The close ties between the House of Morgan and the First National Bank of New York can be seen in the make-up of the latter's board. For example, of the nine outside directors of the First National Bank in 1910, three were high officials of J. P. Morgan & Co., one was president of the Morgan-dominated Chase National Bank, and another (William H. Moore) was a longtime director of the U.S. Steel Corp. And George F. Baker himself was a director of the Astor Trust Co., Chase National Bank, Erie Railroad, Guaranty Trust Co., Liberty National Bank, Manhattan Trust Co., Mutual Life Insurance Co., National Bank of Commerce, and U.S. Steel Corp. However, although many have claimed that the New York Life Insurance Co. was an integral part of the Morgan complex (perhaps because of George W. Perkins' connection with both enterprises between 1901 and 1905), the author does not believe that this big insurance company was under the economic aegis or control of this great banking empire (a statement that also applies to the Equitable Life Assurance Society).

11.   See Thomas C. Cochran, *Business in American Life: A History* (New York: McGraw-Hill, 1972), p. 156. Actually, Cochran extended the period back to 1890, although this is a relatively minor matter about which there is room for disagreement. There were, in any event, very few large banks in any other American city in the first part of the century. While Chicago had two banks which had assets of over $100 million in 1913, there were none of this size in Philadelphia or Boston (although the latter had one that came fairly close), and the combined assets of the two major Mellon banks in Pittsburgh did not greatly exceed that total.

12.   For a comment which reveals much about the deep-seated hostility between J. P. Morgan and John D. Rockefeller, see Edwin P. Hoyt, Jr., *The House of Morgan*, p. 244.

13.   See John K. Winkler, *The First Billion: The Stillmans and the National City Bank* (New York: Vanguard Press, 1934), p. 69 and *passim*. Originally, this bank was dominated by its founder, Moses Taylor, and later by his son-in-law, Percy R. Pyne, which family forces continued to hold an important secondary interest in this institution up to recent times. William Rockefeller, who was until 1911 both president of the Standard Oil Co. of New York and a vice-president of the Standard Oil Co. of New Jersey, served on the board of the National City Bank throughout this period. In his efforts to portray John D. Rockefeller in a favorable light, Allan Nevins has made some statements which are, at best, misleading. For example, he has claimed that "at no time [presumably after 1900] did John D. Rockefeller join William in any important investment outside the oil industry," when, in fact, both served on the board of the Missouri, Kansas & Texas Railway up to 1904. For Nevins' claims, see his *John D. Rockefeller* (New York: Scribner's, 1940), Vol. 2, p. 442.

14.   In 1896 Elsie Stillman married William G. Rockefeller, and in 1901 Isabel Stillman married William Rockefeller's other son, Percy. For more on the manner in which these unions were reportedly arranged, see John K. Winkler, *The First Billion: The Stillmans and the National City Bank*, p. 136.

15.   For example, in 1909 both Rockefeller and Stillman sat on the board of the Hanover National Bank and the United States Trust Co., and their sons and various other relatives and close business associates served as directors of the Farmers' Loan and Trust Co. Also, see John K. Winkler, *The First Billion*, pp. 34, 43, and 60, and Matthew Josephson, *The Robber Barons*, pp. 399–400.

16.   Harriman served as a director of the National City Bank up to his death in 1909. His

principal financial advisor, Kuhn Loeb's Jacob Schiff, who was America's first prominent Jewish investment banker in the 20th century, also sat on this board up to 1915.

17.   See Robert H. Wiebe, *Businessmen and Reform: A Study of the Progressive Movement* (Cambridge, Mass.: Harvard University Press, 1962), *passim;* James Weinstein, *The Corporate Ideal in the Liberal State, 1900–1918* (Boston: Beacon Press, 1968), pp. 3–39; and Philip H. Burch, Jr., "The NAM as an Interest Group," *Politics and Society* (Fall 1973), pp. 97–100. Also, for some insight into the NCF's impact on the thinking of conservative AFL leader Samuel Gompers, see Harold C. Livesay, *Samuel Gompers and Organized Labor in America* (Boston: Little, Brown, 1978), pp. 153 and 157.

18.   See the *National Civic Federation Review* (April 1903), p. 10 and (April 1910), p. 16. In 1903 the public members of this organization's executive committee included Charles W. Eliot (president of Harvard University), Henry C. Potter (bishop of the New York Protestant Episcopal Church), John Ireland (archbishop of the St. Paul Roman Catholic Church), August Belmont (board chairman of the Louisville and Nashville Railroad and a director of the Guaranty Trust Co., Manhattan Trust Co., Republic Iron and Steel Co., and Westinghouse Electric & Mfg. Co.), Cornelius N. Bliss (a director of the Equitable Life Assurance Society and American Cotton Co.), New York City attorney John J. McCook (a director of the Equitable Life Assurance Society, International Banking Corp., and Marconi Wireless Telegraph Co.), James H. Eckels (who, though listed as a Chicago figure, was a director of the Bankers Trust Co. of New York City), David R. Francis (a former Secretary of the Interior, who was a director of the American Cotton Co. and the Chicago and Alton Railway), and several other pro-business figures. Moreover, the chairman of the group was Ohio politico-economic leader Mark Hanna.

19.   Marcus Alonzo Hanna, who largely masterminded and financed McKinley's presidential nominating drive and then oversaw the general election, was a wealthy Cleveland businessman who was prominently identified with various iron companies (primarily through the M. A. Hanna Co.), banking (as the head of the Union National Bank of Cleveland and as a director of other financial institutions in the city), and a number of Great Lakes shipbuilding and operating enterprises. He is also known to have been involved with railroads, municipal transit, and newspaper publishing. Some writers have maintained that he was essentially a Midwestern leader who had only incidental Eastern connections, and that he initially had considerable difficulty raising funds on Wall Street for McKinley's campaign until he accidentally encountered railroad magnate James J. Hill, president of the Great Northern Railway, who, though primarily a St. Paul figure, introduced him to many of the "right" people in Eastern financial circles. This story seems farfetched, for Hanna had some ties with New York financiers and attorneys which were almost as good as Hill's. For example, Hanna had served since 1892 as a director of the Cleveland and Pittsburgh Railroad, along with such influential businessmen as Charles Lanier and Hill's ally, John S. Kennedy, both of whom were closely linked with the House of Morgan. And in 1895 Hanna had been appointed to the board of the Chicago and Erie Railroad (a subsidiary of the Morgan-controlled Erie Railroad), where he came into contact with such men as Samuel Spencer, J. P. Morgan's top railroad man, Francis L. Stetson, Morgan's "attorney general," and Frederic B. Jennings, who was a senior partner in the latter's law firm. For more on Hanna's reported fundraising activities, see Herbert Croly, *Marcus Alonzo Hanna* (New York: Macmillan, 1912), p. 219, and for his connection with the Chicago and Erie Railroad, see *Poor's Manual of Railroads: 1896*, p. 538.

20.   A former Congressman, Bryan had recently served (mostly *in absentia*) as editor of a major Omaha newspaper, which had been bought by two wealthy silver miners, William Clark and Marcus Daly, with a view to building up this progressive agrarian as a presidential candidate. See Charles M. Wilson, *The Commoner: William Jennings Bryan* (Garden City, N.Y.: Doubleday, 1970), pp. 195–204. For an incisive account of the exodus of pro-corporate leaders from the Democratic party following Bryan's famous "Cross of Gold"

speech and dramatic capture of the presidential nomination, see John M. Dobson, *Politics in the Gilded Age,* pp. 180–81.

21. The McKinley forces probably spent about ten times as much as the Bryan-led Democratic party and, contrary to the stories about Hanna's fundraising problems in the East, more than half of this money came from New York City. Indeed the Republicans apparently collected more money from the Rockefeller and Morgan interests than the Democrats were able to gather from *all* sources. See Harold U. Faulkner, *Politics, Reform and Expansion: 1890–1900* (New York: Harper & Row, 1959), pp. 203–04: George Thayer, *Who Shakes the Money Tree?,* pp. 50–51; and George Wheeler, *Pierport Morgan and Friends,* p. 205.

22. The McKinley administration will be treated without reference to the election of 1900, since there were very few changes after his victorious return match with William Jennings Bryan. The basic difference between McKinley's first four years in office and his brief, ill-fated second term was that New York's ebullient Theodore Roosevelt was chosen to serve as Vice President in place of Garret A. Hobart, who had died in November 1899.

23. Partly because of the impression conveyed by Herbert Croly in his biography of Mark Hanna, it has long been thought that Eastern business interests had a mixed or hostile view to McKinley's candidacy. Now it is true that such potent figures as J. P. Morgan had serious reservations about McKinley initially, largely because of his "softness" on the money question. But Myron Herrick had a lengthy meeting with J. P. Morgan in 1896 in which they " . . . discussed the matter of the nomination, and especially McKinley's candidacy, in every detail." And this was followed by another conclave, which Hanna attended, on Morgan's yacht, where many of these politico-economic differences were resolved. See T. Bentley Mott, *Myron T. Herrick* (New York: Doubleday, Doran, 1929), p. 68; Herbert L. Satterlee, *J. Pierpont Morgan* (New York: Macmillan, 1939), pp. 316–17; and for the misleading portrayal, see Herbert Croly, *Marcus Alonzo Hanna,* p. 219.

24. Because he had countersigned for the notes of an old friend who subsequently failed in business, McKinley found himself $130,000 in debt in 1893 and on the brink of bankruptcy, when a small group of friends, led by Hanna, Herrick, William R. Day, and Chicago newspaperman H. H. Kohlsaat, managed to raise the requisite funds through the solicitation of many of McKinley's political and economic supporters, among whom were John Hay, Samuel Mather, James Pickands, J. H. Wade, James H. Hoyt, Charles Taft, Andrew Carnegie, Henry Clay Frick, Philander C. Knox, George M. Pullman, Philip Armour, and the Illinois Steel Co. See Herbert Croly, *Marcus Alonzo Hanna,* p. 170, and H. Wayne Morgan, *William McKinley and His America* (Syracuse, N.Y.: Syracuse University Press, 1963), pp. 169–74.

25. McKinley's first choice for Secretary of the Treasury was Maine's longtime Congressman (and Lewiston newspaperman) Nelson Dingley, Jr., but this influential leader could not be persuaded to enter the Cabinet. Then, reportedly at the suggestion of Mark Hanna (who was on close terms with Jay C. Morse, board chairman of the Illinois Steel Co. and a partner in Cleveland's Pickands Mather & Co.) and Chicago newspaperman Herman Kohlsaat, McKinley selected the able and conservative Gage, a former Cleveland Democrat. Bliss, a major Republican party fundraiser, would seem an odd choice for Secretary of the Interior, and was apparently picked to restore peace in New York's badly divided GOP ranks. The post was first offered to New York lawyer John J. McCook, who was also a trustee of the Equitable Life Assurance Society, but he had wanted a different Cabinet seat. See Margaret Leech, *In the Days of McKinley* (New York: Harper & Row, 1959), pp. 106–07.

26. In addition, Sherman's son-in-law, Colgate Hoyt, who was a former financial advisor to John D. Rockefeller, served on the board of the Missouri, Kansas & Texas Railway and various lesser enterprises in the 1890s.

27.   For more on Long's influential politico-economic backing, see Carolyn W. Johnson, *Winthrop Murray Crane: A Study in Republican Leadership, 1892–1920* (Northampton, Mass.: Smith College, 1967), p. 14.

28.   Stanford probably had much to do with McKenna's appointment to the U.S. Court of Appeals in 1892. In fact, it was Mrs. Stanford who first broke this good news to the McKenna family. For more on this matter, plus some commentary on McKenna's pro-railroad activities as a California Congressman, see Matthew McDevitt, *Joseph McKenna: Associate Justice of the United States* (Washington, D.C.: Catholic University of America Press, 1946), pp. 23–24 and 78–79, and Leon Friedman and Fred L. Israel (eds.), *The Justices of the United States Supreme Court, 1789–1969,* Vol. III, p. 1723. Actually, this Cabinet post was first offered to well-connected Pittsburgh lawyer Philander C. Knox, who turned it down for financial reasons, although he was appointed Attorney General four years later. See George Harvey, *Henry Clay Frick: The Man* (New York: Scribner's, 1928), pp. 290–91.

29.   See Leland L. Sage, *William Boyd Allison,* p. 284, and Margaret Leech, *In the Days of McKinley,* p. 106. Allison was reportedly McKinley's first choice to be Secretary of State, but he decided to remain in the Senate where he represented a powerful force.

30.   Day's father-in-law, Louis Schaefer, had also been a board member of the Cleveland and Canton Railroad briefly in the late 1880s. However, the primary reason Day was appointed to the State Department was because he was an intimate friend and political advisor of McKinley. He was also on good terms with Mark Hanna. Over the years Day had reportedly been retained as an attorney by a large number of economic enterprises, including the Baltimore and Ohio Railroad. See H. Wayne Morgan, *William McKinley and His America,* pp. 50–51, and for more on the heavily corporate character of the law practice of Lynch and Day, see Leon Friedman and Fred L. Israel (eds.), *The Justices of the United States Supreme Court,* Vol. III, p. 1775, and Vernon W. Roelofs, "Justice William R. Day and Federal Regulation," *Mississippi Valley Historical Review* (June 1950), p. 42.

31.   The Federal Steel Co., which was created in 1898, was probably controlled by the Morgan interests prior to its merger into the United States Steel Corp. in 1901, for its outside directors included J. P. Morgan, Robert Bacon (a partner in J. P. Morgan & Co.), and Samuel Spencer (one of Morgan's most trusted advisors). Moreover, the vice-president of this big steel company was Charles MacVeagh, who was a partner in the "Morgan" law firm which by this time was known as Stetson, Jennings and Russell. For more on Hay's socio-economic background, see Kenton J. Clymer, *John Hay: The Gentleman as Diplomat* (Ann Arbor: University of Michigan Press, 1975), p. 44, and Howard I. Kushner and Anne Hummel Sherrill, *John Milton Hay: The Union of Poetry and Politics* (Boston: Twayne, 1977), pp. 68–75.

32.   See Margaret Leech, *In the Days of McKinley,* p. 174.

33.   According to one recent study, this post was first offered to Joseph H. Choate, a Wall Street lawyer who was then serving as American Ambassador to Great Britain, but he chose to stay on in London. See Bingham Duncan, *Whitelaw Reid: Journalist, Politician, Diplomat* (Athens: University of Georgia Press, 1975), p. 214.

34.   It is true that Root had married the daughter of a fairly prominent New York City lawyer, Salem H. Wales, but Root was clearly the more able and aggressive of these men and soon overshadowed his father-in-law in corporate and legal affairs. Root also outshone all his law partners in the post–Civil War period.

35.   The president of this concern was Levi P. Morton, who was a longtime intimate friend of J. P. Morgan and a director of the Guaranty Trust Co., Equitable Life Assurance Society, and Panama Canal Co. of America. Other prominent members of the board of the Morton Trust Co. were George F. Baker (president of both the Astor National Bank and First National Bank of New York), Richard A. McCurdy (president of the Mutual Life Insurance Co., vice-president of the International Bell Telephone Co., Ltd., and a director

of the Guaranty Trust Co. and National Bank of Commerce), Frederic Cromwell (treasurer of the Mutual Life Insurance Co. and a director of the Guaranty Trust Co. and National Bank of Commerce), Walter G. Oakman (president of the Guaranty Trust Co.), and William C. Whitney (who was a member of the board of the Mutual Life Insurance Co., National Bank of Commerce, and the recently formed Cuba Co.).

36. See Richard W. Leopold, *Elihu Root and the Conservative Tradition* (Boston: Little, Brown, 1954), pp. 15–17, and Philip C. Jessup, *Elihu Root* (New York: Dodd, Mead, 1938), Vol. I, pp. 132 and 206. According to the latter source (p. 216), New York Republican boss Thomas C. Platt acquiesced in Root's replacement of his friend and business associate, Russell Alger, in the Cabinet only after Ryan persuaded him to do so.

37. Secretary of Agriculture James Wilson obviously had the fewest economic connections of these thirteen Cabinet members. McKinley's first Attorney General, Joseph McKenna, apparently also had no formal ties with business interests, although he had been quite friendly with California railroad magnate Leland Stanford. The other eleven Cabinet officials all had various noteworthy economic links, both direct and indirect. Curiously, most of the second-ranking officers in the administration did not have such associations.

38. See Harvey O'Connor, *The Astors,* pp. 164–68, 226, 255, and 276, and Allan Nevins, *John D. Rockefeller,* pp. 118 and 147.

39. The overall American investment in Cuba was estimated to be between $30 million and $50 million. The annual volume of trade before the insurrection was around $100 million, but this total dropped sharply as the conflict worsened. By 1897 sugar imports from Cuba had fallen off by about 80 percent, and the big American Sugar Refining Co. was compelled to buy huge quantities of this commodity from other sources at substantially higher prices. See David F. Healy, *The United States in Cuba, 1898–1902* (Madison: University of Wisconsin Press, 1963), pp. 11–12, and Ernest R. May, *Imperial Democracy: The Emergence of America as a Great Power* (New York: Harcourt Brace Jovanovich, 1961), p. 115.

40. A letter from the president of the Spanish-American Iron Co. to the Secretary of State (cited in Julius Pratt's *Expansionists of 1898* [Baltimore: Johns Hopkins Press, 1936], p. 251), makes this very point. And it may have been given considerable weight by McKinley's advisors since two of the directors of this concern, Rockefeller advisor Frederick T. Gates and Colgate Hoyt (a son-in-law of former Secretary of State John Sherman) were also associated with the American Steel Barge Co., the vice-president of which was Samuel Mather, John Hay's brother-in-law. Certain American businessmen were, understandably, very much concerned about conditions in Cuba, and a New York–based group known as the Cuba junta (whose chief spokesman was Wall Street lawyer John J. McCook, a political ally of McKinley) did make a serious, albeit unsuccessful, attempt to purchase Cuba from Spain, but this was a far cry from the advocacy of hostile action.

41. Although some historians have argued that it was primarily business influence rather than rampant "yellow" journalism and concomitant Congressional pressure which eventually forced McKinley to take the provocative steps which led to the Spanish-American War, most scholars contend that economic forces played only a secondary role in this dispute. On the basis of the available literature, the author is inclined to agree with the latter analysis. True, many business (or pro-business) figures, such as Elihu Root, finally came to feel that war with Spain was inevitable, but this was largely because of the belligerent climate of public opinion created by various major newspaper publishers, particularly Hearst and Pulitzer, neither of whom was closely linked with the business community. Also, it is interesting to note that although McKinley's (pre-war) Ambassador to Spain, Stewart L. Woodford, has usually been described as just a Brooklyn lawyer, he was actually the longtime general counsel for and a director of the Metropolitan Life Insurance Co. Since this official, like many others in the administration, labored strenuously to preserve peaceful relations between Spain and the United States, this lends additional credence to the thesis

that until early 1898 American business interests were, on the whole, opposed to our involvement in the Cuban conflict.

42. For more on this transformation in American thinking, see Julius W. Pratt, *Expansionists of 1898*, pp. 252–78, and Walter LaFeber, *The New Empire: An Interpretation of American Expansion, 1860–1898* (Ithaca, N.Y.: Cornell University Press, 1963), *passim*.

43. One of the much-prized "revokable" permits granted by Secretary of War Elihu Root was awarded to the Cuba Co., a company created to develop a major rail system in this depressed country. Four of the eight directors of this concern—Edward J. Berwind, George G. Haven, Thomas Fortune Ryan, and William C. Whitney—had similar ties with the Morton Trust Co. (of which Root himself was a board member), and the treasurer of the Morton Trust Co., W. Redmond Cross, held the same position with the Cuba Co. For more detail and background on this matter, see David F. Healy, *The United States in Cuba, 1898–1902*, pp. 191–93.

44. See John Morton Blum, *The Republican Roosevelt* (Cambridge, Mass.: Harvard University Press, 1954), p. 56. According to Blum (pp. x and xi), Roosevelt was neither a liberal nor a conventional conservative, but, as he puts it, a conservative progressive who was " . . . seeking ways to accommodate American institutions to advancing industrialism. . . ."

45. See Gabriel Kolko, *The Triumph of Conservatism* (Glencoe, Ill.: Free Press, 1963), especially pp. 57–138.

46. The Oyster Bay Roosevelts are descended from Johannes (or John) Roosevelt, who was a brother of Jacobus (or James) Roosevelt, the pre-Revolutionary War founder of the Hyde Park branch of the family. Although the latter Roosevelts amassed considerable money as New York merchants in the late 18th and early 19th centuries, the Oyster Bay Roosevelts, thanks largely to the efforts of Cornelius V. S. Roosevelt, who at his death in 1871 was regarded as one of the five richest men in New York, more than made up for lost time and, through banking and other business endeavors in the mid- and late-19th century, accumulated wealth far in excess of their Hyde Park cousins.

47. See Stephen Hess, *America's Political Dynasties*, pp. 172–73.

48. James A. Roosevelt, who was the top executive in the family banking firm of Roosevelt & Son in the post–Civil War era, served as a vice-president of this railroad up to 1886, when the hostile Harriman forces apparently took it over. He was also president of the Wabash Railway in the late 1870s and sat on the board of a number of other railroad and business concerns. Theodore Roosevelt's father died prematurely in 1878, cutting short what might otherwise have been a promising business career.

49. Although little attention has thus far been paid to W. Emlen Roosevelt, he was, as one authority has pointed out, on very close terms with his politically famous cousin, Theodore, and acted as " . . . his financial adviser before, during, and after his two terms as President." See William T. Cobb, *The Strenuous Life: The "Oyster Bay" Roosevelts in Business and Finance* (New York: William E. Rudge's Sons, 1946), p. 64, and also Allen Churchill, *The Roosevelts* (New York: Harper & Row, 1965), p. 211.

50. As evidence that Roosevelt was well regarded and warmly supported by big business, over 72 percent of the funds collected for his 1904 presidential campaign came from corporate sources, with by far the largest sum being supplied by men associated with the House of Morgan. See Henry F. Pringle, *Theodore Roosevelt* (New York: Harcourt, Brace, 1931), pp. 357–58. Much of the money raised for the conservative Democratic candidate in 1904, New York judge Alton B. Parker, was reportedly donated by a small set of wealthy Eastern interests led primarily by August Belmont (II) and Thomas Fortune Ryan. See George Thayer, *Who Shakes the Money Tree?*, p. 53; R. Carlyle Buley, *The Equitable Life Assurance Society of the United States, 1859–1964* (New York: Appleton-Century-Crofts, 1964), Vol. I, p. 648; and Ralph M. Goldman, *Search for Consensus: The Story of the Democratic Party* (Philadelphia: Temple University Press, 1979), p. 122.

51. Samuel Mather's brother, William, also sat on the board of the Wheeling and Lake Erie Railroad, a company headed in the early 1900s by the late President McKinley's close friend and political advisor, Cleveland banker Myron T. Herrick. Another one of its directors was Mark Hanna's son, Daniel.

52. Hay's son-in-law, Payne Whitney, served as a director of the Great Northern Paper Co. from at least 1903 through 1905, and his brother, Harry Payne Whitney (who had married a member of the Vanderbilt family), was a director of the Guaranty Trust Co.

53. Knox's former law partner, James H. Reed, was a board member of the U.S. Steel Corp. from 1901 through 1904 and president of the Pittsburgh, Bessemer and Lake Erie Railroad from 1897 through 1904 (during the last four years it was a subsidiary of U.S. Steel). However, in the absence of detailed studies, it is difficult to make a valid assessment of the significance of these links because Knox and Reed (who served on no Mellon bank boards) severed their legal ties in 1901 and never reestablished their law partnership.

54. See Arthur D. Howden Smith, *Men Who Run America* (Indianapolis: Bobbs-Merrill, 1935), p. 222.

55. Both of these posts were first offered to Massachusetts Governor W. Murray Crane, whose brother, Zenas, was a director of the Boston and Albany Railroad, the Chicago and Northwestern Railway, and the New York & New Jersey Telephone Co. (a subsidiary or affiliate of AT&T). See Solomon B. Griffin, *People and Politics* (Boston: Little, Brown, 1923), p. 420. One of the first prominent figures to be appointed by President Roosevelt was Postmaster General Henry C. Payne, a Wisconsin leader on close terms with John C. Spooner and the late Philetus Sawyer. Payne was reportedly selected as part of a plan to break the powerful hold established over the national Republican party by Ohio boss Mark Hanna, who was viewed politically as a Roosevelt adversary. But Payne (who was no relation to the Ohio and New York Paynes of, originally, Standard Oil fame) was also deeply involved in Milwaukee utility and banking affairs and was a longtime director of the North American Co., a big public utility holding company headed by New York City financier Charles W. Wetmore, whose board included such important persons as Robert Bacon, a partner in J. P. Morgan & Co. (and one of Theodore Roosevelt's closest friends), and Edmund C. Converse, the president of the Morgan-dominated Liberty National Bank of New York City.

56. See Leland L. Sage, *William Boyd Allison*, pp. 277 and 283, and Horace S. Merrill and Marion G. Merrill, *The Republican Command*, pp. 103–04.

57. As an attorney in the 1880s, Moody's clients reportedly included electric utilities and various gas, telephone, and paper interests, primarily in eastern Massachusetts. See Leon Friedman and Fred L. Israel (eds.), *The Justices of the United States Supreme Court, 1789–1969*, Vol. III, p. 1804.

58. Much of the pressure for the creation of this new Cabinet post was reportedly exerted by John A. McCall, president of the New York Life Insurance Co., and George W. Perkins, who was a vice-president of the New York Life Insurance Co. and a partner in J. P. Morgan & Co. See Morton Keller, *The Life Insurance Industry*, p. 232, and Horace S. Merrill and Marion G. Merrill, *The Republican Command*, p. 139.

59. Of these seven, only Victor H. Metcalf, a former California Congressman who served first as Secretary of Commerce and Labor and then as Secretary of the Navy, had essentially local economic links. However, on the basis of other (not totally clear) evidence, William Miller has classified Metcalf and four other members of Roosevelt's Cabinet (Knox, Root, Shaw, and Wright) as lawyers with close ties to major economic interests. See William Miller, "American Lawyers in Business and in Politics," *Yale Law Journal* (Jan. 1951), p. 68.

60. See Philip C. Jessup, *Elihu Root*, Vol. I, pp. 431–34. Root had worked in behalf of Morgan's apparently substantial stake in certain railroads in China, but as Secretary of State he reportedly refrained, because of a possible conflict of interest, from any further involvement in these protracted proceedings.

61. Bacon's predecessor, Francis B. Loomis, had a great deal of experience in both diplomacy and journalism. He also had an elitist and pro-business family background.

62. The board of the Manhattan Trust Co. included such key figures as George F. Baker (the president of both the First National Bank of New York and Astor National Bank, a vice-president of the Northern Securities Co., and a director of the Chase National Bank, Guaranty Trust Co., Morton Trust Co., Mutual Life Insurance Co., AT&T, and many other large companies), August Belmont (president of the Interborough Rapid Transit Co.), Henry W. Cannon (head of the Chase National Bank), James J. Hill (president of both the Great Northern Railway and Northern Securities Co., and a director of the Chase National Bank and First National Bank of New York), Oliver H. Payne (the late William C. Whitney's brother-in-law), and Grant B. Schley (a brother-in-law of George F. Baker and a director of the Chase National Bank, Northern Pacific Railway, and numerous other enterprises).

63. Perhaps because of his substantial wealth and investments, Bonaparte served briefly on the board of the Real Estate Trust Co. in Baltimore, an essentially local link which was his only known corporate affiliation. For more on this man, see Eric F. Goldman, *Charles J. Bonaparte: Patrician Reformer* (Baltimore: The Johns Hopkins Press, 1943), pp. 12–14 and 30. It should also be noted that, up to 1903, Bonaparte's brother-in-law, Thomas M. Day, Jr., served as a director of the American Sheet Steel Co., a concern recently merged into the U.S. Steel Corp.

64. Both Roosevelt and Bonaparte served as members of the Board of Overseers of Harvard College in the late 19th and early 20th centuries, an association of probably much importance to Bonaparte in particular.

65. For more on Straus's close informal ties with Roosevelt even before he was appointed to Cabinet office, see Naomi W. Cohen, *A Dual Heritage: The Public Career of Oscar S. Straus* (Philadelphia: Jewish Publication Society of America, 1969), p. 121. Straus's brother, Isidor, was a longtime director of the Hanover National Bank and Second National Bank of New York, both of which were closely allied with the Rockefeller interests.

66. For instance, in the only comment of this kind in his book on Roosevelt, Blum has stated that the President freely borrowed ideas on labor-management relations and the control of corporations from this influential body. See John Morton Blum, *The Republican Roosevelt*, pp. 38–39.

67. Newberry's father, for example, had been the longtime business partner of James McMillan, who late in life had become part of the dominant inner circle of the United States Senate, along with William Boyd Allison and Nelson W. Aldrich. And Newberry's brother-in-law, Henry B. Joy, had recently become president of the Packard Motor Car Co. For more on these Detroit families, see Stephen Birmingham, *The Right People* (Boston: Little, Brown, 1968), p. 142.

68. Toward the end of the Roosevelt administration Taft was succeeded as Secretary of War by his close friend and former governmental associate, Luke E. Wright, who had been a member of the U.S. Philippine Commission in the early 1900s, governor (or governor general) of the Philippines from 1904 to 1906, and Ambassador to Japan in 1906–07. Wright was a prominent Memphis lawyer whose son-in-law, John H. Watkins, was a local financier who served, from at least 1907 through 1909, as a director of the American Cities Railway and Light Co., a largely Southern-owned public utility holding company. For more on Wright's socio-economic ties, see Roger L. Hart, *Redeemers, Bourbons & Populists*, p. 66.

69. Upon the death of her father in 1900, Charles Taft's wife inherited his entire estate, which reportedly amounted to about $15 million. See Stephen Hess, *America's Political Dynasties*, p. 306.

70. See Henry W. Taft, *A Century and a Half at the New York Bar* (New York: privately printed, 1938), pp. 192–97.

71. Moreover, Newell was, up to 1892, a member of the board of the Cincinnati, Wabash and Michigan Railway, which was then headed by the aforementioned Melville E. Ingalls.

72. Cortelyou, who served first as Secretary of Commerce and Labor and later as Secretary of the Treasury, apparently attained high governmental office largely by dint of his own efforts. However, his appointment as Secretary of Commerce and Labor was strongly backed by such influential figures as Richard A. McCurdy, president of the Mutual Life Insurance Co. (and a director of the Guaranty Trust Co., Morton Trust Co., and National Bank of Commerce). See Morton Keller, *The Insurance Industry*, p. 233.

73. Of the "later-appointed" Cabinet members, only two—Victor Metcalf and Luke Wright—had merely local or regional business ties.

74. See John Morton Blum, *The Republican Roosevelt*, p. 37.

75. Toward the end of the Roosevelt regime he was also board chairman of the Pere Marquette Railroad, a director of the Northern Pacific Railway, Bankers Trust Co., and Astor Trust Co., and in 1909 he became a high official of the National Civic Federation. For a sympathetic treatment of this leader, see John A. Garraty, *Right-Hand Man: The Life of George W. Perkins* (New York: Harper & Brothers, 1957), *passim*.

76. Yet another sign that the Roosevelt regime was closely allied with the House of Morgan can be seen in the appointment of certain second-ranking officials. For instance, when Assistant Secretary of the Navy Truman H. Newberry moved up to replace Victor Metcalf as head of this department in the closing months of the administration, he was succeeded by Herbert L. Satterlee, a relatively unknown Wall Street lawyer, who was probably chosen largely because he was J. P. Morgan's son-in-law. Since neither Newberry (who was a Detroit businessman) nor Metcalf (who was an Oakland, California figure) was even remotely associated with J. P. Morgan, this selection must have been made by President Roosevelt himself.

77. This analysis excludes the incumbent Ambassadors to Great Britain, France, and Germany—Joseph H. Choate, a Wall Street lawyer (who served as emissary until 1905), Horace Porter, a former New York–based business executive (who also held office up to 1905), and Andrew D. White, a long-retired Ivy League college president (who resigned his Berlin post in late 1902).

78. For more on Tower's business and governmental endeavors, see Hal Bridges, *Iron Millionaire: Life of Charlemagne Tower* (Philadelphia: University of Pennsylvania Press, 1952), *passim*. Tower's replacement (in 1908) as Ambassador to Germany, David J. Hill, was an apparently wealthy former college president who had held several diplomatic posts since the start of the McKinley administration. For a reference to Hill's financial status, see Aubrey Parkman, *David Jayne Hill and the Problem of World Peace* (Lewisburg, Pa.: Bucknell University Press, 1975), p. 104.

79. Robert S. McCormick himself had married the daughter of Joseph Medill, the longtime publisher of the *Chicago Tribune,* and another member of this wealthy farm equipment family, Harold F. McCormick, had married the daughter of John D. Rockefeller in 1895, so this Chicago clan had ties to both of New York's top economic interests.

80. White's grandmother, the former Mary LeRoy, was also a member of one of the city's early major mercantile and banking families.

81. There were also a number of Northerners who vigorously backed the Nicaraguan route, but, judging from the make-up of the officers and directors of the Nicaragua Co., most of these do not appear to have been very prominent persons.

82. See David McCullough, *The Path Between the Seas: The Creation of the Panama Canal, 1870–1914* (New York: Simon and Schuster, 1977), pp. 260–401; Walter LaFeber, *The Panama Canal: The Crisis in Historical Perspective* (New York: Oxford University Press, 1978), pp. 19–57; Henry F. Pringle, *op. cit.,* pp. 301–38; and Dana G. Munro, *Intervention and Dollar Diplomacy in the Caribbean, 1900–1921* (Princeton, N.J.: Princeton University Press, 1964), pp. 37–64.

83. The other "outside" party heavily involved in these proceedings, Philippe Bunau-Varilla, was perhaps equally enterprising in his own way, but being a Frenchman, he did not have the governmental access and political power of a well-established American operative. According to McCullough, Cromwell exerted extraordinary influence in the Roosevelt administration, especially in the State Department where he " . . .was consulted just about daily." Tyler Dennett claims also that at least one important draft of a proposed treaty between the United States and Colombia was actually written by Cromwell. See David McCullough, *op. cit.,* pp. 336–37, and Tyler Dennett, *John Hay* (New York: Dodd, Mead, 1934), p. 370.

84. See Henry F. Pringle, *op. cit.*, p. 319.

85. See David McCullough, *op. cit.*, pp. 273–76 and 291.

86. Cromwell also sat on the board of the American Bank Note Co. and, up to 1902, the National Tube Co. (about which time this company was merged into the U.S. Steel Corp.). In addition, it should be noted John Hay's brother-in-law, Samuel Mather, had served until 1901 as a director of the Federal Steel Co. and then in a similar capacity with the Lackawanna Steel Co. And as pointed out earlier, John Hay's daughter had recently married one of the sons of New York magnate William C. Whitney, thereby establishing still other links, including some with the Vanderbilt family.

87. W. Emlen Roosevelt was also a director of the Mexican Telegraph Co. (which was closely affiliated with the Central and South American Telegraph Co.) and two other railroads that were part of the Vanderbilt-Morgan complex.

88. See David McCullough, *op. cit.*, pp. 339–53, 363, and 376.

89. With regard to Simmons' relations with Hanna, see Charles D. Ameringer, "The Panama Canal Lobby of Philippe Bunau-Varilla and William Nelson Cromwell," *American Historical Review* (Jan. 1963), p. 350.

90. Among other things, the question of who got the $40 million paid by the American government (through J. P. Morgan & Co.) to the stockholders of the New Panama Canal Co. remains a mystery to this day. However, it seems fair to assume, judging from the make-up of the board of the Panama Railroad and a revealing remark once made by President Roosevelt (see Pringle, *op. cit.*, p. 382), that a substantial part of the money was disbursed to financial and speculative interests in the United States. According to George Mowry, although the President later disclaimed any knowledge as to the various individuals who ultimately received these funds, both he and Attorney General Philander Knox actually had a list (provided by Cromwell) of the names of the stockholders of the New Panama Canal Co. in the early 1900s. But neither Roosevelt nor Knox ever made the names public, and the list unfortunately disappeared from both men's manuscript papers. See George E. Mowry, *The Era of Theodore Roosevelt, 1900–1912* (New York: Harper & Row, 1958), p. 153.

91. It was in the course of this protracted struggle that the Reading's president, George F. Baer, made his now-famous statement that "the rights and interests of the laboring man will be protected and cared for, not by labor agitators, but by the Christian men to whom God in His infinite wisdom, has given control of the property interests of the country."

92. See Robert J. Cornell, *The Anthracite Coal Strike of 1902* (Washington, D.C.: Catholic University of America Press, 1957), pp. 175–76. Though Roosevelt himself was certainly not an archconservative in the realm of labor relations (unlike the NAM), organized labor secured relatively few benefits from the federal government during his administration. Indeed, as Harold Faulkner has pointed out, it took two more major strikes (in 1912 and 1916) before the business community and the country accepted the concept of unionism and the eight-hour day. See Harold U. Faulkner, *Labor in America* (New York: Harper & Brothers, 1944), p. 126.

93. Hanna's son, Daniel, sat on the board of the big Pittsburgh Coal Co., but this was primarily a bituminous coal company and did not have a direct stake in the strike.

94.   See Richard M. Abrams, *Conservatism in a Progressive Era: Massachusetts Politics, 1900–1912* (Cambridge, Mass.: Harvard University Press, 1964), p. 94 and 166, and Carolyn W. Johnson, *Winthrop Murray Crane,* pp. 38–39. That Roosevelt had a high opinion of Crane may also be seen from the fact that he had recently offered him two Cabinet posts, one of which was Secretary of the Treasury.

95.   There were, to be sure, a number of noteworthy accomplishments in the Roosevelt administration. For instance, taking advantage of a previously enacted federal law, Roosevelt, who as a young man had spent much time in the West, set aside almost 150 million acres of unsold government timberland as national forest reserves—more than three times the amount so designated by his three predecessors combined. In addition, prodded by the public clamor created by the publication of Upton Sinclair's sensational novel, *The Jungle,* the government adopted both a federal meat inspection program and the Pure Food and Drug Act. And finally, as a result of the pressure and persuasion of President Roosevelt, Congress passed the so-called Hepburn Act, which was at least a partial victory for progressive forces in that it gave the Interstate Commerce Commission the power to prescribe maximum railroad rates, subject, probably as a conservative check, to judicial review. However, this measure did not give the commission the right to evaluate corporate properties and cost of services so that it could realistically determine reasonable rates. For two very different analyses of this law, see Gabrial Kolko, *Railroads and Regulation, 1877–1916,* pp. 127–54, and Robert H. K. Victor, "Businessmen and the Political Economy: The Railroad Rate Controversy of 1905," *Journal of American History* (June 1977), pp. 47–66. Also, for more on the conservative character of some of its important supporters, see Leland L. Sage, *William Boyd Allison,* pp. 200 and 297–306.

96.   See Richard A. Posner, "A Statistical Study of Antitrust Enforcement," *Journal of Law and Economics* (Oct. 1970), pp. 365–419.

97.   See the U.S. Federal Trade Commission, *The Federal Antitrust Laws* (Washington, D.C.: U. S. Government Printing Office, 1931), pp. 91–125. These ten cases involved the Northern Securities Co., Swift and Co., Armour & Co., the Virginia-Carolina Chemical Co., Standard Oil Co., Reading Railroad (with regard to its coal holdings), E. I. du Pont de Nemours Powder Co., American Tobacco Co., Union Pacific Railroad, and New York, New Haven & Hartford Railroad.

98.   In 1908 Roosevelt even supported an abortive effort to weaken the Sherman Antitrust Act. This bill was backed by the National Civic Federation and was reportedly drafted by J. P. Morgan's lawyer, Francis Lynde Stetson, who was a director of the Erie Railroad, Niagara Falls Power Co., and U.S. Rubber Co., and Wall Street attorney Victor Morawetz, who was chairman of the executive committee of the Atchison, Topeka & Santa Fe Railway and a director of the National Bank of Commerce, Niagara Falls Power Co., and Norfolk and Western Railway. See Arthur E. Johnson, "Antitrust Policy in Transition, 1908: Ideal and Reality," *Mississippi Valley Historical Review* (Dec. 1961), pp. 424–26.

99.   See John Morton Blum, *The Republican Roosevelt,* p. 118; and Samuel E. Morison, Henry S. Commager, and William E. Leuchtenberg, *The Growth of the American Republic,* 6th ed. (New York: Oxford University Press, 1969), Vol. 2, p. 303.

100.   While Duke did sit on the board of two New York City banks which were closely linked with the House of Morgan (the Morton Trust Co. and National Bank of Commerce), he was essentially an independent figure, as was another noted financier, Thomas Fortune Ryan, who was also associated with this enterprise. According to one recent study, even Roosevelt's action against the Standard Oil Co. was largely a politically inspired maneuver, taken because of the clamor created by such famous muckrakers as Ida Tarbell. See Bruce Bringhurst, *Antitrust and the Oil Monopoly: The Standard Oil Cases, 1890–1911* (Westport, Conn.: Greenwood Press, 1979), pp. 69 and 121–141. Two other companies against which antitrust action was taken later in the administration, the Reading Co. and New York, New Haven and Hartford Railroad, are frequently treated as Morgan-dominated firms, but a

careful look at the make-up of their boards of directors indicates that this was probably not the case.

101.   The U.S. Steel Corp. was formed in 1901 through the amalgamation of a sizable number of major metal companies. It was further enlarged in 1907 through the absorption of the big Tennessee Coal, Iron and Railroad Co., in which concern a financially troubled New York City brokerage house, Moore & Schley, had invested substantial funds which it could not recover because of depressed conditions on Wall Street. Although the U.S. Steel Corp. already controlled over 50 percent of the national market, President Roosevelt, who knew relatively little about business matters, was persuaded by several high-ranking Morgan officials to give his blessing to this merger, an action that resolved the fiscal problems of Moore & Schley (whose second partner, Grant B. Schley, was the brother-in-law of Morgan's chief ally, George F. Baker). For more on this topic, see Gabriel Kolko, *The Triumph of Conservatism*, pp. 114–17.

102.   See John Morton Blum, *op. cit.*, p. 58; Gabriel Kolko, *op. cit.*, pp. 79–81; John A. Garraty, *Right-Hand Man*, p. 257; and Matthew Josephson, *The President Makers* (New York: Harcourt, Brace, 1940), pp. 254–58.

103.   See Matthew Josephson, *op. cit.*, p. 127. Although some have cited this action as evidence that Roosevelt clashed at times with the House of Morgan, it should be noted that J. P. Morgan differed with his friend, James J. Hill, in this case and did not share his determination to preserve the Northern Securities Co. See Albro Martin, *James J. Hill and the Opening of the Northwest*, p. 515.

104.   According to one reliable source, during his last four years in office Roosevelt had better relations with the House of Morgan than did his designated conservative successor, Ohio's William Howard Taft. (See Robert H. Wiebe, "The House of Morgan and the Executive, 1905–1913," *American Historical Review* [Oct. 1959], pp. 49–60). Two other authorities maintain that Roosevelt's contribution to Progressivism was essentially educational (to put it another way, largely symbolic). As they astutely observed, "by his platform espousal of the Progressive program he made it as popular as he was himself. But as far as Big Business was concerned, that popularity was comparatively harmless as long as Roosevelt was its keeper." See Thomas C. Cochran and William Miller, *The Age of Enterprise*, p. 287.

105.   See Donald F. Anderson, *William Howard Taft* (Ithaca, N.Y.: Cornell University Press, 1968), p. 33.

106.   See Henry F. Pringle, *The Life and Times of William Howard Taft* (New York: Farrar & Rinehart, 1939), Vol. II, p. 654.

107.   According to Stephen Hess, Charles Taft, who had married one of Ohio's richest heiresses, reportedly spent about $800,000 on his brother's cause. Furthermore, Henry Pringle referred, as early as 1902, to Taft's New York City lawyer-brother, Henry, as "the advance agent for Taft Presidential Prospects, Inc." For more on these and other such efforts, see Stephen Hess, *America's Political Dynasties*, p. 313; Pringle, *op. cit.*, Vol. I, p. 242; and Ishbel Ross, *An American Family: The Tafts—1689–1964* (Cleveland: World Publishing, 1964), pp. 194–95.

108.   See Henry W. Taft, *A Century and a Half at the New York Bar*, pp. 193–97.

109.   Charles Taft had previously served (from 1903 to 1908) as either an officer or a director of the Cincinnati Gas & Electric Co., a fairly sizable operating concern which had entered into a long-term lease with a subsidiary of the Columbia Gas & Electric Co.

110.   Another sign of Taft's alignment with the business community, particularly Eastern financial interests, was shown in his appointment of New York financier George R. Sheldon as treasurer of the Republican National Committee. Sheldon was president of both the New

York and Western Coal Co. and the Electrical Securities Corp. (a fairly small public utility), treasurer of the North American Co. (a big public utility holding company), and a director of the American Locomotive Co., Bethlehem Steel Corp., National Copper Bank of New York City, and Trust Co. of America.

111. In creating his Cabinet, Taft consulted such prominent Republican leaders as Rhode Island's influential Senator Nelson W. Aldrich (who was a director of the Continental Rubber Co. of America, and whose daughter had married John D. Rockefeller, Jr.), conservative Maine Senator Eugene Hale (the son-in-law of wealthy Detroit businessman Zachariah Chandler), Massachusetts Senator Henry Cabot Lodge (a Boston Brahmin and close friend of Theodore Roosevelt), House Speaker Joseph Cannon, the recently resigned Secretary of State, Elihu Root (a man with many well-established business ties), and, interestingly, several powerful economic figures, Wall Street lawyer William Nelson Cromwell, Northwestern railroad magnate James J. Hill, and New York businessman John Hays Hammond. Cromwell served at this time on the board of the American Cotton Oil Co., Central of Georgia Railway, International Nickel Co., Mercantile National Bank of New York City, North American Co., Panama-American Corp. (about which little is known), and United Bank Note Co. (a company headed by Edmund C. Converse, who was president of both New York's Astor Trust Co. and Bankers Trust Co.). James J. Hill was board chairman of the Great Northern Railway, president of the Northern Securities Co. (a concern of now much reduced size), and a director of the Chicago, Burlington and Quincy Railroad, the First National Bank of Chicago, and four New York City financial institutions—Chase National Bank, First National Bank, Manhattan Trust Co., and Mercantile Trust Co. See Donald F. Anderson, *William Howard Taft*, p. 62, and Paolo E. Coletta, *The Presidency of William Howard Taft* (Lawrence: University Press of Kansas, 1973), p. 49.

112. For a harsh, though revealing insight into the nature of Knox's ties with the influential Andrew W. Mellon, see Arthur D. H. Smith, *Men Who Run America*, p. 222. Knox's (post-1901) relations with his former law partner, James H. Reed, who served on the board of both the U.S. Steel Corp. and Gulf Oil Corp., remain something of a mystery, which further research may clarify. The position of Secretary of State was first offered to Elihu Root, who, having held Cabinet office for about eight years, graciously declined, and to Boston Brahmin Henry Cabot Lodge, who chose to remain in the Senate, where he already wielded considerable power.

113. Dickinson also had some elite family links. He was a great grandson of Jacksonian leader Felix Grundy, and he was distantly related to former Supreme Court Justice Howell Jackson. See Roger L. Hart, *Redeemers, Bourbons & Populists*, pp. 63 and 65. Dickinson's Assistant Secretary of War was an Albany, New York figure, Robert S. Oliver, who was first appointed to this post in 1903, shortly after his daughter had married the son of Joseph H. Choate, then American Ambassador to Great Britain and a director of the New York Life Insurance & Trust Co. Oliver's son-in-law, Joseph H. Choate, Jr., was appointed to the board of the Morgan-dominated Mutual Life Insurance Co. sometime in 1910.

114. Actually, this post was first offered to a well-known mining engineer and entrepreneur, John Hays Hammond, who had no formal experience in government, but was a close friend of the President. Hammond was at this time president of the Esperanza Mining Co., vice-president of the Guanajuato Power & Electric Co., and a director of the big Utah Copper Co. and the Guggenheim Exploration Co., a family-controlled firm that had a substantial interest in a number of noteworthy enterprises, including the Yukon Gold Co. Meyer's Assistant Secretary of the Navy was another fairly important figure, New York's Beekman Winthrop, whose uncle (Henry A. C. Taylor) and two cousins (Moses Taylor and Moses Taylor Pyne) all served in 1909 on the board of the Stillman-Rockefeller–dominated National City Bank of New York and the Lackawanna Steel Co.

115. See James Penick, Jr., *Progressive Politics and Conservation: The Ballinger-Pinchot Affair* (Chicago: University of Chicago Press, 1968), pp. 21 and 41–42.

116. Nagel was reportedly the chief attorney for the wealthy Busch family (see Paolo E.

Coletta, *op. cit.*, p. 50). Nagel's brother-in-law, John F. Shepley, who had married a daughter of former Secretary of the Interior Ethan A. Hitchcock, also served as a vice-president and board member of the St. Louis Union Trust Co. up through 1913. Moreover, Nagel's Assistant Secretary of Commerce and Labor, Benjamin S. Cable, was a former (1899–1909) attorney for the Chicago, Rock Island & Pacific Railway, which big line was headed for many years (1885–1902) by his father, Ransom R. Cable. The elder Cable served on this board up to his death in late 1909, and in the early 1900s was a director of the Corn Exchange Bank of New York City. Thus under Taft the Department of Commerce and Labor was run by men friendly to business, rather than union, interests.

117.   The National Civic Federation was no apolitical body, for it reportedly influenced the Taft administration through its ties with Secretary of the Treasury MacVeagh and the President's close friend, John Hays Hammond. See Marguerite Green, *The National Civic Federation and the American Labor Movement, 1900–1925* (Washington, D.C.: Catholic University of America Press, 1956), p. 346.

118.   George W. Perkins, whom some have described as J. P. Morgan's "secretary of state," claims that he alone was responsible for Taft's choice of Franklin MacVeagh as Secretary of the Treasury. See John A. Garraty, *Right-Hand Man,* p. 226.

119.   The board of this newly formed concern included such prominent figures as financier August Belmont (a director of the American-Asiatic Steamship Co., Louisville and Nashville Railroad, and Manhattan Trust Co.), Edward J. Berwind (president of the Berwind-White Coal Mining Co. and a director of the Atchison, Topeka & Santa Fe Railway, International Mercantile Marine Co., Morton Trust Co., and National Bank of Commerce), Solomon Guggenheim (president of the Yukon Gold Co. and a director of the American Smelting and Refining Co., Guggenheim Exploration Co., and Continental Rubber Co. of America), Walter G. Oakman (board chairman of the Guaranty Trust Co. and a director of the American Car and Foundry Co., Louisville and Nashville Railroad, Morton Trust Co., and National Bank of Commerce), and Cornelius Vanderbilt (a director of the Allis-Chalmers Co., American-Asiatic Steamship Co., Illinois Central Railroad, Lacka-wanna Steel Co., Mexican Telegraph Co., Mutual Life Insurance Co., and New York Life Insurance and Trust Co.).

120.   Another sign of the pro-business orientation of either Wickersham or certain members of the Taft family may be seen in the selection of Lloyd W. Bowers, the longtime counsel of the Vanderbilt-dominated Chicago and Northwestern Railway, to serve as Solicitor General. When Bowers died in the latter part of 1910, he was replaced first, for about a year and a half, by Frederick W. Lehman, a St. Louis lawyer about whom relatively little is known, and then in July 1912 by William M. Bullitt, a well-known Kentucky attorney who served on the board of several Louisville banks and the Louisville, Henderson & St. Louis Railroad (a fairly small line affiliated with the big Louisville and Nashville Railroad).

121.   Pringle claims that "Taft did not, *it would seem,* consult Henry W. Taft to any great extent" (italics added). See Henry F. Pringle, *op. cit.,* Vol. I, p. 385. Pringle seems to have been unaware that Wickersham and Henry W. Taft were partners in the same prominent Wall Street law firm.

122.   See *The Autobiography of John Hays Hammond* (New York: Farrar and Rinehart, 1935), Vol. 2, p. 543.

123.   Ironically (because of a later estrangement), the House of Morgan was apparently well pleased with the men initially appointed to Taft's Cabinet. According to Melvin Urofsky, George W. Perkins told J. P. Morgan that all the Cabinet posts ". . . are filled to our entire satisfaction." See Melvin L. Urofsky, *Big Steel and the Wilson Administration* (Columbus: Ohio State University Press, 1969), p. 18.

124.   See Elting E. Morison, *Turmoil and Tradition: A Study of the Life and Times of Henry L. Stimson* (Boston: Houghton Mifflin, 1960), pp. 12, 22, and 67–73.

125. See E. E. Morison, *op. cit.*, pp. 95 and 144. Indeed, according to Richard Leopold, Root and Stimson were on such intimate terms that ". . . for over a quarter of a century the two men conferred together on every major issue, domestic and foreign." See Richard W. Leopold, *Elihu Root and the Conservative Tradition,* p. 189.

126. Ogden Mills had also previously served for many years as a director of the big Chicago, Rock Island and Pacific Railway and various lesser concerns.

127. Robert Bacon was on more than friendly terms with J. P. Morgan throughout this period. When he resigned as Ambassador to France, Morgan ". . . insisted that Mr. Bacon should have an adjoining office, and actually forced him into compliance, although Bacon did not need such pretentious quarters for his private affairs." See James Brown Scott, *Robert Bacon: Life and Letters* (Garden City, N.Y.: Doubleday, Page, 1923), p. 70.

128. Herrick had also served as a director of the Bowling Green Trust Co. of New York City up to 1908, and his son, Parmely W. Herrick, sat on the board of New York's Chatham and Phenix National Bank from at least 1911 through 1913. For more on Herrick's business and political career, see T. Bentley Mott, *Myron T. Herrick, passim.*

129. Leishman was generally considered to be a protégé of Frick, who served at this time on the board of the Atchison, Topeka & Santa Fe Railway, Chicago and Northwestern Railway, Pennsylvania Railroad, Reading Co., Union Pacific Railroad, U.S. Steel Corp., and Mellon National Bank. For more on Leishman's relations with Frick, see Robert Hessen, *Steel Titan: The Life of Charles M. Schwab* (New York: Oxford University Press, 1975), p. 67.

130. Another reason for Taft's conservative stance probably stemmed from the fact that he relied heavily on the advice of such business-oriented Congressional leaders as Nelson W. Aldrich (who sat on the board of the Intercontinental Rubber Co., and whose daughter had married the son of John D. Rockefeller) and Massachusetts Senator W. Murray Crane, a wealthy paper manufacturer who served as a director of AT&T from 1903 through 1913 (and the General Electric Co. from 1903 to 1909). For more on the latter, see Carolyn W. Johnson, *Winthrop Murray Crane,* especially pp. 38–39 and 43–46.

131. The relations between these Eastern-based entrepreneurial interests and the Taft administration remain sketchy and vague. A few facts and observations are offered here for those interested in pursuing this matter. The Morgan forces appear to have been represented most conspicuously in the Cabinet by Secretary of the Treasury Franklin MacVeagh, who had a brother who served on the board of the Mutual Life Insurance Co. and a nephew who was a member of the "Morgan" law firm of Stetson, Jennings & Russell. Although of different backgrounds, the Guggenheims were linked to the House of Morgan through the directorship ties of Daniel Guggenheim (who was president of both the American Smelting & Refining Co. and Guggenheim Exploration Co.) to the Morton Trust Co. and National Bank of Commerce of New York, that of his brother, Solomon, with the Interborough-Metropolitan Co. (of which board Attorney General Wickersham had been a member until early 1909), and by virtue of the fact that William P. Hamilton, J. P. Morgan's son-in-law, served as vice-president of the Copper River & Northwestern Railway of Alaska, a director of the Kennecott Mines Co., and possibly president of the Alaska Development & Mineral Co. It is also interesting to note that one of President Taft's close friends, mining engineer John Hays Hammond, who in 1909 had been involved in the efforts to persuade Richard Ballinger to become Secretary of the Interior and was at one point apparently accused of having a stake in the disputed Alaskan coal lands, felt constrained to deny any connection with the Guggenheims during these critical years, although he still served on the board of the Guggenheim Exploration Co. See *The Autobiography of John Hays Hammond,* Vol. II, p. 560.

132. For more on this issue, see James Penick, Jr., *Progressive Politics and Conservation: The Ballinger-Pinchot Affair, passim,* and Alpheus T. Mason, *Bureaucracy Convicts Itself: The Ballinger-Pinchot Controversy of 1910* (New York: Viking Press, 1941), *passim.*

133. The author has no ready explanation as to why this came about, for while the House of Morgan did not have as much influence in the Taft administration as it did in the Roosevelt regime, there still were a number of men in high places who were friendly to its interests. The author is inclined to attribute much of this action to the unusual character of Attorney General George Wickersham, who, although he had some former corporate ties, may have felt compelled, in part because of increasing criticism of U.S. Steel's 1907 acquisition of the Tennessee Coal, Iron & Railroad Co., to enforce the Sherman Antitrust Act in a vigorous and impartial fashion. According to Henry Pringle, President Taft (who apparently allowed Wickersham considerable latitude) never saw the suit prepared against the U.S. Steel Corp. before it was formally filed in court. (After much litigation, the suit turned out to be unsuccessful.)

134. Roosevelt's reemergence was motivated by strong political and emotional considerations. He was offended by Taft's seeming slap at a major governmental error or omission on his part, and he was also distressed by the generally unimpressive record compiled by the Taft regime. Perkins, on the other hand, was influenced mainly by economics. According to George Mowry, the antitrust suits filed by the Taft administration against the U.S. Steel Corp. and International Harvester Co. were ". . . a prime factor in Perkins' willingness to join and finance the Bull Moose crusade." He contributed over a quarter of a million dollars to this cause in 1912 alone, and "in 1914 the Progressive party was able to balance its books solely because of his advances." As Mowry also points out, "it was Perkins who was largely responsible for the abandonment of the trust plank in the 1912 [Progressive party] platform," and he reportedly exerted a predominant influence over party policy. See George E. Mowry, *Theodore Roosevelt and the Progressive Movement* (Madison: University of Wisconsin Press, 1946), pp. 225, 249, and 292–93, and Paolo E. Coletta, *The Presidency of William Howard Taft,* pp. 157–62. Also for more on the highly skewed financial backing of Roosevelt's 1912 presidential campaign, see John Allen Gable, *The Bull Moose Years* (Port Washington, N.Y.: Kennikat Press, 1978), p. 118.

135. See Willard L. King, *Melville W. Fuller,* pp. 64 and 93.

136. See Willard L. King, *op. cit.*, pp. 68 and 94. In addition, Fuller's son-in-law, Hugh C. Wallace, was an influential Washington businessman who served on the board of Seattle's National Bank of Commerce from 1900 through 1910.

137. See Harold F. Williamson and Orange A. Smalley, *Northwestern Mutual Life: A Century of Trusteeship* (Evanston, Ill.: Northwestern University Press, 1957), p. 124. Brewer's uncle, Stephen J. Field, will not be treated here at any length since he resigned in December 1897 because of advanced age. Suffice it to say that he had been a close friend of railroad magnate Leland Stanford, and that his brother, Cyrus W. Field, had been involved in a number of industrial and railroad enterprises in the East up to his death in 1892.

138. See Shepard B. Clough, *A Century of American Life Insurance: A History of the Mutual Life Insurance Company of New York, 1843–1943* (New York: Columbia University Press, 1946), p. 183, and Leo Pfeffer, *This Honorable Court,* p. 235.

139. Although the board of the Northwestern Mutual Life Insurance Co. met much less frequently than those of most such concerns, the author would nonetheless argue that Justice Brewer (who rarely missed a meeting of this company) was bound to have his conservative views reinforced by this kind of affiliation, which many would contend constituted a conflict of interest. And the same, of course, applies to Justice Rufus Peckham, whose brother, Wheeler (who was once nominated for the Supreme Court by President Cleveland), also sat on the board of the Buffalo, Rochester and Pittsburgh Railway from 1881 to 1905.

140. For more on this jurist's early economic links, which reportedly had much to do with his elevation to the high Court, see George Shiras, 3rd, *Justice George Shiras, Jr. of Pittsburgh,* pp. 76–77 and 89–90.

141. John C. Gray, who was also a longtime professor at the Harvard law school, served

as a vice-president of the Brahmin-controlled Massachusetts Hospital Life Insurance Co. from 1888 to 1915. In the early 1900s another member of the firm, Roland Boyden, was a director of the First National Bank of Boston, and his colleague, Thomas N. Perkins, sat on the board of the Suffolk Savings Bank and the National Bank of Commerce (of Boston).

142. Note that while Justice Henry B. Brown had served as a federal judge since 1875, he had earlier been a member of a Detroit law firm whose two chief partners were John S. Newberry, who was closely associated with the potent McMillan and Joy interests, and Ashley Pond, who sat on the board of the Vanderbilt-controlled Michigan Central Railroad up through 1906. However, since these links had been established many years earlier, they may have been of relatively little significance by the turn of the century.

143. Holmes's mother was a daughter of Boston merchant and entrepreneur Patrick Tracy Jackson, who was a brother-in-law of Francis Cabot Lowell, another elite figure. Moreover, Holmes himself married the granddaughter of Nathaniel Bowditch, one of the founders and early prime movers of the Massachusetts Hospital Life Insurance Co. For more on the business opposition to his nomination, see John A. Garraty, "Holmes' Appointment to the U.S. Supreme Court," *New England Quarterly* (Sept. 1949), pp. 292–94.

144. The appointment was first offered to William Howard Taft, who was then serving as president of the U.S. Philippine Commission, but he declined apparently because of the pressing nature of his recently assumed special governmental duty. A few years later, when Associate Justice Henry B. Brown resigned, Taft was again tendered a seat on the Supreme Court, and again refused, this time primarily because of his growing presidential aspirations.

145. Also, according to one source, Day had been retained up to the late 1890s by a large number of business enterprises, the most prominent of which was apparently the Baltimore and Ohio Railroad. See Vernon H. Roelofs, "Justice William R. Day and Federal Regulation," *Mississippi Valley Historical Review* (June 1950), p. 42.

146. Moody was actually Roosevelt's fourth choice for this post. The President first offered this seat to Pennsylvania Senator (and former Attorney General) Philander Knox, who was closely tied to the Mellon banking interests in Pittsburgh, next to Secretary of War William Howard Taft, and then to his Secretary of State, Elihu Root, who had until recently been a director of several major financial institutions in New York City. See Henry J. Abraham, *Justices and Presidents*, p. 153.

147. For more on Moody's former clients, see Leon Friedman & Fred L. Israel (eds.), *The Justices of the United States Supreme Court, 1789–1969*, Vol. III, p. 1804.

148. Although three is too small a number from which to generalize, it would appear that, for whatever reason, Roosevelt's Supreme Court appointees were less closely linked to important business interests than were his major Cabinet officers and chief diplomatic emissaries.

149. White's clients included the New Orleans branch of Lehman Brothers, with which family he maintained close personal and financial ties for many years. See Allan Nevins, *Herbert H. Lehman and His Era*, p. 20. Also see Kenneth B. Umbreit, *Our Eleven Chief Justices* (New York: Harper & Bros., 1938), pp. 369–78, and Marie C. Klinkhamer, *Edward Douglass White: Chief Justice of the United States* (Washington, D.C.: Catholic University of America Press, 1943), pp. 1–20.

150. See Leon Friedman & Fred L. Israel (eds.), *The Justices of the United States Supreme Court, 1789–1969*, Vol. III, pp. 1973–78; Alexander M. Bickel, "Mr. Taft Rehabilitates the Court," *Yale Law Journal* (Nov. 1969), p. 23; and Clarinda Pendleton Lamar, *The Life of Joseph Rucker Lamar* (New York: G. P. Putnam's Sons, 1926), p. 22. This Georgia patrician was a second cousin of Lucius Q. C. Lamar, who had served for three years as Secretary of the Interior under Grover Cleveland and was appointed to the Supreme Court in 1888. Not surprisingly, Joseph Lamar's selection was strongly supported (by means of phone calls to key Cabinet members) by such prominent politico-economic figures as Alexander C. King, who was a senior partner in the Atlanta law firm of King and Spalding

and general counsel to a number of railroads over the years. See John P. Frank, "The Appointment of Supreme Court Justices: Prestige, Principles and Politics," *Wisconsin Law Review* (May 1941), p. 378.

151. See Leon Friedman & Fred L. Israel, *op. cit.*, Vol. III, pp. 1945–48, and Lewis L. Gould, *Wyoming: A Political History, 1868–1896* (New Haven, Conn.: Yale University Press, 1968), pp. 13, 62–63, 79, 126, and 213. For more on Warren's efforts to help secure Van Devanter's appointment to the high Court, see G. Edward White, *The American Judicial Tradition* (New York: Oxford University Press, 1976), pp. 182–83.

152. See Friedman & Israel, *op. cit.*, Vol. III, p. 2002. However, as *Poor's Railroad Manual* shows, Pitney also sat on the board of the (fairly small) East Tennessee and Western North Carolina Railroad from 1902 to 1908, during which period he was a member of the New Jersey Supreme Court.

153 Justice Pitney also was related through his mother, the former Sarah Halsted, to several other important figures such as W. Emlen Roosevelt (who was a vice-president of both the Buffalo, Rochester and Pittsburgh Railway and the Central and South American Telegraph Co., and a director of numerous other concerns), Hamilton F. Kean (who had just been appointed to the board of the Buffalo, Rochester and Pittsburgh Railway), and John Kean (who was a longtime high official of the Manhattan Trust Co.).

154. Justice Lurton apparently did not have any business ties other than his early affiliation with a Clarksville, Tennessee bank. But all authorities have described him as a very conservative person, much concerned about property rights. He belonged to a wing of the state Democratic party that was dominated by an oligarchy of old families. See Roger L. Hart, *Redeemers, Bourbons & Populists,* pp. 62–66; David M. Tucker, "Justice Harold H. Lurton," *American Journal of Legal History* (July 1969), pp. 226–30; and Friedman & Israel, *op. cit.*, Vol. III, pp. 1847–55. In his famous *History of the Supreme Court of the United States,* Gustavus Myers maintained (p. 718) that Lurton had, prior to 1886, been a member of a law firm which was closely linked with railroad interests. The author has found no data to confirm this claim, and even if accurate, it is of such a distant nature as to be of doubtful import.

155. For more on Hughes's early years as a New York lawyer, see Merlo J. Pusey, *Charles Evans Hughes* (New York: Macmillan, 1951), Vol. 1, pp. 74–117, and Robert F. Wesser, *Charles Evans Hughes: Politics and Reform in New York State, 1905–1910* (Ithaca, N.Y.: Cornell University Press, 1967). p. 26. Judging from a statement found in Wesser's work, Hughes and his partners may have been unwelcome outsiders on Wall Street, for Hughes claimed that in the 1880s and 1890s "the giants in the profession were retained in the more important litigation and dominated the legal scene. Their firms were entrenched financially and socially, having as regular clients the large monied institutions and transportation companies. These highly privileged firms seemed to hold in an enduring grasp the best professional opportunities and to leave little room for young aspirants outside the favored groups."

156. For a general treatment of these cases, see Ernest S. Bates, *The Story of the Supreme Court* (Indianapolis: Bobbs-Merrill, 1936), pp. 232–41.

157. For a similar verdict applied to a somewhat longer period (1889–1919), see John R. Schmidhauser, *The Supreme Court: Its Politics, Personalities and Procedures,* p. 31.

158. On the other hand, the NAM, which was controlled essentially by medium-sized and small companies, placed no representatives in high federal posts during this period, a revealing sign of its relative weakness.

CHAPTER 5

The Wilson Administration

The eight-year period from 1913 to 1921 was marked by a number of major changes in the political and economic life of the nation. First, because of a serious split in the Republican ranks created by Theodore Roosevelt's bolt to run as the Progressive party candidate for President in 1912, the Democrats held the reins of executive power in the country for the first eight-year stretch since the Civil War. In the first part of this period a significant number of important governmental and financial reform measures were passed, in sharp contrast to the preceding administrations. But in the latter years, the United States became immersed in a major international conflict, World War I, which resulted in a massive mobilization of the country's military and economic resources and also, almost of necessity, in a curtailment in the government's regulatory and social service efforts. In addition, largely as an outgrowth of the wartime expansion in industrial production and the continuation of certain long-term trends, America's economic structure was altered markedly, with various corporate enterprises reaching new heights in both size and sales.

Nowhere was this growth more striking than in the realm of manufacturing. While about 20 industrial concerns had assets of more than $100 million in 1913, a like number had climbed into the over-$250 million category by 1921, this in the space of just eight years. A list of the nation's 25 largest industrial enterprises, as of 1921, is provided in Table 5. It shows that many industrial concerns grew at such a rapid rate during this period that they now rivaled all but the very largest railroads, such as the Pennsylvania and New York Central.[2] Not only that, these years saw the emergence of a number of major new concerns, many of which had to do with the production and use of automobiles. As a matter of fact, although the giant U.S. Steel Corp. still eclipsed all other industrial enterprises, by 1921, ten of the top 25 firms in the country were either oil or automotive companies. Hence it might be said that these eight years marked the beginning of the modern industrial era.

A number of the nation's key financial institutions also grew at a rather

TABLE 5

America's Top 25 Industrial Concerns in 1921

Rank	Company	1913 Assets ($ millions)	1921 Assets ($ millions)
1.	United States Steel Corp.	1,636	2,339
2.	Standard Oil Co. of N.J.	357	1,102
3.	American Telephone & Telegraph Co.	656	1,050
4.	General Motors Corp.	59	515
5.	Armour & Co.	156	481
6.	Bethlehem Steel Corp.	96	366
7.	Swift & Co.	152	362
8.	Standard Oil Co. of N.Y.	103	348
9.	Ford Motor Co.	35	345
10.	Sinclair Consolidated Oil Corp.	—*	343
11.	United States Rubber Co.	186	340
12.	General Electric Co.	132	339
13.	Texas Co.	68	336
14.	Standard Oil Co. of Ind.	49	306
15.	International Mercantile Marine Co.	194	290
16.	Anaconda Copper Mining Co.	198	281
17.	Standard Oil Co. of Cal.	88	277
18.	Gulf Oil Corp.	43	273
19.	Midvale Steel & Ordinance Co.	17	271
20.	Allied Chemical & Dye Corp.	—†	267
21.	International Harvester Co.	130	267
22.	E. I. du Pont de Nemours & Co.	75	252
23.	Western Union Telegraph Co.	168	249
24.	Phelps Dodge Corp. (its post-1917 name)	57	228
25.	New York Shipbuilding Corp.	under 5	216

*Company created in 1919
†Company created in 1920

striking rate during this critical eight-year period. However, most of those that did so were located in New York City, which by this time had clearly become America's chief economic center. Indeed there were only two commercial banks outside of New York City which had (officially stated) assets of over $300 million as of 1921, as may be seen by a look at Table 6.[3] An examination of the make-up of the officers and directors of these institutions reveals that five of the top ten banks in the country—the Guaranty Trust Co., National Bank of Commerce, First National Bank of New York, Chase National Bank, and Bankers Trust Co.—were either controlled by or closely linked with (the privately-owned) J. P. Morgan & Co., which, since the death of its founder in 1913, had been run mainly by Morgan's able lieutenants Henry P. Davison and Thomas W. Lamont.[4]

TABLE 6

America's Top 10 Banks in 1921

Rank	Bank	Early 1913 Assets ($ millions)	Early 1921 Assets ($ millions)
1.	National City Bank, N.Y.C.	265	1,044
2.	Guaranty Trust Co., N.Y.C.	247	924
3.	National Bank of Commerce, N.Y.C.	195	553
4.	Chase National Bank, N.Y.C.	124	535
5.	First National Bank of N.Y.C.	142	466
6.	Continental & Commercial National Bank, Chicago	201	418
7.	Bankers Trust Co., N.Y.C.	190	413
8.	Mechanics & Metals National Bank, N.Y.C.	84	320
9.	Equitable Trust Co., N.Y.C.	94	318
10.	Union Trust Co., Cleveland	53	311

However, the nation's largest bank, the National City Bank of New York, was still dominated by the Stillman-Rockefeller forces (and to a lesser extent, the Taylor-Pyne interests), although this influence was exerted indirectly after the death of its longtime chief executive, James Stillman, in 1918. In addition, another big concern, the Equitable Trust Co. (of New York City), had come under the control of the Rockefeller family shortly before the start of this period.[5] But this development did not seriously threaten the preeminence of the House of Morgan in the overall economic structure of the country, a crucial position pointed up by the much-publicized revelations of the so-called Pujo Committee.[6]

Some of the major insurance companies also grew markedly during the Wilson years. In fact, two concerns—the Metropolitan Life Insurance Co. and the (Newark-based) Prudential Insurance Co. of America—had expanded so rapidly under unusually able and vigorous management that they had soared to or near the top of the insurance field by 1921, as shown in Table 7.

TABLE 7

America's 5 Largest Life Insurance Companies in 1921

Rank	Company	1913 Assets ($ millions)	1921 Assets ($ millions)
1.	Metropolitan Life Insurance Co.	448	1,116
2.	New York Life Insurance Co.	748	953
3.	Prudential Insurance Co. of America	323	790
4.	Mutual Life Insurance Co.	607	678
5.	Equitable Life Assurance Society	525	655

Although these five firms, which were located in the New York metropolitan area, maintained good working relations with various business enterprises, only one of them was intimately associated with one or the other of the two great financial complexes in the country. That was the Mutual Life Insurance Co., which was still closely linked with the House of Morgan.

There were two other noteworthy developments during this period. One involved the creation of the United States Chamber of Commerce, which was formed in the last part of the preceding administration at the request of President Taft, who reportedly felt the need, along with many economic leaders, for a nationwide body that would represent the interests of all important segments of the business community.[7] Judging by both its fairly substantial membership and the make-up of its board of directors, the Chamber was dominated in its early years by small- and medium-sized concerns, like the NAM. However, its effectiveness as a politico-economic unit has long been an unresolved issue, which probably could best be determined either through a detailed study of its relative success in influencing major governmental policy over time (no easy task for even the most dedicated researcher) or through an analysis of its ability to place its men in high federal office, from whence they could act to further their group interests.[8]

The other important organizational development during this period was the emergence as a major force of the Carnegie Endowment for International Peace, a body created in 1910 with funds provided by the famous steelmaster-philanthropist, Andrew Carnegie, to promote better diplomatic relations in the world.[9] Although this organization could best be described as a civic body (the bulk of its officers and trustees were governmental, ex-governmental, educational, and civic figures), it had a marked pro-business orientation. In 1915, for example, a sizable number of its trustees were influential corporate leaders who had no formal governmental experience, such as Cleveland H. Dodge (a high-ranking official of Phelps, Dodge & Co. and a director of the National City Bank of New York), Samuel Mather (former Secretary of State John Hay's brother-in-law, who was a wealthy Cleveland businessman and sat on the board of the U.S. Steel Corp. and the Lackawanna Steel Co.), and George W. Perkins (a former partner in J. P. Morgan & Co., chairman of the finance committee of the International Harvester Co., and a director of the Erie Railroad, International Mercantile Marine Co., New York Trust Co., and U.S. Steel Corp.). Furthermore, an almost equal number of the trustees of the Carnegie Endowment for International Peace were either former or active governmental officials who had long-standing ties to major business enterprises, such as Elihu Root (whose brother, Oren, was board chairman of the Central States Electric Corp.), Joseph H. Choate (a Wall Street lawyer and onetime Ambassador to Great Britain who served on the board of the New York Life Insurance and Trust Co., and whose son was a director of the Mutual Life Insurance Co.), Robert Bacon (a former partner in J. P. Morgan & Co. and American Ambassador to France who now served as a director of the U.S. Steel Corp.), and Oscar S. Straus (a New York mercantile figure and onetime Cabinet member who graced the board of the New York Life Insurance Co.). Indeed, even some of the Carnegie Endowment's civic and educational leaders had close links with the business community, as may be seen by the fact that one of its (1915) trustees, Henry S. Pritchett, president of the Carnegie Foundation for the Advancement of Teaching, also sat on the board of the Atchison, Topeka and Sante Fe Railway. Judging from this evidence, it might be said that the Carnegie Endowment for International Peace was America's first foreign policy "establishment."

Primarily because of the disastrous split between Taft and Theodore Roosevelt in 1912 over the Republican presidential nomination, America was led, from 1913 to 1921, by Woodrow Wilson, a man of a considerably different stripe than most earlier occupants of the White House. He was a scholar and university president who had turned recently to politics.[10] Wilson was, in fact, the first academic ever to hold the nation's highest office. He was probably best known as the able, reformist-oriented (though economically conservative) president of prestigious Princeton University, a position he held from 1902 to 1910.[11] Yet toward the end of his academic (administrative) career Wilson ran into a sea of controversy over the proposed location and control of a new graduate school and, perhaps more importantly, a planned reorganization of collegiate student life designed, in part, to eliminate the university's socially exclusive eating clubs. The moralistic Wilson firmly backed the latter move, much to the angry opposition of a number of wealthy, potent alumni and trustees. Indeed the reaction to this second plan was so strong that some of the school's most influential trustees, especially Moses Taylor Pyne (who was a major stockholder and longtime director of the big National City Bank of New York), dedicated themselves to work toward the ouster of Wilson as university president.[12] Thus the ambitious Wilson no doubt received a good deal of encouragement from various sources, including some figures closely associated with the university, when certain New York City and New Jersey leaders began to boost him as a gubernatorial candidate in 1910. He readily accepted the Democratic nomination and, with substantial organizational support, went on to score a resounding victory in that fall's statewide election.[13]

Wilson was first promoted as a political candidate by George Harvey, a New York executive who had once been associated in various public utility enterprises with William C. Whitney and Thomas Fortune Ryan, two powerful Wall Street financiers long allied with the Democratic party.[14] Later, around the turn of the century, when the Harper Brothers publishing company fell into serious financial difficulty, he was asked to become its head by J. P. Morgan, who by this time was the firm's principal fiscal backer and a close friend of Harvey's.[15] But after 1906 Harvey devoted much of his time to grooming Wilson first as a Democratic candidate for governor of New Jersey, a goal achieved in 1910, and thereafter as a prime contender for the presidential nomination in a reported effort to counter any drive by the "radical" William Jennings Bryan. However, in the closing months of the 1912 race Harvey's close ties to Wilson were reduced considerably, either because this conservative publisher became somewhat disenchanted with Wilson's increasing progressivism (which started during his years as governor of New Jersey) or because of a growing fear that Wilson would be viewed as a candidate backed by wealthy Eastern corporate interests.[16]

One of Wilson's other influential "behind-the-scenes" advisors was Colonel Edward M. House, a man who joined the New Jerseyan's growing political vanguard in 1911 and became by far his most important political strategist.[17] House had emerged some years earlier as the influential leader of the conservative wing of the Democratic party in Texas, which was much opposed to the progressive movement in the Long Star State.[18] He also apparently had a strong desire to play the role of "president-maker" in national affairs, and he shrewdly discerned in Wilson a promising electoral prospect.[19] Once duly installed in executive office, Wilson continued to rely heavily on House in both major personnel and policy matters. But, according to Arthur Link, House was more than a high-level advisor, for he also served as Wilson's chief informal link with the business and banking worlds.

At first glance, this would appear to have been an unusual role for a Texan, since the state was still considered something of a backwater, both economically and politically.[20] However, a close look at House's background and socio-economic ties reveals that he may well have played such a role. He had inherited a fortune from his father, T. W. House, who had large real estate, mercantile, and other holdings in Texas, and with these resources he had made substantial investments in various state and local (primarily Houston and Austin) businesses.[21] One of the most recent such ventures involved the construction and operation of a fairly sizable rail line in Texas known as the Trinity and Brazos Valley Railway, which was financed largely by money raised by the House family, some close business associates, and certain wealthy Boston Brahmins, and was headed by Colonel House from 1902 to 1908, when it was sold to a bigger company.[22] What's more, House himself served from 1903 to 1905 on the board of one of New York's larger financial institutions, the Equitable Trust Co. (a concern then closely linked with the much-troubled Equitable Life Assurance Society), which affiliation would indicate that, though House was by 1911 primarily a political leader, he was not unknown to Wall Street figures.[23]

Finally, it should be pointed out with reference to Wilson himself that, although he certainly did become more progressive as he became increasingly involved in state and national politics, there is still some question as to how liberal (or conservative) he was at heart. One reason for raising this query is that prior to embarking on his presidential drive Wilson served on two important boards—the Carnegie Foundation for the Advancement of Teaching, an essentially civic body, and the Mutual Life Insurance Co. of New York, a concern closely linked with the Morgan interests.[24] What makes the latter (1909–1911) association intriguing is that it was quite uncommon in those days for college presidents to sit on corporate boards, particularly of this size and nature. In fact, only one academic leader had previously served as a trustee of Mutual Life in the entire history of the company, and that person, Charles King, the mid-19th century president of Columbia College, had been an elite figure in his own right (the son of former Federalist leader Rufus King and the son-in-law of onetime wealthy New York City businessman Archibald Gracie).[25] Though Wilson resigned from the board of the Carnegie Foundation in November 1910 (two months before he assumed office as governor of New Jersey), he did not sever his connection with Mutual Life until July 1911, a curious and perhaps revealing time lag.[26]

Early Major Cabinet and Diplomatic Appointments

Further insight into Wilson's politico-economic leanings may also be gained through an examination of the high-level appointment process of his administration, particularly if one bears in mind the complex of forces which are often at work in such proceedings. The premier post of Secretary of State was extended out of political necessity (it was certainly not to Wilson's liking) to the Democratic party's longtime Western agrarian leader and Nebraska newspaperman, William Jennings Bryan, who had little knowledge of or experience in foreign affairs and was widely regarded as a dangerous radical. But because of Bryan's enormous popular support in the party and his crucial late switch to Wilson at the 1912 Democratic National Convention, the President apparently felt that he had no option other than to offer him a key Cabinet post, with the hope that he would prove amenable to the new administration.[27]

More revealing of the President's preferences was the selection of his Secretary of the Treasury. After considerable deliberation and maneuver, Wilson picked William G. McAdoo, a former New York lawyer and transit executive.[28] McAdoo had been the president of the Hudson and Manhattan Railroad Co. (and its predecessor concern, the New York and New Jersey Railroad Co.) for a little over a decade, during the last two years of which he had developed strong political interests and become quite active in Wilson's presidential campaign. According to Arthur Link, McAdoo was an astute choice, particularly from a political standpoint, for he was ". . . a prominent businessman yet not identified with 'Big Business,' a leading financier yet not allied with 'Wall Street,' " a reassuring view that has long been accepted by American historians.[29] Yet this assessment of McAdoo (which is apparently based on his own dubious, if not self-serving, claim) is simply incorrect. First, with regard to size, it is clear from published records that the Hudson and Manhattan Railroad Co. was a big enterprise, with assets of over $120 million in 1912 (which probably ranked it in the top 100 concerns in the country). Second, and even more important, a detailed analysis of the upper-level organizational structure of this interstate transit firm reveals that William G. McAdoo was, from the very outset, on close terms with various key Wall Street figures, particularly those associated with the House of Morgan. That this is so may be seen by a look at the following breakdown of the top officers and directors of the New York and New Jersey Railroad Co. (its initial name) in 1903:

President   William G. McAdoo

Vice-Presidents   Edmund C. Converse, president of both the Bankers Trust Co. and Liberty National Bank of New York City (also a director of the American Bank Note Co., Bowling Green Trust Co., International Nickel Co., International Steam Pump Co., North American Co., and U.S. Steel Corp.)

Walter G. Oakman, president of the Guaranty Trust Co. (also a director of the American Car & Foundry Co., Clarksburg Fuel Co., Corn Products Co., Interborough Rapid Transit Co., Long Island Railroad, Louisville & Nashville Railroad, Morton Trust Co., and Western National Bank of New York City.)

Outside Directors   Otto T. Bannard, president of the Continental Trust Co. of New York City

Anthony N. Brady, board chairman of the Brooklyn Rapid Transit Co. and president of the New York Edison Co. (also a director of the American Tobacco Co., Consolidated Gas Co. of New York, and Westinghouse Electric & Mfg. Co.)

Elbert H. Gary, board chairman of both the Allis-Chalmers Co. and U.S. Steel Corp. (also a director of the International Harvester Co.)

Frederic B. Jennings, partner in the New York law firm of Stetson, Jennings & Russell, vice-president of the First National Bank of North Bennington, Vt. (also a director of the Continental Trust Co. and the International Paper Co.)

John G. McCullough, president of the First National Bank of North Bennington, Vt. (also a director of the Atchison, Topeka & Sante Fe Rwy., Erie Railroad, and Lackawanna Steel Co.)

G. Tracy Rogers, vice-president of the New York Casualty Co. (also a Binghamton, N.Y. businessman)

David Young, president of Jersey City, Hoboken and Paterson Street Railway Co. (which was merged into the newly formed Public Service Corp. of N.J. in mid-1903)

Edward F. C. Young, president of the First National Bank of Jersey City and the Colonial Life Insurance Co. of America (also a director of the Bowling Green Trust Co., Distilling Co. of America, Jersey City, Hoboken and Paterson Street Railway, and the Liberty National Bank of NYC)

John S. Williams, president of the Richmond Trust & Safe Deposit Co. of Va., Seaboard Air·Line Railway, and the Florida Central & Peninsular RR Co. (also a director of the Bowling Green Trust Co.)

Thus the two vice-presidents of McAdoo's newly formed New York and New Jersey Railroad Co. were, in their primary capacities, the chief executive officers of two of the biggest banks in New York City, both of which were part of the House of Morgan, and at least three of the outside directors of the company were also closely linked with this vast financial complex (one of them was, in fact, a senior partner in the "Morgan" law firm of Stetson, Jennings & Russell).[30] Moreover, many of these interests were still intimately associated with the Hudson and Manhattan Railroad Co. (and its parent concern, the Hudson Companies) in 1912, the last full year in which McAdoo was affiliated with this enterprise. In this latter year, for example, the outside directors of the Hudson and Manhattan Railroad Co. included Frederic B. Jennings; John G. McCullough; Elbert H. Gary; William M. Barnum, president of the Morgan-dominated Pacific Coast Co. (and a director of the American Locomotive Co., Bethlehem Steel Corp., and the Electrical Securities Corp.); Lewis L. Clarke, president of the American Exchange National Bank of New York City (and a director of the American Locomotive Co.); and Pliny Fisk, another New York City banker who sat on the boards of the American Exchange National Bank, American Locomotive Co., Bethlehem Steel Corp., and Electrical Securities Corp.[31] Hence, contrary to what has been claimed, it would appear that McAdoo was basically an ambitious politico-economic figure who until his entry into the Cabinet had been closely linked with the Morgan interests.[32] And shortly after he entered the Cabinet, McAdoo solidified his political position when he married the President's daughter.[33]

After much consultation and negotiation which eliminated more than one prime prospect, President Wilson selected, at the suggestion of his trusted advisor, Colonel House, a onetime Nashville lawyer (and local bank official), James C. McReynolds, to serve as his first Attorney General.[34] McReynolds had acted as an Assistant Attorney General for four years during the Roosevelt administration, and was shortly thereafter appointed to serve as special counsel to the federal government on antitrust matters. Because of the latter role, many mistakenly thought him to be a liberal.[35] However, McReynolds, who later served briefly (in 1912–1913) as a New York City attorney, turned out to be a poor choice at the Justice Department, in considerable part because of his cantankerous personality, which soon led to severely strained relations within the Cabinet. To resolve this problem, he was "kicked upstairs" to a seat on the United States Supreme Court in August 1914—in retrospect, an extremely shortsighted measure. As his replacement, Wilson chose, again at the urging of Colonel House, a former Austin, Texas lawyer, Thomas W. Gregory, who had very little experience in federal affairs, but was a close friend and staunch ally of the influential House. Gregory was also fairly conservative and had at least one corporate link, since he had served on the board of the Citizens Bank & Trust Co., a fairly small local concern with which House had once been affiliated.[36]

As his Secretary of the Navy, Wilson chose, out of deference to Southern interests and the Bryan wing of the party, a longtime Raleigh, North Carolina newspaper publisher named Josephus Daniels.[37] Unlike many Cabinet members, Daniels had no major corporate or family ties and was often at odds with business interests in his home state.[38] Although he reportedly was not an effective administrator, Daniels got along well with President Wilson and was consequently able to resist various devious or subtle efforts to remove him from high federal office.[39]

After much delay (and at least one rebuff), President Wilson chose as his Secretary of the Interior a former San Francisco lawyer and Democratic party leader named Franklin K. Lane, in a move designed largely to placate Western interests. But his selection stemmed basically from pressure exerted by Colonel House, who had important political connections in many sections of the country.[40] In addition, Lane, who had a progressive image, had a fair amount of experience at the federal level of government, having served for the seven preceding years as a member of the Interstate Commerce Commission.[41] Probably also in his favor, up to the early 1900s he had been associated (along with his brother) with the Independent Oil Producers Agency in California, a group which presumably favored the development of the West's petroleum resources.

Wilson selected a second Midwesterner, David F. Houston, as his Secretary of Agriculture. But this man was clearly no Bryan supporter. Although he had no formal governmental experience, Houston apparently appealed to the President partly because he was an able academic, who had served since 1908 as chancellor of Washington University in St. Louis, and before that as president of Texas ·A. and M. and of the University of Texas. Actually, Houston was, because of his former Texas ties, another Cabinet nominee of the influential Colonel House, and also of Walter Hines Page, whom he reportedly met through his work with the Rockefeller-endowed General Education Board and the Southern Education Board.[42] Houston was closely linked to certain St. Louis leaders too, particularly Robert S. Brookings, who, upon his partial withdrawal from business activity, had devoted much of his time as chairman of the board of trustees to overseeing the affairs of Washington University.[43] Whether Brookings played any part in Houston's appointment is unknown. However, Brookings had at least one important link to Washington politico-economic circles, for he had sat for several years on the board of the prestigious Carnegie Endowment for International Peace, along with such prominent figures as former Morgan partner and federal official Robert Bacon, Cleveland businessman Samuel Mather, New York's onetime Cabinet member Oscar S. Straus, and President Wilson's friend, Cleveland H. Dodge. And Houston himself served as a director of the St. Louis Terminal Cupples Station & Property Co. from 1913 to 1916 (when this concern, which was headed by Brookings, was merged into a larger company). Though only one piece of evidence, this association would indicate that Houston's outlook on agriculture was essentially that of a businessman. Indeed, he was strongly opposed to any federal aid to the nation's hard-pressed small farmers or any other underprivileged group.[44]

For the now separate post of Secretary of Commerce, President Wilson made, at the behest of various liberal forces, another serious effort to appoint Boston's well-known and progressive leader, Louis Brandeis. But because of the vehement opposition mounted by important business interests, registered largely through Colonel House and Wilson's much wealthier friend, Cleveland H. Dodge, this idea was ultimately abandoned. The President chose instead a relatively obscure New York Congressman and minor industrial executive named William C. Redfield.[45] Besides serving in the House of Representatives for the last two years, Redfield had held a number of second-echelon management posts with several small or medium-sized concerns over the years, hardly the sort of business credentials one would expect of the first person selected to hold this high "clientele" post. Redfield may, however, have been appointed for another reason, a rarely-noted key secondary connection, for he had been a trustee of the big Equitable Life Assurance Society since 1905.[46]

And finally for the newly created (spin-off) post of Secretary of Labor, President Wilson picked a Pennsylvania Congressman, William B. Wilson, who prior to holding this federal office had served for eight years as the secretary-treasurer of the United Mine Workers of America.[47] Wilson (who was no relation to the President) had also been chairman of the House Labor Committee during his last term in Congress. His appointment, moreover, had been strongly urged by Samuel Gompers, the longtime president of the American Federation of Labor, who, in fact, met with the President-elect to help promote this choice. Partly because of this pressure, and the obvious political logic of the selection, Pennsylvania's William B. Wilson became the first former union official to be accorded a Cabinet position in the nation's history.

In the realm of foreign relations, President Wilson initially offered the premier post of Ambassador to Great Britain to two able, though distinctly conservative men—former Harvard College president Charles W. Eliot (who was born into a wealthy family, married into two others, and sat on the board of the elitist Carnegie Endowment for International Peace) and, even more revealingly, former Cleveland Cabinet member Richard Olney (who was a director of AT&T, the Boston and Maine Railroad, Old Colony Trust Co., and Massachusetts Electric Companies). But for various reasons, both men declined. At this juncture Wilson turned to a longtime friend, Walter Hines Page, who had served since 1899 as a vice-president of the New York publishing concern of Doubleday, Page & Co. (now Doubleday & Co.), in which capacity he had worked largely as a literary editor.[48] Page, who came from a wealthy Southern family, was a highly conservative person who had little use for William Jennings Bryan and other progressive leaders.[49] This bias was probably reinforced by his later association with elitist leaders in New York, particularly those he met while serving as a trustee of the General Education Board, a philanthropic body devoted to improving health and educational conditions in the South, which had been created and financed largely by the Rockefeller interests.[50] In 1912 this organization was headed by the Rockefeller family's primary financial advisor, Frederick T. Gates, who served as a vice-president of the Colorado Fuel & Iron Co. and as a director of such (mostly Rockefeller-controlled) concerns as the American Linseed Co., American Shipbuilding Co., Western Maryland Railway, and up to 1911 the Missouri-Pacific Railway. The board contained many other prominent economic figures such as John D. Rockefeller, Jr. (who was a director of the American Linseed Co., Colorado Fuel & Iron Co., and Delaware, Lackawanna & Western Railroad), Starr J. Murphy (who was a vice-president of the American Linseed Co. and a director of the Colorado Fuel & Iron Co.), and Edgar L. Marston (a New York City banker who served on the board of the Astor Trust Co., Bankers Trust Co., Denver and Rio Grande Railway, Guaranty Trust Co., Missouri-Pacific Railway, and Western Maryland Railway). With these connections and his Anglophile background, Page mixed well with Britain's largely upper-class leaders.

After considerable delay (which stemmed largely from one abortive offer),[51] the President chose a former Ohio Congressman and businessman, William G. Sharp, as his Ambassador to France. Sharp had been a loyal Democratic supporter in the Lower House for the last six years. He had also been president of the fairly sizable Lake Superior Iron & Chemical Co. up to 1910 (and a director of this concern until 1912), but he had no formal links to any other important economic interests. Thus Sharp was apparently picked primarily for political reasons, although he probably had a strong pro-business point of view.

And finally, though initially reluctant to do so, Wilson selected as his Ambassador to Germany former New York state supreme court justice and attorney James W. Gerard, who, as Arthur Link has observed, ". . . contributed heavily to the Democratic war chest in 1912."[52] Gerard had reportedly secured his judicial post largely because of his ties with Tammany Hall. Up to 1908 he had been a member of a moderately prominent New York law firm, Bowers and Sands, and a director of the (medium-sized) Knickerbocker Trust Co. Through his marriage to the daughter of one of the founders of the big Anaconda Copper Mining Co., he had also come into a substantial fortune, which reportedly had much to do with his appointment.[53] However, as often happens with such inexperienced figures, Gerard proved to be a poor diplomat, this unfortunately during an extremely critical period in German-American relations.

Early Important Actions

One of the most crucial actions taken during the early years of the Wilson administration was the creation of the Federal Reserve System. This was done in 1913 in an effort to provide a strong stabilizing force for the nation's currency and general fiscal structure, which had witnessed many major booms and depressions since the Andrew Jackson–decreed demise of the second Bank of the United States in 1836.[54] Actually, the origins of this program go back to at least 1908 when the National Monetary Commission was established by Congressional edict following the great financial panic of 1907, during which J. P. Morgan acted as virtually a one-man national bank in shoring up the nation's shaky economy.[55] This select group, which was headed by wealthy Republican leader Nelson W. Aldrich (who was, up to 1911, a U.S. Senator with many influential connections), made an exhaustive study of this complex problem over a four-year period, and came up with a set of recommendations which called for an essentially privately-operated system of fiscal controls. The incoming Wilson regime initially rejected this plan because it was a Republican proposal and, to many, seemed contrary to sound democratic procedure.[56]

Interestingly enough, the initial response of the Wilson administration was to prepare, with the aid of House banking committee chairman Carter Glass, a Virginian closely linked with small-town interests, what amounted to a decentralized version of the big-banker–backed Aldrich plan, which would place control of the proposed system in private hands. But the more progressive wing of the party, led by Secretary of State William Jennings Bryan, objected vehemently to this scheme and insisted that its primary governing body, the Federal Reserve Board, be controlled by public figures. To this demand President Wilson and his more conservative advisors felt compelled to consent.[57] After much maneuver and debate, a bill was ultimately adopted that apparently satisfied most of the major economic and political parties involved.[58]

This law provided for the establishment of a seven-man Federal Reserve Board, which was to be composed of five persons picked by the President, with the advice and consent of the Senate, to serve for staggered ten-year terms, plus two ex-officio figures—the Secretary of the Treasury and the Comptroller of the Currency. Between eight and twelve Federal Reserve banks (and districts) were also to be created, each to be managed by a board which was to consist of three Class A directors (chosen by the bankers of that district), three Class B directors (chosen by its Federal Reserve members to represent those engaged in commerce or "some other industrial pursuit"), and three Class C directors (public members to be appointed by the Washington-based Federal Reserve Board itself). Though this complex measure fell short of creating a truly national or central bank, such as already existed in various European countries, it has nonetheless been described as ". . . a compromise between what the bankers wanted and what the most advanced progressives said the country needed," and as an outstanding example of "responsible leadership in action," a dual accolade which would seem to be warranted only if this legislation led to a form of fiscal control free from domination by vested interests.[59]

Perhaps the best indication of whether this law really was a soundly conceived compromise among various conflicting groups, and was, in fact, a laudable example of enlightened leadership on the part of the Wilson administration, can be ascertained through an examination of the types of men who were initially appointed to the Federal Reserve Board (in which selection process the President had a good deal of latitude, except that it was originally prescribed that at least two of the non-governmental members had to be persons "experienced in banking or finance" and that he could not pick more than one individual from a single Reserve district). The two ex-officio members were, as prescribed by law, the Secretary of the Treasury, William G. McAdoo, a former New York City lawyer and transit executive with some significant economic ties, particularly to the House of Morgan, and the Comptroller of the Currency (and also recent Assistant Secretary of the Treasury), John S. Williams, who until recently had been a Virginia banker, board chairman of the Raleigh and Charleston Railroad, president of the Georgia and Florida Railway, a director of the big Seaboard Air Line Railway, and, up to 1904, a director of McAdoo's Hudson and Manhattan Railroad Co.[60] The President appointed another of McAdoo's close associates, Assistant Secretary of the Treasury Charles S. Hamlin, a former Boston attorney who had married into a wealthy New York family, as a public member of the Federal Reserve Board.[61] The other openings on the Board were filled largely as a result of the initiative of President Wilson and his influential advisor, Colonel House, and were as follows:[62]

Frederick A. Delano   a Chicago executive who was president of the (New York-controlled) Wabash Railroad and a former director of the National Citizens' League for Sound Banking (a business-dominated group formed to work for major monetary reform in America). His brother, Warren Delano, was a director of the Louisville & Nashville Railroad and the Lackawanna Steel Co.

William P. G. Harding   president of the First National Bank of Birmingham; reportedly appointed at the request of Senator Oscar Underwood, whose father-in-law, Joseph H. Woodward, was a vice-president of this big Alabama bank and president of the fairly sizable Woodward Iron Co.

Adolph C. Miller   a professor of economics at the University of California, who had married the daughter of a once-prominent Chicago businessman, Otho S. A. Sprague, who had served as a director of the Morgan-Vanderbilt-dominated Pullman Co. up to his death in 1909

Paul M. Warburg   a partner in the New York City banking house of Kuhn, Loeb & Co., who had served on the board of the Baltimore and Ohio Railroad, Wells Fargo & Co., Westinghouse Electric & Mfg. Co., and National Bank of Commerce; Warburg had played an important role in the creation of the Federal Reserve System

Thus a vast majority of the nongovernmental figures who were appointed to the Federal Reserve Board were persons who had, directly or indirectly, many major business connections, particularly to important New York and Chicago interests.[63] Indeed, even the one academic among these appointees had key socio-economic ties. Not surprisingly, most of these individuals banded together to form a fairly cohesive group which, with a strong assist from the powerful New York Federal Reserve district, acted not only to create a stable monetary system, but also to promote fiscal policies favorable to banking and business interests.[64]

Another area in which the Wilson regime has received considerable acclaim for its legislative and administrative efforts is in the realm of antitrust activity. The first such measure to be enacted during this period, the Clayton Antitrust Act, tried to make the Sherman Antitrust Act (of 1890) more effective by proscribing a number of "unfair" trade practices, such as pricing action that would lessen competition or create monopolistic conditions, the acquisition by corporations of stock in competing concerns, and interlocking directorates in industrial and financial firms above a certain size.[65] However, because of various gaps and deficiencies, this law was actually quite weak and viewed as inadequate almost from the outset.[66]

Soon pressure was generated for the adoption of a more meaningful measure providing for the creation of a separate institutionalized mechanism for governmental oversight and regulation of (improper) business activity. Indeed, such action had been advocated for some time by a number of major economic interests, particularly the big business–dominated National Civic Federation, which apparently were uneasy about the ambiguous status of many corporations and business practices under the vaguely worded (and erratically enforced) Sherman Antitrust Act of 1890.[67] After much consultation and maneuver, Congress finally passed a law which had been framed largely by (informal) White House advisor Louis D. Brandeis, who was an ardent defender of small business, and perhaps even more importantly, by New York lawyer-lobbyist George Rublee, who was reportedly both a member of the Progressive party and a legislative spokesman for the U.S. Chamber of Commerce.[68] In brief, this measure called for the creation of an independent regulatory body known as the Federal Trade Commission, which was to be directed by a board of five members (no more than three of whom could be from one political party) who were to be appointed by the President, with the advice and consent of the Senate, for seven-year terms. This agency was granted substantial power and was explicitly authorized to investigate and prevent unfair competition through the issuance of "cease and desist" orders, which edits would be enforced by the federal courts. However, as Gabriel Kolko has pointed out, although this law was of a more specific nature than the recently adopted Clayton Antitrust Act, it was still couched in rather general terms that left considerable room for a wide range of administrative action (or inaction) on the part of the commissioners. Thus the initial selection of these officials was a matter of prime importance and a good indication of the strength of Wilson's initial commitment to this cause.[69]

Of the first five commissioners picked to serve on this body, three stood out as especially influential in shaping agency policy during these critical early years. One of these was George Rublee, who had played a vital role in both molding the content and securing the passage of this measure, and hence had special knowledge and insight into its every clause. Although a member of the Progressive party, Rublee was also, interestingly, a director of the fairly sizable American Coal Products Co. from 1913 to 1915, as well as a member of the trust committee of the U.S. Chamber of Commerce.[70] But perhaps even more significantly, he had been a Wall Street lawyer for many years, practicing first (from 1898 to 1910) with a prominent corporate attorney, Victor Morawetz, who served up through 1910 on the board of the Guantanamo Sugar Co., (Morgan-dominated) National Bank of Commerce, Niagara Falls Power Co., and Norfolk and Western Railway (and, up to 1908, as chairman of the executive committee of the Atchison, Topeka & Santa Fe Railway). From 1910 to 1913, Rublee was associated with the New York law firm of Spooner and Cotton, whose last-named partner was a longtime director of the National Railroad Co. of Mexico.[71] Thus Rublee, who only served on the Federal

Trade Commission for a total of fifteen months (he had merely received a "recess" appointment because of intense Democratic opposition), would certainly appear to have been favorably disposed toward business interests.[72]

As the first chairman of the Federal Trade Commission, the President picked a relatively young Madison, Wisconsin lawyer and state Democratic leader, Joseph E. Davies. Little is known about Davies at this stage in his career other than the fact that he had helped to manage Wilson's 1912 campaign in the Middle West, for which effort he was rewarded at the outset of the administration with the position of head of the Bureau of Corporations. Since this agency was in a sense the organizational predecessor of the Federal Trade Commission, Davies's selection was an eminently logical choice. However, Davies was linked with certain influential politico-economic interests in Wisconsin, since he had married the daughter of Ashland entrepreneur John H. Knight, who was for many years a close business and political associate of former state Democratic party chieftain and railroad attorney William F. Vilas, who had been a member of Grover Cleveland's first Cabinet, as well as a major force in various lumber, financial, and real estate enterprises.[73] Though Davies served only briefly as chairman of the Federal Trade Commission, he reportedly worked, as one might expect, to shape this body's policies to suit important business interests, especially by establishing informal advisory channels for such parties.[74]

The third key figure to serve on the Federal Trade Commission in the pre–World War I period was Chicago manufacturer Edward N. Hurley. Unlike Rublee and Davies, Hurley had no previous significant involvement in antitrust (or federal regulatory) matters, but soon after his appointment assumed a very prominent role in agency affairs and was, largely as a result, designated its chairman when Davies stepped down from this position in 1916.[75] Little explanation has been offered as to why Hurley, the apparently able head of the relatively small Hurley Machine Co., was appointed to this body, aside perhaps from the fact that he had recently served as president of the Illinois Manufacturers Association and as United States Trade Commissioner to Latin America (a new and not yet prestigious post). However, another reason for his selection may have been that, although Hurley appeared to be essentially a small business figure, he was a director of the big Chicago Great Western Railroad, whose board included various prominent officials with Chicago or New York City ties.[76] While his railroad connection did not constitute a formal conflict of interest (such concerns were regulated by the ICC), Hurley's link with the Chicago Great Western Railroad brought him into close contact with a number of important business leaders, which may have done much, perhaps unconsciously, to help shape his thinking on antitrust and related trade activities. Given this type of appointment, it is little wonder that the Federal Trade Commission got off to a slow start and exhibited a marked pro-business orientation in the pre–World War I period.[77]

That Wilson and many of his most influential advisors were essentially conservative can also be seen from some of the fiscal policies that were pursued by his administration. For instance, in his annual message to Congress in December 1915, which dealt in part with the need to raise an additional $300 million to pay for the nation's new military preparedness program, the President followed the advice of his Secretary of the Treasury, William G. McAdoo, and recommended a plan in which, according to Arthur Link, the burden ". . . would [fall] much more heavily on the middle and lower classes than upon the rich who paid, relative to their wealth, scarcely any tax at all."[78] However, a number of progressive Democrats in Congress, led by North Carolina's Claude Kitchin, objected strenuously to this scheme, and fought instead for a major increase in the income tax (which was then scaled at a rather modest 1 to 6 percent), the enactment of an inheritance tax to tap other sources of (unearned) wealth, and the imposition of a special levy on the country's munitions manufacturers. As a result of this strong pressure, Wilson was, much to the dismay of conservatives, forced to accept a measure that raised the tax on incomes of over $40,000 a year from the old ceiling of 6 percent to a new maximum of 10 percent, created a federal estate tax (which ranged initially from 1 to 5 percent), and imposed an unprecedented levy of from 5 to 8 percent on the gross earnings of munitions makers. This law was, to again quote Arthur Link, ". . . a landmark in American history, the first really important victory of the movement, begun by the Populists in the 1890's and carried on by progressives in the early 1900's, for a federal tax policy based upon ability to pay."[79] Yet, as even this generally friendly authority has observed, Wilson played a passive, if not reluctant, part in these proceedings.[80]

Later Major Cabinet and Diplomatic Appointments

The conservative character of the Wilson regime was even more emphatically revealed by the type of men the President chose to appoint to high office in the middle and later years of his administration, as the country became increasingly involved in the First World War. In June 1915, following a series of bitter disagreements with the President over America's increasingly close diplomatic and financial ties with two of the Allied countries enmeshed in this great conflict, Britain and France, Secretary of State William Jennings Bryan, who was the most important liberal force in the Cabinet, resigned from the Wilson administration because of its failure, as he saw it, to adhere to a truly neutral foreign policy.[81] Forced suddenly to find a replacement for this popular Democratic leader, whose post could not, without risk, be left vacant for very long, the President turned to the recently appointed counselor to the State

Department, Robert Lansing. This primarily Washington-based attorney had been engaged for many years (up to 1907, when he became associate editor of a prestigious legal journal) in the international law practice of his father-in-law, John W. Foster, who had served briefly as Secretary of State under Benjamin Harrison, but who had devoted much of his life, especially after 1893, to this highly specialized legal field.[82] Lansing himself was a moderately wealthy and distinctly conservative figure, who, though he had no major corporate links, might best be described as a "Grover Cleveland" Democrat.[83] In fact, Lansing's rise in both the legal world and the federal government reportedly stemmed largely from his association with his still influential father-in-law, who served at this time on the board of the elitist-dominated Carnegie Endowment for International Peace, along with such prominent persons as New York Senator and former Secretary of State Elihu Root; Robert Bacon, a former Morgan partner, Assistant Secretary of State, and American Ambassador to France, who was still a director of the U.S. Steel Corp.; St. Louis civic and business leader Robert S. Brookings; President Wilson's close friend, industrialist Cleveland H. Dodge; Samuel Mather, a wealthy Cleveland executive who sat on the board of the Lackawanna Steel Co. and U.S. Steel Corp. (and had been a brother-in-law of former Secretary of State John Hay); and Progressive party leader George W. Perkins, who was chairman of the executive committee of the International Harvester Co. (and a director of the Erie Railroad, International Mercantile Marine Co., New York Trust Co., and U.S. Steel Corp.).[84] Thus, with the apparent backing of America's first foreign policy "establishment," Lansing served as Wilson's chief diplomatic official up through the critical war years to early 1920, when, because of a growing personal breach created partly by the stroke Wilson suffered in his strenuous efforts to secure American support for the League of Nations, he was forced to resign from this high office.[85]

At this late date in the now much-troubled Wilson administration, the President decided to appoint a New York lawyer, Bainbridge Colby, as Lansing's successor. This ambitious man did not have Lansing's elitist connections or his extensive experience in diplomatic affairs, though he had recently served as a member of the U.S. Shipping Board, an ad hoc emergency agency created to help mobilize America's economic and military resources during World War I. To many, Colby's appointment came as a distinct surprise (some even ascribed it to Wilson's severely debilitated condition), for he had until recently been a prominent Republican and Progressive party leader whose motives for switching to the Wilson regime were viewed as suspect. Colby had much earlier served as a director of the American Deposit and Loan Co., which New York concern (known after 1902 as the Equitable Trust Co.) was controlled by the Equitable Life Assurance Society, a faction-ridden firm with whose internal struggles Colby himself became involved, probably to his future detriment. Toward the end of the decade, he also graced the board of the Nevada Smelting and Refining Corp., a fairly small enterprise. These two ties would indicate that although Colby was favorably disposed toward business, he had apparently become something of an economic "outsider" who had turned to politics as a better way to achieve fame and fortune.[86] However, since Colby held office only during the last year of the Wilson administration, when most of the major diplomatic issues had already been resolved, his role as Secretary of State was a relatively minor one.[87]

When Secretary of the Treasury William G. McAdoo resigned from office at the end of the First World War to return to the more lucrative legal profession, the President turned, after much deliberation and one major rebuff, to Virginia's longtime Democratic Congressman, Carter Glass, who had served briefly as chairman of the House Banking and Currency Committee, and in that capacity had played an important part in the establishment of the Federal Reserve System.[88] Glass was a Lynchburg, Virginia newspaperman who was well known for his conservative views, which had probably been reinforced in recent years through his directorship links with two small local banks. Perhaps even more important was the fact that through his work in Congress, particularly in helping to frame the Federal Reserve bill in a way which was basically acceptable to the nation's banking interests, Glass proved to be a man who, while not the first choice of many parties, was still eminently agreeable to major segments of the business community. However, Glass held office for only a little over a year, resigning early in 1920 when he secured a seat in the U.S. Senate. He was replaced by Wilson's able Secretary of Agriculture, David F. Houston, who was a former high-ranking academic official (at Washington University in St. Louis and before that at two Texas universities) and a close friend of both Colonel House and St. Louis business-civic leader Robert S. Brookings, a trustee of the Carnegie Endowment for International Peace. Judging from all accounts (and his lucrative post-Cabinet employment), Houston was, if anything, more conservative than either of his two Democratic predecessors, an appointment trend which was manifest in other areas of the administration as well.[89]

When Colonel House's political ally Thomas W. Gregory resigned as Attorney General in early 1919, he was replaced by a northeastern Pennsylvania lawyer and Democratic leader, A. Mitchell Palmer, who was reputed to be a liberal, but soon exhibited very different qualities. Palmer had served in Congress from 1909 to 1915, and, apparently largely for political reasons, had compiled a rather progressive record. Then from 1917 to 1919 he had acted as Alien Property Custodian for the United States government, a special wartime position.[90] Palmer had been seriously considered for the position of Attorney General at the outset of the Wilson administration, only to lose out because of the strenuous objections of the Bryan forces in the party, who maintained that he should not be appointed to this high office because he represented, as local counsel, both the Delaware, Lackawanna and Western Railroad and the Lehigh Coal and Navigation Co., two sizable concerns.[91] As a result, it was not until after World War I that Palmer was chosen to serve as Attorney General. And with the marked conservative shift in American public opinion after the war, sparked in part by exaggerated fears aroused by the Bolshevik Revolution, it was not long before Palmer, who still served on at least two northeastern Pennyslvania bank boards, turned sharply against all so-called radical forces in the country and, even more significantly, took a clearly hostile line against much union activity. Indeed, according to one reliable source, Palmer gave as Attorney General ". . . an exhibition of antilabor activity unmatched since Richard Olney used the Justice Department to harry Coxey's Army and smash the Pullman strike in 1894."[92]

Another major change in the administration took place in March 1916 when the highly independent Secretary of War, Lindley M. Garrison, resigned because of increasing differences with Wilson and other important leaders over the nation's military preparedness program.[93] As his successor, the President chose a former Ohio lawyer, Newton D. Baker, whom he had once known as a student at Johns Hopkins University, but who had more recently served as a high-ranking, reform-oriented municipal official in Cleveland. In fact, Baker had held governmental office so much since the turn of the century—a total of thirteen years—that he had little time to build up a sizable law practice or establish any important (non-local) corporate ties.[94] Yet while Baker was a civic reformer in the pre–New Deal mold of "honesty and efficiency in government," it should not be assumed that he was hostile to business interests, for the man who served the longest as his top aide, Assistant Secretary of War Benedict Crowell, was a prominent local business executive who sat on the board of the big Cleveland Trust Co. from 1914 to 1917.[95] This, it would seem, was the type of reformer who was attracted to the Wilsonian cause.

Still another Cabinet change occurred in March 1920 when Secretary of the Interior Franklin K. Lane resigned to resume his (long-neglected) California law practice. At this rather late date in the administration, President Wilson turned to a well-known Chicago attorney, John Barton Payne, who had served during the recent war years first as general counsel to both the U.S. Railroad Administration and the U.S. Shipping Board, two emergency ad hoc agencies, and then as chairman of the latter body. However, unlike many of Wilson's top officials, Payne had relatively little experience in governmental affairs, but rather had devoted most of his adult life to the practice of law. In fact, he was a member of one of Chicago's most prominent firms (Winston, Payne, Strawn & Shaw), which represented a number of major corporate interests.[96] Indeed Payne himself had served until 1918 as general counsel of the

Chicago Great Western Railroad (of which line Edward Hurley had been a director prior to his appointment to the Federal Trade Commission) and had sat on the board of the fairly sizable Central Trust Co. of Chicago from 1917 to 1919. Thus it would appear that, in keeping with a trend set earlier in the administration, the appointment of John Barton Payne as Secretary of the Interior represented the selection of a marked pro-business figure in place of one who had no such formal ties.

One of the last major changes in Wilson's Cabinet occurred about the same time as this shift in the Interior Department when, upon the selection of Secretary of Agriculture David F. Houston to take over at the Treasury, the President appointed a pro-agrarian Iowa businessman, Edwin T. Meredith, to assume this position for the remainder of the administration.[97] Although Meredith had no governmental experience, he had been the longtime editor and publisher of a widely read journal called *Successful Farming*. Yet he was clearly the most pro-business figure to occupy this office since J. Sterling Morton, Grover Cleveland's (second-term) Cabinet member, who had been a railroad lobbyist. For example, in addition to running his own fairly substantial business enterprise, Meredith had served up to 1915 as a director of the Iowa Trust & Savings Bank of Des Moines, and, perhaps more importantly, had recently been a (Class B) member of the board of the Federal Reserve Bank of Chicago, which many would view as an Establishment link. Not only that, he had sat on the board of the U.S. Chamber of Commerce from 1915 to 1919 and was the first representative of this organization to receive such a high federal post.[98]

This conservative appointment trend was also at work in the realm of foreign relations, though in less obvious fashion. For instance, when Wilson's friend Walter Hines Page stepped down as Ambassador to Great Britain in October 1918 after a long series of differences with the administration, he was replaced by former West Virginia lawyer and Congressman John W. Davis, who had been acting for the past five years as Solicitor General (the second-ranking post in the Justice Department). Though Davis had no major corporate ties at the time of his diplomatic appointment, he was known to be a staunch conservative who, prior to his election to Congress in 1911, had served as attorney for the Clarksburg Fuel Co. (a concern that had at least one link to New York financial interests) and a number of other West Virginia enterprises, as local counsel for the Baltimore and Ohio Railroad, and as a director of the Union National Bank of Clarksburg. He was also a substantial stockholder in various oil and gas companies in his home state.[99] Probably even more revealing from a socio-economic standpoint was the fact that when Davis relinquished his ambassadorial post in early 1921, he moved almost immediately, thanks to some previous high-level negotiations, into a partnership with the major "Morgan" law firm of Stetson, Jennings and

Russell, which was then renamed Davis, Polk, Wardwell, Gardiner & Reed.[100]

Similarly, when America's Ambassador to France, William G. Sharp, stepped down from office in April of 1919, he was replaced by another former economic (and Democratic political) figure, Hugh C. Wallace, who, however, was from another part of the country.[101] Wallace was, in fact, a longtime Tacoma and Seattle businessman who, though he had retired from most of his entrepreneurial activities, continued to serve on the board of Seattle's big National Bank of Commerce up through 1921 (that is to say, during his nearly two-year stint as American Ambassador to France). That Wallace was probably favorably disposed toward major economic interests can also be inferred from the fact that he was the son-in-law of the former (1888-1910) highly conservative Chief Justice of the U.S. Supreme Court and onetime Chicago corporate lawyer, Melville W. Fuller. In short, the chief diplomatic officials of the latter part of the Wilson administration were hardly liberal or progressive figures.

War Mobilization Efforts

Conservative influences were, not surprisingly, at work during the trying and often hectic years when, given the ominous trend of events in Europe, America decided to embark on an expanded military preparedness program, and then, following the sinking of the *Lusitania,* became enmeshed in World War I itself. In its effort to mobilize the country's vast but uncoordinated economic resources for this great struggle, the Wilson administration created in 1916 a Council of National Defense, which consisted of the Secretaries of War, Navy, Commerce, Labor, Agriculture, and Interior. In addition, it established a special seven-man advisory body, which was headed by Daniel Willard, the president of the Baltimore and Ohio Railroad, and was composed of several other prominent businessmen (chief of whom were Wall Street broker Bernard Baruch and Chicago executive Julius Rosenwald, the president of Sears, Roebuck and Co.), one labor leader (Samuel Gompers of the American Federation of Labor), one academic (Hollis Godfrey, president of Philadelphia's Drexel Institute), and a well-known Chicago surgeon.[102]

Despite the best efforts of these individuals, this agency was not very effective, largely because it lacked real administrative power. Hence on the eve of America's entry into World War I, the Council of National Defense established a General Munitions Board, which was headed by Ohio industrialist Frank A. Scott (who, like Baker's later Assistant Secretary of War, Benedict Crowell, was a director of the big Cleveland Trust Co.), to expedite governmental purchasing in this crucial sphere. But this body was also soon found to have inadequate scope and authority, a dual deficiency that forced the still floundering Wilson regime to abandon the Munitions Board a few months later and replace it with a considerably strengthened War Industries Board.[103] Yet even this agency, which was run briefly by Daniel Willard, did not initially possess the broad policymaking power that was desperately needed to promote the nation's enormous war effort.[104]

In fact, it was not until March 1918, when Bernard Baruch was appointed chairman of this body with a strong personal mandate from the President, that the War Industries Board began to function in a fairly effective fashion.[105] Largely because of Baruch's many contacts in the business community, the Board was finally able to proceed with its assigned task, albeit in a way which was fraught with conflicts of interest. Indeed, judging from the influential character of some of Baruch's top aides (as well as Baruch's own long-term links with the wealthy Guggenheim forces), there is considerable question as to whether the chairman served essentially as an able and efficient coordinator of the nation's first modern wartime economic mobilization, or as a government official who provided a very useful service for America's major economic enterprises through the establishment of a more orderly (and friendly?) military-industrial development and procurement process.[106] For example, one of Baruch's chief staff aides was a well-known Wall Street investor named Eugene Meyer, Jr., who had important ties to both the Guggenheim interests and the House of Morgan (as well as many key family connections), and who served on the board of the (Guggenheim-dominated) Utah Copper Co., Alaska Juneau Gold Mining Co., Inspiration Consolidated Copper Co., Maxwell Motor Co., and the newly formed Pan-American Petroleum & Transport Co.[107] Another of Baruch's trusted assistants was Frederic W. Allen, who was a partner in the primarily Boston-based financial firm of Lee, Higginson & Co. and a director of the (probably New York–controlled) St. Louis–San Francisco Railway, the big Midvale Steel and Ordinance Co., Wright-Martin Aircraft Corp., and Montana Power Co. (a public utility dominated by Eastern interests, although it was officially headed by John D. Ryan, president of the Amalgamated Copper Co.).[108] Thus while Baruch undoubtedly did much to expedite the government's massive war effort, he may also have served as a useful agent for major business forces which had a significant stake in the overall mobilization process.[109] Indeed, according to Robert Cuff, "the members of the WIB [War Industries Board] had their own reasons for inflating Baruch's image. With the 'Zeus of Industry' in the background, they could bring recalcitrant businessmen into line, secure better cooperation from military officials, and gain a cover for their extra-legal activities."[110]

Supreme Court Appointments and Actions

The Supreme Court changed relatively little during this Democratic era, primarily because Wilson had the opportunity to select only three new appointees. Six Justices who had been picked by his more business-oriented Republican predecessors—Edward D. White, Joseph McKenna, Oliver Wendell Holmes, William R. Day, Willis Van Devanter, and Mahlon Pitney—served throughout Wilson's administration, and most of them were of a distinctly conservative persuasion. Justice McKenna had, for instance, once been closely associated with railroad magnate Leland Stanford. Ohio's Justice William R. Day, who had been an intimate friend and political advisor of former President William McKinley, had been a longtime partner of one of Canton's leading corporate law firms, which had represented many large and small business interests in the state; in fact, Day himself had served for at least seven years on the board of one of this city's bigger banks. And while it is true that Wyoming's Justice Willis Van Devanter had held several prominent judicial and administrative posts over the years, he had also been a member of an influential Cheyenne law firm which acted as local counsel for the huge Union Pacific Railroad. Similarly, while New Jersey Justice Mahlon Pitney had held a number of important governmental posts since the late 1890s, he had served up to 1908 as a director of a small Southern railroad and was linked through various family ties with such major enterprises as the Mutual Benefit Life Insurance Co. of Newark.[111] Indeed, even Chief Justice Edward D. White, who had been appointed to the High Court by the Democratic Grover Cleveland and later elevated to the top post by William Howard Taft, was a rather conservative figure, mainly because of his affluent Louisiana background, which included large sugar holdings and a lucrative New Orleans law practice. Thus Wilson had relatively little opportunity to substantially alter the socio-economic (or ideological) make-up of the Supreme Court, if he was so inclined.[112]

The first opening on the Court occurred in July 1914 when Tennessee Justice Horace Lurton died suddenly at the age of sixty. Caught by surprise, Wilson quickly decided to appoint his Attorney General, former Tennessee lawyer and (1903–1912) high Justice Department official James C. McReynolds, to this important post, largely because the irascible McReynolds had been an almost constant source of irritation and trouble within his own Cabinet. However, McReynolds' elevation to the high Court proved to be an even greater mistake than his initial selection as Attorney General, for not only did he interject much ill feeling on the Court, but he soon demonstrated that, despite his recent action on antitrust matters, he was actually a rabid economic conservative.[113]

The second opening on the Supreme Court did not develop until the latter part of Wilson's first term when Georgia's patrician Joseph Lamar died following a long illness. As his successor, the President chose someone who was neither a Southerner nor a conservative. Against the advice of many, he appointed Louis D. Brandeis, a wealthy, well-known Boston lawyer who had once had a largely corporate practice, but later turned into what has generally been described as a "people's lawyer" and an outspoken reformer strongly opposed to "big business."[114] Brandeis had served as a director of the near-monopolistic United Shoe Machinery Corp. up to 1906, and as an attorney and stockholder of this concern until a few years later. But he gradually withdrew from these associations as he came increasingly to believe that such large enterprises possessed too much economic and political power in America.[115] Having undergone a marked transition in his thinking, Brandeis devoted a good deal of his adult life in the pre- and early Wilsonian years to espousing reformist causes, most notably in his famous pro-labor brief in *Muller* v. *Oregon,* and not infrequently attacking various major corporate interests. Scant wonder, then, that when President Wilson nominated him for a seat on the Supreme Court in 1916 vehement objections were raised in many parts of the country. Heading the opposition was William Howard Taft and various leaders of the American Bar Association, which pro-business body clearly revealed that the real basis of its opposition to the progressive Brandeis was not his lack of fitness for high office, but rather his alleged radicalism (or to put it more accurately, his antipathy to the views and goals of big business).[116] And it was only after a vigorous battle in the Senate that Brandeis was confirmed to serve on the Supreme Court, thus capping a struggle which provided much insight into the overall array of politico-economic (and ideological) forces in the country.

Wilson's third opportunity to appoint someone to the Supreme Court occurred shortly thereafter when New York's able and rather liberal incumbent Justice, Charles Evans Hughes, resigned from the bench upon his receipt of the Republican presidential nomination in the summer of 1916. Upon formal notification of this action, Wilson moved promptly to fill this vacancy through the selection of a former longtime Cleveland lawyer and later (1914–1916) U.S. district court judge, John H. Clarke, who was also a well-known Democratic leader in Ohio and a close friend of the recently recruited Secretary of War, Newton D. Baker. Like the latter, Clarke has generally been regarded as a member of the ("good government") reform wing of the party, who, primarily in the immediate pre–World War I years, espoused a number of progressive causes. However, this side of Clarke's life has probably been overemphasized, for he had spent many years in Ohio working, as his biographer put it, as a Grover Cleveland "liberal."[117] Clarke had also devoted most of his time as an attorney to representing corporate clients, particularly the railroad industry, the avowed specialty of his original (1897–1907) firm of Williamson and Cushing. As a matter of fact, Clarke served as the general counsel of the Vanderbilt-dominated New York, Chicago & St. Louis Railroad (a line indirectly controlled by the New York Central system) from 1898 to apparently 1913.[118] Furthermore, although another authority claims that Clarke began to limit his work with the railroads around 1907, it was about this time that he agreed to serve for several years as a director of the medium-sized Cincinnati, Hamilton & Dayton Railway, a concern probably controlled by the Morgan-dominated Erie Railroad (for which Clarke acted as western attorney).[119] Given this background, one might expect Clarke's record on the Court to be quite mixed. Hence it is surprising that he voted on the liberal or moderate side in a significant number of cases, though this might be traced to his later substantial involvement in state and local reformist politics.

The most important case of an economic nature to be heard by the Supreme Court during the Wilsonian era was undoubtedly that of *Hammer* v. *Dagenhart,* which revolved around the limits imposed by the Constitution on the power of Congress to regulate interstate commerce. This was a matter that had been debated once before, in 1895 in the so-called sugar trust case *(United States* v. *E. C. Knight),* in which the Court had ruled in an extremely narrow fashion that the term *commerce* meant essentially transportation, the physical movement of goods following manufacture, and nothing else. In this instance the Court was required to rule on the constitutionality of a 1916 act that attempted to curb the widespread exploitative use of child labor in industry by prohibiting the transportation in interstate commerce of articles made in a factory that employed such help. Unfortunately, because of the relatively slight shift in the overall politico-economic make-up of the Supreme Court during the Wilsonian years, the Court once again ruled, albeit by a much closer (5–4) margin, that the right of Congress to regulate interstate commerce was used improperly to indirectly achieve an entirely different purpose, the elimination of a pernicious labor practice.[120] Thus in the Court's view this act was invalid, although this body had recently sustained somewhat similar legislation enacted to curtail the trade in drugs and prostitution. As Ernest S. Bates has observed, this ruling was made ". . . on the theory that Congress had the right to use its power over commerce to prevent crime, immorality, or the spread of evils disastrous to the whole nation. But the Supreme Court could not see that the health of the nation's youth was in any way a subject of national concern. It was purely a local matter."[121]

The other major set of cases that came before the Court during the Wilsonian years was decided in the latter part of the administration. In response to a growing crisis-inspired spirit of intolerance of the long-hallowed right of free speech, particularly as it related to our involvement in World War I, the Congress passed two repressive espionage acts which placed severe limits on the expression of dissent in our society. These were vigorously enforced by Wilson's last Attorney General, A. Mitchell Palmer. The first major victim of these suppressive measures was the renowned leader of the American Socialist party, Eugene V. Debs, who was convicted and sentenced under this legislation (with the later sanction of the Supreme Court) to ten years' imprisonment for delivering a speech in Canton, Ohio, in which he bitterly described this great world conflict as essentially a "capitalist war."

In another important case *(Abrams* v. *United States)* the Supreme

Court upheld the sentence imposed on five ignorant Russians who, while in New York City, expressed their resentment at the invasion of their native land by American (and other Allied) forces following the First World War in a pamphlet in which they had quoted a few hackneyed phrases from the *Communist Manifesto*. Despite Justice Holmes's strenuous attempt to persuade the Court to adopt the more reasonable (and now well-established) "clear and present danger" doctrine, the recently appointed John H. Clarke, speaking for his conservative colleagues, proclaimed in grossly exaggerated fashion that the Russians' words represented a highly subversive and intolerable appeal to the workers of this country to rise and forcefully overturn the government of the United States. Unfortunately in these and other cases the Court's conservative majority, perhaps cowed to some extent by wartime near-hysteria, chose time and again to ignore the dictum laid down in the earlier (post–Civil War) *Ex parte Milligan* case, in which the Court held that the Constitution of the United States applied at all times and to all people. Thus, in effect, the Supreme Court temporarily nullified the First Amendment of the Constitution.[122]

In retrospect, what judgment can one make about the Wilson administration? Was it, as commonly portrayed, a period in which the federal government was dominated by progressive reformers intent on enacting much-needed economic and social welfare measures? Or has this thesis been vastly overstated? Judging from the recruitment pattern of the Wilson regime, one might conclude that there was indeed a significant shift toward a more reform-oriented government, for in contrast to the three preceding Republican administrations in which close to 92 percent of the chief Cabinet officers and diplomatic officials had key socio-economic ties, only a little over 57 percent had such links during the Wilsonian years.[123] However, this figure is somewhat deceiving, for the drop was due in part to the inclusion of a number of more radical Bryan men in the Cabinet, such as North Carolina's Josephus Daniels, and their selection stemmed largely from certain overriding political considerations rather than a real desire on the part of the President and his major advisors to have such people in the government. In addition, the Wilson regime at various points attracted some extremely ambitious political leaders whose business links were either weak or of little national economic significance, such as Wilson's last Secretary of State, Bainbridge Colby, and Attorney General Mitchell Palmer. Hence it may be a mistake to make too much of the apparent decline in elitist recruitment under Wilson.[124] Indeed, there would seem to have been a marked trend at work during this administration toward the appointment of conservative leaders, which may have reached its peak during the crisis-ridden war years with the establishment of numerous business-dominated ad hoc emergency agencies. As a matter of fact, there was obviously a growing rapprochement with big business interests even before the First World War, as seen in both the creation and the initial staffing of the Federal Reserve Board and the Federal Trade Commission.[125] Thus, one is more or less forced to agree with the findings arrived at by such scholars as Gabriel Kolko, Robert Cuff, and Melvin Urofsky, who contend that, despite its rhetoric and at times reformist tendencies, the Wilson administration was not the progressive regime that many historians have been wont to believe.[126]

Notes

1. Because of this study's federal focus, the author has not included any public utilities of an essentially local or regional nature, such as New York's Interborough Rapid Transit Co. or the North American Co. (a major public utility holding company). However, he has included AT&T and the Western Union Telegraph Co. because of their national scope of operations. For a somewhat earlier and much more extensive list, which may be the first of its kind, see Thomas H. Navin, "Lagniappe: The 500 Largest American Industrials in 1917," *Business History Review* (Autumn 1970), pp. 360–386.

2. These big rail lines, which grew at a considerably slower rate in these years and changed little in their economic ranking, are listed in the first part of Chapter 4.

3. These figures may be considerably understated because of the existence of substantial undeclared trust funds, the magnitude of which has only recently been revealed to federal authorities and the general public.

4. Actually, after 1913 the most important figure in the so-called Morgan complex was probably George F. Baker, the longtime head of the First National Bank of New York, who served throughout this period on the boards of such major enterprises as AT&T, the Consolidated Gas Co. of New York, Erie Railroad, Lehigh Valley Railroad, Mutual Life Insurance Co., New York Central Railroad, Northern Pacific Railway, Pullman Co., and United States Steel Corp. Unfortunately, little has been written about this influential financier.

5. By 1919 the board of the Equitable Trust Co. included such Rockefeller representatives as Walter C. Teagle, president of the Standard Oil Co. of New Jersey, Howard E. Cole, a high-ranking official of the Standard Oil Co. of New York, and Bertram Cutler, a key Rockefeller aide and advisor. Another important Rockefeller figure, Henry E. Cooper, had also served for some years as a vice-president of this enterprise, and one of the family's chief lawyers, George W. Murray (whose partner, E. Parmalee Prentice, had married a daughter of John D. Rockefeller), had graced this board since 1912. Up to about 1905 the Equitable Trust Co. (and its predecessor concerns) had apparently been controlled by the Equitable Life Assurance Society. For more on this point, see Allan Nevins, *John D. Rockefeller*, Vol. 2, p. 617.

6. According to the findings of this Congressional body, there was, early in the century, a vast "money trust" in the United States which controlled much of the nation's wealth and economic resources. The committee claimed that five big closely linked concerns—J. P. Morgan & Co., the First National Bank of New York, Bankers Trust Co., Guaranty Trust

Co., and the National City Bank of New York—held a total of 341 directorships in 112 large corporations, which had overall assets of about $22 billion. In the author's judgment, this was a rather misleading finding, for the last-named firm was dominated by the Stillman-Rockefeller family and certain other friendly forces, and these interests operated quite independently, indeed often as rivals, of the Morgan complex (the core of which consisted of the other four financial enterprises, plus the Chase National Bank, the National Bank of Commerce, and probably the Mutual Life Insurance Co.). The zealous chief counsel of the Pujo Committee was a New York lawyer named Samuel Untermyer, who happened to be the long-trusted attorney for the Guggenheim interests (and a director of the General Development Co., a concern headed by mining magnate Adolph Lewisohn), which relationship raises a question as to whether Untermyer was acting, in part, as the agent for these wealthy rising industrialists who, while they did do business with J. P. Morgan, may have felt that the power of his financial house was so great that it needed to be cut down considerably. See U.S. Congress, *Report of the Committee Appointed Pursuant to House Resolutions 429 and 504 to Investigate the Concentration of Control and Credit* (Washington, D.C.: U.S. Government Printing Office, 1913), *passim;* George Wheeler, *Pierpont Morgan and Friends,* p. 289; and Harvey O'Connor, *The Guggenheims* (New York: Covici Friede, 1937), p. 147 and *passim.*

7.   The U.S. Chamber of Commerce held its first organizational meeting in April 1912, but did not begin to function effectively until at least 1913, so one might date its origins as the early part of the Wilson administration.

8.   Another body, the National Industrial Conference Board, was created around the midpoint of the Wilson regime, but this group, which was initially made up of representatives of twelve other business and trade associations, was too new to be a truly effective force in governmental affairs.

9.   The National Civic Federation also continued to operate throughout the Wilson years, but from a governmental standpoint with apparently much less effect than during the Roosevelt and Taft administrations. However, for a contrary claim, see Gerald Kurland, *Seth Low: The Reformer in an Urban and Industrial Age* (New York: Twayne Publishers, 1971), p. 302.

10.   Having an edge as an incumbent, Wilson was reelected by a very close margin in 1916 over his Republican opponent, Supreme Court Justice Charles Evans Hughes, who ran with the unified backing of his party and many influential businessmen such as former Morgan partner George W. Perkins, who by this time had given up his support of the Progressive cause.

11.   Wilson is generally depicted, even by his most devoted admirers, as a man who, at least until 1908, was of distinctly conservative persuasion. According to Arthur Link, Wilson viewed William Jennings Bryan and other agrarian Democrats as unsound and misguided radicals, labor unions as inimical to the American way of life, and the whole concept of governmental regulation of economic activity as socialistic. Even before he became president of Princeton, Wilson was on close terms with influential economic interests, as may be seen from the fact that he signed a special contract (paying him $2,500 a year over his regular salary) with a small group of wealthy Princeton backers and former college classmates, who were fearful that otherwise he might take a position at another school. See Arthur S. Link, *Wilson: The Road to the White House* (Princeton, N.J.: Princeton University Press, 1947), pp. 26, 32, 111–12, 117–19, 122, and 127, and Henry W. Bragdon, *Woodrow Wilson: The Academic Years* (Cambridge, Mass.: Harvard University Press, 1967), pp. 227 and 277.

12.   See Arthur S. Link, *op. cit.,* p. 71.

13.   Some insight into Wilson's badly strained relations with the university may be gleaned from the fact that, having accepted the New Jersey Democratic gubernatorial nomination in the summer of 1910, one of Wilson's loyal friends on the board of trustees

suggested that this body wait till after the election to accept his resignation. The more numerous anti-Wilson trustees, however, were determined not to lose this opportunity to force Wilson out. They reportedly met in Princeton on the night before the October meeting of the board to confer about this matter, and then sent a delegation, led by industrialist Stephen Palmer, to tell Wilson that he must resign. See Link, *op. cit.*, p. 90.

14. Around 1900 Harvey also sat on the boards of several minor concerns with Walter G. Oakman, who was president of the Morgan-dominated Guaranty Trust Co. and a director of the Morton Trust Co. and Northern Pacific Railway. In addition, Harvey later became head of the relatively small North American Review Publishing Co.

15. For more on this relationship, see Willis F. Johnson, *George Harvey: A Passionate Patriot* (Boston: Houghton Mifflin, 1929), pp. 63, 71, and 75; Francis Russell, *The President Makers: From Mark Hanna to Joseph P. Kennedy* (Boston: Little, Brown, 1976), p. 136; and George Wheeler, *Pierpont Morgan and Friends,* p. 235. One of the apparently pro-Morgan directors of Harper Brothers was Alexander E. Orr, a New York City banker who served, up to 1907, on the board of the Erie Railroad and the Chicago, Rock Island & Pacific Railway (a line headed by Daniel G. Reid, who was a director of the American Can Co., Astor Trust Co., Bankers Trust Co., Guaranty Trust Co., and U.S. Steel Corp.), and, up to 1906, as a director of the National Bank of Commerce. The only other board on which Harvey served for any significant length of time was the relatively unknown Audit Co., a small firm formed to conduct audits and appraisals. The board of this company was studded with such prominent figures as August Belmont (head of the big Interborough Rapid Transit Co.), T. DeWitt Cutler (a Philadelphia banker who served as a director of both the Bankers Trust Co. and Guaranty Trust Co.), Francis L. Hine (president of the First National Bank of New York and a director of the Chase National Bank, Chicago, Rock Island and Pacific Railway, National Bank of Commerce, and Phelps, Dodge & Co.), Cornelius Vanderbilt (who sat on the board of the Illinois Central Railroad, Interborough Rapid Transit Co., Lackawanna Steel Co., and Mutual Life Insurance Co.), and John I. Waterbury (the longtime head of the Manhattan Trust Co. and a director of AT&T, the Chase National Bank, International Mercantile Marine Co., and Western Union Telegraph Co.)

16. According to one source, another key Wilson advisor, Colonel Edward M. House (a Texan who had been recommended to Wilson by Harvey), strove to allay this suspicion by having one of the writers for *Harper's Weekly* publish an article mildly criticizing Wilson. See Arthur Walworth, *Woodrow Wilson: American Prophet* (New York: Longman, Green, 1958), Vol. I, p. 313. Whatever the reason, this break later became permanent.

17. Two other close friends and political counselors of Wilson were Cleveland H. Dodge, a high-ranking official of Phelps, Dodge & Co. and longtime trustee of Princeton University (who, despite his directorship link with the National City Bank of New York, was, unlike Moses Taylor Pyne, a strong Wilson supporter), and George F. Peabody, a New York City banker with substantial holdings in various Mexican enterprises, who reportedly acted as a "statesman without portfolio" throughout much of the Wilson administration. For more on Peabody, see Louise Ware, *George Foster Peabody* (Athens: University of Georgia Press, 1951), especially pp. 161–67.

18. For more on House's role in Texas politics, see Lewis L. Gould, *Progressives and Prohibitionists: Texas Democrats in the Wilson Era* (Austin: University of Texas Press, 1973), pp. 11–101.

19. According to one knowledgeable authority, House's first candidate for the Democratic nomination was New York's Mayor James F. Gaynor, but when the latter's presidential stock dropped sharply in 1911, House shifted his efforts to New Jersey's Woodrow Wilson, with whom he developed an unusually close personal and political relationship. See Arthur Link, *Wilson: The Road to the White House,* p. 333.

20. See Arthur S. Link, *Wilson: The New Freedom,* pp. 94–95.

21. At one time House's father was believed to be the third richest man in Houston, and he owned over a quarter-million acres of land and the biggest wholesale trade concern in the

state, as well as numerous banking and transportation concerns. Upon his father's death in 1890, House's eldest brother, Thomas W., Jr., assumed control of the family's banking interests, another brother, John, took charge of its sugar lands, and Edward M. House agreed to oversee its cotton plantations. See Rupert N. Richardson, *Colonel Edward M. House: The Texas Years, 1858–1912* (Abilene, Texas: Abilene Printing & Stationery Co., 1964), pp. 4–40.

22. Much of the capital for this company was reportedly raised by a syndicate composed of men affiliated with the Old Colony Trust Co. of Boston. Although primarily a Texas figure, Colonel House was obviously on good terms with one of this bank's long-term top officials, T. Jefferson Coolidge, Jr. In addition to his involvement with this rail line, House served on the board of the Citizens Bank & Trust Co. of Austin up to 1907 and as a director of the Union Bank & Trust Co. of Houston up to 1909.

23. One of House's biographers claims that he resigned from this position when he discovered that it would be inconvenient for him to attend its board meetings, but this statement is probably mistaken because House had a fashionable abode in New York City and shuttled back and forth between this metropolis and Texas. (See Arthur D. H. Smith, *op. cit.*, p. 36, and Lewis L. Gould, *Progressives and Prohibitionists*, pp. 15–16.) It should also be noted that in 1912 House's daughter married Gordon Auchincloss, a member of New York's socio-economic elite, one of whose kinsmen (John W. Auchincloss) served at this time as a director of the Illinois Central Railroad and various lesser concerns.

24. Few historians have stressed Wilson's affiliation with the Carnegie Foundation and Mutual Life. Arthur Link, for instance, does not refer to either tie, even though the latter would seem to be of considerable significance. Arthur Walworth does make note of these connections (see *Woodrow Wilson*, p. 211), although he does not draw any politico-economic inference from Wilson's corporate link. David Eakins claims that Wilson also served for several years as an officer of the American Association for Labor Legislation, a moderate reform group backed by a number of wealthy interests, but the dates of this affiliation are unclear. See David W. Eakins, "The Development of Corporate Liberal Policy Research in the United States, 1885–1965" (unpublished University of Wisconsin dissertation, 1966), p. 86.

25. For a complete list of all the trustees of this company from its inception in 1843 to 1943, see Shepard B. Clough, *A Century of American Life Insurance: A History of the Mutual Life Insurance Company of New York*, pp. 347–53.

26. These dates are given in Arthur Walworth, *op. cit.*, pp. 211–12.

27. As further evidence of Bryan's marked Western orientation, one need only note that the "great commoner" (as he was frequently known) picked former Wyoming Governor John E. Osborne to serve as his Assistant Secretary of State—the only man from the Rocky Mountain region ever appointed to this important post. In part to counter this move and Bryan's influence in foreign affairs, the President selected John Bassett Moore, a well-known Columbia University professor of international law, to fill the newly created position of Counselor to the State Department.

28. There were two major rivals for this position, McAdoo and William F. McCombs, a New York lawyer and former (admiring) student of Wilson's at Princeton, who, despite a severe physical handicap and a somewhat abrasive personality, had played a vital role in Wilson's rise to national political prominence. Because of McComb's drawbacks and McAdoo's substantial help in the latter stages of the presidential campaign, Wilson ultimately decided to appoint the latter. It has been asserted that another reason why Wilson did not choose McCombs was that he was too closely linked with Wall Street. However, there was no truth to this charge, for while McCombs did help raise a good deal of money during the campaign, the only company he was connected with at this time was the extremely small Kentwold Co. (which was not even listed in any of the major business manuals). For more on this matter, see Arthur S. Link, *Wilson: The New Freedom*, pp. 9–10, and Arthur D. H. Smith, *op. cit.*, p. 40. According to another source (Louise Ware, *op. cit.*, p. 167), this

Cabinet post was also offered to New York City banker George Foster Peabody, who had extensive business interests in Mexico.

29.   See Arthur S. Link, *Wilson: The Road to the White House,* pp. 330–31. In his biography of McAdoo, John J. Broesamle has referred to some of the other figures involved in the initial financing of the New York and New Jersey Railroad Co., but he does not place them in their proper institutional perspective. See John J. Broesamle, *William Gibbs Mc-Adoo: A Passion for Change, 1863–1917* (Port Washington, N.Y.: Kennikat Press, 1973), pp. 18–19.

30.   Converse became simply an outside director in 1904, but Oakman continued to serve in an important executive capacity in the renamed company up through 1913. John Broesamle merely indicates that McAdoo managed to raise a substantial amount of initial capital for his concern from several of these people, without (except for Gary) pointing out that they also served either as officers or directors of his company. He, however, did acknowledge that Converse and Oakman were both good friends of McAdoo. See John J. Broesamle, *op. cit.,* pp. 18–20, 24, and 38.

31.   The board of the parent company contained a number of other prominent figures, such as William C. Lane, who was a vice-president of the Guaranty Trust Co. and a director of the Electrical Securities Corp., and Grant B. Schley, who was a brother-in-law of the influential George F. Baker, head of the First National Bank of New York.

32.   In addition, McAdoo served as a director of New York's relatively minor Lincoln Trust Co. from 1910 to 1913 and a few years before his Cabinet appointment as a board member of the probably small Long Island Motor Parkway, Inc. (the two top officials of which were William K. Vanderbilt, Jr., and his kinsman, Harry Payne Whitney).

33.   Revealingly, the first two men McAdoo picked to serve as Assistant Secretary of the Treasury were Charles S. Hamlin, a former Boston lawyer and high federal official who had married a member of Albany's Pruyn family, which had been associated with the New York Central Railroad and Mutual Life Insurance Co. in the mid-19th century, and John S. Williams, a prominent Richmond banker and Southern railroadman who had served for many years as the chief executive of the fairly small Georgia & Florida Railway, as either an officer or director of the big Seaboard Air Line Railway, and up to 1904 as a director of McAdoo's Hudson and Manhattan Railroad Co.

34.   The President originally intended to appoint an unusually able and progressive Boston attorney, Louis D. Brandeis, to this key post, but various powerful economic figures induced Wilson's friend and major financial backer, Cleveland H. Dodge, to dissuade Wilson. After weighing at least one other candidate (McReynolds), the President then reportedly decided on former Pennsylvania Congressman A. Mitchell Palmer. However, the Bryan wing of the party strongly objected, largely because Palmer served as local counsel for the Delaware, Lackawanna & Western Railroad and the Lehigh Coal and Navigation Co. The President finally turned, at House's urging, to McReynolds. See Matthew Josephson, *The President Makers,* p. 468; Arthur S. Link, *Wilson: The New Freedom,* p. 116; and Stanley Coben, *A. Mitchell Palmer* (New York: Columbia University Press, 1963), pp. 69–72. For McReynolds' conservative support in Texas, see Lewis L. Gould, *Progressives and Prohibitionists,* pp. 98–102.

35.   See Arthur Walworth, *Woodrow Wilson,* Vol. I, p. 271.

36.   Wilson's Postmaster General, Albert S. Burleson, who was a former Texas Congressman and Austin lawyer, was yet another Cabinet selection by Colonel House, who probably wielded more influence in this high-level recruitment process than any private citizen in American history.

37.   In the closing stages of the Cabinet-making process, after two unsuccessful efforts to find a Secretary of War, Wilson turned in near desperation just one week before his inauguration to one of his chief aides, Joseph P. Tumulty, for help. The latter reportedly thumbed through the *Lawyers' Directory* and came across the name of Lindley M. Garrison,

whom he had known only casually as a resident of his hometown (Jersey City) and as a vice-chancellor of the state of New Jersey. Although he had little pertinent experience, Garrison, who had no recent corporate links, was finally persuaded to accept this Cabinet post. Garrison has not been treated like the other important members of the administration because his largely accidental appointment reveals little about the politico-economic orientation of the Wilson regime. See Arthur S. Link, *Wilson: The New Freedom*, pp. 19–20; and Clarence H. Cramer, *Newton D. Baker* (Cleveland: World Publishing Co., 1961), p. 76.

38.   Daniels's Assistant Secretary of the Navy was a young well-connected New York attorney named Franklin Delano Roosevelt, who had been associated briefly with a comparatively new law firm known as Marvin, Hooker and Roosevelt (one member of which, Henry S. Hooker, served on the board of an aircraft company recently formed, with considerable outside funds, by Orville Wright). One of Roosevelt's uncles, Frederic A. Delano, was president of the big Wabash Railroad, while another kinsman, Warren Delano, was a director of the Atlantic Coast Line Railroad and the Lackawanna Steel Co. Lindley Garrison's Assistant Secretary of War was a young Lexington, Kentucky lawyer, Henry S. Breckinridge, about whom relatively little is known other than that he came from a famous Southern political family. For more on the Roosevelt and Breckinridge clans, see Stephen Hess, *America's Political Dynasties*, pp. 167–216 and 239–72.

39.   In 1916, for example, Colonel House, who had turned hostile to Daniels because he had antagonized certain influential business interests through his rigorous enforcement of sound procurement procedures, asked Wall Street financier Bernard Baruch (who had become an important informal advisor to the President) to urge Wilson to dismiss Daniels, but the effort proved unsuccessful. See Arthur S. Link, *Wilson: The New Freedom*, pp. 124–25.

40.   According to Arthur Link, Wilson ". . . took Lane entirely upon House's recommendation and met him for the first time only on inauguration day." See his *Wilson: The New Freedom*, p. 18, and also Lewis L. Gould, *Progressives and Prohibitionists*, p. 102.

41.   Lane's appointment to the ICC had been warmly recommended to Theodore Roosevelt by Benjamin Ide Wheeler, president of the University of California and a recently-appointed public member of the executive committee of the National Civic Federation, as someone who would protect the interests of shippers. Though widely viewed as a reformer, Lane was actually a member of a pro-mercantile wing of the Democratic party in California which was strongly opposed to the dominant role long played in state affairs by the Southern Pacific Railroad. Lane was closely associated with such political leaders as the wealthy James D. Phelan, who was the president of one local bank and a director of two others, and conservative lawyer Gavin McNab, who sat on the board of the Merchants National Bank of San Francisco. See Keith W. Olson, *Biography of a Progressive: Franklin K. Lane, 1864–1921* (Westport, Conn.: Greenwood Press, 1979), pp. 17–34; Albro Martin, *Enterprise Denied*, p. 178; and George Mowry, *The California Progressives* (Berkeley: University of California Press, 1951), pp. 13–19.

42.   See Arthur D. H. Smith, *Mr. House of Texas* (New York: Funk & Wagnalls, 1940), p. 66; John Milton Cooper, Jr., *Walter Hines Page: The Southerner as Historian, 1855–1918* (Chapel Hill: University of North Carolina Press, 1977), pp. 243–44; and Ross Gregory, *Walter Hines Page: Ambassador to the Court of St. James* (Lexington: University Press of Kentucky, 1970), p. 23. According to the last study, when Houston raised questions about his prospective financial burden as a Cabinet officer, Page solicited enough money from private sources to guarantee him a four-year total of $120,000 (and even more, if necessary).

43.   Indeed, according to his biographer, Brookings *was* the board of trustees. For more on this business and civic figure who essentially founded what later became the Brookings Institution in Washington, see Hermann Hagedorn, *Brookings: A Biography* (New York: Macmillan, 1936), p. 138 and *passim*.

44.   See Arthur S. Link, *Wilson: The New Freedom*, p. 137.

45. See Mathew Josephson, *The President Makers,* p. 468; Arthur Walworth, *Woodrow Wilson,* Vol. I, p. 273; and Arthur S. Link, *Wilson: The New Freedom,* p. 14. According to Link, when Wilson was contemplating appointing Brandeis to this sensitive post, a new anti-Brandeis movement was generated in Boston, led by certain prominent conservative Democrats. "Practically all the party leaders of Massachusetts, bluestocking and Irish alike, rose in rebellion. Thomas P. Riley, Democratic state chairman, and Humphrey O'Sullivan, a party leader in Lowell, visited Wilson in Trenton on February 26, 1913." Even more impressive than their arguments, Link felt, were the letters of protest they brought from Governor Eugene N. Foss (who was, until his election in 1910, a director of the Brooklyn Rapid Transit Co., the Chicago Junction Railway & Union Stock Yards Co., and Massachusetts Electric Companies), Mayor John J. Fitzgerald of Boston, Richard Olney (a director of AT&T, Old Colony Trust Co., and Massachusetts Electric Companies), William A. Gaston (a director of the National Shawnut Bank of Boston and the Gillette Safety Razor Co.), Henry L. Higginson (a director of AT&T, GE, and National Shawnut Bank of Boston), Charles F. Choate, Jr. (a vice-president of the Massachusetts Hospital Life Insurance Co. and director of the National Shawnut Bank of Boston), Sherman L. Whipple (a director of the International Trust Co. of Boston), and Clarence W. Barron (a Bostonian who served as president of New York City's Dow, Jones & Co.)—as Link puts it, "practically the entire Democratic leadership in Massachusetts." Despite this defeat, Brandeis remained an important informal advisor to the President on a number of major domestic matters.

46. Burton Kaufman places greater weight on the fact that Redfield served in 1912 as president of the American Manufacturers' Export Association, a recently formed group whose membership (at most about 1,000) was drawn largely from the New York area. See Burton I. Kaufman, *Efficiency and Expansion: Foreign Trade Organization in the Wilson Administration, 1912–1921* (Westport, Conn.: Greenwood Press, 1974), p. 19. Given the marked corporate (rather than organizational) ties of many high officials in this period, Kaufman's claim seems doubtful, although more research is obviously needed on this point.

47. This new Cabinet seat was first offered to New Jersey Senator and Paterson lawyer William Hughes, who declined but recommended Wilson for the post. According to one source, Wilson was a rather conservative union leader. See Arthur D. Howden Smith, *Mr. House of Texas,* p. 68.

48. According to his most recent biographer, Page probably owed his appointment less to his old acquaintance with Wilson than to his more recently established one with Colonel House. See John Milton Cooper, Jr., *op. cit.,* p. 248.

49. See John Milton Cooper, Jr., *op. cit.,* pp. 46, 105, and 190.

50. For more on Page's adulation of big businessmen and marked aversion to muckraking, see John Milton Cooper, Jr., *op. cit.,* pp. 184–85 and 196. According to Arthur Link, Page could not afford to hold this costly diplomatic post and apparently needed an extra $25,000 a year, which wealthy pro-Wilson mining executive Cleveland H. Dodge kindly supplied. To quote Link, "a system of payment was worked out—Dodge sent money to House, who passed it on to Arthur W. Page, the Ambassador's son, so that Page probably never knew who his benefactor was." Ironically, a few years later when Wilson lost confidence in Page, he tried vainly to get Dodge to take over as our chief emissary to Great Britain. See Arthur S. Link, *Wilson: The New Freedom,* p. 101.

51. Because former Wilson advisor William McCombs waited long before deciding to reject this post (which was offered to allay his anger at not having been appointed Secretary of the Treasury), this position was held until November 1914 by wealthy Cleveland businessman Myron T. Herrick, who, in addition to his banking interests, was up to 1913 the board chairman of the Wheeling and Lake Erie Railroad and a vice-president of the National Carbon Co.

52. See Arthur S. Link, *Wilson: The New Freedom,* p. 101.

53. Gerard's brother-in-law, Marcus Daly, was a member of the board of the big Montana

Power Co., which concern was headed by John D. Ryan, the president of the Amalgamated Copper Co., and was apparently controlled by a largely New York–based syndicate.

54.   The other major fiscal measure of Wilson's early years was the enactment of the Underwood tariff, which represented the first important reduction in the nation's import duties since the Civil War (an overall drop from around 37 percent to about 27 percent). To make up for the anticipated decrease in customs revenue, Congress adopted, after the passage of the 16th Amendment, a graduated income tax, ranging from 1 to 6 percent, on all families and unrelated individuals earning $4,000 or more per year. While it was a significant first step, this act obviously did not take a substantial bite out of the pockets of America's upper classes.

55.   For a recent account of these proceedings, including the role played by such important but unofficial participants as Morgan partner Henry P. Davison, Chicago banker George M. Reynolds, and Harvard professor A. Piatt Andrews, see Robert Craig West, *Banking Reform and the Federal Reserve, 1863–1923* (Ithaca, N.Y.: Cornell University Press, 1974), *passim.*

56.   Although Nelson W. Aldrich was a United States Senator during much of this period (and a father-in-law of John D. Rockefeller, Jr.), he had also been a director since 1907 of the Intercontinental Rubber Co.—or Continental Rubber Co., as it was originally known— which was established with substantial fiscal backing from the Guggenheim brothers, Thomas Fortune Ryan, and Bernard M. Baruch. In 1913, however, it was headed by William C. Potter, a vice-president of the Morgan-dominated Guaranty Trust Co. of New York (and a director of the American Smelting and Refining Co.). Its board then included John R. Morron, president of the Atlas Portland Cement Co. (and a director of the Chicago Great Western Railroad and the Guaranty Trust Co.); Charles H. Sabin, another vice-president of the Guaranty Trust Co. (and a director of the Inspiration Consolidated Copper Co., Montana Power Co., Seaboard Air Line Railway, and Liberty National Bank of New York City); and Allan A. Ryan, a son of Thomas Fortune Ryan and president of the Royal Typewriter Co. (and a director of the Bethlehem Steel Corp. and the National Bank of Commerce of New York City). For more on the initial major backers of this rubber company, see Carter Field, *Bernard Baruch: Park Bench Statesman* (New York: McGraw-Hill, 1944), pp. 64–67.

57.   See Arthur S. Link, *Wilson: The New Freedom,* pp. 205–07.

58.   For more on this complex process, see Arthur S. Link, *op. cit.,* pp. 199–240, and Robert Craig West, *op. cit.,* pp. 91–106. For a more critical analysis which places greater emphasis on the role played by various key economic interests, see Gabriel Kolko, *The Triumph of Conservatism,* pp. 217–54. According to West, Wilson was a close friend of one of the private parties involved in these proceedings, A. Barton Hepburn, who was board chairman of the Chase National Bank (and a director of the Bankers Trust Co., First National Bank of New York, and New York Life Insurance Co.).

59.   See Arthur S. Link, *Wilson: The New Freedom,* pp. 238 and 240.

60.   Williams had also been a director of the Maryland Casualty Co. and at one time a board member of the Bowling Green Trust Co. of New York City. In addition, his brother, R. Lancaster Williams (who took over as president of the Georgia and Florida Railway in (1913), was a director of the International and Great Northern Railway and the Missouri-Pacific Railway, and his Baltimore business partner, J. William Middendorf, was a director of the Maryland Casualty Co., Georgia and Florida Railway, and the Seaboard Air Line Railway.

61.   Hamlin's brother, Edward, was also a fairly prominent Boston businessman. Apparently the offer to Hamlin was made only after the position was refused by the archconservative Boston lawyer (and onetime Cleveland Cabinet member) Richard Olney, who sat on the board of AT&T and three other New England concerns. The influential Olney had already

been asked to serve as Ambassador to Great Britain. See Gerald G. Eggert, *Richard Olney,* p. 318.

62. Invitations had also been extended to Harry A. Wheeler, a second-tier Chicago businessman who was a director of the newly formed U.S. Chamber of Commerce and a member of the National Citizens' League for Sound Banking, and Thomas D. Jones, a former Chicago lawyer and still active director of the International Harvester Co. and the New Jersey Zinc Co. Wheeler declined, and a Senate committee voted against the confirmation of Jones because one of the companies he was associated with had become involved in an antitrust suit with the federal government. For more on the political role of the National Citizens' League, see Robert Craig West, *op. cit.,* pp. 79–80.

63. For more on the conservative and liberal reaction to this set of appointees, see Arthur S. Link, *Wilson: The New Freedom,* pp. 451–52. In 1914 the board of the Alabama-based Woodward Iron Co. included such prominent Northerners as Alvin W. Krech (president of the Equitable Trust Co. of New York City and a director of the National Bank of Commerce, Wabash Railroad, and the Rockefeller-controlled Western Maryland Railway), Boston lawyer William L. Putnam (a director of AT&T, Suffolk Savings Bank, and State Street Trust Co. of Boston), Percy R. Pyne (a member of a wealthy family with a long-standing major interest in the National City Bank of New York), and Sylvanus L Schoonmaker (a director of AT&T, GE, and Chicago Junction Railway and Union Stock Yards Co.) Senator Underwood's brother-in-law, Alan H. Woodward, served from 1913 through 1920 on the board of the Seaboard Air Line Railway, which was dominated throughout this period by New York City interests. Warburg's brother-in-law and banking partner, Jacob H. Schiff, was a director of Wells Fargo & Co., Western Union Telegraph Co., National City Bank, and Central Trust Co. of New York City. Although Miller himself was basically an academic figure, his wife's uncle, Chicago merchant Albert A. Sprague, was a director of the Chicago Telephone Co. (a subsidiary of AT&T), Commonwealth Edison Co., Elgin National Watch Co., Northern Trust Co., and Merchants Loan & Trust Co. of Chicago, and her first cousin, Albert A. Sprague, Jr., sat on the board of the Chicago Great Western Railroad.

64. According to one authority, Warburg, Delano, Miller, and Harding constituted a rather solid and usually dominant bloc on the Federal Reserve Board throughout much of the Wilson regime. It was generally opposed by a pro-administration group led by the ambitious William G. McAdoo, who was eager to establish himself as a national political leader, and his initial high Treasury Department aides, Charles S. Hamlin and John S. Williams. The latter had reportedly been ousted from his position with the Seaboard Air Line Railway by New York City financier Frank A. Vanderlip and his allies, and was thus disgruntled. For more on this split on the Federal Reserve Board, see John J. Broesamle, *William Gibbs McAdoo,* pp. 121–26 and 148–49. The powerful New York Federal Reserve Bank, which played a vital, if not dominant, role in the operation of this financial system up to 1929, was long headed, at the insistence of Morgan interests, by Benjamin Strong, Jr., a former vice-president of the Bankers Trust Co. who had served up to 1914 on the board of the Astor Trust Co., Rock Island Co. (a railroad holding company), Electric Bond & Share Co., GE, International Nickel Co., International Paper Co., and Seaboard Air Line Railway. For more on the role played by Strong and the New York Federal Reserve Bank, see Lester V. Chandler, *Benjamin Strong: Central Banker* (Washington, D.C.: Brookings Institution, 1958), pp. 25, 30, and 39, and Ross M. Robertson, *History of the American Economy,* 2nd ed. (New York: Harcourt, Brace & World, 1964), pp. 498–501.

65. For a more extensive treatment of the subject, see Arthur S. Link, *Wilson: The New Freedom,* pp. 427–42. With America's entry into the First World War, antitrust activity was substantially curtailed. Because of the subsequent conservative Republican domination of the federal government, it was not revived until the more progressive New Deal regime during the Great Depression.

66. Organized labor, however, did receive some noteworthy judicial relief from this measure, although it hardly deserves to be described, as originally acclaimed, as labor's "Magna Carta."

67. See James Weinstein, *The Corporate Ideal in the Liberal State, 1900–1918* (Boston: Beacon Press, 1968), pp. 62–91, and Gabriel Kolko, *The Triumph of Conservatism,* pp. 256–59.

68. Rublee, who was a key figure in these proceedings, has been erroneously described by different sources as a Wisconsin and a New Hampshire lawyer, when in fact he was neither (although he had managed the New Hampshire election campaign of a Republican aspirant for the U.S. Senate). See, for instance, Alan Stone, *Economic Regulation and the Public Interest: The Federal Trade Commission in Theory and Practice* (Ithaca, N.Y.: Cornell University Press, 1977), pp. 38–39; Gabriel Kolko, *op. cit.,* pp. 264–67; and Susan Wagner, *The Federal Trade Commission* (New York: Praeger Publishers, 1971), p. 21.

69. See Gabriel Kolko, *The Triumph of Conservatism,* pp. 267 and 270.

70. The other initial Republican commissioner was William H. Parry, who was a former Seattle businessman (a onetime president of the Morgan Shipbuilding Corp. and recent director of the Seattle-Tacoma Power Co.) and also a prominent local political and municipal official. Parry, who was probably picked to give the West some representation on this regulatory body, had served as a director and treasurer of the Seattle Chamber of Commerce from 1896 through 1915, an affiliation which aided his appointment.

71. Although Rublee's link with the Chamber of Commerce may have been of considerable importance, it should also be noted that the American Coal Products Co. was apparently dominated by an influential group of men associated with the Bon Ami Co. and some Pennsylvania public utilities.

72. Rublee was also a good friend of lawyer Dwight Morrow, who in 1914 became a partner in J. P. Morgan & Co. See Harold Nicolson, *Dwight Morrow* (New York: Harcourt Brace, 1935), *passim*.

73. For more on the extremely close economic, social, and political relationship between these two men, see Horace S. Merrill, *William Freeman Vilas,* pp. 27–29, 54, 115–17, 125, 129, 199, and 216–19. After stepping down from public office, Vilas served on the board of the Wisconsin Central Railway and several financial concerns up to a short time before his death in 1908, and Davies's father-in-law acted as a local attorney for the line apparently until his death in 1903.

74. See, Gabriel Kolko *The Triumph of Conservatism,* pp. 271–72. Kolko claims that the most influential outside consultants of the commission in these critical formative years were Boston's progressive attorney Louis D. Brandeis; Arthur J. Eddy, a Chicago lawyer who served on the board of the American Steel Foundries and was closely linked with various business trade associations; Walker D. Hines, the general counsel of the Atchison, Topeka and Sante Fe Railway; Charles R. Van Hise, the president of the University of Wisconsin, who sat on the board of the Central Wisconsin Trust Co., and Victor Morawetz, George Rublee's former legal mentor, who served at this time as a director of the (Morgan-dominated) National Bank of Commerce, Niagara Falls Power Co., and Norfolk and Western Railway. Of this primarily pro-business group, only Brandeis spoke out against such acts as the commission's decision to give advice (in effect, a form of clearance) to corporations as to the legality of their various proposed practices.

75. Again see Gabriel Kolko, *The Triumph of Conservatism,* pp. 273–74. The fifth person chosen to serve initially on the Federal Trade Commission was a fairly prominent Georgia Democratic leader, William J. Harris, who had been acting since the outset of the administration as director of the Bureau of the Census (a political post). Harris was also a small businessman; he was head of both the Farmers and Mechanics Bank of Cedartown (a town of about 3,500) and the Georgia Fire Insurance Co. (of Atlanta). In all probability, Harris was picked primarily to represent the South on the FTC, and perhaps for that reason he apparently never exerted much influence in administrative proceedings.

76. Of the twelve outside directors of this concern in 1915, four had noteworthy (primary or secondary) New York City connections. These were Charles Steele, who was a partner in J. P. Morgan & Co. (and a director of the Atchison, Topeka and Sante Fe Railway, General Electric Co., International Mercantile Marine Co., Northern Pacific Railway, and Southern Railway); John R. Morron, who was president of the Atlas Portland Cement Co. (and a director of the Baltimore and Ohio Railroad, Guaranty Trust Co. of New York City, and National Bank of the Republic of Chicago); John A. Spoor, who was head of two subsidiaries of the (Eastern-dominated) Chicago Junction Railway and Union Stock Yards Co. (and a director of the First National Bank of Chicago and New York's Guaranty Trust Co.); and Edward F. Swinney, who was president of the First National Bank of Kansas City, Mo. (and a director of the Bankers Trust Co. of New York City). Another factor in Hurley's favor was that he had played a major role in the creation of the National Foreign Trade Council, although some feel that this group may have been too new to carry great weight in high administrative circles.

77. See Arthur S. Link, *Woodrow Wilson and the Progressive Era, 1910–1917* (New York: Harper & Row, 1954), pp. 68–80; Susan Wagner, *The Federal Trade Commission,* pp. 23–24; and Mark J. Green, *The Closed Enterprise System* (New York: Grossman Publishers, 1972), p. 323. For reasons not yet fully explained, President Wilson did select a number of more liberal commissioners (such as Victor Murdock, William B. Colver, and Huston Thompson) in the latter part of the decade. But by this time the administration was engrossed in the war effort and international affairs. And in the 1920s, with the gradual assumption of the archconservative Republican power on the commission, this agency lapsed into relative inactivity.

78. See Arthur S. Link, *Wilson Campaigns for Progressivism and Peace, 1916–1917* (Princeton, N.J.: Princeton University Press, 1965), p. 60.

79. See Arthur S. Link, *op. cit.,* pp. 64–65.

80. Moreover, as Link has noted in another work, Wilson, who was at heart a "laissez-fairist," was never keenly interested in the various efforts made to secure federal social welfare legislation, for he basically did not believe in the efficacy of ambitious governmental programs designed to alleviate the plight of depressed groups. Congress approved three such reform measures in the first part of his administration—the labor provisions of the Clayton Antitrust Act, the LaFollette-Peters (eight-hour workday) Act of 1914, and the Seamen's Act of 1915. But Wilson took no part in their formulation or in their passage, not did he give any support to the women's suffrage movement or the proposed federal child labor law. See Arthur S. Link, *Wilson: The New Freedom,* p. 255.

81. The disagreement was brought to a head by Wilson's response to the German sinking of the *Lusitania,* a British liner carrying both a large number of passengers and a considerable amount of (contraband) military supplies, with an appalling loss of life, including 124 Americans. However, the roots of Bryan's conflict with the President went back much earlier, to numerous other diplomatic matters, particularly with regard to America's wartime relations with Britain and France. See Daniel M. Smith, *Robert Lansing and American Neutrality, 1914–1917* (Berkeley: University of California Press, 1958), pp. 34–90. For a recent revealing treatment of one important aspect of this topic, see Roberta A. Dayer, "Strange Bedfellows: J. P. Morgan & Co., Whitehall and the Wilson Administration During World War I," *Business History* (July 1976), pp. 127–51.

82. Lansing picked a wealthy career diplomat, William Phillips (who had married a member of the Astor family), to serve as his Assistant Secretary of State in place of the Bryanite former governor of Wyoming, John Osborne. Lansing also selected New York lawyer Frank L. Polk, who had been a director of the medium-sized Harriman National Bank, to take over the post of counselor to the State Department. Polk later became the nation's first Under Secretary of State, a position created in the closing part of the Wilson administration to help cope with America's rapidly expanding involvement in world affairs.

83. See Daniel M. Smith, *op. cit.,* pp. 5–6. Though only a local (hometown) business

connection, Lansing did serve, interestingly, as a vice-president of the fairly small City National Bank of Watertown, New York from 1912 through 1920, during most of which years he held high State Department posts.

84. The able John W. Foster died in 1917, following many years of public and private service. However, this was sometime after Lansing's appointment as Secretary of State. That Lansing himself was probably closely linked with this prestigious, business-dominated civic body can be inferred from the fact that, shortly after he stepped down from public office, he was elected to the board of the Carnegie Endowment for International Peace. Moreover, Leonard Mosley claims that Foster became a director of several major Wall Street concerns after he left the federal government, although the author has found no evidence of this. See Leonard Mosley, *Dulles* (New York: Dell Publishing Co., 1978), p. 29.

85. Apparently there was considerable Wall Street support for the nation's entry into the League of Nations, but it failed to convince many skeptical or hostile members of the United States Senate, for in 1920 this body voted, perhaps largely for political reasons, to reject this plan. One indication that important corporate interests probably favored this measure as a way of promoting peaceful international relations and world trade is that, in contrast to the highly partisan Henry Cabot Lodge (who represented essentially old wealth), Massachusetts Republican leader W. Murray Crane, who sat on the board of AT&T and the Morgan-dominated Guaranty Trust Co., lobbied quietly in behalf of this issue. See Carolyn W. Johnson, *Winthrop Murray Crane*, p. 65.

86. See R. Carlyle Buley, *The Equitable Life Assurance Society of the United States, 1858–1964*, Vol. I, pp. 611–99, and Morton Keller, *The Life Insurance Industry*, p. 49. The vice-president of the American Deposit and Loan Co. was James H. Hyde, who was a high official and then-dominant stockholder of the Equitable Life Assurance Society. The board of the first company included such other allied figures as Henry M. Alexander (who was at that time Colby's law partner), Marcellus Hartley, Valentine P. Snyder, and Gage E. Tarbell, all of whom were either officers or directors of Equitable Life. Colby was also closely associated, as an attorney, with newspaper magnate William Randolph Hearst shortly before his appointment to his first federal office. On this point, see Daniel M. Smith, *Aftermath of War: Bainbridge Colby and Wilsonian Diplomacy, 1920–1921* (Philadelphia: American Philosophical Society, 1970), pp. 8–12.

87. That Colby was probably a conservative, despite his checkered background, may also be seen from the fact that he appointed a pro-business figure, Norman H. Davis, as his Under Secretary of State. Davis had served briefly (from 1917 to 1920) in various lesser federal posts, but, more importantly, he had been the chief executive officer of the (fairly small) Trust Co. of Cuba since 1902, and was until 1920 a director of the New York–dominated Central Sugar Corp., Cardenas-American Sugar Corp., and American Foreign Banking Corp., a newly formed concern headed by Albert H. Wiggin, the president of the Morgan-controlled Chase National Bank.

88. Wilson first offered this key Cabinet post to Wall Street's Bernard M. Baruch, who had previously served as an influential informal advisor to the President and as a much-acclaimed governmental mobilizer for the administration during World War I. But Baruch declined because of his wealth, which he feared would lead to accusations of personal bias. Baruch was a financier who had spent considerable time early in the century acting primarily as the agent, first, of the fabled corporate investor, Thomas Fortune Ryan, and then somewhat later, of the enormously wealthy Guggenheim family, by whom he was regarded virtually as "one of the brothers." (See Margaret Coit, *Mr. Baruch* [Boston: Houghton Mifflin, 1957], p. 122.) Baruch was a major stockholder in the Guggenheim-controlled American Smelting and Refining Co., the Utah Copper Co. (another concern in which this family had a sizable stake), and, along with the Morgan interests, the Texas Gulf Sulphur Co. Although one writer claims that Baruch followed a policy of not sitting on corporate boards, he did serve as a director, with Ryan and two of the Guggenheims, of the Continental Rubber Co. around 1907, in which enterprise he had invested about $925,000.

For more on these matters, see Carter Field, *Bernard Baruch: Park Bench Statesman,* pp. 59, 64, and 226, and John Douglas Forbes, *Stettinius, Sr.: Portrait of a Morgan Partner* (Charlottesville: University Press of Virginia, 1974), p. 154.

89. Upon stepping down from office at the end of the Wilson regime, Houston, who had apparently caught the eye of various prominent business figures, became head of a newly formed subsidiary of AT&T.

90. In fact, Stanley Coben went so far as to entitle the second chapter of his biography of Palmer, "The Workingman's Friend," because of his early political action in behalf of the lower classes. See Stanley Coben, *A. Mitchell Palmer,* pp. 16–28.

91. See Stanley Coben, *op. cit.,* pp. 9–10 and 70–71. According to Coben, Palmer served on the board of at least six corporations when he entered Congress, most of which the author has been unable to identify, though all were probably fairly small northeastern Pennsylvania concerns.

92. See Stanley Coben, *op. cit.,* pp. 184 and 189. Palmer's first Solicitor General, Alexander C. King, was a partner in a major Atlanta corporate law firm (King and Spalding), and had served for many years as a director of the Atlanta Trust Co. and as special counsel for the Seaboard Air Line Railway.

93. There were no changes, it should be noted, in the two top posts of the Navy Department during the latter years of the administration. The progressive Josephus Daniels and New York patrician Franklin D. Roosevelt held office for the entire eight years of the Wilson regime.

94. From 1909 to 1913 Baker served, while holding public office, as secretary and treasurer of the Sheffield Land & Improvement Co., a local real estate concern which was headed by Cleveland's famous reformer Tom Johnson up to his death in 1911. However, this was not, from a national or regional standpoint, a very important tie, although it reveals much about the orientation of some municipal reformers.

95. According to Baker's most recent biographer, he was also on friendly terms with such influential figures as Frederick H. Goff, the president of the Cleveland Trust Co., who served on many major corporate boards of directors at this time, and who offered to lend considerable money to the financially strapped Baker while the latter was acting as a Cabinet official (an offer graciously refused). See Clarence H. Cramer, *Newton D. Baker,* p. 165, and especially Daniel R. Beaver, *Newton D. Baker and the American War Effort, 1917–1919* (Lincoln: University of Nebraska Press, 1966), pp. 5–7.

96. One of the other "name" partners, Silas H. Strawn, served on the board of the First National Bank of Chicago, Montgomery, Ward & Co., Chicago Junction Railway (which was controlled by the Chicago Junction Railway and Union Stock Yard Co.), and the Joliet and Northern Indiana Railroad (a subsidiary of the Vanderbilt-Morgan–dominated New York Central system).

97. There was one other, less significant shift in Wilson's Cabinet during his last years in office, and that involved the late 1919 appointment of Joshua W. Alexander, a longtime Missouri Congressman and small-town (Gallatin, Missouri) lawyer, to replace William Redfield as Secretary of Commerce. Unlike his predecessor, Alexander had no known corporate ties.

98. The older NAM, on the other hand, had never had one of its officers or directors appointed to a prominent Cabinet position since it was founded in 1895. This indicates that it had relatively little influence, particularly compared to that exercised by the big-business–dominated National Civic Federation in the preceding Roosevelt and Taft administrations.

99. See William H. Harbaugh, *Lawyer's Lawyer: The Life of John W. Davis* (New York: Oxford University Press, 1973), pp. 46–47, 57–58, and 63–64.

100. For more on these extended partnership negotiations, which dated back to at least September 1920, see William H. Harbaugh, *op. cit.,* pp. 182–88.

101. There was no change in personnel in America's representation to Germany during this period, for former wealthy New York lawyer and judge James W. Gerard held this important post up to February 1917, when the United States formally severed its diplomatic ties to this nation shortly before our entry into World War I.

102. This group was, according to all reports, an unusually active body, for each of its members was given jurisdiction over certain major areas of activity. Willard was responsible for transportation and communications; Baruch for raw materials, minerals, and metals; Howard Coffin (a vice-president of the Hudson Motor Car Co.) for manufacturing, munitions, and industrial relations; Rosenwald for supplies and finished goods; Godfrey for engineering and education; Gompers for labor; and Dr. Franklin Martin (who was secretary general of the American College of Surgeons) for medicine and sanitation. Although Willard did not serve on any important corporate boards at this time, the majority of the "outside" directors of the Baltimore and Ohio Railroad were New York City businessmen, the most prominent of whom were W. Averill Harriman (a vice-president of the Union Pacific Railroad and a director of the Illinois Central Railroad), Leonor F. Loree, president of the Delaware and Hudson Co. (and a director of the Erie Railroad and Southern Pacific Co.), John R. Morron, head of the Atlas Portland Cement Co. (and a director of the Intercontinental Rubber Co. and Guaranty Trust Co. of New York City), Charles A. Peabody, president of the Mutual Life Insurance Co. and vice-president of the Delaware and Hudson Co. (as well as a director of the Illinois Central Railroad, Union Pacific Railroad, and Guaranty Trust Co.), and Felix M. Warburg, who was a partner in Kuhn, Loeb & Co. (and a brother of Federal Reserve Board member Paul M. Warburg).

103. In marked contrast to the unwieldly (and short-lived) 22-man General Munitions Board, the War Industries Board was made up originally of just seven members—Frank Scott, its chairman; Bernard Baruch, commissioner of raw materials; former St. Louis business and civic leader Robert Brookings, commissioner of finished products; Robert S. Lovett, a high official of the Union Pacific Railroad (and a director of the Illinois Central Railroad, New York Central Railroad, and National City Bank of New York), priority commissioner; longtime AFL executive Hugh A. Frayne, labor commissioner; Colonel Palmer Pierce, the U.S. Army representative; and Rear Admiral F. F. Fletcher, Navy representative.

104. There were several other special agencies created by the Wilson administration shortly before or during the First World War, such as the U.S. Shipping Board, which was headed by former Federal Trade Commissioner Edward N. Hurley (now a director of the Central Trust Co. of Chicago), and the War Trade Board, which was dominated by such business figures as New York banker Albert Strauss and longtime Chicago lawyer and Wilson supporter Thomas D. Jones (a board member of the International Harvester Co. and the New Jersey Zinc Co.). But none of these was as important as the War Industries Board.

105. By this time the Board had been expanded to ten members—namely, Bernard Baruch, its chairman; Alexander Legge (the former general manager of the International Harvester Co.), its vice-chairman; Edwin B. Parker (a prominent Houston corporate lawyer), priorities commissioner; Robert Brookings, head of the price fixing committee; George N. Peek (a longtime high official of Deere & Co.), commissioner of finished products; J. Leonard Replogle (the recent head of both the American Vanadium Co. and Wharton Steel Co. and a still active director of the Wabash Railway), steel administrator; the AFL's High Frayne, labor commissioner; Leland L. Summers (a man formerly associated with J. P. Morgan & Co.), technical advisor; General George W. Goethals, U.S. Army representative; and Admiral F. F. Fletcher, Navy representative.

106. While the author feels that business interests did much to shape politico-economic relations during the First World War, he does not subscribe to the view that these relatively brief links were a forerunner of the much more highly structured and enduring connection we have come to call the military-industrial complex. For a sound study of this subject, see Robert D. Cuff, *The War Industries Board: Business-Government Relations during World War I* (Baltimore: Johns Hopkins Press, 1973), *passim;* for a contrary line of analysis, see

Paul A. C. Koistinen, "The 'Industrial-Military Complex' in Historical Perspective: World War I'', *Business History Review* (Winter 1967), pp. 378–403, and his "The 'Industrial-Military Complex' in Historical Perspective: The Interwar Years," *Journal of American History* (March 1970), pp. 819–39.

107. For more on Meyer's early political, economic, and social affairs, see Merlo J. Pusey, *Eugene Meyer* (New York: Alfred A. Knopf, 1974), pp. 3–170. All but one of the companies mentioned in the text ranked in or around the 100 largest industrial enterprises in the country as of 1917. Meyer served as a director of the Inspiration Consolidated Copper Co. and Maxwell Motor Co. until sometime in 1917, and as a director of the Utah Copper Co. and Pan-American Petroleum & Transport Co. until sometime in 1918. Because of their duration, these last two links raise a question of conflict of interest.

108. For a brief description of Baruch's influential governmental staff during these turbulent war years, see Robert D. Cuff, "Bernard Baruch: Symbol and Myth in Industrial Mobilization," *Business History Review* (Summer 1969), pp. 119–20. Allen sat on several of these boards throughout the war years, contrary to all canons of propriety.

109. Although Secretary of War Newton D. Baker was not sympathetic to Baruch's governmental activities, his two Second Assistant Secretaries of War in 1918 were men of a similar sort—Edward R. Stettinius (a recently appointed Morgan executive who served until 1917 on the board of the fairly big International Agricultural Corp.), and then briefly near the end of the war, John D. Ryan (a former Baruch aide who was president of both the Amalgamated Copper Co. and Montana Power Co., a vice-president of the Greene Cananea Copper Co., and a director of the Cuba Cane Sugar Corp., Inspiration Consolidated Copper Co., and Mechanics and Metals National Bank of New York City). Also, for a series of penetrating questions raised about these relationships, see Robert D. Cuff, "Business, the State and World War I: The American Experience," in J. L. Granatstein and R. D. Cuff (eds.), *War and Society in North America* (Toronto: Thomas Nelson and Sons, 1971), pp. 2–3.

110. See Robert D. Cuff, "Bernard Baruch," *Business History Review* (Summer 1969), p. 132. In contrast, Arthur Link has maintained that Baruch was a powerful "economic dictator" as head of the War Industries Board in 1918. See Arthur S. Link, *American Epoch*, 3rd ed. (New York: Knopf, 1967), p. 203. For a further description of the various cooperative, if not collusive, practices established by big business and governmental leaders under the aegis of the War Industries Board, see Robert D. Cuff, *Business, Government and the War Industries Board* (Princeton University, unpublished dissertation, 1966), *passim*.

111. In fact, of the five Republican Justices who served throughout the Wilson administration, only Oliver Wendell Holmes might be said to have been substantially free of deeply ingrained conservative influences, and even he reflected to some extent the biases of his Boston Brahmin background.

112. Of the other three judicial incumbents (Hughes, Lamar, and Lurton), whose service on the High Court was limited to just the first part of this period, only one, Charles Evans Hughes, had a fairly liberal voting record, and this might be explained largely by his desire to obtain still higher public office, which political goal slipped through Hughes's hands by a very narrow margin in the closely contested presidential campaign of 1916.

113. McReynolds had served, while a Tennessee attorney, as a legal advisor to various business enterprises, one of which was the Illinois Central Railroad, and he had also been in the early 1900s a vice-president of Nashville's City Savings Bank. His later work as a New York City lawyer was so brief (about fifteen months in all) as probably to be of little significance. For more on McReynolds' career, see Leon Friedman and Fred L. Israel (eds.), *The Justices of the United States Supreme Court, 1789–1969,* Vol. III, p. 2025.

114. From a historical standpoint, Brandeis was, as one writer has noted, the first Supreme Court Justice whose major (recent) background was that of "counsel for the people." See Ernest S. Bates, *The Story of the Supreme Court* (Indianapolis: Bobbs-Merrill Co., 1936), p. 245.

115. In retrospect, even the admiring Alpheus T. Mason (who was apparently perplexed by Brandeis's early close corporate links) felt compelled to assert that ". . . it is not clear how one so gifted as People's Attorney, so skilled in factual exploration, could unknowingly have become deeply involved with a corporation designed and operated primarily to achieve monopolistic ends." See Alpheus T. Mason, *Brandeis: A Free Man's Life* (New York: Viking Press, 1946), p. 228.

116. See A. L. Todd, *Justice on Trial: The Case of Louis D. Brandeis* (New York: McGraw-Hill, 1964), pp. 69–183, and John R. Schmidhauser, *The Supreme Court: Its Politics, Personalities, and Procedures*, pp. 15–17. Schmidhauser claims, after a careful study of the appointment process, that there is considerable evidence to indicate that the leaders of the bar are often more interested in the ideological assumptions of Supreme Court candidates than in their qualifications or any ideal of objectivity and impartiality. Brandeis, of course, was not a radical, but rather a dedicated reformer who was, at heart, a firm supporter of the nation's free enterprise system (if modified by a number of much-needed changes) and, perhaps because of his corporate legal background, was even ambivalent about the role of organized labor in the United States.

117. See Hoyt L. Warner, *The Life of Mr. Justice Clarke* (Cleveland: Western Reserve University Press, 1959), pp. 9 and 20.

118. According to Warner (*op. cit.*, p. 54), Clarke resigned from this lucrative position in October 1912 so that he could step up his speaking engagements in behalf of presidential aspirant Woodrow Wilson and Ohio Democratic gubernatorial candidate James M. Cox. Yet the 1913 *Poor's Railroad Manual* still listed him as the line's general counsel.

119. See Leon Friedman and Fred L. Israel (eds.), *The Justices of the United States Supreme Court, 1789–1969*, Vol. III, p. 2080, and Hoyt L. Warner, *op. cit.*, p. 31.

120. Of the four dissenting Justices in this case, two, Brandeis and Clarke, were recent Wilson appointees, and a third, Oliver Wendell Holmes, was a highly independent patrician who frequently supported liberal causes.

121. See Ernest S. Bates, *op. cit.*, p. 250.

122. See Ernest S. Bates, *op. cit.*, p. 253.

123. There were some lesser shifts in the other characteristics of Wilson's top officials and those of the three preceding Republican regimes—in all, a drop of about 18 percent in the proportion of those who had college degrees and a 10 percent decline in those who had a considerable amount of governmental experience. No attempt has been made here to compare the Supreme Court recruitment pattern of the various presidential administrations, for this involves a much smaller number of figures who generally serve for long overlapping terms. This matter will not be treated until the concluding chapter of this study.

124. The business-dominated National Civic Federation did not, judging from the available evidence, carry a great deal of weight in Wilson's government, and apparently experienced a significant decline in its overall strength and importance during this period.

125. See, for instance, Robert D. Cuff, "Woodrow Wilson and Business-Government Relations during World War I," *Review of Politics* (July 1969), p. 385.

126. For instance, in his study of the steel industry's record in World War I, Urofsky claims that after our entry into this great conflict, the Wilson administration still had various possible options, ". . . yet in every instance it chose the course most favored by Big Steel. In taxes, priorities, distribution, prices, and controls, the federal government followed the dictates of the Gary committee [the War Industries Board body headed by the top official of U.S. Steel]." See Melvin L. Urofsky, *Big Steel and the Wilson Administration* (Columbus: Ohio State University Press, 1969), p. 336. Even such an admiring authority as Arthur Link conceded at one (early) point in his writings that Wilson's progressivism was essentially of a superficial nature. See Arthur S. Link, *Woodrow Wilson and the Progressive Era, 1910–1917*, p. 80 in particular.

CHAPTER 6

Harding, Coolidge, and Hoover

While the Wilsonian years were marked by a great deal of tension and tumult, the succeeding Republican period has generally been described (up to late 1929) as an era of quietude, a time when most citizens had grown tired of agitation and reform and desired nothing more than a return to "normalcy." The progressive movement had obviously peaked shortly before World War I, and the emotional energies of the nation were so drained by this struggle that when victory came, the great mass of the people sank back into a rather lethargic state from which they could not be shaken by either scandal or massive unmet economic needs.[1]

Yet even as the nation slid into complacancy in the 1920s (from which it was jarred only by the Great Depression), a number of major economic trends were at work that had a marked effect on both business and government in the United States. Thanks in part to a second widespread merger movement, most of the big manufacturing firms in the country continued to grow quite rapidly (at least up to 1929), and thus, despite the impact of the Depression, they were substantially larger in 1933 than they had been at the outset of this period. This may readily be seen by looking at Table 8.[2] Seven of these concerns were big oil companies, which grew at a faster rate than the other enterprises in this elite category. What's more, much of this growth took place outside the United States through the acquisition of lucrative exploration or development rights in such oil-rich areas as the Middle East, in which efforts these companies were often aided, to overcome the opposition of well-entrenched British interests, by high-ranking officials in the federal government.[3]

Of perhaps equal importance was the fact that the vast majority of these top 20 industrial concerns were controlled by major family or entre-preneurial interests, as may be seen from Table 8.[4] Most of these were involved in the establishment and early development of these firms, as in the case of the United States Steel Corp., the Ford Motor Co., the du Pont company, Phelps Dodge Corp., Kennecott Copper Corp. (which was

TABLE 8

America's Top 20 Industrial Firms in 1933

1933 Rank	Company	1921 Assets ($ millions)	1933 Assets ($ millions)	Control Status
1	United States Steel Corp.	2,339	2,103	Morgan interests
2	Standard Oil Co. of N.J.	1,102	1,912	Rockefeller interests
3	General Motors Corp.	515	1,316	du Pont interests
4	Socony-Vacuum Oil Co. (formerly Standard Oil Co. of N.Y.)	348	990	Rockefeller interests
5	International Paper & Power Co.	102	881	probably a management-dominated concern (with, increasingly, the support of the Phipps interests)
6	Anaconda Copper Mining Co.	290	692	probably a management-dominated concern (with the support of some Standard Oil families)
7	Standard Oil Co. of Indiana	306	677	Rockefeller interests
8	Bethlehem Steel Corp.	366	649	probably a management dominated concern
9	Ford Motor Co.	345	639	(Henry) Ford family
10	E. I. du Pont de Nemours & Co.	252	606	du Pont family
11	Standard Oil Co. of Cal.	277	568	Rockefeller interests
12	Texas Corp. (Texaco)	336	498	probably a management-dominated concern
13	Gulf Oil Corp.	273	428	Mellon family
14	Allied Chemical & Dye Corp.	267	412	Eugene Meyer, Nichols, and Belgian Solvay interests
15	General Electric Co.	339	375	J. P. Morgan and certain close-knit Boston Brahmin interests

TABLE 8 (Continued)

1933 Rank	Company	1921 Assets ($ millions)	1933 Assets ($ millions)	Control Status
16	Consolidated Oil Corp. (formerly Sinclair Consolidated Oil Corp.)	343	361	Sinclair interests
17	Armour & Co.	481	356	Armour family (though interest apparently waning)
18	International Harvester Co.	267	349	McCormick family
19	Phelps Dodge Corp.	228	345	Phelps-Dodge and (A. C.) James interests
20	Kennecott Copper Corp.	135	319	Guggenheim and (J. P.) Morgan interests

created by the Guggenheim family in 1915), and the four Standard Oil companies (now formally separated units that were still ultimately dominated by the Rockefeller forces).[5] Other enterprises, however, were taken over later by powerful financial or entrepreneurial interests. One of the most conspicuous of these was the huge General Motors Corp., in which the du Pont family invested sufficient money after World War I to secure a dominant stake, a move which gave this family control over two of the top ten industrial firms in the country.

While the railroads did not expand significantly during this period, they still represented a major force in the economic life of the nation. There was also little change in the overall makeup of the railroad industry, particularly in the top-tier enterprises, which had remained fairly stable since the turn of the century.[6] Unfortunately, by the 1920s it had become very difficult to determine the locus of control in many of these huge lines, as the stockownership pattern became increasingly blurred and complex. Yet certain railroads had clearly fallen under the aegis of such new economic mechanisms as the holding company. The most prominent of these was the Allegheny Corp., which was dominated (after its creation in 1929) by the Van Sweringen brothers of Cleveland and controlled such major lines as the Missouri Pacific Railroad, the Chesapeake and Ohio Railway, and the New York, Chicago and St. Louis Railroad.[7]

One area in which tremendous change did take place in the 1920s and early 1930s was that of the (non-transportation) public utilities. Before World War I there were comparatively few firms in this field which had reached gigantic size. But by the mid-1920s this situation had been altered radically, primarily through the development of huge holding companies and other corporate control devices. Indeed, according to one reliable source, by the end of 1925 the five largest power and light groups in the country controlled nearly half the electricity generated in the United States.[8] By 1933 some enterprises had grown so rapidly that they rivaled the nation's major railroad and industrial concerns in size and importance, as may be seen by a glance at the following list of the top twenty operational or control units in this area.

TABLE 9

America's Top 20 Public Utility Concerns in 1933

Rank	Company	1921 Assets ($ millions)	1933 Assets ($ millions)
1.	American Telephone & Telegraph Co.	1,050	4,940
2.	Consolidated Gas Co. of N.Y.	196	1,352
3.	Cities Service Co. (HC)	402	1,282
4.	United States Electric Power Corp. (HC)	—†	1,152
5.	Commonwealth & Southern Corp.	—†	1,129
6.	Associated Gas & Electric Co. (HC)	7	959
7.	North American Co. (HC)	156	878
8.	United Gas Improvement Co.	121	815
9.	Columbia Gas & Electric Corp.	76	730
10.	Pacific Gas & Electric Co.	219	713
11.	Public Service Corp. of N.J.	136	705
12.	Niagara Hudson Power Corp.	—†	662
13.	United Corp. (HC)	—*	588
14.	International Telephone & Telegraph Corp. (HC)	15	585
15.	International Hydro-Electric System (HC)	—*	581
16.	United Light & Power Co. (HC)	—†	573
17.	Electric Bond and Share Co. (HC)	29	550
18.	American Gas & Electric Co. (HC)	27	458
19.	Commonwealth Edison Co., Ill.	152	446
20.	American Water Works & Electric Co. (HC)	55	422

Note: HC stands for holding company.

*Created in the late 1920s.

†Created in early 1920s

This list is unfortunately somewhat deceiving, for although almost all of these concerns are treated in Moody's and most other business manuals as largely autonomous units, a sizable number were actually closely linked or controlled through certain key corporate devices, the most common of which was the big holding company. For instance, the 13th-ranked United Corp., which was created in 1929 by J. P. Morgan & Co. and allied interests, exercised substantial influence, if not de facto control, over the Commonwealth and Southern Corp., United Gas Improvement Co., Columbia Gas & Electric Corp., Public Service Corp. of New Jersey, and Niagara Hudson Power Corp. (these firms, which ranked in the top twelve, had combined assets of more than $4 billion).[9] Thus, as Cochran and Miller have observed, the House of Morgan, which had established its powerful position in the financial community through the consolidation of many major rail lines around the turn of the century, had turned its efforts by the 1920s to the creation of a number of vast public utility combines.[10]

As a result of this general trend, the overall level of economic concentration had reached the point by 1930 where the top 200 industrial, railroad, and public utility companies controlled nearly half of all corporate wealth in the United States (exclusive of financial institutions), although these huge firms represented only about 0.07 percent of the total number of such enterprises in the country.[11]

The financial field also underwent a great deal of growth and change in the 1920s and early 1930s, in part because of the impact of the Depression, which led to the (forced?) merger of some big banks and the collapse of certain others. That this is true may be seen by a look at the following list of the top ten banks in the country in 1933, five of which had attained such ranking in 1921.[12]

TABLE 10

America's Top 10 Banks in 1933

Rank	Bank	1921 Assets ($ millions)	1933 Assets ($ millions)
1.	Chase National Bank, N.Y.C.	535	1,715
2.	Guaranty Trust Co., N.Y.C.	924	1,420
3.	National City Bank, N.Y.C.	1,044	1,387
4.	Bank of America, Cal.	150	941
5.	Continental Illinois Bank & Trust Co., Chicago	418	747
6.	Bankers Trust Co., N.Y.C.	413	737
7.	Central Hanover Bank & Trust Co., N.Y.C.	251	697
8.	First National Bank, Boston	219	645
9.	First National Bank, Chicago	107	643
10.	Irving Trust Co., N.Y.C.	297	553

Thus in contrast to 1921, when eight of the top ten banks were, in effect, Wall Street concerns, no more than six of the nation's largest financial institutions (excluding insurance companies) were located in New York City by 1933. This noteworthy shift was evidenced most clearly in the sudden rise to national prominence of the Bank of America (or, as it was known until 1930, the Bank of Italy), a California-based firm dominated by a set of distinctly "outside" interests, the A. P. Giannini family. Perhaps even more important, some of the mergers which were consummated during this period led to a change in both the ranking of and the locus of power in certain major financial enterprises. For instance, in 1930 the Rockefeller-dominated Equitable Trust Co. was merged into the considerably larger Chase National Bank. As a result, the Chase, which had long been closely aligned with the House of Morgan, was transformed into a firm in which the key stockownership lay with the influential family of John D. Rockefeller (as revealed in the selection of the bank's new president, Winthrop W. Aldrich, a Rockefeller kinsman).[13] Hence, two of the biggest banks in the country were now controlled by the two major branches of the Rockefeller family—that of the great John D. and that of his lesser-known brother, William. This economic shift marked the beginning of a new era in American banking.[14]

In addition, there were a number of noteworthy developments of an ostensibly civic nature that took place during this period. Because of its long-term impact on American politico-economic affairs, one of the most important of these was the creation of the Council on Foreign Relations, a New York–based group formed in 1921 in response to the country's increasing involvement in international relations.[15] This organization's top leadership was originally composed of a rather well-balanced mix of academic and civic figures, such as geographer Isaiah Bowman and political science professor Stephen P. Duggan, and well-known economic leaders, such as "Morgan" lawyer John W. Davis, our last Ambassador to Great Britain, and Wall Street attorney Paul D. Cravath, who was a director of the Rockefeller-controlled Equitable Trust Co. and Westinghouse Electric & Mfg. Co.[16] However, by the late 1920s the Council had become increasingly dominated by more overt pro-business figures, such as Allen W. Dulles, a partner in the New York law firm of Sullivan and Cromwell and former State Department official (whose brother and professional colleague, John Foster Dulles, served on the board of several major concerns, such as the International Nickel Co. of Canada, Ltd.), Owen D. Young, the board chairman of the General Electric Co., and Charles P. Howland, who was a partner in the Rockefeller-oriented law firm of Murray, (Winthrop W.) Aldrich & Webb. Yet, it should be observed, this body probably still did not have the Establishment status of the older and better-known Carnegie Endowment for International Peace. That organization was headed after 1924 by Columbia University president Nicholas Murray Butler (who was a trustee of the New York Life Insurance Co.), and included among its board members such prominent persons as Elihu Root, an influential lawyer and prewar Cabinet official (whose son was now a director of the American Smelting & Refining Co.), and Frank O. Lowden, a former governor of Illinois who had married into the Pullman family. Thus these two organizations may have provided a key link between the worlds of big business and foreign affairs.[17]

The 1920s, that great era of politico-economic "normalcy," was ushered in by an electoral landslide in which the Republican presidential nominee, Warren G. Harding, won over 60 percent of the popular vote. This lopsided margin represented an emphatic repudiation of the Wilson administration and many of its policies, particularly its ardent support of the ill-fated League of Nations. Although the overwhelming victor, Harding had not been the first choice of the delegates and various influential figures at the party's 1920 national convention. Two more able and appealing business-backed candidates—Illinois Governor Frank Lowden, who had married a Pullman heiress and had previously served on a number of major corporate boards (the most recent of which was the now Morgan-Vanderbilt–dominated Pullman Co.), and the ambitious and highly popular General Leonard Wood, who had the support of many of Theodore Roosevelt's warmest political admirers and certain powerful Eastern economic interests—had much larger followings than the amiable Harding, who was a former Ohio Senator and small-town newspaper publisher.[18] But because of the deadlock that developed over these two top contenders, the power brokers at the convention turned—in considerable part through the efforts of such party leaders as Ohio's Harry M. Daugherty, Myron T. Herrick (both of whom were good friends of Harding), New York publisher George Harvey (a onetime Wilson Democrat), and Pennsylvania's ailing political boss, Boies Penrose—to the handsome, affable, and thoroughly mediocre Warren G. Harding, a man of little stature.[19] Harding had spent most of his adult life publishing a newspaper in his hometown of Marion, Ohio (which had a population of about 4,500). He had held public office at two points in his career, shortly after the turn of the century as a state legislator and lieutenant governor, and later (from 1915 to 1920) as a U.S. Senator. Until the latter part of the preceding decade he had also served on the board of at least three local economic enterprises—the Marion County Bank, Marion County Telephone Co., and Tennessee Timber Co. These ties undoubtedly gave him a pro-business orientation, but hardly one of broad national scope.[20] He thus had few noteworthy links with major corporate executives or financial leaders.[21] Indeed, most of Harding's close friends were ambitious small-time political and economic figures, some of whom apparently had easy scruples.

Harding's Major Cabinet and Diplomatic Appointments

After considerable consultation with a variety of advisors, President Harding appointed the following set of officials (not all of whom were his first choices) as his chief Cabinet members in 1921:[22]

Secretary of State	Charles Evans Hughes, N.Y. (1921 through 1923)	Unsuccessful 1916 Republican presidential candidate; Associate Justice, U.S.

		Supreme Court (1910–1916); governor of New York (1907–1910)
		Partner in New York law firm of Hughes, Rounds, Schurman and predecessor (1917–1921); also partner in Hughes, Rounds & Schurman and predecessor firm (1887–1891 and 1893–1907)
		Trustee of the Rockefeller Foundation (1917–1921)
Secretary of Treasury	Andrew W. Mellon, Pa. (1921 through 1923)	No formal governmental experience
		President of Mellon National Bank, Pittsburgh (up to 1921); vice-president (VP) of the National Union Fire Insurance Co. (up through 1923); VP of the Gulf Oil Corp., Union Trust Co., and Union Savings Bank, Pittsburgh (up to 1921)
		Director of Aluminum Co. of America, Koppers Co., Carbonundum Co., Pittsburgh Coal Co., Standard Steel Car Co., American Locomotive Co., Crucible Steel Co. of America, and National Bank of Commerce, N.Y.C. (all up to 1921)
Attorney General	Harry M. Daugherty, Ohio (1921 through 1923)	Onetime (1890–1894) Ohio state legislator
		Longtime partner in Columbus law firm of Daugherty, Todd & Rarey (up to 1921)
		Director of the (Ohio-based) United States Telephone Co. (at least 1910 to 1914, when merged into a larger company) and Scioto Valley Traction Co. (1915 through 1923)
Secretary of War	John W. Weeks, Mass. (1921 through 1923)	U.S. Senator, Mass. (1913–1919); Mass.

		Congressman (1905–1913); mayor of Boston (1902–1903)
		Partner in Hornblower & Weeks, Boston investment firm (up to 1912); vice-president of the First National Bank of Boston (up to 1912, and a director up to 1913)
		Director of the U.S. Smelting, Refining & Mining Co. (up to 1913)
Secretary of the Navy	Edwin Denby, Mich. (1921 through 1923)	Michigan Congressman (1905–1911)
		Longtime Detroit lawyer (but not with a top-tier firm)
		Director of the (fairly large) National Bank of Commerce, Detroit (up to 1921) and the (considerably smaller) Bankers Trust Co., Detroit (through 1923)
Secretary of Interior	Albert B. Fall, N.M. (1921–March 1923)	U.S. Senator, N.M. (1912–1921); at various earlier points attorney general of New Mexico, associate justice of New Mexico Supreme Court, and state legislator
		Longtime New Mexico lawyer and entrepreneur
		Director of the Rio Grande, Sierre Madre & Pacific RR (up to 1907) and the Greene Gold-Silver Corp. (up to 1905)
Secretary of Agriculture	Henry C. Wallace, Iowa (1921 through 1923)	No formal governmental experience
		Editor or associate editor of (widely read) *Wallace's Farmer* (1896–1921)
		Director of the Central State Bank, Des Moines (1914 through 1923)
Secretary of Commerce	Herbert C. Hoover, Cal. (1921 through 1923)	WWI federal food administrator and postwar relief official

		International mining engineer and entrepreneur, mainly in Asia and Australia (1908–1916); official of Bewick, Moreing & Co., British-controlled international mining and investment concern (up to 1908)
		Director of Burma (Mines) Corp., Ltd. (1906–1919), Chinese Engineering & Mining Co. (1903–1912), Russo-Asiatic Corp. (1913–1916), Zinc Corp., Ltd. (1906–1916), and many other foreign enterprises in pre-WWI period
Secretary of Labor	James J. Davis, Pa. (1921 through 1923)	No formal governmental experience
		President of American Bond & Mortgage Co. Pittsburgh (through 1923)
		Onetime well-known local (Indiana) official of Amalgamated Assn. of Iron, Steel & Tin Workers of America (still a member of national body)

All of these officials had certain links with business interests, although the magnitude and nature of their affiliations varied considerably. Secretary of Agriculture Henry Wallace was the influential publisher of a widely read farm journal and the director of a fairly large Des Moines bank. He was reportedly appointed to this Cabinet post primarily to placate agrarian forces in the Midwest, who were upset by the postwar fall in farm prices and had recently managed to mobilize their political resources effectively through the growing strength of the newly formed American Farm Bureau Federation, which, along with the much older Grange, strongly supported Wallace's selection.[23] Secretary of Commerce Herbert Hoover had served as an officer, director, or sizable stockholder of a substantial number of business concerns (almost all of which were foreign enterprises). But he was apparently chosen mainly because of the tremendous reputation he had acquired as an extraordinarily able and efficient administrator of major food and relief operations during and immediately after the First World War.[24] And the primarily business background of Secretary of Labor James J. Davis (a long inactive labor union man) probably had little to do with his selection, for his financial firm was extremely small and without formal ties to more important economic interests, although Davis belonged, interestingly, to one socially elite local group, Pittsburgh's business-dominated Duquesne Club.[25] Perhaps for good reason, the AFL and most other major unions actually regarded him as a spokesman for business forces rather than for labor. It is indeed revealing that the Harding administration would choose to appoint a person of this nature to such a politically sensitive post.[26]

Two other Cabinet members had economic links of a distinctly different nature. Attorney General Daugherty was a longtime Columbus, Ohio attorney who had served briefly (in the early 1890s) in the state legislature, but having gained this entree and experience, had thereafter devoted the bulk of his time to acting as an influential lawyer-lobbyist and Republican party leader. Such was his reported power in the legislature that large national concerns such as the American Tobacco Co., American Gas & Electric Co., and Armour & Co. chose to retain his services to help pass or kill certain major measures.[27] In addition, Daugherty served on the board of the (locally based) United States Telephone Co. up to 1914, and as a director of the Scioto Valley Traction Co. (another regional enterprise) from 1915 through his years as a Cabinet officer. As a prominent Ohio political leader, the rather unscrupulous Daugherty had devoted himself fairly early to the task of promoting the governmental fortunes of Marion's Warren G. Harding, perhaps partly to improve his own politico-economic prospects. After Daugherty succeeded, with a considerable amount of luck, in securing the presidential nomination for his good friend, Harding rewarded him with the top legal post in the federal government.

The other Cabinet member of questionable, if not unsavory, character was Secretary of the Interior Albert B. Fall, who had been a U.S. Senator from New Mexico. For several years he had sat next to Harding in the Senate, so the two became firm friends. Though Fall had extensive experience in governmental affairs, he was widely known throughout the Southwest as an entrepreneurially oriented lawyer who had represented a number of mining firms and other interests in this area. At one time, in fact, he was closely linked with a major businessman, William C. Greene, who had huge holdings in Mexico and the southwestern section of the United States, the most prominent of which was the Greene Consolidated Copper Co. Indeed, in the first part of the century Fall served on the boards of two sizable concerns, the Greene Gold-Silver Co. and the Rio Grande, Sierre Madre & Pacific Railroad, both of which were run by Greene (these corporate links were, however, severed early by the latter's abrupt economic decline).[28] Fall himself had acquired substantial interests in his home state, chief of which were ranch and land holdings of over 500,000 acres and, with the help of a wealthy syndicate, had secured an important stake in an influential newspaper, the *Albuquerque Morning*

Journal.[29] Obviously, the well-fixed Fall was thoroughly acquainted with the free-wheeling business ways of the West.

The other four members of Harding's Cabinet all had some kind of connections to large Eastern enterprises. Charles Evans Hughes, unknown to many, had undergone a major transformation from a crusading investigator and fairly liberal New York governor and U.S. Supreme Court Justice to a more conservative pro-business lawyer in the four-year period prior to his appointment as Secretary of State.[30] In fact, although the years between Hughes's presidential race in 1916 and his admission to Harding's Cabinet, during which he practiced law in New York, have (except for his many civic activities) been grossly neglected by writers and researchers, it would certainly appear that he established close links during this interval with at least one major American business concern that had a sizable stake in the conduct of the nation's foreign affairs, particularly in the Near East.[31] According to two recent sources, Hughes was an attorney for the huge Standard Oil Co. of N. J. during much or all of this period.[32] As further evidence of this association, Hughes served on the board of the Rockefeller Foundation from 1917 to 1921. While engaged in many humanitarian efforts, this institution also held a substantial block of stock (about 5 percent) in the Standard Oil Co. of N. J., so its economic fortunes were inextricably linked with those of this giant business.[33] Though more research needs to be done on this matter, it is clear then that Charles Evans Hughes was on friendly terms with the chief officers and major stockholders of the nation's largest oil company when he became Secretary of State.

Harding's Secretary of the Treasury, Andrew W. Mellon, was not drawn from the President's intimate circle of Ohio friends, nor was he, like Hughes, a well-known national figure. Mellon was instead an extremely important force in the world of big business. Never before, in fact, had such an influential magnate held a high post of this kind in American government.[34] Indeed, Mellon represented the epitome of wealth and economic power, for although he was virtually unknown to the public at large, he came from one of the richest families in the country, which had built up a huge empire that included the two biggest banks in Pittsburgh (the Mellon National Bank and Union Trust Co.),[35] Gulf Oil Corp., Koppers Co., Pittsburgh Coal Co., Aluminum Co. of America, and various other lesser concerns. These companies had combined assets of over $1 billion in 1921—an aggregate exceeded only by the Rockefeller family and the Morgan interests. As for corporate ties, Mellon had served as president of the Mellon National Bank, vice-president of the Gulf Oil Corp., Union Trust Co., and Union Savings Bank of Pittsburgh, and as a director of the Aluminum Co. of America, Koppers Co., Pittsburgh Coal Co., Standard Steel Car Co., (Mellon-controlled) Carbonundum Co., American Locomotive Co., Crucible Steel Co. of America, American Foreign Securities Co., and National Bank of Commerce (the last two New York City enterprises were dominated by the House of Morgan).[36]

Moreover, although Mellon claimed that he had severed all of his business connections upon entering Harding's Cabinet, he continued to serve (actually up to 1928) as a vice-president and director of the Mellon-controlled National Union Fire Insurance Co., which secondary link kept him in regular contact with some important economic interests and corporate executives who had a sizable stake in the formulation of federal fiscal policy. For this and related reasons, one might well expect that Mellon would take a strongly pro-business point of view as Secretary of the Treasury, and he surely did.[37]

The third member of Harding's Cabinet who had been closely linked with major economic interests was Secretary of War John W. Weeks, who was a former Boston businessman and Massachusetts Congressman and United States Senator. Though originally a Wood supporter at the Republican national convention, he had been rewarded with this high post, in part because of regional considerations and also because of his effective fundraising on behalf of Ohio's amiable compromise candidate, Warren G. Harding. Although Weeks had held federal office for many years (from 1905 to 1919), he was, perhaps more importantly, a wealthy entrepreneur and executive with a number of noteworthy socio-economic ties. He had made his financial fortune, first, as a partner in the Boston investment firm of Hornblower & Weeks (a position he held until 1912) and later as a high official of the First National Bank of Boston, an affiliation he severed when he entered the Senate in 1913. Up to this time he had also been a board member of the big United States Smelting, Refining and Mining Co., along with such other elitist figures as Robert T. Paine, Jr. (who was a director of the General Electric Co., Electric Bond & Share Co., and Old Colony Trust Co.), James J. Storrow (a partner in Lee, Higginson & Co. and a director of the General Motors Corp. and the First National Bank of Boston), and Galen L. Stone (a partner in the well-known securities firm of Hayden, Stone & Co. and a high official of the Atlantic, Gulf and West Indies Steamship Lines). In addition, Weeks's former primary business associate, Henry Hornblower, was a board member of the last-named line up to 1922, and his son's father-in-law, Boston businessman William B. H. Dowse, was a director of the Brahmin-dominated Waltham Watch Co. Hence Weeks, too, was on close terms with many prominent businessmen in the country.

The fourth member of Harding's Cabinet with major business ties was Secretary of the Navy Edwin Denby, a longtime Detroit lawyer and former (1905–1911) Michigan Congressman. Actually Denby was selected, almost as an afterthought, near the end of the Cabinet appointment process, largely at the suggestion of John W. Weeks, with whom he had served in Congress in the pre-Wilsonian years. Denby was apparently a rather mediocre individual who had made no great mark in Detroit legal, business, or governmental circles, but had nonetheless become associated with certain influential people in this now-booming city. Until 1921 he had served on the board of the fairly sizable National Bank of Commerce of

Detroit, an institution long dominated by several prominent families—the Alger, Joy, McMillan, Newberry, and Russell clans, almost all of which were closely linked through marriage and business ties.[38] Indeed, according to Stephen Birmingham, these families were the very heart of Detroit's affluent pre-automotive society and had a substantial stake in a number of financial enterprises in the area.[39] In recent years they had expanded into other ventures, such as a major interest in the Packard Motor Car Co. Thus Denby was another well-connected Cabinet member.[40]

Business forces also apparently wielded considerable influence in the appointment of the three chief diplomatic emissaries of the Harding administration, as may be seen from the following brief biographical summaries:

Ambassador to Great Britain	George Harvey, N.Y. (1921–1923)	no significant governmental experience
		Longtime head of the North American Review Publishing Co. of N.Y.C.; former president of Harper Brothers, N.Y.C. (1900–1915)
		Director of the (fairly small) Audit Co. of N.Y.C. (at least 1899 through 1923) and a number of other concerns in the pre-WWI period
Ambassador to France	Myron T. Herrick, Ohio (1921 through 1923)	Ambassador to France (1912–1914); onetime governor of Ohio (1903–1905)
		Head of Society for Savings, Cleveland (1894–1921); board chairman of Union Carbide and Carbon Corp. (1918 through 1923)
		Director of the New York Life Insurance Co. (1917 through 1923), Erie Railroad (1918–1921), and various other concerns in the pre-WWI period
Ambassador to Germany	Alanson B. Houghton, N.Y. (1922 through 1923)	New York Congressman (1919–1922)
		High official of (still fairly small) Corning Glass Works in western New York (1910 through 1923)

Director of the Metropolitan
Life Insurance Co. (1913
through 1923)

Herrick and Houghton were clearly linked with major economic interests in both their home areas and New York City. Ambassador Herrick, Harding's longtime friend and political supporter, was not only head of a big savings bank in Cleveland, but he was also a director of the huge New York Life Insurance Co. and the top official of the Union Carbide & Carbon Corp., a large enterprise which included among its directors Charles A. Coffin, the board chairman of the General Electric Co. (and a director of the American International Corp., Montana Power Co., and Electric Bond & Share Co.), George W. Davison, the president of New York's Central Union Trust Co. (and a director, up to 1920, of the Sinclair Oil & Refining Corp.), Andrew Squire, a prominent Cleveland attorney, and George M. Reynolds, a key Chicago banker who served on the board of the New York Life Insurance Co.[41] Ambassador Alanson B. Houghton was a former New York Congressman and high official in the Corning Glass Works, which then had assets of only about $14 million. Houghton was probably appointed because of his important secondary tie, for he was a longtime director of the Metropolitan Life Insurance Co., the largest financial institution in the country.

The other major diplomatic representative of the Harding administration, New York publisher (and onetime Wilson promoter) George Harvey, does not appear at first glance to have been closely associated with big business interests. Indeed he is generally thought to have been appointed as American Ambassador to Great Britain primarily because of his dedicated efforts to help win the presidential nomination for Harding.[42] While this is largely true, it should also be pointed out that one of the enterprises with which Harvey had been linked for many years, Harper & Brothers, had once been rescued from severe fiscal straits by the banking house of J. P. Morgan & Co., and that Harvey himself was a longtime friend of this great financier until Morgan's death in 1913.[43] In addition, Harvey had been a director for over twenty years of a relatively obscure New York firm known as the Audit Co., which included among its directors such potent figures as August Belmont (the board chairman of the Interborough Rapid Transit Co. and a director of the Louisville and Nashville Railroad), Cornelius Vanderbilt (a director of the Illinois Central Railroad, Interborough Rapid Transit Co., Mutual Life Insurance Co., and Central Union Trust Co. of New York City), John I. Waterbury (the onetime head of the Manhattan Trust Co., who served on the board of AT&T and the Louisville and Nashville Railroad), and Philadelphia lawyer-executive T. DeWitt Cuyler (who was a director of the Bankers Trust Co., Equitable Life Assurance Society, Equitable Trust Co., Guaranty Trust Co., Interborough Rapid Transit Co., Pennsylvania Railroad, and Atchison, Topeka & Santa Fe Railway). Moreover, at the

Republican National Convention Harvey is reported to have been in close touch with four J. P. Morgan partners, who were there presumably to lend support to the right type of candidate (Harding apparently was one of a number of acceptable choices).[44] Though not exactly an Establishment emissary, Harvey was still on good terms with many of the major economic leaders in the country.

Major Issues and Action of the Harding Administration

The domination of the Harding administration by wealthy and corporate interests can probably best be seen in the various fiscal policies that were pursued by high-ranking officials during this period. As a result of the extraordinary military demands placed upon the government by our involvement in the First World War, the Wilson regime had been forced to adopt a number of key revenue-raising measures, the most important of which were an increase in the recently passed (1913) federal income tax, a sizable boost in the surtax imposed on incomes of over $20,000, the enactment of the first permanent inheritance tax (which ranged from 1 percent on the first $50,000 of an estate to 10 percent on any part over $5 million), and an excess profits tax of 8 percent on the net income and invested capital of corporations and partnerships.[45] Most of these rather progressive measures were thoroughly repugnant to Harding's chief aides and advisors, particularly his influential Secretary of the Treasury, Andrew W. Mellon. Like many men of his economic status, Mellon was convinced that governmental spending was much too high and needed to be cut drastically, and that the tax burden on the wealthy must be sharply reduced (although, in truth, it was not very onerous).[46] Therefore, one of Mellon's first acts upon taking office was to urge Congress to repeal the "loathsome" excess profits tax and to slash the maximum surtax rate from its World War I high of 65 percent (on incomes over $1 million) to 40 percent.[47] Despite his great power and prestige, Mellon, however, was unable to persuade Congress to adopt all the major parts of his regressive tax program (the only people to benefit from the cut in federal surtaxes were those with incomes of over $66,000), largely because of the pressures of the farm bloc and various progressive forces, such as Robert M. La Follette. Consequently, the 1921 tax revision act was something of a compromise measure. Yet Mellon did achieve a partial victory, for after much debate Congress abolished the excess profits tax and lowered the maximum surtax rate to 50 percent, thereby benefiting many wealthy and corporate interests in American society.[48]

Another area in which business forces played an important, albeit quiet, role in national affairs during this period was in the realm of foreign policy. They were especially successful in pressuring responsible federal officials to secure a fair share of the vast oil reserves of the Middle East for certain major American oil companies. With the cessation of hostilities in 1918, and the realization that oil would henceforth be a vital economic and military commodity, the great powers of the world (and big oil companies closely linked with these governments) began a frantic scramble for large exploration and drilling concessions in the critical Middle East.[49] The British government, which had recently obtained valuable grants for such friendly or affiliated concerns as the British Petroleum Co., Anglo-Persian Oil Co., and Royal-Dutch Shell Co., was extremely reluctant to let corporations from other countries gain a foothold in areas where its firms had established a sizable stake. This was especially true in Iraq and Iran (as they are now known) where a band of American oil companies, headed by the Standard Oil Co. of New Jersey and the Standard Oil Co. of New York, was eager to acquire exploration and drilling rights, but was initially rebuffed by British authorities.[50] Both to promote business enterprise—and to protect the nation's long-term economic interest, such sympathetic authorities as Secretary of State Charles Evans Hughes (who had recently served as an attorney for Standard Oil of New Jersey) and Secretary of Commerce Herbert Hoover (who had once been involved in some small-scale oil enterprises) labored assiduously, employing the principle of the Open Door policy, to win a place for certain major American oil companies in the Middle East.[51] While their efforts were initially unproductive, they did succeed by the mid-1920s in securing an agreement which provided adequate entry for many of the nation's top oil companies.[52] Indeed, one authority claims that Hughes and Hoover " . . . began by conferring with oilmen and engineers about obtaining new fields, asked their advice about formulating an international oil policy, and finally allowed businessmen to conduct the oil diplomacy of the United States."[53]

The Harding administration is undoubtedly best known for its involvement in a nefarious domestic matter which also revolved around oil, the famous Teapot Dome scandal. This affair grew out of the long-term grant of lucrative drilling rights on two tracts of federally owned land (at Elk Hills, California, and Teapot Dome, Wyoming) to certain influential private interests—the Pan-American Petroleum & Transport Co. and the Mammoth Oil Co., a subsidiary of the Sinclair Consolidated Oil Corp. This was accomplished in two steps. First, there was an almost unnoticed transfer, by executive order (via Assistant Secretary of the Navy Theodore Roosevelt, Jr.), of the primary leasing authority from Secretary of the Navy Edwin Denby to President Harding's good friend, Secretary of the Interior Albert Fall.[54] The second, more important step was Fall's secret award of these valuable rights, without competitive bidding, to Pan-American and Mammoth in the spring of 1922.

Suspicions were soon aroused in conservationist circles, and as a result of some persistent prodding, these actions were eventually revealed, along with the fact that Pan-American was dominated by Fall's old friend and onetime business associate, Western oilman E. L. Doheny, and that Mammoth was actually controlled (through Sinclair Oil) by another of Fall's major supporters, Harry F. Sinclair. What's more, a Congressional investigation discovered that a number of striking improvements had suddenly been made in Fall's big ranch in New Mexico, which the (then financially depressed) Secretary of the Interior at first claimed stemmed from a $100,000 loan magnanimously extended by a friendly Washington newspaper publisher. But this story was soon proved false when, following President Harding's sudden death, Doheny admitted under oath to a Senate committee that he was the surreptitious source of the loan. Stirred by this damaging disclosure in an election year, Harding's dour New England successor, Calvin Coolidge, after an embarrassing abortive start, appointed two prominent public figures—Atlee Pomerone, a former Democratic Senator from Ohio and recent Cleveland lawyer, and Owen J. Roberts, a well-known Philadelphia attorney and onetime University of Pennsylvania law professor—to serve as special counsel to clean up this vexing affair.[55]

Under the direction of these individuals, especially the more able Roberts, government agents probed into this matter and finally uncovered the existence of a firm known as the Continental Trading Co., a small (and by now, defunct) concern that had been organized in 1921 by Harry Sinclair and several business associates. Within three short years this company had generated an extraordinary profit of over $2 million, most of which had been invested by the participants, in their own names and account numbers, in 3.5 percent Liberty bonds. An extensive examination of the records of all banks in which Fall had accounts in the West also revealed that about $90,000 worth of the bonds that Sinclair had originally purchased (their numbers were easily traced) had been translated into cash and deposited in the account of Albert Fall in the First National Bank of Pueblo, Colorado. The major link in this chain of events was soon established when Fall's son-in-law, M. T. Everhart, was called to testify and finally admitted that in May 1922 Harry Sinclair had turned over to him, as Fall's intermediary, more than $230,000 worth of Liberty bonds and that he had then gone, at Fall's request, to the First National Bank of Pueblo to pay off the latter's ranch debt of $140,500 to the M. D. Thatcher Estates Co. and deposit the rest of the funds in Fall's account in this (out-of-state) bank. In all (there were other substantial gratuities), Fall received more than $300,000 from Sinclair, in addition to the aforementioned $100,000 he got from oilman E. L. Doheny. Because of these revelations, Fall was brought to trial in the late 1920s and was found guilty of having accepted a bribe from Doheny, for which crime he was sentenced to a year in prison and fined $100,000, thereby becoming the first Cabinet officer in the nation's history to be convicted of a felony and placed behind bars. E. L. Doheny was put on trial on similar charges a short time later, but was, curiously, found not guilty, despite the fact that he admitted giving a sizable amount of money to Fall. Sinclair was likewise acquitted of bribery, although he was found guilty of contempt of Congress and trying to tamper with a jury, for which acts he was sentenced to six months in jail. With these proceedings, the Teapot Dome scandal was finally brought to a close.

But is this the entire story? Or is there another, less blatantly corrupt, side to the Teapot Dome scandal, which became submerged and over-looked largely because of the sensational bribery charges and criminal prosecutions, and its activities perhaps aborted by these proceedings? There is a good deal of untapped evidence to indicate that such may indeed have been the case. An examination of the lengthy 1923–1924 Congressional hearings on the subject, and an analysis of the background and affiliations of certain primarily New York–based business leaders, reveals that in addition to the Continental Trading Co., a powerful syndicate was heavily involved in the stockownership and directorship operations of the Sinclair Consolidated Oil Corp. in the early 1920s. This syndicate stood to benefit considerably from the boost in oil reserves and assets which the company gained through the lucrative Teapot Dome lease. According to one source, after the announcement to the public that Sinclair had been granted drilling rights to the Teapot Dome reserves, the value of its stock leaped upward by an aggregate of $57 million.[56] Such returns, if based on advanced "inside" information, would constitute a serious scandal, one which, while less odious than outright bribery, far outweighed the dollar sums involved in illicitly securing the cooperation of Secretary of the Interior Albert Fall.

The make-up of the most conspicuous part of the syndicate probably involved in the Teapot Dome–linked trading in oil stock is best revealed through a brief socio-economic analysis of the officers and especially the outside directors of the Sinclair Consolidated Oil Corp. In the critical waning months of 1921 the top executive and directorship officials of this big oil concern, and their major corporate and family ties, were as follows:[57]

Sinclair Officials		*Other Directorships Held by Sinclair Officials*
Board Chairman	Harry F. Sinclair	Replogle Steel Co. (1920 only)
President	Edward W. Sinclair (a brother of Harry)	
Outside Directors	William E. Corey (board chairman of the Midvale Steel & Ordinance Co.)	Cuba Cane Sugar Corp. Greene Cananea Copper Co., Inspiration Consolidated Copper Co., Mechanics & Metals National Bank, N.Y.C., Montana Power Co.
	Daniel C. Jackling (president of the Nevada Consolidated	Chase National Bank Utah Securities Corp. (to 1920)

Copper Co.; vice-president of the Utah Copper Co. and Chino Copper Co.)

Pacific Steamship Co. (up to 1918)

William P. Philips (partner in J. & W. Seligman & Co., N.Y.C.)

Cuba Cane Sugar Corp.
Pere Marquette Rwy.

John A. Spoor (head of subsidiary of the Chicago Junction Rwys. and Union Stock Yards Co.)

Guaranty Trust Co., N.Y.C.,
Pere Marquette Rwy.,
Montgomery, Ward & Co.,
 Chicago

William B. Thompson (former head of the Inspiration Consolidated Copper Co.)

Chase National Bank
Pacific Steamship Co. (up
 through World War I)
Utah Copper Co. (and its
 subsidiary, the Nevada
 Consolidated Copper Co.,
 up through World War I)

Edward R. Tinker (president of the Chase Securities Corp., an affiliate of the Chase National Bank)

American Motor Body Co.
Otis Steel Co., Cleveland
Pan-American Petroleum &
 Transport Co. (Doheny's
 concern)
Power Securities Corp. (an
 apparent affiliate of the
 Utah Securities Corp.)
U.S. Smelting, Refining &
 Mining Co., Boston
Vanadium Corp. of America
White Motor Co., Cleveland
Willys-Overland Co.
Wilson & Co., Chicago

Elisha Walker (president of Blair & Co., N.Y.C. securities firm)

American Motor Body Co.
Otis Steel Co., Cleveland
Pan-American Petroleum &
 Transport Co.
Willys-Overland Co.
Wilson & Co., Chicago

Harry Payne Whitney (N.Y.C. financier who married a daughter of Cornelius Vanderbilt)

Guaranty Trust Co., N.Y.C.
Cuba Cane Sugar Corp.
Montana Power Co.
Vanadium Corp. of America
 (up to 1921)
Replogle Steel Co. (1920)

The pattern of association revealed here is rather striking and can hardly be accidental. Of the twelve outside directors, six served on the board of one or more of a trio of institutions—the Chase National Bank, Cuba Cane Sugar Corp., and Montana Power Co. (the last two companies were very closely linked).[58] If the count is carried further to include both family ties and such other important concerns as the Guaranty Trust Co., it can be shown that the vast majority of the outside directors of the Sinclair Oil Corp.—and all the outside members of its executive committee—were affiliated with a close-knit set of major business enterprises, more than a few of which were controlled by (or allied with) the House of Morgan. For instance, William Boyce Thompson, a pro-Morgan man, was one of the biggest stockholders in the Chase National Bank, the second largest stockholder in the Nevada Consolidated Copper Co., and apparently an influential figure in the affairs of the Inspiration Consolidated Copper Co., Midvale Steel & Ordinance Co., and Cuba Cane Sugar Corp.[59] Another prominent member of the Sinclair board in the preceding year (1920) was Albert H. Wiggin, board chairman of the Chase Securities Corp., president of the Chase National Bank, and a director of the Inspiration Consolidated Copper Co., Midvale Steel & Ordinance Co., Montana Power Co., and (up to 1918) Pacific Steamship Co. And in 1919, to move back yet another year in time, the board of directors of the Sinclair Oil & Refining Corp. (as it was then known) contained a significant number of other Easterners, the most conspicuous of whom was, interestingly, Theodore Roosevelt, Jr., who two years later played a fairly prominent role, as Assistant Secretary of the Navy, in the early phases of the Teapot Dome affair.

Although comparatively little has been made of any economic ties on the part of Theodore Roosevelt, Jr. or his close kinsmen, there is good reason to think that this may be a serious oversight. For one thing, not only did Roosevelt serve on the Sinclair board from 1916 to 1919, but one of his brothers, Archibald, was placed on the Sinclair payroll in August 1919 to serve as a vice-president of one of its many subsidiaries (the Union Petroleum Co.) and he remained in that position until the day before he was called to testify by the Senate Committee on Public Lands and Surveys in January 1924.[60] What is more, prior to winning a seat in the New York state legislature in 1919, the younger Theodore Roosevelt himself had other notable directorship links with a number of people associated, directly or indirectly, with the Sinclair oil syndicate. From 1916 to 1918 he was a member of the board of the White Motor Co. (of Cleveland), as was Edward Tinker, a vice-president of the Chase National Bank, and J. Horace Harding, a New York investment banker who reportedly served as one of the co-managers in the creation of the Sinclair stock syndicate (along with Theodore Schulze, William Boyce Thompson's son-in-law).[61] At the same time Roosevelt was a director of both the Associated Gas & Electric Co. (a holding company apparently dominated by the J. G. White engineering and financial interests) and the J. G. White Management Corp. (a subsidiary of J. G. White & Co.), two concerns that had close ties to Morgan interests. Thus it seems fair to say that Theodore Roosevelt, Jr. was on good terms with a number of persons involved in the Teapot Dome-linked Sinclair oil syndicate.[62]

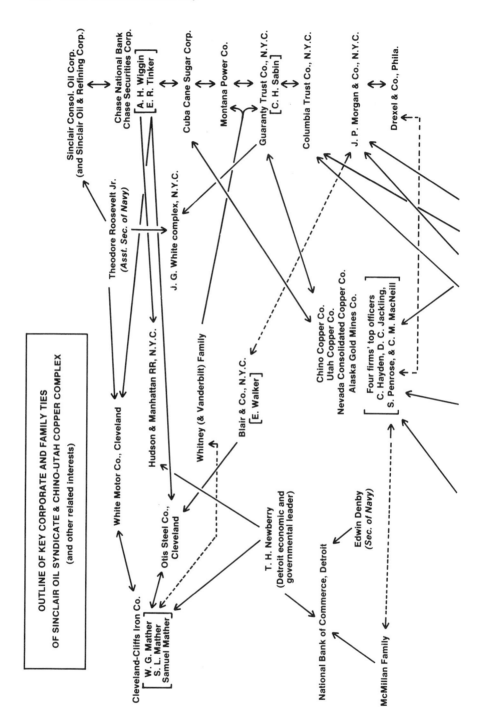

OUTLINE OF KEY CORPORATE AND FAMILY TIES
OF SINCLAIR OIL SYNDICATE & CHINO-UTAH COPPER COMPLEX
(and other related interests)

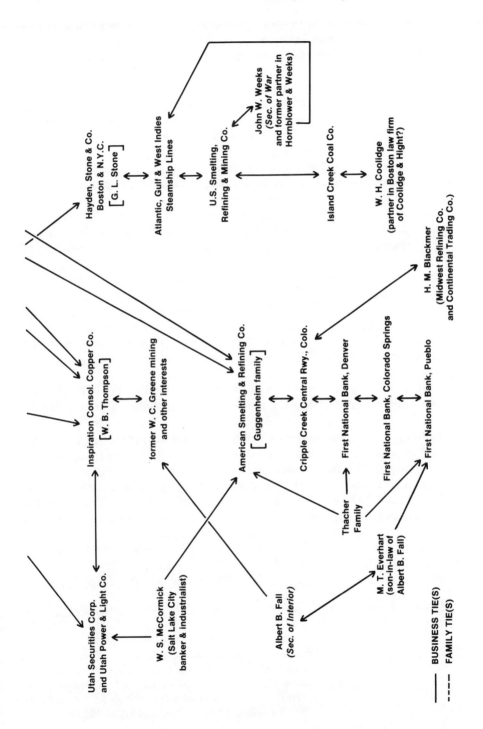

Hayden, Stone & Co.
Boston & N.Y.C.
[G. L. Stone]

Atlantic, Gulf & West Indies
Steamship Lines

U.S. Smelting,
Refining & Mining Co.

John W. Weeks
(Sec. of War
and former partner in
Hornblower & Weeks)

Island Creek Coal Co.

W. H. Coolidge
(partner in Boston law firm
of Coolidge & Hight?)

H. M. Blackmer
(Midwest Refining Co.
and Continental Trading Co.)

Inspiration Consol. Copper Co.
[W. B. Thompson]

former W. C. Greene mining
and other interests

American Smelting & Refining Co.
[Guggenheim family]

Cripple Creek Central Rwy., Colo.

First National Bank, Denver

First National Bank, Colorado Springs

First National Bank, Pueblo

Thacher
Family

Utah Securities Corp.
and Utah Power & Light Co.

W. S. McCormick
(Salt Lake City
banker & industrialist)

Albert B. Fall
(Sec. of Interior)

M. T. Everhart
(son-in-law of
Albert B. Fall)

—— BUSINESS TIE(S)

---- FAMILY TIE(S)

But there is more to this unexplored side of the Teapot Dome scandal than the action and associations of Theodore Roosevelt, Jr., since he was apparently only a secondary figure in the overall affair, which centered mainly around Albert Fall. In all accounts to date it has been assumed that Fall's only significant ties to any of the participants (or beneficiaries) were those of long-standing friendship with his onetime fellow prospector, E. L. Doheny, and his more recently established relationship with Harry F. Sinclair. Fall, however, had other politico-economic interests and associations which, when closely scrutinized, place the entire Teapot Dome scandal in a very different, and even more unfavorable, light. For largely buried in the voluminous 1923–1924 Senate hearings on the subject is the seemingly inconsequential, but actually highly illuminating, disclosure by the former pro-Democratic publisher of the *Albuquerque Morning Journal,* Carl Magee, that in 1920 he had purchased the previously staunchly Republican newspaper from a syndicate which included (then) Senator Fall. The make-up of this group is rather intriguing, for although Magee's memory was marred by one partial omission, it encompassed a very revealing and seemingly diverse set of interests—the Chino Copper Co., the El Paso & Southwestern Railroad, a Boston firm whose name started with Coolidge (this was the minor gap in Magee's testimony), and two wealthy individuals, Harding's New England fundraiser (and future Secretary of War), John W. Weeks, and Cleveland steelman Price McKinney.[63]

Most, if not all, of these interests had significant direct or indirect ties to one another, but the largest of these—the closely linked Utah Copper Co. and Chino Copper Co. complex (which had combined assets of over $100 million)—clearly stood out as being of central importance in this group, primarily because of the make-up of its high officials and their links to other economic enterprises or political figures involved in some way in the Teapot Dome scandal. The top executives and certain directors of these two concerns appear to have formed the center of an even greater set of interlocking mining and financial interests, one that had connections with virtually all the primary and secondary parties in this dubious affair. Through all or part of the period from 1916 through 1923, the three highest-ranking officials of these two firms and their most important affiliations were as follows (with partial periods so specified):

Charles M. MacNeill	President of both the Chino Copper Co. and Utah Copper Co.
	Vice-president of the Replogle Steel Co.
	Director of the Nevada Consolidated Copper Co. (a longtime subsidiary of the Utah Copper Co.), Alaska Gold Mines Co., First National Bank of Denver (up to 1918), Liberty National Bank of N.Y.C. (up to 1920), and Vanadium Corp. of America (1920–1923)
Daniel C. Jackling	Vice-president of the Chino Copper Co., Utah Copper Co., Alaska Gold Mines Co., Ray Consolidated Copper

Co., and Nevada Consolidated Copper Co. (also in the early 1920s, its president)

President of the Utah Power & Light Co. (1916–1920)

Director of the Chase National Bank of N.Y.C., Pacific Steamship Co., Sinclair Consolidated Oil Corp. (1920–1923), and Utah Securities Corp. (up to 1920)

Charles Hayden (senior partner in Hayden, Stone & Co., Boston and N.Y.C. banking firm)

Vice-president of the Chino Copper Co., Utah Copper Co., and Ray Consolidated Copper Co.

President of the Alaska Gold Mines Co.

Director of the Nevada Consolidated Copper Co. (also in early 1920s, a vice-president), First National Bank of Denver (up to 1917), Cuba Cane Sugar Corp. (1921–1923), Pere Marquette Rwy. (1919–1923), Chicago, Rock Island & Pacific Rwy. (also in early 1920s, its board chairman), Utah Power & Light Corp., and Utah Securities Corp.

In addition, Hayden's other name partner, Galen L. Stone, served as a high official of the big Atlantic, Gulf and West Indies Steamship Lines, a director of the Chase Securities Corp., and had once been associated with the Island Creek Coal Co. and the U.S. Smelting, Refining & Mining Co. Other prominent members of the board of the Utah Copper Co. included, during much or all of this period, several members of the Guggenheim family (which held a dominant interest in both the American Smelting & Refining Co. and Kennecott Copper Corp.); two "mining" brothers of Boies Penrose, the powerful Republican Senator from Pennsylvania who played a much-discussed behind-the-scenes role in the nomination of Warren G. Harding in 1920; William P. Hamilton, a partner in both J. P. Morgan & Co. and its Philadelphia affiliate, Drexel & Co. (and a vice-president of the Kennecott Copper Corp.); Thomas Cochran, a recently appointed partner in J. P. Morgan & Co. (and a director of the Chase Securities Corp.); and Theodore Schulze, a son-in-law of the aforementioned William Boyce Thompson (and a director of the Chase National Bank and Inspiration Consolidated Copper Corp.). Two of the more important outside directors of the Chino Copper Co. were Spencer Penrose, one of Boies Penrose's brothers, who was a founder of the Utah Copper Co. (and one of its top officials up to 1917), and, up to 1920, Mark L. Sperry, who, though a New England industrialist, had served some years earlier as a vice-president of both the Greene Consolidated Copper Co. and the Greene Gold-Silver Co.[64] And it should be noted that by World War I the Inspiration Consolidated Copper Co. was closely affiliated with the Greene Cananea Copper Co. (the successor company of the Greene Consolidated Copper Co. and several other operations), since the same persons, William D. Thornton and Joseph W. Allen, served, respectively, as vice-president and secretary-treasurer of both concerns.[65] This association with the mining interests established by William

C. Greene may be significant, for Albert Fall served as general counsel for Greene and his various business enterprises through most of the first decade of the century. In fact, Fall sat on the board of this ill-fated entrepreneur's Greene Gold-Silver Co. in 1905, along with Mark L. Sperry and Galen L. Stone, Charles Hayden's primary business partner (and a director of the Greene Consolidated Copper Co.), and certain other business figures, mostly from the Northeast. Hence it is clear that a number of the people who had a significant stake in the Teapot Dome affair had more than a nodding acquaintance with New Mexico's Albert Fall.

Three of the principal figures in the Utah-Chino copper complex—Charles MacNeill, Charles Hayden, and Spencer Penrose—also served on the boards of a number of noteworthy nonmetallurgical concerns in the West. Probably even more important, Charles MacNeill sat on the board of the First National Bank of Denver until 1918, as did Charles Hayden up to the preceding year. These affiliations take on special significance only when it is realized that the First National Bank of Denver and seventeen other financial institutions in the state, including the First National Bank of Pueblo, were controlled by the wealthy Thatcher family, whose longtime acknowledged head, Mahlon D. Thatcher, was linked through directorship ties, until his death in early 1916, with the Guggenheim-dominated American Smelting & Refining Co., which interests had major holdings in the Utah Copper Co. and many other mining concerns in the West.[66] Not only did R. C. Thatcher and M. D. Thatcher (the brother and son of Mahlon D.) serve as chairman and president of the First National Bank of Pueblo from 1916 through 1923, but they also sat on the board of the First National Bank of Denver, plus another closely allied local enterprise, the International Trust Co. In addition, H. J. Alexander, who was president of the First National Bank and vice-president of the International Trust Co., served as one of the relatively few outside directors of the First National Bank of Pueblo. Another outside director of this Colorado bank was a New Mexico man by the name of M. T. Everhart, a rather curious selection since his father-in-law was Albert Fall, the central figure in the Teapot Dome scandal. Thus it seems fair to say that both Everhart and Fall, who borrowed a substantial amount of money from the Thatcher interests (which was later repaid using Harry Sinclair's bribe-tainted Liberty bonds), were on fairly close terms with the well-connected Thatcher family.[67]

The identity of one of the other parties reported to be associated with the pre-1920 ownership of the *Albuquerque Morning Journal* has not, unfortunately, been fully established. Carl Magee's memory was somewhat faulty at this point. The best that he could recall for the Senate committee was that it was a Boston firm by the name of "Coolidge and something."[68] A search of the *Directory of Directors in the City of Boston and Vicinity* (supplemented by *Who's Who in America*) reveals that there were only a few concerns in this metropolitan area which started with the name "Coolidge," and that only one was likely to be involved in business affairs, with one or more partners serving on various boards of directors. This was the Boston law firm of Coolidge and Hight, and the author is strongly inclined to think that this was the concern to which Magee was referring. One of its partners, William H. Coolidge, served up to 1921 on the board of the Alaska Gold Mines Co., of which company Charles Hayden served as president, Daniel C. Jackling as vice-president, and Charles MacNeill as an outside director. What's more, Coolidge served as board chairman of the Island Creek Coal Co., and his law partner, Clarence A. Hight, was a vice-president of this big concern, on whose board Charles Hayden's major partner, Galen Stone, also served up to 1919 as a director, thereby establishing yet another link in this rather intriguing chain of corporate interrelations.

The fourth party involved in the pre-1920 ownership of the *Albuquerque Morning Journal* was John W. Weeks, a former Boston businessman and U.S. Senator from Massachusetts. Around the time of the sale of the newspaper to Carl Magee, Weeks was temporarily out of both business and government office and was serving as one of Harding's political advisors and major fundraisers in his 1920 presidential campaign, (for which efforts he was soon rewarded with an appointment as Secretary of War.) Prior to his election to the Senate in 1913, Weeks had been a partner in the prestigious State Street banking house of Hornblower & Weeks, and had served up to the same time as a vice-president of the big First National Bank of Boston. In addition, until early 1913 he had served on the board of the U.S. Smelting, Refining & Mining Co., along with Clarence A. Hight, Charles Hayden's major partner, Galen Stone (who sat on the board of the Atlantic, Gulf & West Indies Steamship Lines), and many of the directors of the First National Bank of Boston. Weeks's former primary business partner, Henry Hornblower, was also a board member of this shipping line from 1909 through the early 1920s (by which time Galen Stone had become its highest official).[69] Hence John W. Weeks was probably well acquainted with the partners of the Coolidge and Hight law firm and the two top officials of Hayden, Stone & Co., one of whom (Hayden) was a key figure in the Chino-Utah copper complex and the other (Stone) later became a director of the Chase Securities Corp.[70]

Now that a substantial number of the links among many of the parties with an interest in the Teapot Dome lease have been described, it is essential to analyze the background and affiliations of the special officials chosen to clean up this scandal, bearing in mind that the inquiry could have extended to other unsavory aspects of this affair, such as lucrative syndicate operations based on "inside" knowledge.[71] As briefly noted elsewhere, President Coolidge originally nominated a former (1914–1919) Democratic Attorney General, Thomas W. Gregory, and a prominent Republican lawyer, Silas H. Strawn, as dual counsel to handle this explosive case, but their names were soon withdrawn. Gregory, it was discovered, had been retained in recent years as an attorney by E. L. Doheny, a primary figure in the Teapot Dome affair, a disclosure which quickly eliminated him. The legislative objections to Strawn, a Chicago lawyer who was a partner of Fall's Cabinet predecessor, John B. Payne, were never fully specified. However, it is just as well that he did not act in any investigative capacity, for a look at various business manuals reveals that Strawn had a number of ties to parties involved in the Sinclair Oil syndicate. He served, for instance, as chairman of Montgomery, Ward & Co., whose board had many links with the Continental & Commercial National Bank of Chicago, and also included as directors Francis D. Bartow, a vice-president of the First National Bank of New York, and John A. Spoor, head of the relatively small Chicago Junction Railways Co. (and perhaps more importantly, a director of the Pere Marquette Railway, Sinclair Consolidated Oil Corp., and Guaranty Trust Co. of New York). In addition, Strawn himself graced the board of the Chicago Junction Railways Co., along with E. V. R. Thayer, a former (1918–1921) president of the Chase National Bank now serving as a vice-president of both the line's parent company, the Chicago Junction Railways & Union Stock Yards Co., and the Punta Alegre Sugar Co. (and as a director of AT&T, Pere Marquette Railway, and Sinclair Consolidated Oil Corp.).[72] Furthermore, until the early 1920s Strawn served as a director of the Joliet and Northern Indiana Railroad, a subsidiary of the Michigan Central Railroad, which was, in turn, controlled by the Vanderbilt-Morgan-dominated New York Central system.[73] Thus, although these links were not explored by federal officials, it is fortunate that the nomination of Silas Strawn was withdrawn.

Following these abortive efforts (which would indicate that Coolidge may not have been a "Puritan in Babylon"), the President managed to secure Senate approval of the appointment of two other well-known lawyers, Atlee Pomerene, a recently defeated (1911–1923) Democratic Senator from Ohio and onetime Canton lawyer, and Owen J. Roberts, a Philadelphia attorney and former (1898–1918) University of Pennsylvania law professor, to serve in Gregory's and Strawn's places.

The Democratic special counsel, Atlee Pomerene, had, upon his departure from the Senate, severed his legal and residential ties with the city of Canton and taken a position with the prestigious Cleveland law firm of Squire, Sanders & Dempsey, an affiliation he maintained throughout the five-year (1924–1929) investigation and trial period. Unknown to almost all parties at the time, the senior partner of this firm had very close ties to a number of persons at least indirectly associated with the Sinclair syndicate. Andrew Squire, for instance, served as president of the Cleveland and Pittsburgh Railroad (a board graced up to 1918 by William G. Mather, a distant relative of New York financier Harry Payne Whitney), and as a director of the city's big Union Trust Co. (with which Myron T. Herrick's son and several members of the Mather family were also connected) from at least 1911 through 1929, and the probably Herrick-controlled Union Carbide & Carbon Corp. (on whose board sat George W. Davison, a recent Sinclair director, Chicago banker George M. Reynolds, and Charles A. Coffin, a longtime Montana Power Co. director) from 1917 through 1929. Moreover, the second-ranking partner in this important firm, William B. Sanders, served from 1918 to 1927 as a vice-president of the Society for Savings (which had long been headed by Myron T. Herrick) and as a director, with William G. Mather, of two other lesser concerns, the Kelley Island Lime & Transport Co. and the Guardian Savings & Trust Co. In addition, up to 1920 Sanders was a member of the board of the Mather-dominated Otis Steel Co., along with such Sinclair syndicate figures as New York financiers Edward R. Tinker and Elisha Walker. And Pomerene himself served on the board of the Guardian Savings & Trust Co. from early 1924 through 1929. Thus a serious question could be raised about Pomerene's ability and willingness to deal thoroughly and fairly with all possible aspects of the Teapot Dome affair.

The Republican special counsel was Owen J. Roberts, an able and energetic man who did much more, according to all accounts, than Pomerene to bring about the indictment and conviction of Albert Fall for the gross criminal act of bribery. But Roberts had close ties to certain segments of the business world (some of which were established after his selection to this key post). Sometime in late 1923 or early 1924 (it is impossible to ascertain the exact date from available business directories), he was elected to the board of the Franklin Fire Insurance Co., a Philadelphia subsidiary of the larger Home Insurance Co. of New York.[74] The board of the latter concern contained a number of persons on friendly terms with various members of the Sinclair syndicate, and the president of both the parent and subsidiary company, Eldridge G. Snow, served on the board of the American Exchange National Bank of New York (which was headed by Morgan ally Lewis L. Clarke) and the New York Life Insurance Co. (which counted among its directors Chicago banker George M. Reynolds and President Harding's longtime political advisor and Ambassador to France, Myron T. Herrick.[75] In addition, Roberts had some key professional and family ties. His Connecticut-born wife was the sister of the first wife of the prominent Philadelphia-bred financier, Thomas S. Gates, who by the early 1920s had become one of the senior partners in the two formally affiliated banking firms of Drexel & Co. and J. P. Morgan & Co.[76] And although Gates's first wife had died in 1906, he and Roberts apparently remained close friends, for Roberts' Philadelphia law firm had frequently been retained to represent Drexel & Co. (the city's premier banking firm since the downfall of Jay Cooke), the Bell Telephone Co. of Pennsylvania, and many other large concerns.[77] Such elitist links may well have restrained Roberts, perhaps subconsciously, from pursuing a thorough and wide-ranging investigation of all aspects of the Teapot

Dome affair, particularly those which might have involved certain powerful economic interests. It is thus not surprising, given the many interlocking links of the influential Sinclair oil syndicate, that this perhaps equally important side of the Teapot Dome scandal was not uncovered by government officials.[78]

The Coolidge Administration

Upon the sudden death of the politically harassed Harding in the summer of 1923, Vice President Calvin Coolidge entered the White House. Coolidge had been elected governor of Massachusetts in 1918, and two years later made a determined bid for the Republican presidential nomination. He had been awarded the second spot on the ticket partly for geographical reasons and partly because of the strong political forces behind his ambitious electoral drive. Coolidge has generally been depicted as an extremely colorless and taciturn man with a rather limited mind (or imagination) and a highly conservative philosophy, who, thanks to the backing of certain powerful leaders, climbed steadily up the Republican party ladder of his state and, as governor, received widespread acclaim for breaking the Boston police strike. To many people, he had much appeal because he was a small-town (Northampton) lawyer with a modest practice that involved only minor business concerns, and he apparently had been catapulted to fame largely by a combination of luck and perseverance, plus the dedicated efforts of Boston merchant (and fellow Amherst graduate) Frank W. Stearns.[79]

This picture is, however, rather misleading. True, Stearns was an ardent political and financial supporter of Coolidge after their first meeting in 1915, but two other, much less publicized men played critical roles in Coolidge's rise to power in both state and national affairs. One of these was longtime Republican leader W. Murray Crane, who served as Coolidge's influential mentor and primary political backer from very early in his career until about the time he secured the vice presidential nomination.[80] Though the state's top party chieftain, the wealthy Crane (whose family had a substantial paper business in western Massachusetts) actually had more important economic ties to New York City than to Boston. Up to his death in late 1920, he served as a director of AT&T, a once Brahmin-controlled concern that had come increasingly under the sway of Morgan interests, and the Morgan-dominated Guaranty Trust Co. of New York.[81]

Coolidge's other influential political supporter was not a Massachusetts man, but a college classmate, Dwight W. Morrow, who became a Wall Street lawyer and then (in 1914) a partner in J. P. Morgan & Co. After lending his services to the federal government during World War I, Morrow returned to private life in 1919 and almost immediately threw himself into a dedicated effort to promote Calvin Coolidge as a presidential candidate, although because of his Morgan connections he felt compelled to operate in an extremely quiet, behind-the-scenes fashion. According to all accounts, Morrow labored hard at this endeavor, at one point, early in the proceedings, even inviting Coolidge admirer (and former Amherst graduate) Frank Stearns down to New York to discuss these plans.[82] When Morrow and fellow Morgan partner Thomas Cochran went to the Republican National Convention in Chicago in 1920, they continued to lobby strenuously (at a distance) in behalf of Massachusetts' "favorite son."[83] And though they did not succeed, these activities show that Coolidge was quite acceptable to some high officials in the House of Morgan, and presumably to other influential economic interests as well.[84]

Upon being thrust abruptly into the Presidency, Coolidge chose initially to retain all of Harding's Cabinet members, both the good and the not-so-good. Some of these men continued to hold office up to the late 1920s, long after Coolidge had won the 1924 election over Democratic candidate John W. Davis (and Progressive party nominee Robert M. La Follette).[85] For instance, Coolidge kept for the duration of his administration both the conservative Secretary of Labor, James J. Davis, a onetime union official who had become a minor Pittsburgh financial figure, and the more able and extraordinarily rich Secretary of the Treasury, Andrew W. Mellon, who, despite his claim to have severed all corporate ties, served as a vice-president of the fairly small, family-controlled National Union Fire Insurance Co. of Pittsburgh up to 1928.[86] Another pair of Harding officials—Secretary of Commerce Herbert Hoover, a wealthy former mining engineer turned high wartime federal executive, and Secretary of the Interior Hubert Work, a longtime Pueblo (Colorado) physician and state party leader who had replaced the disgraced Albert Fall in early 1923—held their posts under Coolidge up to the summer of 1928, when both resigned to take key roles in the 1928 presidential campaign.[87]

However, two other members of Harding's administration—Secretary of the Navy Edwin Denby and Attorney General Harry Daugherty—were replaced by President Coolidge soon after he assumed the reins of leadership, primarily because of their at least indirect linkage with recent highly publicized scandals (Denby with the Teapot Dome affair, Daugherty with other, less important machinations). In what may have been a move made to improve the tarnished image of this post, Coolidge appointed a prominent California jurist, Curtis D. Wilbur, to succeed Denby. Wilbur had been a state superior court judge from 1902 to 1918, and a justice of the California Supreme Court from 1919 to 1924.[88] His reputation was also probably enhanced by the fact that he was the brother of Ray Lyman Wilbur, the president of prestigious Stanford University.[89]

Another official appointed early in the Coolidge administration in an obvious effort to rid the regime of its aura of graft and corruption was Attorney General Harlan Fiske Stone. Although he did not know the

President well, the new head of the Justice Department was a fellow alumnus of Amherst College. Stone had an unusual dual background, for he had served as dean of the Columbia Law School from 1910 to 1923 (and before that as a professor at this institution), and for an even longer period as a partner in the New York law firm of Satterlee, Canfield & Stone (and its predecessor concern).[90] Some scholars tend to dismiss or deemphasize the latter relationship, claiming that Stone rarely handled key cases for influential economic interests.[91] But the author, while agreeing that Stone's close links with the Columbia Law School probably had a marked effect on his outlook, also believes that Stone's other affiliation was of more significance than many may realize. Though not mentioned in most accounts, Stone served from 1909 to 1924 as a director and secretary of the fairly small New York–controlled Atlanta & Charlotte Air Line Railway, a concern whose other three top officers were George F. Canfield (Stone's longtime law partner), John A. Middleton (who was, more importantly, a vice-president of the Lehigh Valley Railroad), and John W. Platten (a high-ranking official in the Gulf States Steel Co. and a director of the Morgan-dominated Hudson & Manhattan Railroad and International Mercantile Marine Co.). Canfield was also board chairman of the Bradstreet Co. (a small real estate firm) and a director of the Montana Power Co. (on whose board sat various parties closely linked with the Sinclair syndicate).[92] The other name partner in Stone's longtime law firm, Herbert L. Satterlee, was, interestingly, the late J. P. Morgan's son-in-law (although he does not appear to have been a very active legal or economic figure). Thus although Stone apparently had little or nothing to do as a Cabinet official with the Teapot Dome investigation, it would certainly seem that this able attorney, and particularly his former law partners, were on friendly terms with a number of persons involved in the Sinclair syndicate.

Stone served as Attorney General for only about a year when, for a variety of reasons, he was nominated by President Coolidge to fill an opening on the Supreme Court.[93] After his first attempt to replace Stone with a Detroit figure was rejected by the Senate because of certain controversial business connections, President Coolidge chose an old family friend, a Ludlow, Vermont lawyer and onetime state attorney general, John G. Sargent, to take over at the Justice Department.[94] Sargent was a little-known small-town attorney whose firm (Stickney, Sargent & Skeels) acted as general or local counsel for a rather surprising number of business concerns, such as the American Railway Express Co., Boston and Maine Railroad, Vermont Hydro-Electric Co., and Rutland Railway, Light & Power Co. (the last two were subsidiaries of the New York-based General Gas & Electric Co.).[95] Moreover, although hardly a major business figure, Sargent served on the board of the fairly small Vermont Valley Railroad up to his appointment as Attorney General.[96] Hence Sargent might best be described as essentially a personal selection who, because of certain economic associations, probably had a pro-business bias.

Coolidge was extremely eager to retain the services of the able Charles Evans Hughes as Secretary of State, which he was able to do until March 1925, when Hughes decided to return to his lucrative law practice. To replace him, Coolidge chose Frank B. Kellogg, a man of much lesser stature. Kellogg had recently served briefly as American Ambassador to Great Britain, and before that as a United States Senator from Minnesota (from 1917 to 1923). But he was primarily a wealthy St. Paul lawyer with numerous prominent economic ties, the most longstanding of which was his directorship with the big Merchants National Bank of that city (a link he maintained throughout his years in Coolidge's Cabinet). Before his election to the Senate, Kellogg had served as general counsel for the U.S. Steel Corp. in Minnesota and several other states in the region, and as attorney for the Chicago Great Western Railroad and the influential James J. Hill's vast rail enterprise in the Northwest (a magnate on close terms with the House of Morgan).[97] In addition, Kellogg's longtime intimate friend and law partner, Cordenio A. Severance, was a board member of the elitist Carnegie Endowment for International Peace until his death in May 1925, an association which may have had much to do with both Kellogg's appointment to the State Department and his preceding ambassadorial post.[98] Despite his Establishment ties, Kellogg did not prove to be a very effective Secretary of State, and was frequently forced to rely on the advice of such more able, but equally pro-business, figures as Elihu Root and Charles Evans Hughes.[99] Indeed, according to one authority, Kellogg was so overwhelmed by perplexing diplomatic problems in the late 1920s that he ". . . virtually surrendered the control of both policy and operations in the two important areas of Mexican and Nicaraguan relations to Dwight W. Morrow and Henry L. Stimson" (two men closely identified with Morgan interests).[100]

Coolidge also retained Harding's Secretary of War, John W. Weeks, up to the latter part of 1925 when this former Boston businessman and U.S. Senator was forced to resign from office because of a serious illness. As his replacement, the President chose Dwight F. Davis, who had served for the two preceding years as Weeks's chief assistant (following a brief stint with the War Finance Corp.).[101] Davis was a wealthy St. Louis leader whose family had amassed a considerable fortune in the dry goods trade in the late 19th century and had later been content to play primarily an investment role in business affairs. Davis had himself served as a director of the State National Bank of St. Louis from around 1909 to 1926, and one of his brothers, John T. Davis, sat on the board of the big St. Louis Union Trust Co. and First National Bank of St. Louis. In addition, various members of the family had long been associated with the fairly sizable Houston Oil Co. of Texas. But perhaps even more important from a national standpoint was the fact that Dwight F. Davis (a onetime famous tennis star) had served, shortly before his appointment as Assistant Secretary of War, on the board of overseers of Harvard University (the was one of the few Midwesterners on this elitist body). There he came into contact with such influential figures as Henry Cabot Lodge and Thomas W. Lamont, one of the senior partners in J. P. Morgan & Co.[102] In short, Davis was well integrated into the "right" social circles in America.[103]

Some of the top diplomatic officials of the Coolidge administration were, like many of the Cabinet members, carryovers from the Harding regime. But several were not. The American Ambassador to Great Britain, George Harvey (a New York publisher turned major presidential strategist), resigned in November 1923, apparently because of the State Department's dissatisfaction with his performance. After two abortive efforts to secure a more able successor, President Coolidge appointed Frank Kellogg, a well-established St. Paul corporate lawyer who had recently served a six-year term in the U.S. Senate.[104] After a little over a year at the Court of St. James, Kellogg was asked to become head of the State Department. Coolidge then persuaded our business-oriented Ambassador to Germany, Alanson Houghton, a former high executive of the (then medium-sized) Corning Glass Works and apparently still active director of the huge Metropolitan Life Insurance Co., to take over the diplomatic reins in London, a position he held for the duration of the administration. As Ambassador to France, Coolidge decided to retain President Harding's longtime friend and political advisor, Myron T. Herrick, who was an influential Ohio and national businessman. In fact, even while Ambassador, Herrick continued to serve as president of Cleveland's Society for Savings, as board chairman of the big Union Carbide & Carbon Corp. (up to 1925, when he reverted to a less active directorship status), and as a trustee of the New York Life Insurance Co. Finally, as Houghton's replacement as Ambassador to Germany, Coolidge picked former Cornell University president Jacob G. Schurman, who, upon his retirement from this academic post, had become American Minister to China. Schurman had at least one major socio-economic tie (other than those forged through civic and academic channels), for his younger brother, George, was a partner in the New York law firm headed by Charles Evans Hughes.[105] Thus most of America's top diplomatic officials during this period were closely linked with big business.

By far the most important actions taken by the federal government during the Coolidge years were in the realm of domestic finance.[106] The Harding administration had been partially thwarted in its pro-wealthy tax reduction efforts by the strong opposition of various liberals and farm leaders in Congress in the early 1920s. President Coolidge, urged on by Andrew Mellon, resumed the battle in 1924 when he strongly recommended that Congress adopt the highly regressive tax program still advocated by his rich Secretary of the Treasury. Mellon, not surprisingly given his background, was thoroughly addicted to the idea of reducing the tax burden of the wealthy interests in America, on the debatable grounds that only they could provide the necessary capital to finance the nation's desired economic growth. But again, because of bitter resistance in Congress, the Mellon-Coolidge administration (a not inaccurate phrase) was only partially successful. It was able to gain a noteworthy cut in the maximum surtax rate imposed on incomes above a certain level (now specified as that portion of a person's income over $500,000 a year) from 50 down to 40 percent, which was one of Mellon's 1921 goals. However, this was achieved, much to the dismay of the Pittsburgh magnate, primarily at the price of a significant increase in the recently adopted federal estate tax of from 25 percent to 40 percent (on any part of an estate over $10 million in value) and also, in an effort to help curb widespread evasion of the latter levy, the enactment of a federal gift tax, ranging from 1 to 25 percent (with the higher rate being applied to any portion of a gift which exceeded $10 million).[107] Indeed, although not a resounding victory for the Mellon-led forces, these measures resulted, according to one authority, in an overall lightening of the tax burden of the wealthy of some $700 million.[108]

This Republican regime scored a more impressive and rewarding triumph in 1926 when, following the lopsided electoral mandate of 1924 (and the death of such stalwart defenders of the public interest as Robert M. La Follette), a major revenue measure was passed which drastically reduced both the rate of the federal estate tax and the (among the rich, much-despised) income surtax from 40 to 20 percent and completely abolished the federal gift tax.[109] In addition, and perhaps even more important in the long run, the Coolidge-Mellon administration managed, with the help of various key figures in Congress, to secure a tremendous boost in the depletion allowance granted to extractive industries (mostly oil and mining firms) since 1913.[110] It went up from an average of about 5 percent of these concerns' gross income (the actual cost incurred in the discovery and development of these resources) to an unwarranted and arbitrarily arrived at 27.5 percent, a dubious provision which remained in effect for almost 50 years. It is little wonder that many rich and powerful interests in American society were wont to describe Andrew Mellon as the greatest Secretary of the Treasury since Alexander Hamilton.

The Hoover Administration

With the announcement by the laconic Coolidge in late 1927 that he did not choose to run for another term of office, a number of ambitious claimants made serious bids to capture the Republican presidential nomination. The winner was Herbert Hoover, who had served as Secretary of Commerce under both Harding and Coolidge, in which role he had done much to build up this department as well as the nation's foreign and domestic trade. Before entering Harding's Cabinet, Hoover (who, unlike most major governmental executives, was a former engineer) had compiled an enviable record as a federal administrator during the First World War, and then as an extremely efficient and humane relief official in war-ravaged Europe. Given this national recognition, it was not difficult for him to secure the Republican presidential nomination and go on to win an overwhelming victory over his Democratic opponent, New York's more plebeian Governor, Alfred E. Smith, in the 1928 election.[111]

Now Hoover, who was a self-made man, has been described in some quarters as an ill-fated progressive with either poor or mixed relations with Eastern financial interests, whose politico-economic world collapsed around him in the Great Depression of the early 1930s (hence his harsh treatment by many later historians).[112] There is, of course, a certain amount of truth to this line of argument. There can be no doubt, for instance, that many of the political and economic values long firmly held by Hoover, such as a faith in the principles of laissez faire and rugged individualism, were rendered obsolete by the financial debacle which was precipitated by the great stock market crash in October 1929. And most authorities are quite willing to concede that Hoover was more liberal than the vast majority of high officials who served under Harding and Coolidge, hardly a severe standard.

However, it should also be emphasized that while Hoover was an engineer by training and early experience, he had, by the time he severed his former business and professional ties with the British firm of Bewick, Moreing & Co. in 1908, emerged as both a very wealthy man (his fortune soon reached a total of over $4 million) and, as one economic journal described him, a noteworthy capitalist in his own right.[113] Although most of Hoover's many later (1908–1919) links with mining, financial, and extractive enterprises were with foreign-based, if not foreign-controlled, concerns, these were basically business rather than engineering affiliations, and they must have had a marked and probably enduring effect on his general politico-economic outlook.[114] Thus it seems more accurate to treat Hoover not as a liberal or progressive (although he may have looked the part compared to other prominent Republicans of the period), but rather as an able engineer and administrator who held strongly conservative and pro-business views throughout his years of federal executive service. Indeed, if Hoover was a progressive—or as some would have it, an enlightened moderate—one wonders why during his first years in office he felt compelled to talk (over the phone) at least three times a week with Morgan partner Dwight W. Morrow.[115]

An even better insight into Hoover's overall orientation may be gained from a look at the following brief biographical analysis of the men he chose to appoint or retain as his chief Cabinet officers at the outset of his administration:

Secretary of State	Henry L. Stimson, N.Y. (1929–1933)	Governor General of Philippine Islands (1927–29); special U.S. envoy to Nicaragua (1927); Secretary of War (1911–13)
		Longtime partner in New York law firm of Winthrop, Stimson, Putnam & Roberts (and predecessor concerns)
		Director of the American Superpower Corp. (1925–1927)
Secretary of the Treasury	Andrew W. Mellon, Pa. (1929–February 1932)	Secretary of the Treasury (1921 through 1929)
		Vice-president of National Union Fire Insurance Co., Pittsburgh (up to 1928); President of the Mellon National Bank (up to 1921); vice-president of the Gulf Oil Corp. and Union Savings Bank (up to 1921)
		Director of the Aluminum Co. of America, American Locomotive Co., Carbonundum Co., Crucible Steel Co. of America, Koppers Co., Pittsburgh Coal Co., Standard Steel Car Co., and National Bank of Commerce of N.Y.C. (all up to 1921)
Attorney General	William D. Mitchell, Minn. (1929–1933)	U.S. Solicitor General (1925–1929)
		Longtime partner in St. Paul law firm of Mitchell, Doherty, Rumble, Bunn & Butler (and predecessor concern of Butler, Mitchell & Doherty)
		Director of the Capital Trust & Savings Bank, St. Paul (1917–1925)
Secretary of War	James W. Good, Ill. (March–November 1929)	Iowa Congressman (1909–1921); Western manager of Hoover's 1928 campaign

		Partner in Chicago law firm of Good, Childs, Bobb & Wescott (1921–1929); partner in Cedar Rapids law firm of Deacon, Good, Sargent & Spangler (1908–1921)
		Apparently no notable corporate ties
Secretary of Navy	Charles F. Adams, Mass. (1929–1933)	No significant governmental experience
		Longtime Boston lawyer; former president of Fifty Associates, Boston (a Brahmin-dominated investment group); also vice-president of Provident Institution for Savings, Boston (around 1910 through 1933)
		Director of the Old Colony Trust Co. (1910–1929), John Hancock Mutual Insurance Co. (1918 through 1933), AT&T (1912–1928), American Sugar Refining Co. (1921–1928), Massachusetts Gas Companies (at least 1905 through 1933);, and Edison Electric Illuminating Co. of Boston (1918–1928)
Secretary of the Interior	Ray L. Wilbur, Cal. (1929–1933)	No significant governmental experience
		President of Stanford University (1916–1929)
		Trustee of Rockefeller Foundation (1923 through 1933)
Secretary of Agriculture	Arthur M. Hyde, Mo. (1929–1933)	Governor of Missouri (1921–1925)
		Longtime Princeton and Trenton (Mo.) lawyer; also president of Sentinel Life Insurance Co., Kansas City (1927–1928) apparently no other formal corporate ties

Secretary of Commerce	Robert P. Lamont, Ill. (March 1929–August 1932)	No significant governmental experience President of American Steel Foundries, Chicago (1912–1929) Director of Armour & Co. (1923–1929), American Radiator Co. (1925–1928), Dodge Bros., Inc., (1925–1928), International Harvester Co. (1924–1928), Montgomery, Ward & Co. (1925–1929), Illinois Bell Telephone Co., subsidiary of AT&T (1928–1929), and First National Bank of Chicago (1917–1929)
Secretary of Labor	James J. Davis, Pa. (March 1929–December 1930)	U.S. Secretary of Labor (1921–1929) Former president of American Bond & Mortgage Co. (small Pittsburgh concern) No other corporate ties, but a still active member of the Iron, Steel and Tin Workers of America Member of Pittsburgh's Duquesne Club

Thus of Hoover's nine major Cabinet officers, seven were new appointees and two were carryovers from the preceding Republican regimes of Harding and Coolidge. One of the latter officials was the conservative Secretary of Labor, James J. Davis, who, judging by all accounts, was not much of a union man and did little to advance the cause of the workingman during his years in office.[116] The other Cabinet carryover was a much more important person, Secretary of the Treasury Andrew W. Mellon, whose family controlled a huge complex of corporations embracing oil, metals, coal, banking, and insurance.[117] While Mellon had by this time severed all his overt corporate ties, the other members of this rich clan (especially his brother, Richard) had not only taken over most of the posts he once held, but had established still other links with such companies as the Pennsylvania Railroad, Westinghouse Air Brake Co., and Guaranty Trust Co. of New York. Hence, even though President Hoover reportedly did not rely on Mellon's advice nearly so much as his less able and more compliant predecessors, one can hardly view the retention of this archconservative at Treasury until early 1932 as a sign of progressive thought and action.[118]

Perhaps the most important of Hoover's own appointees was Secretary of State Henry L. Stimson, who has generally been depicted primarily as an extremely able and dedicated public servant, both in this and later presidential regimes.[119] Actually, up to the late 1920s, Stimson, who was once Elihu Root's protégé, had spent less than five years in the federal government, all in the pre-Wilsonian period (two as Secretary of War under Taft). In 1927 he was asked, first, to assume the post of special envoy to the financially troubled state of Nicaragua, and then, having resolved that problem, he was persuaded to accept the position of Governor General of the Philippine Islands. Hence his reputation, as of 1929, as a prominent federal official.

But there is another side to Stimson's career, and that is his role as a well-connected corporate lawyer. Stimson had, after all, spent the bulk of his adult life as a senior partner in a Wall Street law firm known by the late 1920s as Winthrop, Stimson, Putnam & Roberts, which, according to his biographer, represented such sizable concerns as the Bristol-Myers Co., Singer Manufacturing Co., and a number of (unidentified) public utility companies.[120] A look at certain business directories reveals, furthermore, that Stimson himself served, from 1925 to 1927, as a director of the American Superpower Corp. (a big public utility holding company closely linked with the Morgan-oriented Electric Bond and Share Co.), along with his law partner, George Roberts.[121] Two of Stimson's cousins, Alfred L. Loomis and Landon K. Thorne (both of whom were high-ranking figures in Bonbright & Co., a New York financial firm on friendly terms with the House of Morgan), also served either as officers or directors of American Superpower, which reinforced Stimson's links with this major enterprise.[122] It therefore seems fair to say that Stimson was a highly conservative, pro-business official, firmly predisposed to defend America's economic interests abroad.[123]

Another member of Hoover's Cabinet who has been described as essentially a non-economic figure was Attorney General William D. Mitchell, who had served as Solicitor General during the last four years of the Coolidge administration, and was thus widely viewed as an "inside" selection. However, this is a misleading assessment, for Mitchell had been a longtime partner in a prominent St. Paul corporate law firm known until the early 1920s as Butler, Mitchell & Doherty, and thereafter, following the appointment of Pierce Butler to the U.S. Supreme Court, as Mitchell, Doherty, Rumble, Bunn & Butler. As David Danelski's work shows, this law firm represented various important economic interests in the Northwest, especially big railroads.[124] In fact, Mitchell had served, up to 1925, as a director of the Capital Trust & Savings Bank of St. Paul, which institution and its larger affiliate, the Capital National Bank, counted many of the city's major business figures among its board members. Hence Mitchell probably also had a profoundly conservative, pro-corporate orientation.

Yet another of Hoover's clearly elitist Cabinet officials was Secretary of the Navy Charles F. Adams, who prior to his appointment had no real governmental experience, but had instead been a wealthy Boston lawyer and financier.[125] Not surprisingly given his Brahmin background, Adams had a number of key socio-economic links. For example, he had served as president of an entrepreneurial group known as the Fifty Associates (which was probably a direct descendant of the once-famous Boston Associates), as vice-president of the city's prestigious Provident Institution for Savings, and as a director of the Old Colony Trust Co., John Hancock Mutual Life Insurance Co. of Boston, AT&T, and American Sugar Refining Co. In addition, his daughter had married J. P. Morgan, Jr., who, following in the footsteps of his long-deceased father, was by 1929 board chairman of the U.S. Steel Corp. and a director of the International Mercantile Marine Co. and Pullman, Inc. Thus, despite the claims of some ill-informed observers, Adams, who was New England's only representative in the Cabinet, was obviously on intimate terms with many of the nation's most powerful economic interests.[126]

There were some members of Hoover's Cabinet who do not appear to have been chosen primarily because of their business connections. One was Hoover's first Secretary of War, James W. Good, who was a former Chicago (and Cedar Rapids, Iowa) lawyer and onetime (1909–1921) Iowa Congressman. Good's most recent major political activity was his work as director of Hoover's 1928 campaign in the Midwest, for which effort he was soon rewarded with a Cabinet post.[127] But Good died shortly after he took office. He was succeeded by his recently selected top aide, Patrick J. Hurley, another Midwestern (Tulsa, Oklahoma) lawyer who had served as a high-ranking official in both Hoover's 1928 pre-convention and general election campaigns. This was presumably the principal reason for his appointment.[128]

Another person who was most likely picked for non-economic reasons was Secretary of the Interior Ray Lyman Wilbur, who, as the longtime president of Stanford University (Hoover's alma mater), was the only Cabinet member to be recruited from the Far West. Wilbur was also a very close friend of the President, who had served as a trustee of this prestigious school since 1912. As president of Stanford, Wilbur was probably on friendly terms with many major business leaders and, no doubt, shared many of their views. But, given his background, it would appear that he was picked primarily for geo-political and personal reasons.[129] Similarly, Secretary of Agriculture Arthur M. Hyde, who was a former governor of Missouri and essentially a small-town lawyer and businessman, would certainly seem to have been chosen because of sectional considerations, for by this time the Midwest had managed to establish a firm hold on this position.[130] Indeed, both Interior and Agriculture were departments which, with the growing strength of Western and farm interests in American politics, no well-advised chief executive would contemplate turning over to overt big business figures.

Hoover's penchant for appointing important economic (or politico-economic) leaders to high office was also manifested in the realm of foreign affairs. As American Ambassador to Great Britain, he selected Charles G. Dawes, who had served as Vice President of the United States during the last four years of the Coolidge administration, and briefly in the early 1920s as the first director of the Bureau of the Budget. Dawes was also a major business executive with a number of noteworthy socio-economic links. He had served, most conspicuously, as head of the fairly large (probably family-dominated) Central Trust Co. of Chicago since its creation in 1902, and at times as a director of various sizable concerns, most recently of the Chicago Great Western Railroad (from 1923 to 1925). In addition, one of his three brothers, Beman Dawes, had acted as president of the big family-controlled Pure Oil Co. up to 1924, at which point he became board chairman of the firm when another brother, Henry, took over this executive position.[131] Dawes held this prestigious diploma-tic post until the end of 1932, when he returned to the United States to assume the presidency of the newly formed Reconstruction Finance Corp. (a product of the Depression). He was replaced in London by the rich and influential Andrew Mellon, who took over this role both to advance his own oil interests and because his relations with Hoover had become somewhat strained.[132]

Hoover's Ambassador to France, Walter Edge, was a less overt pro-business figure than either Dawes or Mellon, and had spent much more time in government than either man. Edge had, in fact, served for ten years (1919–1929) as a United States Senator from New Jersey, and before that as both a governor and state legislator. However, he was also a longtime Atlantic City newspaper publisher who had certain key socio-economic ties. For example, he had served up to 1923 as a director of the Crex Carpet Co., a fairly small New York City firm that was closely linked with the larger Cerro de Pasco Corp., which was dominated by wealthy mining interests (of which Under Secretary of the Treasury Ogden Mills had until recently been an integral part).[133] And perhaps even more important, Edge was a very close friend and relative of the president of the Standard Oil Co. of N.J., Walter C. Teagle, a potent force in the business world.[134]

Similarly, when Jacob G. Schurman resigned as American Ambassador to Germany, he was replaced by a prominent politico-economic figure from Kentucky, Frederic M. Sackett, who had served for five years in the United States Senate, but who also had a number of noteworthy business links. Until the late 1920s, he had been president of two small (apparently privately-owned) coal companies and a vice-president of the locally based Louisville Cement Co. Moreover, prior to his election to the Senate, he had been a board member of the Louisville branch of the Federal Reserve Bank of St. Louis (which many would regard as an Establishment tie) and a director of the American Tar Products Co., a fairly small concern in which the Mellon family had a substantial interest.[135] Hence it seems fair to say that Hoover's top diplomatic officials were men with a variety of important (direct or indirect) links with the business community.

It is also true that the generally conservative nature of the Hoover administration had much to do with the ineffective way in which it responded to the Great Depression. This grievous decline was touched off by the near-total collapse of the stock market in October 1929, which was followed by a series of other shocks that plunged the nation into a terrible downward spiral. Within a short period of time, in fact, the American people were confronted with a major economic disaster, the likes of which they had never before experienced. Millions of investors lost their savings, and thousands of people were forced into bankruptcy. Prices and trade dropped sharply, most factories drastically curtailed production (many went out of business entirely), owners and management cut back on wages, and a vast number of people were simply thrown out of work. By the early 1930s more than seven million Americans were unemployed, and over 5,000 banks had closed their doors. In short, the nation was in desperate straits.

Yet Hoover's reaction to this unprecedented debacle was of a distinctly limited (and sometimes inconsistent) nature. He was hampered by the conservative counsel he constantly received from his chief advisors and his own firm belief as a wealthy businessman in "rugged individualism," the importance of voluntary action, and the undesirability of government intervention in the economy. Although he did step up federal spending for public works projects to increase employment, establish new farm purchasing programs to try to shore up agricultural prices, and create the Reconstruction Finance Corp. to extend loans to hard-pressed business concerns, these measures were, as several historians have observed, ". . . largely nullified by other policies. Committed to budget-balancing, Hoover took away with one hand what he gave with the other."[136] The increase in federal public works spending was, for example, so modest that it was more than offset by the drastic Depression-induced cuts in state and local spending. And while Hoover's Federal Farm Board did make many loans to agricultural cooperatives around the country, farm prices continued to drop, primarily because of Hoover's unwillingness to impose any kind of production controls. Moreover, as the Depression deepened, Hoover spurned appeals for more vigorous federal action. He remained strongly opposed to granting direct relief to America's many needy citizens because he clung to the archaic view that this financial burden was the sole responsibility of private charity and the state and local units of government. In other words, because of his own business background and the conservative, pro-corporate orientation of his principal advisors, the President acted on much too small a scale and was simply too inflexible a figure to deal effectively with the Great Depression.

For his failure, he lost the support of the vast majority of the American people.

Supreme Court Appointments and Actions

The Supreme Court during this twelve-year period of Republican hegemony was likewise dominated by conservative politico-economic forces, in considerable part because of the carryover of a substantial number of pro-business figures from the earlier Taft, Roosevelt, and McKinley administrations. Their influence far outweighed the mild infusion of reformist thinking introduced by the Wilsonian regime, primarily through the appointment of the progressive Louis D. Brandeis. Of the nine men sitting on the high Court in March 1921, six had been picked at least a decade before by Presidents who, whatever their differences, were fairly closely linked with corporate interests. Only one of these six, Boston Brahmin Oliver W. Holmes, could be said to exert a moderate or liberal influence on the Court. The rest, men such as Joseph McKenna (a former friend and political ally of railroad magnate Leland Stanford) and Willis Van Devanter (a onetime attorney for the Union Pacific Railroad), could generally be counted on to support the position of the wealthy and more powerful groups in American society.

The first opening on the Supreme Court in the 1920s occurred only a matter of months after Harding took office when Chief Justice Edward D. White, a wealthy Louisiana conservative, died suddenly. In keeping with a promise made earlier, President Harding appointed one of the most prominent Republican leaders in the country, former President William Howard Taft, who had long coveted this post. Since his retirement from executive office in 1913, Taft had been acting as a professor of law at Yale University, his alma mater. Yet although undoubtedly devoted to the law, he was hardly a neutral figure on most issues affecting business and government. For one thing, as pointed out before, he came from a wealthy Cincinnati family, and various close kinsmen, such as his brother, Henry W. Taft, and his half-brother, Charles P. Taft, were still intimately associated with several major business concerns.[137] Moreover, Taft himself served as a "public" member of the executive committee of the business-dominated National Civic Federation from 1907 up to the time of his appointment to the Supreme Court. But perhaps even more revealing was the network of influential friends and allies he had built up in the business and corporate legal worlds over the years. According to one reliable source, these included Chicago attorney Max Pam, a director of the fairly large American Steel Foundries, and Taft's old Yale friend, Nathaniel T. Guernsey, who was general counsel of AT&T.[138] These relationships indicate quite clearly that Taft was a staunch conservative.

Taft presided as Chief Justice up to early 1930, when, having become old and ill, he reluctantly resigned. He was quickly replaced by President Hoover with another well-known and exceedingly able Republican leader, Charles Evans Hughes, who had served as an Associate Justice of the Supreme Court from 1910 to 1916 (he stepped down to run for the Presidency), as Secretary of State from 1921 to 1925, and since 1929 as a judge of the Permanent Court of International Justice—a most impressive governmental record. However, for about four years both before and after his term as Secretary of State, he had been a senior partner in a prominent New York law firm known as Hughes, Rounds, Schurman & Dwight; as such, he had often represented Standard Oil Co. of N. J. and, during the late 1920s, the American Petroleum Institute. In short, by the time of his return to the high Court, Hughes was closely associated with the business world.[139] Not surprisingly, as Chief Justice he took a conservative stance on most major economic (but not civil rights) issues that came before this august body during the much-troubled 1930s.

Harding made three other appointments to the Supreme Court during his relatively brief term in office. The first of these occurred in September 1922 when Associate Justice John H. Clarke, a onetime railroad lawyer and Ohio Democratic leader with a strong idealistic bent, stepped down from the high Court to devote more time to the then-promising world peace movement. As his successor, Harding selected a onetime (1893–1917) Salt Lake City lawyer and former (1905–1917) U.S. Senator from Utah, George Sutherland, who had also acted as one of the President's most important political advisors during the 1920 pre-convention and general election campaign. A man with long-established ties to Utah, Sutherland had nonetheless chosen, since his enforced retirement from the Senate in 1917, to practice law in Washington, D.C., perhaps because he had been elected president of the American Bar Association about that time. Sutherland was, above all, a conservative, almost a Social Darwinist—a philosophy some have attributed to his early reading and complete acceptance of the writings of Herbert Spencer.[140] But Sutherland's rightist views more likely stemmed largely from his various business-oriented affiliations over the years. For example, he had served, along with Utah Senator Reed Smoot, as a director of the Mormon-dominated Deseret Savings Bank in Salt Lake City from around 1910 to 1922 (during the last five years of which time he was a Washington attorney), and also as a vice-president of the much smaller Home Trust Co. of Salt Lake City from 1910 to 1926 (four years after he became a Supreme Court Justice). Not only that, he sat on the board of the business-dominated Carnegie Endowment for International Peace from 1920 to 1925, an association that may have reinforced his conservative thinking on many subjects. Whatever the reason, Sutherland was one of the most reactionary men appointed to the Supreme Court in the entire post–Civil War era.

The next opening on the Court occurred just two months later when another elderly Associate Justice, Ohio's William R. Day, resigned after almost two decades on this important body. After much behind-the-scenes maneuver and high-level consultation involving many leading businessmen, President Harding selected a wealthy St. Paul corporate lawyer, Pierce Butler, who, unlike most recent Supreme Court appointees, had no formal judicial experience and relatively little in major governmental affairs.[141] Butler had instead devoted the bulk of his adult life to building up a lucrative law practice in partnership with William Mitchell, who later became Hoover's Attorney General. Much of this work was done for various large concerns, such as (up to at least 1905) the Chicago, St. Paul, Minneapolis & Omaha Railway, a line controlled by the Vanderbilt-dominated Chicago and Northwestern Railway. Indeed, according to one authority, Butler became, in the course of his career, perhaps the foremost railroad lawyer in the Northwest.[142] In light of these links, it is little wonder that he proved to be one of the most conservative figures on the High Court until the crucial late New Deal years.

Harding's last appointment to the Supreme Court was made in the first part of 1923 when, following the resignation of New Jersey's Mahlon Pitney, he chose, a longtime Tennessee judge, Edward T. Sanford, to replace him. Having served in a judicial capacity for fifteen years (and briefly before that as an Assistant Attorney General), Sanford had no noteworthy corporate ties in recent years, although he had served as a director of the East Tennessee National Bank of Knoxville for five years before his appointment to the federal bench. Sanford came from a moneyed background, for his father was a rich local businessman who up to the early 1900s had been president of the Knoxville and Ohio Railroad (a subsidiary of the big Southern Railway system) and a director of the Southern Car & Foundry Co. His brother, Alfred F. Sanford, also served (apparently taking Edward's place) on the board of the East Tennessee National Bank from 1909 through 1930. Thus, Sanford was essentially a conservative, with only occasional liberal leanings.[143]

Although President Coolidge held office for about six years, he had only one opportunity to make an appointment to the high Court, and that choice, as indicated earlier, was Harlan Fiske Stone, a former New York lawyer who had served briefly (1924–1925) as U.S. Attorney General, in which capacity he had instituted a number of important actions, including one perhaps politically ill-advised antitrust suit against the Mellon-dominated Aluminum Co. of America (this reportedly was one reason why he was elevated to the Supreme Court). Stone actually had a rather unusual background in that he had been both a Wall Street lawyer and the (1910–1923) dean of the prestigious Columbia University Law School. He had served for about six months in 1923–1924 as a partner in the major corporate law firm of Sullivan & Cromwell, and for many years before that he had been a partner in the less influential firm of Satterlee, Canfield & Stone.[144] However, this latter connection was always, according to

Alpheus T. Mason, a secondary affiliation, for the able and industrious Stone apparently found the less conservative academic environment more to his liking.[145] Much to the disappointment of many of his former wealthy friends and supporters, this assessment may well have been correct, for in his later years on the bench Stone proved to be a fairly liberal Justice.

President Hoover, for his part, made two appointments to the Supreme Court besides that of Chief Justice Hughes. The first of these occurred in 1930, when the death of Edward Sanford presented the President with an opening which he first attempted to fill with an allegedly anti-labor Southern judge (John J. Parker). Failing in this endeavor, he then nominated a well-known Northern lawyer, Owen J. Roberts, who had built up a national reputation through his investigation and prosecution of the notorious Teapot Dome scandal. Though Roberts had established his name through these proceedings, he was basically a well-fixed Philadelphia lawyer with many key economic ties. He had served as a director of the fairly small Franklin Fire Insurance Co. (which was a subsidiary of the much larger New York–based Home Insurance Co.) from 1924 to 1930, as a board member of the (fourth-ranked) Equitable Life Assurance Society of the United States from 1926 to 1930, and as a director of the Bell Telephone Co. of Pennsylvania from 1926 to 1929, at which point he was elected to the board of its parent company, AT&T.[146] Although Roberts, too, had once been associated with a prominent law school (as, until 1918, a part-time faculty member of the University of Pennsylvania), this affiliation apparently did little to lessen his pro-corporate orientation since he soon showed that he would be a strongly conservative force on the High Court.

Hoover's second appointee to the Supreme Court was, happily, a very different type of person. Heeding the advice of many enlightened legal and political leaders, the President picked, upon the resignation of New England's aged able Oliver Wendell Holmes, a renowned New York jurist, Benjamin Cardozo, who had served on that state's court of appeals for a total of eighteen years.[147] Cardozo was generally regarded as the most distinguished judge on any state court in the country. Indeed, he had, after practicing with his brother for a number of years, literally devoted his life to the law, writing various works on the subject, in addition to performing his weighty judicial duties. Neither he nor any members of his family had any significant ties in recent years to corporate or wealthy economic interests (though, unlike Brandeis, he was no crusading civic reformer). Hence he soon became identified with the more liberal minority faction on the Court, which until the late 1930s was confined to registering a set of vigorous dissents from the decisions handed down by the conservative-minded majority.

During the business-dominated 1920s and early 1930s the Court gave ample evidence of its highly rightist nature. Among other things, it vastly increased the rate at which it overturned acts of Congress with which it disagreed constitutionally, and often philosophically. In no decade prior to this time had the Supreme Court nullified more than nine laws adopted by the legislative and executive branches of government. Yet it did so nineteen times during the 1920s. For instance, in the controversial case of *Adkins* v. *Children's Hospital,* the Court ruled that the Congress had no legal right to establish minimum wages for women working in the District of Columbia, thereby ignoring the judgment rendered in two previous decisions (*Muller* v. *Oregon* and *Bunting* v. *Oregon*) and, in effect, resurrecting the outmoded and unfair "freedom of contract" doctrine. It also proceeded to emasculate many of the regulatory efforts made by a (temporarily) revitalized Federal Trade Commission, with the result that the Clayton Antitrust Act was rendered as weak, if not useless, as the original Sherman antitrust statute. Indeed the record of the Supreme Court during the 1920s and early 1930s was in many respects worse than that of its predecessors, for as one observer has pointed out, the conservatism of the Fuller Court (1888–1910) was not, at least initially, noticeably behind the overall economic thinking and general temper of its time, whereas the Court was by the post–World War I period an obvious political anachronism in its reactionary attempts to restore the laissez-faire and heavily pro-business conditions of a bygone era.[148]

What overall assessment, then, can be made of the Harding, Coolidge, and Hoover administrations, particularly in comparison to the preceding Democratic and Republican regimes? For one thing, it is clear that these governments continued to rely heavily on people who had both a considerable amount of education and significant governmental experience prior to their appointment to high federal office; 70 percent had graduated from college, and about 55 percent had previously held important administrative or diplomatic posts. Perhaps even more important, over 80 percent of these high administrative and diplomatic officials had key socio-economic ties. This is considerably more than the 57 percent total of the Wilson regime, but somewhat less than the 92 percent found during the McKinley, Roosevelt, and Taft administrations. But the first of these figures should not necessarily be taken as evidence that the Harding, Coolidge, and Hoover administrations were less closely linked to major economic interests than the three previous (1897–1913) Republican regimes. Though there was probably more small-business representation in the federal government in the post–World War I period (through such people as Harry Daugherty and John G. Sargent), much of the difference may be traced to the fact that, prior to Wilson, the position of Secretary of the Interior was filled largely by men with many pro-corporate connections (such as Cornelius N. Bliss, E. A. Hitchcock, and James R. Garfield), whereas by the 1920s and early 1930s it was politically imperative to recruit more purely Western leaders (i.e., Albert Fall, Hubert Work, and Ray Lyman Wilbur). If proper allowance is made for these and other geo-political developments (the appointment of four Secretaries of Agriculture, most of whom were linked with big farm interests), there is scarcely any difference in the overall politico-economic nature of the presidential administrations which held power during these two periods.[149]

There were, however, some noteworthy changes in the kinds of business forces which were represented in these Republican regimes. While the House of Morgan continued to wield considerable influence in governmental circles in both eras, the Mellon interests had emerged by the 1920s as a major force in Republican affairs, as seen in the appointment and long (11-year) tenure of Andrew W. Mellon as Secretary of the Treasury. In what was probably the most important policy action of this period, Mellon worked assiduously, with the aid of others, to drastically curtail federal spending, which had risen sharply in World War I, and to reduce the tax burden of the rich; in both of these endeavors he was ultimately quite successful. But the Great Depression later posed a tremendous problem for the Hoover administration, which because of its conservative make-up proved completely unable to deal with the burden, and thus led to its own demise.

Notes

1. In 1929, as Arthur Link has pointed out, about 71 percent of the families in the United States had incomes of under $2,500 a year, the sum then estimated as being necessary to maintain a decent standard of living. Yet conversely, the 36,000 wealthiest families (which made up only a little over 0.1 percent of the population) had an aggregate income almost equal to that received by the 11,653,000 households (or roughly 42 percent of the population) earning less than $1,500 a year. See Arthur S. Link, *American Epoch,* 3rd ed., p. 257.

2. The vast majority of these firms were considerably larger in 1929 than they were in 1933, by which time the Depression had taken a significant economic toll. Of the top twenty industrial concerns in 1921, only five—U.S. Steel, U.S. Rubber, International Mercantile Marine, Armour, and Swift—had declined in overall size, and one former major company, Midvale Steel & Ordinance, had merged with Bethlehem Steel in 1923. Shell Oil was excluded from this ranking because it was basically a subsidiary of a much larger foreign-controlled concern.

3. For more on this complex (and often overlooked) struggle for control over valuable oil resources, see Gerald D. Nash, *United States Oil Policy, 1890–1964: Business and Govern-*

ment in Twentieth Century America (Pittsburgh: University of Pittsburgh Press, 1964), pp. 49–71, and Joan Hoff Wilson, *American Business and Foreign Policy, 1920–1933* (Lexington: University Press of Kentucky, 1971), pp. 184–200.

4. As indicated in the author's *The Managerial Revolution Reassessed* (Lexington, Mass.: Heath, 1972), pp. 116–27, many of these findings are at variance with those arrived at in Adolf Berle and Gardiner Means's noted study of *The Modern Corporation and Private Property* (New York: Macmillan, 1932), pp. 95–114. However, the author believes that his data, which are based on later information, are more accurate.

5. By control, the author means *ultimate* control, in the sense of having the power to direct overall corporate affairs, rather than involvement in the day-to-day management of a concern. This type of control was, for instance, demonstrated by the Rockefeller interests in the late 1920s when, after considerable effort, they finally ousted the well-entrenched but scandal-tainted chief executive officer of the Standard Oil Co. of Indiana (who had been installed with their backing).

6. In 1900, for example, the top fifteen railroads were as follows (in order of overall assets): the Achison, Topeka & Sante Fe Railway; Northern Pacific Railway; New York Central Railroad; Pennsylvania Railroad; Southern Railway; Erie Railroad; Baltimore & Ohio Railroad; Union Pacific Railroad; Chicago, Burlington & Quincy Railroad; Southern Pacific Co.; Chicago, Milwaukee, and St. Paul Railroad; Chicago and Northwestern Railway; Great Northern Railway; Reading Co.; and Illinois Central Railroad. In 1933 the top fifteen included all the preceding concerns except the Reading Co. and Erie Railroad, which had been replaced by the Chesapeake and Ohio Railway and the Missouri-Pacific Railroad.

7. For an elaborate diagram outlining these relationships, see Adolf A. Berle and Gardiner C. Means, *The Modern Corporation and Private Property,* p. 79.

8. See Edward C. Kirkland, *A History of American Economic Life,* p. 483.

9. Moreover, the big Electric Bond and Share Co., which was on friendly terms with the United Corp. and its Morgan-backed interests, also controlled the (18th-ranked) American Gas & Electric Co., a holding company whose major arms had assets of over $2.8 billion. According to *Moody's Public Utility Manual,* the United Corp. was controlled by J. P. Morgan & Co., Drexel & Co. (its Philadelphia affiliate), Bonbright & Co. (another New York financial concern), and the Morgan-oriented American Superpower Corp. In the early 1930s the "outside" directors of the United Corp. included Harold Stanley and George Whitney (two partners in J. P. Morgan & Co.), Edward Hopkinson, Jr. (a senior partner in Drexel & Co.), and the top officials of four of the five public utility (operating) units listed in the text. The board of the Electric Bond and Share Co. counted among its members George H. Howard (president of the United Corp.), William C. Potter (president of the Guaranty Trust Co. of New York), and S. Sloan Colt (president of the Bankers Trust Co.).

10. See Thomas C. Cochran and William Miller, *The Age of Enterprise,* p. 309. Another sizable complex was that assembled by Chicago's ambitious entrepreneur, Samuel Insull. It included at its peak (around 1930) the Commonwealth Edison Co. and at least five other large concerns, with combined assets of almost $2 billion. However, Insull's empire, which apparently rested on rather shaky foundations, collapsed in the early 1930s, reportedly much to the satisfaction of rival Eastern interests.

11. See Adolf A. Berle and Gardiner C. Means, *The Modern Corporation and Private Property,* pp. 28–32.

12. Two of the top ten banks in 1921—the Equitable Trust Co. and National Bank of Commerce of New York City—disappeared because of major mergers around 1930 (the former into the Chase National Bank and the latter into the Morgan-dominated Guaranty Trust Co.). The First National Bank of New York and Union Trust Co. of Cleveland had both dropped out of the top ten rankings by 1933, although the former was still a major financial institution. Though obviously a potent force in American business affairs, the firm of J. P. Morgan & Co. was itself of somewhat lesser size than the economic giants listed in

Table 10, for it had assets of only about $344 million in 1934 (the first year such figures were published in *Moody's* financial manual). The figures in Table 10 are considerably understated because of the omission of bank trust funds, which were estimated to be about $25 billion in 1933, and were primarily held by big institutions. For more on this matter, see Herman E. Krooss and Martin R. Blyn, *A History of Financial Intermediaries*, p. 150.

13. Of the five largest (over $1 billion) life insurance companies in the United States, one, Metropolitan Life, was also closely linked (through directorship rather than stock-ownership ties) with the Chase National Bank, a working relationship established before the Rockefeller forces took over this bank. The Morgan interests were on friendly terms with the Mutual Life Insurance Co. and, to a somewhat lesser extent, the Newark-based Prudential Insurance Co. of America. In the author's opinion, the New York Life Insurance Co. was not really allied with either of these great economic complexes; the status of the Equitable Life Assurance Society was unclear.

14. Apparently these two banks did not work together frequently, although various high officials of the major Standard Oil companies served on one or another of the two boards of directors (and not those of other New York City banks) well into the post–World War II period. Two of the other banks on the top ten list—Guaranty Trust and Bankers Trust—were still controlled by the Morgan interests, which continued to have more economic (and political) power than the Rockefeller forces.

15. According to Edward C. Kirkland, there were about 800 important national or international trade organizations in the United States by the early 1920s, although they apparently did not carry great weight in American government.

16. Of the fifteen officers and directors of the Council on Foreign Relations in 1921, seven were academic or civic figures, six were noted economic leaders who had extensive recent experience in high-level diplomatic or governmental posts, one was a major corporate lawyer (Cravath), and one was a prominent New York banker, Otto H. Kahn of Kuhn, Loeb & Co.

17. Two somewhat similar organizations had also recently been created—the Boston-based World Peace Foundation, which was dominated by educational and (non-business) civic figures, and the New York–headquartered Foreign Policy Association, which grew out of the abortive League of Free Nations Association. The first group has apparently had little influence in American government, while the latter body has never attained the power and prestige of the more illustrious Council on Foreign Relations.

18. The well-financed Wood forces spent about four times as much in their presidential nomination efforts as Frank Lowden, who reportedly supplied most of his own money. One of the biggest contributions to Wood's cause came from William C. Procter, the wealthy head of Cincinnati's fairly sizable Procter and Gamble Co., who reportedly put up at least $700,000. Though an Ohioian, Procter served on the board of the Rockefeller-dominated National City Bank and the Cincinnati, New Orleans & Texas Pacific Railway (which was controlled by the Baltimore and Ohio Railroad and Southern Railway.). Other major contributors to Wood's campaign were Ambrose Monell, former president of the International Nickel Co. (who was now a director of the American International Corp. and the Midvale Steel & Ordinance Co.), New York magnate William Boyce Thompson (a director of the Chase National Bank, Metropolitan Life Insurance Co., and Sinclair Consolidated Oil Corp.), California oilman E. L. Doheny, and Harry F. Sinclair, head of the Sinclair Consolidated Oil Corp. (and a director of the newly formed Replogle Steel Co.). See Wesley M. Bagby, *The Road to Normalcy* (Baltimore: Johns Hopkins Press, 1962), p. 26, and Andrew Sinclair, *The Available Man* (New York: Macmillan, 1965), p. 134.

19. Daughterty, Herrick, and Harvey were rewarded with high diplomatic or Cabinet posts. The patrician Penrose, who was then slowly succumbing to a fatal disease, had a brother, Spencer, who was a vice-president of the (Colorado-based) Cripple Creek Central Railway and a director of the big Utah Copper Co. and the considerably smaller Holly Sugar Corp. Another brother, Charles Penrose, had married into the Drexel family, which had long

been allied with the Morgan interests. For more on Penrose's economic investments and friendly relationships with such potent western Pennsylvania businessmen as Andrew W. Mellon and Henry Clay Frick, see Robert B. Bowden, *Boies Penrose* (New York: Greenberg Publisher, 1937), pp. 164–65 and 244.

20.   Harding had married the daughter of wealthy Marion businessman Amos Kling, but the two did not get along well, at least until the last part of Kling's life.

21.   One such tie is worthy of mention. As a Senator, Harding was clearly on friendly terms with U.S. Steel head Elbert H. Gary, who obliged him by finding a place in his big company for Harding's mistress, Nan Britton. See Francis Russell, *President Harding: His Life and Times, 1865–1923* (London: Erye & Spottsiwoode, 1969), p. 290, and Samuel H. Adams, *Incredible Era: The Life and Times of Warren Gamaliel Harding* (Boston: Houghton Mifflin, 1939); pp. 103–04.

22.   The position of Secretary of State was first offered to Columbia University's politically active president, Nicholas Murray Butler (who was a board member of both the New York Life Insurance Co. and Carnegie Endowment for International Peace), but he refused to consider the idea. The Cabinet posts of War and Navy were extended, in an effort to allay intraparty divisions stemming from the 1920 Republican national convention, to General Leonard Wood and Frank O. Lowden. However, neither would settle for these positions. Harding's first preference for Secretary of the Treasury was Chicago banker-businessman (and party stalwart) Charles G. Dawes. But the outspoken Dawes was apparently viewed with strong disfavor by powerful Eastern financial interests, so he was shunted over to the newly created post of director of the Bureau of the Budget.

23.   The more liberal National Farmers Union, on the other hand, was apparently opposed to Wallace, probably because of his close links with the wealthier, commercially-oriented Farm Bureau. Wallace has sometimes been described as a progressive, mainly because he had backed various farm causes and frequently fought the food processing and railroad industries, which he felt exploited agricultural interests. See Donald L. Winters, *Henry Cantwell Wallace as Secretary of Agriculture, 1921–1924* (Urbana: University of Illinois Press, 1970), pp. 25, 53, and 73, and Orville M. Kile, *The Farm Bureau Through Three Decades* (Baltimore: Waverly Press, 1948), p. 124.

24.   Hoover had amassed a considerable fortune (later estimated to be over $4 million) as a mining engineer and entrepreneur, particularly in Asia and Australia. He had served until recently as an officer or director of the Russo-Asiatic Corp., Chinese Engineering & Mining Co. (the biggest single prewar commercial venture in that country), the Burma Corp., Ltd. (a major mining complex), and the Zinc Corp., Ltd., which was a part of Australia's big Broken Hill development. Hoover, interestingly, had close links with relatively few major American businessmen (the most prominent of whom was apparently Morgan partner Thomas W. Lamont), and owed his appointment largely to his highly publicized administrative achievements in the latter part of the preceding decade. However, Hoover did serve in 1921 as a trustee of an elite-dominated, Washington-based organization known as the Institute for Governmental Research, which was headed by former St. Louis businessman Robert Brookings (and was later named, after a merger with two other groups, in his honor). For more on Hoover's prewar economic holdings and business connections, see "The President's Fortune," *Fortune* (August 1932), pp. 33–37 and 82–90; Walter W. Liggett, *The Rise of Herbert Hoover* (New York: H. K. Fly Co., 1932), pp. 146–99 and 365–71; and Geoffrey Blainey, *The Rush That Never Ended: A History of Australian Mining* (Melbourne: Melbourne University Press, 1963), pp. 265–78. Hoover's early politico-economic backing is described in Gary D. Best, *The Politics of American Individualism: Herbert Hoover in Transition, 1918–1921* (Westport, Conn.: Greenwood Press, 1975), pp. 54–66.

25.   Despite the limited scale of his banking, real estate, and commercial activities, Davis was reportedly a wealthy man. For more on the exclusive, highly conservative character of the Duquesne Club, see E. Digby Baltzell, *The Protestant Establishment* (New York:

Random House, 1964), pp. 362–66, and Osborn Elliott, *Men at the Top* (New York: Harper & Bros., 1959), pp. 159–66.

26.   Not surprisingly, under Davis the Department of Labor atrophied in the 1920s and ceased to provide any leadership in this important area. Davis also later served two terms in the Senate as, to quote one authority, "... a loyal Mellon Republican." See Robert H. Zieger, *Republicans and Labor, 1919–1929* (Lexington: University of Kentucky Press, 1969), pp. 57–59.

27.   See James N. Giglio, *H. M. Daugherty and the Politics of Expediency* (Kent, Ohio: Kent State University Press, 1978), pp. 38–42.

28.   According to the 1905 *Moody's Railway & Corporate Securities* (p. 1973), the Greene Consolidated Copper Co. owned 10,000 acres of mining property and 475,000 acres of land in the Southwest, and the Greene Gold-Silver Co. had the exclusive mining rights to some 4,000 square miles in Mexico prior to the social revolution in that country. For more on the Greene-Fall relationship, see Francis Russell, *President Harding: His Life and Times*, p. 266.

29.   For a brief account of Fall's land holdings in New Mexico, see Francis Russell, *op. cit.*, p. 492.

30.   Because of his earlier liberal governmental record and his more recent strong support of the League of Nations, the now conservative Hughes's appointment was strongly opposed initially by the GOP's Old Guard.

31.   There is no reference to any such corporate links in Merlo Pusey's two-volume biography of Hughes, his 1917–1921 chapters being entitled "Civilian War Worker," "Champion of Liberty" (which is devoted largely to Hughes's involvement in various major civil rights cases), and "Fight over the League of Nations." About the closest Pusey came to describing the new Hughes was to say that "his reputation entitled him to the cream of the legal business, and his energy enabled him to take a thick skimming." Similarly, in another study, Dexter Perkins confined his attention during this period to Hughes's participation in the bitter domestic fight over the League of Nations. See Merlo J. Pusey, *Charles Evans Hughes* (New York: Macmillan, 1951), Vol. I, p. 384, and Dexter Perkins, *Charles Evans Hughes and American Democratic Statesmanship* (Boston: Little, Brown, 1956), pp. 71–94.

32.   See Joan Hoff Wilson, *American Business and Foreign Policy, 1920–1933*, p. 298, and Richard O'Connor, *The Oil Barons* (Boston: Little, Brown, 1971), p. 244. Wilson maintains that Hughes also acted as legal counselor for the American Petroleum Institute, but since this organization had only been created in 1919, it probably was not as potent a force as the big Standard Oil Co. of N. J. At one point Pusey himself noted (*op. cit.*, p. 384) that John D. Rockefeller retained Hughes for important estate matters. For more evidence on this point, see Timothy N. Pfeiffer and George W. Jaques, *Law Practice in a Turbulent World* (New York: Charles P. Young Co., 1965), p. 28.

33.   See any of the annual reports of the Rockefeller Foundation during this period. Although none of its top officers or trustees had any overt connection with the Standard Oil Co. of N. J., these holdings may have constituted an important part of an indirect control mechanism. For example, in 1929, when the Rockefeller forces moved to oust Robert W. Stewart, the scandal-tainted but well-entrenched chief executive of the Standard Oil Co. of Indiana, they apparently used the foundation's 5 percent interest in this concern in the big battle waged against him. See Arthur M. Johnson, *Winthrop W. Aldrich: Lawyer, Banker, Diplomat* (Boston: Harvard University, Graduate School of Business Administration, 1958), p. 62.

34.   One reported reason for Mellon's selection was that Harding did not want someone connected with Wall Street to hold this key post. Ironically, Mellon was as influential and conservative as any New York banker, and had served on the boards of two financial enterprises located in that city.

35.   These two banks and the Mellon-controlled Union Savings Bank had assets which, had they been combined into one institution, would have ranked in or close to the top ten in the country.

36.   The Mellon interest in all but the last four firms was maintained through substantial family stockownership and the influential role played by close kinsmen as either officers or directors of these concerns. In all, Mellon is reported to have been a director of some fifty corporations at the time he was appointed to Harding's Cabinet, but this is a misleading figure since many of these were subsidiaries of other larger units, such as the Gulf Oil Corp. For one such list (which does not include a few of the firms named in the text), see David E. Koskoff, *The Mellons* (New York: Thomas Y. Crowell 1978), pp. 165–66.

37.   As his top aide, Mellon retained former Wall Street lawyer S. Parker Gilbert, who had served in various Treasury Department posts in the latter part of the Wilson regime. Perhaps the most prominent of Mellon's three assistant secretaries was Eliot Wadsworth, who had been a high-ranking figure in the American Red Cross since 1916 and a former executive of the big Boston-based utility investment and management concern of Stone and Webster, Inc. (as well as a recent director of the Franklin Savings Bank of Boston).

38.   Denby also served as a director of the much smaller Bankers Trust Co. of Detroit from 1917 through 1924 (that is to say, throughout his years as a high federal official).

39.   See Stephen Birmingham, *The Right People*, p. 168. Two members of this group, Russell Alger and Truman H. Newberry, had served as Cabinet members in the McKinley and Roosevelt administrations.

40.   Denby's Assistant Secretary of the Navy was another elite figure, Theodore Roosevelt, Jr., a former (1919–1921) New York state assemblyman, who served, until his assumption of public office, as a director of the Sinclair Oil & Refining Corp., White Motor Co. (of Cleveland), Associated Gas & Electric Co., and the J. G. White Management Corp. (which last two concerns were allied with Morgan interests).

41.   For more on Herrick's role in the development of the Union Carbide & Carbon Corp., see T. Bentley Mott, *Myron T. Herrick: Friend of France* (Garden City, N.Y.: Doubleday, Doran, 1929), p. 92. Herrick's son, Parmely, was also a director of the Union Trust Co. of Cleveland, Harriman National Bank of New York, and New York, Chicago & St. Louis Railroad.

42.   Harvey, who had little diplomatic or governmental experience, was appointed over the opposition of Secretary of State Charles Evans Hughes, who felt he was not suited for the post. See Robert K. Murray, *The Harding Era* (Minneapolis: University of Minnesota Press, 1969), p. 134.

43.   See Willis F. Johnson, *George Harvey: A Passionate Patriot* (Boston: Houghton Mifflin, 1929), pp. 71 and 75.

44.   See, for instance, Francis Russell, *President Harding,* p. 361, and Wesley M. Bagby, *The Road to Normalcy,* p. 86.

45.   For a fuller treatment of this marked shift in fiscal policy, see Sidney Ratner, *American Taxation: Its History as a Social Force in Democracy* (New York: W. W. Norton, 1942), pp. 341–421 and appendix.

46   According to one scholar, Mellon's regressive tax plan was actually devised largely during the latter stages of the Wilson regime by Assistant Secretary of the Treasury Russell Leffingwell, who was a former partner in the New York law firm of Cravath and Henderson (now Cravath, Swaine & Moore), and S. Parker Gilbert, who had been associated with the same concern (and in 1921 was appointed to the second-ranking post in the Treasury Department). However, given Mellon's immense influence and status in the business world, it seems doubtful that he would have accepted a financial plan proposed by two relatively young Wall Street attorneys if he had not fully agreed with its basic features. It is also interesting to note that both Leffingwell and Gilbert later became partners in J. P. Morgan &

Co. See Lawrence L. Murray, "Bureaucracy and Bi-partisanship in Taxation: The Mellon Plan Revisited," *Business History Review* (Summer 1978), pp. 212–25.

47. Indeed, such was Harding's faith in Mellon's financial wisdom that he reportedly backed his able Secretary of the Treasury in this important matter without really knowing why. See Robert K. Murray, *The Harding Era,* p. 186.

48. At this time Mellon was still vice-president of the National Union Fire Insurance Co., which stockownership enterprise clearly benefited from the repeal of the excess profits tax, and economist Ben Seligman has claimed that the Mellon family gained about $1 million through this massive tax cut. However, because the farm bloc and other interests in Congress had to be mollified, the tax on the *net* profits of corporations was raised by 2.5 percent, and, as a sop to the lower-income groups, the allowance for dependents and the exemption for heads of families with incomes of $5,000 or less was increased by $200 and $500, respectively. During the Harding administration the national debt and federal spending were both reduced by over $2 billion under Mellon's fiscal policies. See Ben B. Seligman, *The Potentates* (New York: Dial Press, 1971), pp. 300–01, and John D. Hicks, *Republican Ascendancy,* p. 54.

49. Indeed, John DeNovo dates the beginning of an "oil-oriented" American foreign policy as the end of World War I. See his "The Movement for an Aggressive American Oil Policy Abroad, 1918–1920," *American Historical Review* (July 1956), pp. 854–76.

50. The Mellon-controlled Gulf Oil Corp. was also a member of this potent group, along with the Atlantic Refining Co., (American-dominated) Mexican Petroleum Co., Sinclair Consolidated Oil Corp., and Texas Co. But none of these concerns took a leading role in this endeavor, and most eventually dropped out of the lengthy negotiations.

51. According to Joan Hoff Wilson, American officials applied the principle of the Open Door policy in the Middle East and Far East after World War I because it suited our economic interests, but in Central and South America, where we were well entrenched, federal authorities chose to pursue a "closed door" policy. Professor Wilson claims that Hoover was quite inconsistent in another way, in that he supported the Open Door policy as a means of gaining access to rich foreign oil fields, but did not object when a development was monopolized by one or two large firms, so long as one was American. See Joan Hoff Wilson, *American Business and Foreign Policy, 1920–1933,* pp. 9 and 186.

52. Both men would undoubtedly have pushed hard for the American oil firms simply to help supply the nation's future need, but Hughes may have exerted unusual pressure because of his former association with the Standard Oil Co. of N. J. This clearly is a topic which needs further research.

53. See Joan Hoff Wilson, *op. cit.,* p. 189.

54. Denby was out of Washington at this time, so this action was taken (with Denby's approval) by his chief aide and advisor, Theodore Roosevelt, Jr.

55. As bipartisan special investigators, Coolidge originally selected, subject to Senate approval, two well-known lawyers, Thomas W. Gregory, a Texan who had been Attorney General under Wilson, and Chicago corporation lawyer Silas H. Strawn. Both names were quickly withdrawn when it was discovered that Gregory had recently served as an attorney for Doheny and Strawn was reportedly associated with various major banks, business concerns, and oil enterprises. See Burl Noggle, *Teapot Dome* (Baton Rouge: Louisiana State University Press, 1962), p. 108, and M. R. Werner and John Starr, *Teapot Dome* (New York: Viking Press, 1959), p. 152.

56. See Morris R. Werner, *Privileged Characters* (New York: R. M. McBride & Co., 1935), p. 68. One of the pools organized by certain well-informed entrepreneurs, such as Harry Sinclair and the top officials of the Chase Securities Corp. (an affiliate of the Chase National Bank), is reported to have made a tidy profit of over $12 million through the prescient purchase and trading of Sinclair oil company stock.

57. There were seven less significant vice-presidents and four other less influential directors of the Sinclair Consolidated Oil Corp. The latter were: Edward H. Clark, president of the Homestake Mining Co. of California; Samuel L. Fuller, a partner in the Morgan-oriented securities firm of Kissel, Kinnicutt & Co.; Francis Steinhardt, head of the Havanna Electric Railway, Light & Power Co.; and Richard T. Wilson, a wealthy New Yorker, one of whose daughters married Cornelius Vanderbilt III.

58. Alfred Jaretski, a partner in the Wall Street law firm of Sullivan & Cromwell, served from 1916 through 1921 as a vice-president of both the Cuba Cane Sugar Corp. and Montana Power Co., a dual role also played in the latter year by Frederick Strauss, a partner in J. & W. Seligman & Co.

59. See Herman Hagedorn, *The Magnate: William Boyce Thompson and His Time* (New York: Reynal & Hitchock, 1935), pp. 130, 145, 165, 171, and 189. The frequent references made here to the House of Morgan should not be construed to mean that all or even a substantial number of the high officials of this complex were involved in this venture. Many may have had no knowledge of this affair, and those who did participate may have been acting in a completely independent entrepreneurial capacity.

60. The length and character of this employment raises a serious question as to its purpose and necessity, for during much of this period Archibald Roosevelt also served as a vice-president of the newly formed, yet sizable (apparently privately-owned) Roosevelt Steamship Co.

61. See U.S. Senate, Committee on Public Lands and Surveys, 68th Congress, 1st Session, *Leases upon Naval Oil Reserves* (Washington, D.C.: U.S. Government Printing Office, 1924), p. 3112.

62. There is no evidence that Theodore Roosevelt, Jr. or any of the other outside directors of Sinclair Oil had any knowledge of or complicity in the tainted Doheny and Sinclair gifts to Secretary Fall; these sophisticated men would probably not have stooped to such brazen and illicit tactics.

63. See U.S. Senate, Committee on Public Lands and Surveys, *Leases upon Naval Oil Reserves,* pp. 831 and 2122.

64. Spencer Penrose had also married a member of the wealthy McMillan family of Detroit, which was linked, through elitist marriage ties, to the influential Joy, Newberry, and Russell clans. This close-knit group clearly dominated Detroit's National Bank of Com-.nerce, which was the only significant board on which Secretary of the Navy Edwin Denby served prior to his appointment to high federal office.

65. Other notable directors of the Inspiration Consolidated Copper Co. were William E. Corey, president of the Midvale Steel & Ordinance Co. (and a director of the Sinclair Consolidated Oil Corp.); Charles H. Sabin, president of the Guaranty Trust Co. (and a director of the Chase Securities Corp., Cuba Cane Sugar Corp., Midvale Steel & Ordinance Co., and Montana Power Co.); and Albert H. Wiggin, president of the Chase National Bank (and a director of the Midvale Steel & Ordinance Co. and Montana Power Co.).

66. For more on the Thatcher interests, see Leroy R. Hafen, *Colorado and Its People* (New York: Lewis Historical Publishing Co., 1948), Vol. IV, p. 729.

67. As pointed out earlier, another of the major parties allied with Albert Fall and the Chino Copper Co. in the syndicate which owned the *Albuquerque Morning Journal* up to 1921 was the El Paso and Southwestern Railroad. This fairly sizable concern was headed by Thomas M. Schumacher, a former official of the American Smelting & Refining Co. and Chicago, Rock Island & Pacific Railroad, who in 1921 was made a director of the Vanadium Corp. of America. This company's board included the aforementioned Charles MacNeill, Edward R. Tinker, president of the Chase Securities Corp. (and a director of both the Pan-American Petroleum & Transport Co. and the Sinclair Consolidated Oil Corp.), and Harry Payne Whitney, who served on the board of the Cuba Cane Sugar Corp., Montana Power Co., Sinclair Consolidated Oil Corp., and Guaranty Trust Co. of New York City.

68. See the U.S. Senate Committee on Public Lands and Surveys, *op. cit.,* p. 2122. When Secretary of the Interior Albert Fall resigned under a cloud of scandal in early 1923, he was replaced by the recently appointed Postmaster General, Hubert Work, a prominent Colorado political leader and physician who had lived for a long time in Pueblo (which had a population of about 45,000), where he may well have known various members of the influential Thatcher family.

69. The U.S. Smelting, Refining & Mining Co. was closely linked with the Island Creek Coal Co., since the latter's president and vice-president were William H. Coolidge and Clarence A. Hight (and Galen Stone was a director up to 1919).

70. The one remaining member of the syndicate involved in the pre-1920 ownership of the *Albuquerque Morning Journal* was Cleveland executive Price McKinney, the head of the big privately-owned (but faction-ridden) McKinney Steel Co. Curiously, he did not serve on any major corporate boards in Ohio. In fact, as far as the author has been able to determine, the only board on which he served as an outside director was that of the Continental & Commercial National Bank of Chicago. This major financial institution was apparently dominated by its two chief executive officers, the brothers Arthur and George M. Reynolds. These two Chicago bankers, with whom McKinney was presumably friendly, had a number of key corporate ties in the East. In the early 1920s, for example, Arthur Reynolds served on the board of both the Asia Banking Corp. and Foreign Bond and Share Corp., two New York–based concerns controlled largely by such powerful and closely linked interests as the Guaranty Trust Co., Bankers Trust Co., J. & W. Seligman & Co., and Cuba Cane Sugar Corp. And George M. Reynolds served on the board of the Union Carbide & Carbon Corp., which was dominated by Harding's friend and newly appointed Ambassador to France, Myron T. Herrick, as well as the Continental Insurance Co. of New York City, which was headed by Henry Evans, an executive close to the Morgan interests. Continental's board included the influential Carl J. Schmidlapp, a vice-president of the Chase National Bank (and a director of the Montana Power Co.); Daniel G. Reid, board chairman of the American Can Co. (and a director of the Chase Securities Corp.); and George W. Davison, a New York City banker (and former director of Sinclair Oil). For more on Henry Evans's economic relations, see Merlo J. Pusey, *Eugene Meyer,* p. 42.

71. One possible reason for the laggard rate at which the Senate investigating committee moved initially was that it was chaired from 1921 to 1923 by Utah Republican leader, Reed Smoot, who was in private life the president of the Provo Commercial & Savings Bank. The vice-president of this concern was C. E. Loose, who served, with the aforementioned Charles Hayden, on the board of the Utah Power & Light Co., whose president (up to 1920) was Daniel C. Jackling, a vice-president of both the Utah Copper Co. and Chino Copper Co. (and a director of the Chase National Bank and Sinclair Consolidated Oil Corp.).

72. Other outside directors of this Chicago rail line were: William C. Lane, a vice-president of both the Guaranty Trust Co. and Asia Banking Corp. (and a director of the Electric Bond & Share Co., which controlled the Utah Power & Light Co.); Charles B. Wiggin, a director of the Punta Alegre Sugar Co. (along with Galen Stone and Henry Hornblower's son, Ralph), and apparent kinsman of Chase National Bank president Albert H. Wiggin; and Frederick L. Ames, a Bostonian who sat on the board of the (Utah-Chino-linked) Alaska Gold Mines Co.

73. According to one authority, Strawn actually served as an attorney for the Morgan interests in Chicago. See Benjamin R. Twiss, *Lawyers and the Constitution: How Laissez Faire Came to the Supreme Court* (Princeton, N.J.: Princeton University Press, 1942), p. 242.

74. Roberts had also served since about 1920 as a director of both the Board of City Trusts (which administered the big estate of the long-deceased Stephen Girard) and the Real Estate Title Insurance & Trust Co. of Philadelphia, but from a national standpoint these were less important concerns.

75. Other noteworthy outside directors of the Home Insurance Co. were New York banker Lewis L. Clarke, Cornelius N. Bliss, Jr. (a director of the New York Life Insurance Co., Morgan-dominated Bankers Trust Co., and, up to 1917, Cuba Cane Sugar Corp.), and William S. Gray (up to 1923, a director of J. G. White & Co.).

76. Gates was by late 1925 or early 1926 a member of the board of the Public Service Corp. of New Jersey, in which the Philadelphia-based United Gas Improvement Co. and New York–based American Superpower Corp. had a substantial interest. He was also a director of the big Baldwin Locomotive Works (along with Sinclair syndicate leader William E. Corey) and the Philadelphia Savings Fund Society (where he came into contact with Spencer Penrose's patrician physician brother, Charles B. Penrose, who had married the niece of the late Anthony J. Drexel, the longtime senior partner of this prestigious banking house).

77. See Drew Pearson and Robert S. Allen, *The Nine Old Men* (Garden City, N.Y.: Doubleday, Doran, 1937), pp. 147–48. In either late 1925 or early 1926 Roberts was elected to the board of the Equitable Life Assurance Society of New York (a firm with few significant ties to Teapot Dome interests) and the Bell Telephone Co. of Pennsylvania, an operational subsidiary of the giant Morgan-Brahmin–dominated AT&T (to which board Roberts himself was added sometime in 1928).

78. Although not formally involved in the Teapot Dome investigation, the Solicitor General from 1921 to 1925 was, interestingly, still another friendly official, James M. Beck, a former Philadelphia and New York lawyer, who served from 1908 through 1925 on the board of the Morgan-dominated Mutual Life Insurance Co. and, up to early 1922, as a director of the Mechanics & Metals National Bank of New York, along with such prominent men as William E. Corey, board chairman of the Midvale Steel & Ordinance Co. (and a director of the Inspiration Consolidated Copper Co., Montana Power Co., and Sinclair Consolidated Oil Corp.), and John D. Ryan, head of both the Anaconda Copper Mining Co. and Montana Power Co. (and until 1922 a director of the Inspiration Consolidated Copper Co.).

79. See Donald R. McCoy, *Calvin Coolidge: The Quiet President* (New York: Macmillan, 1967), pp. 41, 51, and 63. Coolidge had served as an attorney, director, and later high official of the Nonotuck Savings Bank of Northampton, but this was a small concern of little significance even in predominantly rural western Massachusetts. Most historians have been content to treat Stearns as merely the head of a Boston dry goods firm, R. H. Stearns & Co. (which had assets of only about $3.5 million). However, he sat on the board of the medium-sized American Trust Co. and the big Provident Institution for Savings, two Boston enterprises dominated by Brahmins. Two of Coolidge's distant relatives, Louis A. Coolidge and T. Jefferson Coolidge, were also connected with certain prominent Boston concerns, the former as a board member of the American Trust Co. and the latter as a director of the Old Colony Trust Co.

80. See Carolyn W. Johnson, *Winthrop Murray Crane, passim*; Claude M. Fuess, *Calvin Coolidge* (Boston: Little, Brown, 1940), pp. 99–100, 115, and 157; Donald R. McCoy, *op. cit.*, p. 37; and Francis Russell, *The President Makers: From Mark Hanna to Joseph P. Kennedy* (Boston: Little, Brown, 1976), pp. 241–58. After having done much to boost Coolidge's political prospects over the years, Crane died after a brief illness in October 1920, about a month before election day, and thus exerted no influence on Coolidge in national affairs, except through certain long-established indirect links which may have carried over from the pre-1920 period. As evidence of such influence, one of Coolidge's first acts as chief executive was to appoint William M. Butler, Crane's chief aide, as chairman of the Republican National Committee in 1923. According to one reliable source, Butler was by this time the president of nine corporations (mostly New England textile mills), a director of six other concerns, and legislative counsel (i.e., a lobbyist) for the Boston Gas Light Co., American Woolen Co., and Metropolitan Life Insurance Co. See Carolyn W. Johnson, *op. cit.*, p. 61.

81. Crane was, moreover, a member of the executive committee of AT&T and even had his own office at the company's headquarters in New York City. He also served, up to a few years before his death, on the board of the American Bank Note Co. and the big New York, New Haven and Hartford Railroad. For more on Crane's major corporate links, see Carolyn W. Johnson, *op. cit.*, pp. 38–39.

82. It was Morrow who, several years earlier, apparently arranged for Stearns (who had attended Amherst at a different time) to meet Coolidge, then a lesser politician. See Claude M. Feuss, *op. cit.*, p. 130.

83. Perhaps the best description of the true roles played by the primary figures (other than Murray Crane) involved in this campaign is provided by Harold Nicolson, who noted that, fearing their association with Wall Street might prejudice or doom Coolidge's cause, "Morrow and Thomas Cochran, although moving spirits in the whole drive, remained in the background. The foreground was filled by the large, the devoted, the imperturbable figure of Frank Stearns." See Harold Nicolson, *Dwight Morrow* (New York: Harcourt, Brace, 1935), p. 232.

84. It is possible to explain Morrow's role on the basis of friendship. However, the more important Cochran (who was a director of the Bankers Trust Co., Chase Securities Corp., New York Trust Co., Texas Gulf Sulphur Co., and Utah Copper Co.) was a former Midwesterner who had not gone to Amherst, and thus had little or no reason to support Coolidge (except perhaps as a personal favor to Morrow, a rather unlikely prospect). Although some observers have claimed that Coolidge did not rely significantly on Morrow for aid or advice during his administration, the author finds this unconvincing. If, as reported (see Nicolson, *op. cit.*, p. 269), President Hoover (a more able man) telephoned Morrow at least three times a week during his first years in office, one can safely assume that Coolidge was even more dependent on his counsel.

85. Coolidge's major political opponent in this campaign was a compromise candidate, John W. Davis, who was finally agreed upon after 103 ballots had been cast at the Democratic national convention. Davis, who had been Solicitor General and Ambassador to Great Britain under the Wilson administration, was by this time a senior partner in the principal law firm of the House of Morgan (which was now known as Davis, Polk, Wardwell, Gardiner & Reed) and a director of the United States Rubber Co. and the Morgan-dominated National Bank of Commerce of New York. Davis thus became the only Democratic "dark horse" candidate ever produced by the Morgan interests.

86. Various close relatives of Mellon, especially his brother (Richard) and two nephews (William L. and Richard K.), were still very much involved in such family-controlled firms as the Aluminum Co. of America, Carbonundum Co., Gulf Oil Corp., Koppers Co., and Standard Steel Car Co., five companies which had a substantial stake in the fiscal policies pursued by the federal government. Mellon's first Under Secretary of the Treasury in the Coolidge regime was Chicago lawyer Gerald B. Winston, who had been a director of the Joliet and Northern Indiana Railroad subsidiary of the (Vanderbilt-dominated) New York Central system and a partner of Silas Strawn, the board chairman of Montgomery, Ward & Co. and a director of numerous other enterprises. When Winston resigned in 1927, he was succeeded by New York financier (and former Congressman) Ogden L. Mills, who had been a board member of the Mergenthaler Linotype Co., New York Trust Co., and Atchison, Topeka & Sante Fe Railway (and whose father was a director of the Cerro de Pasco Corp., Farmers Loan & Trust Co. of New York, New York Central Railroad, Southern Pacific Railroad, and United States Trust Co. of New York).

87. Hoover was succeeded by a Massachusetts businessman and longtime Coolidge supporter, William F. Whiting, who was the head of a family-owned paper company in the western part of the state (and a director, along with Frank Stearns, of the Brahmin-dominated American Trust Co. of Boston and the American Surety Co., a minor New York City concern). Work's place was taken by Chicago attorney and Illinois Republican leader

Roy O. West, who served as a director of the small South Side Trust & Savings Bank (and whose law partner's father, Bernard A. Eckhart, was a board member of Armour & Co., the Continental National Bank & Trust Co. of Chicago, Erie Railroad, and Montgomery, Ward & Co.).

88. Theodore Roosevelt's successor as Assistant Secretary of the Navy was, ironically, his first cousin, T. Douglas Robinson, one of whose kinsmen, W. Emlen Roosevelt, was a director of the Bank of New York, Central Union Trust Co., and Chemical National Bank, while another, George Emlen Roosevelt, sat on the board of the (Morgan-dominated) National Bank of Commerce.

89. Ray Lyman Wilbur was a trustee of the Rockefeller Foundation, although the author is not sure whether this tie was of any politico-economic significance or was strictly a civic-academic link.

90. Stone severed both of these ties in the fall of 1923 when he joined the well-established Wall Street law firm of Sullivan & Cromwell, whose senior partner, William Nelson Cromwell, served as a director of such major concerns as the American Bank Note Co., American Water Works & Electric Co., and International Nickel Co. However, this association was of such short duration (about six months) that the author is not inclined to place much weight on it.

91. See, for instance, Alpheus T. Mason, *Harlan Fiske Stone: Pillar of the Law* (New York: Viking Press, 1956), pp. 88–89.

92. The treasurer of the Bradstreet Co., Charles M. Clark, also set on the board of the Montana Power Co. and the aforementioned Utah Securities Corp., along with Charles Hayden of the Chino-Utah copper complex.

93. Reportedly, one of the primary reasons Stone was offered this post was that he was seriously contemplating instituting an antitrust suit against the monopolistic Aluminum Co. of America, which rumored action quickly aroused Coolidge's influential Secretary of the Treasury, Andrew Mellon, whose family controlled this concern. See, for instance, Alpehus T. Mason, *op. cit.,* pp. 182–85.

94. Coolidge's initial nominee, Charles B. Warren, was rejected primarily because he had served as president of the Michigan Sugar Co., which under a previous administration had been charged, along with the New York–based American Sugar Refining Co. (which owned 34 percent of the former's stock), with a gross violation of the federal antitrust laws. The board of the American Sugar Refining Co. was made up of such prominent people as Chase National Bank head Albert H. Wiggin and Chicago executive James H. Douglas, whose son had recently been made a member of Silas Strawn's law firm. The American Sugar Refining Co. also owned 28 percent of the stock of the Great Western Sugar Co., whose treasurer was Mahlon D. Thatcher, president of the First National Bank of Pueblo, Colorado. Also, although largely unnoticed, Warren served up to 1925 as a director of the National Bank of Commerce of Detroit (the same board on which Harding's compliant Secretary of the Navy, Edwin Denby, served until 1921).

95. See the *National Cyclopaedia of American Biography,* Vol. A, p. 12.

96. In addition, Sargent's law partner, William W. Stickney, was a director of the National Life Insurance Co. of Vermont and president of the extremely small Ludlow Savings Bank & Trust Co., of which Coolidge's father was a vice-president.

97. Hill (who had built up the Great Northern Railway and later took over the Northern Pacific Railway) had long graced the board of the Chase National Bank and the First National Bank of New York, both of which were firmly in the Morgan camp. And according to Kellogg's biographer, "much of the legal business connected with Mr. Hill's railroad enterprises was done in the offices of Mr. Kellogg's firm, and much of it by Mr. Kellogg himself." Moreover, Kellogg served as president of the Wisconsin, Minneosta & Pacific Railroad up to 1906, when he was appointed a Special Assistant Attorney General in charge

of the government's antitrust case against the Harriman-dominated Union Pacific Railroad (an action that must have pleased the rival Morgan interests). For more on Kellogg's relations with James J. Hill (who died in 1916) and U.S. Steel, see David Bryn-Jones, *Frank B. Kellogg* (New York: G. P. Putnam's Sons, 1937), pp. 36–39, 52, 68, and 108.

98.   Severance was one of the few figures from the western part of the country to serve on the (roughly 25-man) board of the prestigious Carnegie Endowment for International Peace.

99.   See L. Ethan Ellis, *Frank B. Kellogg and American Foreign Relations, 1925–1929* (New Brunswick, N.J.: Rutgers University Press, 1961), p. 233.

100.   See L. Ethan Ellis, *op. cit.,* p. vii. At the time of his appointment as Ambassador to strife-torn Mexico in 1927, Morrow was a partner in J. P. Morgan & Co. (and a director of the Bankers Trust Co. and GE), while Stimson, who was asked about the same time to take charge of our Nicaraguan affairs, was a partner in the Wall Street law firm of Winthrop, Stimson, Putnam & Roberts (and a director of the American Superpower Corp., a large Morgan-oriented public utility holding company). Kellogg had initially wanted Morrow as his Under Secretary of State, but this idea was quickly dropped because of the latter's well-known connection with the House of Morgan. Instead Kellogg chose to retain career diplomat (and Boston Brahmin) Joseph C. Grew in this important post. Ironically, he too was linked, through family ties, to Morgan and other prominent economic interests, for his cousin had married the son of the late J. P. Morgan and his uncle, Henry S. Grew, sat on the board of the fairly large Suffolk Savings Bank of Boston.

101.   Before the war Davis had been a prominent St. Louis municipal and civic official, perhaps in the best sense of *noblesse oblige.* The patrician, much-experienced Davis was certainly not a geo-political selection, because there were already two Midwesterners in the Cabinet, Secretary of Agriculture William Jardine and Frank Kellogg.

102.   Davis's successor as Assistant Secretary of War was an Iowa leader, Hanford MacNider, who was a former national commander of the American Legion (one of the few representatives of this group ever to hold such a high federal office). MacNider had been president of both the First National Bank of Mason City, Iowa, and the small Northwestern States Portland Cement Co. His more prominent father, Charles H. MacNider, was a director of the big Chicago, Milwaukee & St. Paul Railroad, Alpha Portland Cement Co., Michigan Sugar Co., Mason City and Fort Dodge Railroad (an affiliate of the Chicago Great Western Railroad), and Federal Reserve Bank of Chicago. The position of Assistant Secretary of War for Air was created in 1926, and was filled for the duration of its existence (six years) by a well-connected New Yorker, F. Trubee Davison, whose brother, Henry P. Davison, was a partner in J. P. Morgan & Co. (and a director of the New York Trust Co. and the newly formed Time, Inc.).

103.   President Coolidge also initially retained Harding's Secretary of Agriculture, Henry C. Wallace, who had played a prominent role in the creation of the (now powerful) American Farm Bureau Federation. When this Iowa leader died in October 1924, he was replaced, largely at the urging of the Farm Bureau, by West Virginia's agrarian spokesman, Howard M. Gore, who held office for only about six months before he was elected governor of his home state. Gore's successor was a Midwesterner, William M. Jardine, who had served first (from 1913 to 1918) as director of the experiment station at the Kansas College of Agriculture, and then for the next seven years as president of this institution. This general recruitment pattern indicates that the American Farm Bureau Federation exerted great influence on this arm of the federal government during the 1920s. For more on some of these ties, see Orville M. Kile, *The Farm Bureau Through Three Decades* (Baltimore, Md.: Waverly Press, 1948), pp. 124–25.

104.   This post was first offered to New York lawyer (and onetime Cabinet member) Elihu Root, a well-known spokesman for influential corporate interests, and then to former Illinois Governor Frank Lowden, who had married a member of the Pullman family and had been connected with various major business concerns. Both refused it.

105. One member of this firm, Richard E. Dwight, was associated with a number of New York area business concerns, the most important of which was probably that established in 1927 when he was appointed to the board of Merck & Co. Jacob Schurman was also apparently a close friend of John D. Rockefeller. See Allan Nevins, *John D. Rockefeller,* pp. 455–56.

106. It is true that a number of seemingly significant international agreements were entered into by the United States during the 1920s and early 1930s. Most of these had to do with disarmament. Unfortunately, in the long run they did little to ease ill feeling and tension among certain nations.

107. For more on these (and many other fiscal) measures, see Sidney Ratner, *American Taxation, passim,* but especially pp. 400–21.

108. See Ben B. Seligman, *The Potentates,* pp. 300–1, and for a recent account of Mellon's overall record as Secretary of the Treasury, see David E. Koskoff, *The Mellons,* pp. 171–353.

109. The best the liberal opposition in Congress could do at this juncture was, by acceding to certain major concessions, to preserve the federal estate tax at an at least respectable level (although one, unfortunately, marked by many loopholes), for a number of conservative leaders would have liked to have eliminated this levy too. The corporate income tax was maintained throughout most of this period at a rather modest rate of about 12 or 13 percent. During Mellon's first eight years in office, well over a billion dollars was refunded, under other fiscal programs, to various corporations, including almost $20 million to two Mellon-controlled concerns (Gulf Oil and Alcoa). See Jules Abels, *In the Time of Silent Cal* (New York: G. P. Putnam's Sons, 1969), pp. 218–19.

110. At the reputed urging of the Mid-Continent Oil and Gas Association (a Southwestern-based group), Senator David A. Reed of Pennsylvania managed to include a resolution in the Finance Committee's report to the Upper House that the minimum depletion allowance be pegged at 25 percent. The recommendation was later raised to 30 percent, from whence a compromise figure of 27.5 percent was finally reached. The reported origin of this set of events is, however, open to another line of explanation or analysis, for Senator Reed was, apparently unknown to many, a director of the Mellon National Bank and (family-controlled) Union Trust Co. of Pittsburgh, and his father and law partner, James H. Reed, had served on the board of the Mellon-dominated Gulf Oil Corp. since at least 1909. The rationale for this much higher rate was that it was then costing oil operators roughly this amount to develop this vital natural resource, a calculation (or claim) which soon proved to be a colossal error. For more on the first matter, see Gerald D. Nash, *United States Oil Policy, 1890–1964* (Pittsburgh: University of Pittsburgh Press, 1968), p. 86; and Ronnie Dugger, "Oil and Politics," *Atlantic Monthly* (Sept. 1969), p. 70; also for a somewhat different version, David E. Koskoff, *The Mellons,* p. 161.

111. Although Smith was originally a liberal on most major governmental issues, there is some question as to his politico-economic views by the late 1920s, for by this time he had begun to associate with a number of wealthy Irish and Jewish businessmen in New York City, such as William F. Kenny, who was a big local contractor (and a director of the Chrysler Corp.). Evidence of Smith's increasing conservatism may be found in the fact that he chose as his campaign manager (and chairman of the Democratic National Committee) a well-known Catholic business executive, John J. Raskob, who was a vice-president of both the E. I. du Pont de Nemours & Co. and the (du Pont–controlled) General Motors Corp., as well as a director of the (Morgan-dominated) Bankers Trust Co. of New York and the Missouri-Pacific Railroad. For more on Smith's ideological shift in the mid-1920s, see Richard O'Connor, *The First Hurrah: A Biography of Alfred E. Smith* (New York: Putnam, 1970), pp. 154–63 and 241.

112. Nowhere is this Hoover-as-a-progressive thesis more explicitly espoused than in Joan Hoff Wilson's book, *Herbert Hoover, Forgotten Progressive* (Boston: Little, Brown,

1975), as seen by her chapter headings: "The Progressive as Domestic Dynamic" (Chapter IV) and "The Progressive in Time of Depression" (Chapter V).

113. See "The President's Fortune," *Fortune* (August 1932), p. 86.

114. Most writers have chosen to ignore or gloss over the lengthy list of Hoover's corporate and stockownership ties presented in the *Fortune* article (pp. 82–88) and in the appendix of Walter Liggett's *The Rise of Herbert Hoover*. Hoover's connections with various domestic business interests, unfortunately, remain shrouded in mystery, which future research will hopefully do much to rectify. Some insight into Hoover's relations with Eastern financiers may be gained from the fact that in 1928 the chairman of the Republican National Committee was former Secretary of the Interior, Hubert Work (a Colorado physician about whom relatively little is known), the vice-chairman was New Jersey's Daniel Pomeroy (who was a high official of the American Brake Shoe Co. and a director of the Bankers Trust Co.), the treasurer was Joseph R. Nutt (a Cleveland banker who was also board chairman of the Fort Worth Power & Light Co. subsidiary of the American Power & Light Co., vice-president of the New York, Chicago & St. Louis Railroad, and a director of the Cleveland and Pittsburgh Railroad, McKinney Steel Co., Quaker Oats Co., and White Motor Co.), and the Eastern treasurer was New York financier Jeremiah Milbank (who was a director of the Allis-Chalmers Manufacturing Co., Chase National Bank, Corn Products Refining Co., Metropolitan Life Insurance Co., and Southern Railway).

115. See Harold Nicolson, *Dwight Morrow*, p. 269. Although Morrow served as Ambassador to Mexico and as a delegate to the London Naval Conference during much of this period, apparently many of these calls were made on other than diplomatic matters.

116. See Robert H. Zieger, *Republicans and Labor, 1919–1929*, pp. 58–59. When, upon his election to the Senate, Davis resigned from the Cabinet in late 1930, he was promptly replaced by Willian N. Doak, who was a longtime official of the Brotherhood of Railroad Trainmen. Like Davis, Doak was not backed by the AFL, which would have much preferred the appointment of its more aggressive John L. Lewis.

117. Although it is not clear when, Hoover offered this Cabinet post to his close friend and informal advisor, Henry M. Robinson, who was president of the Los Angeles–First National Trust and Savings Bank (and a director of the General Electric Co., Pacific Mutual Life Insurance Co., Southern California Edison Co., and the Union Oil Co. of California). But Robinson could not be persuaded to enter the federal government.

118. Hoover relied extensively on the opinion of Under Secretary of the Treasury Ogden L. Mills, with whom he was able to establish a warmer relationship, and who eventually replaced Mellon as department head. But this wealthy New York lawyer was also closely linked with the business community, for he had served, until assuming high federal office, on the board of the New York Trust Co., International Paper Co., Crex Carpet Co., and Atchison, Topeka & Sante Fe Railway. Also, his father was, until his death in 1929, a director of such prominent concerns as the New York Central Railroad and Southern Pacific Railroad. One of Mills's conservative top aides initially was New York attorney Walter E. Hope, who had been a board member of the Borden Co. When he stepped down in 1931, he was replaced by Arthur Ballantine, a partner in the Wall Street law firm of Root, Clark, Buckner & Ballantine.

119. See Richard N. Current, *Secretary Stimson: A Study in Statescraft* (New Brunswick, N.J.: Rutgers University Press, 1954), *passim*. Stimson was not, please note, Hoover's first choice for this post, for, after Kellogg declined to stay on, it was offered to the able Charles Evans Hughes (who had recently been serving as an attorney for the Standard Oil Co. of N. J.), Supreme Court Justice (and onetime Coolidge Cabinet member and New York lawyer and law school dean) Harlan Fiske Stone, career diplomat Hugh Gibson, Idaho Senator William E. Borah, and also, perhaps, J. P. Morgan partner (and recent Mexican envoy) Dwight W. Morrow. See David Burner, *Herbert Hoover* (New York: Alfred A. Knopf, 1979), pp. 209–10.

120. See Elting E. Morison, *Turmoil and Tradition: A Study of the Life and Times of Henry L. Stimson* (Boston: Houghton Mifflin, 1960), p. 268. Stimson was an extremely wealthy man by this time; he paid $825,000 for his home in Washington upon his appointment as Secretary of State in 1929 (when the dollar was worth much, much more than it is today).

121. Roberts, who was also a vice-president of Bonbright & Co., was elected shortly thereafter to the board of two other large enterprises, the American & Foreign Power Co. and Niagara Hudson Power Corp.

122. Thorne, furthermore, served as a director of the Morgan-dominated Bankers Trust Co. from 1923 through 1933, and Loomis was elected to this board in the early 1930s. Both men were part of the Morgan-oriented group which created the huge United Corp. in 1929. See *Fortune* (June 1940), p. 130.

123. As Richard Current once aptly put it, Stimson's brand of progressivism ". . . could be summed up as little more than a belief in powerful and efficient government. It was the progressivism of Alexander Hamilton'' (see Richard N. Current, *op. cit.,* pp. 12–13). Additional evidence of Stimson's conservatism may be found in the choice of his top aides. His first Under Secretary of State, Joseph P. Cotton, was a former New York lawyer who served up to the late 1920s on the board of the New York Railways Corp., Willys-Overland Co., and Farmers Loan & Trust Co. of New York. When Cotton died suddenly in 1931, he was replaced by William R. Castle, Jr., a wealthy career diplomat whose family had substantial business holdings in Hawaii. And Castle's successor as Assistant Secretary of State was a longtime Boston attorney, Harvey H. Bundy, who had served as a director of the Brahmin-dominated State Street Trust Co. and had married the daughter of another prominent Bostonian, William Lowell Putnam, who had sat on the board of AT&T up to his death in 1924.

124. See Davis J. Danelski, *A Supreme Court Justice Is Appointed* (New York: Random House, 1964), *passim.*

125. Hoover's Secretary of Commerce, Robert P. Lamont, was, predictably, an avowed spokesman for influential corporate interests, for not only had he been head of Chicago's American Steel Foundries for many years, but he had also served as a director of various large Midwestern business concerns.

126. In her biography of Hoover, Joan Hoff Wilson claims that he gave a number of Cabinet posts to conservative, wealthy businessmen primarily to mollify those interests in the Republican party that most distrusted him, namely Eastern economic leaders and the Old Guard. But she also maintains that he made some exceptions, such as in the appointment of Henry L. Stimson, William D. Mitchell, Ray Lyman Wilbur, and Charles F. Adams, a dubious statement (except for Wilbur). See Joan Hoff Wilson, *Herbert Hoover,* p. 134. For a more accurate assessment of the make-up of this Cabinet, see Harris G. Warren, *Herbert Hoover and the Great Depression* (New York: Oxford University Press, 1959), p. 53.

127. Since the author has not found that Good had any important economic ties, he is inclined to treat this official as essentially a political figure (although later research may show this to be in error).

128. Hurley, who was a well-established lawyer with many clients in the state's oil industry, did serve as a director of the First National Bank of Tulsa in the late 1920s and in a like capacity with the Paragon Refining Co. of Ohio in the early 1920s. But neither of these enterprises was a truly important national concern. For more on this controversial figure, see Don Lohbeck, *Patrick J. Hurley* (Chicago: Henry Regnery Co., 1956), pp. 40 and 76–80, and Russell D. Buhite, *Patrick J. Hurley and American Foreign Policy* (Ithaca, N.Y.: Cornell University Press, 1973), pp. 37–38.

129. Wilbur had also served on the board of the Rockefeller Foundation since 1923, but the author is not sure what inference should be drawn from this affiliation, which may have been forged purely for professional reasons.

130. Hyde's relations with the American Farm Bureau Federation remain something of a mystery, although the author would assume that they were on at least cordial terms. According to one source, Hoover offered this post to U.S. Senator (and Salem, Oregon lawyer) Charles McNary and apparently several other persons before turning to Hyde. See David Burner, *Herbert Hoover*, p. 210.

131. Henry M. Dawes was also a director, in the mid-and late-1920s, of the Central Trust Co., the Chicago Great Western Railroad (apparently taking his brother's place when he became Vice President of the United States), and the Metropolitan Gas & Electric Co. of Ohio, which was headed until 1929 by still another brother, Rufus Dawes.

132. Mellon reportedly did much as Ambassador to help secure a large concession in Kuwait for the Gulf Oil Corp., which his family controlled, an act of dubious propriety. See David E. Koskoff, *The Mellons*, pp. 295–98.

133. Edge had also been a director of the Marine Trust Co. of Atlantic City up to the mid-1920s, but this was a very small concern of no national or even regional significance.

134. In the late 1920s Teagle was a director of the (Rockefeller-controlled) Consolidation Coal Co. and the smaller White Motor Co. of Cleveland. For more on Edge's relationship with Teagle, see Bennett H. Hall and George S. Gibb, *Teagle of Jersey Standard* (New Orleans: J. G. Hauser, 1974), *passim,* and Walter Evans Edge, *A Jerseyman's Journal* (Princeton, N.J.: Princeton University Press, 1948), pp. 44, 121–22, and 148.

135. The Mellon-dominated Koppers Co. formally took over the management and operation of this company shortly after Sackett stepped down from its board of directors.

136. See Samuel Eliot Morison, Henry Steele Commager, and William E. Leuchtenburg, *The Growth of the American Republic*, 6th ed. (New York: Oxford University Press, 1969), Vol. II, p. 475.

137. His Wall Street lawyer-brother, Henry W. Taft, served as a trustee of the big Mutual Life Insurance Co. from 1906 through the last year of Taft's labor on the High Court, and his more entrepreneurially-inclined half-brother, Charles P. Taft, was a director of both the Columbia Gas & Electric Co. and the Cincinnati & Suburban Bell Telephone Co. (a subsidiary of AT&T) up to the late 1920s.

138. See David J. Danelski, *A Supreme Court Justice is Appointed*, pp. 47 and 80. Although this remarkably thorough study does not focus primarily on Taft, much light is nonetheless shed on this matter because of Taft's key behind-the-scenes role in the appointment of conservative St. Paul lawyer Pierre Butler to the High Court in the early 1920s.

139. See Joan Hoff Wilson, *American Business and Foreign Policy, 1920–1933,* p. 298, and George Sweet Gibbs and Evelyn H. Knowlton, *The Resurgent Years* (New York: Harper, 1956), p. 615. Hughes was also reported to have been senior counsel to Dillon, Read & Co. in the late 1920s, and counted many other major business concerns among his clients. See Martin Mayer, *Emory Buckner* (New York: Harper & Row, 1968), p. 238, and Drew Pearson and Robert S. Allen, *The Nine Old Men*, p. 88. In addition, Hughes served as one of the twenty councillors (economic advisors) of the big-business–dominated National Industrial Conference Board, a research-oriented group created back in 1916.

140. See Joel Paschal, *Mr. Justice Sutherland: A Man Against the State* (Princeton, N.J.: Princeton University Press, 1951), *passim.*

141. For an unusually thorough and incisive analysis of the various figures contacted to mobilize support for Butler's nomination to the High Court, see David J. Danelski, *A Supreme Court Justice is Appointed, passim.* Note especially the elaborate diagrams found on pages 157 and 161, which show an intriguing pattern of influence exerted in behalf of Butler's candidacy. Among the prominent people involved in this endeavor were Charles W. Bunn, general counsel for the Northern Pacific Railway; Hale Holden, president of the Chicago, Burlington & Quincy Railroad; Marvin Hughett, board chairman of the Chicago and Northwestern Railway; John D. Ryan, board chairman of the Anaconda Copper

Mining Co.; and lumber magnate Frederick E. Weyerhaeuser. In the author's judgment, Danelski's work stands as a model of sound research, which, if it were applied to the appointment of many other high federal officials, would probably reveal the existence of various potent politico-economic forces in the administrative and diplomatic recruitment processes.

142.   See Leon Friedman and Fred L. Israel (eds.), *The Justices of the United States Supreme Court, 1789–1969,* Vol. III, p. 2184. Up to the early 1920s, Butler also served as a director of such lesser concerns as the Capital National Bank of St. Paul and the St. Paul Gas Light Co. (a subsidiary of the New York–based American Light & Traction Co.).

143.   See Ernest S. Bates, *The Story of the Supreme Court,* p. 262.

144.   As already noted, one of Stone's longtime law partners, George F. Canfield, was a high-ranking official of the small Atlanta & Charlotte Air Line Railway (with which line Stone was also associated up to 1924), and as a director of the New York–dominated Montana Power Co. Stone's other, apparently less active, partner, Herbert L. Satterlee, was a son-in-law of the late J. P. Morgan.

145.   See Alpheus T. Mason, *Harlan Fiske Stone,* p. 89.

146.   Roberts is also reported to have had close ties with the Pennsylvania Railroad (although the author has no evidence on this matter) and at least one high-ranking figure (Thomas S. Gates) in the Philadelphia banking house of Drexel & Co., which had long been linked with J. P. Morgan & Co. See Henry J. Abraham, *Justices and Presidents,* p. 189, and Drew Pearson and Robert S. Allen, *The Nine Old Men,* pp. 147–48.

147.   Because there were already two New Yorkers and one Jew on the Supreme Court, Hoover was initially reluctant to appoint Cardozo, but finally yielded to the pressure exerted by such men as Harlan Fiske Stone.

148.   See Ernest S. Bates, *op. cit.,* p. 264.

149.   Labor's lack of power in the 1920s was amply demonstrated by the appointment of a token figure as Secretary of Labor—James J. Davis, a minor Pittsburgh financial official who was a member of the elitist Duquesne Club.

CHAPTER 7

Summary

This study, which is the second part of a three-volume work, consists of a detailed historical analysis of the recruitment pattern and selected governmental actions of the nation's chief Cabinet and diplomatic officials and Supreme Court Justices between 1861 and 1933. As initially indicated, it was undertaken as a means of assessing the distribution of power in the country at different points in time, proceeding primarily on the premise that a President may be judged by the type of men he picks to serve as his chief aides and advisors. It is therefore essential to summarize the massive amount of data which has been collected in this research effort and place it in proper historical perspective, to see whether there were any major patterns or important trends at work that deserve special emphasis.

As one might expect, there were a number of important changes in the federal recruitment pattern between the Civil War, which is generally thought to have marked the beginning of the Industrial Revolution in America, and the New Deal, during which watershed period the country underwent a series of major shifts that, in effect, ushered in a new era in politico-economic relations. One of the most striking developments was the emergence of New York City as a key source of high administrative and diplomatic talent. In contrast to the pre–Civil War period when New York state supplied about 10 percent of such governmental officials (one-third of whom were upstate leaders), close to 23 percent were drawn from the Empire State between 1861 and 1933, and the vast majority of these were from New York City (see Table 11).[1] However, at no time after about 1870 did New York state have more than roughly 10 percent of the nation's population, with New York City providing about half of that total. In short, this shift in federal recruitment was not basically a demographic development, but one which was related primarily to New York City's rapidly rising economic influence.[2]

Conversely, certain other states experienced a sharp decline in their geopolitical power during this period, at least as measured by their ability

TABLE 11
Percentage of High Federal Posts Held by People from Different States or Regions 1861–1933

Major Cabinet and Diplomatic Posts

Presidential Administration	Mass.	Other New England States	N.J.	N.Y.	Pa.	Va.	Other Southern States	North-Central States	Mid-western States	Rocky Mountain States	Pacific Coast States	Dist. of Columbia
Lincoln	7.7	15.4	7.7	7.7	15.4	—	7.7	30.8	7.7	—	—	—
A. Johnson	5.5	5.6	—	27.8	5.6	—	11.1	22.2	5.6	—	—	16.7
Grant	14.8	3.7	3.7	18.5	7.4	—	7.4	33.3	3.7	—	3.7	3.7
1861–1877 TOTAL	10.4	6.9	3.4	19.0	8.6	—	8.6	29.3	5.2	—	1.7	6.9
Hayes	15.4	—	—	15.4	15.4	—	—	30.8	23.1	—	—	—
Garfield	—	16.7	—	—	16.7	—	16.7	16.7	33.3	—	—	—
Arthur	8.3	8.3	8.3	25.0	8.3	—	—	16.7	8.3	8.3	8.3	—
Cleveland	8.3	8.3	—	25.0	—	—	41.8	8.3	8.3	—	—	—
B. Harrison	7.1	14.3	—	28.6	—	—	7.1	41.8	7.1	—	—	—
Cleveland	14.3	—	7.1	7.1	—	—	35.7	21.4	14.3	—	—	—
1877–1897 TOTAL	9.9	7.0	2.8	18.3	5.6	—	16.9	22.5	14.2	1.4	1.4	—
McKinley	5.9	—	5.9	29.4	5.9	—	—	35.3	11.8	—	5.9	—
T. Roosevelt	9.7	—	—	38.7	6.4	—	9.7	19.4	9.7	—	6.4	—
Taft	6.7	—	—	33.3	13.3	—	—	26.7	13.3	—	6.7	—
1897–1913 TOTAL	7.9	—	1.6	34.9	7.9	—	4.8	25.4	11.1	—	6.3	—
Wilson	—	—	4.0	20.0	8.0	4.0	16.0	16.0	20.0	—	8.0	4.0

Harding	7.7	—	—	23.1	—	15.4	—	23.1	7.7	15.4	7.7	—
Coolidge	8.7	4.3	—	21.8	—	8.7	4.3	17.4	21.8	4.3	8.7	—
Hoover	5.6	—	5.6	16.7	—	16.7	11.1	27.8	11.1	—	5.6	—
1921–1933 TOTAL	7.4	1.9	1.9	20.4	—	13.0	5.6	22.2	14.9	5.6	7.4	—
1861–1933 TOTAL	8.1	3.7	2.6	22.9	0.4	8.5	10.0	24.0	12.2	1.5	4.4	1.8

Supreme Court Posts

Political Period

1861–1877 TOTAL	—		11.1	11.1	—	11.1	—	44.4	11.1	—	11.1	—
1877–1897 TOTAL	7.7		—	15.4	—	7.7	38.4	23.1	7.7	—	—	—
1897–1913 TOTAL	20.0		10.0	10.0	—	—	30.0	10.0	—	10.0	10.0	—
1913–1921 TOTAL	33.3		—	—	—	—	33.3	33.3	—	—	—	—
1921–1933 TOTAL	—		—	37.5	—	12.5	12.5	12.5	12.5	12.5	—	—
1861–1933 TOTAL	9.3		4.7	16.2	—	7.0	23.2	23.2	7.0	4.7	4.7	—

Note: The Supreme Court totals were aggregated on a broader basis than presidential administrations because of the smaller number of people involved and their often long, overlapping terms of office.

to have their leaders appointed to high federal office. For instance, Virginia, one of the key states in the Confederacy, suffered a disastrous drop after the Civil War in its (non-legislative) representation in the upper echelons of the federal government. Only one of its leaders, Congressman Carter Glass, was appointed to an important Cabinet or diplomatic post during this 72-year period, and that was during the latter part of the perhaps atypical Wilson administration. Indeed, the heavily Democratic South fell sharply out of favor during these largely Republican-dominated years (actually, if it had not been for the efforts of the Cleveland and Wilson regimes to build up party support in the South, this region's rather modest total would have been reduced even further).[3] Thus the Civil War not only broke the political power of the South, but dealt it such a devastating blow that it did not recover for generations.

Another state that suffered a serious decline in its ability to secure key federal positions after the Civil War was, somewhat surprisingly, Pennsylvania. This state has, of course, long been looked upon as perhaps the very heart of American industry—the home, for example, of both Bethlehem Steel and (in terms of its major base of operations) the United States Steel Corp. Yet it did not fare well in its high-level (non-legislative) representation, dropping from an average of about 16 percent of all key Cabinet and diplomatic posts in the pre–Civil War years to little more than 8 percent between 1861 and 1933. This was chiefly because Philadelphia, which had once been the financial center of the country, fell precipitously in both economic and political influence following, first, Andrew Jackson's destruction of the Biddle-dominated second Bank of the United States, and then the collapse of the financial house of Jay Cooke & Co. in the early post–Civil War years.[4] To be precise, of Pennsylvania's total of 23 major Cabinet and diplomatic appointments from 1861 to 1933, four represented two men (one of whom was a three-time carryover) selected to serve, because of their union background, as Secretary of Labor, and thus, from the standpoint of business-government relations, they should probably be excluded from these calculations. Of the remaining aggregate of 19, ten represented Pittsburgh figures (seven of these were accounted for by Andrew Mellon and his attorney, Philander C. Knox, each of whom served under three administrations); one was from northeastern Pennsylvania; and four, all chosen well before the turn of the century, were either relatives of, or lawyers for, the then state Republican party boss Simon Cameron, who was a central Pennsylvania leader. Hence, although it was one of the nation's very largest cities, Philadelphia—unlike Boston, Cleveland, and Chicago—obviously carried little weight in high Washington circles in the post–Civil War period.

There was a similar shift in the pattern of appointments to the Supreme Court between 1861 and 1933. Again, the greatest drop was in the South, which declined from 57 to 23 percent in its share of Supreme Court seats (although this loss was not as marked as that which it experienced in the administrative and diplomatic area, where it fell off from about 50 percent to a little over 10 percent). The biggest gain, on the other hand, was that registered by the north central section of the country, which jumped from about 3 to 23 percent in its representation on the high Court. And perhaps equally important, of the six Chief Justices picked during this period, four were from this region, with Ohio faring particularly well; it received three of these selections.

As America emerged from its pre-industrial state to become a major economic power in the 1861-to-1933 period, there was also, not surprisingly, a continuation of the educational trends that had been at work in the recruitment of high federal officials in the pre–Civil War years. There was a gradual, albeit uneven, decrease in the percentage of major Cabinet and diplomatic officers who had never attended college, while the proportion of men who had secured at least some college education held almost constant (see Table 12). But after the late 1860s the percentage of Ivy League graduates who were appointed to high office rose sharply up to the Wilson regime (although it fell off thereafter).[5] However, this trend was offset to a considerable extent by the recruitment of men who had gone to other prestigious schools such as Stanford and Amherst, with the proportion provided by other lesser-known private colleges climbing even more sharply. Perhaps equally significant was the emergence toward the end of this era of the publicly supported institutions of higher education as a noteworthy source of executive and diplomatic talent. Also, although only about 3 percent of the male population went to college during the first third of the century, the proportion of men with college degrees who were appointed to major Cabinet and diplomatic posts remained about the same as it has been in the pre–Civil War period, around 67 percent.

The Supreme Court Justices who were chosen between 1861 and 1933 were, interestingly, of an even higher educational status than the men picked to hold key administrative and diplomatic posts. Over 85 percent were college graduates (see the last part of Table 12), and those who were not had either secured some college education or had engaged in a good deal of other closely supervised study to meet professional standards. Close to 40 percent had gone to an Ivy League college (in contrast to a little under 35 percent in the pre–Civil War years), and nearly 14 percent had attended other fairly prestigious private schools. In short, from an educational standpoint, the recruitment pattern of Supreme Court Justices between 1861 and 1933 was of a highly elitist nature. In fact, only one of the 43 justices appointed during this period (Ohio's William R. Day) went to a state university or other public college—a rather revealing commentary on the nation's still badly skewed economic opportunity structure.[6]

Another important factor in the federal recruitment process was the amount of government experience America's top officials had prior to their appointment to a major Cabinet, diplomatic, or Supreme Court post.

TABLE 12

Educational Background of High Federal Officials
1861–1933

Major Cabinet and Diplomatic Officers

Presidential Administration	No College Education	Some College Education	Total with a College Degree	Harvard, Yale, or Princeton	Other Ivy League College	Other Private College	Public College	College Education Abroad
Lincoln	38.4%	15.4%	46.2%	15.4%	7.7%	23.1%	—	—
A. Johnson	11.1	22.2	66.7	16.7	—	33.3	16.7%	—
Grant	20.8	4.2	75.0	41.7	12.5	16.7	4.2	—
1861–1877 TOTAL	21.8	12.7	65.5	27.3	7.3	23.6	7.3	—
Hayes	46.2	15.4	38.4	30.8	7.7	—	—	—
Garfield	33.3	16.7	50.0	33.3	—	16.7	—	—
Arthur	25.0	16.7	58.3	25.0	—	25.0	8.3	—
Cleveland	25.0	8.3	66.7	25.0	—	25.0	16.7	—
B. Harrison	28.6	—	71.4	28.6	7.1	21.4	14.3	—
Cleveland	23.1	23.1	53.8	15.4	7.7	23.1	7.7	—
1877–1897 TOTAL	30.0	12.9	57.1	25.6	4.3	18.6	8.6	—
McKinley	31.3	—	68.7	18.8	6.3	31.3	12.5	—
T. Roosevelt	18.5	11.1	70.4	33.3	7.4	25.9	3.7	—
Taft	6.7	13.3	80.0	26.7	—	53.3	—	—
1897–1913 TOTAL	19.0	8.6	72.4	27.6	5.2	34.4	5.2	—
Wilson	20.8	25.0	54.2	—	4.2	41.7	8.3	—

Harding	23.1	15.4	61.5	7.7	7.7	15.4	30.8	—
Coolidge	10.0	10.0	80.0	10.0	5.0	25.0	35.0	5.0%
Hoover	17.6	17.6	64.8	17.6	5.9	17.6	17.6	5.9
1921–1933 TOTAL	16.0	14.0	70.0	12.0	6.0	20.0	28.0	4.0
1861–1933 TOTAL	22.2	13.2	64.6	21.4	5.4	25.7	11.3	0.8

Supreme Court Justices

Political Period								
1861–1877 TOTAL	11.1	—	88.9	22.2	11.1	55.5	—	—
1877–1897 TOTAL	7.7	7.7	84.6	38.4	7.7	38.4	—	—
1897–1913 TOTAL	—	10.0	90.0	30.0	10.0	40.0	10.0	—
1913–1921 TOTAL	33.3	—	66.7	—	—	66.7	—	—
1921–1933 TOTAL	—	—	100.0	25.0	37.5	37.5	—	—
1861–1933 TOTAL	4.7	9.3	86.0	25.6	14.0	41.9	4.7	—

Note: The Supreme Court totals were aggregated on a broader basis than presidential administrations because of the smaller number of people involved and their often long, overlapping terms of office.

As indicated in Volume I, it was relatively rare for a person without a long record of prominent government service to be appointed to such positions in the pre–Civil War era. But this practice changed noticeably after this epic conflict, particularly with regard to Cabinet and high diplomatic officials. After 1861 the nation's chief executives relied to a significant extent on men who had either little or no governmental experience, but were drawn directly (or almost directly) from outside sources, usually from the worlds of business and corporate law. In remarkably consistent fashion, at least 40 percent of the men appointed to high office in both the late 19th and early 20th centuries came in as virtual political neophytes. They were generally chosen for reasons of economic influence, geography, or other essentially non-governmental factors. The post–Civil War era also produced an increase in the proportion of Supreme Court Justices who were selected with little or no judicial or governmental experience. It was roughly the same percentage of people (about 40 percent) appointed without significant prior service to important Cabinet or diplomatic posts.

Another major facet of the federal recruitment process involved the occupational and economic status of these high officeholders. Up to the post–Civil War period large landowning and slaveholding interests had been strongly represented in the federal government. However, after 1861 this recruitment pattern underwent a profound shift. As a result of the Civil War and the defeat of the South, there were, understandably, very few appointees, be they lawyers or other leaders, who derived a substantial part of their wealth and income from plantation or other landholding interests. In addition, there was, around the turn of the century, a significant decrease in the proportion of lawyers tapped for such important posts, especially after the Wilson regime. Yet there was also, paradoxically, a sharp rise in the percentage of corporate (or pro-business) lawyers recruited for key positions.[7] This pattern was most clearly seen with reference to the office of Secretary of State, which was occupied at various times in the pre–Civil War period by such essentially non-corporate leaders as James Monroe (a member of the Virginia dynasty), John Quincy Adams (an ex-Federalist political outcast), John Forsyth (an Augusta, Georgia lawyer), and James Buchanan (a onetime Lancaster, Pennsylvania lawyer); in the late 19th and early 20th centuries, however, this post was held by such business-oriented attorneys as Hamilton Fish, William M. Evarts, Frederick T. Frelinghuysen, Richard Olney, Elihu Root, Philander C. Knox, and Henry L. Stimson, all of whom had previously served on one or more major corporate boards.[8]

There was also a marked increase in the appointment of important business executives during post-Civil War period. This trend reached its pre–World War II peak during the Harding, Coolidge, and Hoover regimes, when close to half of all high federal officials were recruited from such sources.[9] Furthermore, for the first time in American history a significant number (19) of newspapermen were appointed to high administrative or diplomatic office. But a majority of these were really wealthy business (or pro-business) figures, such as John Hay (who served, up to 1900, as a director of the Western Union Telegraph Co.), Whitelaw Reid (who had married into the enormously rich Mills family), and Walter Evans Edge (who was the best friend of the president of the Standard Oil Co. of New Jersey).[10] And as part of a modest trend, an almost equal number of academic and literary figures were appointed to high office during these years, some of whom also had strong corporate ties.[11]

Yet another aspect of the federal recruitment process which deserves special attention is the economic elite status of America's top governmental officials in the Civil War-to-New Deal period.[12] As one might expect, there were some interesting shifts in the proportions of elite and non-elite figures appointed to high office in the United States. For instance, after the highly elitist (and probably pro-railroad) Lincoln administration, there was a significant increase in the relative number of non-elite persons named to important executive and diplomatic posts during the presidential regime of Andrew Johnson, perhaps because he himself was a man of modest means and humble origins (see Table 13). However, this pattern did not continue during the administration of former Army general Ulysses S. Grant, most likely because, following his triumphant role in the Civil War, he had been catapulted into a position of national fame that brought him into close contact with various influential economic and political leaders. Similarly, in the judicial realm almost all (nearly 90 percent) of the men who were elevated to the Supreme Court during this critical period were elite figures.

In the course of the next 20 years, from the administration of Rutherford B. Hayes through Grover Cleveland's second term, there was remarkably little change in the relative amount of elite and non-elite representation in the upper ranks of the federal government. Although there was some variation, all of these administrations were dominated by wealthy or well-connected (mostly railroad and/or banking) figures, who made up an average of 88 percent of the key executive and diplomatic appointees during this period—a higher percentage than that for the Civil War and Reconstruction years. Actually, excluding the brief, ill-fated Garfield regime, the greatest proportion of economically elite officials was picked by New York Democrat Grover Cleveland (during his first presidency) and Benjamin Harrison, while the largest number of non-elite selections was made during the administration of Rutherford B. Hayes and, curiously, during the second term of Grover Cleveland. One possible reason for Cleveland's less overt reliance on elite figures during his second term may be that, upon relinquishing office in 1889, this conservative leader became affiliated with the "Morgan" law firm of Bangs, Stetson, Tracy and MacVeagh (as it was then known) in New York City, and may have had less need to rely during his second term on the formally proferred advice of economically elite Cabinet and diplomatic officials. A

TABLE 13

General Occupational Background and Elite (or Non-Elite) Status of High Federal Officials
1861–1933

Major Cabinet and Diplomatic Officers

Presidency	Large Landowner, Farmer, or Land Speculator	Lawyer and Large Land-owner	Lawyer	Big Business	Small Business	Government Service	Other	No. of Elite Appointees	Percentage Elite Appointees	Number of Non-Elite Appointees	Number, Indeterminate Status
Lincoln	—	—	10	1	—	—	2	12	92.3	1	—
A. Johnson	—	—	9	1	—	4	4	11	68.7	5	2
Grant	—	—	17	4	—	1	2	20	83.4	4	3
1861–1877 TOTAL	—	—	36	6	—	5	8	43	81.1	10	5
Hayes	—	—	8	1	—	—	4	9	75.0	3	1
Garfield	—	—	5	—	—	1	—	6	100.0	—	—
Arthur	—	—	8	3	—	—	1	9	81.8	2	1
Cleveland	—	—	11	1	—	—	—	11	91.7	1	—
B. Harrison	—	—	6	5	1	1	1	11	91.7	1	2
Cleveland	—	—	9	2	—	—	2	11	84.6	2	1
1877–1897 TOTAL	—	—	47	12	1	2	8	57	86.8	9	5
McKinley	—	—	8	5	—	—	3	15	93.8	1	1
T. Roosevelt	—	—	10	8	—	3	5	24	88.9	3	4
Taft	—	—	7	5	—	—	3	13	92.9	1	1
1897–1913 TOTAL	—	—	25	18	—	3	11	52	91.7	5	6

Wilson	—	—	12	6	—	12	57.1	9	4
Harding	—	—	3	7	—	3	9	81.8	2	2
Coolidge	—	1	7	8	—	4	16	80.0	4	2
Hoover	—	—	5	8	—	4	13	81.2	3	2
1921–1933 TOTAL	—	—	15	23	1	11	38	80.9	9	6
1861–1933 TOTAL	—	—	135	65	11	44	202	83.5	40	26
			(52.7%)	(25.4%)		(17.2%)			

Supreme Court Justices

Political Period

1861–1877 TOTAL	8	88.9	—	—
1877–1897 TOTAL	11	84.2	1	—
1897–1913 TOTAL	8	100.0	—	2
1913–1921 TOTAL	1	50.0	1	1
1921–1933 TOTAL	7	87.5	1	—
1861–1933 TOTAL	35	87.5	5	3

Note: The first (occupational) part of this table has been compiled according to the number of people who held high federal office, while the second part, dealing with economic elite (or non-elite) status, has been compiled on the basis of the number of appointments made, because the status of some later (post-New Deal) officeholders changed between their periods of government service. The "other" occupational column includes academic figures, newspapermen, and various other types of persons. The last category was established because there was not enough background data to classify some officials. No occupational background data were presented for the Supreme Court justices since they were all lawyers. Their elite (and non-elite) totals were, with one exception, aggregated on a broader basis than presidential administrations because of the smaller number of people involved and their often long, overlapping terms of office.

highly elitist pattern was also maintained in the selection of Supreme Court Justices throughout this 20-year period, for almost the same percentage (83 percent) of these figures had important corporate (usually railroad) ties or pro-business backgrounds.

Actually, the practice of making elitist Cabinet and diplomatic appointments reached its post–Civil War peak in the years between 1897 and 1913. In this era, ironically, there was a great deal of progressive sentiment in the country, which found much support, according to many historians, in the administration of Theodore Roosevelt, an ambitious patrician turned civic reformer. Yet, interestingly, there was not much difference between the percentage of elitist appointments of the Roosevelt regime and that found in either the McKinley or the Taft administration (see Table 13). Thus Gabriel Kolko and various other authorities were apparently right when they described Theodore Roosevelt as essentially a fairly conservative figure who, through his often colorful rhetoric and occasional reformist actions, probably did more to defuse than to advance the progressive movement in America.[13] Similarly, during this period all of the men appointed to the high Court (about whom sufficient information exists) were elite leaders.

During the Wilson regime, on the other hand, the number of non-elite people appointed to major Cabinet and diplomatic posts increased markedly, from about 8 percent in the McKinley-through-Taft period to a high of 43 percent under this New Jersey Democrat.[14] This was by far the highest level yet reached in the recruitment of such officials since the founding of the Republic, and it would seem to signify a major shift in American politico-economic relations. However, the overall impact of this appointment policy was apparently muted considerably by the fact that both President Wilson and his chief influential informal advisor, Colonel House, were essentially conservative. As one might expect, there was a similar pattern in the selection of Supreme Court Justices during this period, though the number of such officials picked was extremely small—only three.

In the Republican-dominated 1920s and early 1930s there was a sharp increase in the proportion of elite figures appointed to important office. But for all their conservatism, the administrations of Harding, Coolidge, and Hoover did not climb back completely to the high levels of elite appointments set by many previous Republican presidents, such as Roosevelt and Taft. Overall, the proportion of elite leaders appointed to high executive and diplomatic posts during these years averaged about 80 percent.[15] Curiously, an even larger percentage of economically elite figures was elevated to the high Court under Harding, Coolidge, and Hoover than was appointed to major Cabinet and diplomatic posts—a policy in marked contrast to that followed by many later administrations.[16]

The strong influence of business interests in the federal government between 1861 and 1933 can also be seen in many of the actions taken by different presidential regimes, regardless, as a rule, of which party was in power. For instance, it was probably no accident that the largest railroad land grants in American history were given out while Abraham Lincoln, a former Illinois Central Railroad lawyer, was in office. That railroad forces, which represented the nation's first "big business" (but were not monolithic body), wielded considerable influence in the Democratic party was revealed even more vividly some 30 years later by the way in which the second Cleveland administration handled the famous Pullman strike of 1894. In this bitter dispute President Cleveland was persuaded by his conservative Attorney General (and Boston corporate lawyer) Richard Olney to send in federal troops to break the widespread, at times violent, strike, even though no such action was requested by Illinois' Governor John Peter Altgeld. From a politico-economic standpoint, the most intriguing aspect of this affair was the fact that, although an influential Cabinet official, Olney had continued to serve as a director and general counsel of two major railroads, one of which was based in Chicago and very much a party to these proceedings.

A number of the actions taken by Theodore Roosevelt, on the other hand, have been interpreted by many historians as evidence of the increasing influence of reform interests. In considerable part this was because of Roosevelt's verbal assaults against the "malefactors of great wealth" in America and his much-publicized steps against certain vast business combines; for these, he has often been extolled as the "great trustbuster." However, a close look at Roosevelt's record in office reveals that he actually initiated a much smaller number of antitrust suits, especially against big companies, than his conservative successor, William Howard Taft, who only served one term as President. Moreover, Roosevelt made a curious distinction between what he regarded as "good trusts" and "bad trusts." Yet upon further inspection, the good trusts usually turned out to be Morgan-dominated concerns, while the bad ones were what might be referred to as "non-Morgan trusts," such as the Rockefeller-controlled Standard Oil Co. and E. H. Harriman's Union Pacific Railroad.

Although the Wilson administration was, partly because of the strength of the Bryan forces in the Democratic party, of a less elitist nature than any of the Republican regimes, a number of the actions taken during this period reflected the influence of corporate interests too. This was seen both in the creation and early operation of the Federal Reserve System and the Federal Trade Commission, the top positions of which bodies were initially dominated by pro-business figures.

In the 1920s the most important measures taken by the federal government were in the realm of domestic finance. To the surprise of some, the Harding administration was initially thwarted by liberal forces in Congress in its attempts to reduce the fairly sizable tax burden that had been imposed for the first time on both rich people and major corporate interests by the Wilson regime to help finance America's involvement in World War I. But in the mid-1920s President Coolidge and Secretary of the Treasury Andrew Mellon were able to overcome this resistance and secure the passage of a key fiscal measure which drastically reduced the rates of both the federal estate (i.e., inheritance) tax and the progressively conceived income surtax, and completely abolished the recently enacted federal gift tax.

In addition, and perhaps even more important in the long run, the Coolidge-Mellon administration, as some have described it, managed, with the help of certain key figures in Congress, particularly Pennsylvania's Senator David A. Reed (who was closely allied with the Mellon interests), to obtain a tremendous boost in the depletion allowance granted to extractive industries, mostly oil and mining firms, since 1913. In 1926 this subsidy was raised from an average of about 5 percent of these corporations' gross income to a lucrative, arbitrarily arrived at 27.5 percent, a rate that remained in effect for over 40 years.

Both these governmental acts and the highly skewed federal recruitment process show that elite interests wielded great influence in American government in the Civil-War-to-New-Deal years. This was true even during the Progressive era when the political reform movement was widely believed to be at its peak.

Notes

1. Of the New York (1861–1933) appointment total of 58, eight were from the northern part of the state. Half of this aggregate consisted of two prestigious ex-college presidents, Andrew D. White and David J. Hill, each of whom held two diplomatic offices. The other half was made up of Auburn lawyer William H. Seward (who served as Secretary of State under two administrations) and Corning Glass Works owner Alanson B. Houghton (who held diplomatic posts under both Harding and Coolidge). Even these two latter men had ties to New York City—Houghton through his directorship with the Metropolitan Life Insurance Co. and Seward through his longtime legal and political association with the entrepreneurially oriented Richard M. Blatchford.

2. The major Cabinet and diplomatic representation of the rapidly growing (and increasingly industrialized) north central section of the country—Ohio, Illinois, Indiana, Michigan, and Wisconsin—also jumped sharply during this period, more or less in line with its share of the nation's population and overall economic output. On the other hand, although New England's proportion of high-level federal appointments fell off somewhat after the Civil War, the decline was not as severe as one might have expected, in large measure because Boston itself continued, as a major financial hub, to wield considerable influence in American politics.

3.   Even though Texas had become by far the largest state in the South shortly before the turn of the century, it did not receive its first Cabinet seat (or diplomatic post) until the Wilson administration. And that no doubt stemmed from the influence of the President's intimate informal advisor, Colonel House.

4.   In like manner, the city of Baltimore, which had once claimed a significant number of major Cabinet and diplomatic posts (a total of ten in the pre–Civil War era), fell off sharply, obtaining only two between 1861 and 1900, and the same small number in the first third of the 20th century. Both of the latter were held by the same person, the patrician reformer Charles J. Bonaparte, who was probably picked primarily because he was a member of the executive committee of the then-influential National Civic Federation.

5.   Some may find it rather curious that Woodrow Wilson, a former Ivy League college president, did not recruit more heavily from such institutions, but he may not have felt free to do so because of strong party and other pressures.

6.   Although a number of other Justices (such as Harlan, McKenna, Miller, and Van Devanter) attended relatively unknown private colleges (such as DePauw and Transylvania), they represented a fairly small percentage of the total number of Supreme Court Justices appointed during this period.

7.   Although various authorities have aptly described the period from the 1860s to roughly the turn of the century as "the great age of American railroads," remarkably few entrepreneurs or executives associated with this industry were appointed to high federal office during these years. Instead, this influential sector made its weight felt in governmental affairs through the selection of lawyers and political leaders who were closely linked with the railroads, usually through directorship ties.

8.   There were, of course, some staunchly pro-business figures who served as Secretary of State in the pre-industrial era, such as Daniel Webster and William L. Marcy, but these were the exception rather than the rule. After the 1860s, on the other hand, even such statesmen as John Hay and James G. Blaine (both of whom were former newspapermen rather than attorneys) were closely linked with influential economic interests. And the same may be said of Delaware's patrician Senator Thomas F. Bayard, who was a longtime friend of New York financier August Belmont.

9.   The 25 percent business-recruitment figure for the Wilson administration may be somewhat deceiving because two-thirds of these officials served in a diplomatic capacity rather than in a Cabinet post, which appointment pattern was not maintained in either the preceding or succeeding Republic regimes.

10.   Not all newspapermen appointed to high office during this period were pro-business; two of those selected by the Wilson administration, William Jennings Bryan and Josephus Daniels, were clearly progressive leaders.

11.   In addition, a small number of men appointed to important Cabinet and diplomatic posts during this (1861–1933) period had spent most of their lives in some form of government service. But the majority of these were former Army generals who were appointed shortly after the Civil War when such figures were still extremely popular.

12.   As indicated in the first chapter, the term *economic elite* has been used to describe someone who held an important (executive or directorship) post in a major business enterprise and/or whose family had considerable wealth or like executive or directorship ties at or around the time of his appointment to high federal office. In terms of numbers, this rich or well-connected segment of the population probably never constituted more than about 0.5 or 1 percent of the people in the country, and clearly represented the core of America's upper class.

13.   See Gabriel Kolko, *The Triumph of Conservatism* (Glencoe, Ill.: Free Press, 1963), *passim*.

14.   Four Wilson appointees were, because of a mixed background or a lack of sufficient biographical data, placed in the indeterminate status category (see Table 13, and for more

detail Appendix A). If most of these people were, upon further analysis, adjudged to be non-elite, the 43 percent figure would, of course, increase.

15.   If these (1921–1933) non-elite figures were analyzed on the basis of length of time served in office (another perhaps equally important yardstick), the above totals would in each case be reduced by about 5 percentage points.

16.   In fact, only the last of the Supreme Court Justices appointed during this period, New York's Benjamin Cardozo, was clearly a non-elite figure. Overall, if one excludes "indeterminate status" cases, about 87 percent of the Supreme Court appointees between 1861 and 1933 could be classified as elite figures, compared to about 84 percent of the major Cabinet and diplomatic officers (the latter total represented a 12 percent drop from the pre–Civil War period).

Appendix A

Primary Background Data of Major Cabinet
and Diplomatic Officials:
1861–1933

ABBREVIATIONS

BD	board of directors
BT	board of trustees
BC	board chairman
VC	vice-chairman
CEC	chairman of executive committee
P	president
VP	vice-president
GC	general counsel
Sec.	secretary
ptr.	partner
off.	official
dir.	director
adm.	administrator
E	elite status
NE	non-elite status
?	indeterminate status

Note: Because of a lack of sufficient data, a number of officials have been classified with less certainty, as probably elite (E?) or probably non-elite (NE?). A few carryover officials served so briefly that they were not counted in the concluding chapter's summary analysis and are indicated by n/c in the last column of the tables. Persons holding office at the start of an administration (or time period), or serving into another, are indicated by an italicized date.

LINCOLN ADMINISTRATION (1861–1865)

Officeholder	College Education	Prior Governmental Experience	Primary Occupation	Important Secondary Economic Affiliations	Family and Other Social Ties	Other Pertinent Information	Elite or Non-Elite Status
President							
Abraham Lincoln, Ill. (March 1861–April 1865)		Prominent Ill. political leader (first as a Whig and later as a Republican); Illinois Congressman (1847–49); former state legislator (mid-1830s and early 1840s)	Springfield, Ill. lawyer (1837–61)				E
Secretary of State							
William H. Seward, N.Y. (March 1861 through 1865)	Union College	U. S. Senator, N.Y. (1849–61); Governor of New York (1838–42); also former state legislator (1830–34)	Auburn, N.Y., lawyer (1823–60); partner, Blatchford & Seward, Auburn and N.Y.C. law firm (1845–50; of counsel, 1850–60); nephew, Clarence Seward, ptr., Blatchford, Seward & Griswold, N.Y.C. law firm (1854 on)	Blatchford a director or officer of the New York Central RR (1861–67), and a director of Saratoga & Whitehall RR (early 1860s)	Married daughter of Elijah Miller, who, though he died in 1851, had much to do with creation of Auburn & Syracuse RR; Seward's father also wealthy		E

Sec. of Treasury					
Salmon P. Chase, Ohio (March 1861–June 1864)	Dartmouth College	Prominent Republican and abolitionist leader; Governor of Ohio (1856–60); U. S. Senator (1849–55 and March 1861)	Cincinnati, Ohio lawyer (1830 on)	Third (now deceased) wife the wealthy daughter of one of the founders of Cincinnati (with major landholdings)	E?
William P. Fessenden,* Maine (July 1864–March 1865)	Bowdoin College	U. S. Senator, Maine (1854–64); Maine Congressman (1841–43); also former state legislator	Portland, Maine lawyer (1827 on)	Married daughter of James Deering, well-to-do Portland merchant	E
Attorney General					
Edward Bates, Missouri (March 1861–Nov. 1864)		Judge, St. Louis Land Court (1853–56); Mo. Congressman (1827–29); also former state legislator; U. S. attorney, Mo. (1821–26)	St. Louis, Mo. lawyer (1842 on), represented mainly wealthy business and landholding interests; Charles County, Mo. lawyer (1828–42)		E?

*Fessenden's successor, Hugh McCulloch (who took office in March 1865), is treated under the Andrew Johnson administration.

LINCOLN ADMINISTRATION (continued)

Officeholder	College Education	Prior Governmental Experience	Primary Occupation	Important Secondary Economic Affiliations	Family and Other Social Ties	Other Pertinent Information	Elite or Non-Elite Status
James Speed, Kentucky (Dec. 1864–1865)	St. Joseph College, Ky.	Ky. state legislator (1847–49 and 1861–63)	Louisville, Ky. lawyer (1833–64); also law professor, Univ. of Ky. (1856–58)	BD of Louisville & Nashville RR (at least 1856–65)		brother of Joshua Speed, a longtime close friend of Lincoln	E
Secretary of War							
Simon Cameron, Penn. (March 1861–Dec. 1862)		U. S. Senator and Republican party leader, Penn. (1857 on); Democratic U. S. Senator, Penn. (1845–49)	Central Penn. businessman; founder and longtime head of rail system later known as the Northern Central RR; also dominant figure in Bank of Middletown (Penn.)	P of Lebanon Valley RR (1853 on)	Son, J. D. Cameron, P of Northern Central RR, Penn. (1863 on)		E
Edwin M. Stanton, Penn. (Jan. 1862 through 1865)	Kenyon College (not complete)	U. S. Attorney-General (1860–61); special counsel, U. S. Government (late 1850s)	Washington, D. C. lawyer (1856–60); Pittsburgh, Penn. lawyer (1847–1856); Steubenville, Ohio lawyer (1839–47)		Married (in 1856) Ellen Hutchison, daughter of a wealthy Pittsburgh merchant		E?

	Education	Government career	Business/professional career	Economic/financial	Family background	Political	
Secretary of Navy							
Gideon Welles, Conn. (March 1861 through 1865)		Chief, Bureau of Provisions for Navy (a minor U.S. post, 1846–49); Hartford Postmaster (1836–41); former state govt. official (late 1830s and early 1840s); Conn. state legislator (1827–35)	High official, *Hartford Evening Press* (1856–61); part-owner and editor of *Hartford Times* (1826–36)	BD of Hartford National Bank (1855–60)	Father a well-to-do Conn. merchant	Rep. Natl. Committeeman, Conn. (1856–64)	E
Secretary of the Interior							
Caleb B. Smith, Ind. (March 1861–Dec. 1862)	Miami Univ. (not graduate)	U. S. Mexican Claims Commissioner (1849–1851); Indiana Congressman (1843–49); also former state legislator (1832–37 and early 1840s)	Cincinnati, Ohio lawyer (1851–54); P of Cincinnati & Chicago RR (1854–58); Indiana lawyer (1828–51 and 1859–61, latter years in Indianapolis)				E

Officeholder	College Education	Prior Governmental Experience	Primary Occupation	Important Secondary Economic Affiliations	Family and Other Social Ties	Other Pertinent Information	Elite or Non-Elite Status
John P. Usher, Ind. (Jan. 1863–May 1865)		U. S. Asst. Sec. of the Interior (1862–1863); Ind. Attorney-General (1861); former state legislator (1850–51)	Terre Haute, Indiana lawyer (1840 on); represented both Lake Erie, Wabash & St. Louis RR and Leavenworth, Pawnee & Western RR before Civil War		Brother-in-law, Demas Deming, on BD of Terre Haute & Richmond RR (at least 1856–65)		E
Minister to Great Britain							
Charles F. Adams, Mass. (May 1861 through 1865)	Harvard Univ.	Mass. Congressman (1859–61); also former state legislator (1835–40)	Boston (Brahmin) author and historian		Brother-in-law, Peter C. Brooks, VP of Mass. Hospital Life Insur. Co. (1865–70, P thereafter); late father-in-law, P. C. Brooks also P of this company (1840s); brother-in-law (by marriage) of former Secretary of State Edward Everett		E

Minister to France					
William L. Dayton, N.J. (May 1861–Dec. 1864)	Princeton Univ.	N. J. Attorney General (1857–61); U. S. Senator, N.J. (1842–51); member, N.J. Supreme Court (1838–41)	Trenton, N.J. lawyer (1841 on)	Grandson of Elias Dayton, former wealthy New Jersey merchant	N-E?

Minister to Germany					
Norman B. Judd, Ill. (July 1861–Sept. 1865)		Illinois state legislator (1844–60)	Chicago, Ill. lawyer (1836 on); P of Peoria and Bureau Valley RR (at least 1856 on?)	BD of Chicago and Rock Island RR (at least 1856–62) and Mississippi and Missouri RR (at least 1856–59)	E

JOHNSON ADMINISTRATION (1865–1869)

Officeholder	College Education	Prior Governmental Experience	Primary Occupation	Important Secondary Economic Affiliations	Family and Other Social Ties	Other Pertinent Information	Elite or Non-Elite Status
President							
Andrew Johnson, Tenn. (April 1865–March 1869)		Vice-President of the United States (March–April 1865); military governor of Tenn. (1862–65); U.S. Senator, Tenn. (1857–62); Governor of Tenn. (1853–57); Tenn. Congressman (1843–53); also former state legislator	Longtime Greeneville, Tenn. tailor				N-E

	College	Position	Career	Railroad connections	Notes	
Secretary of State						
William H. Seward, N.Y. (1865–1869)	Union College	Sec. of State (1861–65); also see earlier Lincoln administration entries	Auburn, N.Y. lawyer (1823–60); ptr., Blatchford & Seward, Auburn and N.Y.C. law firm (1845–50, of counsel 1850–60; nephew, Clarence Seward, ptr., Blatchford, Seward & Griswold, N.Y.C. law firm (1854 on)	Richard M. Blatchford, a director or officer of New York Central RR (1861–67); also on BD of Saratoga & Whitehall RR (up to 1865); son, W. H. Seward, Jr., on BD of Southern Central RR (1867 on)	Married daughter of Elijah Miller, who died in 1851, but had much to do with the organization and early operation of Auburn & Syracuse RR	E
Secretary of Treasury						
Hugh McCulloch, Ind. (1865–1869)	Bowdoin College (2 years)	U. S. Comptroller of Currency (1863–65)	P of State Bank of Indiana (1856–63); mgr. of Ft. Wayne branch of State Bank of Indiana (1835–56)			N-E?

JOHNSON ADMINISTRATION (continued)

Officeholder	College Education	Prior Governmental Experience	Primary Occupation	Important Secondary Economic Affiliations	Family and Other Social Ties	Other Pertinent Information	Elite or Non-Elite Status
Attorney General							
James Speed, Kentucky (April 1865–July 1866)	St. Joseph College, Ky.	U.S. Attorney General (Dec. 1864–April 1865); Ky. legislator (1847–49 and 1861–63)	Louisville lawyer (1833–64); law prof., Univ. of Kentucky (1856–58)	BD of Louisville & Nashville RR (at least 1856 to 1865)			E
Henry Stanbery, Ohio (July 1866–March 1868)	Washington & Jefferson College, Penn.	Ohio Attorney General (1846–53)	Cincinnati lawyer (1853–66); Lancaster, Ohio lawyer (1824–46)				?
William M. Evarts, N.Y. (July 1868–March 1869)	Yale Univ.	Asst. U.S. attorney, southern dist., N.Y. (1849–53); also held other special ad hoc posts	Partner, Evarts, Choate & Southmayd, N.Y.C. law firm and predecessor firms (1842 on)				E

Secretary of War

Name, State (dates)	Education	Prior office	Career	Family	
Edwin M. Stanton, Penn. (April 1865–August 1867)	Kenyon College (not complete)	Sec. of War (1862–65); see earlier Lincoln administration entry	Washington, D.C. (and Pittsburgh) lawyer (1856–60); Pittsburgh lawyer (1847–56); Ohio lawyer (1839–47)	Married (in 1856) Ellen Hutchison, daughter of a wealthy Pittsburgh merchant	E?
Ulysses S. Grant, Ill. (August 1867–Jan. 1868)	U.S. Military Academy, West Point		Commander of Union army during Civil War; U.S. Army officer (1843–54; Mo. and Ill. farmer and small businessman (1854–60)		N-E?
Lorenzo Thomas, Del. (Feb.–June 1868)	U.S. Military Academy, Wt. Point		U.S. Army officer (1823 on)		N-E
John M. Schofield, Ill. (June 1868–March 1869)	U.S. Military Academy, West Point		U.S. Army officer (1853–60 and 1861–68); prof. of physics, Washington Univ., St. Louis (1860–61)		N-E

JOHNSON ADMINISTRATION (continued)

Officeholder	College Education	Prior Governmental Experience	Primary Occupation	Important Secondary Economic Affiliations	Family and Other Social Ties	Other Pertinent Information	Elite or Non-Elite Status
Secretary of Navy							
Gideon Welles, Conn. (1865–69)		Sec. of the Navy (1861–65); see earlier Lincoln administration entry	High official, Hartford Evening Press (1856–61); part-owner and editor of Hartford Times (1826–36)	BD of Hartford National Bank (1855–60)	Father a well-to-do Conn. merchant	Rep. Natl. Committeeman, Conn. (1856–64)	E
Secretary of Interior							
James Harlan*, Iowa (May 1865–Sept. 1866)	DePauw Univ.	U.S. Senator, Iowa (1855–65)	Iowa City and Mount Pleasant, Iowa lawyer (1848 on); P of Iowa Wesleyan Univ. (1853–55); Harlan also a former lobbyist for T. C. Durant, organizer and early high official of the Union Pacific RR			Member of Des Moines Regency till late 1860s (when fell out of favor)	E?

*Lincoln incumbent, John P. Usher, served till May of 1865

Orville H. Browning, Ill. (Sept. 1866–March 1869)	Augusta College (not graduate)	U. S. Senator, Ill. (1861–63); also former longtime state legislator	Quincy, Ill. lawyer (1831 on); Washington, D.C. lawyer and lobbyist (1863–66); attorney for Chicago, Burlington & Quincy RR (1869 on, and perhaps also in late 1850s or mid-1860s)	Law partner, N. Bushnell, P of Northern Cross RR until merger with Chicago, Burlington & Quincy RR	E

Minister to Great Britain

Charles F. Adams, Mass. (April 1865–May 1868)	Harvard Univ.	U. S. Minister to Great Britain (1861–65)	SEE EARLIER LINCOLN ADMINISTRATION ENTRY		E
Reverdy Johnson, Md. (Sept. 1868–May 1869)	St. John's College, Md.	U.S. Attorney General (1849–50); U.S. Senator, Md. (1845–49 and 1863–65)	Longtime Baltimore lawyer (1817 on); counsel for B & O RR since about 1830	Kinsman, Oden Bowie, P of Baltimore & Potomac RR (1860 on); another relative, Wm. D. Bowie, also a member of this railroad's BD	E

JOHNSON ADMINISTRATION (continued)

Officeholder	College Education	Prior Governmental Experience	Primary Occupation	Important Secondary Economic Affiliations	Family and Other Social Ties	Other Pertinent Information	Elite or Non-Elite Status
Minister to France							
John Bigelow, N.Y. (April 1865–Dec. 1866)	Union College	U.S. Consul-General in France (1861–65)	Part-owner and editor, *New York Post* (1848–61); also onetime New York lawyer				?
John A. Dix, N.Y. (Dec. 1866–May 1869)	College of Montreal (not complete)	U.S. Sec. of Treasury (1861); U.S. Senator, N.Y. (1845–49); also former state govt. official	P, Union Pacific RR (1863–66); NYC lawyer (1861–63); P of Mississippi & Missouri RR (1854–at least 1859); P of Chicago & Rock Island RR (1853–54); Albany lawyer (1840–53)	BD of South Side RR, N.Y. (a small concern, at least 1867 through 1869)	Married daughter of John Morgan, wealthy upstate N.Y. landowner		E
Minister to Germany (Prussia)							
Joseph A. Wright, Ind. (Sept. 1865–May 1867)	Indiana Univ. (2 years)	U.S. Senator (1862–63); U.S. Minister to Germany (1857–61);	Rockville, Ind. lawyer (1829 on)				N-E?

Officeholder	College Education	Prior Governmental Experience	Primary Occupation	Important Secondary Economic Affiliations	Family and Other Social Ties	Other Pertinent Information	Elite or Non-Elite Status
		Governor of Indiana (1849–57); Ind. Congressman (1843–45); also former state legislator					E
George Bancroft, N.Y. (orig. Mass.) (Aug. 1867 through 1869)	Harvard Univ.	Minister to Great Britain (1846–49); U.S. Sec. of Navy (1845–46)	New York-based historian and writer (1849 on); before 1845, a Boston historian		Nephew, J. C. Bancroft Davis, on BD of Erie RR (at least 1865 on)		E

GRANT ADMINISTRATION (1869–1877)

Officeholder	College Education	Prior Governmental Experience	Primary Occupation	Important Secondary Economic Affiliations	Family and Other Social Ties	Other Pertinent Information	Elite or Non-Elite Status
President							
Ulysses S. Grant, Ill., orig. Ohio (1869–1877)	U.S. Military Academy, West Point	U.S. Sec. of War (1867–68)	U. S. Army officer (1843–54, 1861–69); appointed commander of Northern army in later stages of Civil War; Ill. and Mo. farmer and small businessman (1854–61)				N-E?

Officeholder	College Education	Prior Governmental Experience	Primary Occupation	Important Secondary Economic Affiliations	Family and Other Social Ties	Other Pertinent Information	Elite or Non-Elite Status
Secretary of State							
Elihu B. Washburne, Ill. (one week, March, 1869)	Attended Maine Wesleyan Seminary for a few months	U. S. Congressman, Ill. (1853–69); former longtime Whig and Republican leader from Ill.	Galena, Ill. lawyer (1840 on)			SEE LATER BRITISH AMBASSADORIAL ENTRY FOR MORE ON THE ECONOMIC TIES OF VARIOUS OTHER MEMBERS OF THIS FAMILY	E
Hamilton Fish, N. Y. (March 1869–March 1877)	Columbia Univ.	U. S. Senator, N.Y. (1851–57); Governor of New York (1849–50); N.Y. Congressman (1843–45)	Longtime NYC lawyer (1830 on)	Dir. (or off.) of New Jersey RR (1851–72?), Bank for Savings in N.Y.C. (1860–69), and New York Life Ins. & Trust Co. (1854 through 1877)	Brother-in-law, John Kean, on BD of Central RR of N.J. (1874–at least 77); mother a member of Stuyvesant family; long-deceased father was a former high official of the Mohawk & Hudson RR		E

Secretary of Treasury						
George S. Boutwell, Mass. (March 1869–March 1873)		Mass. Congressman (1863–69); Sec. State Board of Education (1855–61); Gov. of Mass. (1851–52); also former state legislator (1842–44 and 1847–50)	Suffolk Co., Mass. lawyer (1862 on)		Bd. Overseers, Harvard College (1853–56)	?
William A. Richardson, Mass. (March 1873–June 1874)	Harvard Univ.	Asst. Sec. of Treasury (1869–73); Mass. state judge (1856–69); former Whig-Rep. politician, Mass.	Lowell, Mass. lawyer (1846–55, as ptr. of brother, Daniel S. Richardson)	Brother, Daniel S. Richardson, P of Vermont & Massachusetts RR (at least 1865–74; brother also on BD of Nashua & Lowell RR (least 1859–74)	Bd. Overseers, Harvard College (1863–75)	E
Benjamin H. Bristow, Kentucky (June 1874–June 1876)	Jefferson College, Penn.	Asst. U.S. attorney and U.S. Attorney for Kentucky (1865–69); U.S. Solicitor-General (1870–72)	Louisville, Ky. lawyer (1873–74); law ptr. of John M. Harlan (1868–70); P of California & Texas Construction Co. sub of Texas & Pacific RR (1872–73); Elkton and Hopkinsville, Ky. lawyer (1853–61)	Cousin, John L. Helm, P of Louisville and Nashville RR (up to 1860)	Union army officer, Civil War	E?

GRANT ADMINISTRATION (continued)

Officeholder	College Education	Prior Governmental Experience	Primary Occupation	Important Secondary Economic Affiliations	Family and Other Social Ties	Other Pertinent Information	Elite or Non-Elite Status
Lot. M. Morrill, Maine (July 1876–March 1877)	Colby College (one year)	U.S. Senator, Maine (1861–76); Governor of Maine (1858–61); also former state legislator	Augusta, Maine lawyer (1841 on); longtime law partners were James W. Bradbury and Richard D. Rice	BD of Somerset & Kennebec RR (mid-1850s)	Brother, Anson P. Morrill, on BD of Androscoggin & Kennebec RR (mid-1850s) and P or other high official of Maine Central RR (1867–74); A. P. Morrill also owner of Readfield woolen mill	Chrm. State Dem. Committee, Me. (1849–56)	E
Secretary of War							
John A. Rawlins, Ill. (March–Sept. 1869)			Galena, Ill. lawyer (1854–60)			Close friend of General U. S. Grant; also former Civil War officer	N-E

William T. Sherman, Ohio, orig. (Sept.–Oct. 1869)	U.S. Military Academy, West Point	U.S. Army officer (1840–53); off., Calif. branch of St. Louis bank (1853–57); Leavenworth law ptr. of T. & H.B. Ewing (1857–58); supt., La. military college, (1859–61)			Brother, U.S. Senator John Sherman, on BD of Pittsburgh, Ft. Wayne and Chicago Rwy. (1866 thru 1869) and also on BD of Atlantic and Great Western Rwy. (up to 1866); W. T. Sherman married daughter of Thomas Ewing, former Ohio Whig leader	Famous Civil War general	E?
William W. Belknap, Iowa (Dec. 1869–March 1876)	Princeton Univ.	U.S. Collector of Internal Revenue for Iowa (1865–69); also former Iowa state legislator (1857–58)	Keokuk, Iowa, lawyer (1851–61)			Civil War officer (highest rank, Brigader-General)	N-E
Alphonso Taft, Ohio (March–May 1876)	Yale Univ.	Cincinnati judge (1865–72)	Cincinnati lawyer (1838–65 and 1872–76)	BD of Little Miami RR (least 1856 to 1868); also BD of Cincinnati & Hillsboro RR (1856) and Marietta & Cincinnati RR (1859)	Son, Charles P. Taft, married daughter of David Sinton, one of the wealthiest men in Cincinnati		E

Officeholder	College Education	Prior Governmental Experience	Primary Occupation	Important Secondary Economic Affiliations	Family and Other Social Ties	Other Pertinent Information	Elite or Non-Elite Status
J. Donald Cameron, Penn. (June, 1876–March, 1877)	Princeton Univ.		Central Penn. businessman; longtime P of Bank of Middletown, Penn.; P of Northern Central RR (1863–74)	BD of Wilmington, Columbia & Augusta RR (1869–77), Wilmington & Weldon RR (1870–75), and Columbia & Port Deposit RR (least 1867 to 1873)	Married daughter of James McCormick, a wealthy Harrisburg businessman	Father, Simon Cameron, Repub. party boss in Penn. and U.S. Senator, Penn. (1867 on)	E
Attorney General							
E. Rockwood Hoar, Mass. (March 1869–July 1870)	Harvard Univ.	Mass. Supreme Court Justice (1859–69); Mass. state judge (1849–55); also former state legislator	Boston, Mass. lawyer (1855–59, the last two years as a partner of Horace Gray); Concord, Mass. lawyer (about 1840 to 1849)		Member of one of Boston's top 50 families; cousin, Wm. M. Evarts, a Wall Street lawyer and former (1868–69) U.S. Attorney General	Bd. Overseers, Harvard College (1857–58 and 1868–80); Fellow, Harvard College (1857–68)	E

Name	College	Government positions	Law practice	Business	Notes	N-E
Amos T. Akerman, Georgia (July, 1870–Jan., 1872)	Dartmouth College	U.S. attorney for Ga. (1869–70)	Elberton, Ga. lawyer (up to Civil War and perhaps briefly thereafter)		Confederate Army officer, Civil War	N-E
George H. Williams, Oregon (Jan. 1872–April 1875)		U.S. Senator, Oregon (1865–71); Chief Justice, Oregon territory (1853–57); Iowa judge (1847–52)	Portland, Ore. lawyer (1857 on); former general counsel to Alaska Improvement Co.			?
Edwards Pierrepont, N. Y. (May 1875–May 1876)	Yale Univ.	U. S. attorney, southern district, N.Y. (1869–70); N. Y. C. judge (1857–60)	NYC lawyer (1846 on)	Treasurer and director of Texas and Pacific Rwy., a line headed by T. A. Scott of Penn. RR (1871–74)		E
Alphonso Taft, Ohio (June 1876–March 1877)	Yale Univ.	U. S. Sec. of War (March–May, 1876); Cincinnati judge (1865–72)	Cincinnati lawyer (1838–65 and 1872–76)	BD of Little Miami RR (least 1856 to 1868), Cincinnati & Hillsboro RR (1856), and Marietta & Cincinnati RR (1859)	Son, Charles P. Taft, married daughter of David Sinton, one of the wealthiest men in Cincinnati	E

347

Officeholder	College Education	Prior Governmental Experience	Primary Occupation	Important Secondary Economic Affiliations	Family and Other Social Ties	Other Pertinent Information	Elite or Non-Elite Status
Secretary of Navy							
Adolph E. Borie, Penn. (March–June 1869)	U. of Penn.		Longtime Phila. merchant (McKean, Borie & Co.) and financier (P of Bank of Commerce, Phila. 1848–60, and a director thereafter)	BD of Philadelphia & Reading RR (at least 1865–69), Reading & Columbia RR (at lease 1865–69), Eastern Penn. RR (at least 1865–69), and Phila. Savings Fund Society (1848 through 69)	Member of one of Philadelphia's top 50 families		E
George M. Robeson, N.J. (Dec. 1869–March 1877)	Princeton Univ.	N.J. Attorney General (1867–69); Camden County prosecutor (1858–61)	Jersey City lawyer (1850–58)	BD of Belvidere-Delaware RR (1867 up to 1873)		Civil War Brig.-General	E

Secretary of Interior					
Jacob D. Cox, Ohio (March 1869–Oct. 1870)	Oberlin College	Governor of Ohio (1866–68); former state legislator (1859–61)	Warren, Ohio lawyer (1853–61); Cincinnati lawyer (1868–69)	Civil War general	N-E
Columbus Delano, Ohio (Dec. 1870–Sept. 1875)		Ohio Congressman (1845–47 and 1865–69)	Mt. Vernon, Ohio lawyer (1831–50); ptr., NYC banking firm of Delano, Dunlevy & Co. (1850–55); wealthy Ohio farmer (1855–64?)	BD of Springfield, Mt. Vernon and Pittsburgh RR (1856); also BD of Western and Atlantic RR (1873 through 1875), his son also on BD in this period	E
Zachariah Chandler, Mich. (Oct. 1875–March 1877)		U.S. Senator, Michigan (1857–75)	Wealthy former Detroit merchant, banker and land speculator		E

GRANT ADMINISTRATION (continued)

Officeholder	College Education	Prior Governmental Experience	Primary Occupation	Important Secondary Economic Affiliations	Family and Other Social Ties	Other Pertinent Information	Elite or Non-Elite Status
Minister to Great Britain							
John L. Motley, Mass. (June 1869–Dec. 1870)	Harvard Univ.	Onetime state legislator (1849–50)	Longtime Boston historian and writer		Member of one of Boston's top 50 families; father, Thos. Motley (a wealthy Boston merchant), on BD (1823–53) and VP (1854–60) of Mass. Hospital Life Insur. Co.; niece, Anna L. Motley, married son of late Abbott Lawrence (textiles and other interests)		E
Robert C. Schenck, Ohio (June 1871–March 1876)	Miami Univ.	Ohio Congressman (1863–71); Minister to Brazil (1851–53); Ohio Congressman (1843–51); former state legislator (1839–43)	Dayton, Ohio lawyer (early 1830s on); VP of American Central Rwy. (1856)				?

350

Edwards Pierrepont, N.Y. (July 1876–Dec. 1877)	Yale Univ.	U.S. Attorney General (1875–76); U.S. attorney, southern dist., N.Y. (1869–70); N.Y.C. judge (1857–60)	N.Y.C. lawyer (1846–75)	BD of Texas and Pacific Rwy., a line headed by T. A. Scott of Penn. RR (1871–74)

Minister to France

Elihu B. Washburne, Ill. (May 1869–Sept. 1877)	Maine Wesleyan Seminary (few months)	Ill. Congressman (1853–69); former longtime Whig and Republican leader, Ill.	Galena, Illinois lawyer (1830 on)	Washburne's kinsman, C.P. Chouteau, on BD of Illinois Central RR and Missouri-Pacific RR (late 1850s) and BD of Syracuse, Binghamton & New York RR (1865–69); another kinsman, Chas. Hempstead, on 1859 BD of Galena & Chicago Union RR; brothers, C.C. and W.D. Washburn, high officials, Minneapolis Mill Co. (1856 through 1877); W.D. Washburn on BD of Minnesota Valley RR (mid-1860s), Lake Superior & Miss. RR (early 1870s), P of Minneapolis & Duluth RR (early 1870s), and VP (1870–75) and P (1875 on) of Minneapolis & St. Louis RR

GRANT ADMINISTRATION (continued)

Officeholder	College Education	Prior Governmental Experience	Primary Occupation	Important Secondary Economic Affiliations	Family and Other Social Ties	Other Pertinent Information	Elite or Non-Elite Status
Minister to Germany							
George Bancroft, N.Y., orig. Mass. (1869–June 1874)	Harvard Univ.	U.S. Minister to Germany (1867–69)	SEE EARLIER ANDREW JOHNSON ADMINISTRATION ENTRY				E
J. C. Bancroft Davis, N.Y. (August 1874–Sept. 1877)	Harvard Univ.	Asst. Sec. of State (1869–74); former state legislator (1868–69); sec. American Legation, Great Britain (1849–52)	N.Y.C. lawyer (1844–49 and 1852–62); Amer. correspondent, *London Times* (1854–61)	BD of Erie Railway (at least 1865 to 1868)	Married daughter of James G. King (son of Rufus King); nephew of George Bancroft		E

HAYES ADMINISTRATION (1877–1881)

Officeholder	College Education	Prior Governmental Experience	Primary Occupation	Important Secondary Economic Affiliations	Family and Other Social Ties	Other Pertinent Information	Elite or Non-Elite Status
President							
Rutherford B. Hayes, Ohio (1877–81)	Kenyon College	Governor of Ohio (1868–72 and 1876–77); Ohio Congressman (1865–67)	Fremont, Ohio lawyer (1845–49); Cincinnati lawyer (1849–61); Fremont lawyer (1872–75)		Uncle, Sardis Birchard, a former wealthy Ohio businessman; brother-in-law, William A. Platt, on BD of Scioto Valley RR (1877)	High-ranking Civil War officer	E?
Secretary of State							
William M. Evarts, N.Y. (1877–81)	Yale Univ.	U. S. Attorney General (1868–69); see Andrew Johnson administration entry for other data	Ptr., NYC law firm of Evarts, Choate & Southmayd (1842 on)	BD of Consolidation Coal Co. (1872 to 1877)	Ptr., Charles F. Southmayd, on BD of New York Life Insur. & Trust Co. (1875 on); brother of other partner, Charles F. Choate, P of the Old Colony RR (1877 on, but BD and GC before that)		E

HAYES ADMINISTRATION (continued)

Officeholder	College Education	Prior Governmental Experience	Primary Occupation	Important Secondary Economic Affiliations	Family and Other Social Ties	Other Pertinent Information	Elite or Non-Elite Status
Secretary of Treasury							
John Sherman, Ohio (1877–81)		U. S. Senator, Ohio (1861–77); Ohio Congressman (1855–61)	Mansfield, Ohio lawyer (1844 on)	BD of Pittsburgh, Ft. Wayne and Chicago RR (1866 through 1881) and Atlantic and Great Western RR (at least 1865 up to 1866)		Brother of famous Civil War general	E
Attorney General							
Charles Devens, Mass. (1877–81)	Harvard Univ.	Mass. Superior or Supreme Court judge (1867–77); also former state legislator and govt. official	Worcester, Mass. lawyer (1854–61?); originally a Northfield and Greenfield, Mass. lawyer		Former law partner, Senator George F. Hoar, a close friend and nephew of William M. Evarts	Civil War officer (1861–66)	?

George W. McCrary, Iowa (March 1877–Dec. 1879)	Iowa Congressman (1869–77); former state legislator (late 1850s and 1861–65)	Keokuk, Iowa lawyer (1856 on)	BD of Des Moines Valley RR (up to 1868)	E
Alexander Ramsey, Minn. (Dec. 1879–March 1881)	Lafayette Col. (not complete)	U. S. Senator, Minn. (1863–75); Governor of Minnesota (1859–63); also former state legislator; governor of Minn. territory (1849–53); Penn. Congressman (1843–47) — St. Paul, Minn. lawyer (1853 on); Harrisburg, Penn. lawyer (1839–49?)	BD of Western RR of Minn. (1879 and perhaps previous years); before Civil War, BD of Minnesota & Northwestern RR; also one of the original incorporators of Northern Pacific Rwy.	E?

Secretary of Navy

Richard W. Thompson, Ind. (March 1877–Dec. 1880)	Ind. judge (1867–69); Ind. Congressman (1841–43 and 1847–49); former state legislator (mid-and late-1830s and 1840s)	Bedford, Ind. lawyer (1834–43); Terre Haute, Ind. lawyer (1843 on)	BD of Jeffersonville, Madison and Indianapolis RR, headed by T. A. Scott of PRR (1871 through 1880)	E

HAYES ADMINISTRATION (continued)

Officeholder	College Education	Prior Governmental Experience	Primary Occupation	Important Secondary Economic Affiliations	Family and Other Social Ties	Other Pertinent Information	Elite or Non-Elite Status
Nathan Goff, Jr. W. Va. (Jan.-March 1881)	Georgetown Univ. (not complete)	U. S. attorney for W. Va. (1868–81)	Clarksburg, W. Va. lawyer (1867 on?); also had coal, oil, gas, and real estate holdings			Civil War officer; unsuccessful Rep. candidate for governor of West Va. (1876 and 1880)	E?
Secretary of Interior							
Carl Schurz, Missouri (and Wisc.) (1877–81)		U. S. Senator, Mo. (1869–75); U.S. Minister to Spain (1861–62)	St. Louis newspaperman (late 1860s on); also popular public speaker			Civil War officer; also longtime Midwestern liberal Repub. (and abolitionist) leader	N-E
Minister to Great Britain							
John Welsh, Penn. (Dec. 1877–Aug. 1879)		Local govt. offl. (mid-1850s to at least early 1870s)	Longtime Phila. merchant (1820s on)	BD of Phila. Natl. Bank (1857 through 1879), Phila. Contribution-ship for Ins.	Father on BD of Phila. Natl. Bank (1803–54); son, J. Lowber Welsh, on BD of Erie RR and one of its successor companies, the New York, Lake Erie		E

				of Homes from Loss by Fire (1866 through 1879), Lehigh & Susquehanna RR, sub. of Lehigh Coal & Navigation Co. (late 1860s on)	& Western RR (1875 through 1879) and Syracuse, Geneva & Corning RR (up to 1876)
					Prominent Civil War officer E
James Russell Lowell, Mass. (March 1880 through 1881)	Harvard Univ.	U. S. Minister to Spain (1877–80)	Longtime Boston writer; Harvard Univ. prof. (1855 on); editor, *Atlantic Monthly* (1857–61) and editor of *North American Review* (1864–66)	Member of one of Boston's top 50 families; cousin, John A. Lowell, a longtime officer and dir. of the Boston Mfg. Co., Merrimack Co., Boott Mill, and Massachusetts Mutual Ins. Co.; BD of Suffolk Bank (1822–81) and Massachusetts Hospital Life Insur. Co. (1834–78), also at one time on BD of the Boston & Lowell RR; another cousin, Francis C. Lowell, on BD of Massachusetts Hospital Life Insur. Co. (1846–73); another kinsman, John Lowell Gardner, on BD of Chicago, Burlington & Quincy RR (1878 on)	

HAYES ADMINISTRATION (continued)

Officeholder	College Education	Prior Governmental Experience	Primary Occupation	Important Secondary Economic Affiliations	Family and Other Social Ties	Other Pertinent Information	Elite or Non-Elite Status
Minister to France							
Edward F. Noyes, Ohio (Sept. 1877–Aug. 1881)	Dartmouth College	Governor of Ohio (1871–73); Cincinnati solicitor and judge (late 1860s)	Cincinnati lawyer (1859 on?)			Prominent Civil War officer; also a friend and strong political backer of Hayes	N-E?
Minister to Germany							
Bayard Taylor, Penn. (May–Dec. 1878)		Sec. legation under U.S. Minister to Russia (1862–63)	Longtime author and translator; non-resident prof. German literature, Cornell Univ. (1870s)				N-E?
Andrew D. White, N.Y. (June 1879–Aug. 1881)	Yale Univ.	New York state legislator (1864–67)	First president of Cornell Univ. (late 1860s on); prof. of history, Univ. of Michigan (1857–63)	BD of New York Central RR (1866) and merchants Nat'l Bank & Trust Co., Syracuse (1863–66)	Father, Horace White, was a Syracuse banker and big holder of railroad securities; both father and uncle (Hamilton White) were former directors of the New York Central RR and the Buffalo and State Line RR		E

GARFIELD ADMINISTRATION (March–Sept. 1881)

Officeholder	College Education	Prior Governmental Experience	Primary Occupation	Important Secondary Economic Affiliations	Family and Other Social Ties	Other Pertinent Information	Elite or Non-Elite Status
President							
James A. Garfield, Ohio (March–Sept. 1881)	Williams College	Ohio Congressman (1863–81)	Hiram (?), Ohio lawyer (1865 on); P of Hiram College (1859–61)			Prominent Civil War officer	?
Secretary of State							
James G. Blaine, Maine (March–Dec. 1881)	Washington College, Pa.	U. S. Senator, Maine (1876–81); Maine Congressman (1863–76); also former state legislator (1859–62)	Augusta, Maine newspaperman (1854–60)	BD of Richmond & Allegheny RR (about 1880) and West Virginia Central & Pittsburgh Rwy. (June 1881 on)			E

359

GARFIELD ADMINISTRATION (continued)

Officeholder	College Education	Prior Governmental Experience	Primary Occupation	Important Secondary Economic Affiliations	Family and Other Social Ties	Other Pertinent Information	Elite or Non-Elite Status
Secretary of Treasury							
William Windom, Minn. (March-Nov., 1881)		U. S. Senator, Minn. (1870–81); Minn. Congressman (1859–69)	Winona, Minn. lawyer (1855 on)	BD of Northern Pacific RR (1869–74)			E?
Attorney General							
Wayne MacVeagh, Penn. (March-Nov. 1881)	Yale Univ.	U. S. Minister to Turkey (1870–72); dist. att., Chester Co., Penn. (1859–64)	Harrisburg, Penn. lawyer (1865–76); Phila. lawyer (1876–81)	BD of Northern Central RR, a subsidiary of the PRR (1875–77, GC thereafter)	Son-in-law of longtime Penn. Repub. party boss, Simon Cameron		E
Secretary of War							
Robert T. Lincoln, Ill. (March through Sept. 1881)	Harvard Univ.		Ptr., Chicago law firm of Isham, Lincoln & Beale (1872–81); ptr. in Scammon & Lincoln law firm (1867–72)	Recently appointed to BD of Pullman's Palace Car Co.(?)			E?

Position / Name	Education	Career	Notes	
Secretary of Navy				
William H. Hunt, La. (March 1881–April 1882)	Yale Univ. (not complete)	Assoc. judge, U.S. Court of Claims (1878–81); La. Attorney General (1876–77)	New Orleans lawyer (1844–78)	E?
Secretary of Interior				
Samuel J. Kirkwood, Iowa (March 1881–April 1882)		U. S. Senator, Iowa (1877–81); Governor of Iowa (1876–77); U.S. Senator (1866–67); Governor of Iowa (1860–64); also former state legislator (1856–59)	Longtime Iowa City lawyer; P of the Chicago, Omaha & St. Joseph RR (1870–75)	E?

As indicated in the text, President Garfield also appointed one major diplomatic official, Levi P. Morton, but since this figure served largely under President Arthur, he will be treated in the next part of this appendix.

ARTHUR ADMINISTRATION (Sept. 1881–1885)

Officeholder	College Education	Prior Governmental Experience	Primary Occupation	Important Secondary Economic Affiliations	Family and Other Social Ties	Other Pertinent Information	Elite or Non-Elite Status
President							
Chester A. Arthur, N. Y. (Sept. 1881–March 1885)	Union College	Vice-President of the United States (1881); Collector of Port of New York (1871–78)	N.Y.C. lawyer (1854–60, 1863–71, and 1878–81)			Former longtime political ally of state Repub. party boss, Roscoe Conkling	N-E
Secretary of State							
Frederick T. Frelinghuysen N. J. (Dec. 1881–March 1885)	Rutgers Univ.	U. S. Senator, N.J. (1871–77 and 1866–69); N.J. Attorney General (1861–66)	Newark, N. J. lawyer (1839 on)	BD of Central RR of N. J. (at least 1856 up to 1881), Mutual Benefit Life Ins. Co. (1878–85), Howard Savings Inst. of Newark (1857–85), Great Western RR of Ill. (1862–65); also GC (and director in early 1870s and possibly other years) of the Morris Canal & Banking Co.	Brother-in-law, J. N. A. Griswold, on BD of Chicago, Burlington & Quincy RR (1874 through 1885		E

Secretary of Treasury					
Charles J. Folger, N. Y. (Nov. 1881–Sept. 1884)	Hobart College	New York state judge (1870–81); U.S. Asst. Treasurer, NYC (1869–70); state legislator (1861–69); New York local govt. official (1844–55)	Geneva, N. Y. lawyer (1840 to 1869?)	Longtime ally of New York Repub. boss, Roscoe Conkling	?
Walter Q. Gresham, Ind. (Sept.–Oct. 1884)	Indiana Univ. (1 year)	U. S. Postmaster General (1882–84); U. S. district court judge, Ind. (1869–82); former state legislator (1860–61)	Corydon, Ind. lawyer (1873–82); New Albany, Ind. lawyer (1865–69)	Civil War officer	N-E?
Hugh McCulloch, N.Y. (orig. Ind.) (Dec. 1884–March 1885)	Bowdoin College (less than 2 years)	Member, U. S. Tariff Commission (1882–84); U.S. Sec. of Treasury (1865–69); U.S. Comptroller of Currency (1863–65)	Head, McCulloch & Co., N.Y.C. (1873–82); ptr., Jay Cooke & Co. (1869–73); P of State Bank of Indiana (1856–63); off. Fort Wayne branch of State Bank of Ind. (1835–56)	BD of Northern Pacific RR (1879–81) and Bowery Savings Bank, NYC (1880–81); also BD of Richmond & Allegheny RR (1879–81)	E

Officeholder	College Education	Prior Governmental Experience	Primary Occupation	Important Secondary Economic Affiliations	Family and Other Social Ties	Other Pertinent Information	Elite or Non-Elite Status
Attorney General							
Benjamin H. Brewster, Penn. (Jan. 1882–March 1885)	Princeton Univ.	Penn. Attorney General (1867–68; special prosecutor, Star Route fraud (1881)	Philadelphia lawyer (1838 on); longtime counsel of Penn. Repub. party boss, Simon Cameron			Married daughter of former Sec. of Treasury, Robert J. Walker	E
Secretary of War							
Robert T. Lincoln, Ill. (Sept. 1881–March 1885)	Harvard Univ.	U.S. Sec. of War (March–Sept., 1881)	Member, Chicago law firm of Isham, Lincoln & Beale (1872–81)	BD of Pullman's Palace Car Co. (1880–?)		Son of former President Abraham Lincoln	E?
Secretary of Navy							
William E Chandler N. H. (April 1882–March 1885)	no college (but grad. of Harvard Law School)	Asst. Sec. of Treasury (1865–67); high Repub. party official thereafter (Sec., Rep. Natl. Com., 1876 and 1880); also former state legislator (1863–65)	Lobbyist for Union Pacific RR (1867–80) and Northern Pacific RR (late 1860s to least mid-1870s)		Close friend of Austin Corbin, head of Long Island RR		E?

Interior					
Henry M. Teller, Colo. (April 1882–March 1885)	Alfred Univ., N.Y.	U. S. Senator, Colo. (1876–82)	Central City, Colo. lawyer (1861 on); P of Colorado Central Rwy. (1872–76, BD before that); also legal rept. of Union Pacific RR in Colorado (early 1870s, if not even later)		E?
Minister to Great Britain					
James Russell Lowell, Mass. (1880–May 1885)	SEE HAYES ADMINISTRATION ENTRY				E
Minister to France					
Levi P. Morton*, N.Y. (August 1881–May 1885)		N.Y. Congressman (1879–81)	P of Morton, Bliss & Co., N.Y.C. banking firm (1869 on); head of own N.Y.C. banking firm (1863–69)	BD of Delaware & Hudson Canal & RR Co. (1877–81), Burlington, Cedar Rapids & Northern RR (1876–77), New Orleans & Texas RR (1876–77), Milwaukee & St. Paul RR (1869–74), and Union Pacific RR (early 1870s)	E

*Actually appointed by Garfield, but served largely under Arthur.

ARTHUR ADMINISTRATION (continued)

Officeholder	College Education	Prior Governmental Experience	Primary Occupation	Important Secondary Economic Affiliations	Family and Other Social Ties	Other Pertinent Information	Elite or Non-Elite Status
Minister to Germany							
Aaron A. Sargent, Calif. (May 1882–June 1884)		U. S. Senator, Calif. (1873–79); Calif. Congressman (1861–63 and 1870–73)	Nevada City, Calif. lawyer (1854 on); also former Calif. newspaperman			Close friend and political ally of Calif. railroad magnate, Collis P. Huntington	E?
John A. Kasson, Iowa (Sept. 1884–June 1885)	Univ. of Vermont	Iowa Congressman (1863–1866, 1873–77, and 1881–84); U.S. Minister to Austria-Hungary (1877–81); also former state legislator (1868–72)	Des Moines, Iowa lawyer (1857 on); St. Louis, Mo. lawyer (1850–57)			Foe through most of 1870s of the Des Moines Regency	N-E?

FIRST CLEVELAND ADMINISTRATION (1885–1889)

Officeholder	College Education	Prior Governmental Experience	Primary Occupation	Important Secondary Economic Affiliations	Family and Other Social Ties	Other Pertinent Information	Elite or Non-Elite Status
President							
Grover Cleveland, N.Y. (1885–89)		Governor of New York (1883–85); mayor of Buffalo (1882–83); also former local government official	Ptr., Buffalo law firm of Cleveland & Bissell (1877–83); ptr., Bass, Cleveland & Bissell law firm (1873–77); ptr., Laning, Cleveland and Folsom law firm (1869–73)				?
Secretary of State							
Thomas F. Bayard, Del. (1885–89)		U.S. Senator, Del. (1869–85); U.S. attorney for Delaware (1853–54)	Wilmington, Del. lawyer (1851 on, except for a few years in Phila.)			Longtime close friend and ally of N.Y.C. financier August Belmont	E

FIRST CLEVELAND ADMINISTRATION (continued)

Secretary of Treasury

Officeholder	College Education	Prior Governmental Experience	Primary Occupation	Important Secondary Economic Affiliations	Family and Other Social Ties	Other Pertinent Information	Elite or Non-Elite Status
Daniel Manning, N.Y. (March 1885–Feb. 1887)			Longtime official, Albany newspaper, *Argus*; VP or P of the National Commerce Bank, Albany (early to mid-1880s, BD from 1873 on); VP or P, Nat'l. State Bank, Albany (1880–82)	BD of National State Bank, Albany (1869–80); BD of the Albany & Susquehanna RR (1880–81, public director from 1882 to 1884)		Longtime close friend and political ally of Samuel J. Tilden; Chrm., Dem. State Committee (1881–83)	E
Charles S. Fairchild, N.Y. (April 1887–March 1889)	Harvard Univ.	N. Y. Attorney-General (1876–78); Asst. Sec. of the Treasury (1885–87)	NYC lawyer (1880–85); Albany lawyer (1866–76)		Married niece of former Democratic presidential candidate, Horatio Seymour; father, S. T. Fairchild, for many years an attorney for the New York Central RR; father also on BD of Erie & Pittsburgh RR (1878 through 1889) and Union Trust Co. of N.Y.C. (at least 1881 up to 1888)		E

Office / Name	Education	Government positions	Legal career	Banking	Business / family	Other	Code
Attorney General Augustus H. Garland, Ark. (1885–89)	St. Joseph's College, Ky.	U.S. Senator, Ark. (1877–85); Governor of Arkansas (1874–76)	Little Rock, Ark. lawyer (1856 on, except for the Civil War years)		BD of Memphis and Little Rock Rwy. (1873–74)		E?
Secretary of War William C. Endicott, Mass. (1885–89)	Harvard Univ.	Mass. Supreme Court justice (1873–82)	Salem, Mass. lawyer (1850–73); P. Salem Bank (1858–64); some time shortly thereafter, P of Salem Nat'l. Bank	BD of Salem Savings Bank (apparently some time in 1870s through 1889)	Member of one of Boston's top 50 families; married daughter of George H. Peabody, nephew of the late banker, George Peabody; uncle, Francis B. Crowninshield, P of both the Boston & Lowell RR and the Nashua & Lowell RR (up to late 1870s) and also on BD of Suffolk Bank (1856–77)	Bd. Overseers, Harvard College (1875–82 and 1883–85); unsuccessful Democratic candidate for governor of Mass. (1884)	E

FIRST CLEVELAND ADMINISTRATION *(continued)*

Officeholder	College Education	Prior Governmental Experience	Primary Occupation	Important Secondary Economic Affiliations	Family and Other Social Ties	Other Pertinent Information	Elite or Non-Elite Status
Secretary of Navy							
William C. Whitney, N.Y. (1885–89)	Yale Univ.	N.Y.C. corporation counsel (1875–82)	N.Y.C. lawyer (1865 on); NYC traction figure (1884–on)	BD of New York, Chicago & St. Louis Rwy. (1882–84) and New York, Ontario & Western RR (1879–80)	Married sister of O. H. Payne, treas. of the Standard Oil Co. till 1884 (BD thereafter); father-in-law, Henry B. Payne, on BD of Lake Shore & Michigan Southern Rwy. (1869–83, and BD of one of its predecessor lines before that); H. B. Payne also on BD of Atlantic & Great Western RR (1880–81), Cincinnati, Wabash & Michigan Rwy. (1880–84), and Valley Rwy. (1879 through 1889)		E
Secretary of Interior							
Lucius Q. C. Lamar, Miss. orig. Ga.	Emory Univ., Ga.	U.S. Senator, Miss. (1877–85); Mississippi	Oxford, Miss. lawyer (1854 on); also prof. of law,	BD of Mississippi Central RR		Member of prominent Southern family	E

(March 1885–Jan. 1888)	Univ. of Mississippi (immediate pre- and post-Civil War years)	Congressman (1857–60 and 1873–77)		(1867–74) and its successor company, the New Orleans, St. Louis & Chicago RR (1874–76)		
William F. Vilas, Wisc. (Jan. 1888–March 1889)	Univ. of Wisconsin	U.S. Postmaster-General (1885–88)	Madison, Wisc. lawyer (1860 on); prof. of law, Univ. of Wisconsin (1868–85); Wisc. attorney for Chicago & Northwestern Rwy. (1874–84); also P of the Superior Lumber Co. (1885)	BD of Madison Mutual Insur. Co. (1875–80)	Democratic Natl. Committeeman of Wisc. (1876–86)	E

Secretary of Agriculture

Norman J. Colman, Missouri (one month, 1889)	no college (but grad. of Univ. of Louisville Law School)	U.S. Commissioner of Agriculture (1885–89); former Mo. state legislator; member Mo. State Board of Agriculture (1865 on)	Former (pre-1861) St. Louis, Mo. lawyer and, after Civil War, publisher of rural newsletter		Head of many agricultural organizations	N-E

FIRST CLEVELAND ADMINISTRATION (continued)

Officeholder	College Education	Prior Governmental Experience	Primary Occupation	Important Secondary Economic Affiliations	Family and Other Social Ties	Other Pertinent Information	Elite or Non-Elite Status
Minister to Great Britain							
Edward J. Phelps, Vt. (May 1885–Jan. 1889)	Middlebury College	2nd Comptroller of the U.S. Treasury (1851–53)	Burlington, Vt. lawyer (1845 on); prof. of law, Yale College (1881–85)	BD of Harlem Extension RR and (Vt.) predecessor line (up to 1870)		Longtime Vermont Democratic leader; P of American Bar Assn. (1880)	E?
Minister to France							
Robert M. McLane, Maryland (May 1885–May 1889)	U.S. Mil. Academy, West Point	Governor of Maryland (1883–85); Md. Congressman (1879–83 and 1847–51); Minister to Mexico (1859–61); United States Commissioner to China (1853–54)	Baltimore lawyer (1843–51 and late 1860s on); western counsel, Western Pacific RR (late 1850s to early or mid-1860s)	Brother, James L. McLane, P of Western Maryland RR (early 1870s) and BD of Baltimore & Ohio RR (1884 through 1889)	Father, former Del. pol. leader, Cabinet official, Minister to Great Britain, and president of B & O RR (last tie, 1837–48)		E

Minister to
Germany

Officeholder	College Education	Prior Governmental Experience	Primary Occupation	Important Secondary Economic Affiliations	Family and Other Social Ties	Other Pertinent Information	Elite or Non-Elite Status
George H. Pendleton, Kentucky (June 1885–April 1889)	Entered, but did not graduate from college	U.S. Senator, Ohio (1879–85); Ohio Congressman (1857–65); also former (pre–Civil War) state legislator	Cincinnati, Ohio lawyer (1847 on); P of Kentucky Central RR (1869–77)	BD of Kentucky Central RR (1877–80) and BD of Dayton & Cincinnati Shore Line RR (around 1856)	Nephew, Elliott H. Pendleton, on BD of Kentucky Central RR (through 1889) and BD of Commercial Bank, Cin. (1888–90)		E

HARRISON ADMINISTRATION (1889–1893)

Officeholder	College Education	Prior Governmental Experience	Primary Occupation	Important Secondary Economic Affiliations	Family and Other Social Ties	Other Pertinent Information	Elite or Non-Elite Status
President Benjamin Harrison, Ind. (1889–93)	Miami Univ.	U.S. Senator, Ind. (1881–87)	Indianapolis lawyer (1854–89)				?

Officeholder	College Education	Prior Governmental Experience	Primary Occupation	Important Secondary Economic Affiliations	Family and Other Social Ties	Other Pertinent Information	Elite or Non-Elite Status
Secretary of State							
James G. Blaine, Maine (March 1889–June 1892)	Washington College, Penn.	U.S. Senator, Maine (1876–81); U.S. Sec. of State (1881); Maine Congressman (1863–76)	Augusta, Maine newspaperman (1854–60)	BD of West Virginia Central and Pittsburgh Rwy. (1881–85 and Jan. 1891 on); also BD of Richmond & Allegheny RR (around 1880)	Son, Emmons Blaine, married (in Sept. 1889) sister of Cyrus H. McCormick, head of the International Harvester Co. (as it is now known)	Unsuccessful Republican presidential candidate (1884)	E
John W. Foster, Ind. (June 1892–Feb. 1893)	Indiana State Univ.	Several special diplomatic posts (1st part of Harrison administration); U.S. Minister to Spain (1883–85); Minister to Russia (1880–81); Minister to Mexico (1873–80)	Washington, D.C. lawyer (1885 to early 1890s); editor, *Evansville Daily Journal* (mid-1860s to early 1870s); Evansville, Ind. lawyer (late 1850s)			Former Indiana Repub. party leader	N-E

	Education				
Secretary of Treasury					
William Windom, N.Y., orig. Minn. (March 1889–Jan. 1891)		U.S. Sec. of the Treasury (1881); U.S. Senator, Minn. (1870–81 and 1881–83); Minn. Cong. (1858–69)	N.Y.C. lawyer (1883–89); P of Winona and Southwestern RR (1888–89); Winona, Minn. lawyer (1855–83)	BD of Northern Pacific Rwy. (1869–74)	E
Charles Foster, Ohio (Feb. 1891–March 1893)		Governor of Ohio (1879–83); Ohio Congressman (1871–79)	Fostoria, Ohio merchant; P (1874–79) and VP (about 1870 to 1874) of Lake Erie & Louisville RR	BD of Lake Erie & Western Rwy. (1880–83), Ohio Central RR (1879–82), Columbus, Hocking Valley & Toledo RR (1890 on), Cincinnati, Jackson & Mackinow RR (1888), and New York, Chicago & St. Louis RR (1882)	E
Attorney General					
William H. H. Miller, Ind. (1889–93)	Hamilton College, N.Y.		Indianapolis law partner of Benjamin Harrison (1874–89); Ft. Wayne lawyer (1866–74)		?

HARRISON ADMINISTRATION (continued)

Officeholder	College Education	Prior Governmental Experience	Primary Occupation	Important Secondary Economic Affiliations	Family and Other Social Ties	Other Pertinent Information	Elite or Non-Elite Status
Secretary of War							
Redfield Proctor, Vermont (March 1889–Nov. 1891)	Dartmouth College	Governor of Vermont (1878–80); Lt. Gov. (1876–78); also former state legislator (four years before Civil War and 1888–89)	P of Vermont Marble Co. (1880 on); also P (up to 1889) of Clarenden & Pittsford RR; Rutland lawyer (late 1860s)				E?
Stephen B. Elkins, W.Va. (Dec. 1891–March 1893)	Univ. of Missouri	New Mexico Congressman (1873–77); U.S. attorney, N.M. (1867–70); also former N.M. local government official	VP of West Virginia Central & Pittsburgh Rwy. (1881 through 1893); P of Santa Fe. Nat'l. Bank (1864–77); former N.M. lawyer and mine owner	BD of St. Louis Southwestern Rwy. (1891)	Married daughter of Henry G. Davis, wealthy W. Va. businessman and U.S. Senator (1871–83)	Close friend and political associate of James G. Blaine	E
Secretary of Navy							
Benjamin F. Tracy, N.Y. (1889–93)		New York state judge (1881–83);	N.Y.C. law partner in firm of Tracy,	BD of (small) Brooklyn &		Longtime friend of New York	E

		U.S. attorney, eastern district, N.Y. (1866–73); also former state legislator	MacFarland, Boardman & Platt (1885 on); N.Y.C. lawyer (1865 on, except years in government service); upstate N.Y. lawyer (late 1850s)	Brighton Beach Rwy. and predecessor firms (1878–89); also BD of American Loan & Trust Co., N.Y.C. (1890)	Rep. party boss, Thomas C. Platt
Secretary of Interior					
John W. Noble, Missouri (1889–93)	Yale Univ.	U.S. attorney for Eastern district, Mo. (1867–70)	St. Louis, Mo. lawyer (1865 on); Keokuk, Iowa lawyer (1856–61)	Brother, Henry C. Noble, on BD of Columbus & Hocking Valley RR (1874–81) and Columbus & Toledo RR (early 1870s)	E?
Secretary of Agriculture					
Jeremiah M. Rusk, Wisc. (1889–93)		Governor of Wisconsin (1882–89); Wisc. Congressman (1871–77); former state legislator and local government official	Owner, Wisc. stage line and various other enterprises; also co-owner of a Wisc. bank.		?

HARRISON ADMINISTRATION (continued)

Officeholder	College Education	Prior Governmental Experience	Primary Occupation	Important Secondary Economic Affiliations	Family and Other Social Ties	Other Pertinent Information	Elite or Non-Elite Status
Minister to Great Britain							
Robert T. Lincoln, Ill. (May 1889–May 1893)	Harvard Univ.	U.S. Sec. of War (1881–85)	Ptr., Chicago law firm of Isham, Lincoln & Beale (1872–81 and 1885–89)	BD of Pullman's Palace Car Co. (1880–81 and 1885–89?)			E
Minister to France							
Whitelaw Reid, N.Y. (May 1889–March 1892)	Miami Univ., Ohio		Editor or publisher of *New York Tribune* (1869 on); also P of Mergenthaler Linotype Co.	BD of Mercantile Trust Co., N.Y.C. (1888 on)	Father-in-law, Darius O. Mills, P of Virginia & Truckee RR, Nevada (1886–93) and on BD of Metropolitan Trust Co., N.Y.C. (at least 1887–92), Farmers Loan & Trust Co., N.Y.C. (at least 1889–92), Lake Shore & Michigan Southern Rwy. (1879 through 1893), Chicago & Northwestern Rwy. (1879 up to 1888), Duluth & Iron Range RR (1887–93), Minnesota		E

E

Name / Dates	Education	Government	Business	Directorships	Social / Family	Other
T. Jefferson Coolidge, Mass. (June 1892–May 1893)	Harvard Univ.	Commissioner, Pan-American Congress, 1889 (a special ad hoc appointment)	Boston financier and entrepreneur; longtime treas. of Amoskeag Mfg. Co., Lawrence Mfg. Co., and Boott Mills	BD of Boston & Lowell RR (1875 Chicago, Burlington & Quincy RR (1876 through 1893), Kansas City, Ft. Scott & Memphis RR (1884–93), St. Paul Minneapolis & Manitoba RR (1888), Merchants Nat'l. Bank, Boston (around 1890), Massachusetts Hospital Life Insur. Co. (1878 through 1893), and Old Colony Trust Co., Boston (1890 on) Iron Co. (at least 1887 on) and Bank of New York (1881 on); brother-in-law, Ogden Mills, on BD of New York, Lake Erie & Western RR (1884–1893), Chicago & Eastern Ill. RR (1886–88)	Member of one of Boston's top 50 families; married daughter of William Appleton; son, T. J. Coolidge, Jr., P of Old Colony Trust Co. (1890 on) and BD of Manhattan Trust Co., N.Y.C. (at least 1888 through 1893) and GE (1892 on)	Bd. Overseers, Harvard Univ. (1886 through 1893)

Officeholder	College Education	Prior Governmental Experience	Primary Occupation	Important Secondary Economic Affiliations	Family and Other Social Ties	Other Pertinent Information	Elite or Non-Elite Status
Minister to Germany							
William W. Phelps, N.Y. (Sept. 1889–June 1893)	Yale Univ.	N.Y. Congressman (1873–75 and 1883–89); U.S. Minister to Austria–Hungary (1881–82)	Manager, family business interests and investments (1869 on); N.Y.C. lawyer (up to 1869)	BD of Delaware, Lackawanna & Western RR (1867–88), New Haven & Northampton RR (late 1860s–82), International & Great Northern RR (1880–81), Farmers Loan & Trust Co., N.Y.C. (1869–93), U.S. Trust Co., N.Y.C. (at least 1883 through 1893), and National City Bank N.Y.C., (up through 1893)	Long-deceased father, J. J. Phelps, a long-time major railroad figure	Longtime friend and political ally of James G. Blaine	E

SECOND CLEVELAND ADMINISTRATION (1893–1897)

Officeholder	College Education	Prior Governmental Experience	Primary Occupation	Important Secondary Economic Affiliations	Family and Other Social Ties	Other Pertinent Information	Elite or Non-Elite Status
President							
Grover Cleveland, N.Y. (1893–97)		President of the United States (1885–89); Governor of New York (1883–85); also former local government official	Member (either partner or "of counsel") of N.Y.C. law firm of Bangs, Stetson, Tracy & MacVeagh (1889–93); ptr. in Buffalo law firm of Cleveland & Bissell and its predecessor concern (1873–83)				E
Secretary of State							
Walter Q. Gresham, Ind. (March 1893–May 1895)	Indiana Univ. (1 year)	U.S. Circuit Court judge (1869–82 and 1884–93); U.S. Sec. of Treasury (one month, 1884); Postmaster-General (1883–84)	New Albany, Ind. lawyer (1865–69); Corydon, Ind. lawyer (1854–60)			Former prominent Repub. leader who bolted to the Democratic party in 1892	N-E?

Officeholder	College Education	Prior Governmental Experience	Primary Occupation	Important Secondary Economic Affiliations	Family and Other Social Ties	Other Pertinent Information	Elite or Non-Elite Status
Richard Olney, Mass. (June 1895–March 1897)	Brown Univ.	U.S. Attorney General (1893–95); Mass. state legislator (one term, 1870s)	Boston corporation lawyer (1859 on)	BD of Old Colony Trust Co., Boston (1890 through 1897); see Attorney General entry for other railroad directorship ties			E
Secretary of Treasury							
John G. Carlisle, Kentucky (1893–97)		U.S. Senator, Ky. (1890–93); Ky. Congressman (1877–90); Lt.-Gov. of Ky. (1871–75); also former state legislator	Covington, Ky. lawyer (1858 on)				N-E?
Attorney General							
Richard Olney, Mass. (March 1893–June 1895)	Brown Univ.	Mass. state legislator (1873–74)	Boston corporation lawyer (1859 on)	BD of Boston & Maine RR (1884 through 1897) and one of its predecessors, the			E

Judson Harmon, Ohio (June 1895–March 1897)	Denison Univ.	Municipal judge, Ohio (1878–87)	Cincinnati lawyer (about 1870 on); ptr. in law firm known as Hoadly, Johnson & Colston (1887–95)	BD of Dayton, Ft. Wayne and Chicago RR (1889–90), Ohio Southwtn. RR (1893–94), and Cincinnati, Washington & Baltimore RR (1887–89, when merged into B & O RR); also GC of Baltimore & Ohio Southwestern RR (1890–94)

Eastern RR (1879–84), the Chicago, Burlington & Quincy RR (1889 through 1897), the Portland and Rochester RR (1883–86), Philadelphia, Wilmington & Baltimore RR (1877–81), and Old Colony Trust Co. (1890 through 1897)

E

SECOND CLEVELAND ADMINISTRATION (continued)

Officeholder	College Education	Prior Governmental Experience	Primary Occupation	Important Secondary Economic Affiliations	Family and Other Social Ties	Other Pertinent Information	Elite or Non-Elite Status
Secretary of War							
Daniel S. Lamont, N.Y. (1893–97)	Union College (not complete)	Private secretary, Governor and President Cleveland (1883–89); chief clerk, N.Y. Dept. of State (1875–82)	N.Y.C. business figure (1889–93); P of Houston, West Street and Pavoma Ferry RR (1889–90)	BD of New York Security & Trust Co. (1889–93), Continental Nat'l. Bank, N.Y.C. (1891–93), Penna. Steel Refining Co. (up to 1893), and Tennessee Coal, Iron & RR Co. (1889–90)			E
Secretary of Navy							
Hilary A. Herbert, Ala. (1893–97)	Univ. of Alabama (2 years)	Alabama Congressman (1877–93)	Montgomery, Ala. lawyer (1872 on); Greenville, Ala. lawyer (1856–61 and 1864–72)			Close friend of Mayer Lehman	E?

Secretary of Interior

Name	Education	Occupation	Business	Other connections	Political	Party
Hoke Smith, Ga. (March 1893–Aug. 1896)		Owner and publisher, *Atlanta Journal* (1887 on); Atlanta lawyer (1873 on)	BD of Georgia, Carolina & Northern RR (at least 1890 to 1893) and Capital City Bank, Atlanta (at least 1890–1893)	Married niece of former Secretary of the Treasury, Howell Cobb	Cleveland supporter at 1892 Democratic Nat'l. Convention	E
David R. Francis, Missouri (Sept. 1896–March 1897)	Washington Univ., St Louis	Governor of Missouri (1888–92); mayor of St. Louis (1885–87)	St. Louis merchant (1870s on); VP of Mississippi Valley Trust Co., St. Louis (up to 1896)	BD of Merchants-Laclede Natl. Bank, St. Louis (1894–96)	Father-in-law, John D. Perry, P of Kansas Pacific Rwy. (1867–70, BD from 1870 to 1877), BD of Illinois & St. Louis RR & Coal Co. (1880–88), Mississippi Valley Trust Co. (up through 1897), and Merchants-Laclede Natl. Bank, St. Louis (early and mid-1890s)		E

Officeholder	College Education	Prior Governmental Experience	Primary Occupation	Important Secondary Economic Affiliations	Family and Other Social Ties	Other Pertinent Information	Elite or Non-Elite Status
Secretary of Agriculture							
J. Sterling Morton, Nebraska (1893–97)	Union College, N.Y.	Former (pre–Civil War) Neb. state legislator; P of Nebraska State Bd. of Agriculture (1873–75, board member before that); onetime (1857–61) secretary of the Nebraska territory	Nebraska newspaperman (1854 on)		Son, Paul Morton, VP of Atchison, Topeka & Santa Fe Rwy. (1896 on), BD of Colorado Fuel & Iron Co. (1890–96) and Indiana, Illinois and Iowa RR (1893 through 1897); son, Joy Morton, head of Joy Morton & Co. (1885 on) and BD of American Trust and Savings Bank, Chicago (at least 1893 on)	Longtime Democratic state party leader	E
Ambassador to Great Britain							
Thomas F. Bayard, Del. (June 1893–March 1897)		U.S. Sec. of State (1885–89); U. S. Senator, Del. (1869–85)	Wilmington, Del. lawyer (1871 on)		Member of longtime prominent Delaware family; son-in-law, S. D. Warren, a partner in S. D. Warren & Co., a major New England paper mfg. enterprise		E

Ambassador to France						
James B. Eustis, La. (May 1893–May 1897)	Harvard Univ.	U. S. Senator, La. (1877–79 and 1885–91); also former state legislator	New Orleans, La. lawyer (1856 on); law prof. (1879–84) at Univ. of Louisiana (now Tulane)	Married daughter of prominent La. planter	Major Cleveland supporter in 1892	E?
Ambassador to Germany						
Theodore Runyon, N. J. (June 1893–Jan. 1896)	Yale Univ.	Chancellor of New Jersey (1873–87); mayor of Newark (1864–65); Newark corp. counsel (1856–64)	Newark, N.J. lawyer (1846–56, 1865–73, and 1887–93); P of Manufacturers Natl. Bank, Newark (1871–73)	BD of Newark Gas Light Co. (at least 1869 to 1893)		E
Edwin F. Uhl, Mich. (May 1896–1897)	Univ. of Michigan	Asst. Sec. of State (1893–96); mayor of Grand Rapids, Mich. (1890–92)	Ptr., Grand Rapids law firm of Norris & Uhl (1876–93); P of Grand Rapids Natl. Bank (roughly 1880 to early or mid-1890s); Ypsilanti, Mich. lawyer (1864–76)	BD of Detroit, Eel River & Illinois RR (1874–77)		?

McKINLEY ADMINISTRATION (March 1897–Sept. 1901)

Officeholder	College Education	Prior Governmental Experience	Primary Occupation	Important Secondary Economic Affiliations	Family and Other Social Ties	Other Pertinent Information	Elite or Non-Elite Status
President							
William McKinley, Ohio (March 1897–Sept. 1901)	Allegheny College, Penn. (not complete)	Governor of Ohio (1892–96); Ohio Congressman (1877–83 and 1885–91); prosecuting attorney, Stark County, Ohio (1869–71)	Canton, Ohio lawyer (1867 on)	BD of Central Savings Bank, Canton (1895–96)	Married daughter of James A. Saxton, prominent Canton businessman		E?
Secretary of State							
John Sherman, Ohio (March 1897–April 1898)		U. S. Senator, Ohio (1861–77 and 1881–97); U. S. Secretary of the Treasury (1877–81); Ohio Congressman (1855–61)	Mansfield, Ohio lawyer (1844 on)	BD of Pittsburgh, Fort Wayne and Chicago Railroad (1866–98)	Son-in-law, Colgate Hoyt, on BD of the Missouri, Kansas & Texas Rwy. (1890 thru 1898), Chicago Terminal Transfer Railroad Co. (1897–98), and Spanish-American Iron Co. (least 1897 on)		E

Name	Education	Position	Other	Business affiliations	Notes	
William R. Day, Ohio (April-Sept. 1898)	Univ. of Michigan	Asst. Sec. of State (1897–98); municipal judge, Canton (1886–87)	member, Canton law firm of Lynch & Day (1872–97)	BD of City National Bank, Canton (at least 1893 through 1898)	Father, former Chief Justice, Ohio Supreme Court; married daughter of Louis Schaefer, Canton businessman; ptr., Wm. A. Lynch, on BD of Connotton Valley RR (1880–83 and Cleveland & Canton RR (1887–88), off. of Pittsburgh, Akron & Western RR (early 1890s); pres. of Canton & Massillon Elec. Rwy. (1896)	Longtime close friend of William McKinley	E?
John Hay, Ohio (Sept. 1898 through 1901)	Brown Univ.	U.S. Ambassador to Great Britain (1897–98); Asst. Sec. of State (1879–81); also held number of minor diplomatic posts (late 1860s); N.Y. journalist, *New York Tribune* (early 1870s); also former writer and author	Overseer of deceased father-in-law's investments (1883–97); Ohio businessman (1875–83); asst. private sec. or aide, President Lincoln (1861–65)	BD of Western Union Telegraph Co. (1880–1900) and Cleveland, Lorain & Wheeling RR (1884–85)	Former father-in-law, Amasa Stone (died 1883), longtime dir. of Lake Shore & Michigan Southern RR (up to 1883); brother-in-law, Samuel Mather, longtime high off. of Pickands, Mather & Co., VP of American Steel Barge Co., P of Minnesota Steamship Co., and dir. of Federal Steel Co., Lorain Steel Co., and many major banks in Cleveland		E

Officeholder	College Education	Prior Governmental Experience	Primary Occupation	Important Secondary Economic Affiliations	Family and Other Social Ties	Other Pertinent Information	Elite or Non-Elite Status
Secretary of Treasury							
Lyman J. Gage, Ill. (1897 through 1901)			P of 1st National Bank of Chicago (1891–97, VP from 1882 to 1891)			P, American Bankers Assn. (1883); a Democrat; former head of Chicago predecessor of National Civic Federation	E
Attorney General							
Joseph McKenna, Calif. (March 1897–Jan. 1898)	Benicia Collegiate Inst., Cal. (early college years in Penn.)	Judge, U.S. Circuit Court of Appeals (1892–97); Calif. Congressman (1885–92); district attorney, Solano Co. (1866–70): also former state legislator	Fairfield and Benicia, Calif. lawyer (1865–92)			Longtime friend and associate of late Leland Stanford and William McKinley	?

John W. Griggs, N.J. (Jan. 1898–March 1901)	Lafayette College	Governor of New Jersey (1896–98); also former longtime state and local govt. official	Paterson, N.J. lawyer (1871 on); also P of Paterson Natl. Bank (1894–1901, BD before that)	BD of Morris County Railroad (1891–95)	E
Philander C. Knox, Penn. (April 1901 on)	Mt. Union College, Ohio	Pittsburgh lawyer (1875 on); partner of James H. Reed (1877–1901)	GC, Carnegie Steel Co.; BD of Pittsburgh Natl. Bank of Commerce (at least 1888 through 1901), Union Trust Co., Pittsburgh (1895 through 1901), Pittsburgh & Lake Erie RR (1897 through 1901)	Ptr., Jas. H. Reed, president of Bessemer & Lake Erie RR (1897 through 1901) and BD of Lake Shore & Michigan Southern RR (1891–98)	E

Officeholder	College Education	Prior Governmental Experience	Primary Occupation	Important Secondary Economic Affiliations	Family and Other Social Ties	Other Pertinent Information	Elite or Non-Elite Status
Secretary of War							
Russell A. Alger, Mich. (March 1897–August 1899)		Governor of Michigan (1885–87)	Longtime Mich. businessman; Grand Rapids lumber business (1860 on); P of Detroit & Rio Grande Cattle Co.; P of Detroit, Bay City & Alpena RR (1884–94); P of Alpena & Northern RR, sub. of Detroit & Mackinac RR (1895)	BD of Manistee Lumber Co. (at least 1897 on), Union Lumber Co., Cleveland (at least 1897 on), State Savings Bank of Detroit (1894 on), U.S. Express Co., N.Y.C. (at least 1897 on), Detroit Savings Bank (1895 through 1899), Mansitique Rwy. (1889 through 1899), and Detroit Natl. Bank (at least 1888–97)			E

E

Name	Education	Government	Law/Business	Directorships	Family
Elihu Root, N.Y. (August 1899 through 1901)	Hamilton College	U.S. attorney for southern district of N.Y. (1883–85)	N.Y.C. lawyer, various firms (1867 on); ptr., N.Y.C. law firm of Root, Howard, Winthrop & Stimson (1897–99)	BD of National Bank of North America (at least 1888–1901), Morton Trust Co. (1900 on), Bank of New Amsterdam (at least 1888 on), State Trust Co., NYC (at least 1899–1900), Louisville, New Albany & Chicago RR (1885–89), and Hannibal & St. Joseph RR (1879–83)	Married daughter of Salem H. Wales, N.Y.C. lawyer

Officeholder	College Education	Prior Governmental Experience	Primary Occupation	Important Secondary Economic Affiliations	Family and Other Social Ties	Other Pertinent Information	Elite or Non-Elite Status
Secretary of Navy							
John D. Long, Mass. (1897 through 1901)	Harvard Univ.	Mass. Congressman (1883–89); Governor of Mass. (1880–83); Lt. Gov., Mass. (1879–80); also former state legislator (1873–77)	Boston lawyer (1862 on)	BD of U.S. Trust Co., Boston (early 1901 on)			E?
Secretary of Interior							
Cornelius N. Bliss, N.Y. (March 1897–Feb. 1899)			Head, mercantile firm of Bliss, Fabyian & Co., N.Y.C. (1866 on); VP, Fourth Natl. Bank, N.Y.C. (at least 1891 up to 1897, BD through 1899)	BD of Equitable Life Assur. Society (1884 through 1899), Central Trust Co., N.Y.C. (at least 1889 through 1899),		Treasurer of Rep. Natl. Committee (1892); Chrm., Rep. State Com. (late 1880s); P, American Protective Tariff League	E

Ethan A. Hitchcock, Missouri (Feb. 1899 through 1901)	U.S. Ambassador to Russia (1897–99)	Longtime prominent St. Louis businessman; P of Crystal Plate Glass Co. (1888 till 1895 when merged into Pittsburgh Plate Glass Co.); P of Chicago & Texas RR and predecessor concern, Grand Tower and Carbondale RR (1876 to 1898, when merged into Illinois Central RR)	BD of Merchants Bank, St. Louis (at least 1888 to 1897) and Pittsburgh Plate Glass Co. (1895 to 1900)	Home Insur. Co., N.Y.C. (late 1890s, and perhaps earlier), and American Cotton Co. (late 1890s)	Brother, Henry Hitchcock, on BD of Mississippi Valley Trust Co., St. Louis (1894 to 1900), and Continental Trust Co., N.Y.C. (up to early 1890s)

Officeholder	College Education	Prior Governmental Experience	Primary Occupation	Important Secondary Economic & Organizational Affiliations	Family and Other Social Ties	Other Pertinent Information	Elite or Non-Elite Status
Secretary of Agriculture							
James Wilson, Iowa (1897 through 1901)	Iowa College (later known as Grinnell)	Iowa Congressman (1873–77 and 1883–1885); member Iowa Railroad Commission (1878–83); also former state legislator (1867–71)	Head, agricultural experiment station, Iowa State College (1891–97; also longtime Iowa farmer			friend of Wm. B. Allison	N-E?
Ambassador to Great Britain							
John Hay, Ohio (May 1897–Sept. 1898)	Brown University	SEE PRECEDING SECRETARY OF STATE ENTRY					E
Joseph H. Choate, N.Y.	Harvard Univ.		Ptr., N.Y.C. law firm of Evarts,	BD of N.Y. Life Insur. &	Brother, Chas. F. Choate, P of Old Colony	Prominent N.Y.C. civic	E

396

(March, 1899 through 1901)

Choate, Sherman & Leon (and predecessor firms, about 1860 on)

Trust Co. (1898 on); longtime attorney for Astor interests

RR until merger in 1893 into N.Y., New Haven & Hartford RR (of which then a dir. through 1905); also VP or dir. of Mass. Hospital Life Insur. Co. (1889–1900)

and Repub. leader (but no formal govermental office)

E

Ambassador to France

Horace Porter, N.Y. (May 1897 through 1901)

U.S. Military Academy

Private sec. to President U.S. Grant (1869–72)

VP of Pullman's Palace Car Co. (1872–96)

BD of Equitable Life Assurance Society (1872–97), Atlanta, Knoxville & Northern RR (1897 through 1901), St. Louis and San Francisco Rwy. (1880–89), and Hannibal & St. Joseph RR (1877–81)

397

Officeholder	College Education	Prior Governmental Experience	Primary Occupation	Important Secondary Economic Affiliations	Family and Other Social Ties	Other Pertinent Information	Elite or Non-Elite Status
Ambassador to Germany							
Andrew D. White, N.Y. (June 1897 through 1901)	Yale Univ.	U.S. Ambassador to Russia (1892–94); also Minister to Germany (1879–81)	P of Cornell University (1867–85)				E

THEODORE ROOSEVELT ADMINISTRATION (Sept. 1901–March 1909)

Officeholder	College Education	Prior Governmental Experience	Primary Occupation	Important Secondary Economic Affiliations	Family and Other Social Ties	Other Pertinent Information	Elite or Non-Elite Status
President							
Theodore Roosevelt, N.Y. (Sept. 1901–March 1909)	Harvard Univ.	Vice-President of the United States (March–Sept. 1901); Governor of New York (1899–1900); Asst. Sec. of Navy (1897–98); president of N.Y.	Former writer (history) and N.Y.C. civic leader		Brother-in-law, Douglas Robinson, on BD of Astor Natl. Bank (1902–09) and Atlantic Mutual Insur. Co. (1902–09); cousin, W. Emlen Roosevelt, on BD of Astor Natl. Bank (or Trust Co., 1899–1906),		E

		Board of Police Com'rs. (1895–97); member, U.S. Civil Service Board (1889–95); former New York Assemblyman (1882–84)			Chemical Natl. Bank least 1894–1909), Gallatin Natl. Bank (at least 1893–1909), N.Y. Life Insur. & Trust Co. (1893–1909), Union Trust Co. (least 1894–1909), Mexican Telegraph Co. (at least 1894–1909), Central & South American Tel. Co. (1905–08, 1909 VP), Mobile & Ohio RR (1900 through 1909), and New York, Chicago & St. Louis RR (1900–07)
Secretary of State					
John Hay, Ohio (1901–July, 1905)	Brown Univ.	U.S. Sec. of State (1898–1901); Ambassador to Great Britain (1897–98); Asst. Sec. of State (1879–81)	Overseer of deceased father-in-law's investment (1883–97); Ohio businessman (1875–83); journalist, *N.Y. Tribune* (early 1870s); also former writer and author	BD of Western Union Telegraph Co. (1880–1900) and Cleveland, Lorain & Wheeling RR (1884–85)	Brother-in-law, Samuel Mather, high off. in Pickands, Mather & Co., and dir. (or EC member) of Lackawanna Steel Co. (1902 on), National Civic Federation (1903–05), Federal Steel Co. and Lorain Steel Co. (1899–1901), and many major banks in Cleveland; W. G. Mather on BD of Wheeling and Lake Erie RR (1900–05);

THEODORE ROOSEVELT ADMINISTRATION (continued)

Officeholder	College Education	Prior Governmental Experience	Primary Occupation	Important Secondary Economic Affiliations	Family and Other Social Ties	Other Pertinent Information	Elite or Non-Elite Status
					daughter, Helen Hay, wed (in 1902) Payne Whitney, son of Wm. C. Whitney; Payne Whitney on BD of Great Northern Paper Co. (1903–05); his brother, H. P. Whitney (who married a member of Vanderbilt family) on BD of Guaranty Trust Co. (1899–1905); Wm. C. Whitney on BD of Mutual Life Insur. Co. (1895–1904), Morton Trust Co. (at least 1901–04), Natl. Bank of Commerce (at least 1901–04), Western Natl. Bank (1903), Consolidated Gas Co. of N.Y. (1900–04), and Cuba Co. (1900–04)		

400

					E
Elihu Root, N.Y. (July 1905–Jan. 1909)	Hamilton College	U.S. Sec. of War (1899–Feb. 1904); U.S. attorney for southern district of N.Y. (1883–85)	BD of Mutual Life Insur. Co. (1901–05) Natl. Bank of Commerce (1903–05), Morton Trust Co. (1900–05), Continental Ins. Co., N.Y.C. (1902–05), and a number of other banks and railroads before 1901		E
Robert Bacon, N.Y. (Jan.–March 1909)	Harvard Univ.	Asst. Sec. of State (1905–09)	Ptr., J. P. Morgan & Co. (1894–1903); ptr., E. Rollin Morse & Brother, Boston (1883–94)	BD of Federal Steel Co. (1898–1903), U.S. Steel Corp. (1903–05), Amalgamated Copper Co. (1899–1903), National City Bank, N.Y.C. (1897–1902), Northern Securities Co. (1902–05), Manhattan Trust Co. (1905 through 1909), Bank for Savings in N.Y.C. (1903 through 1909), North American Co. (1901–05), Erie RR (1901–05), Hocking Valley Rwy. (1901–05), Northern Pacific RR (1896–1901), and National Tube Co. (1899–1903)	Close friend of Theodore Roosevelt E

THEODORE ROOSEVELT ADMINISTRATION (continued)

Officeholder	College Education	Prior Governmental Experience	Primary Occupation	Important Secondary Economic Affiliations	Family and Other Social Ties	Other Pertinent Information	Elite or Non-Elite Status
Secretary of Treasury							
Lyman J. Gage, Ill. (Sept. 1901–Jan. 1902)		Sec. of Treasury (1897–1901)	P of 1st National Bank of Chicago (1891–97, VP from 1882 to 1891)				E (n/c)
Leslie M. Shaw, Iowa (Jan. 1902–March 1907)	Cornell College, Iowa	Governor of Iowa (1898–1902)	Ptr., Denison, Iowa law firm of Shaw and Kuchnle (up to 1898); also former P of Bank of Denison (1890–1902)				?
Geroge B. Cortelyou, N.Y. (March 1907–March 1909)		U.S. Postmaster General (1905–07); Sec. of Commerce & Labor (1903–04); exec. assistant to both Presidents Cleveland and McKinley (1895–1903); clerk and stenographer, U.S. Customs Service and Post Office Dept. (1887–95)					N-E?

Attorney
General

Philander C. Knox, Penn. (1901–June 1904)	Mt. Union College, Ohio	U.S. Attorney General (April, 1901 on)	Pittsburgh lawyer (1875 on); partner of James H. Reed (1877–1901)	Former GC, Carnegie Steel Co.; BD of Pittsburgh National Bank of Commerce (at least 1888 through 1904), Union Trust Co. of Pittsburgh (1895 through 1904), and Union Savings Bank (1903–04), and Pittsburgh & Lake Erie RR (1897–1901)	Ptr., J. H. Reed of Pittsburgh, on BD of Bessemer & Lake Erie RR (1897 through 1904) and U.S. Steel Corp. (1902 through 1904)	E
William H. Moody, Mass. (July 1904–Dec. 1906)	Harvard Univ.	Sec. of Navy (1902–04); Mass. Congressman (1895–1902); U.S. attorney for eastern district, Mass. (1890–95)	Haverhill, Mass. lawyer (1878 on)	BD of Shoe & Leather Natl. Bank, Boston (1891–93)		E?

Officeholder	College Education	Prior Governmental Experience	Primary Occupation	Important Secondary Economic Affiliations	Family and Other Social Ties	Other Pertinent Information	Elite or Non-Elite Status
Charles J. Bonaparte, Md. (Dec. 1906–March 1909)	Harvard Univ.	Sec. of Navy (1905–06); member, U.S. Bd. of Indian Commissioners (1902–04)	Baltimore lawyer (1874 on)	BD of Real Estate Trust Co., Baltimore (1899–1900)	Brother-in-law, Thomas M. Day, Jr. on BD of American Sheet Steel Co. (up to 1903), sub. since 1901 of U.S. Steel Corp.	Exec. com. of Natl. Civic Federation (1900–08); Chrm., Civil Service Reform League (up to 1905); Bd. Overseers, Harvard Univ. (1891–1903)	E
Secretary of War							
Elihu Root, N.Y. (1901–Feb. 1904)	Hamilton College	Sec. of War (1899–1901); U.S. attorney for southern district of N.Y. (1883–85)	N.Y.C. lawyer, various firms (1867 on); ptr., N.Y.C. firm of Root, Howard, Winthrop & Stimson (1897–99)	BD of Morton Trust Co. (1900–04), Continental Insur. Co. (1902–05), Western Natl. Bank (1903), and a number of other banks and railroads before 1900			E

William H. Taft, Ohio (Feb. 1904–June 1908)

Yale Univ.

President, U.S. Philippine Commission (1900–04); U.S. Circuit Court judge (1892–1900); U.S. Solicitor-General (1890–92); Ohio Superior Court judge (1887–90)

Dean, Univ. of Cincinnati Law School (1896–1900); Cincinnati lawyer (1880–87)

Brother, Henry W. Taft, N.Y.C. lawyer, on BD of National RR of Mexico (1901–03) and Mutual Life Insur. Co. (1906 on); half-brother, Charles P. Taft, on BD of Little Miami RR (1891 through 1908), Cincinnati & Suburban Bell Tel. Co. (at least 1904–08), and Cincinnati Gas & Electric Co. (1903–08); C. P. Taft's daughter's father-in-law, M. E. Ingalls, P of Chesapeake & Ohio Rwy. (1889–99), P of Cincinnati, Wabash & Michigan Rwy. (1890–93), P of Cleveland, Cincinnati, Chicago & St. Louis Rwy. (1899 through 1908), and BD of Equitable Life Assurance Society (1891–1905) and Cincinnati, New Orleans & Texas Pacific Rwy. (1896–1908)

THEODORE ROOSEVELT ADMINISTRATION (continued)

Officeholder	College Education	Prior Governmental Experience	Primary Occupation	Important Secondary Economic Affiliations	Family and Other Social Ties	Other Pertinent Information	Elite or Non-Elite Status
Luke E. Wright, Tenn. (July 1908–March 1909)	Univ. of Mississippi (not grad.)	Ambassador to Japan (1906–07); governor-general of Philippines (1904–06); member, U.S. Philippine Commission (1900–04); attorney general of Tenn. (1870–78)	Memphis, Tenn. lawyer (1868 on, except for years abroad); ptr., Memphis law firm of Wright, Folkes & Wright (up to 1886); ptr., law firm of Wright & Turley thereafter		Son-in-law, John H. Watkins, on BD of American Cities Rwy. & Light Co. (at least 1907 through 1909)		E?
Secretary of Navy							
John D. Long, Mass. (Sept. 1901–May 1902)	Harvard Univ.	U.S. Sec. of Navy (1897–1901)	SEE PRECEDING MCKINLEY ADMINISTRATION ENTRY				E?
William H. Moody, Mass. (May 1902–June 1904)	Harvard Univ.	SEE ABOVE ROOSEVELT ADMINISTRATION ENTRY					E?
Paul Morton, Ill. (July			VP of Atchison, Topeka & Santa Fe	BD of Iowa Central Rwy.	Son of former Sec. of Agriculture J. Sterling		E

				E	?

Name / Dates	Education	Position	Law/Business	Banking	Other Affiliations
1904–July 1905)			Rwy. (1896–1904)	(1901–05), Great Western Cereal Co. (1904), Colorado Fuel & Iron Co. (1890–95), Indiana, Illinois & Iowa RR (1893–95 and 1899–1901), and Commercial Natl. Bank, Chicago (1902 to 1904)	Morton; brother, Joy Morton, longtime P of Joy Morton & Co., VP of Great Western Cereal Co. (1901–05), VP of Indiana, Illinois & Iowa RR (1899–1901), and BD of Corn Products Co. (1902–05), American Trust & Savings Bank, Chicago (at least 1893 through 1905), and North American Trust Co., N.Y.C. (1902–05)
Charles J. Bonaparte, Md. (July 1905–Dec. 1906)	Harvard Univ.	SEE ABOVE ROOSEVELT ADMINISTRATION ENTRY			
Victor H. Metcalf, Calif. (Dec. 1906–Dec. 1908)	Yale Univ. (not complete)	U.S. Sec. of Commerce and Labor (1904–06); Calif. Congressman (1899–1903)	Ptr., Oakland law firm of Metcalf and Metcalf (1879 to 1903)	BD of First Natl. Bank of Oakland (early 1900s) and Cal. Bank, Oakland (mid- and late 1890s)	

THEODORE ROOSEVELT ADMINISTRATION (continued)

Officeholder	College Education	Prior Governmental Experience	Primary Occupation	Important Secondary Economic Affiliations	Family and Other Social Ties	Other Pertinent Information	Elite or Non-Elite Status
Truman H. Newberry, Mich. (Dec. 1908–March 1909)	Yale Univ.	Asst. Sec. of Navy (1905–08)	P of Detroit Steel & Spring Co. (1887–1901); also off. or dir. of Michigan State Telephone Co. (1904–06)	BD of Packard Motor Car Co. (1903 on), Parke, Davis & Co. (at least 1904 on), Cleveland Cliffs Iron Co. (at least 1904 on), Railway Steel Spring Co., N.Y.C. (1902–04), Union Trust Co. (1896–1909), and State Savings Bank, Detroit (early 1900s)	Father, John S. Newberry, former founder of Michigan Car Co. and dir. of Natl. Bank of Commerce, Detroit (up to late 1890s) and Detroit, Bay City & Alpena RR (up to late 1880s); brother-in-law, Henry B. Joy, P of Packard Motor Car Co. (1906 on); father-in-law, James F. Joy, dir., Wabash Rwy. (up to mid-1880s) and number of other railroads		E

Secretary of Interior					
Ethan A. Hitchcock, Missouri (1901–March 1907)		Sec. of Interior (1899–1901); U.S. Ambassador to Russia (1897–99)	Prominent St. Louis businessman; former P of Crystal Plate Glass Co. and Chicago & Texas RR	BD of Pittsburgh Plate Glass Co. (1895–1900 and 1905 on) and Merchants Bank, St. Louis (early and mid-1890s)	E
James R. Garfield, Ohio (March 1907–March 1909)	Williams College	Commissioner of Corporations, U.S. Dept. of Commerce and Labor (1903–07); member, U.S. Civil Service Commission (1902–03); state legislator (1876–77)	Ptr., Cleveland law firm of Garfield & Garfield (1888–1902)	Brother and former law ptr., Harry A. Garfield, on BD of Cleveland Trust Co. (1895 through 1909); father-in-law, John Newell, P of Pittsburgh & Lake Erie RR (1883–1894), P of Lake Shore and Michigan Southern Rwy. (1883–94), and BD of Cincinnati, Wabash & Michigan Rwy. (1886–92) and Cleveland, Lorain & Wheeling RR (1885–94)	E
Secretary of Agriculture					
James Wilson, Iowa (1901–09)	Iowa College	Sec. of Agriculture (1897 through 1901)	SEE PRECEDING MCKINLEY ADMINISTRATION ENTRY		N-E?

Officeholder	College Education	Prior Governmental Experience	Primary Occupation	Important Secondary Economic Affiliations	Family and Other Social Ties	Other Pertinent Information	Elite or Non-Elite Status
Secretary of Commerce and Labor							
George B. Cortelyou, N.Y. (Feb. 1903–June 1904)	SEE ABOVE ROOSEVELT ADMINISTRATION ENTRY						N-E?
Victor H. Metcalf, Calif. (July 1904–Dec. 1906)	Yale Univ. (not complete)	SEE ABOVE ROOSEVELT ADMINISTRATION ENTRY					?
Oscar S. Straus, N.Y. (Dec. 1906–March 1909)	Columbia Univ.	U.S. Minister to Turkey (1887–89 and 1898–1900); member, Permanent Court of Arbitration, Hague (1902–06)	Longtime high off., L. Straus & Sons, N.Y.C. mercantile concern (1880–87, 1889–98, and 1900–06)	BD of New York Life Insurance Co. (1894–1905)	Brother, Isidor Straus, on BD of Hanover Natl. Bank, N.Y.C. (1897–1909) and Second Natl. Bank, N.Y.C. (at least 1888–1909)	VP or VC of National Civic Federation (1900–06)	E
Ambassador to Great Britain							
Joseph H. Choate, N.Y.	Harvard College	Ambassador to Great Britain	SEE PRECEDING MCKINLEY ADMINISTRATION ENTRY				E

Whitelaw Reid, N.Y. (June 1905 through 1909)	Miami Univ., Ohio	U.S. Minister to France (1889–92)	Publisher of *New York Tribune* (1872 on); editor of *New York Tribune* (1869–72)	BD of Mergenthaler Linotype Co. (least 1898 through 1909)	Father-in-law, Darius O. Mills, on BD of Bank of New York (1881 through 1909), Erie Railroad (1895–1907), Farmers Loan & Trust Co. (1890 through 1909), International Paper Co. (at least 1899 through 1909), Lackawanna Steel Co. (1902 through 1909), Lake Shore & Michigan Southern Rwy. (1880 through 1909), Madison Square Garden Co. (1896 through 1909), Mergenthaler Linotype Co. (at least 1898 through 1909), Morton Trust Co. (1900 through 1909), New York Central & Hudson River RR (1900 through 1909), U.S. Trust Co. of N.Y. (1896 through 1909), and Equitable Life Assur. Society (1898–1905); brother-in-law, Ogden Mills, on many of same BD's, plus Chicago, Rock Island & Pacific Rwy. (1898 through 1909)

Officeholder	College Education	Prior Governmental Experience	Primary Occupation	Important Secondary Economic Affiliations	Family and Other Social Ties	Other Pertinent Information	Elite or Non-Elite Status
Ambassador to France							
Horace Porter, N.Y. (1901–May 1905)	U.S. Military Academy	SEE PRECEDING MCKINLEY ADMINISTRATION ENTRY					E
Robert S. McCormick, Ill. (May 1905–March 1907)	Univ. of Virginia (not grad.)	Ambassador to Russia (1902–05); Minister to Austria-Hungary (1901–02); sec., American legation, London (1889–92)			Member of prominent Chicago family (associated with International Harvester Co.); son, Joseph Medill McCormick, married daughter of Mark Hanna (1903); married daughter of Joseph Medill, longtime owner of *Chicago Tribune*		E
Henry White, N.Y., orig. Md. (March 1907–Nov. 1909)		Longtime career diplomat (1883 on); Ambassador to Italy (1905–07)			Married daughter of L. M. Rutherford, prominent N.Y.C. family; wife's cousin, Winthrop Rutherford, on BD of Morton Trust Co. (1904–09); originally member of wealthy Baltimore family		E

Ambassador to Germany

Name	University	Government positions	Business positions	Business affiliations	Notes	
Andrew D. White, N.Y. (1901–Nov. 1902)	Yale Univ.	SEE PRECEDING MCKINLEY ADMINISTRATION ENTRY				E?
Charlemagne Tower, Penn. (Dec. 1902–June 1908)	Harvard Univ.	Ambassador to Russia (1899–1902); Minister to Austria-Hungary (1897–99)	VP of Finance Co. of Pa. (1887–91); gen. mgr. of Minnesota Iron Co. (1882–87); P of Duluth & Iron Range RR (1882–87)	BD of Northern Pacific Rwy. (1896–97), Philadelphia, Reading & New England RR (and predecessor line, 1889–98), Duluth and Iron Range RR (1888–97), and Lehigh Coal & Navigation Co. (1891–97)	Deceased father also once a director of Northern Pacific Rwy. (1872–79)	E
David J. Hill, N.Y. (June 1908 through 1909)	Bucknell Univ.	U.S. Minister to Netherlands (1905–07); Minister to Switzerland (1903–05); Asst. Sec. of State (1898–1903)	P of University of Rochester (1888–96); P of Bucknell Univ. (1879–88); prof., Bucknell Univ. (1874–79)			?

413

Officeholder	College Education	Prior Governmental Experience	Primary Occupation	Important Secondary Economic Affiliations	Family and Other Social Ties	Other Pertinent Information	Elite or Non-Elite Status
President							
William H. Taft, Ohio (1909–13)	Yale Univ.	Sec. of War (1904–08); president, U.S. Philippine Commission (1900–04); U.S. Circuit Court judge (1892–1900); U.S. Solicitor-General (1890–92)	Dean of Univ. of Cincinnati Law School (1896–1900); Cincinnati lawyer (1880–87)		Brother, Henry W. Taft, N.Y.C. lawyer, on BD of National RR of Mexico (1901–03 and 1909), Mutual Life Insur. Co. (1906 through 1913), and American Hawaiian Steamship Co. (1909–11); half-brother, Charles P. Taft, on BD of Little Miami RR (1891 through 1913), Cincinnati Gas & Elec. Co. and successor firm, Columbia Gas & Elec. Co. (1903–13), and Cincinnati & Suburban Bell Tel. Co. (at least 1904 through 1913); C. P. Taft's daughter's father-in-law, M. E. Ingalls, P of Cleveland, Cincinnati, Chicago & St. Louis Rwy. (1889–1912),	Off. or exec. com. member. Natl. Civic Federation (1907 through 1913)	E

Secretary of State					
Philander C. Knox, Penn. (1909–13)	Mt. Union College, Penn.	U.S. Senator, Penn. (1904–09); U.S. Attorney General (1901–04)	Longtime Pittsburgh lawyer, ptr. in law firm of Knox and Reed (1877–1901)	Up to 1901, GC of Carnegie Steel Co.; BD of Pittsburgh & Lake Erie RR (1897–1901), and Pittsburgh National Bank of Commerce (at least 1888 to early 1900s) Union Trust Co. (1895–1913), and Union Savings Bank, Pittsburgh (1903–13)	Former law ptr., James H. Reed, P of Pittsburgh, Bessemer & Lake Erie RR, since 1904 sub. of U.S. Steel Corp. (1897–1913); BD of U.S. Steel Corp. (1902 through 1913) and Gulf Oil Corp. (at least 1909 through 1913) and BD of Cincinnati, New Orleans & Texas Pacific Rwy. (1896–1912) and Equitable Life Assurance Society (1891–1905)

TAFT ADMINISTRATION (continued)

Officeholder	College Education	Prior Governmental Experience	Primary Occupation	Important Secondary Economic Affiliations	Family and Other Social Ties	Other Pertinent Information	Elite or Non-Elite Status
Secretary of Treasury							
Franklin MacVeagh, Ill. (1909–13)	Yale Univ.		Head, Franklin MacVeagh & Co., Chicago wholesale grocery concern (1871 on)	BD of Commercial Natl. Bank of Chicago (1881–1909)	Father-in-law, Henry F. Eames, founder and longtime president of Commercial Natl. Bank of Chicago; brother, Wayne MacVeagh, a Phila. lawyer, on BD of Mutual Life Insur. Co., N.Y.C. (1903 through 1913); nephew, Charles MacVeagh, ptr. in Stetson, Jennings & Russell and predecessor firm, N.Y.C. (1883–94 and 1896 through 1913), sec. of Internatl. Traction Co. (1901–04), and BD of Allis-Chalmers Co. (1908–11), Bethlehem Steel Corp. (1902–03), American Steel Hoop Co. and National Steel Co.,	Employer rept., exec com., Natl. Civic Federation (1900–09, public member up through 1913)	E

Office / Name	Education	Career positions	Business positions	Notes	Code
Attorney General					
George W. Wickersham, N.Y. (1909–13)	Lehigh Univ. (not complete)	Partner in N.Y.C. law firm of Strong & Cadwalader (1887–1909)	BD of Mexican Central Rwy., Ltd. (1909), Interborough-Metropolitan Co. (1906–09), American-Hawaiian Steamship Co. (1906–09), and National Railroad Co. of Mexico (1902–05)	Law ptr., Henry W. Taft, who was the President's brother, on several already noted boards; both subs of U.S. Steel Corp. (1902–03), also VP of Federal Steel Co. (1899–1902)	E
Secretary of War					
Jacob M. Dickinson, Ill., orig. Tenn. (March 1909–May 1911)	Univ. of Nashville	Asst. U.S. Attorney General (1895–97); member, Tenn. Superior Court (1891–93)	Gen. Solicitor or GC, Illinois Central RR (1899–1909); gen. att., Louisville & Nashville RR (1897–99); Nashville lawyer (1874 to 1899); BD of Bon Air Coal & Iron Co., Tenn. (1902–10)		P, American Bar Assn. (1907–08) E

Officeholder	College Education	Prior Governmental Experience	Primary Occupation	Important Secondary Economic Affiliations	Family and Other Social Ties	Other Pertinent Information	Elite or Non-Elite Status
Henry L. Stimson, N.Y. (May 1911–March 1913)	Yale Univ.	U.S. attorney for southern district of N.Y. (1906–09)	Member, N.Y.C. law firm of Winthrop & Stimson (1901–11); member of N.Y.C. law firm of Root, Howard, Winthrop & Stimson (1893–1901)		Law ptr., Bronson Winthrop, on BD of Morton Trust Co. (1909–10)		E
Secretary of Navy							
George von L. Meyer, Mass. (1909–13)	Harvard Univ.	U.S. Postmaster General (1907–09); U.S. Minister to Russia (1905–07); Minister to Italy (1900–05); former state legislator (1892–97)	Longtime member of Linder & Meyer, Boston mercantile concern	BD of Amoskeag Mfg. Co. (mid-1890s through 1913), Provident Inst. for Savings, Boston (1897–1913); BD of Ames Plow Co. (at least 1905 through 1913), and Old Colony Trust Co. (1891–1908)	Married daughter of Charles H. Appleton, whose sister had wed son of former wealthy textile magnate, Abbott Lawrence		E

Secretary of Interior					
Richard A. Ballinger, Wash. (March 1909–March 1911)	Williams College, Mass.	U.S. Commissioner of General Land Office (1907–08); mayor of Seattle (1904–06); Wash. Superior Court judge (1894–97)	Longtime Seattle lawyer and in recent years a partner in law firm of Ballinger, Ronald, Battle & Tennant	BD of Scandanavian-American Bank, Seattle (1900–09)		E
Walter L. Fisher, Ill. (March 1911–March 1913)	Hanover College, Ind.	Member, Federal Railroad Securities Com. (1910–11)	Ptr., Chicago law firm of Matz, Fisher & Boyden (1888–1911)	Ptr., Rudolph Matz, on BD of United Shoe Machinery Corp., Boston (1899 through 1913) and Chicago Savings Bank & Trust Co. (at least 1903 through 1913); ptr., W. C. Boyden, on BD of Western Trust & Savings Bank and predecessor concern, Chicago (at least 1909 through 1913) and Bd. Overseers, Harvard College (1911 on)	1908 P of Conservation League of America; 1910 P of National Conservation Assn.	E?

Officeholder	College Education	Prior Governmental Experience	Primary Occupation	Important Secondary Economic Affiliations	Family and Other Social Ties	Other Pertinent Information	Elite or Non-Elite Status
Secretary of Agriculture							
James Wilson, Iowa (1897–13)	SEE INITIAL MCKINLEY ADMINISTRATION ENTRY						N-E?
Secretary of Commerce and Labor							
Charles Nagel, Missouri (1909–13)	Wash. Univ., St. Louis	St. Louis city councilman (1893–97); also former state legislator (early 1880s)	Ptr., St. Louis law firm of Nagel, Kirby & Shepley (1905 on); St. Louis lawyer (1873 on)	Off. or dir. of American Diesel Engine Co. (1904–06)	Brother-in-law, J. F. Shepley, VP and BD of St. Louis Union Trust Co. (through 1913); Shepley had married a daughter of E. A. Hitchcock, a former St. Louis businessman and Sec. of the Interior	Rep. Natl. Committeeman (1908–12)	E
Ambassador to Great Britain							
Whitelaw Reid, N.Y. (1909–Dec. 1912)	Miami Univ., Ohio	Ambassador to Great Britain (1905 on)	SEE PRECEDING ROOSEVELT ADMINISTRATION ENTRY				E

Ambassador to France						
Robert Bacon, N.Y. (Dec. 1909– April 1912)	Harvard College	Sec. of State (brief period, early 1909); Asst. Sec. of State (1905–09)	Ptr., J. P. Morgan & Co. (till 1903)	BD of Bank for Savings in N.Y.C. (1903 through 1912), Manhattan Trust Co. (1905–09), U.S. Steel Corp. (1903–05), North American Co. (1901–05), Erie RR (1901–05), and other large concerns earlier.		E
Myron T. Herrick, Ohio (April 1912 thru 1913)	Ohio Wesleyan Univ. (2 years)	Governor of Ohio (1904–06); former Cleveland city councilman (mid-1880s)	P of Society for Savings, Cleveland (1894 through 1913; Sec. & Treas., 1886–94); BC, Wheeling & Lake Erie RR (1900 through 1913); VP of National Carbon Co. (1902 through 1913)	BD of Quaker Oats Co. (at least 1901 through 1913), Citizens Trust & Savings Bank, Columbus (through 1913), Missouri, Kansas & Texas Rwy. (up to 1909),	son, P. W. Herrick, on BD of Chatham & Phenix Natl. Bank, NYC (at least 1911 through 1913)	1901 P of the American Bankers Assn.	E

TAFT ADMINISTRATION (continued)

Officeholder	College Education	Prior Governmental Experience	Primary Occupation	Important Secondary Economic Affiliations	Family and Other Social Ties	Other Pertinent Information	Elite or Non-Elite Status
Ambassador to Germany							
David J. Hill, N.Y. (1909–Sept. 1911)	Bucknell Univ.	Ambassador to Germany (1908 on)	SEE PRECEDING ROOSEVELT ADMINISTRATION ENTRY	Bowling Green Trust Co., N.Y.C. (up to 1908), Trust Co. of America, N.Y.C. (up to 1905), and Central Colorado Power Co. (up to 1911)			?
John G. A. Leishman, Penn. (Oct. 1911 through 1913)		Ambassador to Italy (1909–11); Ambassador to Turkey (1900–09); Ambassador to Switzerland (1897–1900)	VP, Carnegie (Phipps) steel works (1886–92); P of Carnegie Steel Co. (1892–97)				E

WILSON ADMINISTRATION (1913–1921)

Officeholder	College Education	Prior Governmental Experience	Primary Occupation	Important Secondary Economic & Organizational Affiliations	Family and Other Social Ties	Other Pertinent Information	Elite or Non-Elite Status
President							
Woodrow Wilson, N.J. (1913–21)	Princeton Univ.	Governor of New Jersey (1911–13)	President of Princeton University (1902–10); prof. of history and government, Princeton Univ. (1890–1902); prof. of history and govt., Bryn Mawr College and Wesleyan Univ. (1885–90)	BT of Mutual Life Insur. Co., N.Y.C. (1909–11)			E
Secretary of State							
William J. Bryan, Nebraska (1913–June 1915)	Illinois College	Unsuccessful Democratic candidate for President of U.S. (1896, 1900, and 1908); Nebraska Congressman (1891–95)	Editor, Lincoln (Neb.) *Commoner* (1901 on), and Omaha *World-Herald* (1894–1901)			Longtime leader of progressive agrarian wing of national Democratic party	N-E

423

WILSON ADMINISTRATION (continued)

Officeholder	College Education	Prior Governmental Experience	Primary Occupation	Important Secondary Economic Affiliations	Family and Other Social Ties	Other Pertinent Information	Elite or Non-Elite Status
Robert Lansing, Wash., D.C., orig., N.Y. (June 1915–Feb. 1920)	Amherst College	Counselor, U.S. State Dept. (1914–15)	Assoc. editor, American Journal of International Law (1907–1914); Washington, D.C. law practice with former Sec. of State (and father-in-law), John W. Foster (1889–1907)	VP of City National Bank, Watertown, N.Y. (1912 through 1920; before that, a director)	Son-in-law of former (1892–93) Secretary of State, John W. Foster, who served, up to death in 1917, on BT of Carnegie Endowment for International Peace		E
Bainbridge Colby, N.Y. (March 1920–March 1921)	Williams College	Member, U.S. Shipping Board (1917–19), Vice-Chariman of its Emergency Fleet Corp.; former state legislator (1901)	Longtime N.Y.C. lawyer (partner of Henry M. Alexander in early 1900s)	BD of Nevada Smelting & Mining Corp. (1908–10) and American Deposit & Loan Co., N.Y.C. (1900–01)		Former Republican and Progressive party leader	?

Secretary of Treasury

William G. McAdoo, N.Y. (March 1913–Dec. 1918)	Attended Univ. of Tennessee (briefly)	P of Hudson & Manhattan RR Co. and predecessor concern, New York & New Jersey RR Co. (1902–12); N.Y.C. lawyer 1892–1902); P of Chattanooga Hoe & Tool Co. (up to early 1890s); Chattanooga lawyer (1885–92); P of Knoxville Street Railroad Co. (1889–92)	BD of Lincoln Trust Co., N.Y.C. (1910–13) and Long Island Motor Parkway, Inc. (1907–10)	Married daughter of President Wilson (1914)	E
Carter Glass, Va. (Dec. 1918–Feb. 1920)	Va. Congressman (1902–18); also former state legislator	Lynchburg, Va. newspaper editor (1888 on)	BD of Peoples Natl. Bank of Lynchburg (1917–18) and United Loan & Trust Co., Lynchburg (1914–18)		N-E?

WILSON ADMINISTRATION (continued)

Officeholder	College Education	Prior Governmental Experience	Primary Occupation	Important Secondary Economic Affiliations	Family and Other Social Ties	Other Pertinent Information	Elite or Non-Elite Status
David F. Houston, Missouri, orig. Texas (Feb. 1920–March 1921)	College of South Carolina	U.S. Secretary of Agriculture (1913–20)	Chancellor, Washington University, St. Louis (1908–16); president, Texas A. & M. and Univ. of Texas (1902–08); prof. of political science, Univ. of Texas (1897–1902)	BD of St. Louis Terminal Cupples Station & Property Co. (1913–16)			E?
Attorney General James C. McReynolds, Tenn. (& later N.Y.) (March 1913–August 1914)	Vanderbilt Univ.	Spec. counsel to U.S. Attorney General on antitrust matters (1907–12); Asst. U.S. Attorney General (1903–07)	Individual N.Y.C. lawyer (1912–13); Nashville, Tenn. lawyer (1885–1903); Vanderbilt Univ. law prof. (1900–03)	VP City Savings Bank, Nashville (early 1900s)			N-E?

Thomas W. Gregory (August 1914–March 1919)	Texas Southwtrn. Presbyt. Univ., Tenn.	Spec. asst. to U.S. Attorney General on antitrust matters (1913–14)	Member of Austin, Texas law firm of Gregory, Batts & Brooks (1900–14)	BD of Citizens Bank & Trust Co., Austin (1906 to 1913)	?
A. Mitchell Palmer, Penn. (March 1919–March 1921)	Swarthmore College	Alien Property Custodian, U.S. govt. (1917–19); Penn. Congressman (1909–15)	Stroudsburg and northeastern Penn. lawyer (1893–1917)	BD of Stroudsburg Natl. Bank (1912 through 1921) and Scranton Trust Co. (1906 through 1921)	?
Secretary of War					
Lindley M. Garrison, N.J. (March 1913–Feb. 1916)	Harvard Univ. (1 year)	Vice-Chancellor of New Jersey (1904–13)	Jersey City lawyer (1898–1904); Camden, N.J. lawyer (1888–98)	BD of newly-formed Lancaster County Rwy. & Light Co. (1902–04)	N-E?
Newton D. Baker, Ohio (March 1916–March 1921)	Johns Hopkins Univ.	Mayor of Cleveland (1912–16); Cleveland city solicitor (1903–12)	Ptr., newly-formed Cleveland law firm of Baker, Hostetler & Sidlo (2 months, 1916); Cleveland lawyer (1897–1902)	Sec., treas., and dir. of the Sheffield Land & Improvement Co. (1909–1913)	N-E?

427

Officeholder	College Education	Prior Governmental Experience	Primary Occupation	Important Secondary Economic Affiliations	Family and Other Social Ties	Other Pertinent Information	Elite or Non-Elite Status
Secretary of Navy							
Josephus Daniels, N.C. (1913–21)	Wilson Collegiate Inst.		Publisher and editor, Raleigh *News and Observer* (1895 on)			Prominent N.C. Democratic party leader (a Bryan man)	N-E
Secretary of Interior							
Franklin K. Lane, Calif. (March 1913–March 1920)	Univ. of California (2 years)	Member and later chairman, ICC (1906–13); city and county attorney of San Francisco (1899–1904)	San Francisco lawyer (1895–99); editor, Tacoma *Daily News* (1891–95)	Member, Independent Oil Producers Agency, Calif. (up to early 1900s)			N-E?
John B. Payne, Ill. (March 1920–March 1921)		Chrm., U.S. Shipping Board (1919–20); GC, U.S. Shipping Board and U.S. Railroad Adm. (1917–19); Chicago judge (1893–98)	Ptr., Chicago law firm of Winston, Payne, Strawn & Shaw (1902–17); Chicago lawyer (1882–93 and 1898–1902)	GC (but not BD) of Chicago Great Western RR (up to 1918); BD of Central Trust Co., Chicago (1917–19)			E

Secretary of Agriculture

Name / Term	Education	Career	Directorships	Note
David F. Houston, Missouri, orig. Texas (March 1913–Jan. 1920)	College of South Carolina	SEE ABOVE SECRETARY OF THE TREASURY ENTRY		E?
Edwin T. Meredith, Iowa (Feb 1920–March 1921)	Highland Park Coll., Iowa, now Des Moines Univ. (not complete)	Longtime publisher and editor, *Farmers' Tribune*, Iowa	BD of Iowa Trust & Savings Bank, Des Moines (1908 to 1915); BD of Federal Reserve Bank of Chicago (1918–20)	E

Secretary of Commerce

Name / Term	Education	Career	Directorships	Note
William C. Redfield, N.Y. (March 1913–Nov. 1919)	N.Y. Congressman (1911–13); local govt. official (1902–03)	VP, American Blower Co. of Mich. (1909–13); VP, Fuller & Reuman Co. (1901–09); T of J. H. Williams Co. (up to 1901)	BD of Equitable Life Assur. Society of N.Y. (1905–13); BD of U.S. Chamber of Commerce (1915–19)	E

WILSON ADMINISTRATION (continued)

Officeholder	College Education	Prior Governmental Experience	Primary Occupation	Important Secondary Economic Affiliations	Family and Other Social Ties	Other Pertinent Information	Elite or Non-Elite Status
Joshua W. Alexander, Missouri (Dec. 1919–March 1921)	Christian Univ., Mo. (now Culver Stockton Coll.)	Mo. Congressman (1907–19); also former longtime state and local govt. official	Longtime Gallatin, Mo. lawyer				N-E
Secretary of Labor							
William B. Wilson, Penn. (1913–21)		Penn. Congressman (1907–13)	Sec.-Treas., United Mine Workers (1900–08)				N-E
Ambassador to Great Britain							
Walter Hines Page, N.Y. (May 1913–Oct. 1918)	Randolph-Macon Coll. and Johns Hopkins Univ. (but not complete)		VP of Doubleday, Page & Co., N.Y.C. publishing firm (1899–1913); editor, *Atlantic Monthly* (1895–99)			Longtime friend of President Wilson; BT of General Education Board (1902–18)	E?

Name	Education	Public office	Business/other	Banking	Notes	
John W. Davis, W.Va. (Dec. 1918–March 1921)	Washington & Lee Univ.	U.S. Solicitor-General (1913–18); W. Va. Congressman (1911–13); also former state legislator	Longtime Clarksburg, W. Va. lawyer			?

Ambassador to France

SEE ENTRY FOR THIS POST IN THE PRECEDING TAFT ADMINISTRATION

Name	Education	Public office	Business/other	Banking	Notes	
Myron T. Herrick, Ohio (1912–Nov. 1914)	Ohio Wesleyan Univ. (2 years)					E
William G. Sharp, Ohio (Dec. 1914–April 1919)	Univ. of Michigan	Ohio Congressman (1909–1914)	P of Lake Superior Iron & Chemical Co. Detroit (up to 1910, BD 1911–12)			E
Hugh C. Wallace, Wash. (April 1919–March 1921)			Former Tacoma, Wash. banking, business, and real estate figure	BD of National Bank of Commerce, Seattle (1900 through 1921)	Prominent Washington state Democratic leader; son-in-law of former Chief Justice Melville W. Fuller	E

WILSON ADMINISTRATION (continued)

Officeholder	College Education	Prior Governmental Experience	Primary Occupation	Important Secondary Economic Affiliations	Family and Other Social Ties	Other Pertinent Information	Elite or Non-Elite Status
Ambassador to Germany							
James W. Gerard, N.Y. (Oct. 1913–Feb. 1917)	Columbia Univ.	Assoc. Justice, New York Supreme Court (1908–13)	Member, N.Y.C. law firm of Bowers and Sands (1892–1908)	BD of Knickerbocker Trust Co., N.Y.C. (1904–08)		Son-in-law of former head and founder of Anaconda Copper Mining Co., (deceased) Marcus Daly; brother-in-law, Marcus Daly, on BD of Montana Power Co. (at least 1913–17)	E

HARDING ADMINISTRATION (1921–July 1923)

Officeholder	College Education	Prior Governmental Experience	Primary Occupation	Important Secondary Economic Affiliations	Family and Other Social Ties	Other Pertinent Information	Elite or Non-Elite Status
President							
Warren G. Harding, Ohio	Ohio Central College	U.S. Senator, Ohio (1915–21); Lt.-Gov., Ohio	Publisher, *Marion Daily Star* (1884 on)	BD of Marion County Bank (up to 1920),			N-E

	Education	Political/Career	Business	Additional	Foundation	Code
(1921–July 1923); state legislator (1899–1903)			Marion County Telephone Co. (up to at least 1916), and Tennessee Timber Co. (at least 1911 up to 1918)		BT of Rockefeller Foundation (1917–21)	E

Secretary of State

	Education	Political/Career	Business	Code
Charles Evans Hughes, N.Y. (1921 through 1923)	Brown University	Republican presidential candidate (1916); Assoc. Justice, U.S. Supreme Court (1910–16); Governor of New York (1907–10); chief counsel and investigator, N.Y. insurance company scandals (1905–06)	Ptr., N.Y.C. law firm of Hughes, Rounds, Schurman & Dwight (1917–21); also ptr., Hughes, Rounds & Schurman and its predecessor firm (1887–91 and 1893–1907)	

Secretary of Treasury

	Education	Political/Career	Business	Directorships	Family	Code
Andrew W. Mellon, Penn. (1921 through 1923)	Univ. of Pittsburgh, originally known as Western Univ. (not complete)		P (1902–21) of the Mellon Nat'l. Bank; VP of the Nat'l. Union Fire Insur. Co., Pittsburgh (at least 1908–23) VP of the Gulf Oil Corp., (at least 1910 to 1921), Union	BD of Alcoa (at least 1910 to 1921), Koppers Co. (probably 1915 to 1921), Carbonundum Co. (probably	Brother of R. B. Mellon, P of Mellon Nat'l. Bank (1921 on), VP of both Union Trust Co. and Union Savings Bank, Pittsburgh (1921 on), and off. or dir. of Alcoa (at least 1910 through 1923), Gulf Oil Corp. (at least 1910 through 1923),	E

Officeholder	College Education	Prior Governmental Experience	Primary Occupation	Important Secondary Economic Affiliations	Family and Other Social Ties	Other Pertinent Information	Elite or Non-Elite Status
			Trust Co. (1895–1921), and Union Savings Bank, Pitts. (1903–21)	1915 to 1921), American Locomotive Co. (1915–21), Crucible Steel Co. of America (1920–21), Pittsburgh Coal Co. (1899–1921), Standard Steel Car Co. (1905–21), Nat'l Bank of Commerce of N.Y.C. (1904–21), and N.Y.C.-based American Foreign Securities Co. (up to 1921)	Koppers Co. (at least 1921 through 1923), Pittsburgh Coal Co. (1921 through 1923), Carbonundum Co. (at least 1910 through 1923), and Standard Steel Car Co. (1903 through 1923)		
Attorney General Harry M. Daugherty, Ohio (1921 through 1923)	Univ. of Michigan	Onetime Ohio state legislator (1890–94)	Longtime ptr., Columbus, Ohio law firm of Daugherty, Todd & Rarey (up'to 1921)	BD of Scioto Valley Traction Co. (1915 through 1923) and			N-E?

					both the U.S. Telephone Co. and the closely linked Columbus Citizens' Telephone Co. (at least 1910 to 1914)	E
Secretary of War						
John W. Weeks, Mass. (1921 through 1923)	U.S. Naval Academy	U.S. Senator, Mass. (1913–19); Mass. Congressman (1905–13); also mayor of Boston (1902–04)	Longtime ptr., Hornblower & Weeks, Boston banking firm (up to 1912); VP (up to 1912) and BD (up to 1913) of the First National Bank of Boston	BD of U.S. Smelting, Refining & Mining Co. (1908 to 1913)		
Secretary of Navy						E
Edwin Denby, Mich. (1921 through 1923)	Univ. of Michigan	Mich. Congressman (1905–11)	Longtime Detroit lawyer; one of founders of Hupp Motor Car Co. (an officer or director from 1914 to 1918); also a VP of the Denby Motor Truck Co. (up through 1923)	BD (up to 1921) of the National Bank of Commerce, Detroit; also BD of smaller Bankers Trust Co., Detroit (1917–23)		

435

Officeholder	College Education	Prior Governmental Experience	Primary Occupation	Important Secondary Economic Affiliations	Family and Other Social Ties	Other Pertinent Information	Elite or Non-Elite Status
Secretary of Interior							
Albert B. Fall, N.M. (1921 through March 1923)		U.S. Senator, N.M. (1912–21); Attorney-General, N.M. on two separate occasions (late 1890s and late 1910); assoc. justice, N.M. Supreme Court (mid-1890s); also former state legislator	Longtime N.M. lawyer and entrepreneurial figure	BD of Rio Grande, Sierra Madre & Pacific RR (1906–07) and Greene Gold-Silver Co. (probably 1902 up to 1905)	Son-in-law, M. T. Everhart, on BD of First National Bank of Pueblo, Colo. (1917 through 1923)		?
Hubert Work, Colo. (March 1923 on)	Univ. of Michigan, and M.D. from U. of Penn.	U.S. Postmaster General (1922–23); Asst. Postmaster General (1921–22)	Longtime Pueblo, Colo. physician (mid-1890s to 1921)			President, American Medical Assn. (1921–22); Rep. Nat'l Committeeman, Colo. (1913–19)	N-E?

Secretary of Agriculture					
Henry C. Wallace, Iowa (1921 through 1923)	Iowa State College		Editor or assoc. ed., *Wallaces' Farmer* (1896 on)	BD of Central State Bank, Des Moines (1912 through 1923)	E
Secretary of Commerce					
Herbert C. Hoover, Calif. (1921 through 1923)	Stanford Univ.		Off., Bewick, Moreing & Co., British mining and investment concern (up to 1908); mining engineer and entrepreneur, mainly in Australia and Asia (1908–16); BC of Santa Gertrudis, Ltd. and Camp Bird, Ltd. (1914–16)	BD of Burma Corp. (1906–19), Zinc Corp., Ltd. (1906–16), Messina Development Co. (1915–16), Tanalyk Corp. and Irtysh Corp. (1914–16), Russo-Asiatic Corp. and Kyshtim Corp. (1912–16), LaLune Oil Blocks, Trinidad (1911–13), Lagunitas Oil Co. (1910–14), Chinese Engineering & Mining Co. (1903–12), London & Western Australian Exploration Co.	E

HARDING ADMINISTRATION (continued)

Officeholder	College Education	Prior Governmental Experience	Primary Occupation	Important Secondary Economic Affiliations	Family and Other Social Ties	Other Pertinent Information	Elite or Non-Elite Status
				(1904–07), Oroya Brownhill (1904–07), Talisman Consolidated (1904–07), Lancefield Gold Mining Co. (1904–07), and Australian Smelting Corp. (1905–07)			
Secretary of Labor							
James J. Davis, Penn. (1921 through 1923)	Sharon Business College (not complete)		Longtime P, American Bond & Mortgage Co., Pittsburgh			Member, Amer. Assn. of Iron, Steel & Tin Workers of America: dir. gen., Loyal Order of Moose (1907 on); also member of the Duquesne Club	?

438

Position / Name	Education	Public Office	Business	Directorships	Notes	
Ambassador to Great Britain						
George Harvey, N.Y. (May 1921–Nov. 1923)			P of Harper Brothers, N.Y.C. (1900–15); then head of North American Review Publishing Co. (up to 1921)	BD of Audit Co., N.Y.C. (at least 1898 through 1923); also BD of Cuba Electric Co. and Mechanics & Traders Bank, N.Y.C. (in first years of century)	One of Harding's chief advisors at 1920 Repub. Nat'l. Convention	E?
Ambassador to France						
Myron T. Herrick, Ohio (July 1921 through 1923)	Ohio Wesleyan Univ. (not complete)	Ambassador to France (1912–14); Governor of Ohio (1904–06)	P or BC, Society for Savings, Cleveland (1894–1921); BC, Union Carbide & Carbon Corp. (1918 through 1923, VP of National Carbon Co. before that); BC, Wheeling & Lake Erie Rwy. (up to 1915)	BD of New York Life Insur. Co. (1917 through 1923) and Erie RR (1918–21)	Son, P. W. Herrick, on BD of New York, Chicago & St. Louis RR (1918–22), Harriman Nat'l. Bank, N.Y.C. (1915 through 1923), and Union Trust Co. and predecessor company, Cleveland (1914–23)	A major Harding supporter at 1920 Repub. Nat'l. Convention E

Officeholder	College Education	Prior Governmental Experience	Primary Occupation	Important Secondary Economic Affiliations	Family and Other Social Ties	Other Pertinent Information	Elite or Non-Elite Status
Ambassador to Germany							
Alanson B. Houghton, N.Y. (April 1922 through 1923)	Harvard Univ.	New York Congressman (1919–22)	BC, CEC, or P of the Corning Glass Works (1911 through 1923); VP of Corning Glass Works (1902–10)	BD of Metropolitan Life Insurance Co. (1913 through 1923)			E

Officeholder	College Education	Prior Governmental Experience	Primary Occupation	Important Secondary Economic Affiliations	Family and Other Social Ties	Other Pertinent Information	Elite or Non-Elite Status
President							
Calvin Coolidge, Mass. (August 1923–1929)	Amherst College	Governor of Mass. (1919–21); Lt.-Gov., Mass.(1916–18); state legislator	Northampton, Mass. lawyer (1897–1921), ptr. with Ralph W. Hemenway				N-E

Secretary of State					
Charles Evans Hughes, N.Y. (August 1923–March 1925)	Brown Univ.	Sec. of State (1921–23)	(1907–08 and 1912–15)	(1916–21); P of Nanotuck Savings Bank, Northampton (1918–21, VP and BD before that)	SEE PRECEDING HARDING ADMINISTRATION ENTRY — E
Frank B. Kellogg, Minn. (March 1925–March 1929)		American Ambassador to Great Britain (1923–25); U.S. Senator, Minn. (1917–23); spec. counsel, federal govt., Standard Oil and Union Pacific RR antitrust cases (1906–11)	Ptr., St. Paul law firm of Davis, Kellogg, Severance & Morgan and predecessor concerns (up to 1923); also P of Wisconsin, Minnesota & Pacific RR (up to 1907, when became part of Chicago Great Western RR)	BD of Merchants Nat'l. Bank of St. Paul (1897 through 1929)	E

COOLIDGE ADMINISTRATION *(continued)*

Officeholder	College Education	Prior Governmental Experience	Primary Occupation	Important Secondary Economic Affiliations	Family and Other Social Ties	Other Pertinent Information	Elite or Non-Elite Status
Secretary of Treasury							
Andrew W. Mellon, Penn. (August 1923 through 1929)	Univ. of Pittsburgh (not complete)	Sec. of the Treasury (1921–23)	P of Mellon Nat'l. Bank and VP of Gulf Oil Corp., Union Savings Bank, and Union Trust Co. of Pittsburgh (up to 1921); VP of National Union Fire Insur. Co. (up to 1928)	SEE PREVIOUS ENTRY FOR OTHER ECONOMIC LINKS	Brother, R. B. Mellon, on BD of Alcoa, Gulf Oil Corp., Pittsburgh Coal Co., and Koppers Co. (up through 1929); other family members also still involved in Carbonundum Co. and Standard Steel Car Co.		E
Attorney General							
Harry M. Daugherty, Ohio (August 1923–April 1924)	Univ. of Michigan	U.S. Attorney General (1921–23)	Former Columbus, Ohio lawyer and lobbyist	BD of Scioto Valley Traction Co. (up through 1924)			N-E?

442

Harlan Fiske Stone, N.Y. (April 1924–March 1925)	Amherst College		Ptr., Sullivan & Cromwell, N.Y.C. law firm (1923–24); ptr., N.Y.C. law firm of Satterlee, Canfield & Stone (and predecessor firms, 1901–23); dean, Columbia Law School (1910–23, law school prof., before that)	Sec. and dir., Atlanta & Charlotte Air Line Rwy. (1909–24)	E?
John G. Sargent, Vermont (March 1925–March 1929)	Tufts Univ.	Vermont Attorney General (1908–12)	Ptr., Ludlow, Vt. law firm of Stickney, Sargent & Skeels (1892–1925)	BD of Vermont Valley RR (1916–25)	N-E

Secretary of War

John W. Weeks, Mass. (August 1923–Oct. 1925)	U.S. Naval Academy	U.S. Sec. of War (1921–23)	SEE PRECEDING HARDING ADMINISTRATION ENTRY	E

443

COOLIDGE ADMINISTRATION (continued)

Officeholder	College Education	Prior Governmental Experience	Primary Occupation	Important Secondary Economic Affiliations	Family and Other Social Ties	Other Pertinent Information	Elite or Non-Elite Status
Dwight F. Davis, Missouri (Oct. 1925–March 1929)	Harvard Univ.	Asst. Sec. of War (1923–25); also former WWI officer and prominent St. Louis municipal and civic official	Sec. or mgr., Davis estate, St. Louis (both before and after WWI)	BD of State National Bank of St. Louis (at least 1909 through 1926)	One or both of brothers, J. T. Davis and S. C. Davis, St. Louis merchants, on BD of St. Louis Union Trust Co. and First Natl. Bank of St. Louis (up through 1929); one or more members of family also on BD of Houston Oil Co. (up through 1929)	D. F. Davis on Board of Overseers, Harvard Univ. (1915–21 and 1926 on)	E
Secretary of Navy							
Edwin Denby, Mich. (August 1923–March 1924)	Univ. of Michigan	U.S. Sec. of the Navy (1921–23)	Former Detroit lawyer and VP of Denby Motor Truck Co.	BD of National Bank of Commerce, Detroit (up to 1921) and BD of Bankers Trust Co., Detroit (up through 1924)			E (n/c)

Curtis D. Wilbur, Calif. (March 1924–March 1929)	U.S. Naval Academy	Chief Justice, Calif. Supreme Court (1922–24); Assoc. Justice, Calif. Supreme Court (1919–22); judge, Calif. Superior Ct. (1902–18)	Los Angeles lawyer (1890–1902)		Brother, R. L. Wilbur, P of Stanford Univ. and on BT of Rockefeller Foundation (since 1923)	E
Secretary of Interior						
Hubert Work, Colo. (August 1923–July 1928)	Univ. of Michigan, and M.D. Univ. of Penn.	Sec. of the Interior (March-August, 1923); Postmaster General and Asst. Postmaster General (1921–23)	Longtime Pueblo, Colo. physician (mid-1890s to 1921)		Repub. Natl. Committeeman, Colo. (1913–19)	N-E?
Roy O. West, Ill. (July 1928–March 1929)	DePauw Univ.		Ptr., Chicago law firm of West, Eckhart & Taylor (1902–28)	BD of South Side Trust & Savings Bank, Chicago (1923–29)	Prominent Ill. Repub. leader	E?
Secretary of Agriculture						
Henry C. Wallace, Iowa (August 1923–Oct. 1924)	Iowa State College	Sec. of Agriculture (1921–23)	Longtime publisher, *Wallaces' Farmer*, Iowa	BD of Central State Bank, Des Moines (1912 up to 1924)		E

COOLIDGE ADMINISTRATION (continued)

Officeholder	College Education	Prior Governmental Experience	Primary Occupation	Important Secondary Economic Affiliations	Family and Other Social Ties	Other Pertinent Information	Elite or Non-Elite Status
Howard M. Gore, W.Va. (Nov. 1924–March 1925)	West Virginia Univ.	Member W.Va. Bd. of Education (1920–24); minor federal official in WWI	Ptr., H. M. Gore & Brothers (farm, livestock and mercantile concern)	BD of Clarksburg Trust Co. (1915–24)		Important figure, American Farm Bureau Federation; P, Wt. Va. Livestock Assn. (1912–16)	E?
William M. Jardine, Kansas (March 1925–March 1929)	Agricultural College of Utah		P of Kansas College of Agriculture (1918–25); dean of agronomy & dir., exper. station, Kansas Col. of Agriculture (1913–18)				N-E?
Secretary of Commerce							
Herbert C. Hoover, Calif. (August 1923–August 1928)	Stanford Univ.	U.S. Sec. of Commerce (1921–23)	SEE PRECEDING HARDING ADMINISTRATION ENTRY				E

William F. Whiting, Mass. (August 1928–March 1929)	Amherst College	Longtime P, Whiting Paper Co., Holyoke, Mass. (1911–28)	BD of American Trust Co., Boston (1920 through 1929) and American Surety Co., N.Y.C. (about 1910 through 1929)	E

Secretary of Labor

James J. Davis, Penn. (August 1923 through 1929)	U.S. Sec. of Labor (1921–23)	SEE PRECEDING HARDING ADMINISTRATION ENTRY	?

Ambassador to Great Britain

George Harvey, N.Y. (August–Nov. 1923)	Ambassador to Great Britain (1921–23)	SEE PRECEDING HARDING ADMINISTRATION ENTRY	E? (n/c)

Frank B. Kellogg, Minn. (Dec. 1923–Feb. 1925)	SEE ABOVE COOLIDGE ADMINISTRATION ENTRY	E

COOLIDGE ADMINISTRATION (continued)

Officeholder	College Education	Prior Governmental Experience	Primary Occupation	Important Secondary Economic Affiliations	Family and Other Social Ties	Other Pertinent Information	Elite or Non-Elite Status
Alanson B. Houghton, N.Y. (April 1925–March 1929)	Harvard Univ.	Ambassador to Germany (1922–25); N.Y. Congressman (1919–22)	High off. of Corning Glass Works, western N.Y. (1911 through 1929); Corning Glass works VP (1902–1910)	BD of Metropolitan Life Insur. Co. (1913 through 1929)			E
Ambassador to France							
Myron T. Herrick, Ohio (August 1923–March 1929)	Ohio Wesleyan College (not complete)	Ambassador to France (1912–14 and 1921–23); also Governor of Ohio (1904–06)	P or BC, Society for Savings, Cleveland (1894–1929); BC, Union Carbide & Carbon Corp. (1918–25, dir. till 1928)	BD of New York Life Insur. Co. (1917 through 1929) and Erie RR (1918–21)	Son, P. W. Herrick, on BD of Harriman National Bank, N.Y.C. (1915 through 1929) and Union Trust Co., Cleveland (1914 through 1929)		E
Ambassador to Germany							
Alanson B. Houghton, N.Y. (August 1923–Feb. 1925)	SEE ABOVE COOLIDGE ADMINISTRATION ENTRY						E

Officeholder	College Education	Prior Governmental Experience	Primary Occupation	Important Secondary Economic Affiliations	Family and Other Social Ties	Other Pertinent Information	Elite or Non-Elite Status
Jacob G. Schurman, N.Y. (June 1925 through 1929)	Univ. of London	U.S. Minister to China (1921–25)	P of Cornell Univ. (1892–1900); prof. of philosophy, Cornell Univ. (1886–92)		Younger brother, George W. Schurman, a partner in the N.Y.C. law firm headed by Charles Evans Hughes		?

HOOVER ADMINISTRATION (1929–1933)

Officeholder	College Education	Prior Governmental Experience	Primary Occupation	Important Secondary Economic Affiliations	Family and Other Social Ties	Other Pertinent Information	Elite or Non-Elite Status
President Herbert C. Hoover, Calif. (1929–33)	Stanford Univ.	Sec. of Commerce (1921–August 1928); WWI federal food administrator and postwar relief official	Mining engineer and entrepreneur, mainly in Australia and Asia (1908–16); off., two small mining concerns (1914–16); off., Bewick, Moreing & Co., British mining and investment concern (up to 1908)	Director of many mining and extractive concerns, abroad (up to around WWI)		BT of Stanford Univ. (1912–33)	E

449

Officeholder	College Education	Prior Governmental Experience	Primary Occupation	Important Secondary Economic Affiliations	Family and Other Social Ties	Other Pertinent Information	Elite or Non-Elite Status
Secretary of State							
Henry L. Stimson, N.Y. (1929–33)	Yale Univ.	Governor general of Philippine Islands (1927–29); special U.S. envoy to Nicaragua (1927); Sec. of War (1911–13)	Longtime ptr. in N.Y.C. law firm of Winthrop, Stimson, Putnam & Roberts (and predecessor concern of Root, Howard, Winthrop & Stimson)	BD of American Superpower Corp. (1925–27)	Cousin, A. L. Loomis, a VP of Bonbright & Co., an off. or dir. of American Superpower Corp. and affiliated concerns (1925 through 1933) and BD of Central Hanover Bank & Trust Co., N.Y.C. (1930 on); another cousin, L. K. Thorne, P of Bonbright & Co., off. or dir. of American Superpower Corp. (1925–33) and BD of Bankers Trust Co., N.Y.C. (1923 through 1933) and Federal Insur. Co. (1930 on)		E

Secretary of Treasury						
Andrew W. Mellon, Penn. (March 1929–Feb. 1932)	Univ. of Pittsburgh (not complete)	U.S. Sec. of the Treasury (1921 through 1929)	P of Mellon National Bank, Pitts. (up to 1921); VP of Gulf Oil Corp., Union Trust Co., and Union Savings Bank, Pitts. (up to 1921); VP of Natl. Fire Insur. Co. (up to 1928)	BD of Alcoa, Carbonundum Co., American Locomotive Co., Crucible Steel Co. of America, Koppers Co., Pittsburgh Coal Co., Standard Steel Car Co., and Natl. Bank of Commerce, N.Y.C. (up to 1921)	Brother, R. B. Mellon, P of Mellon Natl. Bank (up through 1932), VP of Union Trust Co. and Union Savings Bank, Pitts. (up through 1932), dir. of Alcoa, Carbonundum Co., Gulf Oil Corp., Pittsburgh Coal Co., and Crucible Steel Co. of America (up through 1932), Westinghouse Air Brake Co. (1925–33), Guaranty Trust Co., N.Y.C. (1926 through 1932), and PRR (1927 through 1932); other family members on number of above boards; nephew, R. K. Mellon, on BD of Standard Steel Car Co. (up to 1930) and Pullman, Inc. (1930–33)	E
Ogden L. Mills, N.Y. (Feb. 1932–March 1933)	Harvard Univ.	Under Sec. of the Treasury (1927–32); New York Congressman (1921–27)	Longtime N.Y.C. lawyer and financial figure	BD of New York Trust Co. (1917–26), International Paper Co. (1911–26),	Father, Ogden Mills, on BD of New York Central RR, Southern Pacific Co., Farmers Loan & Trust Co., U.S. Trust Co. of N.Y.C., Cerro de Pasco	E

Officeholder	College Education	Prior Governmental Experience	Primary Occupation	Important Secondary Economic Affiliations	Family and Other Social Ties	Other Pertinent Information	Elite or Non-Elite Status
				Atchison, Topeka & Santa Fe Rwy. (1917–26), Crex Carpet Co. (1911–27), Mergenthaler Linotype Co. (1910–31), and New York Tribune, Inc. (at least 1915 to 1931)	Corp., and Mergenthaler Linotype Co. (up to death in Jan. of 1929)		E
Attorney General William D. Mitchell, Minn. (1929–33)	Univ. of Minnesota	U.S. Solicitor General (1925–29)	Ptr. in St. Paul law firm of Butler, Mitchell & Doherty, later known as Mitchell, Doherty, Rumble, Bunn & Butler (1904–17 and 1919–25)	BD of Capital Trust & Savings Bank, St. Paul (1917–25)			

Secretary of War

Name	College	Government experience	Career	Business affiliations	Other	Campaign	
James W. Good, Ill. (March–Nov. 1929)	Coe College, Iowa	Iowa Congressman (1909–21)	Ptr., Chicago law firm of Good, Childs, Bobb & Wescott (1921–29); ptr., Cedar Rapids, Iowa law firm of Deacon, Good, Sargent & Spangler (1908–21)			1928 western manager, Hoover presidential campaign	N-E?
Patrick J. Hurley, Okla. (Dec. 1929–March 1933)	Bacone Jr. College, Okla. (not complete)	Asst. Sec. of War (March–Dec. 1929)	Longtime Tulsa, Okla. attorney (1911–29, accept WWI years)	BD of First National Bank, Tulsa (1927–29) and Paragon Refining Co. of Ohio (1921–22)		1928 Hoover campaign official	E?

Secretary of Navy

Name	College	Government experience	Career	Business affiliations	Other	Campaign	
Charles F. Adams, Mass. (1929–33)	Harvard Univ.		Longtime Boston lawyer; also P of Fifty Associates, Boston; VP, Provident Inst. for Savings, Boston (around 1910 to 1933, before that a trustee)	BD of Old Colony Trust Co., Boston (1910–29), John Hancock Mutual Life Insur. Co. (1918 through	Daughter married J. P. Morgan, Jr., who was BC of U.S. Steel Corp. (1928–31, dir. both before and after) and BD of Pullman, Inc. (1914 through 1933) and International Mercantile Marine Co. (1914–31)		E

Officeholder	College Education	Prior Governmental Experience	Primary Occupation	Important Secondary Economic Affiliations	Family and Other Social Ties	Other Pertinent Information	Elite or Non-Elite Status
				1933), A. T. & T. (1912–29), American Sugar Refining Co. (1921–28), Massachusetts Gas Companies (1905–33), Edison Electric Illuminating Co. of Boston (1918–28), and Puget Sound Power & Light Co. (1916–29)			
Secretary of Interior Ray L. Wilbur, Calif. (1929–33)	Stanford Univ.		P of Stanford Univ. (1916–29); dean, Stanford Univ. medical school (1911–16)			BT of Rockefeller Foundation (1923 through 1933)	E

Secretary of Agriculture

Name	Education	Prior Govt. Service	Business Affiliations	
Arthur M. Hyde, Missouri (1929–33)	Univ. of Michigan	Governor of Missouri (1921–25)	Longtime Mo. lawyer (first Princeton and Trenton, Mo.); also P of newly formed Sentinel Life Insur. Co., Kansas City (1927–28)	N-E?

Secretary of Commerce

Name	Education	Prior Govt. Service	Business Affiliations	
Robert P. Lamont, Ill. (March 1929–August 1932)	Univ. of Michigan		P of American Steel Foundries, Chicago (1912–29) BD of Illinois Bell Tel. Co., sub. of A. T. & T. (1928–29), First Natl. Bank of Chicago (1917–29), Armour & Co. (1923–29), American Radiator Co. (1925–28), Dodge Bros., Inc. (1925–28), International Harvester Co. (1924–28), and Montgomery Ward & Co. (1925–29)	E

Officeholder	College Education	Prior Governmental Experience	Primary Occupation	Important Secondary Economic Affiliations	Family and Other Social Ties	Other Pertinent Information	Elite or Non-Elite Status
Roy D. Chapin, Mich. (Dec. 1932–March 1933)	Univ. of Michigan (not complete)		P, Hudson Motor Car Co. (1909–23; BC, 1923–32)	BD of First National Bank, Detroit (1914–30)			E
Secretary of Labor							
James J. Davis, Penn. (March 1929–Dec. 1930)			SEE PRECEDING HARDING AND COOLIDGE ADMINISTRATION ENTRIES				?
William N. Doak, W.Va. (Dec. 1930–March 1933)	Business college, Bristol, Va. (not complete?)		Longtime off., Brotherhood of Railroad Trainmen				N-E
Ambassador to Great Britain							
Charles G. Dawes, Ill. (June 1929–Dec. 1931)	Marietta College, Ohio	Vice President of the United States (1925–29); dir., Bureau of the Budget (1921–22);	P or BC of Central Trust Co., Chicago (1902–25, BD early 1929)	BD of Chicago Great Western RR (1923–25)	One brother, Beman Dawes, P of Pure Oil Co. (up to 1924, BC thereafter); another brother, Henry M.		E

Name / Dates	Education	Government Position	Occupation	Business Affiliations	Kinsman	
		Comptroller of Currency, Treasury Dept. (1898–1901)		Dawes, P of Pure Oil Co. (1924 through 1933) and BD of Central Trust Co., Chicago (1920–31), Chicago Great Western RR (1925–33), and Metropolitan Gas & Electric Co., Ohio (up to 1929); third brother, Rufus C. Dawes, P of Metropolitan Gas & Electric Co. (up to 1929)		E
Andrew W. Mellon, Penn. (April 1932–March 1933) / Ambassador to France	Univ. of Pittsburgh (not complete)	Sec. of the Treasury (1921–32)		SEE PRECEDING HOOVER, COOLIDGE, AND HARDING ADMINISTRATION ENTRIES		
Walter E. Edge, N.J. (Dec. 1929–April 1933)		U.S. Senator, N.J. (1919–29); Governor of New Jersey (1917–19); also former state legislator	Longtime Atlantic City newspaper publisher	BD of Crex Carpet Co., N.Y.C. (1919–23) and Marine Trust Co., Atlantic City (1911–27)	Kinsman, Walter C. Teagle, P of Standard Oil Co. of N.J. (1918 through 1933) and a dir. of the White Motor Co. (1924 through 1933) and Consolidation Coal Co. (1929 through 1933)	E?

Officeholder	College Education	Prior Governmental Experience	Primary Occupation	Important Secondary Economic Affiliations	Family and Other Social Ties	Other Pertinent Information	Elite or Non-Elite Status
Ambassador to Germany							
Jacob G. Schurman, N.Y. (1929–Jan., 1930)	SEE PRECEDING COOLIDGE ADMINISTRATION ENTRY						?
Frederic M. Sackett, Kentucky (Feb. 1930–March 1933)	Brown Univ.	U.S. Senator, Ky. (1925–30)	VP of Louisville Cement Co. (up to 1929) and head of two small (apparently privately-owned) coal companies	BD of American Tar Products Co. (1913–24) and Fidelity & Columbia Trust Co. and predecessor company, Louisville; (1911–24) also BD of Louisville branch of Federal Reserve Bank of St. Louis (1917–24)			E

Appendix B

Primary Background Data of
Supreme Court Justices:
1861–1933

SUCCESSION OF U.S. SUPREME COURT JUSTICES (1861–1933)

Chief Justice	Associate Justices								
Roger B. Taney (1836–1864)	James M. Wayne (1835–1867)	John McLean (1829–1861) / Noah H. Swayne (1862–1881)	John Catron (1837–1865)	Samuel Nelson (1845–1872)	Robert C. Grier (1846–1870)	Nathan Clifford (1858–1881)	Samuel F. Miller (1862–1890)	David Davis (1862–1877)	Stephen J. Field (1863–1897)
Salmon P. Chase (1864–1873)				Joseph P. Bradley (1870–1892)					
Morrison R. Waite (1874–1888)		Stanley Matthews (1881–1889)		Ward Hunt (1872–1882)	William Strong (1870–1880) / William B. Woods (1880–1887)	Horace Gray (1881–1902)		John M. Harlan (1877–1911)	

460

Melville W. Fuller (1888–1910)

David J. Brewer (1889–1910)

Samuel Blatchford (1882–1893)

Lucius Q. C. Lamar (1888–1893)

Joseph McKenna (1898–1925)

Henry B. Brown (1890–1906)

George Shiras, Jr. (1892–1903)

Howell E. Jackson (1893–1895)

Edward D. White (1894–1910)

Rufus W. Peckham (1895–1909)

William R. Day (1903–1922)

Oliver Wendell Holmes (1902–1932)

William H. Moody (1906–1910)

Joseph R. Lamar (1911–1916)

Mahlon Pitney (1912–1922)

Harlan F. Stone (1925–1933)

Edward T. Sanford (1923–1930)

Louis D. Brandeis (1916–1933)

Horace H. Lurton (1909–1914)

James C. McReynolds (1914–1933)

Willis Van Devanter (1910–1933)

Charles E. Hughes (1910–1916)

John H. Clarke (1916–1922)

George Sutherland (1922–1933)

Pierce Butler (1922–1933)

Edward D. White (1910–1921)

William H. Taft (1921–1930)

Charles E.
H...

Benjamin N.
C...

Owen J.

Officeholder	College Education	Prior Governmental Experience	Primary Occupation	Important Secondary Economic Affiliations	Family and Other Social Ties	Other Pertinent Information	Elite or Non-Elite status
Chief Justice							
Roger B. Taney, Md. (1836–Oct. 1864)	Dickinson College	Chief Justice, U.S. Supreme Court (1836 on); Sec. of Treasury (1833–34); U.S. Attorney General (1831–33)	Baltimore lawyer (1823–31 and 1834–36); Frederick, Md. lawyer (1801–23)	Former senior or general counsel, B&O RR; counsel and director of number of local Maryland banks (prior to 1851)			E
Assoc. Justice							
John Catron, Tenn. (1837–May 1865)		Chief Justice, Tennessee Supreme Court (1831–34); Tennessee Judge (1824–31)	Former Nashville lawyer (1818–24), a lucrative practice				E

Officeholder	College Education	Prior Governmental Experience	Primary Occupation	Important Secondary Economic Affiliations	Family and Other Social Ties	Other Pertinent Information	Elite or Non-Elite Status
James M. Wayne, Ga. (*1835*–July 1867)	Princeton Univ.	U.S. Congressman, Ga. (1829–35); Georgia judge (1824–29)	Former longtime Savannah, Ga. lawyer	R. R. Culyer, former law partner and father of son-in-law, former longtime P of Central Georgia RR and Southwestern RR	Father a former major planter and Savannah merchant		E
Samuel Nelson, N.Y. (*1845*–Nov. 1872)	Middlebury College	Chief Justice, N.Y. Supreme Court (1837–45); Justice, N.Y. Supreme Court (1831–37); N.Y. judge (1823–31)	Cortland, N.Y. lawyer (1817–23)				N-E?
Robert C. Grier, Penn. (*1846*–Jan. 1870)	Dickinson College	Judge, Pa. district court (1833–46)	Central Pa. lawyer (1817–33)		Married daughter of John Rose, former wealthy Williamsport figure		

Nathan Clifford, Maine (*1858*–July 1881)	U.S. Minister to Mexico (1848–49); U.S. Attorney General (1846–48); Maine Congressman (1839–43) also longtime state govt. official	Portland, Maine lawyer (1849–58); Newfield, Maine lawyer (1824–46)	John B. Brown, father-in-law of two of Clifford's children, P of Portland Sugar Co. and on BD of Atlantic & St. Lawrence RR (prob. at least 1856–81), Portland & Kennebec RR and successor company, Maine Central RR (at least 1865–81), Toledo, Peoria & Warsaw RR (at least 1865–apparently 1873), Portland, Saco & Portsmouth RR (late 1860s), and New York, Lake Erie & Western RR (1875–77)	E
Noah H. Swayne, Ohio (Jan. 1862–Jan. 1881)	U.S. attorney for district of Ohio (1830–39)	Columbus, Ohio lawyer (1839 on)	Son, Wager Swayne, on BD of Atlantic & Lake Erie RR (1872–75), Mansfield, Coldwater & Lake Michigan RR (1873–75), and Toledo, Tiffin & Eastern RR (1874–76); another son, Noah H. Swayne, Jr. on BD of Wheeling & Lake Erie RR (1882 on)	E?

Officeholder	College Education	Prior Governmental Experience	Primary Occupation	Important Secondary Economic Affiliations	Family and Other Social Ties	Other Pertinent Information	Elite or Non-Elite Status
Samuel F. Miller, Iowa (July 1862–Oct. 1890)	Transylvania Univ.		Keokuk, Iowa lawyer (1850–62)			Longtime Iowa Rep. party leader (but never held any major public office)	N-E?
David Davis, Ill. (Dec. 1862–March 1877)	Kenyon College	Illinois state judge (1848–62); also former state legislator	Bloomington, Ill. lawyer (1836–48); also a wealthy former real estate speculator		Illinois cousin, Levi Davis, a director or officer of St. Louis, Alton & Terre Haute RR (at least 1856 through 1877)	Longtime close friend of Lincoln	E?
Stephen J. Field, Calif. (March 1863–Dec. 1897)	Williams College	Judge, Calif. Supreme Court (1857–63); also former state legislator (early 1850s)	Marysville, Calif. lawyer (1849–57); N.Y.C. lawyer, with brother, D. D. Field (1841–48); also former Calif. real estate speculator		Brother, Cyrus Field, head of Atlantic Telegraph Co. (early 1860s on); P of N. Y. Elevated RR (late 1870s); also BD of New York Central and Hudson River RR (1879–92), Manhattan Rwy. (1879–92), and Western Union Telegraph Co. (1881–92); brother, Dudley D. Field, counsel for Jay Gould and Jim Fisk in Erie RR suit	Close friend of Calif. governor and railroad entrepreneur, Leland Stanford	E?

						E
Chief Justice						
Salmon P. Chase, Ohio (Dec. 1864–May 1873)	Dartmouth College	U.S. Secretary of Treasury (1861–64); Governor of Ohio (1856–60); U.S. Senator, Ohio (1849–56); former prominent Republican and abolitionist leader	Cincinnati lawyer (1830 on)	Son-in-law, R.I. Senator William Sprague, on BD of New Orleans, Mobile and Chattagoona RR (1868) and his brother, Amasa Sprague, on BD of Kansas Central RR (1871 on)	Third (now deceased) wife the wealthy daughter of one of the founders of Cincinnati (with major landholdings)	E
Assoc. Justice						
William Strong, Penn. (Feb. 1870–Dec. 1880)	Yale Univ.	Judge, Penn. Supreme Court (1857–68); Penn. Congressman (1847–51)	Phila. lawyer (1868–70); Reading, Penn. lawyer (1832–57)	Former counsel, Philadelphia & Reading RR; BD of Lebanon Valley RR (1856); also former BD of Farmer's Bank of Reading		E

Officeholder	College Education	Prior Governmental Experience	Primary Occupation	Important Secondary Economic Affiliations	Family and Other Social Ties	Other Pertinent Information	Elite or Non-Elite Status
Joseph P. Bradley, N.J. (March 1870–Jan. 1892)	Rutgers Univ.		Newark, N.J. lawyer (1839 on); P of New Jersey Mutual Life Insur. Co. (1865–69); actuary, Mutual Benefit Life Insur. Co. (1851–63)	BD of Camden & Amboy RR (at least 1865 to 1870), Morris and Essex RR (at least 1865 up to 1870), and Second National Bank of Newark (mid-1860s up to at least 1876)	Son-in-law of former N.J. Chief Justice, Joseph C. Hornblower; nephew, William B. Hornblower, on BD of New York Life Insurance Co. (1891 on)		E
Ward Hunt, N.Y. (Dec. 1872–Jan. 1882)	Union College	N.Y. state judge (1865–72); former state legislator (1838–39)	Utica, N.Y. lawyer (early 1830s–1865)	BD of Schenectady and Utica RR (1868–72) and Mohawk Valley RR (early 1850s)	Father, a former longtime off. of 1st Nat'l. Bank of Utica	Close friend of N.Y. Republican boss, Roscoe Conkling	E

Chief Justice

Morrison R. Waite, Ohio (Jan. 1874–March, 1888)	Yale Univ.	American consul, Geneva arbitration proceedings (early 1870s); former state legislator (1849–50)	Toledo, Ohio lawyer (1850–74); also Maumee, Ohio lawyer (1839–50)	Director (at least 1859 to 1873) and VP (1868–73) of Dayton and Michigan RR; also on BD of Toledo Gas Light and Coke Co. (1854–74), Toledo Nat'l. Bank (1855 on?), and Toledo Street Rwy. (1860 on?)	Son, C. C. Waite, VP of Cincinnati, Hamilton & Dayton RR (1882 through 1888), P of Dayton & Union RR (1883 through 1888) and BD of Chicago & Atlantic RR (1883 through 1888); also asst. to P, New York, Lake Erie & Western RR (1881–82) and sec. and treas., Cincinnati & Muskingum Valley RR (1875–81)	E

Assoc. Justice

John Marshall Harlan, Kentucky (Nov. 1877–Oct. 1911)	Centre College, Ky.	Kentucky Attorney General (1864–67); also former county judge (1858–59)	Frankfort, Ky. lawyer (1853–61); Louisville lawyer (1861–64 and 1867–1877), with Benj. Bristow (1868–71)		Prominent Kentucky Repub. party leader; key late supporter of Hayes for Rep. presidential nomination in 1876	N-E?

Officeholder	College Education	Prior Governmental Experience	Primary Occupation	Important Secondary Economic Affiliations	Family and Other Social Ties	Other Pertinent Information	Elite or Non-Elite Status
William B. Woods, Ala., orig. Ohio (Dec. 1880–May 1887)	Yale Univ. / Emory Univ., Ga.	U.S. Circuit Court judge (1869–80); Ala. State Chancellor (1868–69); former Ohio state legislator (pre-Civil War period)	Mobile and Montgomery, Ala. lawyer (1866–68); Newark, Ohio lawyer (1848–61)				N-E?
Stanley Matthews, Ohio (May 1881–March 1889)	Kenyon College	U.S. Senator, Ohio (1877–79); local judge (mid-1860s); also former state legislator; U.S. attorney, southern district, Ohio (1858–61)	Cincinnati lawyer (1844 on, except for Civil War and immediate postwar years)	BD of Knoxville & Ohio RR (at least 1877 up to 1881); GC for the Cincinnati, Hamilton & Dayton RR (1868 to at least 1878); Midwestern counsel for Jay Gould		Sister married brother-in-law of Rutherford B. Hayes	E

Horace Gray, Mass. (Dec. 1881–Sept. 1902)	Harvard Univ.	Massachusetts state supreme court justice (1864–81)	Boston lawyer (1851–64, the last 7 years as ptr. of Ebenezer R. Hoar)		Member of one of Boston's top 50 families; grandfather, William Gray, a wealthy Boston businessman; half-brother, John C. Gray, ptr. in the major Boston law firm of Ropes & Gray (and a VP of the Massachusetts Hospital Life Insur. Co., 1851–6? and 1888 on)	E
Samuel Blatchford, N.Y. (March 1882–July 1893)	Columbia Univ.	U.S. district judge (1867–72); U.S. Circuit Court judge (1872–82)	Member, Seward & Blatchford law firm (N.Y.C., 1842–45 and 1854–67; Auburn, 1845–54)		Married member of wealthy Appleton family of Boston; late father, Richard M. Blatchford, a prominent N.Y.C. lawyer, political ally of Wm. H. Seward, and former officer or director of the New York Central & Hudson River RR	E
Lucius Q. C. Lamar, Miss., orig. Ga. (Jan. 1888–Jan. 1893)	Emory Univ., Ga.	U.S. Secretary of the Interior (1885–88); U.S. Senator, Miss. (1877–85); Miss. Congressman (1857–61 and 1873–77)	Oxford, Miss. lawyer (1849–52 and 1855 on); also prof. of law, Univ. of Mississippi (1866–70); Covington, Ga. lawyer (1847–49)	BD of Mississippi Central RR (1867–74) and successor company the New Orleans, St. Louis & Chicago RR (1874–76)	Member of prominent Southern family (Ga. and Texas); cousin of former U.S. Supreme Court Justice, John A. Campbell	E

Officeholder	College Education	Prior Governmental Experience	Primary Occupation	Important Secondary Economic Affiliations	Family and Other Social Ties	Other Pertinent Information	Elite or Non-Elite Status
Chief Justice							
Melville W. Fuller, Ill. (July 1888–July 1910)	Bowdoin College		Chicago lawyer, largely corporate practice (1856 on)		Deceased father-in-law, Wm. F. Coolbaugh, longtime P of Union Nat'l. Bank, Chicago and BD of Equitable Life Assur. Society of N.Y.C. (1876–77), Chicago, Rock Island & Pacific RR (1867–68), and Burlington & Missouri River RR (at least 1856 up to 1865); son-in-law, Hugh C. Wallace, on BD of National Bank of Commerce, Seattle (1900 through 1910)		E

Assoc. Justice							
David J. Brewer, Kansas (Dec. 1889–March 1910)	Yale Univ.	Judge, U.S. Circuit Court of Appeals (1884–89); Kansas state supreme court justice (1870–84); Leavenworth city attorney (1869–70); Kansas state and local judge (1862–69)	Leavenworth, Kansas lawyer (1859–61)	BT of Northwestern Mutual Life Insur. Co. (1872–1910)	Nephew of U.S. Supreme Court Justice, Stephen J. Field, and entrepreneur, Cyrus Field		E
Henry B. Brown, Mich. (Dec. 1890–May 1906)	Yale Univ.	U.S. district court judge (1875–90); asst. U.S. attorney, Mich. (1863–68)	Detroit lawyer (1860–75), partner of Ashley Pond (mid-or late 1860s to mid-1870s)		Married daughter of wealthy Mass. lumberman		E?
George Shiras, Jr., Penn. (July 1892–Feb. 1903)	Yale Univ.	Former U.S. marshal and municipal judge (early 1860s)	Pittsburgh lawyer (1858–92)	BD of Safe Deposit & Trust Co., Pittsburgh (1891–92)	Married daughter of Robert T. Kennedy, Pittsburgh manufacturer; brother, O. P. Shiras, an Iowa law partner of Congressman David B. Henderson; son, W. K. Shiras, on BD of Safe Deposit & Trust Co. (1893 through 1903)	Member of Duquesne Club	E

Officeholder	College Education	Prior Governmental Experience	Primary Occupation	Important Secondary Economic Affiliations	Family and Other Social Ties	Other Pertinent Information	Elite or Non-Elite Status
Howell E. Jackson, Tenn. (Feb. 1893–Aug. 1895)	West Tennessee College	Judge, U.S. Circuit Court of Appeals (1886–93); U.S. Senator, Tenn. (1881–86); state judge (1875–78); former state legislator	Memphis lawyer (1858–61 and 1865–74); Jackson, Tenn. lawyer (1878–86, 1874–75 and mid-1850s)		Father a former large plantation owner in Tenn.		E
Edward D. White, La. (Feb. 1894–Dec. 1910)	Georgetown Univ. (not complete)	U.S. Senator, La. (1891–94); Louisiana state supreme court justice (1879–80); former state legislator (1874–79)	New Orleans lawyer (1868 on); also had a 1,600-acre beet sugar plantation		Married daughter of Romanzo Montgomery, New Orleans banker; father a former La. Congressman and Governor		E

Name, state (term)	Education	Judicial/political career	Legal practice	Business connections	Family connections	Political connections	
Rufus W. Peckham, N.Y. (Dec. 1895–Oct. 1909)		Judge, N.Y. Court of Appeals (1886–95); justice, N.Y. Supreme Court (1883–85); Albany corporation counsel (1881–83); Albany county district attorney (1869–72)	Albany, N.Y. lawyer (1859–83?)	BD of Mutual Life Insur. Co., N.Y.C. (1884–1905)	Married daughter of D. H. Arnold, P of Mercantile Bank of N.Y.C.; brother, Wheeler H. Peckham, on BD of Buffalo, Rochester & Pittsburgh RR and predecessor concern (1881–1905); father a former New York State Supreme Court Justice		E
Joseph McKenna, Calif. (Jan. 1898–Jan. 1925)	Benicia Collegiate Inst., Cal. (early college years in Penn.)	U.S. Attorney General (1897–98); judge, U.S. Circuit Court of Appeals (1892–97); Calif. Congressman (1885–92); former state legislator	Fairfield and Benicia, Calif. lawyer (1865–92)			Longtime friend of William McKinley (and deceased railroad magnate, Leland Stanford)	?
Oliver Wendell Holmes, Mass. (Dec. 1902–Jan. 1932)	Harvard Univ.	Mass. Supreme Court Justice (1883–1902)	Member, Boston law firm of Shattuck, Holmes & Munroe (1873–82)		Member of one of Boston's top 50 families		E

Officeholder	College Education	Prior Governmental Experience	Primary Occupation	Important Secondary Economic Affiliations	Family and Other Social Ties	Other Pertinent Information	Elite or Non-Elite Status
William R. Day, Ohio (Feb. 1903–Nov. 1922)	Univ. of Michigan	Judge, U.S. Circuit Court of Appeals (1899–1903); Sec. of State (6 months, 1898); Asst. Sec. of State (1897–98)	Member of Canton law firm of Lynch and Day (1872–97)	BD of City National Bank, Canton (at least 1893 to 1900)			E?
William H. Moody, Mass. (Dec. 1906–Nov. 1910)	Harvard Univ.	U.S. Attorney General (1904–06); Sec. of Navy (1902–04); Mass. Congressman (1895–1902); U.S. attorney for eastern district, Mass. (1890–95)	Haverhill, Mass. lawyer (1878–1902)	BD of Shoe & Leather Natl. Bank, Boston (1891–93)			E?

Horace H. Lurton, Tenn. (Jan. 1910–July 1914)	Univ. of Chicago (not complete)	Judge, U.S. Circuit Court of Appeals (1893–1910); Tenn. Supreme Court Justice (1886–93); Tenn. State Chancellor (1875–78)	Prof. of law, Vanderbilt Univ. (1898–1910, dean of law school, 1905–10); Clarksville, Tenn. lawyer (late 1860s–86); P of Farmers & Mechanics Natl. Bank, Clarksville (late 1870s–1886?)	E?
Charles Evans Hughes, N.Y. (May 1910–June 1916)	Brown Univ.	Governor of New York (1907–10); counsel for Armstrong Insurance Commission investigation (1905–06)	Ptr., Hughes, Rounds & Schurman and predecessor firm of Carter, Hughes & Dwight (1887–91 and 1893–1907); prof. of law, Cornell Univ. (1891–93)	E?

Chief Justice

Edward D. White, La. (Dec. 1910–May 1921)	Georgetown College (mat grad)	Assoc. Justice, U.S. Supreme Court (1894–1910); U.S. Senator, La. (1891–94); also former state govt. official	New Orleans lawyer (1868–94); also owner of large beet sugar plantation	E

Officeholder	College Education	Prior Governmental Experience	Primary Occupation	Important Secondary Economic Affiliations	Family and Other Social Ties	Other Pertinent Information	Elite or Non-Elite Status
Associate Justice							
Willis Van Devanter, Wyoming (Dec. 1910 through 1933)	DePauw Univ., Ind.	Judge, U.S. Circuit Court of Appeals (1903–10); Asst. U.S. Attorney General (1897–1903); Chief Justice, Wyoming Supreme Court (1889–91)	Longtime Cheyenne, Wyo. lawyer; ptr., law firm of Lacey and Van Devanter (1891–97)				E
Joseph R. Lamar, Ga. (Jan. 1911–Jan. 1916)	Bethany College, W.Va.	Georgia Supreme Court Justice (1903–05); also former state legislator (late 1880s)	Augusta law partner of E. H. Callaway (1905–10); Augusta law ptr. of Henry C. Foster (1880–90) Augusta lawyer (1890–1902)		Father, Joseph Lamar, a wealthy Ga. planter		E

Mahlon Pitney, N.J. (March 1912–Dec. 1922)

Princeton Univ.

Chancellor of N.J. (1908–12); member, N.J. Supreme Court (1901–08); N.J. state legislator (1899–1901); N.J. Congressman (1895–99)

Morristown, N.J. lawyer (1889–1901); Dover, N.J. attorney (1882–89)

Off. or dir., Cranbury Iron Co. (1882–89); BD of East Tennessee and Western North Carolina RR (1902–08)

Brother, John O. H. Pitney, longtime ptr. in Newark, N.J. law firm of Pitney, Hardin & Skinner; off. or dir., P. Ballantine & Sons (1903–13), and BD of National Newark Banking Co. (1901–17), Mutual Benefit Life Insur. Co. (1903 through 1922), and American Insurance Co. (1902 through 1922); J. O. H. Pitney's father-in-law, Robert F. Ballantine, up to death in 1905, P of P. Ballantine & Sons, VP of Howard Savings Inst., Newark, and BD of Mutual Benefit Life Insur. Co. and Farmers Loan & Trust Co., N.Y.C.; 2nd cousin's husband, W. Emlen Roosevelt, a VP of Buffalo, Rochester & Pittsburgh Rwy. (1908 through 1922) and Central & South American Telegraph Co. (1909–18,

Officeholder	College Education	Prior Governmental Experience	Primary Occupation	Important Secondary Economic Affiliations	Family and Other Social Ties	Other Pertinent Information	Elite or Non-Elite Status
					when became BC), and BD of Mexican Telegraph Co. (up to 1919), Mobile & Ohio RR (1900 through 1922), New York Life Insur. & Trust Co. (1893 through 1922), Hanover Natl. Bank (1912–16), and Central Union Trust Co. of N.Y.C. (at least 1894 through 1922); another 2nd cousin's husband, Hamilton F. Kean, a partner in Kean, Taylor & Co., on BD of Buffalo, Rochester & Pittsburgh Rwy. (1912 through 1922), and many New Jersey companies; his kinsman, John Kean, a longtime high official of Manhattan Trust Co., N.Y.C.		

James C. McReynolds, Tenn., and later N.Y. (August 1914 through 1933)	Vanderbilt Univ.	U.S. Attorney General (1913–14); special counsel to U.S. Attorney General on antitrust matters (1907–12); Asst. U.S. Attorney General (1903–07)	Individual N.Y.C. lawyer (1912–13); Nashville, Tenn. lawyer (1895–1903); Vanderbilt Univ. law prof. (1900–03)	VP, City Savings Bank Nashville (early 1900s)		N-E
Louis D. Brandeis, Mass. (June 1916 through 1933)		Ptr., Boston law firm of Brandeis, Dunbar & Nutter (1897–1916)		BD of United Shoe Machinery Corp. (1899 to 1906)	Counsel for and advocate of many progressive causes (1906–16); VP, American Asson. for Labor Legislation (1910 and possibly later)	?
John H. Clarke, Ohio (July 1916–Sept. 1922)	Western Reserve College	U.S. district court judge (1914–16)	General counsel, New York, Chicago & St. Louis RR (1898–1913); ptr., Cleveland law firm of Williamson & Cushing (1897–1907); ptr., Youngstown law firm of Hine & Clarke (1885–97)	BD of Cincinnati, Hamilton & Dayton Rwy., in which line the Erie RR had a substantial stake (1906–09)		E

Officeholder	College Education	Prior Governmental Experience	Primary Occupation	Important Secondary Economic Affiliations	Family and Other Social Ties	Other Pertinent Information	Elite or Non-Elite Status
Chief Justice							
William Howard Taft, Ohio (June 1921–Feb. 1930)	Yale Univ.	President of the United States (1909–13); Secretary of War (1904–08); U.S. Circuit Court judge (1890–92); Ohio superior court judge (1887–90); also co-chairman, War Labor Board (1918–19)	Prof. of law, Yale Univ. (1913–20); dean, Univ. of Cincinnati law school (1896–1900); Cincinnati lawyer (1880–87)		Brother, Henry W. Taft, on BD of Mutual Life Insur. Co. (1906 through 1930); half-brother, Charles P. Taft, on Columbia Gas & Electric Co. and predecessor concern (at least 1904 to 1926) and Cincinnati & Suburban Bell Telephone Co., sub of A. T. & T. (at least 1904 to 1929)	Member of exec. committee of National Civic Federation (1907 to 1920)	E
Associate Justice							
George Sutherland, Utah (Sept. 1922 through 1933)	Brigham Young Univ.	U.S. Senator, Utah (1905–17); Utah Congressman (1901–03)	Salt Lake City lawyer (1893–1917); Washington, D.C. lawyer (1917–22); VP of Home Trust & Savings Co., Salt Lake City (1910 to 1926)	BD of Deseret Savings Bank, Salt Lake City (at least 1909 to 1922), and Home Trust & Savings Co. (1927)		BT of Carnegie Endowment for International Peace (1920–25); also P of the American Bar Assn. (1917)	E

Pierce Butler, Minn. (Dec. 1922 through *1933*)	Carleton College	Spec. Asst. to Attorney General to handle certain antitrust cases (few years, Taft administration)	Ptr., St. Paul law firm of Butler, Mitchell & Doherty (1893 to 1922)	BD of Capital National Bank, St. Paul (1917–23 and St. Paul Gas Light Co., a sub. of the American Light & Traction Co. (1919 to 1923)	Son, Pierce Butler, Jr., on BD of Capital National Bank, St. Paul (1923–24); another son, Francis D. Butler, on BD of Northwestern Trust Co., St. Paul (1930–1933)	E
Edward T. Sanford, Tenn. (Jan. 1923–March 1930)	Univ. of Tennessee and Harvard Univ.	Federal district court judge (1908–23); Asst. Attorney General (1907–08)	Knoxville, Tenn. lawyer (1890–1907)	BD of East Tennessee Natl. Bank, Knoxville (1904–09)	Father, E. J. Sanford, a wealthy Knoxville merchant, was P of the Knoxville & Ohio RR, a part of the Southern Rwy. system (up to 1901) and BD of Southern Car & Foundry Co. (up to 1904), East Tennessee Natl. Bank (up to 1903); and Virginia & Georgia RR (up to 1892); brother, A. F. Sanford, on BD of East Tennessee Natl. Bank (1909 through 1930)	E?

Officeholder	College Education	Prior Governmental Experience	Primary Occupation	Important Secondary Economic & Organizational Affiliations	Family and Other Social Ties	Other Pertinent Information	Elite or Non-Elite Status
Harlan Fiske Stone, N.Y. (Feb. 1925 through 1933)	Amherst College	U.S. Attorney General (1924–25)	Ptr., Sullivan & Cromwell, N.Y.C. law firm (1923–24); ptr., N.Y.C. law firm of Satterlee, Canfield & Stone (up to 1923); dean, Columbia Univ. Law School (1910–23)	Off. or dir. of Atlanta & Charlotte Air Line Rwy. (1909–24)			E?
Chief Justice							
Charles Evans Hughes, N.Y. (Feb. 1930 through 1933)	Brown Univ.	Judge, Permanent Court of International Justice (1929–30); U.S. Secretary of State (1921–25); U.S. Supreme Court Justice (1910–16); Governor of New York (1907–10)	Ptr., Hughes, Rounds, Schurman & Dwight (1917–21 and 1925–29)			BT of Rockefeller Foundation (1917–21 and 1926–28); also Councillor, National Industrial Conference Board (late 1920s)	E

Associate Justice					
Owen J. Roberts, Penn. (May 1930 through 1933)	Univ. of Penn.	Investigating and prosecuting off., Teapot Dome scandal (1924–29)	Ptr., Phila. law firm of Roberts & Montgomery and predecessor concern (1902–30); prof., Univ. of Penn. law school (1898–1918)	BD of Equitable Life Assur. Society of N.Y.C. (1926–30), Bell Telephone Co. of Pa. (1926–29), A.T. & T. (1929–30), and Franklin Fire Insur. Co., aff. of Home Insur. Co., N.Y.C., (1924–30)	E
Benjamin N. Cardozo, N.Y. (March 1932 through 1933)	Columbia Univ.	Chief judge, U.S. Court of Appeals (1928–32); judge on same court (1914–28)	N.Y.C. lawyer (1892–1914); ptr., Cardozo Brothers (up to 1903); then with Simpson, Werner & Cardozo		N-E

Index